Hans Christian
Andersen

Hans Christian
Andersen

a new life

Jens Andersen

Translated from the Danish by Tiina Nunnally

OVERLOOK DUCKWORTH
NEW YORK • WOODSTOCK • LONDON

First published in 2005 by
Overlook Duckworth, Peter Mayer Publishers, Inc.
New York, Woodstock & London

NEW YORK:
141 Wooster Street
New York, NY 10012

WOODSTOCK:
One Overlook Drive
Woodstock, NY 12498
www.overlookpress.com
[for individual orders, bulk and special sales, contact our Woodstock office]

LONDON:
90-93 Cowcross Street
London EC1M 6BF
inquiries @duckworth-publishers.co.uk
www.ducknet.co.uk

Library of Congress Cataloging-in-Publication Data

Andersen, Jens, 1955–
[Hans Christian Andersen. English]
Hans Christian Andersen : a new life / by Jens Andersen ;
translated from the Danish by Tiina Nunnallly.
p. cm.
Includes bibliographical references and index.
1. Andersen, H. C. (Hans Christian), 1805-1875.
2. Authors, Danish—19th century—Biography. I. Title.
PT8119.A7155 2005   839.8'136—dc22 [B]   2004065985
ISBN 1-58567-642-X (hc)   ISBN 0-7156-3361-9 (UK hc)
ISBN 1-58567-737-X (pb)   ISBN 0-7156-3375-9 (UK pb)

Book design and type formatting by Bernard Schleifer
Printed in the United States of America
3 5 7 9 8 6 4 2

"Dear Reader, simply become a child again, yet do not forget everything you have read since you became a big, sensible person . . ."

—HANS CHRISTIAN ANDERSEN, *Walking Tour*, 1829

Contents

Translator's Note

SINCE THIS BOOK IS INTENDED for English-speaking readers, the titles of all of Hans Christian Andersen's works are presented in English, even though some may not be currently available in English translation. A list of the original Danish titles can be found at the end of the volume. All translations of passages from Andersen's diaries, letters, and writings are my own, including quotes from his stories, most of which are cited from my translations in *Fairy Tales* by Hans Christian Andersen, published by Viking (2005). I am also responsible for the translations of other Danish and German passages included in the text.

Translating poetry is always a difficult task, and even more so if the poems are written with specific rhyme schemes. In this biography, Andersen's poems are often used to illustrate aspects of his life and psyche. For this reason I felt it was important to stay as close to Andersen's Danish as possible, which meant sacrificing the rhymes in favor of the content. Consequently the English translations, rendered in blank verse, may not do full justice to Hans Christian Andersen as a poet.

I would like to thank Jens Andersen for his willingness to answer my questions while I was translating his magnificent biography. I also received invaluable linguistic assistance from Steven T. Murray. And I am grateful to Editors David Mulrooney and Caroline Trefler, and Associate Publisher Tracy Carns at The Overlook Press for their continuing support of my work.

—TIINA NUNNALLY
Albuquerque, New Mexico
December 2004

Foreword

*I*N A MODEST DISPLAY CASE at the Bakkehus Museum in Frederiksberg, a suburb of Copenhagen, there is a piece of paper on which Hans
Christian Andersen describes in his nearly illegible script how he, at an
early stage of his life, fortified his self-confidence and dream of fame
by making a list of "clever people whose names end in '-sen.'" This list
shows Andersen's own name appearing as number three, after Marsk Stig
Andersen and Jens Andersen Beldenak, the bishop of Odense.

The name "Andersen" was and is a terribly common name in
Denmark, and thus an outward sign of anything but originality or noble
ancestry. For a person such as Hans Christian Andersen, who at quite a
young age was aware how different he was and fervently wished to put the
social milieu of his childhood behind him, the name "Andersen" was also
a stigma. It was a constant reminder of the reality and background from
which it was impossible to escape, even though the writer tried to do so
in many of his stories.

And yet he never forgot his connection with the common people, folk
tales, or his childhood by the river out in God's nature, to which the name
"Andersen" had once given him access. This was the basis for all of his
writing, his genius, and his distinctive character. Andersen never suppressed
this profound truth, just as he never changed his name, and he regularly
defended everything that was original in himself with great zeal. Any time
one of his many mentors in the higher social circles would come too close
to the folksy core he possessed by expressing critical admonitions, the
instinctual reply from the man and the poet was always: "Take me as I am!"
And if anyone entered into a conversation with him and questioned this
edict, his answer was always (even in the years when he was utterly

dependent on the goodwill and charity of the upper class): "It's against my nature to be any different than I am."

The purpose of this book is to depict Hans Christian Andersen "as he was." As a human being, a man, and a writer. Ever since Andersen's death in 1875, an immense amount has been written about his life and work. Many of the assertions with which we've grown up, which have been used for generations to evaluate Andersen, are based on a number of myths that the author himself helped to devise and perpetuate, partially to create a romantic distance to his true background, as mirrored in his last name.

In this book I will attempt a thorough investigation of these myths. Not to expose Andersen as a liar, but rather to understand the forces he was up against, both internal and external.

Some readers may be offended by the fact that in specific sections of the book I closely examine Andersen's puzzling sexuality, which even in our enlightened and emancipated times may seem bizarre or downright abnormal to certain people. Let me say that my intention here is not to pull Andersen down from his pedestal or to point fingers or to cause a sensation. Enough of that has already been done in regard to Andersen. Instead, I've tried to take him as he was, showing respect for all the multiplicities and caprices of human nature. This was something that Andersen himself supported, and which he expressed in his travel book *Shadow Pictures* from 1831, when he went out into the world for the first time and encountered humanity:

> "Since no leaf on a tree is a copy of another, should a human being, in all his naturalness, be a copy?"

Even though a life most often begins with a scream and ends with a sigh, I have chosen to organize my story of Andersen's life in such a way that it begins with the date that he fondly called his birthday: September 6, 1819. That was the day when he, at the age of fourteen, arrived in Copenhagen and when, as he said, the fairy tale of his life began. The reader will have to wait to hear about the author's childhood until Chapter Seven, which concerns the 1840s, when Andersen decided for the first time to make public a detailed account of his childhood. This occurred in his 1847 autobiography *The True Story of My Life*, which was first published in German and became the basis for *The Fairy Tale of My Life* in 1855.

Chapter Ten, which is the last chapter of my book, gathers up all the important threads of Andersen's life and work that are addressed in the previous chapters. It includes topics such as his relationship to art, to love and to both sexes, to faith and science and nature, and to the child within.

Hans Christian Andersen was tremendously aware of the educational trends of his day. This was especially true because in the 1820s he was enrolled in a school and subjected to an extensive, intellectual learning process in which his ungovernable emotions were constantly subordinated to the demand for reason and self-discipline. He managed to survive this culture shock too, and he actually learned a great deal. Quite prophetically, he wrote in one of his essay books from that period: "Free and pure—the way we imagine an angel—is how a human being starts out on his life's path; but things become strangely linked together; everything is involved in an eternal struggle and ferment."

The fact that I quote from original sources is not meant to make things difficult for the reader or to distance Andersen from our own time. Rather, it's an attempt to preserve an authenticity, to respect the speech patterns and writing styles of the Golden Age in Denmark, and at the same time to reflect Hans Christian Andersen's deeply personal and not always proper use of language. His writing style was often labeled by contemporaries as "unaesthetic," since it was much too colloquial and colored by imagination. It usually placed greater value on the content than on the demand for a specific form. Spelling mistakes and errors in punctuation were abundant in Andersen's work. In this area, as well, he was the way he was, and he took pride in it.

Each chapter in this book begins with a section in italic, which presents a little scene from Andersen's life that in biographical and scholarly terms is different from the rest of the book. There are ten such tableaux; they may not have been played out exactly as I relate them, and yet they do contain factual material, factual experiences, and factual statements. The sources and dates of these scenes—as with all other references cited—can be found in the Notes at the end of the book. Readers may choose to skip these italicized sections or to consider them as appetizers for the individual chapters.

I've never undergone a better education than during the four years it took me to write this book. In addition to the subject himself, I wish to thank a hundred years of inspiring Andersen research, to which this book is deeply indebted, as evidenced by the notes and bibliography. I would also like to thank the following institutions and individuals for making this project possible and for helping me along the way with discussions, criticism, and guidance:

The Carlsberg Foundation, The San Cataldo Association, The Association for Danish-Norwegian Cooperation, The Royal Library, Odense City Museums, *Berlingske Tidende*, Inger Andersen, Ida Collin, Gertrud Collin, Benedicte Collin Frederiksen, Kirsten Dreyer, Karsten Eskildsen, Joakim Garff, Lars Handesten, Johan de Mylius, Niels Oxenvad, Jørgen Skjerk, Ane Grum-Schwensen, Bruno Svindborg, and Henrik Wivel.

An especially warm thanks to Tom Alsing, Einar Askgaard, Klaus P. Mortensen, Johannes Riis, Mogens Rüdiger, my entire circle of family and friends, as well as Anders, Kathrine, Mathias, and—as always—Jette.

Jens Andersen
August 2003

Chapter One

Arrival (1819-1822)

"Please pay us a visit this evening, and you'll have a chance to see a young genius!"

These are the words of the invitation to Dr. Carl Otto sent by Fru Belfour on Norgesgade on an autumn day in 1819. The young doctor, who earlier in the year had defended his doctoral dissertation with bravura, promptly accepts the invitation, even though he is pressed for time. He's in the midst of final preparations for a European cultural tour which, over the next couple of years, will bring him into contact with many of the great artists and natural scientists of the day: Goethe, Jean Paul, Humboldt, and, in particular, the surgeon Guillaume Dupuytren, whose operations in Paris are witnessed by hundreds of French medical students. They all wait for the ritualistic moment when the flamboyant doctor cuts something off the patient, which he then, with a carefully calculated gesture, flings up to the rows of benches where the cheering students throw themselves on the treasures dripping with blood.

In his own medical practice, Carl Otto seldom reaches for the scalpel. Like the ancient Greeks who studied the earth or the sky with the naked eye and the power of the mind, he dreams of mapping human nature by means of clinical studies. The young doctor swears by phrenology, and he is completely convinced that by using a "craniometer"—to measure and feel the distances between the frontal bone and the parietal bone, the back of the skull and the temple—he can determine the most important aspects of an individual's psychological character. The young doctor is in the process of assembling a scientific collection of human skulls, and not many years will pass after his cultural tour before he has also started a journal for phrenology and published several books containing studies of craniums, some of which are those of criminals. These include the poisoner Peder Hansen Nissen, who killed his in-laws with rat poison; the five-time child murderer Ane Nielsdatter; and seven men who joined forces to set fire to an orphanage in Copenhagen. All of these heads are obtained by the doctor offering money under the table to the hangman out at Amager Commons after the executions.

Dr. Carl Otto belongs to the Romantic zeitgeist—a collector with a sense for the freaks of nature. He is convinced that it's not among the great masses of average Philistines but among the psychopaths, eccentrics, and those who are inclined toward "Genius-Fever" that he will find human destinies which diverge from the times and can tell him something fundamentally new about nature. For that reason he has taken a seat in the front row of Widow Belfour's apartment on Norgesgade on this autumn day in 1819, so as to "ad oculos" measure the skull of the youth whom his hostess has enthusiastically labeled "a pure young man," recently arrived in the city. He is hoping that this boy possesses the sort of genius nature that Henrich Steffens, the natural philosopher, has discussed: an individual who breaks through all rules thrown before him and who always blazes his own trail.

The doctor will not be disappointed. The ungainly boy is nearly six feet tall, lanky and loose-limbed, awkward in his movements. A type straight from the lowest strata of society, wrapped in a worn brown coat with sleeves that do not properly cover his long arms and fingers, which point down to a pair of enormous boots full of holes. He is wearing a gaudy cotton scarf, wound so tightly around his long neck that it looks as if his head with the blond hair is about to separate from his body. There is something apelike about the pale, gaunt face with the narrow, deep-set eyes. His cranium looks as if it could never have had the soft round shape of an infant's head. Dr. Otto judges the circumference of the skull to be approximately twenty-five inches and the mass of his brain to weigh three pounds, more or less evenly distributed between the back of the head, where the bestial instincts reside, and the front of the head, where the centers of intelligence, morals, and an individual's spiritual constitution are to be found.

The boy is remarkably spontaneous and openhearted. With the greatest innocence he declaims snippets from various comedies and poems, untroubled by the fact that he is being observed and studied. He sings, recites, and improvises wildly from the depths of his being. The Widow Belfour's guests are compelled to follow along with the boy's favorite dramatic scenes. When the guests are finally allowed to get up and go in to dinner, the boy stumbles over a door sill. And at the table he blithely stuffs sandwiches into his mouth and several times drops his knife and fork as he looks around in bewilderment, rattling off a steady, feverish stream of words.

"Geniuses are mysterious hieroglyphs," writes Dr. Otto many years later in his memoirs,[1] thinking about the head he would have liked to include in his huge collection of Danish craniums from the 19th century, which he donated to the University of Copenhagen. On that autumn evening in 1819 it's abundantly clear that the boy with the large, deeply etched physiognomy and the small, sunken eyes is not merely one of the many charlatans and conjurers of the day. He's not the kind who, at the marketplace, can make a roasted sheep's head bleat or snowballs burn, who can swallow bucketfuls of fire and ask riddles such as: "While you look for me and use your head to find my whereabouts, I am something. But as soon as you find me, I am nothing. Who am I?"

*Y*ES, WHO WAS HE, THIS STRANGE BOY? Where had he come from, and where was he going? That's what one of Dr. Carl Otto's good friends, the writer Just Mathias Thiele, asked himself one day as he sat in his lodgings on Gammel Strand and wrote out some of the folk legends and tales he had collected from the peasantry. Suddenly there was a loud knock on the door.

"Come in!" said Thiele, who was sitting with his back to the door and continued to write. Someone knocked even harder, and a moment later the door opened. In came, or practically fell, a tall, gaunt lad with a highly peculiar appearance. He stopped just inside the door and looked at Thiele, but then abruptly threw off his cap and flung out his arm. "May I have the honor of expressing my feelings for the theater in a poem which I myself have written?"

Before Thiele could manage to reply, his guest was in the midst of reciting a poem. He brought the last verse to an end with a sweeping bow, and without any sort of pause or transition, much less an introduction, he began performing a scene from Adam Oehlenschläger's play *Hagbarth and Signe*, acting out all the roles himself. Thiele sat there utterly speechless, astonished and enchanted. The youth was oblivious to his surroundings, becoming more and more lost in the world of illusions. At a breathless tempo he came to the end of the scene. The improvised epilogue that rounded out the whole performance was concluded with a deep theatrical bow, whereupon he grabbed his cap from near the door and vanished down the stairs without another word.[2]

The folklorist never forgot that astonishing encounter with the importunate but naively endearing person who—like Thiele himself—was a messenger between the inexhaustible imagination to be found in the folk tales from the countryside and the salons of the big city, where people with a certain affectation had begun to cultivate the historical and natural roots of humanity.

It wasn't until a couple of days after this unannounced visit that Thiele realized who the strange boy was. At a dinner given in town, other guests happened to mention similar unannounced visits made by a fourteen-year-old boy calling himself "Hans Christian Andersen" and claiming to be the son of a deceased shoemaker. He had recently left behind his poor mother in Odense, carrying a knapsack over his shoulder, which contained nothing more than dreams of performing at the Royal Theater and a child's faith in both Our Lord and the tales in which the hero always triumphs in the end. To be an actor was the only thing in life that he desired, he said. If that failed, then ballet or singing would have to be his profession. At any rate, he was determined to go on stage.

The theater's leading dancer of the day, Anne Margrethe Schall (also known as "Madame Schall"), the poet and critic Knud Lyne Rahbek, and Lord Frederik Conrad von Holstein—both of whom sat on the board of the Royal Theater—all received visits from the boy. His frail, sickly exterior quickly proved to be inversely proportional to his outspoken manner and the almost mulelike will that he exhibited whenever he planted his big boots full of holes on the doorsteps of the city's better families and was granted an interview. The solo dancer turned him away, convinced that he was more of a lunatic than a genius. The theater directors also had little patience with him. Holstein didn't think such a gaunt figure was suited to go on stage, to which the young Andersen boldly replied—as he tells it in his memoirs—that if His Lordship would hire him at a salary of 100 *rigsdaler* per year, he would undoubtedly make haste to grow fat!

Last but not least, the boy from Odense sought out the theater's newly appointed choirmaster and conductor, Giuseppe Siboni, at his home on Vingårdsstræde. On that day Siboni happened to be hosting a large dinner party with prominent guests such as the poet Jens Baggesen and the composer C. E. F. Weyse. At five o'clock, just as the guests were sitting down at the table, the boy knocked on the front door and was immediately shepherded out to the kitchen, where he was offered something to eat. This also gave him the opportunity to confide in the choirmaster's housekeeper, who was given the short version of his long, touching life story. Like most romantic stories, it was both edifying and, like the amber heart the boy wore on a string around his neck, full of faith, hope, and charity. It was his intention, the boy said, to be hired by the Royal Theater. That was actually the reason why he was now sitting in Choirmaster Siboni's kitchen, wearing his brown confirmation jacket, which had been made from the coat of his late father. He also wore a pair of trousers with the legs tentatively tucked into the tops of his boots, though they kept creeping up; an enormous ruffle on his shirt; and a hat that looked as if it had been plucked from the street and was now constantly falling over the boy's small eyes.

Hans Christian, as the boy was called, told his story of the humble, impoverished, but happy shoemaker's home in Odense, where he had come into the world fourteen years before in a marriage bed that had been constructed from the remnants of a deceased count's catafalque. With a few coins in his pocket and a bundle of clothes over his shoulder he had recently left his hometown. The boy talked about his kind old paternal grandmother back in Odense who had stood at the city gates to wave farewell on the day he left. She had always said that the boy should try to become a clerk because "that was rather distinguished." And at least he could win promotions and become something better than his wretched paternal grandfather. It's true that his grandfather had once had his own farm out in the country, but he had lost his mind and now roamed the streets of Odense, wearing an emperor's crown made of gold paper and trying to sell the strange little figurines he carved out of wood. The boy's father, who had died several years ago, was a kind and clever man who thought his son should never be forced into anything, but should become whatever he liked. For his own part, the father had preferred to read books all day long and go to war for Napoleon rather than sit year after year cobbling together wooden clogs in the low-ceilinged room that served as bedroom, parlor, and workshop. The boy's mother, who had now married another shoemaker, was of the opinion that Hans Christian should become a carpenter, tailor, or bookbinder, and thus had quite a different view of his upbringing. She had only allowed her son to leave home because one of the wise women, in whom she had great faith, had foretold at the boy's confirmation that the capital of the island of Fyn would one day be lit up by a gigantic torchlight procession in honor of her Hans Christian.

It was quite a fairy tale the lanky boy had to tell. After the housekeeper had dried her eyes, she went to the dining room to clear the table, and she then whispered to Siboni what she had just heard. Soon everyone at the table had voted to take a closer look at this curiosity.

This was the age not only of absolute monarchy but also philanthropy. Among the well-educated and the intellectuals there was a sophisticated sense and an alert eye for what was extraordinary in individual people. The highest honor that could be given anyone during this period, which was both rationalistic and romantic, was to call the person in question "a genius" or "an original."[3]

That was the main reason why the poor boy in Siboni's kitchen—and at many other places in Copenhagen where he would suddenly appear during September 1819—was not promptly thrown out amidst a hail of curses and abuse. That was what he was accustomed to back home in the streets of his childhood town, where he was often subjected to the derision and scorn of his peers because he was different. There was one thing

this boy had learned early on: if he gained admittance to the better bourgeois homes or to the palace, he would find a completely different understanding of and interest in a personality such as his. As the men at Siboni's
house said to each other while the dishes were cleared from the table, he
might be a "genuine savage."

A Son of Nature

Young Andersen must have done a remarkable job of promoting himself at Siboni's house on that evening in September 1819. At any rate, the
boy's appearance in the parlor was of decisive importance for his fate and
his career, which had been in imminent danger of ending before it even
began. The last of his money was gone, and a return home to Odense with
all the incumbent humiliations was fast approaching. It was all or nothing,
so the improviser put his heart and soul into it when he was allowed to
speak in the home of the choirmaster. His potpourri of songs, poems, and
drama on that evening was presumably a mixture of highbrow culture and
marketplace playacting. This was something that Andersen was fond of,
both as a young man and later in life, and he often made use of it in his
art. This was especially true whenever it was a matter of a stage performance, such as in *Preamble to the Carnival*, written for the popular Casino
Theater in 1853:

> Ladies and gentlemen, humble and great,
> Here comes a man you have to know
> My name resounds through Europe's streets
> My great-great-great-great grandfather
> Was Doctor Philippus Aureolus
> Theophrastus Bombastius Paracelsus . . .
> I am of his lineage, but more a genius,
> And without any boasting I say this. [4]

The fourteen-year-old Andersen probably didn't present himself in
such a self-confident or practiced manner, but the boy's repertoire on
that evening was a quaint blend of the high and the low: an aria from a
ballad opera, which he had learned back home in Odense from a visiting Frøken Hammer; a couple of ample scenes from plays by Ludvig
Holberg; as well as some home-brewed poems that no doubt sounded
both provincial and pathetic. According to Andersen's memoirs, he

ended up bursting into tears, utterly overwhelmed by the goodwill that was suddenly showered upon him on that fateful day. But isn't it also possible that the young improviser was overcome by his own art and emotions? At any rate, the manner in which he presented his texts personified the words of Herder, who says that song is a reflection of the savage himself:

> "All uncivilized peoples sing and take action; whatever they do, they sing, and they sing treatises . . . Nature has given them a single solace for the many words that oppress them, and a single substitute for the numerous so-called blessings that we enjoy: their love of freedom, their idleness, merriment, and song."[5]

Siboni's guests that evening included, as mentioned, the poet Jens Baggesen. He was one of the stars of Danish literature in the period 1800-1820 who had lost the battle to become Denmark's poet laureate to Adam Oehlenschläger. After the performance by the peculiar child of nature, the poet took the boy by the hand and asked him whether he wasn't afraid of being laughed at or criticized. The lad, still sniffling, shook his head vigorously, and then Baggesen looked around at the other guests and said in a deliberate and solemn voice: "I predict that he's going to make something of himself one day! But don't let it go to your head when the whole audience applauds you!" And everyone nodded in agreement when Baggesen concluded that such a rare guest was reminiscent of the pure, true naturalness that is lost with age and in human discourse.[6] Siboni promised at once to train the boy's bright, clear voice, which was not without possibilities. And the rest of the evening a deep plate was passed around, enabling Weyse to collect 70-80 *rigsdaler* for the strange songbird, who had landed at one of the city's fashionable parties in such an astonishing manner. The composer also took upon himself the responsibility of ensuring that the money would be paid out to the boy in allotments and that he would receive lessons in the German language and the educational basics. This, according to Choirmaster Siboni, was an essential prerequisite for succeeding at the king's theater.

No doubt the cosmopolitan Giuseppe Siboni—who was also a political refugee—knew what he was talking about. As a former tenor singer he had performed in Vienna, London, and at La Scala in Milan. He kept his word and provided free singing lessons and tried to train the boy's voice. The project had to be given up the following year when young Andersen's voice began to change, but until then the boy found a sort of home twice a week when he came "for leftovers" at Siboni's house. He ate the leftovers from the table of the choirmaster and conductor, and he was served meals up in the maids' room after running various errands in the city for Siboni, his Italian cook, and the servant girls of the house. One day when Andersen was told to carry a platter to the dinner table, Siboni stood up and went out to the kitchen to inform his staff that Andersen was not a servant. That was a great day, and from then on the boy appeared more often in the parlor, growing closer to Siboni and his family, including the choirmaster's niece, who was fond of drawing. She found an amusing model in the odd boy, especially when she dressed him in Siboni's sky-blue tunic with a purple, gold-embroidered toga. The stout lord of the house had worn the costume in Mozart's opera *Titus* when he performed for the first time in Copenhagen in January 1819. Now that Hans Christian had been admitted to the parlor, the boy also had an opportunity to listen to the choirmaster and to follow along with the music when the royal singers gathered for rehearsals, or Siboni directed various scenes from an opera.[7] The free German lessons, which had been one of Siboni's requirements, were arranged by Weyse through an agreement with a teacher named Bruun on Farvergade. He, like many others, was enchanted by the boy's fantastic stories and so—as it turned out later—he even neglected to ask for payment for the lessons.

As he stood there in Siboni's drawing room the young Hans Christian Andersen must have seemed like one of the wild-looking children that people during the Enlightenment loved to take in and cultivate as symbols of the Noble Savage. Outwardly filthy, ragged, and bestial; inwardly purer and nobler than so-called civilized people. It was almost as if all civilization had glanced right off this young lad with the talent for brilliant improvisation. He seemed utterly unaffected by—and ignorant of—everything having to do with breeding, morals, Christianity, and traditional conventions. In this son of nature there was apparently no inherited or innate refinement, but rather sheer, unadulterated sincerity. His hallmark was his primitiveness. As Jens Baggesen had been the first to point out, this presented a rare opportunity to test all the liberal, humane teachings of Rousseau and Fichte, which had very briefly found expression in Denmark's Struensee era in the late 18th century. Back then they had also exposed the paltry view of humanity held by the absolute monarchy, as well as its numerous repressive measures.

In the 1770s Rousseau had interpreted the natural state of the wild child—both in terms of the individual adult and the entire time period— as something that had been lost. The boy from Fyn was quite simply a Danish variation of the 18th century "Peter of Hannover," who was once found near Hannover, Germany, and then taken to the court of England's George I. There the wild boy was kept as a sort of pet and jester figure, and he attracted a great deal of attention from the authors, philosophers, and scientists of the Enlightenment. An even more recent example was "the wild boy of Aveyron"—a boy of ten or eleven who in 1800 emerged from the woods in the south of France and was brought to Paris, where every conceivable natural scientist, doctor, pedagogue, and anthropologist in Napoleonic France attempted to study and then civilize the boy. The same was later done with the mysterious foundling Kaspar Hauser. Both cases aroused great attention in the Romantic era and revived the discussions from the Enlightenment about the relationship between humans and animals. The debate was particularly fueled by the explorers who returned home from expeditions to the far corners of the world with new, fascinating reports of orangutans (which were thought to be human), savages and barbarians, Hottentots, and children who had been raised by animals.[8]

This fourteen-year-old boy, at once inept and talented, with the romantic destiny, who now stood in the elegant bourgeois home, presented an extremely interesting and welcome challenge in the blasé, slightly indolent spiritual and social life of the capital. After decades of absolute monarchy, Denmark's humiliating defeats in the war with England in 1807, and the national bankruptcy of 1813, Copenhagen had become a city in which people lived in a spiritual prison. As it says in the biography of another of the young artists of the day:

> "We harbored no doubts about the wisdom of the government, but held our hats in hand and our backs bowed to its officials. We quietly accepted what was inevitable or what was in any case impossible to avoid, and submitted to a patient, contented torpor, under which nothing ever happened and little was accomplished."[9]

The artists and scientists had all the more reason, sentiment, desire, and will to see possibilities in a boy with a natural though raw and unpolished talent. Here was something for observation and discussion in the absolute monarchy's Copenhagen, something that interested the rationalists, republicans, and Romantics, including the professor and poet Frederik Høegh-Guldberg. He was the brother of one of the boy's greatest benefactors back home in Odense, Lieutenant Colonel Christian Høegh-Guldberg, and at one time he took up his own collection in Copenhagen on behalf of Andersen. On that occasion the boy had again aroused attention when he insisted on going around to thank in person all his benefactors, most often giving them a spirited little improvisation, exactly as he had done for Just Mathias Thiele. If he was clever enough to squeeze his big foot in the door, he was also smart enough to show his gratitude, in keeping with one of the popular tunes of the day: "My son, if you want to get ahead in the world, then bow!"

All these strategic forays swiftly brought Andersen out to "Bakkehus," the meeting place and cultural hub of the intellectual circles. Everyone associated with the Danish Golden Age of art and science frequently gathered there with the owners of the house, the artist couple Kamma and Knud Lyne Rahbek. At the time, Bakkehus stood outside Copenhagen's ramparts, a refreshingly long walk away from the city center, out in God's free nature near Valby Hill, where everyone, regardless of social class or ancestry, could enjoy the same sunshine and the same fresh air. On his way to this paradise, Hans Christian had to walk through Vesterbro, past all the comedy theaters, menageries, shooting galleries, and carnival booths with strongmen and giant women, live seal pups in tubs, calves with two heads, and lambs with five legs. Farther out, he passed the house where Oehlenschläger was born, the restaurants on Pile Allé, and Frederiksberg Castle, where half of Copenhagen would gather on Sundays to listen to music outside the palace and watch the royal family sail along the canals with King Frederik VI, dressed in his admiral's uniform, at the tiller.[10]

Not far from there, out in the open and with a view of the city, stood Bakkehus, where everyone was in many ways refreshingly free from the omnipresent repression of ideas and deeds under the absolute monarchy. And out there it was easy to entertain the heretical thought that nature certainly could—yes, perhaps even ought to—replace the law books and the Bible. In their home the Rahbeks had created an indoor and outdoor salon culture, in which the zeitgeist was more or less always being debated. Out there Rationalism and Romanticism were not incompatible opposites. And for the majority of the writers, painters, philosophers, politicians, and scientists who came to Bakkehus, "emotion" ranked equally with "reason." Spirit resided in nature, as it was expressed by one of the regular guests, the physicist H. C. Ørsted, who discovered electromagnetism in 1820. Beauty and truth were to be found in the mountains, the sea, the woods, as well as in lightning and thunder, magnetism, and the human body and soul. This was something known and acknowledged by most of the luminaries who convened out there at Bakkehus. Participants included Adam Oehlenschläger; Ørsted and his brother, the jurist Anders Sandøe Ørsted; the writer Johan Ludvig Heiberg; and the composer C. E. F. Weyse. From the civil servant class came the ever-diligent and respected businessman and philanthropist Jonas Collin with all his well-mannered children: Ingeborg, Gottlieb, Edvard, Louise, and Theodor, who were so cultivated that Kamma Rahbek instantly dubbed them "The Thousand Thank-yous." [11]

It was among this cultured company, which in many ways was a microcosm of the Danish Golden Age, that the young Hans Christian Andersen now made his entrance. He was a real provincial "Clumsy Hans" who—as it says in one of his mother's letters from the 1820s—"lands on his head right in the middle of the big world." [12] He was exactly like some of the fairy-tale characters in his later works and in his colorful paper-cuts, who also tumble around in the modern world after having been released from underground. The goal was to create a new life for himself, and a new identity. The basis for this was to be the irresistible fairy tale of his romantic childhood, which all the distinguished Copenhagen citizens swallowed whole. They did so primarily because the extraordinary story of the boy's life fit hand in glove with the prevailing ideas and educational ideals of the milieu to which the determined boy sought admittance. The perception of being a "Son of Nature" and an "Aladdin," as the favorite of the ages was called in Oehlenschläger's play, was one of the era's great illusions, and Andersen gladly played along with this perception. As he later wrote in his memoirs: "I must have been a remarkable child of nature, quite a unique revelation, not to mention a 'presence.'" [13] With an astonishingly clear insight into the zeitgeist and a well-developed sense for who should be influenced, where, when, and how, the fourteen-year-old boy from Fyn threw himself into the greatest and most important endeavor of his life: to establish contacts with the leading citizens of Copenhagen and learn how to create and make a name for himself in their art and culture.

According to Andersen himself, his very first foray was directed at the solo dancer Anna Margrethe Schall, who lived on Bredgade. He brought her a recommendation from the book printer and newspaper publisher Herr Iversen, who may have been an important man in Odense but was largely unknown in Copenhagen. At any rate, he was unknown to the solo dancer, who had never heard of the publisher of the newspaper *Fyens Stifts Avis*. In *The Fairy Tale of My Life* and in other, shorter memoirs, Andersen describes the astounding scene when he went to visit the solo dancer and immediately pulled off his boots so he could sing and dance the tender part of the female lead in Isouard's popular ballad opera *Cendrillon*. A contemporary critic described the opera as a noble and "ingratiating expression of naïveté, childish innocence, deep emotion, chivalrous spirit, and beautiful, outlandish reverie."[14] The play, which recounts the story of Cinderella, had taken Copenhagen by storm in the 1812-13 season. The following summer it became a nationwide triumph, with performances in other cities, including Odense. That was where the young Hans Christian witnessed all the songs and dances of the opera, because he had finagled himself a part as an extra, dressed as a page in red silk trousers.

This stood him in good stead in Madame Schall's parlor in 1819, where every single scene, line, dance step, and tap on the tambourine—and here the boy had to use his hat—was performed inside and out, with sweeping, expressive gestures and emotion. Little leaps and loud slaps on his hat emphasized the painful subtext—also for Andersen—of the key words: "What do riches mean, / what is splendor and magnificence?"[15] That was not something Madame Schall could tell him, and she was equally uncomprehending and alarmed when confronted with this strange person and his terribly primitive interpretation of a classic ballerina role, with which the dancer was quite familiar. Surely the boy was mad. She quickly ushered him out with a few words about speaking to director Bournonville on his behalf. With tears in his eyes, the boy thanked her, offering to run errands in town for her in the future if she would help him.[16]

The Courage to Have Talent

"It takes courage to have talent," wrote the young Danish critic Georg Brandes in a brilliant essay about Hans Christian Andersen published six years before the death in 1875 of the world-famous author of fairy tales.[17] Brandes was the highly gifted man of letters who was quite familiar with the international literary scene and would soon become the standard-bearer for Naturalism and "The Modern Breakthrough." In his articles he dared to reproach the world-famous author of fairy tales by saying that there was no other writer in the entire kingdom who had damaged Danish literary criticism as much as he had, primarily because he had always had the courage to have talent. Right from the start.

When a poor, fatherless, and introverted boy of fourteen—"a pup so tall that you could break him in half and make two pups out of him," as it says in Andersen's last novel from 1870[18]—conceives the idea that he's going to be famous and, trusting in the abilities that Our Lord has given him, then sets out in the world to realize his dream, his life will be shaped as a series of tests. Achieving fame is seldom a smooth process, especially for someone who is destitute. No matter how brilliant his talents, he has to have an unfailing faith in his calling and abilities. Without certain physical and psychological strengths, his talent will be crushed under the struggles of life. Andersen himself has told the story many times, for instance in the novel *Only a Fiddler* from 1837. In his portrait of Christian the musician, we have quite a precise description of an individual who never manages to realize his brilliant potential because he lacks the will and the courage to have talent—not to mention benefactors. Andersen described his own departure from Odense in early September 1819, which became increasingly shrouded in legend over the years, in his first autobiography from 1832. This book, which was not intended for publication, was first discovered fifty years after the author's death and published in Denmark.

"I then decided, like the heroes in all the tales I had read, to set off, all alone, out into the world. I was quite calm because I trusted blindly in Our Lord, who would undoubtedly look out for me. After all, things always went well in the comedies and stories."[19]

Hans Christian was confirmed in April 1819, and by then he had reached a point in his life where he had to do what was right for himself, even if it might be dangerous and require courage. So in early September of that year, he left Odense with a few possessions, a travel pass, and a letter of recommendation from Herr Iversen the book printer. After the voyage across the Great Belt in the pitching sloop and the subsequent long coach ride from Korsør to Copenhagen, Hans Christian quickly encountered everything that was cause for alarm in a big city, although there were also a few comforting signs. For example, the Royal Theater opened its season on September 6—the same day on which the boy arrived. He was deposited outside the city gates, and then found lodgings at an inn on Vestergade.

From the ramparts surrounding Copenhagen, it was possible to see all the way to the Swedish coast to the east, while to the north there was a view of Svanemølle Bay, Charlottenlund, and—in good weather—the copper dome of Bernstorff Castle. Farther out to the north was the rolling countryside with farms and small towns, Bispebjerg Mill on Frederikssund highway, and the estate Bellahøj. People with exceptional eyesight claimed that to the west they could also catch a glimpse of the slender spire of Roskilde Cathedral.

In contrast to its picturesque surroundings—the sea, the green ramparts, lakes, fields, and forests—the interior of Copenhagen was not an attractive sight in 1819. It's true that in certain ways Copenhagen was a small, securely sleepy city of approximately 100,000 inhabitants. On the other hand, there were four times as many rats and thousands of other larger animals. Horses and cows lived in such great numbers within the city gates that in some buildings it was necessary to construct stables on the second floor, which meant that the animals had to be hoisted up and down. Fierce, thin dogs could be seen roaming everywhere. People and animals were crowded together in wretchedly paved streets with no sewers, where the deep gutters were always filled with rainwater, food scraps, and excrement, which at regular intervals would pour into the cellar living quarters whenever there was a heavy rain. This meant that countless numbers of epidemic diseases flourished in Copenhagen around 1820. Contemporary descriptions of the city mention "gastric and typhoid fever, measles, roseola, influenza, catarrh, diarrhea, and dysentery." Yet the doctor was rarely called in; for the most part he belonged to the upper classes. If one of the doctors for the poor was summoned, he had to be prepared to crawl on his knees to tend to the sick, who lay packed together in dark garret rooms.

In other words, if a person did not spend his daily life behind the elegant facades of the palaces, estates, and bourgeois abodes surrounding Kongens Nytorv, the Danish capital was an unspeakably filthy and unhealthy place. All those human beings crowded into such a small space, less than ten square meters per person, meant that Copenhagen was always teeming with people and animals, who were all penned in for a large part of the time. Between nine at night and seven in the morning, no one was allowed to pass through the city gates and ramparts, which marked the border between city and countryside. In the narrow dark streets lined with shops, the view was limited to the walls of the buildings and street corners. Signs hung from the facades with symbols for all sorts of professions: scissors for tailors, boots for shoemakers, keys for locksmiths, horseshoes for smiths, and basins for barbers.[20]

Also prevalent among the urban populace were the more bestial instincts. Morals were as lax as might be expected in a capital with so many unemployed and idle individuals, including soldiers, servant girls, apprentices, drunks, whores, and pickpockets of both sexes and all ages. Drunkenness, fornication, fraud, gambling, theft, and the fencing of stolen goods were all the order of the day. Prostitution was on the rise in the early 19th century, as was divorce, and illegitimate births made up more than one-fourth of all births in Copenhagen. Casual relationships between the sexes had, in other words, become an ingrained part of social life, in both the lowest and the highest classes.

When Andersen arrived in Copenhagen on September 6, 1819, it was as a "stowaway," which did not mean that he had cheated, but that he had paid the lowest fare of three *rigsdaler*. And for that reason he was set down outside Vesterport. He then took his time walking to the top of Frederiksberg Hill, where he could see and count all the towers in the king's city. Some of them had been standing for years, while others had been rebuilt after the heavy bombardment by the British in 1807, when shells and firebombs had rained down upon the city. The national bankruptcy in 1813, after the humiliating wars with England and the subsequent economic crisis, had left its mark on the city and the country. A sharp line between rich and poor had been drawn in Denmark—a line that the paternal King Frederik VI was intent on maintaining. Young Andersen had once seen the absolute monarch in Odense when the king was passing through. That was in June 1818. The shoemaker's son had climbed up on the church wall and, awestruck, had peered at the mighty man. But he was disappointed because the king wore neither gold nor silver but was dressed in a simple blue cape and a red velvet collar, making him look more like a soldier. It was only as an old man that Andersen first spoke of this encounter with the king, after which he had said to his mother: "Oh, but he's just a human being!" The pious and loyal woman had promptly hushed the lad, who was starting to take too much after his liberal-minded and outspoken father. She said, "Have you lost your mind, boy!"[21]

The Royal Theater in Copenhagen served as both a symbolic and tangible stage in the whole illusion about what life was like for Danes under God and the rule of the kings in their native country, and governed by the lords, who, in spite of the abolition of serfdom in 1788, still wielded great influence and power in the countryside. Night after night during the long, boring winter, plays were performed at the theater for the upper classes. The king sat in his customary, elevated seat in the theater, and just below him sat the nobility, ministers, and government officials, as well as writers such as Adam Oehlenschläger, B. S. Ingemann, and—in time—Johan Ludvig Heiberg, Henrik Hertz, and Hans Christian Andersen, who could all make the people forget about the economic recession and enjoy themselves for a few hours. The Royal Theater was the only public theater, and there were performances nine months of the year, up to six times a week. The theater could seat 1,300 to 1,400 people. In addition, the drama school students, including at one time the dance pupil Hans Christian Andersen, gave a number of Sunday matinées during the year at the Court Theater in Christiansborg Castle. Several private theaters also existed, as well as traveling troupes, whose actors were often amateurs. It was truly the age of the theater! Everyone performed comedies, and that's what everyone wanted to see. As a historian expressed it in the 1890s as he attempted to describe the theater mania around 1820:

> "Quite a good interplay exists between the stiltedness that character-izes the whole public tone of the day and the passion not only to see but to act in comedies. The naïve and the artificial entered into an insepara-ble union and determined the tastes of the time." [22]

The world of the theater did not open for Andersen quite as easily as he may have imagined it would after his first successful performance at the home of Choirmaster Siboni in September 1819. The boy's perception of his own artistic potential and limitations had no basis in reality. At any rate, there was an enormous gulf between the cozy parlors in Odense belong-ing to Widow Bunkeflod and Lieutenant Colonel Høegh-Guldberg, who had always praised and encouraged the boy, and the drama school at the king's own theater, where the law of the jungle reigned every hour of the day. Back home in Odense, Hans Christian's mother had actually known what she was talking about when she once told him that the theater path was no bed of roses but rather a laborious process. You risked starving to death to be light on your feet, and you were given oil to drink to make your limbs supple. [23]

At the theater's drama school the shoemaker's son was no longer the gifted only child but merely one more talented young person among many others with greater talent. And, for the most part, they were much more expressive and genuine on stage than he was. Young Andersen, with his naive faith in the good Lord and his own boundless abilities, had not taken this into account. He discusses this in his novel *Only a Fiddler*, in which the talented young violinist Christian tries his luck in Copenhagen. He too has become enamored of the theatrical world. At his first encounter with this mecca on Kongens Nytorv, it's said that he might well have gone over to the ticket office and stuck his head all the way inside the window, in the belief that the ticket window was the very framework and space in which he would see the comedy.[24] In spite of everything, the fourteen- or fifteen-year-old Andersen did not have quite such a primitive concept of what the theater was like. But he had no idea at all what was required to become a dancer or singer at the Royal Theater. Time after time he made himself ridiculous on stage during 1820–21. He was also humiliated, mocked, and tormented by teachers and students alike at the theater. With expert eyes they universally appraised him as a creature who lacked all mastery of his movements, and it quickly became clear that he could be used only close to the wings, where it was a matter of keeping his mouth shut and concentrating on carrying torches, weapons, and flower bouquets without dropping them or stumbling in his costume.

Back in Odense the boy had always playacted. In fact, daily life *was* a theater for such a sensitive and imaginative boy, who needed only a piece of cloth and a stick to transform himself into a knight battling dragons. Down by the river he would improvise his little nature dramas with numerous roles, all of which he played himself. When he visited the pastor's kindly widow, Fru Bunkeflod, who lived right across from Shoemaker Andersen on Munkemøllestræde, he heard not only about the art of poetry and read many classic dramas, but he also learned to sew costumes for his puppets. Andersen grew up in the spotlight of the lively, "real" theater. Odense had a theater of its own, and during the summer months many traveling theater companies came to town. They always found a large and appreciative audience in Denmark's second-largest city, even though the quality of the performances varied, ranging from the professional summer tours of the Royal Theater to amateur troupes from both Denmark and abroad, offering dilettante productions, dance, juggling, and acrobatics.

During his childhood Andersen had many opportunities to take a look at the work of the more or less professional actors who came to Odense, performing plays by Holberg, Wessel, and Kotzebue. Occasionally he would go to a play with a local actor, also a clerk at the prefect's office, who had taken an interest in the peculiar lad with his fondness for the theater. Or Hans Christian might sneak into the wings and beg for a job as an extra, which meant not only that he would be admitted free but that he would also be rewarded with a place up on stage. In all his memoirs, Andersen describes his most celebrated childhood role in the aforementioned *Cendrillon* when, dressed as a page in red silk trousers, he had ample opportunity to study all the dance steps that he later performed in such an original fashion in his stocking feet at the home of Madame Schall, the solo dancer in Copenhagen. On another occasion a visiting acting troupe advertised for extras. The children were supposed to present themselves in long white shirts with black borders, and the six- or seven-year-old Andersen performed for two evenings in this costume. After the play, when several ladies out on the street laughed at the boy's attire, Hans Christian's mother, both offended and proud, replied: "He's an actor in a comedy at the real theater!"[25]

Another way to gain free admittance to the various theaters in Odense was to become a placard carrier. That was why, early on, the boy allied himself with the town's placard carrier, Peter Junker. Even if this didn't give him a ticket to a seat in the promised land, he could still sit at home in a warm corner with the placard. And with the help of the plays' exotic titles and the actors' melodious names, he could conjure up a drama, the likes of which the world had never seen. "This was my first unconscious attempt at writing," Andersen says in *The Fairy Tale of My Life*, in which he also talks about whole plays that he would memorize or piece together in the course of a day. In terms of his own productions, Hans Christian was not only the author, director, and set designer, but also the tailor, dresser, and press officer. In the back of his father's military account book for 1812-13, the seven-year-old budding dramatist lists the titles of no less than twenty-five plays that he has either written or—for the most part—intends to write. In his memoirs Andersen mentions his tragedy *Abor and Elvire*, in which all the characters of the play die, one after the other, because that's what always happened in the plays he had seen and read! The intrigue for this play was taken from an old ballad about Pyramus and Thisbe in a school textbook:

> "Elvire awaited her Abor, but when he did not come, she hung her necklace on a hedge to show that she had been there and went for a short walk. Abor arrived, thought that Elvire had been killed by a wild animal, and killed himself. Then Elvire appeared and was supposed to die of grief, but since the whole play didn't yet fill more than half a page, I made a hermit come in to tell her that his son had seen her in the forest and had fallen in love with her. To touch Elvire's heart, and because I didn't know any better, I made him speak exclusively in scriptural passages taken from *Balle's Catechism*. Then the son appeared and killed himself because of love. Elvire followed suit, and the old man exclaimed: 'Death do I apprehend / in all my limbs!' whereupon he too succumbed. I was particularly fond of this work and read it to anyone who would listen."[26]

One of the people to whom young Andersen read his play was the neighbor woman on Munkemøllestræde. She sarcastically suggested that he call it "Perch and Cod" [the Danish word for perch is *aborre*]. When he indignantly told his mother about the neighbor's remark, she told Hans Christian not to mind—the woman was merely jealous because her own son would never be able to write such a play. Otherwise the neighbors offered both help and inspiration. Another play, which the shoemaker's boy never completed, was supposed to include numerous royal personages, but unfortunately he was not at all sure how he should present the more refined speaking style that royalty would use. Hans Christian then sought the advice of his neighbors, who felt that kings and queens would undoubtedly speak in many foreign languages. The pragmatic young dramatist instantly acquired an old lexicon containing scores of German, English, and French phrases, and all of a sudden he was able to speak on behalf of royalty. Stylistic concerns, also relating to grammar and punctuation, had no effect on the boy's imagination, so the play opens with the princess offering a nonsensical morning greeting to her father. The splendid line, with its childish appetite for the whole world, is so unmistakably typical of Andersen, and it anticipates the cosmopolitan—and at times Babel-like—embrace of the globe embodied by his later life and work:

"*Guten Morgen, mon père!* Have you had good *sleeping?*"[27]

Dance Pupil

Many of Andersen's childhood dreams and illusions were shattered during his first years in Copenhagen as he, Apollo-like, tested his forces and sought transfiguration in the art of the theater. Yet there were some bright moments in the gathering darkness. In 1821 the stubborn young man seized upon hope when Crown Princess Caroline herself heard rumors about the odd, talented boy and expressed her desire to see and hear him at Frederiksberg Castle. It was an unforgettable day. Hans Christian Andersen sang and declaimed so it was sheer delight, and afterwards he was rewarded with fruit and cakes, as well as a paper twist filled with candy and ten shiny *rigsdaler*. He promptly dropped the paper twist, and the candy rolled across the floor at the feet of the princess. Utterly unperturbed, as if he were out on the street, the boy threw himself onto his hands and knees and scooped up the sweets, which merely amused the Crown Princess all the more. Happy and bearing his rewards, Andersen then strolled home through Frederiksberg Gardens, where he sat down under one of the budding beech trees. He sampled his treats and then impulsively threw his arms around a tree, kissed the bark, and spoke to the branches, the birds, and the flowers, proceeding to sing joyfully at the top of his lungs. "At that moment I was a child of nature," the adult Andersen recounts in his memoirs. Others didn't take quite as positive a view of the happy Pan. "Are you out of your mind?" shouted a stable boy to Andersen, who slunk homeward in embarrassed silence.[28]

In a physical sense he often suffered great need during the period 1820-21. There were times when he didn't have proper food, but he was familiar with deprivation from his childhood, and he managed to get by, though he was often on the verge of starvation. There was nothing new about being tormented, impoverished, or hungry, or in living right next door to criminals and prostitutes. During the first turbulent days after his arrival in 1819, when Hans Christian had spent all his money and was try-ing to gain an audience with those in power at the Royal Theater, he also sought out a certain Madame Hermansen. They had been fellow travelers in the mail coach to Copenhagen, and she not only offered the shoemak-er's boy from Odense food and lodging, she helped him figure out how he could most quickly earn some money. At that time he had not yet encoun-tered any goodwill among the theater people, and so he had few choices. Either he would have to find a skipper to take him back to Fyn or he would have to become an apprentice to a Copenhagen craftsman. The boy chose the latter on September 17, 1819, when Madame Hermansen showed him a little announcement in the newspaper *Adresseavisen*: "Sturdy fellow of honest parents who wishes to learn the cabinetmaking profession should report to Borgergade 104, second floor."

In his memoirs, the adult Andersen recounts that he arrived, "bashful as a maiden," at the cabinetmaker's workshop at six the next morning. But his sensitive skin soon collided with a harsh and filthy wall of Copenhagen journeymen with an endless repertoire of raw and vulgar jokes. The new apprentice was a tasty morsel for the taunts of the apprentices and jour-neymen. What a shrimp and sissy he was; he couldn't even manage to pull the big saw! This was all too reminiscent of what he had experienced back home at the clothing factory in Odense when a workman heard him singing in his clear, delicate voice and suddenly said: "That's no boy, it's a little maiden!" Whereupon all the others had lifted Hans Christian up onto a table and pulled down his pants.

"I screamed and wailed, the other workmen found the vulgar joke amusing, they held me by the arms and legs. I shrieked, wild with fear, and shy as a girl I dashed out of the building and home to my mother, who promised me at once that I would never have to go back there again."[29]

But in 1820-21 in Copenhagen, there was no mother for Hans Christian to run home to, nor was he suited to be a cabinetmaker, and so he was forced to depend on charity and live in wretched conditions in one of Copenhagen's red-light districts. Andersen found lodgings with a Madame Thorgesen, who owned a four-story building at the narrow, infamous end of Ulkegade (later named Holmensgade and today known as Bremerholm). His room was a pantry with no window and barely enough space for a bed. Whenever he wasn't at the theater or the drama school he would sit in this pantry with books from J. C. Lange's Lending Library and daydream his way into much larger worlds. Or he would reconstruct his childhood puppet theater and sew puppet costumes from scraps of silk and velvet he had begged as fabric samples from the elegant shops on Østergade. Like many of the other women in the building, Madame Thorgesen lived a mysterious night life. Men of all ages came and went— some more refined and incognito than others—as the sixteen-year-old boy looked on, apparently uncomprehending. Judging by the memoirs of the adult Andersen, he had no awareness of the shady, unsavory side of love as it was being practiced right outside the door of his pantry.

"I lived in happy dreams, paying almost no attention to the demoralizing surroundings that daily intersected with my life . . . only now, as a grown-up, do I realize what an abyss it was, in the true sense of the word, where I played and dreamed."[30]

Madame Thorgesen was a stern, no-nonsense widow who, in contrast to all the refined acquaintances the poor boy had made, refused to be charmed by the boy's touching life story when he had no money for the exorbitant rent. From the beginning she stood firm with her demand for 20 *rigsdaler* a month for room and board. Andersen had been forced to give as good as he got and use his magic to get the rent lowered. He fixed a penetrating stare on the picture of Madame Thorgesen's deceased husband, which hung in her parlor, and prayed to the dead man in the painting, who actually looked quite kind and gentle, asking him to persuade his wife: "I even rubbed some of my tears on the eyes of the painting so he could feel how bitterly I was crying."[31]

Andersen lived for a year and a half in that pantry on the second floor of Madame Thorgesen's house, but in September 1821 her finances became so tenuous that she advised the boy to seek food and lodging up on the third floor with Madame Henckel, who was the wife of a coxswain.

Uncertainty soon spread to all areas of the boy's life in the capital. Choirmaster Siboni had long since ended his agreement with young Andersen when the boy's voice suddenly began to change. Nothing was working out for him at the ballet school or at the Court Theater, either, where Andersen had wormed his way in as a "dance pupil" during the 1820-21 season. Yet all the toil was worth it for the theater-obsessed lad, because as a dance pupil he had free admittance every third evening to the female dance pupils' gossip-box on the fourth floor of the theater on Kongens Nytorv. There he would sit in "peculiar company and often hear peculiar things, but my soul was pure and my thoughts lived and breathed nothing but the theater."[32] The ballet and acting pupil was proud of his free access, and no less of his tights in his musician's role for the ballet *Nina*, which was one of Madame Schall's most celebrated parts. Andersen was allowed to perform in this ballet, primarily due to his height, on January 11, 1821. It was his debut, and by early afternoon he was already in costume. Pleased as punch, and wearing long red stockings and thin-soled ballet slippers, he pranced across Kongens Nytorv to the home of the royal watchmaker Jürgensen on Østergade. The boy was accustomed to visiting Jürgensen's mother now and then, so she could see and admire the pupil in his musician's outfit.[33]

Even back then Andersen was a great poseur. Many years later—in a conversation with one of his young traveling companions—he described another, special evening at the theater during his time as an aspiring dancer. The king was in his box that night, and Andersen, wearing his lovely new tights, slowly worked his way forward during one act, all the way to the front of the stage, so that His Majesty up in the royal box would be able to have a good look at him. The king peered down with astonishment at the odd boy, who was not in the least embarrassed or bashful under the king's scrutiny. This was primarily because the boy himself was preoccupied with studying Adam Oehlenschläger; he had suddenly caught sight of the great writer in the orchestra seats and had fallen in love with him.[34]

The ballet training was hard on Andersen. The usual pedagogical practice was to let the youngest pupils learn from the older ones ahead of them. It demanded great concentration and discipline from the pupils, both of which were in short supply at the Royal Ballet around 1820. Threats of being confined to their quarters or expelled outright constantly hung over the heads of those young dancers who, as it said in a decree posted in the Court Theater, "waste time with games and noise, and forget the esteem they owe to those who have been appointed by the king as their teachers and closest authorities."[35] It's not difficult to imagine the ambitious but impatient Andersen occasionally skipping over the tedious practice sessions as well as the ranks of pupils ahead of him in order to move as quickly and as high up in the theater as possible. In his typical impetuous style, and with his equally sure sense for finding a sympathetic and tender maternal heart, he pushed his way to the very forefront of the ranks in the home of ballet master Dahlén and his family on Badstuestræde. Here the young Andersen promptly lay siege to the ballet master's kindly wife, who was an actress. For a period in 1821 he was an almost daily visitor, dining with the family and playing with the Dahlén daughters, who loved Andersen's puppet theater performance of *Rolf Bluebeard*, which he had rewritten as an opera.

But even with these private gestures of support, and in spite of many mornings spent on the ice-cold stage of the Court Theater, where the ballet school practiced, with fifteen-year-old Andersen standing at the long barre, trying to stretch his legs and do a *battement*, he never managed to be more than a fierce troll in ballet master Dahlén's four-act ballet *Armida*. A bit more fire and "vivacity," as the older and more experienced dancers said, would presumably have brought the boy to a more prominent position on stage in Dahlén's ballet, which had its premiere on April 12, 1821. August Bournonville attended the performance with his father, and many years later he described it in his memoirs as a huge fiasco, also declaring Carl Dahlén to be a hopelessly superannuated dancer and "ballet director," whose talent had consisted primarily of engaging scores of new pupils so as to dress them as cupids and trolls in his own large-scale ballet productions.[36]

In the program for *Armida*, Andersen's name finally appeared in print for the first time. In the right-hand column at the bottom, it says "Trolls . . . Herr Andersen." Other dancers included: "Cupids . . . Johanne Petcher." This misspelled maiden name belonged to Johanne Luise Heiberg (née Pätges), who would eventually become the great Danish star of the stage. Several decades later, she would make life miserable for the dramatist Hans Christian Andersen, but that's something we'll return to in Chapter Six. The month of April in 1821 was a stellar moment for the young extra, whose name had finally appeared in print.

> "It was a milestone in my life when my name was printed; I thought it signified a nimbus of immortality. All day long at home I kept looking at the printed letters. I took the ballet program to bed with me that night, lay near the light, and stared at my name, putting it down only to pick it up again; what bliss!"[37]

Armida was a so-called heroic ballet in four acts that, in addition to war and love, dealt with "seeing your fate in the mirror of truth." The rather sensationalist play took place in a harsh landscape in a distant, heathen time and made generous use of themes from Homer, including the story of the sorceress Circe, who uses cunning to detain the men on their way home to their families. In Dahlén's play the sorceresses are named Armida and Ismene. They live on an island that is one day attacked by hostile soldiers, led by Ubaldo, who is searching for his lost friend and comrade-in-arms Rinaldo. It turns out, of course, that he has fallen into the clutches of Armida, and Ubaldo then sets out to drive out the many agile sorcerers guarding the island.[38] And it was here that Andersen the dance pupil suddenly came into the picture. In the heat of the battle, he and the other sorcerers, "with loud shrieks," were supposed to flee through the grove, which meant diagonally across the stage, and then disappear in all directions. This was just the thing for an improviser like Andersen. Things went splendidly, up until the grand finale. Huge boulders were supposed to crash down onto the stage while all the sorcerers performed their finale dance, which according to the script would end with them "falling among the piles of rocks in various ghastly positions and groups." Unfortunately, Andersen fell so hard and with such drama at the premiere that, as Bournonville reported, he plunged headfirst into a crack in the rocks. And that's where he remained when the curtain went down and the majority of the audience waited in hushed expectation.

Bournonville, who was the same age as Andersen, remembered that the final reaction to the play "was not marked by any clear expressions of displeasure, but with an ominous snickering." The fiasco could not be blamed entirely on a single unfortunate pupil, however, since the main roles had been put in the hands of such experienced forces as Madame Schall, who according to Bournonville "had ceased to look young or lovely." As for ballet master Dahlén, it was said with even more deadly effect that he "had already long since acquired the privilege of arousing merriment."[39]

Other performances that Andersen gave as an extra also had unfortunate results. His voice was changing, and in 1820-21 he had to settle for a couple of chances to be a "choir extra," which simply meant that he would walk on stage with the choir but would keep his mouth shut while the others sang. He was there merely to fill up space and make the choir look bigger, to mime and gesticulate along with the real singers. Here again the boy was plagued, teased, and mocked, both when the curtain was up and when it was down. A malicious singer stuffed the boy's mouth with snuff when he was supposed to perform and beat him when Andersen later complained to the directors. To be a pupil at the Royal Theater's drama school was, on the whole, a hellish experience. Especially for those, like Andersen, who were there because of outside patronage and went on stage only in a pinch, as pages, shepherds, halberdiers, trolls, peasants, and soldiers, with no lines to speak, although on lucky occasions they might carry a weapon or help pull a triumphal wagon. The tone behind the curtain was raw and vulgar, and—as theater historian Thomas Overskou writes—the interaction between male and female members was "spiced with lurid improprieties." Many of the men drank like pigs, while the women, in particular the scantily clad ballerinas, were the lovers of distinguished and powerful men. There was a good deal of whispering in the corners about orgies with one of the king's adjutants. Another open secret was the scandalous relationship between Madame Schall and Privy Councilor Frederik Julius Kaas, who most assuredly was married, though not to the solo dancer.[40]

The relationship between the established artists and the aspiring pupils was particularly tense. After one of his first performances in the fall of 1820, when Andersen had been shoved out on stage with practically anyone who could be found among the pupils, machine operators, and random stage-hands to fill out a marketplace scene, the older actor Johan Daniel Bauer heavily ridiculed the tall, thin extra with the comical appearance. He took Andersen by the hand and led him up to the footlights to face the huge theater, which was now empty. There Bauer gestured grandly and shouted: "Allow me to introduce you to the Danish people, sir!"

The terrified drama pupils and the older, self-confident actors, singers, and dancers formed two widely different castes, and the old-timers treated the young people like slaves. They might suddenly decide to jab a pin deep into the calf of a student, making him practically leap on stage in his flesh-colored tights. Afterwards the student would be met with the scornful, cold remark: "So . . . his calves are genuine, after all; I didn't believe it!" This was reported by Thomas Overskou, who once appeared with Hans Christian Andersen in 1821 in the exotic opera *Lanassa*, which was set in the East Indies during the reign of Henry IV.[41] Along with other choir students, the two young men were supposed to play Indian sacrificial priests, and Crown Princess Caroline attended the premiere. On an earlier occasion, when Andersen paid a visit to Frederiksberg Castle and dropped his paper twist of candy, she had pleased the boy by saying that in profile he looked like Schiller. Later she told Andersen, however, that the extras, rather than resembling Schiller or Indian sacrificial priests, looked more like flayed cats and scalded pigs. Andersen had to agree:

> "Our costumes were terrible. Tight-fitting, flesh-colored fabric over our whole body, with only a little belt; otherwise our back and chest were naked. Our hair was pulled up into what looked like a little whip. We looked dreadful. People laughed and booed. I was so monstrously thin that I felt properly ashamed, and that made me seem comical. For the next performance we were more covered up."[42]

By the autumn of 1821 Andersen's stage appearances at the Royal Theater were coming to an end. After having tried his luck for a year and a half as a dancer, singer, and actor, while taking private lessons from Ferdinand Lindgren—who at the same time was responsible for the training of a pupil as gifted as Ludvig Phister—his options seemed exhausted. Lindgren quite bluntly told his peculiar student, who had proclaimed at his very first lesson that he was only interested in playing "touching" leading roles, that tall, skinny heroes were something that provoked laughter. But he then added that a young person such as Hans Christian Andersen, who had both a heart and a brain, might be advised to consider a different profession: "You shouldn't run around here, wasting your time; you should study. You're not suited to be an actor, but there are also other glorious and great things besides this art!" Andersen replied, "I'm not suited? Not even for comedy? Oh, God, I'm so unhappy! What will become of me?"[43]

In Lindgren's opinion, Andersen ought to learn as quickly as possible some Latin grammar, and when he had accomplished that, people would undoubtedly take him seriously and do more for him. But things didn't go well with Latin grammar, either, in 1821. Andersen played hooky from the boring lessons provided by a student named Bentzen, which had been arranged by the good Professor Høegh-Guldberg. Young Andersen preferred to go to the theater, give puppet shows, or spend more time working on the plays he had started to write. In some respects, the boy's whole life had become one big play, which was now drawing to a close because he had been found out. There was no substance behind his role. Høegh-Guldberg, at any rate, felt he had been used when he discovered that Andersen was skipping his Latin lessons, which were so essential for the boy's education. The professor gave the starry-eyed Andersen an earful when he showed up to apologize at the professor's country home in

Nørrebro and, as usual, pretended to be miserable. "Miserable!" said Høegh-Guldberg to Andersen. "What a screed of a comedy you're spouting! I've heard this before. I refuse to do anything for you. I still have thirty *rigsdaler* that belong to you, and you can come to get ten of them each month, but I'm through with you!"[44]

As a result, Andersen was living on borrowed time in the winter of 1821-22, and he realized that something radical would have to happen during 1822. And this was even before the Royal Theater notified him in the summer of 1822 that he was no longer welcome at any of their drama schools. His desperation is evident in the sentimental New Year's scene he later included in all of his autobiographies, in which the young man, on January 1, 1822, sneaks onto the theater's empty stage and says the Lord's Prayer in a loud voice, hoping that higher powers than those in the candelabras will listen and guide his talent in the right direction.[45] Other signs in the year that had just passed also indicated that Andersen's future was about to be made clear, as well as the fact that his opportunities for a stage breakthrough had not yet been exhausted. But initiative was required of him. "Our Lord may provide the nuts, but He does not crack them open!" Andersen wrote many years later in the story "The Ice Maiden." And in regard to the demonstrable article of faith that moves like a pulse throughout the fairy-tale author's entire life and work, the stage was now set for the decisive act. The nuts that had to be cracked were some of the period's most important representatives of Danish cultural life: Adam Oehlenschläger; H. C. Ørsted; Knud Lyne Rahbek; and Jonas Collin, who was one of Frederik VI's most trusted officials. And Collin, along with Rahbek, sat on the board of the Royal Theater.

Entering the Golden Age

In January 1821, the king appointed Jonas Collin the new managing director of the Royal Theater, primarily so that he would tend to the theater's precarious finances. Andersen, at the urging of Professor Frederik Høegh-Guldberg, immediately paid a call on the newly appointed manager at his residence on Bredgade. Andersen conscientiously waited to introduce himself during the busy man's office hours, but the exceedingly brief audience didn't offer him much hope. Collin's brusque, official manner was not at all to Andersen's liking, and so he decided on his sixteenth birthday, April 2, 1821, to send a letter and a poem to the powerful man, in which he intensified his pleas to become a more permanent member of the Royal Theater. The letter is unmistakably typical of Andersen, with its pathos and careless errors, which reveal not only the sender's youth and lack of education but also something about how hastily he had sent off the enclosed poem. And yet the poem was not so personal that it had prevented him from sending it to other potential benefactors, such as Grundtvig and B. S. Ingemann, who had each received a copy six months earlier.[46] Andersen did not even ensure that the recipient's name and title were correctly spelled. "Herr Privy Concillor Kolin" is what it says above the poem to Jonas Collin, which is a pompous invocation of a paternally sympathetic power that might bring the distressed poet's ship to land, preferably to Kongens Nytorv at the foot of the theater steps—Thalia's temple:

The temple of art I see in the distance
Among cliffs in the lap of the sea
Thither do I hasten, oh! so eagerly
That shipwreck and all peril I ignore.
These wrecks do not frighten me, I see
The ones the wild waves play with,
For in my heart has long blazed
The hope of reaching this dear shore . . .
I will ascend the steep cliffs.
Then I will see Thalia's temple near.
No one then, even among the joyous,
Will be as joyous as I, No! No one . . . .[47]

In this way Collin received a powerful reminder of the peculiar boy who, in his craving to be heard and win acclaim in the summer of 1821, had sought out Kamma and Knud Lyne Rahbek at Bakkehus in Frederiksberg to read from his new work, *The Forest Chapel*. It was a play based on a German short story, which had been published in the magazine *Brevduen* in 1819. Like so many other Shakespeare-inspired dramas of the day, Andersen's rollicking play was written in blank verse, meaning without rhymes and very close to colloquial speech.

Kamma Rahbek had instantly perceived the droll and poetic side of Andersen. As the critic Georg Brandes wrote in 1870 in an essay about the first lady of Bakkehus and the early Golden Age: "She saw the weak and human sides of geniuses and laughed at these aspects without being impressed. But she also had such insight into what was brilliant that she recognized it when it was still in bud. She realized who among her con-temporaries carried the future within."[48] She was the one who immedi-ately saw the quality of Danish writers such as J. P. Mynster, J. L. Heiberg, and Poul Martin Møller. She was also one of the first to pay serious atten-tion to the peculiar young boy named Andersen, who kept on showing up with comedies and tragedies in five acts. And she was the first to call him "a poet." One day, when Kamma Rahbek recognized long passages from plays by Oehlenschläger and Ingemann in the middle of one of Hans Christian's readings, she pointed out this unrestrained and poorly con-cealed borrowing, whereupon Andersen—quite typically—replied: "Yes, but they're so lovely!"[49]

From the summer of 1821 and for the next year, up until June 1822, when Andersen published his first book, *Youthful Attempts*, under the curi-ous pseudonym "Villiam Christian Walter," a shift occurred in his life as he finally became aware of the limitations of his dramatic talents. Andersen realized that the strength of his gift for improvisation lay not in the per-formance but in the creation of the drama, and he understood that his path to the stage must take a roundabout route, via writing. But his sole objec-tive was still to conquer the theater, and he had no doubt whatsoever about his God-given talent. Yet he knew that it was essential for something to happen, since all the other art forms at the Royal Theater had closed their doors to him in the spring of 1822. The only remaining untested possibil-ity was writing.

By the fall of 1821 Andersen was already considering submitting his play *The Forest Chapel* to the theater, but he resisted doing so when Frederik Høegh-Guldberg urged him not to send it, although the boy was greatly surprised at the professor's advice. It's indicative of young Andersen's perception of himself that he was convinced Høegh-Guldberg's advice was prompted, first and foremost, by jealousy and chagrin that the professor had never written anything comparable.[50] In early 1822, when the self-confident Andersen, now almost seventeen, finished his patriotic tragedy *The Robbers of Vissenberg on Fyen*, inspired by a local folktale, he could no longer restrain himself and anonymously sent the play to the Royal Theater. It was received in March, after having gone through a thorough process of read-ing and correcting by others, although this time not by Høegh-Guldberg. He had by now had enough of the intractable Andersen, who simply went his own quixotic way with no comprehension of what was required to become an artist. But Andersen, who never seemed to run out of patrons, helpers, or people to feed him during the years 1819–22, had now pulled a new assistant out of his hat. Her name was Laura Tønder-Lund. They had been confirmed together in Odense in 1819, and she was as childlike and good-natured as Hans Christian. She was now living in Copenhagen. Frøken Tønder-Lund stepped forward to help Andersen, offering him both money and a copyist. As the author explains in his memoirs: "She paid someone to write out a more legible copy than mine; besides, we thought it was important that my handwriting not be recognized. And then the tragedy was submitted."[51]

Today only a single but particularly spectacular scene remains of *The Robbers of Vissenberg*, which was another highly dramatic play in blank verse. In this scene we indirectly witness a murderous attack by robbers on a traveling coach filled with civilians. The brutal Jørgen Klo seizes an infant by the legs and smashes the child against the coach so that "its brains spray over all you other pale ghosts."[52] The play was, of course, flatly rejected. In the middle of June 1822, the theater management—which consisted of Knud Lyne Rahbek, Jonas Collin, Frederik Conrad von Holstein, and Gottsche H. Olsen—reported in a brief, emphatic letter of rejection that the play was "entirely unsuited for the stage." It was furthermore made clear to the author, whose attempt at anonymity had utterly failed, that the play was a mishmash completely lacking in refinement and the most elementary structure. Then the management added, in several ambiguous phrases, that it was about time for the author's "friends and benefactors" to make an effort to take this bewildered soul in hand, since his chaotic talent was in severe need of being constrained within the more solid framework of an education. The rejection was crystal clear, but the enigmatic closing lines held an admission of a certain distinction and talent. Did this mean that a door stood partway open? That was enough for Andersen. He made a new resolution and set in motion one of the most optimistic book publications ever seen in the history of Danish literature. With a cool-headed, strategic sense, the first-time author took charge of all aspects of launching his book. And over a couple of extremely hectic months, he became simultaneously the author, publisher, publicist, reviewer, and bookseller of his book.

"I found myself in the midst of the mysteries of Copenhagen, but I didn't understand how to read them," the older Andersen says in *The Fairy Tale of My Life*. To this we might add that the seventeen-year-old may well have been uncomprehending about the love life of men and women, but

he was no fool when it came to furthering his own ambitions and perceiving propitious opportunities in the big city. He had come up with the
idea of publishing a book with three different texts that he had completed. Even before Andersen received the final rejection for *The Robbers of
Vissenberg*, he had finished and sent off a new play titled *Alfsol* to the management of the Royal Theater. This play was also—as the theater's advisers
later wrote—a collection of "words and tirades with no dramatic plot,
structure, or distinction, full of all sorts of reminiscences, parts taken from
Ewald and Oehlenschläger, Icelandic mixed with contemporary German,
ordinary phrases in ordinary rhymes." But other, less-refined luminaries
liked it very much, including Frederik Carl Gutfeld, dean of Holmen's
Church, who had urged Andersen to send the play to the theater. And then
there was the kind-hearted Widow Jürgensen, the old mother of the royal
watchmaker on Østergade, who had applauded all of Andersen's ballet costumes and enjoyed his readings, including the five-act play *Alfsol*.
Afterwards she told him quite prophetically, "I won't live another ten years,
but mark my words: by then the world will regard you differently than it
does now. Oehlenschläger won't always be the foremost writer; other men
will come along!"[53]

In June 1822, after *Alfsol* had been submitted for consideration, Andersen
began to put his plan into motion. As soon as he received the refusal of *The
Robbers of Vissenberg* on June 16, Andersen managed to get a scene from the
rejected drama accepted by the respected journal *Harpen*, and six weeks
later, on August 9, 1822, it was published on the front page. This meant that
a scene from the rejected play could be read at the same time as the management of the Royal Theater was still digesting its assessments of *Alfsol*.
They had not yet entirely decided how to formulate another clear dismissal
of "the crazy lad from Fyn," or how to quell his compulsion to write in
the future. In a sense, the seventeen-year-old upstart had put pressure on
the entire management. Not only because of the publication in *Harpen*,
where the whole elite of Copenhagen could see what Messieurs Rahbek,
Collin, Holstein, and Olsen had rejected, but also because Andersen stuck
another knife in the back of the board of directors during that busy summer. On July 12, 1822—three weeks after receiving the first rejection of
his play—it was reported in the daily papers that a young man, whose
name was not mentioned although it was unlikely to be anyone other than
the ubiquitous Hans Christian Andersen, would soon publish a book entitled *Youthful Attempts*.

Andersen had paid a visit to the critic Henrik Proft at the newspaper

Dagen, given him a thorough account of the situation, and even shown him the manuscript. Proft then chose to report this strange book publication, which still balanced on a thread since the financial and technical printing aspects were far from resolved. Yet all of Copenhagen could read in *Dagen* on July 12 about a forthcoming book project. The book, along with its talented unknown author, received excellent free promotion, even though the whole article was based on the fact that Andersen had not yet found the required number of subscribers demanded by the book printer to cover expenses. But the advance notice in *Dagen* was sure to solve this problem. The whole arrangement—because the course of events was certainly not a series of coincidences—demonstrates better than anything else the determination and ability of the young and far from insecure Andersen to promote himself.

The more or less conscious intent of the first-time author was to force upon the theater management further proof of his abilities and to argue for the acceptance of *Alfsol*. The management would not be able to sit by passively while they sent another letter of rejection urging the author's many friends and benefactors to handle the matter. Because of Andersen's renewed pressure during the summer of 1822, the management had to step forward and make a crucial decision: either for or against the "crazy lad from Fyn." The management's decision had to have a deeper impact and reach farther than all the superficial confrontations that could be anticipated in the coming years if Andersen continued to bombard the theater with all these "scribbled tragedies," as his future nemesis, Headmaster Simon Meisling, called the impulsive, hastily produced works that Andersen never outgrew. Improvisation was and continued to be a substantial part of his artistic nature and manner of expression. This meant that even as an older, more mature author who could afford to take his time, Andersen would feel that he was done with a text once the basic idea had been conceived, even if entire acts or chapters weren't yet fully realized. New ideas, projects, and challenges would already be knocking at his brain, demanding to be put on paper. "I don't know how to write according to rules; that would be too tedious. The pen has to run and the heart dictate," Andersen writes to Ingemann in 1826.[54] And it's easy to imagine that the young author of *The Forest Chapel* would choose the brief Goethe quote: "*Die Kunst ist lang; / und kurz ist unser Leben*" [*Ars longa, vita brevis*] as a motto for himself and his future life and work.[55] How was Andersen ever going to achieve everything he wanted to do? As they said back home on the island of Fyn, a person had to be "quick to his feed and quick to his work."

The result of the *Alfsol* episode was that Jonas Collin, who had overall responsibility for the finances and activities of the theater's management, recommended to King Frederik VI that funds from the Royal Foundation *Ad usus publicos* should be used to provide further education for Hans Christian Andersen. Crucial to this decision was Knud Lyne Rahbek's objective and precise assessment of *Alfsol*. It was as if, over the course of the summer, Rahbek had changed his evaluation of the young man's dramatic talent and suddenly could sense the glimmerings of a writer, the likes of which the world had never seen. For that matter, many years would pass before other critics managed to dissect Andersen as accurately as Rahbek did in his strong evaluation. First he completely tore *Alfsol* apart as a dramatic work, calling it "unusable for the stage," and then he acknowledged the numerous gems, in whose disjointed scraps an artist might be found after all:

> "On the other hand, when one takes into consideration the fact that this play is the product of a person who can barely manage decent penmanship, who knows nothing of orthography or Danish grammar, who is utterly lacking in the most essential of notions, and furthermore possesses in his brain a hodgepodge of good and bad all jumbled together, from which he indiscriminately pulls things out at random, and yet one can find in his work individual glimpses ... one can't help but wish that an attempt might be made to see what this singular mind, with education, might become."[56]

On September 6, 1822, on the third anniversary of Andersen's arrival in Copenhagen, Rahbek presented his evaluation to his colleagues at the theater's weekly board meeting. A majority was now in favor of sending Andersen on to the king, even though Gottsche Olsen was strongly opposed to "this highly tasteless youth" and repeated his ultra-brief opinion, which said that *Alfsol* "exhibits more of decline rather than progress in the outlandish literary path of the writer."[57] But the majority had spoken, and it was decided at the meeting that Jonas Collin would request as soon as possible a verbal assurance from His Majesty regarding free education for Andersen, starting with the next school year, which was just about to begin. Furthermore, it was decided to summon Hans Christian Andersen to the following week's board meeting. There the young man accepted, with gratitude and a bow, the offer of free schooling, as well as food and lodging, during the coming years. Rahbek was the spokesman, while Collin agreed to take charge of the practical matters necessary for carrying out the plan, including the rather important issue of selecting a school and headmaster. But the first task was to submit the application, directed to the Royal Foundation *Ad usus publicos*, in which it was emphasized that the young man would be "unhappy and lost to proper society if he were allowed to idle away his time." It was also mentioned that there was reason to hope that the young man, through a scholarly education, would leave behind this "straying literary path" and most likely become a useful citizen.[58] The request was for 400 *rigsdaler* annually for three years, to pay for living expenses and schooling. This was quite a significant sum in light of the economic crisis in which the country now found itself after the bankruptcy of 1813. Subsequently everyone was expected to show great frugality. The king took the lead, making do with a few worn uniforms, and going from shop to shop in the capital—it was said—to find the least expensive snuff. But the application was approved, and toward the end of the year, when "the aforementioned Andersen, who is entirely bereft of means," as it said in the documents, was sitting on a school bench in Slagelse, the agreement was finally signed and sealed.

In other words, Andersen's great summer plan had reaped rewards. The only disappointment, of course, was that none of his plays had been accepted by the Royal Theater, but he had also taken this into account, since the projected publication of *Youthful Attempts* was to serve as the framework for at least one of the rejected plays. And his bold plan for his debut book, which had to be sold before it could be printed, was certainly not to be abandoned or postponed just because Andersen was now going to attend school. On the contrary. Now it was important to line up everything quickly, both the artistic and the financial aspects, before his departure. He was headed for Slagelse Grammar School and not—as Andersen had hoped up to the very last minute—Sorø Academy.[59]

The plans for his first book were truly on a grand scale, including even the pseudonym, which we will return to in a moment. Young Andersen was prepared to gamble everything. And we shouldn't forget that he had a great deal to lose. Rahbek, Collin, and the other members of the board had made it quite clear from the beginning that the awarding of a royal stipend presupposed that Andersen would spend his time on his studies and the school syllabus, and *not* on all sorts of artistic "idling," to use Collin's own word in this connection, which reveals his extremely rational and practical temperament.

As the day for his departure approached, Andersen continued, undaunted, to put his publication plans into motion. He fortified and spread the myth about himself and his debut via the subscription drive he had started in June, whereby a signature would commit an individual to buy a copy of Andersen's book. Publication was planned for the end of 1822, provided that the young writer would be able to acquire the number of subscribers required by the Copenhagen printer before the presses would be inked and start printing. Andersen quickly acquired many prominent names on his subscription list. Enthroned at the top was Her Royal Highness, Crown Princess Caroline, who had kindly agreed to pay in advance for all of five copies, which was quite impressive when enticing other, lesser-known buyers to subscribe.[60] But right up to the last minute, there must have been a dearth of buyers for the nebulous product, since book printer Cohen required fifty subscribers for one print run of *Youthful Attempts*. More rounds of sales letters were distributed during August and September, and to the wording of the last letters Andersen added news of his latest triumph, of course: the royal stipend for his schooling. Bishop J. P. Mynster was among those who received the following letter, replete with spelling errors, along with a subscription list that also functioned as a sort of enumeration of the excellent company he could join by ordering this book and paying in advance:

> "Having spent everything on my studies, I find it necessary (at an age of slightly more than 17 years) to publish my first attempt. Since I would be unable to pay for the expenses without a subscription, I am emboldened to request that you take a copy. The price of the copy is 9 Marks. If you permit, I would with pleasure read some of my work for you, at a time that you designate. The management of the Royal Theater has found so much good in my work (*Alfsol*), that they have decided to pay my expenses for several years at Sorøe Academy. Respectfully, H. C. Andersen."[61]

Hans Christian Andersen's Debut

Amazingly enough, the book was published. Listed on the title page, in addition to the author's pseudonym and the title, was a notice that the book had been published by the Author's Publishing Company and printed by E. M. Cohen's Widow in 1822. Not a single copy was sold beyond those the subscribers had purchased in advance. With Andersen's departure for Slagelse Grammar School at the end of October, the manuscript and the remaining copies were left behind with the printer. New owners later found them, and in 1827—to the great regret of a now older and more self-critical author—they tried to sell the work with a new title page. The obscure debut work no longer pleased the more learned Andersen in the late 1820s, and decades later, in his autobiography *The Fairy Tale of My Life*, he chose to sweep the work under the carpet with the words: "The whole thing is, as it must be, a highly immature work."[62]

Yes and no. This Hans Christian Andersen book, today largely unknown to the general public, is undoubtedly an immature and uneven literary hodgepodge, as debut books often are. But *Youthful Attempts* is also a highly charming work with quite a few colorful characters, witty dialogue, and hints of the modern fairy-tale style that Andersen would develop in the 1830s. Within its genre, his fairy-tale style would signal a revolution in world literature. This is a topic we will return to in Chapter Five. Some of those who are most knowledgeable about the life and work of the young Hans Christian Andersen have also asserted that his debut book cannot be viewed in terms of the writer's inner life, that it seems impersonal, and that it should not be taken as a true expression of the seventeen-year-old's literary ability or point of view.[63] This assessment is both unjust and inaccurate. His debut book is in every respect an example of the young Andersen's formidable ability to place his art and himself in a mutually stimulating relationship, in which life becomes writing and the written text, in turn, makes its mark on the young author's life.

That was also the reason why his first book was furnished with an author pseudonym, for which the adult Andersen, in his memoirs, seems to want to blame the book printer. With the pseudonym, we see how the aspiring author, who was anything but shy or humble, elevates himself to the status of two of the stars of world literature. Behind the pseudonym Villiam Christian Walter are concealed the names of William Shakespeare (Villiam) and Walter Scott (Walter), while the middle Christian stands for Andersen himself. About this conceited and self-mocking device Andersen later said in his memoirs:

> "I had given myself a [pseudonym] which at first glance seems to signify the most staggering vanity, and yet that was not the case; rather, it was love, the kind a child might feel and thus name his doll after the person for whom he has the greatest affection. I loved *William* Shakespeare and *Walter* Scott, and of course I also loved myself."[64]

So we should not allow ourselves to be deceived by the adult Andersen's snobbish disavowal of his first book. There was certainly no reason to be embarrassed about *Youthful Attempts*. It offers a glimpse into Andersen's youthful nature during 1820-22, and in that sense it also provides an honest documentation of the writer who was beginning to stir. The book consists of three parts. First, a brief autobiographical prologue written in verse, in which we are introduced to the young author, his birthplace, and his background. Next comes a longer historical tale, "The Apparition at Palnatoke's Grave." And finally, a Norse tragedy in five acts, the aforementioned *Alfsol*, which had been rejected by the Royal Theater.

The book's use of three widely different literary genres should not be viewed or interpreted as proof of the young author's limited literary inventory. The categorical spreading and mixing of genres and styles was a typical aspect of Romanticism and of Hans Christian Andersen's earliest writing. Throughout Andersen's long career as an author, it's possible to trace his need to express himself in many different literary forms and directions. This might be interpreted as restlessness or a compulsion for variety, but it can also be seen as a strong inner desire to experiment and to shake up the established literary rules—the "aesthetics," which was one of the terms that Andersen hated. In a literary career that would last more than fifty years—from 1822 to 1875—Andersen often wrote in a proper, attractive style that followed the norms. At the same time, he could put on a more inquisitive and adventurous face, intent on challenging the "aesthetics" and all the Danish critics, as he dashed in and out of a handful of different genres and literary forms in a single text. He had a deep wish to try out everything that was new and to see where the boundaries might be for a story, a novel, a poem, a travel account, a play, a diary, or a letter. One of the most lucid examples of this tendency can be found in Andersen's first novel, published in 1829. In one of the last chapters of *Walking Tour from Holmen's Canal to the Eastern Point of Amager in the Years 1828 and 1829*, Andersen has his first-person narrator reach the boundary of his tour: the eastern point of the island of Amager. There he has the urge to continue across to the island of Saltholm, but he is confronted at the water's edge by a hideous merman of a critic with pens sticking out of his hair and a tail made from the spines of old books. He speaks like Knud Lyne Rahbek, and he tells the narrator and author, who are one and the same, that a person should never overstep the boundaries of his own book: "'You've titled your book *Walking Tour to the Eastern Point of Amager*,' exclaimed the man, 'and now you dare to go farther!'"[65] That's the voice of the guardians of aesthetics. Yet the young author does manage, all the same, to burst the framework of his book. We'll return to this topic in Chapter Three.

This same sense of curiosity, along with a desire to explore the established boundaries and his own abilities, is evident in *Youthful Attempts*. The first-time author, at seventeen, cannot be said to have a weak view of himself. In addition to the imposing pseudonym, the prologue introduces us to a new author and a budding literary career. This is done with the help of the goddess Dana. She takes the stage and presents an intensely sentimental biographical portrait of the young genius who is about to enter Danish literature. The three pages of blank verse cover eight years, starting in May 1814, when Hans Christian, as a sweet and innocent nine-year-old, sits on the bank of the Odense River and is endowed with divine poetic gifts. The verse ends when he is a seventeen-year-old in the Danish capital—meaning in 1822, when the book was actually written—and the lyrical embers have become an uncontrollable element that others will now have to help him to steer and refine:

> Now I am already seventeen, deep
> Inside me burns high a mighty flame,
> Which I am much too weak to subdue;
> A spirit drives me, and yet I tremble
> When my hand touches the harp's golden strings!
> Oh, if I dare, will they receive me,
> Receive such a young, such a weak singer?[66]

But we also meet the harp-loving youth when he was nine, sitting near his childhood's idyllic river, which is one of the great mythological landscapes and visionary tracks in Andersen's works. "Memory is the only paradise from which we cannot be driven out." This is one of his favorite quotes during the 1820s, stemming from the German Romantic writer Jean Paul. For Andersen, the banks of the Odense River remained eternally fresh and fertile; he could always return there in his thoughts and in his writing. Here we see him through the eyes of the goddess Dana, who is on her way across Fyn (Fiona):

> Then did I wander through Fiona's lands
> And met a boy of nine, playing
> Not with the other hale and lively boys,
> But weaving lovely flower wreaths,
> Which he regarded with proud satisfaction
> As he placed them on his little head.
> And, so that they would not wither,
> He plaited from the green reeds

> A little boat, decorated with wreaths,
> And like a poet's ship from fantasy's realm
> It sailed on the flowing crystal,
> Surrounded by curious small fish
> Who nipped at the green flower ships![67]

This boy is not at all like "the other hale and lively boys." He is exceptional, never plays with his peers, and would rather sit by himself out in nature, adorning his own remarkable works. In the midst of this pastoral, narcissistic idyll, where the boy is about to put to sea another little vessel laden with dreams, he is visited by an extraordinary omen. Into the scene near the river steps a little fairy, and her mission is to bestow on the chosen boy a remarkable gift of grace:

> Then a friendly little fairy girl
> Came down from old Nonnebakke; she
> Was Imagination, and she pressed
> Her hot kiss on the boy's mute lips,
> And then fluttered away on light wings.[68]

It's important to make clear that this providential and magical gift does not come from God on high, up in heaven, but from below, on the earthly plane. From the surrounding nature and from the cloister "Nonnebakke," which was rumored on Fyn to have housed women who, during the night, were busy with many things other than praying to God. It's significant that the symbolic presentation of the boy's poetic gifts does not occur in a heavenly transfigured light but on a lower, more earthbound, and slightly muddy plane. The emphasis is on himself as a human being, and on some basic powers in his writer's nature that come from the common people. Here on the banks of the Odense River, in 1814, it is not angels who float down, offering an inviting ladder to heaven. The inspiration comes from nature itself—from fish, birds, flowers, trees, and forest creatures like fairies, which in both beautiful and demonic forms have always been closely tied to the peasants' faith in nature. They were also a frequently used motif in German Romantic writing—for example, in the work of Andersen's great mentor Ludwig Tieck. The fairy is an ether-borne creature, a spirit of both land and air, who can be found in many different sizes and can move along the same muddy track as an earthworm, a dung beetle, and a mole, yet at the same time can dash off like a bird, a bee, or a spider. The fairy girl's hot kiss is so filled with imagination that it turns the boy into a poet. Both in thought and body he becomes—as it says in the prologue—"A fairy with the white wings of innocence / Childishly I exclaimed: 'I too wish to rise / And light up like a friendly little star / That adorns the sky in the dim night!'"

According to the nature mythology that Andersen often uses in his stories, the fairy is first and foremost a spreader of joy. With this decisive fairy kiss on the banks of the Odense River, young Hans Christian is given the task here in life to spread happiness and joy among his fellow humans with the beautiful fairy song—the art of poetry! Yet he can do so only as long as he continues to be good and childlike and is able to preserve his "white wings of innocence." It is on this promise that the whole business of his upbringing rests. If the boy should one day lose his fairy wings, or if they lose their special dust, he will at once be stripped of the special talents and powers that reside in the gift of imagination.

A Heathen Sense of Nature

What makes *Youthful Attempts* particularly interesting is the deep, and occasionally heathen, sense of nature that exists in the book, along with the author's carefully structured attempts to draw the reader farther and farther away from reality. From the first page to the last, the narrator displays a remarkably intelligent interest in everything in human life that cannot be seen but can be sensed. All three texts exhibit a youthful, alert, and inquisitive mind, with its sensory apparatus attuned to both the physical and metaphysical sides of nature. If we follow the path of the seventeen-year-old Andersen through the entire book without allowing too many criticisms along the way, *Youthful Attempts* becomes a journey through time that is deepened and prolonged by means of the sequence and themes of the texts. If read in order, the prologue, the saga, and the Norse drama gradually move away from the present reality of the year 1822. From the prose poem's initial introduction of the young poet and his fairy creature in Odense and Copenhagen, the book then branches off to move backwards in both time and space. The reader is suddenly wearing seven-league boots and leaping into a saga, "The Apparition at Palnatoke's Grave," which takes place in 17th-century Fyn. Then the reader digs in his toes again and takes another big leap back in time with the play *Alfsol*, which is set in Denmark and Norway around 900 A.D.

"The Apparition at Palnatoke's Grave" takes place in the time of Christian IV, with the landscape of Fyn and the island's folklore shaping the story's content and framework. It must be assumed that Andersen's retelling of the story is more or less in tune with the old, oral source that he heard as a child. He then added various literary borrowings from secondary readings of both old tales and legends in books and journals, such as the more recent stories of Adam Oehlenschläger, B. S. Ingemann, and Jens Baggesen. At any rate, the story is quite entertaining, and the plot practically drips with red and black blood. Andersen never got over his thirst for horror and splatter, and the thirty-page tale contains a murder by poisoning, several spectacular suicides, falls, and hangings, as well as the abduction of an infant. The whole thing is embellished with a couple of violently drunk peasants, demented women who smash in each other's skulls, flashing knives, rattling prison keys, and a dozen ominously alive apparitions!

The story itself has to do with how the orphan Sophia, in spite of a brutal start, manages to achieve a good and beautiful life. In the end she is united with her sweetheart, Johannes, at the lovers' hill in Aasum, near the river just outside of Odense. There the jealous rival, Jochum, in an attempt to murder the sweethearts, ends up being crushed by the huge boulder that he intended for Sophia and Johannes. It may not be a perfect love story, but the author, "Villiam Christian Walter," was only seventeen, after all. The reader may look in vain for the sound of the older, more experienced Hans Christian Andersen, who nurses and plays with the language, yet there is never any doubt who the author is here. In *Youthful Attempts* we meet for the first time in his writing the treasure chest and peddler's box full of folk poetry and Fyn folklore from which Andersen's fairy tales would draw so many years later. This is particularly evident in the portrait of Stine of Broby, called "the crazy beast" and the mother of the story's heroine, Sophia. Sophia is taken as an infant from her mother and, wrapped in "cold sheets," placed in the Odense River. But that same evening she is rescued by a farmer, who takes the child home to his wife and eventually sees to her happiness. The raving mad Stine, who holds the precious secret of the true identity of Sophia's father, is described as follows:

> "Now she was seen in all her finery, a tattered and torn coat hung loosely around her large, gaunt limbs; all over it she had fastened withered meadow violets with the help of several thorns. Her hair was adorned with cloth scraps of all colors, concealed under a dirty old straw hat decorated with long rooster feathers." [69]

It's apparent that here the young writer is on home turf. But the Andersen at seventeen could also be satirical. In the middle of the story we have a splendid snapshot of a smug deacon standing in the pulpit in church. This is comedy of a high order, and there's definitely a Holberg type of humor at work when the young author writes of the fire-and-brimstone preacher that his gestures "are so natural, as if he had learned to gesticulate in the cradle, and his lovely white cuffs flutter back and forth just like the wings of a big wild goose; and when he pounds the pulpit, the congregation jumps up in terror, as if at the sound of the final trumpet."[70]

We also catch glimpses of the later, brilliant master of the art of dialogue, especially in the little, terse, idiomatic phrases: "Don't stand there staring like a cow on the moon!" and "You stink like a heathen, old Mother Rat Poison!" Both point to the future fairy-tale writer, who can also be seen in the proverbs and wordplay in this early story: "Wherever Sister Gossip slips inside, Brother Lie is not far behind." Yet the future writer is most apparent in the saga's assiduous use of the whole creepy-crawly life of the earth's surface. Some of the vermin belong to the sphere of zoology, while others are definitely part of the mythological world. At any rate, we find sea toads, elves, water sprites, harlots, and the Devil—both with and without his great-grandmother—whom neither the young nor the old Hans Christian Andersen could ever do without. In the robber story from 1822 the Devil shows up for the first time, with his diabolically long fingers, and steals himself a wife, making her queen with a crown of big, fat, lively spiders.

Last but not least, "The Apparition at Palnatoke's Grave" contains an interesting social collision between the poor and the rich, the peasant and the lord, which would eventually appear quite frequently in Andersen's writings, although not in such gruesome or realistic portrayals. But the poor in both the countryside and the city were always measured against the nobility and civil servant class. This is most evident in some of Andersen's last tales, such as "The Porter's Son," "What the Thistle Experienced," "What A Person Can Think Up," and "The Gardener and the Lord." These stories were all written during the last decade of Andersen's life. In a cheerfully mischievous manner he skewers a number of self-righteous, one-dimensional people, who time after time fail to measure up to ordinary but exceedingly practical and down-to-earth farmers. The learned gentlemen and ladies of the big city could not survive out in nature. This is what we learn in 1822 in "The Apparition at Palnatoke's Grave," when the elegant, distinguished deacon's wife, Madame Steffens, one day gets stuck in the bog. She soon finds out that muddy water on Fyn is ice-cold, but then she is pulled out by an exceptionally drunk fiddler from Dalum. Of course, with all the ignorance of her class hatred, she mistakes the man for the Devil himself.

In these more or less voluntary confrontations between the poor and the upper classes there is a fundamental social conflict which Andersen, as a proletarian and child of humble parents, was particularly qualified to portray. And he was never able to let it go, although for obvious reasons he was forced to conceal and camouflage his original, destitute beginnings. We're talking about a social instinct that Andersen possessed, which deep down was never blunted in spite of the fact that from 1825 until his death in 1875 he was a member of the elite in Denmark. For extended periods every year he also lived free of charge at various Danish manor houses, while in the capital he had a permanent weekly dinner schedule. This meant that on each weekday in the late afternoon he would dine with one of the city's finest families before he rushed off to his permanent seat at the Royal Theater or the Casino. The author socialized privately with all these individuals who, in terms of social class, were far better situated and—on the surface—more cultivated and learned than he was. At the same time, he would surreptitiously study them at close range and then weave them into his stories, where they can be found in all their falseness, hiding behind various effective disguises. In this sense it can be said that Andersen, no matter how conservative and loyal he may have presented himself outwardly, was something of a social rebel. Not with loud guns or red banners or big, revolutionary speeches, but—to use his own implacable definition of a good story—by holding "a merry judgment day over appearance and reality."

It seems as if he should have felt himself to be a traitor to his class or at least somewhat torn. But that was not the case. A splendid example of how relatively untroubled Andersen felt about being a poor man in a baron's bed can be seen in the 1840s when he spent several years working on his novel *The Two Baronesses*. He began writing the book while staying with a duke in Germany and finished it at the Glorup estate on Fyn. There he slept with the nine-pointed crown of the count above his head, with silk wrapped around his feet, and with an abundance of daily services and comforts. None of this is apparent from the power structure in the universe of his novel. Here we don't see the world for even a second from the comfortable point of view of the lord or squire. Instead, we find ourselves among peasants who are about to die of hunger and oppression. The novelist's attitude toward the relationship between the peasantry and the upper classes was also enormously far from that of the many ingratiating letters that he simultaneously sent out to all his noble, aristocratic hosts and hostesses in Denmark and abroad. These letters often began with such phrases as: "Most Gracious Duchess" or "Dear, Blessed Lady Countess."[71]

An awareness of what it meant to be rich and poor was deeply rooted in Andersen's character, and was especially tied to the way people behaved toward and treated one another. In 1819-22, when Andersen pestered the best families of Copenhagen with all his longings for the theater and showed up in his ridiculous clothes and let them laugh as he sang and danced for hours, the "son of nature" was at the same time observing his audience with his small, deep-set eyes. And occasionally, but not always, he would see through these people and discover how false and ignorant they actually were. One evening during the 1820s at the home of Adam Oehlenschläger, after everyone had once again made fun of part of young Andersen's dramatic reading that failed to hide his provincial accent, Oehlenschläger had to console the boy, who was wounded by the laughter. Denmark's great poet also admonished his young guest. Yet he couldn't resist poking fun at the poor boy himself by reportedly saying: "How strange it is that the Fyn dialect is still less respected than the dialect of Jutland. And yet people say that Our Lord speaks Fynsk with his angels, but only on Sunday!"

The fact that laughter often depends on social status was something that Andersen learned during his first years in Copenhagen, when people laughed uproariously at his expense. This was documented in a letter from the seventeen-year-old daughter of a rural dean from Fyn. In 1822 she was in Copenhagen visiting her aunt, who had ties to the Collin family. She reports in her letter that in Copenhagen social circles, people looked down on the boy from Fyn, and she could easily understand why. Even a pastor's daughter from Vester Skerninge had to cringe at the primitive poet:

> "Ask Otillie if she can remember the little shoemaker's son from Odense who performed comedies for them. He's in the city right now, writing tragedies and stories, which he sometimes reads aloud for us. There are occasional beautiful places in them, but in general it's all such dreadful nonsense ... Tomorrow he's coming over again to read. I'm looking forward to it, if only I can stop myself from laughing, but that's practically impossible because he behaves so foolishly."[72]

Apparent in even an early text such as "The Apparition at Palnatoke's Grave" are Hans Christian Andersen's recognition and awareness of the fact that simple, naturally attuned people could possess and radiate more riches on the spiritual level than any nobles, aristocrats, landowners, or lords. With a flawless sense for the pictorial and dramatic possibilities inherent in social conflict and confrontation, Andersen invests all his sympathy in the sons and daughters of nature—in this case in Jørgen. In one delightful scene, Jørgen has a discussion with Madame Steffens, who can speak *French*, but whose superficial learning and knowledge quickly prove to have little value in the countryside. In contrast, the farm hand Jørgen is practically a philosopher when he claims at one point that animals have just as much common sense as humans and that no one denies animals their common sense—except for humans, because they're so proud and prejudiced. And with that, Madame Steffens is effectively put in her place.

This is a very early and vigorous version of Hans Christian Andersen the fairy-tale writer. He never forgot that animals can sometimes be just as sensible as people, and occasionally can possess much more emotion. The fact that he also remembered that the North had once been united under Freya, Thor, and all the gods of Valhalla is evident in the last text of his first book.

The Gentle Power of Love

The play *Alfsol*, which deals with an "exalted and steadfast love in the North," presents a precise impression of the young playwright, even though it's true that the blank verse may sound a bit false. And some of the more flamboyant juxtapositions of the meter may transform a scene into an utter comic strip.

We find ourselves in the early Middle Ages, sometime around 1000 A.D., when Harald Bluetooth has begun to Christianize the heathen Danes. The king's daughter, Alfsol, from northern Jutland is sent by her father, a grieving widower, to Norway to seek advice from the holy Norns about her own marriage prospects. The journey proves fatal, because up in the rugged mountains the lovely girl—this "fragile stalk of a lily"—arouses the passions of two men, turning the rugged warrior heads of the fearless young Harald and the grizzled old Sigurd Ring. By means of various cunning intrigues, which young Andersen manages to insert quite successfully into the plot via the rogue Snær, the drama moves swiftly through all five acts, in which the beautiful, good thoughts about love are transformed into ruined kinship relations, family feuds, and war.

As is so often the case in stories from saga times, the play ends with the violent death of all concerned. Love is war, and in the final scene a burning ship weighs anchor, loaded with sulfur, pitch, and the mutilated bodies of warriors. In the midst of this inferno of flame and smoke, one of the rejected suitors stands over the body of the bride—Alfsol—whom no one managed to win because she committed suicide. "Thus it doth befit a king / To die and visit Odin in Valhalla." Curtain.

But before Ragnarok and before the curtain falls, we are introduced in detail to one of the most beautiful betrothed couples in all of Hans Christian Andersen's work: Alfsol and Harald. They're from a phase of Andersen's life when he was still a boy and so innocent and ignorant, so unaware of the extent and nature of his own sexuality, that he did not feel a fierce, instinctive fear of the opposite sex. For this reason, in *Alfsol*, we have a rare, utopian and profoundly beautiful depiction of the loyal, gentle power of love between a man and a woman. But there is no mating between a man and a woman in Andersen's work without a certain emotional distortion between the sexes. "Gentle sex," says the old commander Sigurd at one point. With these words in mind, we see Harald and Alfsol as two virgins who possess not only innocence but also the potential of both sexes within themselves. He is a womanly man, and she is a manly woman. Harald is the sensitive, thoughtful male; in fact, at times he is bursting with so many emotions that Alfsol has to remind him that, in spite of everything, he is indeed a man. "Stand up! Kneeling does not become a hero!" And he complies, because Alfsol is a woman above all others. She is described by both men in the tragedy as the indescribably beautiful sister of Freya, who nevertheless has blustering masculine gods like Thor and Odin in her female blood. And that's why she is capable of taking action based on her own free will. "I dare do anything! The girls of the North / can also die a hero's death!"

This is how Andersen's first book ends: with plenty of wars, sex, love, and heroic deaths on a burning ship in the North Sea. Along the way, Alfsol's clever brother, Inge, has tried to gather up and explain the tragedy's brutal, random dissipation of life and death in a profound examination of the human condition. He speaks of sorrow and joy, which wander hand in hand through life as siblings. This "linked wisdom," says Inge, is something that we humans ought not to break. Instead, we should learn to live with it. "What would joy be if we did not know sorrow!"[73] These words would become a mantra in Andersen's diaries.

Hans Christian Andersen's colorful debut in 1822, which so beautifully reflects the three most important literary genres of his career—autobiography, fairy tale, and drama—never received a single review. Perhaps his benefactors, by now many in number, had unanimously agreed to maintain utter silence and thus suppress Villiam Christian Walter's *Youthful Attempts*. Perhaps Knud Lyne Rahbek managed to use his power and influence within the literary establishment of the day to quash any mention or review. That kind of publicity would have just put more ideas into the bewildered boy's head, which now—on a platter—was delivered to the learned headmaster Simon Meisling at the grammar school in Slagelse. This was the same school once attended by Jens Baggesen and B. S. Ingemann. The headmaster had been enjoined to educate this Andersen, whose head had impressed both the phrenologists and the philanthropists. After all, behind the high forehead were not only conceited dreams but also poetry, courage, and the will to assert himself. He possessed a drive that, in the seventeen-year-old's first book, found expression through the masculine maiden Alfsol: "By Freya, Thor, and all the gods of Valhalla, / I swear. Either Harald or death."[74]

That was quite a line to leave behind as he left the capital. And now a new chapter in the young man's fairy-tale life was about to begin. On October 26, 1822, he set off by mail coach in the beautiful autumn weather, headed for Slagelse to start his education among boys who were only eleven or twelve. Before leaving he went to say farewell to Jonas Collin, calling on him at his home near Kongens Nytorv, with Collin's son, Edvard, and his daughters, Ingeborg and Louise, scowling from beneath the courtyard gallery. Andersen's new benefactor told him, "Don't hesitate to write and tell me what you need, and to let me know how things are going!"[75]

He didn't have to say this twice.

Chapter Two

In the House of Education (1822-1827)

"Go to hell!" resounds through the dimly lit room. The words are flung at the twenty-two-year-old Andersen who, on an April morning in 1827—happily freed from the tailcoat and rough gray fabric of his school clothing—has stepped inside the library on the second floor of Helsingør's grammar school to say goodbye and to thank the headmaster for all the kindness that was shown to him over the years.

But the stout little man at the end of the room, who in Andersen's eyes looks like a jelly doughnut with legs, doesn't move a muscle. With his hands stuffed in his pockets, Headmaster Meisling fixes an angry glare on the spines of the books and refuses to turn around to face the odious, gangly young man with the huge nose and elephant feet who, for the past five years, has been his most hated student and favored target during class.[1]

The evening before, the headmaster had sent the maids, one after the other, down to Andersen's room to ask him to return his pillow, then his quilt, his blanket, and finally the mattress, which were to be taken over by the new boy in the house. That made it hard for Andersen to get through the night, which was just as long and bewildering as the one during the previous week, when the headmaster was in Copenhagen. That's when Fru Meisling once again had a visit from a gentleman in uniform and "by mistake" gave Andersen the key to the woodshed instead of the house. But the following day she had apologized and reminded him that a person's good name was the most precious thing he owns.

The Devil take it all! He had long ago announced his departure for Copenhagen with the day's first coach from the town on the sound, and he can already hear the clamor of the post-horn from the highway. The mighty Jonas Collin in Copenhagen has finally issued his decree, and Headmaster Meisling is to be left behind, humiliated.

On his way out of the library, the young man who is no longer a pupil receives one last versified slap on the back of the head: "You may think you have fantasy, yet it is nothing but poseury! A genius is what you may envision, but you'll end up mad and in a prison!"

Yet it's quite clear that this Andersen is, in fact, a genius. Headmaster Meisling no longer has any doubts about that. At the same time, the lad is also a damn sissy who has never been able to control his body or soul. And he cries at the drop of a hat, which means that the headmaster has had to pound even harder on the table and demand that he wipe his prosaic eyes.

Time after time over the past five years the headmaster has had to discipline this conceited, daydreaming boy when he hadn't learned his Greek and Latin lessons properly or had once again defied the ban against writing and declaiming poetry. The intolerable whelp can't go near a refined group of people without feeling compelled to perform. And nothing can make a classical philologist more irritated than hearing a young man start sniveling over "the helplessness of a child in a mother's arms."[2]

No, Andersen's poem written for the headmaster's installation at the school in Helsingør wasn't half bad. It sounded almost beautiful when all the pupils in the Cloister Church began singing the salutary, edifying words: "Teach us then strength and virtue / And your wage shall be blissful joy."[3]

If Andersen had more time, his parting words to the headmaster would have included the story about the promoters of education who rarely have any life in them because they neither resist nor object to anything. But now the post-horn is sounding; Copenhagen is calling!

Many years later, after the student has become a famous and esteemed author all over Europe, although he still has nightmares about his old headmaster, this little story is finally told on stage:

> Once upon a time there were two brothers who went out into the world because they wanted to seek their fortune. In the middle of the road stood a big house, and on the sign it said that this was a house of education where you had to stay for seven years, but by then you would be properly educated.
>
> "I'm heading through the woods," said one of the brothers, and off he went. "And I'm going into the house of education!" said the other.
>
> "In here you have to learn to stand properly on your own two feet," they told him inside. "First position!" And he took up the first position.
>
> "Speech is silver, but silence is golden!" they told him, and then he kept perfectly still.
>
> "Don't let anyone see that you're thinking about yourself. Eyes forward!" And then he fixed his eyes forward.
>
> "Don't move your legs like that when you walk!"
>
> "I'd better fasten a string to them!" he said, and he promptly had a string fastened to them.
>
> "And don't move your arms like that!" they now said. "Fasten a string to them!"
>
> And the strings were pulled, making him gesticulate, and then he was educated![4]

*I*T WAS DURING THE PERIOD 1822-27 that Simon Meisling and Hans Christian Andersen collided in a teacher-student relationship of some renown because Andersen—with his usual sense for tending to and promoting his own myth—recorded their conflict in world literature. In *The Fairy Tale of My Life* in the 1850s, Andersen depicts his school years under Headmaster Meisling at the grammar schools in Slagelse and Helsingør as one prolonged martyrdom. He compares his fate before the altar of education with the distressed state of all the boys in the books of Charles Dickens. Andersen even takes the liberty of presuming that if Dickens had heard about the Danish author's fate in the 1820s and "knew about what I had endured, what I had felt and suffered, he would not have found my story any less difficult or humorous to describe."[5]

Month after month, class after class, for five long years, the screw was tightened again and again, if we are to believe Andersen. This was done partially through renewed verbal attacks, partially through constant ridicule from Meisling, who kept reminding the young man that he was utterly lacking in the most basic qualifications to become an educated person; for that very reason, any future as a writer was unthinkable. Meisling constantly emphasized that if Andersen could not better govern his imagination and emotions, he would remain a simple outhouse-poet.

"'Recite for me a single verse, a single line of poetry that your empty brain has created. You have no feelings, they're nothing but drivel; you have no imagination, except the kind possessed by the inmates of Bistrup madhouse, and your intelligence I won't even discuss. Recite for me a poem you've written!' I wept, I could not reply. My poem, 'The Dying Child,' was 'drivel, that any outhouse poet could slap together!'"[6]

That's what Andersen writes in his private autobiography from 1832, and it's this same negative image of both his teacher and the entire educational process during the period 1822 to 1827 that he presents to us in his later, published autobiographies from 1847 and 1855. In *The Fairy Tale of My Life*, his portrayal of the five years under Headmaster Meisling sounds like an account of how to ruin the soul of a child. But in reality this educational process was much more complicated. The student years in Slagelse and Helsingør became a catalyst for the whole stream of literature that poured out of Hans Christian Andersen in the late 1820s; within a year he had made his debut as a novelist, playwright, and poet.

In Andersen's more private writings from the Slagelse years, consisting of diaries and letters in which the words "straight from my heart into my pen" often occur, a more nuanced account appears.[7] In all the letters that he showered on his friends and benefactors in Copenhagen, Sorø, and Odense, Andersen had not yet shaped the massive framework of suffering around his life's story, with which we are so familiar and which became concentrated in fairy-tale "punch lines" such as "a person must first endure such dreadful evil—and then he becomes famous!" Andersen had not yet begun to fill up his autobiography with all the sighs and complaints that simplified and distorted the truth about him.

As we will see, in reality it was a matter of a prolonged and fierce mental battle between the two, which ended with the victim drawing the longer straw. In addition, he had the pleasure of seeing his tormentor emphatically put in his place as a pedagogue, patriarch, and poet. In the struggle and subsequent rupture between these two intransigent individuals, we see crystallized two different physiognomies and temperaments. Yet we also sense a collision of epic proportions, since the two men represented different eras, educational ideals, and views of art. Keeping in mind the deep and fundamentally incompatible differences that were constantly hovering over the curriculum, examinations, and grade books, we can better understand the relationship between the choleric headmaster and his daydreaming pupil, who was subjected to such contrived nicknames as "Poetus longus est Abekattus rectus" [the tall poet is a regular monkey].[8] The relationship developed into a battle for power that turned out to be decisive not only for Andersen but also for Meisling. After the rupture in the spring of 1827, Andersen took his headmaster's bitter words of farewell to heart and in an artistic sense actually did "go to hell" in his first published novel, *Walking Tour of Amager*, which he wrote in the fall of 1828 while he was taking his final exams. At the same time, Meisling slowly but surely lost faith in his own pedagogical ideals. Simon Meisling's decline began on that April day in 1827, when the oddest and most remarkable student a Danish headmaster had ever confronted left Helsingør. Quietly and calmly Meisling sank deeper and deeper into Greek and Roman antiquity, the punch bowl, and a steadily increasing number of grievances of one sort or another filed against him. This meant that eventually he had to give up his headmaster's post and return to Copenhagen, where one of his few remaining pleasures was to castigate his former pupil. In the 1830s Andersen had begun to make a name for himself in the Students' Association, which was academician Meisling's old domain. In a conversation with another former pupil from Slagelse and Helsingør, which must have taken place in Copenhagen around 1835, Meisling supposedly said of Andersen: "And who is it who admires and idolizes this genius? A number of hysterical females; a few minor poets who, like him, are intent on self-adoration; and children, who don't even understand him."[9]

Simon Meisling, Bachelor of Theology and Doctor of Philosophy, was a frequent visitor at the Students' Association beginning in the mid-1820s. At that time older members of the association, who now held official government positions all over Sjælland, started coming to the capital to seek diversion among their nostalgic fellow lodge brothers. Such was also the case for Meisling, who was enrolled as a "member at large of the Students' Association."[10] And in the 1830s the headmaster must have encountered his former pupil on many occasions, when Andersen performed at the meetings. According to the records, Andersen often used the opportunity to jump up on stage and perform a scene from a play, declaim, or read from his own texts. Revenge must have been particularly sweet for Andersen one evening in the fall of 1830 when Meisling witnessed his former pupil present a tremendously funny and deeply ironic short story, "The Beautiful Grammatica." In a marvelous, nonsensical format, the story makes fun of the vile, unimaginative classical grammar ("Herr von Cicero's Compulsory Teachings") and starts off in the following way:

> "Dear fathers and mothers! You who have been given a book entitled *Baden's Latin Grammar*. It is to these perilous, overwrought lessons directed at a daydreaming heart that I wish to draw your attention. Never let this book fall into the hands of your daughters; it's worse even than *Claurens* and all his successors. Oh yes, I know it well! I know what effect it has had on me and on others! And it's even more dangerous for ladies, since it's written throughout in prose and only in the most incisive passages adorned with spiritual verses in classic drapery. I am astonished that none of the hyper-sensitive poets, if I might use such an adjective, has ever made use of this rich gold-mine; here is something worth watering down! What a colorful world of the imagination lies beneath the whole Latin grammar! What a colossal image of a touching *Liebes-Geschichte!*" [love story][11]

Later in the 1830s Andersen read aloud, in addition to various minor plays and sketches,[12] his novel *Only a Fiddler* and the tale "The Galoshes of Fortune." The author was always well-groomed and at times his attire, according to the records, included silk stockings, a white satin vest, and a French hat. Oh yes, a certain elegance was in order after having escaped

Meisling's clutches. Yet Andersen never mentions in *The Fairy Tale of My Life* any of the spectacular occasions at the Students' Association when he would note with great satisfaction the presence of his former headmaster in the audience. In Andersen's memoirs Meisling was not allowed admittance to the Students' Association. On the other hand, Andersen didn't hide the fact that the headmaster, after leaving Helsingør Grammar School in the 1830s, had to drag through the rest of his days as a head teacher like some sort of fool in a Holberg play. Eventually Meisling became such a regular, abject figure on the streets of Copenhagen that in 1854 the Students' Association published in its newsletter, *Vrøvleblade*, the following piece about the slovenly, foul-smelling private teacher:

> "Whenever a crowd of people gathers on the streets of Copenhagen, in one out of a hundred cases the reason will be: Professor Meisling has acquired a new pair of boots. In zero out of a hundred cases: Professor Meisling with a new suit."

Headmaster Meisling may have once harmed a talented young boy in an emotional sense, what the aged Hans Christian Andersen characterizes as "an extraordinary cruelty, without knowing it."[13] But at the same time, with the strict classical form and content of his teachings, didn't he also provide a more solid and stable basis for the young man's brilliant but chaotically flighty nature? Didn't Meisling create the balustrades and foundation that were so essential, making it possible for the intellectually flighty Hans Christian Andersen to develop as a writer during the period 1822-27? There is reason to believe this was true, especially if you read Andersen's more sober analyses of himself and his situation in various letters to Jonas Collin during the 1820s:

> "Put yourself in my position, my first education, imagine your head filled with foolishness and a stock of jumbled poems and novels, all the flawed abilities and the vile inconstancy with which I have done my daydreaming; you are the best one to judge me . . ."[14]

The question is whether Hans Christian Andersen ever would have become the immortal writer he dreamed and exclaimed about in the early 1820s, after he had demonstrated his lack of talent as a singer, actor, and ballet dancer, if an academic tormenter named Simon Meisling had not turned his world upside down with his Latin grammar and time after time tried to prevent Andersen from becoming an artist. With his ironically derisive teaching method, he often drove his pupil into a corner from which neither God nor Jonas Collin nor any other paternal providence, but only the talent of the boy's own "Rhyming Demon," could free him. Meisling was one of the reasons that Andersen became a writer. I say this not out of sympathy for Meisling's pedagogical method but in light of the impossible task he had been given and agreed to undertake.

The Art of Instilling an Education

It was more likely the role of a watchdog rather than a monster that Jonas Collin had intended for the teacher who would take Hans Christian Andersen in hand. During the negotiations about Andersen's future, the young man was called Collin's "poetic client,"[15] which was not entirely a misnomer, even though Knud Lyne Rahbek was actually the one who, with his evaluation of *Alfsol*, had put the stamp of approval on the decision.

The fact that Jonas Collin showed any interest at all in the peculiar youth in 1821-22 was due to an old fondness for the works of Jean-Jacques Rousseau and Johann Gottlieb Fichte, which Collin, as a young man, had cultivated and translated to Danish in the 1790s.[16] As one of Frederik VI's most trusted officials during the period of absolute monarchy in the early 19th century, Collin had to develop this humanistic-philanthropic side of his nature under more discreet and cautious forms, especially when it occurred in the service of the state. But behind the decision of this practical and diligent man to participate in the education and cultivation of Hans Christian Andersen during the 1820s was a solid knowledge of Rousseau's view of humanity's noble propensity for freedom. He was also familiar with Fichte's ideas in *The Vocation of the Scholar*, which include arguments against punishing or mocking people without telling them how they might improve themselves. As a young man, Jonas Collin had also attended lectures on the philosophy of Immanuel Kant at Copenhagen University in the 1790s. He had written a five-hundred-page compendium that couldn't avoid touching on the German philosopher's ideas regarding "the art of instilling an education." The central message was that a person is neither more nor less than his upbringing makes of him, and thus he has a need for solicitude, training, and discipline; he has to learn to submit to the rules of reason:

> "A human being is given by nature such a great propensity for freedom that once he has become accustomed to it for a period of time, he will sacrifice anything for it. That is precisely why discipline, as mentioned, must also be employed quite early; if this is not done, it is difficult

afterwards to change a person. Then he will follow every whim of his own. It can also be seen among savage peoples that even if they have served Europeans for some time, they never grow accustomed to European ways of life ... If allowed to have his way when young and not offered any opposition, a person will retain a certain savageness through-out his entire life."[17]

Collin, the highly respected department head and cultivator of com-mon sense, was at heart quite content to be able to follow—at a slight dis-tance and more or less covertly—an interesting philanthropic "experi-ment" such as Hans Christian Andersen. Whereas a proclaimed universal Romantic like H. C. Ørsted wished to see Andersen make his way as an artist, for Collin—this "catalyst between theory and practice"[18]—it was a matter of making a good, productive citizen out of the wild boy from Fyn. Jonas Collin directed his application to Herr Mynster, who later became bishop but at the time was a member of the board for the university and grammar schools. With Mynster's help, in September 1822, Collin began to look around for someone who could take on this pedagogical project. At first Mynster was disinclined, even unwilling, to participate in the experi-ment. This was partly because Andersen had paid a visit to Mynster to tell him what the theater management had said, and that he ought to go to Sorø Academy, which was just enrolling its first class of students. Among the teachers was the kind, gentle B. S. Ingemann, whom Andersen had got-ten to know in Copenhagen.[19] Of course this was out of the question for a boy so utterly lacking in social position as Hans Christian Andersen. Instead, Mynster suggested Simon Meisling, the high-principled, newly appointed head of Slagelse Grammar School, who from a professional standpoint was a very capable teacher. He had taken his final university exams in theology at the young age of twenty; that same year he won the university's gold medal, and a mere two years later he was awarded a doc-toral degree.

The former head teacher at the prestigious Metropolitan School in Copenhagen was known for his ability to initiate his students into classical scholarship and culture. Surely he would be the perfect choice for bring-ing a dreamer like Andersen down to earth and taming his fluttering, wild nature. In Copenhagen, Meisling was also respected as a knowledgeable and diligent classical philologist who had produced countless retellings of the works of antiquity's Greek and Latin authors, as well as a series of trans-lations of plays by Shakespeare and Gozzi. In terms of translation, Meisling's ambitions and diligence speak for themselves, considering his long list of publications. In the five-year period during the 1820s when he was Hans Christian's headmaster and teacher, and also responsible for administrative work, Meisling still managed to produce more than ten translations of Greco-Roman poetry, complete with copious, discerning notes. On the negative side were a couple of reprimands he received for overly difficult exams and several complaints about questionable methods of punishment. On occasion during 1820-21 at the Metropolitan School he was said to have placed pupils who could not answer correctly at the back of the classroom on a special bench marked with the sign: "Particularly Inept Subjects."[20]

The case was clear, as far as Meisling was concerned, when Jonas Collin appealed to him in October 1822. King Frederik, Jonas Collin, Mynster, and for that matter even Hans Christian Andersen, were not to be refused. Taking them in reverse order, Andersen was a welcome challenge, from a professional and spiritual point of view, for a classically oriented pedagogue like Simon Meisling. At a time when everything was streaming more and more toward a rush of emotion and the worship of Nature, Meisling saw it as his primary goal to put a stop to the cultural dilution and to recover the pure lines of art—by cutting straight through the distortions of the Baroque, Rococo, and Romantic eras.

But of course there were other important although more covert motives behind Meisling's decision to accept the proposal of Mynster, Collin, and the king. His reasons had to do with prestige and money. As a Copenhagener living in a province of Sjælland, Meisling always had a need for contact with someone like Jonas Collin, an influential government official. Collin was not only trusted by the king, he also held central positions in the management of the Royal Theater and with the foundation *Ad usus publicos*, where he was secretary and could thus keep an eye on the monthly stipend for Andersen's room and board in Slagelse. This vital foundation was also the source of ready funds for artists in an impoverished Denmark under absolute monarchy. It was possible to send in applications—as Simon Meisling did several times during the 1820s—to seek support for translations.[21] As a classical philologist, the headmaster of a faltering provincial school, and the father of five, Meisling had good use for any kind of support from the national treasury.

Yet during the first years of Andersen's sojourn in Slagelse, the royal funds did not go directly into Meisling's pocket. This was because the private pupil took lodging, which included his meals and mending, with Madame Erikke Henneberg. She was the widow of a district judge and didn't know a thing about art. She thought that Herr Shakespeare—who sounded like such a nice person—was an older gentleman whom Andersen knew from Copenhagen. Madame Henneberg had plenty of maternal solicitude left over for her sensitive and strangely innocent lodger. Andersen always grew so alarmed and frightened whenever the other lodger, a pupil who was the not particularly pious son of a pastor from Ringsted, would come staggering home in the wee hours of the morning. The two lodgers shared a bed, and whenever the pastor's son would have an urge to snuggle up to Andersen to tell him lewd stories, Hans Christian would flee upstairs to his landlady, who would let him sleep on her sofa. Not until the following day could he confess his innocence to his diary and pray to the higher powers to give him more strength the next time the pastor's son came home drunk and told him stories. "We're all flesh and blood. God help me not to yield to temptation."[22] But this maternal security came to an end in 1825 when Meisling, who for a long time had been taking advantage of Andersen's talents as a babysitter, began to cast an eye on all those *rigsdaler* that were being paid to Madame Henneberg for his pupil's room and board.

There is one thing that is often overlooked in the relationship between Meisling and Andersen. The fact is that during the five years when Andersen knew the headmaster as his teacher and landlord, Meisling was not the utter swine that Andersen often makes him out to be in his memoirs, especially in *The Fairy Tale of My Life*. For extended periods Meisling could be kind and friendly toward Andersen, occasionally even entertaining or helpful. Sundays were often quite pleasant, when Meisling was in the habit of putting aside his teacher role and headmaster mask; for a few hours he would become a child again, both for his own sake and for that of his children. In that role he was even, according to Andersen, more of a child than his own brood. All the desks would be hastily moved out of the classroom so the Meisling family and Andersen could have baby carriage races. They would dash wildly through the classroom, up and down the corridors, with Meisling pushing and Andersen squeezed inside the carriage with his long legs dangling over the side! Afterwards they would all catch their breath with a puppet show, the card game Rambus, or a game of chess, unless they decided to play with tin soldiers, read newspapers and magazines, or settle down to have some sweets. The sense of being part of the family, for better or worse, is evident in various entries in Andersen's diary from 1825. His days were not solely full of terror and torment. For instance, on one dark and stormy Sunday in November, after Andersen had been treated kindly and he could sit down in peace and quiet to pour out his heart, he wrote: "A terrible storm outside, the table is shaking, but I'm fond of storms, when nature comes alive, especially when I have doughnuts, apples, and punch in front of me . . ."[23]

So it was not only a diet of bread and water that he received in the Meisling household. And if we take a closer look at Andersen's diary and his letters from the period 1822-27, we have a much more nuanced impression of the plump little headmaster than in *The Fairy Tale of My Life*. In the memoirs Meisling exclusively plays the role of the tormenter while Andersen appears as the eternally persecuted and deeply unhappy young man who only survived those five years with Simon Meisling through the will of God and the vigilance of Jonas Collin. In reality, for almost two years—from the fall of 1824 to the summer of 1826—Andersen encountered a much more sympathetic and obliging Meisling than the stern headmaster and teacher who had terrified him when he started his schooling. It was as if Meisling, for a year and a half, became more fatherly, friendly, amenable, and empathetic toward Andersen, who was no doubt astonished at this sudden transformation in his teacher. What could he be after?

This gives rise to the idea that Meisling's plans for moving to Helsingør to take over the vacant headmaster position—plans that he told Andersen about in 1825—may have prompted the change in his attitude toward his pupil with the royal stipend. Young Hans Christian Andersen, who, as an educational project, must not result in a defeat for Simon Meisling, was presumably an important element in the headmaster's tactical planning for his own future. Meisling couldn't possibly allow Andersen to stay behind in Slagelse, no matter how much he would have liked to do so, because then the headmaster would lose his warm ties to Collin and the foundation *Ad usus publicos*. For that reason, he decided to persuade Andersen to move into his home as a lodger, which he succeeded in doing in the fall of 1825, after nine months of relatively lenient treatment in the classroom. His royal private pupil acted as both his shield and prod toward the school authorities in Copenhagen as well as Jonas Collin. Meisling was worried that they might criticize a headmaster, who had not yet acclimated himself to his position in Slagelse, for suddenly applying for a post in Helsingør, which had become vacant upon the death of the previous headmaster in 1825.[24] On the other hand, it was conceivable that Collin—aided by a couple of animated letters from Andersen, who spoke more favorably of his headmaster than he ever had before—would use his influence with Mynster and the other members of the school system.

We can't be certain if that was the actual situation, but it's possible. At any rate, Meisling won his new job and moved to Helsingør in May 1826. And it's a fact that from the fall of 1824 to the summer of 1826, Andersen experienced a relatively peaceful time in school, with almost no torment or persecution from Meisling, and he could thus write to Jonas Collin:

"I'm particularly happy that I have won over the good heart of that man who last year seemed quite intent on trampling me and was filled with dissatisfaction about me; he not only wants to take me into his home, but wishes me to follow him."[25]

During Christmas in 1825, the twenty-year-old Andersen was the guest of Commodore Wulff and his lively sons and daughters. The family lived at the Naval Academy in one wing of Amalienborg Palace. One evening Andersen stood in one of the four royal palaces, looking down at the palace square cloaked in winter darkness. He felt like Aladdin in the sultan's palace. Of course, he was there for only a few days at Christmas, and Peter Frederik Wulff, who was head of the Naval Academy, was certainly no sultan. On the other hand, his sweet wife and their children— Henriette, Ida, Christian, and Peter—had given Andersen three volumes of Shakespeare's plays as a Christmas present. Later that evening, when Andersen sat with his diary and tried to digest all the happy impressions— including the long drive from Slagelse with the Meisling family, and the magical lights in the palace square—he ended up writing:

"Thousands of emotions are streaming through me—oh, what hasn't God done for me? Things are happening for me as they did for Aladdin, who says at the end of the play as he looks out the window at the palace . . . Five or six years ago I was walking around down there, didn't know a single person in the city, and now here I am, visiting a dear and esteemed family, enjoying myself with my Schekspear—oh, God is good; a drop of the honey of joy makes me forget all bitterness. Oh, God will not desert me—He has made me so happy."[26]

It is no coincidence that Andersen, during the edifying period of his schooling from 1824 to 1826, should have Aladdin's fate burned into his soul as a way of life and a personal motif. A certain sense of peace and harmony had settled over him. This meant that Andersen could surrender to his faith in providence, which took further nourishment from his religious training and from his more or less covert reading of the Romantic literature of the day, as well as biographical portraits of great mentors in various magazines. He eagerly sought examples in both Jesus and Aladdin.

Gradually he saw himself as one of the chosen; surely Headmaster Meisling would soon allow him to rub the wonderful lamp, which, for every day that passed, became more and more filled with a wild poetic spirit that clamored to be free.

From Heaven to Hell and Helsingør

The almost idyllic mood lasted the entire autumn of 1825. In a letter from September, Andersen couldn't get the headmaster's positive attitude and behavior in recent months to jibe with what he had experienced during the same time the previous year. Now Latin and Greek were downright fun, Andersen maintained, because "the headmaster gives us so many interesting notes," and was in general "so kind and gentle toward me." This is what he wrote in October 1825 when without any particular difficulties he was promoted to the fourth level.[27] It's true that Meisling did attempt to rein in Andersen a bit during the aforementioned Christmas holiday in Copenhagen in 1825, when Andersen slept in Amalienborg Palace as a guest of the Wulff family and, much against Meisling's wishes, paid calls on other families to read from his plays and poems. But other than that, a fundamentally positive tone and atmosphere continued between the two in early 1826. Yet for a long time Andersen had felt—as he confided to Collin in a letter—a persistent fear of Meisling, which meant that he could never feel entirely comfortable in the Meisling household: "If my heart can't completely open to him, if I can't love him, I am still deeply grateful for his interest in me."[28] Andersen had written something similar in his Christmas diary at Amalienborg, when a potentially deeper friendship with Meisling was assessed with the true words of a man of nature: "I would dearly like to love him with all my heart, but I can't create my own feelings."[29] Yet when Andersen dreamed about his headmaster during Christmastime, Meisling suddenly became kind and amenable in his dream!

In May 1826, when Andersen had to decide whether to accompany the headmaster's family to Helsingør, he acknowledged it would probably cost him too much if he did *not* accompany Meisling because he was "unlikely to find a headmaster who would take such an interest in me as he has, especially lately."[30] And up until July 1826, after they had left Slagelse in favor of Helsingør, the peaceful, idyllic mood continued. Almost like father and son, or two friends, Andersen and Meisling took walks together on a couple of Sundays, having such intimate, heart-to-heart conversations that Andersen learned something quite different than he had in the classroom. He received an insight into himself which he later reported to Collin:

> "Day after day I do my utmost to know myself, but considering my abilities and strengths, I am not particularly successful, no doubt because I feel that awful vanity sneaking into the act; and if in a dark moment I judge myself a bit too harshly, for the most part I would like to think better of myself. Yet Meisling has prompted me to realize that there is something terribly flimsy about my nature, something restless and hasty about my spirit that makes it doubly difficult for me to penetrate the [ancient] languages."[31]

So far, so good. But in July and August 1826 the disagreements, hatred, and fear began to grow. What exactly happened, we don't know for sure. Possible causes might include Meisling's financial and marital problems, which were now backing him into a corner. But a more likely source of the conflicts and confrontations that now arose between the headmaster and his private student was Andersen's repeated provocation and breach of the promise he had given to the board of the Royal Theater, Jonas Collin, Lieutenant Colonel Høegh-Guldberg back home in Odense, and Fru Wulff at Amalienborg, who regularly wrote to Andersen and kept an eye on him and his studies. Even in a letter to Collin from early July 1826, Andersen once again, on his honor, assured his benefactor that he would "extinguish every spark of this spiritual fire." But this was much easier said than done, and during that very month Andersen's name appeared in the magazine *Nyeste Skilderie af Kjøbenhavn*. Rasmus Nyerup, a professor of literature, had submitted a literary contribution entitled "Fragment of an Excursion from Roeskilde to Helsingør," written by a most promising student by the name of Hans Christian Andersen.

Andersen was permitted to write poetry and prose during his holidays, but to submit a summertime letter, formatted as a topical travel account, to a number of people with ties to the literary milieu, including Rasmus Nyerup, was a very bold thing for Andersen to do. We might wonder how he dared; but, as usual, he had played his cards with great cleverness. He didn't send the travel account directly to the magazine with a request that it be published. Instead, Andersen no doubt hoped that his text, in the guise of a pleasant, informative summer letter to friends and acquaintances—of its own accord, so to speak—would land exactly where it did. What a professor of literature did with the communiqués he received was not of concern to Andersen. Copyright laws had not yet been invented, and private letters to the newspapers' associates were more or less always in danger of ending up in a larger and more public forum. Such was also the case with Andersen's little travel sketch written in a Romantic mode, which completely disregarded Meisling and his family, even though the headmaster most certainly took part in the excursion, and in any case was the one who had paid for it. On the other hand, the article's gallant young narrator included all the ladies in the mail coach, who, in his account, have to balance on the backs of chairs to descend from the coach when they reach the one-horse town of Slagelse. And when the coach departs once again, heading for Frederiksborg Castle, the ride is so uncomfortable that the narrator's heart practically "dances a solo." It must have been an unusually difficult article for the headmaster to read. He was banished from his own expensive excursion by mail coach from Roskilde to Helsingør by a poetic lout, who now presented it like a Romantic man of the world and shouted to the coachman, urging him to show a little more haste with a spirited line from an early poem by Goethe: "*Spute dich, Schwager Kronos!*" [Make haste, coachman Chronos!][32]

During July and August of 1826, everything changed and became just as oppressive and tense as it had been at the start of Andersen's "Plaguelse," as he called Slagelse in a letter to B. S. Ingemann. The atmosphere was even more oppressive because three times a day Andersen had to sit down for meals with Meisling. As he wrote in a letter to Collin in September 1826: "For fourteen days he hardly spoke to me at the table, barely returned my greeting, and seized every opportunity to quarrel; only yesterday did he speak to me briefly, but as yet I dare not trust in any improvement."[33]

Once again Andersen had to put up with being called "a monster," and in the presence of the entire class he was addressed as "an idiot, an utterly, brutishly stupid boy."[34] Even worse were the headmaster's sudden and totally unpredictable mood swings, which meant that at one moment Andersen might be psychologically terrorized and the next praised and encouraged. This was something that Andersen's already nervous temperament simply couldn't bear. He would barricade himself behind new complaints and a self-pity that sought solace in the theory of the genius who must always be carefully handled, and who requires constant affirmation and admiration. As Andersen wrote in his diary the year before, after being utterly absorbed by Lord Byron's biography: "Oh, he resembled me, right down to his penchant for gossip. My soul is as ambitious as his and feels happy only when admired by everyone; even when the most lowly does not do so it can make me despondent."[35]

The tense relationship wasn't ameliorated in the fall of 1826 by the fact that Meisling seemed to have used Andersen for some pedagogical double-dealing. Jonas Collin, in several comments and reports, was informed that things were going splendidly with his private student, who was both intelligent and industrious. Yet to Andersen, who in the headmaster's opinion would benefit from as little praise as possible, he said just the opposite. He also tightened the reins with even more grammar and syntax pedantry, more lessons in rhetoric, and Danish essays every two weeks, with topics that were nearly always stated as a question regarding the pupil's educational process, such as: *"Does the person who makes good use of the years of his youth need to be anxious about his future?"* To this, Andersen cleverly replied "no," expanding his answer with words that directly reflected his own unhappy situation:

> "Order, regularity, and diligence combined with integrity are what make a youth amiable . . . yet this zeal in a youth may take a wrong turn; the soul is constantly at work shaping a future for itself, and then it may be a simple matter for the images to become dark and menacing. Then a fevered restlessness shudders through the youth. A harmful apprehension steals into his soul that consumes his roots and strength. His striving becomes mechanical. He strives out of fear, his blood is in ferment, flowing heavily through his frightened mind . . ."[36]

If the headmaster had a difficult time perceiving his pupil's true nature and understanding the ferment in his blood, Andersen, on the other hand, was quick to categorize Meisling. At one point the student was supposed to write an essay on irascibility and what means should be employed to tone down a much too choleric nature. No one had any doubt where the essayist had found his inspiration at the school:

> "An insignificant incident may arouse [the choleric temperament], and then it's as if fire were flowing through the veins, as if a satanic force had tensed all the nerves; the blood rises to the head, the veins and muscles swell, the features now become convulsively distorted, and a wild fire seems to flash from the eyes. At that moment he is almost unaware of himself. The person then becomes an animal, passion is the absolute monarch, because reason is stifled at that moment by the choleric fire . . . Then he might murder himself or others. If he is in a position of influence, his iras-

cibility often causes him to commit extreme acts, harmful in their consequences to both society and himself."[37]

Under a pedagogue with an entirely different view of human beings
and life, Andersen's temperament might have developed quite differently
during the 1820s. With all his substantial and repeated demands for
Andersen to restrain the feminine side of his character, Simon Meisling,
with the support of Andersen benefactors such as Christian Høegh-
Guldberg and Fru Wulff, was partially to blame for the fact that Andersen,
as an erotic being, remained at the child stage during the 1820s. It was a
sensitive issue, but Lieutenant Colonel Høegh-Guldberg bellowed from on
high in Odense and clearly expressed his attitude, and that of others,
toward Andersen's oddly sexless nature: "Fear the sickliness your imagination suffers from, and fight against it! . . . Fix your eyes forward like a man,
and do not whimper like a woman who does not have a man's courage."[38]
The following year Høegh-Guldberg's spirited command resounded anew
to the sensitive, feminine Andersen: "Young friend! Put your hand to your
chest and see how great a role vanity still plays in you . . . No, lower your
eyes and work strenuously against yourself!"[39]

But Andersen learned neither to put his hand to his chest nor to salute
in the mid-1820s. At that time, in the eyes of those around him, he should
have entered the ranks of adults in terms of his sexuality, like his two extroverted friends from Sorø Academy, Carl Bagger and Fritz Petit, whom he had
met in 1823 when he was visiting Ingemann. But Andersen merely listened
to their merry tales of dissipation while he remained a boy whose desires and
yearnings were directed toward the first and only woman in his life. And that
bond became the basis for Andersen's first real, completely wrought poems:
"To My Mother" and "The Dying Child." He wrote them under Meisling's
stern rule, which did not permit expression of the young man's ethereal
nature. On the contrary, certain aspects of Andersen's nature were considered—in Høegh-Guldberg's words—"sickly," and the youth's ears were filled
with advice on how to suppress these aspects. Although previously he may not
have felt that he was "sickly," he did so now. It's quite clear that in the fall of
1826, in letters to Jonas Collin and B. S. Ingemann, Andersen suddenly started
to question his sexuality and talk about "my womanish, tedious character."

But it was not only Meisling and other adults who, from the start, kept a
watchful eye on the softer side of Andersen's personality—"this gushing," as the
headmaster called it. His fellow pupils, who were much younger, also noticed,
as one of them later reported, that Andersen was "vanity incarnate, from the
top of his head to the soles of his feet."[40] And it's evident from Andersen's diary

entries and letters from 1825 to 1827 that again and again, without any sort of help from his friends, he was forced to examine his own unusual nature. As he wrote to Ingemann in September 1826: "I suppose I'm also a bit childish and tears quickly appear in my eyes whenever the wind blows a bit harshly, even though I know that life can't be an eternal May day ... I don't really understand myself, but I can tell that I'm much too feminine and weak."[41]

It's clear that during the 1820s Andersen's psyche received some serious abrasions that caused him as a man to withdraw further into himself. His innocence became a means of defense for the wounded young man who refused to grow up. In his covert writings, he had begun to perceive and understand himself in the idyllic image of a little, untouched child.

If the psychological aspect of Meisling's pedagogy was catastrophic for Hans Christian Andersen, the years in Slagelse and Helsingør under the strictures of the stern headmaster did have a positive impact on Andersen's art, since most of his writing had to be done in secret. It was precisely this sort of heightened opposition that the improviser needed. During the period 1822-27, Andersen created an entire subculture of poetry, which developed with almost catapult-like force when he finally escaped from his teacher and mentor in 1827. Even in the 1820s Andersen had a notion of how important it was for him as a writer to experience intellectual and aesthetic opposition. He touches on this subject in many of his school essays, and without having to play the nice, clever boy for his benefactors in Copenhagen, the budding young poet could suddenly say: "Only through strife will the world endure; only through the fiery flames will the metal be purified; and it is only through battles that the soul wins strength and dignity."[42] The twenty-year-old Andersen certainly had quite a clear and conscious awareness of the laws of opposition. In an essay with the edifying title "Why should a human being not want constant happiness in life?," he took the idea further than he could actually vouch for when he categorically stated that it is only through suffering that a person becomes educated. Later in the essay he elaborated on this point of view:

> "Through opposition and struggle everything achieves its existence; that was the manner in which chaos was given order. It is through the power of fire that base metals are purified, and so it is that only through suffering can a human being be purified for true bliss, which can only be grasped and hoped for when the agonies of earthly life have opened his inner gaze."[43]

In his book about Andersen, Edvard Collin, who later became the writer's friend and adviser regarding both financial and aesthetic matters, emphasized how absolutely essential it was for a radical evolution to take place in Andersen's internal writer during the 1820s. At that time everything inside him was jumbled up, like these lines of verse he wrote in January 1823 to Madame Henneberg's daughter, which Collin used to illustrate his point in 1882: "With dark moss on the sacred head, / Majestically grieving, peering down / The ivy encircled / Crumbling pillar; / Pointing toward mortality."[44]

Collin used this quote in his book to defend the educational methods for which Simon Meisling—and in part even his own father, Jonas Collin—was responsible. Edvard Collin called the headmaster "an old-fashioned schoolmaster" in the positive sense, because for the most part Meisling had been faithful to the task entrusted to him by Jonas Collin as well as to his superiors in Copenhagen and to his vocation as a teacher. Edvard Collin wrote that it was necessary to understand that the obligations of Meisling's position required him to act as he did, to educate his students in accordance with the demands of the university, which could not simply be modified for widely differing and exceptional individuals such as Andersen. The scholarly learning that went on in Denmark's grammar schools in the early 19th century was primarily intended to prepare students for the university. This meant that the inevitable requirement—as Collin emphasized—was for a pupil to know not only "that" something was true, but also "why" it was so. And in this sense, Edvard Collin concluded that Meisling did what he could for Andersen, even though he never succeeded in forcing his pupil with the royal stipend to get to the bottom of Danish grammar. For Hans Christian Andersen, pedantry was like water running off a duck's back, as Collin wrote. He also pointed out that throughout his life, Andersen continued to label grammar and syntax as "the backbone of the language, which, like a vile skeleton, keeps laughing at me."[45]

A Potpourri of Poetry

One of Edvard Collin's important points is that Andersen, in spite of the fact that he never "learned to learn properly," absorbed a great deal of knowledge about a wide range of subjects during his five years under Meisling's pedagogical supervision. In addition to lessons in the classical languages, the curriculum included a comprehensive, systematic examination of the history of culture, art, and religion—most of which was utterly new to Andersen. Concurrently, the studious Andersen familiarized himself, whenever he had the opportunity, with smaller doses of modern Danish, German, French, and English literature.

The extent and breadth of Andersen's reading during his school years of 1822-27 are vividly reflected in the collection of quotes that he secretly assembled during his years in Slagelse and Helsingør, copying them into a little notebook. On the outside he wrote the label: *Pourpuri*.[46] "Potpourri" was a popular notion of the times, a symbol of the mixture of tones, moods, genres, and styles that was cultivated during the Romantic era. Potpourri was not just a stew made from various kinds of meat; it was also a blend of fragrant dried flowers placed in a jar, or a collection of melodies loosely tied together with an interlude. And Andersen's potpourri of ideas from the time became shaped into lengthy excerpts from the books he devoured during the 1820s. He wrote down these quotes in his own hand ("runes" as he called his penmanship in a letter to B. S. Ingemann) because they made an immediate impression on him, they were beautiful and inspiring, or they aptly applied to him, to his life situation and fate.

In "Pourpuri," Andersen wrote down the opinions of others regarding such topics as the art of writing, love, bravery, or finding fault with one's fellow human beings. He also included quotes about childishness, such as Oehlenschläger's "Where there are children, there is a perpetual Christmas." Yet most of the quotes have to do with a person's individuality and an essential respect for the peculiarities that we all possess. For instance, he cited the following quote from the Norwegian writer Claus Frimann, in which the student in Slagelse and Helsingør must have seen himself reflected, not to mention Herr and Fru Meisling: "Each is cast from his own form, / Each thus has his own worm." This was how his collection of quotes functioned. Later Andersen also made frequent use of it in his kaleidoscopic debut novel, *Walking Tour*, from 1829. In the novel the quotes formed an intellectual hall of mirrors through which Andersen could move and observe his mysterious first-person narrator in the words and thoughts of others. During his school years he also collected life histories about great men whose destiny seemed to resemble his own—figures no less than Shakespeare, Lord Byron, Leonardo da Vinci, Alexander the Great, Napoleon, and Jesus. In a school essay comparing Alexander the Great to Napoleon, young Andersen touches on the possible shared destiny of people who demonstrate similarities in intellect, ambition, and deeds, and whose souls "in many respects perform with the same colors," as the twenty-year-old Andersen writes.[47]

In particular, it was the destinies of the great writers that inspired Andersen and gave him the courage to begin his own clandestine literary endeavors in the mid–1820s. Andersen encountered Lord Byron in the magazine *Nyt Aftenblad* in the spring of 1825 when a portrait of the Romantic hero, translated from English, was presented in several consecutive issues. The "half poet and half schoolboy"[48] in Slagelse swallowed it all whole. Later that same year we see that William Shakespeare has become the standard for Andersen's explorations and attempts to understand himself. In Andersen's interpretation, it almost sounds as if it were Shakespeare who had copied Hans Christian Andersen, who always found it terribly difficult to spell the Englishman's name properly:

> "In the evening I read for the Wulffs William Skakspear. The writer has portrayed him straight from my own soul; in Act I William's lines perfectly matched my feelings. He intends to become a poet, he decides not to write verse. Oh, tears came to my eyes, in bed all my despondency awoke, but with faith in God and the awareness that I have worked according to my abilities, I fell asleep."[49]

Only a couple of weeks later, in January 1826, it's suddenly the biography of Leonardo da Vinci that seems vividly alive to Andersen, inspiring him to dream of writing a play about the Italian genius who was both manly and as gentle as a woman. All his life Leonardo worked patiently and tirelessly to gain knowledge of nature's secrets, and he never adopted any form of religion, because he considered it greater to be a philosopher than a Christian or Muslim. He was without doubt an artist worth emulating, thought Andersen, who writes that even during his lessons at the grammar school he would hear his imagination whispering lines to him. In the midst of all the pedantry he would picture the magnificent life before him: "Leonardo di Vinci's story hovers before me; what a tragedy I could write about him, but be off, be off—I dare—and I ought not."[50]

Part of Simon Meisling's pedagogical method, as mentioned, was to stifle any poetical tendencies in the young man, but as Andersen writes in his memoirs, this merely strengthened his determination to become a writer:

> "Meisling thought he could force me forward more quickly by continually prostituting me, which frequently made me despair; I often wept with loneliness at home . . . I had a great propensity for daydreaming, which increased all the more; I felt an urge to write. Several times I wrote down various outbursts, and then despaired once again because Collin was against it, of course."[51]

"I can write too!" the headmaster thundered with his hateful irritabil-
ity when the eccentric pupil was once again caught spending his free time
writing instead of devoting extra hours to Greek and Latin grammar. "I'm
a writer myself, and I certainly know what that means. But what you possess is confusion, foolishness, and lunacy!"[52] And the punishment came
swiftly each time the pupil was caught declaiming poetry at gatherings in
Sorø or Slagelse, or during his vacations in Copenhagen, where
Andersen—in Meisling's view—played the role of the provincial clown.
With his Fyn accent he swallowed every single "d" in the Danish language.
Yet most often these charming little errors in pronunciation were over-
shadowed by the affectations of the young reciter. For some people, including the maternal Fru Wulff, it could be excruciating to be repeatedly forced
to listen with a cultivated ear to Andersen's eager recitations.

> "Permit me to say that your reading of German is quite poor, but
> even worse is your reading of Danish. The fact is that you declaim in such
> an affected manner and presume that you are presenting impressions and
> feelings. I must be cruel and tell you: Everyone is laughing at you, though
> you don't realize it. But it is no longer possible for me to keep quiet about
> this; I must make you aware, my good Andersen, how necessary it is for
> you to alter your outward demeanor. Your noble heart is too good not to
> be better protected from the satire of others . . . I have often, my good
> Andersen, both verbally and in writing, given you a hint, but you are so
> preoccupied with yourself, as you are with everything that you undertake,
> that you haven't been able to hear it . . . For God's sake, wake up, dear
> Andersen, and stop dreaming about becoming immortal; because that will
> no doubt merely lead to ridicule."[53]

In other words, Andersen did not exactly bring honor to the grammar school with his performances. Yet they were absolutely essential for
him in his stifled life at school, where poetry writing and daydreaming
were strictly forbidden. That was why Andersen would eagerly seize any
"legal" opportunity to let loose this inner force of nature, about which he
wrote an entire poem in 1826. Later this force of nature was allowed to
speak on the first page of Hans Christian Andersen's first poetry collection in 1830:

> Know that as far back as my mind reaches
> Alas! All my days
> I see a little demon leading me;
> He lives inside me, around me, everywhere,

> Though I cannot describe his form,
> Yet awake and in dreams, at any time
> He is the reason that I must—rhyme.[54]

His "Rhyming Demon" is what Andersen called this delightful, surreptitious sinner who appeared and spoke for the first time in the poem of the same name, under a Hebrew motto, which means "Lead us not into temptation." This Rhyming Demon was Andersen's spirit of civil disobedience, an anarchical joker who defied all authorities, including a headmaster who couldn't understand that a poet was not something a person became by reading the work of other poets; it was something *innate*. The Rhyming Demon was a manifestation of the writer's vocation within Andersen that could no longer be controlled.

> That's how it is. Wherever I turn
> It ends with verse,
> That's why they scold
> And angrily shout at me at every hour:
> "Stop your rhyming!"
> Yes, dear God! I would prefer that, by far,
> But I was born under an ill-fated star.[55]

Written secretly—developed like a whole little subculture from the 1820s—we find more than fifty poems, verses, and songs that illustrate how Andersen seized every imaginable opportunity during his first years in Slagelse to fire off a poem, preferably in writing. The earliest of these Andersen poems were originally written down on various kinds of paper and then stitched together with twine into a booklet. The fourteenth and last page of the booklet ended with a drawing of the rolling landscape near Slagelse.[56]

During these first years, and behind Headmaster Meisling's back, Andersen sought out various benefactors and arbiters of taste around Sjælland, especially those who had ties to journals and magazines. Among them was Pastor H. Bastholm of Slagelse, who was known for his enormous library. He also edited the newspaper *Den Vest-Siællandske Avis*. In his *Annals for the Year 1823*, Bastholm reports that among many bothersome visitors he had also turned away a certain pupil named Andersen from the grammar school, "who was constantly appearing at my door with his mediocre verses, and whom I had to dismiss."[57] Among the fifty early rhymed deviltries from Andersen's pen we find texts written for Meisling's induction as headmaster, for the funeral of Dean Gutfeldt, for the sweet daughter of Madame Henneberg, for the pastor's wife Fru Fuglsang, and birthday greetings for various male friends, including Commodore Wulff's son Christian. In this latter poem, the elegant colloquial tone of the future fairy tale slips into the rhyme and rhythm of the verses. Down the river it goes with full fairy-tale force, heading for Copenhagen and Christian at Amalienborg Palace:

> Though my word is not comely nor in fashion,
> You will excuse me—It is truly meant. —
> But how did my little verse come about,
> In what manner—the manner was this:
> A ship I made of reeds and leaves
> And fairies bore it on the briny wave.
> Now here is the poem!—Just a humble gift.[58]

In addition to the more or less lively poems written for specific occasions, such as weddings and funerals, there are also a number of autobiographical sketches, which in concentrated form repeat the Romantic tale about the budding genius poet, which had already carried Andersen quite far. In Copenhagen the young Andersen had recited the prose story of his childhood to get his foot in the door with potential benefactors and patrons. Similarly, he now writes a long poem to the wife of Pastor Fuglsang, intended to arouse the family's sympathy and interest in the sender, whose brilliance has finally been taken in hand from on high: "Then noble men did hear the fragile tones, / And listened to the child's feeble song / . . . They took the child from his nature free / And set him behind the temple's dark wall."

In the midst of this autobiography in verse, Andersen saw his chance to take a poke at Headmaster Meisling: "I have heard an esteemed voice once say / That I was a stupid, confused dreamer." And then he nicely and effectively finished off his plea for a little maternal understanding and solicitude with: "Yet surely you won't misconstrue my little song? / Smile then, but laugh not at its childish sound." The whole thing was sent off, signed "Faithfully yours, Andersen."[59]

In comparison to what Andersen later produced as a poet, most of these poems are quite disjointed, lacking in color and contour, sentimental ("easily the heart may bleed / in the poet's bosom"), and filled with ponderous metaphors ("the genius of hunger" and "the angel of despondency dressed in nightly fog"). They are, as they must be, frail attempts written by a young, openhearted poet who had not yet found his own rhythm and pulse but was still imitating everything around that was called great poetry. But in the midst of yet another heavy-handed and not particularly imaginative picture of nature's vibrancy, young Andersen suddenly takes up a stance in the center of the landscape and waves to the reader, who in this case was Madame Henneberg's twenty-five-year-old daughter. He speaks in the self-mocking tone that would later become an inseparable part of Andersen's poetic voice: "When Boreas with his storms / visits Sjølund's lovely regions / And you spy a scarecrow / Standing in the naked field alone, / Then think of me!"[60]

A lonely scarecrow on a bare, windswept field in winter—what an ice-cold but precise and clear self-portrait! In another place, in the midst of numerous praises of the good Lord and Romantic lamentations over the lost land of childhood, we find another admission from the nineteen-year-old scarecrow, this one dealing with eternal innocence. Here, in the poem "The Youth and the Old Man," it is the erotically excluded Andersen who for the first time in his literary career speaks about the sensual side of love, "the fire of pure deity," which was now in the process of searing all the narrator's peers. As for the "I" of the poem, he is not exactly a pyromaniac. So far he is familiar only with a child's forms of love.

> Love for God is all I know,
> For my mother and those close to me;
> Love, you heavenly strong maiden
> Alas, of your image I cannot sing.
> My heart swells, my thoughts fade,
> You only as portent do I see.[61]

These fifty early poems from the period 1822-25 were all links in a crucial maturation process that took place in secret. The uneven, unfinished poems indicate the slow and difficult path toward more concentrated and completely wrought poems in the years 1825-27. The later poems included "Poetry," "The Soul," "To My Mother," and the truly epochal "The Dying Child," which along with many others from his school days in Helsingør was included in Andersen's first poetry collection in 1830 and swiftly became known abroad.

Religious and Poetic Maturation

In spite of the ban on writing poetry, Andersen managed to satisfy both his urge to write and his poetic yearnings. This is evident in the whole colorful spectrum of poems from the period 1822-27, as well as in various prose pieces that he wrote. The latter included the extensive fragment of a historical novel, written during the same period, in which Andersen once again skewered his nemesis of a headmaster by presenting him as a little pasty-faced devil.[62] We also find Andersen's compulsion to write in the steady stream of letters to all the friends and acquaintances he was attempting to make or keep as his allies. When Hans Christian truly hit his stride and had something exciting to report—such as a good grade or some new rudeness on the part of Meisling—he could write up to fourteen pages a day. The flood of communiqués was primarily directed at Jonas Collin and quickly became much more intense and intimate in tone than Collin had envisioned. The letters can be read like one long umbilical cord of paper, to which Andersen steadfastly clings, preoccupied solely with himself and insisting on this natural right, whether he is begging, complaining, or bragging about his grades and enclosing a particularly good school essay. But beneath all the smugness, the moaning, and the rhetorically well-formulated pleas for funds to pay for clothing, books, and resoling his shoes, it's also possible to hear a young man's cry for help—stemming from both material need and spiritual desperation.

This is a cry that also resounds throughout the more than seventy school essays that Andersen submitted during 1822-28. They offer a scattered but very lively glimpse of how the Rhyming Demon was stirring within young Andersen, side by side with his faith in the good Lord. The fact that both a poetic and a religious maturation occurred inside of him at more or less the same time during the 1820s is evident from Andersen's diary from those years, when he often—indirectly—prays that God and the Rhyming Demon might soon find each other and become reconciled. During the fall of 1825, his urge to start writing once again arises so strongly that Andersen fears his vigorous imagination might soon send him to the madhouse or lead him to suicide.[63] He then prays that this violent force he feels inside him might give his soul the courage to break free. "Fill my heart until you burst!" is the watchword one day. The following day, when he suddenly has doubts and begins to fear this rebellious tendency and anarchical urge within, he prays for the good Lord to take charge and govern what is ungovernable inside of him:

> "You want the best for me; with my faith in You, all-merciful God, I accept my fate. God, let happiness accompany me! If it is Your will that I should become a poet, surely You will not weaken my courage and rob me of everything. My soul breathes solely for the art of poetry. I thought

I could detect Your hand in the governance of my fate; do not rob me of faith; God my Father, my only One, hear Your weak child!"[64]

This great internal struggle that took place in Andersen around 1825 found great sustenance in his reading of a textbook that was widely used at the time in the grammar schools throughout Denmark: *Catechism on the Christian Religious and Moral Philosophy*. It was written in 1818 by Peter Krog Meyer, who later became a Norwegian bishop and professor. The book was a systematic examination of the fundamentals of the Christian religion, presented in brief but rather ponderous paragraphs, to which the pupils were indirectly supposed to refer in the essays they wrote.[65] The topics of the assignments were often of such a philosophical character that today they would be considered more appropriate for older theology students than for a pupil of eighteen. There was never any question of allowing a student to choose his own essay topic, since the point was—especially in the case of Andersen—to use the essay assignment to curb the wilder flights of fancy in a young man and to force the leaping associations of the person in question onto more stable and rigorous paths.

Hans Christian Andersen, who was never brilliant in Greek or Latin, was both an attentive and avid pupil during the lessons in religion. Like most people, from childhood he had shown a natural interest in religion, and he also felt impelled to search for the basis and purpose of life. In addition, he possessed a talent for thinking, reasoning, and for formulating his religious ideas. In other words, Andersen was not afraid of faith. His piousness also contained a healthy skepticism toward excessive piety, since he had grown up in an impoverished home with an exceedingly superstitious mother and a rationalistic father.

The religious lessons in Slagelse were administered by Jeppe Quistgaard. He was a kind and gently earnest sort of teacher, who, unlike Simon Meisling, was not a supporter of fatuous pedantry. He saw it as a much more exalted task to lead his pupils to a personal and well-considered Christian point of view. That was what Andersen acquired during those years. He ended up with a sort of combination and amalgam of what Quistgaard, through Krog Meyer's book, taught him, and everything he had learned back home in Odense—which, roughly speaking, consisted of equal parts superstition and rationalism. Andersen, who was both attentive and interested, proved to be a challenging student, and Jeppe Quistgaard quickly took an interest in the reflective young man. By refusing to handle Andersen with the sternness that Meisling usually practiced, the religion teacher, at Andersen's request, became a sort of father confessor to the young man who had a talent for believing in and talking about God. Whether Andersen was in fact pleased with this quiet and often melancholy teacher, or whether Quistgaard was simply one of the few people at the grammar school to whom the eighteen-year-old could open his heart, is not clear in the letter he sent to his religion teacher right before exams during his first year at the school in Slagelse. In any case, Andersen did encounter a sympathetic person in the figure of his religion teacher:

> "Dear Teacher. Your kindness toward me at school draws me to you, and I hope that this will not cause you to misunderstand or in any way have wrong thoughts about me. *In this town* I am utterly without any guide or true friend . . . From your religious lessons I think I know you well enough to see that you are a man who feels and wants to help someone who is striving. Do not be angry if my letter seems a bit long, but I find it impossible to explain to you in only a few words what my thoughts are."[66]

With Krog Meyer's textbook in hand, Quistgaard made himself a spokesperson for a view of humanity and life that put God in the absolute center. And, as we can read in Andersen's essays, this was a lesson that spoke to the essayist's heart and mind. As he points out—quite lucidly, we might add—in an essay about the proof of God's existence:

> "Only a fool says in his heart: 'There is no God.' Marked by the omnipotent, the inscrutable, even the smallest vermin in the cheese stands on the farthest planet in the universe and on the smallest mite in the deep."[67]

It's not surprising that Andersen, who was both fatherless and without a family, should be so strongly preoccupied with the idea of God as the loving father of every individual. Since he, as a child, had presumably often eaten spoiled food or had no food whatsoever, Andersen would inevitably covet better and cleaner conditions when he finally escaped from Odense, the filthy and unhealthy site of his childhood. For that reason, there is a direct link between the cautious attempts in the young Andersen's first essays to include his own fate in a larger, divine pattern and the older Hans Christian Andersen's unshakable faith in God as the merciful, paternal Providence who—as Andersen wrote in one school essay—governs "the great order that we can trace in all of nature."[68] As early as the 1820s, we can speak of a faith with roots in the writer's piety and skepticism, as well as in Krog Meyer's textbook and the Romantic era's philosophy of nature. Over the next decades, partially under the influence of the physicist H. C. Ørsted, this would all merge in the adult Andersen's attempt to write tales about "the spirit in nature," in which he explained the world as an outpouring from God—as it's so beautifully stated in one of his school essays.

> "The human soul is a spark from the eternal flame. The storm is His voice, the clouds and waves His raiment, and the whole earth a humble flower in His glorious crown."[69]

In spite of the inspiration from Krog Meyer's book, there is reason to question what the young Hans Christian Andersen believed in most during his school years: Was it the good Lord up in heaven, or was it the fairy down on earth by the Odense River? Andersen gives what might be an answer in an essay from 1825 in which he was supposed to discuss the relationship between emotion and reason. We have here a fine example of how, in Andersen's eyes and ears, the lessons of Christianity were not a collection of dead facts, as the lessons in grammar and geometry were. Instead, they represented vivid realities about which he felt compelled, both as a young man and as an artist, to form an opinion, even though it might be a divided one.

In Andersen's view, the essay was so good that he chose to enclose it in a letter to Jonas Collin.[70] At first reading, the sender seems to be a confused person who can't govern his own impressions or ideas and has great difficulty in organizing his material, even within a few pages. That's why the clear threads are quickly lost in the prelude's lively introduction of the merry young *Fantasy* and his serious and rather boring big brother, *Reason*. Halfway through the essay, the whole argument seems to come to a halt, and the narrator suddenly realizes that he is not a great writer but merely a schoolboy and essayist who has set off in the wrong direction. After that the essay straightens out and the text shifts from the fairy-tale-like opening into a more theological explication of the basis for the Creation and the greatness of the human spirit. Even though the initial fairy-tale aspects now disappear entirely from the text, the deliberations presented in the rest of the essay are no less original. The young essayist says, for instance, that the power behind the Creation can be defined as "the childlike spirit that animated the first humans, the almighty God, who so miraculously developed everything more and more. Aren't the ideas about the creation of the earth childlike?"[71]

Young Andersen doesn't hesitate to set an equal sign between "God" and "childlike spirit," and in the rest of the essay we hear that it is not bor-ing, adult reason, but rather the child's sparkling imagination that has marked the development of all cultures and peoples. The twenty-year-old Andersen hails *homo ludens*—the playful human—and the essay's mature message is quite simply that grown-ups must learn to kneel before the child. Only in that way will their small, down-to-earth worlds expand. As early as 1825 we are at the very root of a familiar Andersen theme: the cold, adult sagacity versus the simple, warm child-hearts of Gerda and Kai in "The Snow Queen."

As a fairy tale, the sophisticated school essay about the relationship between reason and emotions was far from complete. But young Andersen's boldness speaks for itself in his way, in writing, of presenting powers within himself and in his closest importunate surroundings. Once again we see an example of Andersen's exceptional courage, in a stifling and extremely stressful situation, to confront all the fathers and big brothers of reason and in his parting words—literally in the first sentence of the very last paragraph—to challenge the teachers of all the grammar schools in Denmark: "In the currents of time, everything mediocre top-ples. Only what is exceptionally great can endure."[72] This was something even the headmaster had to understand: Pedagogues disappear, geniuses endure.

During the course of his five years in school, Andersen became an underground poet. While ostensibly doing his lessons—including writing essays—Andersen poured out a number of brief poetic texts, which, like their author, wanted to go farther out into the world, to be heard and find their way into print. The fact that all ploys were valid in this difficult process was the most natural thing in the world for an impoverished improviser like Hans Christian Andersen. For him, poetry was the natural ticket for admittance into the better circles. Literature was not something to be piled up in notebooks or locked drawers, waiting for better times or more advantageous trends. Literature was a natural link in a larger, uni-versal cycle that was beyond birthright and social class. This worldwide, invisible kingdom—"the spirit's Hindustan"—was described in one of Andersen's first truly successful poems, "Poetry." In this poem he also intro-duced some of his own poetics—such as his belief that fairy tales spring from the present moment and ordinary life—which would become the lifelong basis for the way he lived and wrote.

There is a glorious land,
Poetry it is called!
It reaches to the sky,
Is wrapped up in a rosebud,
And the heart's melody
Dwells on its green shore

        . . .

There, to a poem of beauty
Is exalted daily life;
You feel that God is near.
Bygone times live there;
Forceful thoughts do tremble,
So grand it is here, so rich!

        . . .

The spirit's Hindustan,
Home of the melody,
Land of God's Covenant,
That will stand when worlds are ravaged,
Its name is *Poetry,*
Fatherland of the light.[73]

Andersen felt like a chosen sovereign in this realm. By using his Romantic view of art, which in some respects seemed to be innate, through his poetry he would now teach the whole world that there is another world—invisible to most people—that is much more glorious than the one in which we live. And for this journey toward the spirit's Hindustan, Andersen the poet would be the medium through which the true, beautiful, and good spoke and would now "wrap our earth in glory," as he writes in the fourth stanza of "Poetry."

Nearly all the poetic texts that Andersen wrote during 1824-27 were intended to be put into lyrical circulation, either enclosed in letters or sent out in public to be recited or printed as quickly as possible. As a rule his new texts, which might go farther out into the world, were first cautiously aired in letters to the proper recipients outside of school, such as B. S. Ingemann in Sorø. Or they might be given a trial reading for the right circles, for instance for the Wulffs at Amalienborg, for Oehlenschläger, Ørsted, Collin, or Madame Jürgensen in Copenhagen.

His inner Rhyming Demon, like a genie in a bottle when it finally escapes its imprisonment, needed to get out into the world. An example of this occurred in January 1824, after the nineteen-year-old Andersen had a refreshingly long Christmas vacation in Copenhagen, where he received wonderful gifts, such as the collected works of Sir Walter Scott and *New Poems* by Adam Oehlenschläger. Back home in Slagelse, the thumbscrews of reason were immediately applied. Yet Andersen takes the time to write a lengthy letter to Herr Iversen, the book printer in Odense. He has come up with the idea to publish some of his own poems from the period before and after his arrival in Slagelse in 1822. Andersen writes that he's not interested in money, if only he might have sixteen free copies of the book, which, in the eyes of the budding poet, would be worth their weight in gold. He could use them as thank-you gifts and to introduce himself, and they would send his poetry out into circulation around the world. The rest of the copies the book printer could use as he pleased:

> "During the holidays I have now read through them and selected the best, which I have read for Ølenslæger and other men who can judge such things, and they told me that I might venture to offer them to the public. For that reason I am sending you the poems, and if you will read through them and print them, you may (indeed, if not before, then after they are sold) give me whatever you like for them, after you have been paid for your trouble. If you would merely give me 16 copies, which I will give to friends, I will leave the rest to you."[74]

Yet the good Iversen could not see any profit in such an undertaking, and the fact that the book was never published is no doubt something that the mature writer of fairy tales scarcely regretted. Instead Andersen found new expression for his suppressed artistic impulses in 1824 with his long poem "The Soul," in which the poetic narrator appeals to a mysterious, multi-voiced "you," who is initially juxtaposed with the power the narrator feels inside and wants to express: "O power that resides within us / But cannot be interpreted in words."[75] The fact that this was more than just a physiological and psychological stirring is evident in the poem's next lines, in which the narrator asks whether this indefinable urge inside is "a divine spirit, / That errantly fell from heaven." The answer is somewhat nebulous; we're told that at issue is a great and highly remarkable order, whose power always evades any type of contact or explanation: "No one knows you, O most High! / Nor do you understand yourself. / Dreams hover before your eye / And an eternity portends you."[76]

The word in human speech that unifies and approaches what this power stands for is also the title of the poem, "The Soul." And in our striving to obtain even a tiny bit of knowledge about the soul's secret powers, the poem's narrator must not only ask about the truth of our spiritual life after death but also acquire knowledge about the intentions of this power. What is its purpose as it roams around like that inside a person? Is it to sing a song in honor of "The Almighty"? the narrator asks. Or is it simply to make itself known and to reel boldly through five stanzas and thirty lines of verse? For whom does this soul-power speak? God or the Rhyming Demon? In either case, it is remarkable.

The Dying Child

The corrosive battle between Andersen the poet and Headmaster Meisling entered its final stage in 1826-27, as a consequence of the poem about the soul, the school essay about the relationship between feeling and reason, and, in particular, the aggravating description in a magazine of the headmaster's family trip by horse-drawn carriage from Slagelse to Helsingør in May 1826. After a truce that had lasted a year and a half, the headmaster once again began to use every imaginable opportunity to chase off Andersen's Rhyming Demon. From August 1826 until April 1827, Andersen was besieged around the clock with the demand to come to his bourgeois senses.

Right before Andersen's arrival in Helsingør, Lieutenant Colonel Høegh-Guldberg in Odense had sent him a sharply admonishing letter, in which he commented on the young man's desperate pronouncement in a previous letter: "Poet or nothing!" The colonel wrote that under no circumstances should he allow himself to say such a thing, and he told Andersen to leave such decisions to Our Lord. The boy should also tend to his schoolwork, and in the future he should ensure that he had a dictionary close at hand whenever he wrote letters![77] From the opposite point on the compass thundered Fru Wulff, issuing similar warnings and admonitions to Andersen about continuing to control his awkward demeanor and pay attention to his lessons instead of constantly climbing onto his Pegasus:

"You are neither more nor less than a pupil who must attend school to learn and learn and complete your schooling quickly without believing that you are or will become something brilliant, a poet or any such thing, or take into consideration what the state or private individuals are doing for you. You are not the first, nor will you be the last, for whom something similar is done. Therefore, show your gratitude with modesty, and don't think it's because there is anything more remarkable about you than about thousands of others."[78]

During that period a couple of classmates even began offering advice to the self-absorbed and stubborn Andersen, telling him to banish all fantasies from his body. In early 1827, Andersen received a letter from Jens Hviid, a former friend at the school in Slagelse, who now urged his classmate to keep his dream life in check and find his way to "the center lane of life," where it's possible to dream without "falling into the ditch." Jens Hviid also offered a good old folk remedy for Andersen's wild imagination: "When you start dreaming again, take a stick and whip your poor hide until the dreaming disappears; but don't hit too hard, because then it might hurt."[79]

But it was all to no avail. Andersen kept on writing, and eventually, during the winter of 1826–27, he dared go so far as to lift the veil which for many years had hidden his poetic impulse and production from all his friends and benefactors in Copenhagen, who might at any time report back to Meisling. It was also possible that they might withdraw both their own and the king's support. In other words, Hans Christian Andersen was playing a highly risky game with his future. But as he once wrote in a school essay about overstepping one's own limitations: "When duty invites a person to act, and he does so, even though the act is associated with danger, then he shows courage."[80]

And it was at this level that Andersen acted when, shortly after his arrival in Helsingør in 1826, he wrote the simple, perfectly formed poem "The Dying Child," which was also translated into German. The following year, both versions were published on the front page of the newspaper *Kjøbenhavnsposten*, after Andersen had finally escaped from Meisling and no longer felt that he was, well, a dying child.[81] Yet this short, touching poem with its slow, forward-moving rhythm and clear syntax ought to be read as a work of art all on its own. And in the larger context of literature and cultural history, "The Dying Child" is an epochal text because Andersen's poetic elevation of the child's thoughts and speech, which carry the poem's structure, broke with all the norms of how a good and proper literary text should look in the 1820s. Such a deep and thorough prostration before a child's nature had never been attempted by any other poet in the world—not even Goethe in his poem about the *Erlkönig* from the late 18th century.

Mother, I am tired, I want to sleep,
Let me fall asleep by your heart;
But do not weep, first promise me that,
For your tears are burning on my cheek.
It is cold in here, outside the storm threatens,
But in dreams, all is so beautiful,
And I see the sweet angel children
When I close my weary eyes.

Mother, do you see the angel at my side?
Do you hear the lovely music?
Look, he has two beautiful white wings,
Our Lord surely gave them to him;
Green, yellow and red hover before my eye,
Flowers that the angel scatters!
Will I too have wings while I live,
Or, Mother, will I have them when I die?

Why are you pressing my hands?
Why are you placing your cheek on mine?
It is wet, and yet it burns like fire,
Mother, I will always be yours!
But now you must no longer sigh,
If you weep, I will weep with you.
Oh, I am so tired!—Must close my eyes —
Mother—look! Now the angel is kissing me![82]

On the threshold of death, in his feverish dream, the child sees an entrance to the divine realm about which the pious mother—we have to imagine—once told her child. At the same time that the childish imagination is allowed to determine the course of the poem with its sense perceptions, reflections, and inquisitive, naïve questions—"Will I too have wings while I live?"—Andersen manages in very little space to give us quite an expansive look at a child's spiritual and intellectual resources. Even on the verge of death, there is room for empathy and solace when the dying child puts his arm around his sobbing mother and says:"If you weep, I will weep with you."

Previously, the child had always been a silent and static object in literature, but in Andersen's poem in 1826, the child became a subject who spoke and acted—a person *sui generis*. Even in the Romantic era around

1800, which was so fond of children, and in the wake of Rousseau's discovery of childhood as something inherently valuable, it was still the eyes
and ears of the adult that dominated and determined the form and content
of a work of art. Yet, as we see in the three verses of Andersen's poem, the
adult is suddenly transformed to a shadow by the child, and the mother's
shape and presence are depicted exclusively through the words of the child.
The roles were switched, and the ancient balance of power was thus upset
by a twenty-one-year-old Danish poet, who had magnificently transposed
the solemn gravity of death to the natural perceptions of a little child.

The consistent adherence to the child's point of view was no coincidence but rather a conscious, poetic act on Andersen's part. This is evident
from a draft of the poem, in which the poet, in his first attempt, considered making use of an adult voice—the mother's—to begin the poem with
the words: "Sleep, beloved child, you are so tired / My arms rock you so
warm and so close, / Sleep sweetly, you will awake again." Then the dying
child would be allowed to speak.[83] But when the poem was published, after
Andersen had spent a winter in Helsingør and then returned to
Copenhagen in 1827, the radical decision had been made to tell the poem
exclusively from the child's naïve and fearless point of view.

The word "naïve" had a positive connotation during the Romantic
period. For that reason, it was not difficult for the German-speaking
world, in which many educated people understood Danish and read
Danish newspapers, to see the qualities of "Das sterbende Kind" [The
Dying Child], which appeared on September 15, 1827, on the front page
of *Kjøbenhavnsposten* in both Danish and German. Andersen had his poem
translated to German with the assistance of Ludolph Schley, a secretary at
the Swedish Consulate in Helsingør. And with that, he took the first small
step toward world fame. In 1834, when he was away on his cultural journey to Italy, Andersen stated in a letter that even at the distant latitudes of
Naples, his "dying child" had won him praise, since people knew of the
poem in a French translation. But farther north, and primarily in
Germany, the poem had already achieved acclaim by 1830. At any rate,
Andersen tries to convince the reader of this in the tenth chapter of his
travel book *Shadow Pictures* (1831), when we're on our way with the
express mail coach from Leipzig to Dresden and listen as the young Danish
poet is questioned by an older German traveler who is interested in Danish
literature. Could this Andersen sitting across from him be related to the
author of the poem "The Dying Child"? When the young traveler confirms this, the older man wants to know how such a young, inexperienced

writer could write such a wise poem. Had he perhaps suffered the loss of a little child himself? Andersen replies truthfully that the poem was composed during a foreign-language class at school. In the very midst of conjugating the Hebrew word for "to kill," he had "felt and written" those three verses.[84]

Liberation

It's not hard to understand why Andersen, by the winter of 1826-27, had finally had enough of Meisling and his whole motley family, which included five children ranging in age from one to thirteen, a housekeeper, and a couple of maids—in all, more than ten mouths to feed. The circumstances in the headmaster's home during that first year after the move to Helsingør had begun to develop in a disastrous direction. Simon Meisling's marriage to the quick-witted and promiscuous Fru Inger Cathrine, who, according to Andersen's memoirs written in 1832, had bedded most of the garrison in both Slagelse and Helsingør, had become an absurd situation, nothing but a travesty. "I developed no good ideas about women, and the mistress assured me that they were all just like her, but I was so divertingly innocent for my age."[85]

It is primarily in *Hans Christian Andersen's Autobiography 1805–1831*, from which the above quotation was taken, that Andersen reports the shocking experiences in Meisling's home during 1826-27, when everything fell apart and the shameless filth overtook both the management of the household and the conduct of Herr and Fru Meisling. The loose-living Fru Inger Cathrine flirted with everyone, even the innocent Andersen, while every evening her pigheaded, introverted, and slovenly husband would retreat with the punch bowl and his Greco-Roman classics. As Andersen maliciously remarks in his memoirs, it was as if Meisling, after they had moved to Helsingør, washed his hands only by squeezing lemons into his sweet, soothing evening drink.

On October 26, 1826, Andersen for the first time spoke candidly in a long letter that was both sober and restrained. In contrast to his many other letters from previous years, this one was not merely crammed full of "Jeremiads and Werther." It cut right to the heart of the matter, meaning Simon Meisling. "Every day he expresses his displeasure toward me, and on Sunday morning when I bring my Latin essay, he shakes my soul at every mistake, speaking the most awful truths. That he wishes the best for me, I have no doubt, but everything arouses his displeasure, and I live in the most horrid tension."[86]

Andersen then rattled off all the monstrous, degrading remarks with which he was being bombarded, and Collin must have found it very hard to believe. At the time the headmaster called this pupil who had been entrusted to him by King Frederik VI and Jonas Collin "a person without feeling or honor" and "an awkward, stupid creature" and a lunatic who ought to be put in a "curiosity cabinet inside a cupboard to speak Greek" (because then crowds of spectators would come). Even the hesitant Collin could now see that things had gone quite wrong, but as the loyal government official and diplomat that he was, he did not immediately spring to his feet like a jack-in-the-box. Headmaster Meisling, on the other hand, did just that when he received Collin's letter at the end of November 1826, inquiring about the situation. This was the first time—officially—that Meisling's pedagogical methods were questioned. These were the very methods that Collin, as the foundation's secretary, had supported and defended, especially to Andersen whenever they met during the Christmas or Easter holidays in Copenhagen. He always gave the young man, who would have preferred to stay in the city, some of the usual encouraging words, such as: "Every land its plague, as it says in King Solomon; you must make do with your fate!"[87]

Headmaster Meisling lived up to his local reputation, both as the watchdog and the monster, when he read Collin's letter in November. His reply was prompt. The sharp tone of his voice was unprecedented, and his arguments were downright shameless, or at least inflammatory. From the very first sentence, Meisling's letter hinted that Jonas Collin ought to mind his own business since he had such a poor understanding of such matters: "I have always believed that the pedagogue resembles the artist, at least in the sense that he continues to perform his best when no one is looking at his fingers with anxious fastidiousness."[88]

This letter was in sharp contrast to the servile application for an extension of funding for Andersen's room and board from the foundation *Ad usus publicos*, which Meisling had sent to Collin three months earlier. In the application there was no limit to Andersen's merit. But with the November letter the headmaster virtually signed his own dismissal notice. His unrestrained dipping into the inkwell because of "a sickly, pampered creature," who was Andersen, signified the beginning of the end to Simon Meisling's pedagogical and academic career. Collin's reply two days later was as brief and direct as Meisling's, though of course not nearly as rash. On the same day Andersen received word from Collin that a change in his living and study situation would most likely soon take place. Yet this change did not become a reality until Easter 1827, after Andersen had fed Collin a steady diet of new horror stories about Meisling as teacher and landlord during that trying winter. For instance, the headmaster had now started saving money by refusing to heat Andersen's room, and the young man froze like a Spaniard, constantly shuffling around in his tiny room like flies in the sunshine. At the same time, all laundering was suspended and the meals—like his hosts— became more and more unappetizing.

Christian Werliin was a newly hired teacher at the school who was the same age as Andersen and taught Hebrew. During the winter of 1826-27 he observed the disgraceful situation, and at Easter he went to Copenhagen specifically to report the truth—face to face with Jonas Collin—about Meisling's decline and the methods he was using with Andersen. Only then, after several months of consideration, did Collin give in and take action. Around the first of April 1827, the headmaster was informed by letter that Andersen, as of the 14th, would be leaving for Copenhagen, where a fourth-floor room had been rented for him at Vingaardstræde 131 (the present-day number 6). There the last eighteen months of his studies leading to his final exams would be supervised by the private tutor, Ludvig Christian Müller. He was a young theological student who lived in Christianshavn and had been recommended by Christian Werliin. For the immediate future, Andersen's meals would be provided, in turn, by the Collin, Wulff, Ørsted, and Balling families, as well as others.[89] When the despondent Andersen in Helsingør heard about Collin's intercession, he was so happy that he nearly jumped out the window of his room in the school building. A classmate who happened at that moment to come out of the entrance on Kongensgade heard Andersen yelling loudly: "I'm leaving the school! I'm going to Copenhagen!"

But for Meisling, things were headed in only one direction: downhill. Several years later his marriage came to an end, and over time the Helsingør Grammar School acquired such a bad reputation that pupils stopped enrolling, and the school was forced to close. Over the years, Meisling's lack of polish, tolerance, and basic social manners had brought him into conflict with everyone in Helsingør, where they had to put up with a headmaster who ran around with a hip flask sticking out of the pocket of his perpetually filthy and foul-smelling clothes.

★ ★ ★

Even many years after Meisling's death, his old pupil continued to think about—and especially dream about—his former tormenter. In 1867, Andersen, now a Councilor of State, had a long dream about Meisling, who was transformed into both Jonas Collin and his son Edvard. All of them gave the author such a stern lecture that at last he woke up:

> "Last night I had a vile dream; it's thoroughly psychological that I should still have such dreams. I thought I was in Meisling's house. Everything was just the same, in every detail, except that Meisling called me, in all his bitterness and scorn: Sir Councilor. Yet one thing had changed with me; I stood up from the school bench, flung my books at him, and left the room . . . I find it quite strange that so long after that early period I should so often in my dreams be carried back to those circumstances. It shows how deeply affected, how oppressed, how dependent I felt! It gives an impression of being born a slave."[90]

In reality, over the years Andersen managed to fling quite a few books at Simon Meisling through his writing. In many places in his poems, novels, plays, and fairy tales written over a period of forty years, there are more or less undisguised references to the headmaster. They are often quite blunt, such as the ode in "The Swines," from 1830, where Andersen, with an elegant reference to the headmaster's Greco-Latin snout, manages to trample him with the words: "Many a mighty man was transformed to a swine, / We can read about that in both Greek and Latin."[91] Even in his first real attempt to write a novel in 1824-25, Andersen had clothed Meisling as an executioner and described him as a big, strong, and meaty man with "an African face, a flat nose, and big, protruding, thick lips; how strangely his tiny green vampire eyes stuck out from under his bushy red eyelashes."[92] But this terrifying image was too shamelessly good to be left in an abandoned novel fragment, so Andersen used it again in his debut novel *Walking Tour* in 1829. In the book's eleventh chapter the young author goes down to hell and meets a schoolmaster who, with his bristly hair and purplish face, his curses and his cheap jokes, is a vile image. "Suddenly he looked up and noticed me, and at that moment he raised one arm, which grew until it reached the glass vault on which I stood. I thought I could feel him tickling the soles of my feet. My blood rose to a fevered heat; in desperation I cried: 'God save me from the claws of Satan!' and then dashed off."[93]

Only at the very end of his life was Hans Christian Andersen freed from Meisling, but it took a good-sized cup of morphine to do it. This was in December 1874, when the old fairy-tale writer lay ill with bronchitis. He was coughing badly and reached for the medicine bottle. Not until the following day did he return to reality and his diary:

> "The morphine must have had a strong effect. I had lovely dreams and one was especially nice, in which I, diligently and cheerfully, was taking an exam and Meisling came in, and I announced that he should not listen to me during the exam because then I would feel so pressured that I would give stupid answers, which is exactly what I did. A little later I was taking a walk with Meisling. He started in on his sort of humor. I felt cheerful and lively. Soon we happened to talk about art and all things beautiful, and in the end we became quite good friends. He seemed to value me, as I did him. When I woke up I felt very happy about this conciliatory dream."[94]

It was so beautiful and merciful that the good Lord must have nodded with recognition at the old writer bending over his diary as Andersen apparently managed to bury his nemesis at the end of his own life and career. Yet it should also be remembered that after Simon Meisling's death in 1856, a group of literati wished to honor the old headmaster's memory, and they took up a collection for his headstone. For that reason they paid a call on his famous pupil to ask him for a small contribution. Although they weren't exactly told to go to hell, they did receive a definite no.[95]

Chapter Three

Wild Like a Poet (1827-1832)

"Hold on tight to the star up there, because that fire will never be put out!"

That's what his father once said, and after that the boy did nothing else but collect falling stars, milky ways, and other ancient heavenly artifacts. He saw the big comet in 1811 from St. Knud's Cemetery along with his mother and several neighbor women. Everyone said the Judgment Day was at hand, and that the mighty ball of fire with its great glittering tail would smash the earth into bits and pieces. The boy's father, who happened to come past, shook his head and loudly pronounced it all nonsense.

By 1827 his father has been dead for many years, and the boy has become a young man and student, but he still isn't certain what he should believe. The moon has accompanied him to Copenhagen, where it often peers into his low-ceilinged room and tells stories that the student writes down. "Paint what I tell you and you'll have quite a fine picture book," the moon says on its first visit to the garret room on Vingaardstræde. From that vantage point there is a view over the rooftops of Holmensgade and Slagterboderne, out to Vesterport, the windmills on the ramparts, and the green fields outside the city.

One night he's lying in bed dreaming about a fat little devil with round spectacles who is stuffing tufts of hair down the throats of the pupils with his filthy fingers, which stink of lemon and rum. The student wakes up, covered in sweat and with a wildly pounding heart. The moon is shining into the cramped room, and someone is rattling the small, low door. Is it the elf that the distiller down in the cellar has seen sneaking up and down the stairs, wrapped in one of the landlady's big shawls and peering in at keyholes? The student swings his legs out of bed beneath the slanting wall and reaches for the candle in the holder standing on the deal table amid Homer, Horace, a pen and inkwell, and papers covered with both elegant poetry and more prosaic scribblings. Then he walks over to the door. He finds neither an elf nor his landlady on the threshold, and when the pale student in the skimpy nightshirt—so tall and thin that the stars can shine right through him—turns around and takes three steps toward the window, the moon begins its story:

"Once upon a time there was a headmaster who was visited by three friends. They set about discussing two small books by two promising young authors, which the headmaster was supposed to review. 'I've just received one of them,' said the headmaster. 'I haven't read it yet, but it's beautifully bound. What do all of you think of the contents?'

"'Oh,' said one of his friends, 'it's quite good, perhaps a bit verbose, but good Lord, that young poet is already an esteemed man. No doubt the verses could have been a little better; the ideas are sound enough, but so ordinary. Well, what should I say? It's not always possible to come up with something new. You can indeed praise him!'

"'No, that's going too far!' said one of the other friends. 'There's nothing worse in poetry than mediocrity, and this author is never going to get beyond that!'

"Then the headmaster picked up the other book. 'I hear that this one is being praised by everyone. They say the poet is a genius. What do you think?'

"'Everyone is screaming genius,' said his first friend. 'And this is certainly wild, the punctuation is especially brilliant! He could use a good hauling over the coals, and suffer a few setbacks, or else he'll undoubtedly start getting a big head!'

"'Let's not brood over minor errors,' exclaimed the third friend, who until now hadn't said a word. 'Instead, let's rejoice at what is good, and there is truly a great deal of that here! This young poet certainly beats all the rest of them.'

"'God save us, if he's such a genuine genius, as you say, then surely he can stand some neglect!' said one of the others. 'I've heard that there are plenty of people who are praising him in private. Let's not add to his madness!'

"'Unmistakable talent,' wrote the headmaster, 'but with the usual carelessness. The fact that he can also write deplorable verse is evident on page twenty-five, which contains two hiatuses. A study of the ancients is thus recommended.'

"At the home of the esteemed poet, a crowd of invited guests were celebrating the young man's new book. In the meantime the wild poet was attending a party given by one of his benefactors, and at that moment they were discussing the other poet's book. 'I'm going to read yours too,' said the wild poet's biggest patron. 'You know that I always tell you my honest opinion. I don't expect much from your book; you have too much imagination for me!'

The moral is that what is unique ends up in the mud, while what is ordinary is raised to the sky. It's an old story that is always new."[1]

I<small>N</small> J<small>ANUARY</small> 1830, Hans Christian Andersen's first poetry collection was published with the exceedingly modest and brief title: *Poems.* The Danish critics were exceptionally kind, even though the approximately forty poems presented a rather uneven reading experience for most of them. Christian Molbech, who would later become one of Andersen's most hateful critics, stated in the distinguished journal *Maanedsskrift for Literatur* [Monthly Journal of Literature] that the young poet showed potential. But, according to the critic, his lyrical images were still much too fleeting and diffuse. There was also, of course, one serious fault: that such a young and immature person did not show the requisite respect for everything classical and correct in poetry. Huge, ugly grammatical errors and various orthographic failures were not becoming to a poetry collection in the year of our Lord 1830.

It's easy to understand Molbech's reservations. Like so many other hastily produced texts by Andersen during that period, *Poems* vacillates between the sublime and the slipshod. The reader encounters magnificently concentrated metaphors, only to run up against the pure "nonsense-compote," as Andersen called the most flighty sections of his improvisations, which often contained a number of strained rhymes.[2] Nevertheless, this nonsense-compote was an inseparable part of Andersen's poetic nature and practice; it is abundantly present throughout his writings, appearing in the form of party songs, poems written for specific occasions, vignettes and brief poems intended for dance cards, Christmas gifts, and masquerades. All these pleasant songs and little witticisms frequently offered a counterbalance to the gravity, anxiety, and melancholia that were also part of his nature. As he writes: "'You must laugh!' was my refrain, / Laughter mutes every sorrow; / believe me, many whom we praise, / Found in laughter their happiness!"[3] This nonsense-compote also reflected the poet's desire to challenge high-brow culture with his banal outpourings to the moon:

> I would gladly sigh for you in Spanish,
> But I have no skill in grammar.
> Alas, I can barely manage to speak Danish,
> My heart sinks into my coat pocket.
> If you do not soon grant my heart ease,
> I will surely play *Werther* number two.[4]

Some people might call verses like the one above literary trifles, but aesthetic concerns never much worried Andersen. He had finally managed to speak, and his goal was to try out all possible styles, themes, points of view, and stage-sets in the belief that it is only by overstepping boundaries that a person will learn where the boundaries are. For that reason the first poetry collections from Andersen's hand possess an irresistible pace and power. And what a wealth of variations the young poet brings to light during 1830-32! He writes nature poems, portrait and adventure poems, romances and ballads. And in the midst of everything the young poet even sneaks a single prose text into the stream of poetry, ending *Poems* with the long story entitled "The Ghost," which eventually became known and loved under the title "The Traveling Companion." This type of genre deviation was no accident, but a link in a larger and deliberate plan, which Andersen repeated in his next poetry collection, *Fantasies and Sketches*, from 1831. In this volume a prose text also appeared among all the poetry.[5] These two experiments were wholly in keeping with the idea of Romantic poetry concerning a dissolution and merging of artistic genres and styles. It also reflected the freedom of form that represented the release of the young, newly baked student and poet during the years 1829-31. The whole flood of poetry that had piled up inside him under Meisling's tyrannical yoke was now allowed to pour out in all directions under the slogan: "Loose the bonds of form, for real poetry / In prose itself as poetry will glow."[6]

Andersen's first three poetry collections (1830-32) express his enormous yearning to develop his own lyrical persona in all its many possible facets. In terms of style and theme, the range, as mentioned, is impressive even though the sublime and the banal often go hand in hand throughout the more than one hundred texts in *Poems, Fantasies and Sketches*, and *The Twelve Months of the Year*. It's understandable that at one point Andersen would consider calling his second poetry collection a "Poetic Hodgepodge" since both the form and content of the poems went off in so many different directions and attempted so much. For instance, in one poem dealing with the tyranny of form and reason, Andersen not only dares to use mathematical formulas as a narrative device, he even makes use of arithmetical symbols within the poem itself. He also uses part of the poem as a blackboard to tell a story about how form is what has become rigidified and speaks only to reason, while content is what is real—what is alive and pulsing—that always speaks to and *is* the emotions.

Behind these wild experiments and all the nonsense-compote in the first three poetry collections, we also find the more serious and concentrated poet in his purest and finest distillation. These poems are from a time in Hans Christian Andersen's life and work when he was not yet caught up in the role of permanent provider of cantatas to the royal family and party songs to various colonels and Privy Councilors. When the poet, barely twenty-five years of age, struck the gold vein of poetry, he could make a poem sparkle and resound in a condensed language that could hardly be matched in literary history even a couple of decades later. More than twenty years before the French poet Charles Baudelaire became the godfather of modern art—which has been defined as "the ability, in the wasteland of the big city, not only to see the decline of humanity, but also to sense a hitherto undiscovered beauty"[7]—Hans Christian Andersen was already in full swing, boiling down his experiences of tumultuous big-city life to the smallest fragments of the language. One result was a stroboscopically flickering poem about the modern metropolis. It's true that there are not as many impressive and infernal big-city tableaux in the young Andersen's *Poems* from 1830 as there are in Baudelaire's *Les Fleurs du Mal* from 1857, but the Dane could also make Østergade's "colorful multitudes" flash with the beauty of the new age:

> Oh, what life! ha, merry and bright!
> Parting and meeting,
> Pushing and shoving,
> Wearing out life, boots and shoes,
> Fluttering ribbons and fluttering women,
> Painted hearts and painted cheeks,
> Horse teams of four and horse teams of two;
> Pious matrons,
> Tiny barons,
> Rich man and beggar,
> Merry in hansoms, coaches and gigs;
> Noises shall roll!
> God bless my soul![8]

This energetic, gripping, big-city poem, "Østergade, Poetically Observed," was, as mentioned, written twenty-five years before Baudelaire became intoxicated by the crowds of people on the sidewalks of Paris and talked about how the reader, along with the poet, had to delve into the unknown in order to find the new. But here it is Hans Christian Andersen who is pervaded by the presence of the city—"All of life, just as it is / And goes"—seeking an ideal world behind everything that is swiftly flickering, shimmering, and colorful on Østergade. The women entice, the beggars lurk, and the fruit seller "beckons" with apples, raisins, almonds, and grapes, electrifying the poet:

> There's such an odd tickle in marrow and bone,
> You feel yourself turning quite strange.
> You talk about longing in your breast,
> About "silk like blue violets,"
> Silver clouds and the coast of light,
> And the arrow and pistols of pain,

And before you even know it
You're a poet. ——
Electricity sparks in your hair;
Into the newspaper office
You rush now; all your pockets stuffed
Full of poet flowers.
——Then it goes quickly in youth's happy flight;
All so beautiful,
In harmony the great whole dwindles,
From trashman to the nine goddesses.[9]

In *Poems*, which was published in January 1830, Andersen sought to express his gratitude to "My dear benefactor, the esteemed Privy Councilor J. Collin, Deputy of Finances, President of the Royal Agricultural Society, Knight of the Dannebrog, and recipient of the Silver Cross of the Order of the Dannebrog." With this pompous dedication at the front of his book, the young Hans Christian Andersen was pointing out to the world that he was no longer just some boy who had been gathered up in 1819 in Copenhagen and helped on his way; he was now considered virtually a son in the Collin household.

Andersen used this same ploy in his next two poetry collections. In *Fantasies and Sketches*, which appeared in 1831, the poet expresses his gratitude to another father figure in the circle of acquaintances that by now had become quite elite. This time it's the scientist H. C. Ørsted who is thanked with "devotion and esteem" for "his hearty encouragement and fatherly advice." And in 1832, *The Twelve Months of the Year* was dedicated to King Frederik VI himself, who thus became part of the circle of great Danish father figures surrounding the young poet—this time with a few loving verses at the front of the volume:

A poor child was I, and no one knew me,
But in my heart burned the poet flame;
It drove me bravely on in the world's bustle,
Though I had It alone and God in heaven.

To Denmark's king they led my feet,
I felt merely that I stood before a father,
Who gave my heart courage, my thoughts wings. ——
And to the father heart I safely bring my song;
I do not see the throne where I kneel,
But in your eye: fatherly love.

Father Collin

Fatherly love was at the top of Andersen's wish list around 1830. Again and again in his school essays during the period 1822-27 he wrote about how he longed for and dreamed his way into a family network, governed by an almighty, kind, and fair-minded patriarch by the name of "father." In one of these essays, which Andersen wrote after he had returned to Copenhagen in the spring of 1827 and had begun to be a regular visitor to the Collin household, he imagines himself once again to be a member of a larger brotherhood and says: "Let the most intimate bonds of brotherly love embrace us, as it embraced the apostles."[10]

It is noteworthy that at this time—more than five years before his mother died in 1833, living among the old, sick, and drunken paupers back home in Odense—Andersen already considered himself to be a poor orphan. In the essay his thoughts are never directed at Odense or his mother, to whom he had written fewer and fewer letters in recent years. Instead, he let the grandiose school essay end with a revelation about the happy family, which other chosen loners, such as the apostles and Jesus, had once had:

> "If we're left abandoned in this world, if father and mother are resting in their graves, and we, with no family or guide, must wander alone on the difficult road of this earthly life, then the apostles may be our example. Like us, they too were abandoned by their friend, their father; but with faith and belief they became the mightiest pillars in the great edifice of eternity . . . With faith and charity, frugality and patience, let us follow the holy chosen ones; then shall the community—as in the first years of Christendom—become one family. Like the children of one father we will then live together, and approach closer and closer to the ideal of holiness, God and Christ."[11]

Jonas Collin was the perfect father figure. He was a refined person and an influential man in Danish society, who was not swept up in the pleasures of life but managed his fortune as sensibly as he did his family. In contrast to H. C. Ørsted, the other father figure in Andersen's adult life to whom we will return in Chapter Eight, Jonas Collin was a man grounded in reality to a much greater extent than in dreams. Whereas the gentle Ørsted pampered the genius in Andersen, the busy and pragmatic Collin took a firmer and more demanding hold on the poet's persona, although he was not at all blind to the interesting possibilities of Andersen's distinctive character.

As mentioned earlier, Collin was a child of the Enlightenment. He became a university student at the young age of sixteen, and three years later—in 1795—he could list Bachelor of Law on his calling card. At that point the talented young man was employed in his father's lottery office. At the same time he attended various university lectures in philosophy, mathematics, physics, astronomy, botany, and geology. It was typical of young Collin—and of the concerns of the time, which had resulted from the French Revolution and Struensee's battle for citizens' rights under absolute monarchy in Denmark—that the first written work by the young law student should be: "A Method for Spreading Knowledge Among the Peasantry." It was printed in the newspaper *Den danske Tilskuer* in 1794, and it expressed the eighteen-year-old's vision for general education and to "move the honest peasant class farther along in knowledge." Young Collin proposed, for example, that libraries be established for the peasants and that a popular, easy-to-read mini-newspaper be created that would twice a week act as a sort of pedagogical insert in the large, widely read newspaper *Adresseavisen*.

Jonas Collin wrote other articles during this period of his life around 1800, when he also made a name for himself as a translator and author, became a member of "Dreyer's Club," and met intellectuals such as the Ørsted brothers, J. P. Mynster, Adam Oehlenschläger, Henrich Steffens, and Knud Lyne Rahbek. These articles had both a specifically legal aspect and a general moral-ethical point of view. It was during these years of seeking and pondering in the 1790s that a solid and versatile groundwork was laid for one of the more discreet legends of the Danish Golden Age: Jonas Collin, Senior. He was a fiery diplomatic soul, an administrator and initiator during the period 1800-50, with a rare ability to talk to, influence, and act on the behalf of such diverse social groups as tradesmen, peasants, and writers. In the midst of the administrative machinery of the absolute monarchy, Jonas Collin worked tirelessly in all corners and niches of Danish society. His energy and diligence from 1800 to 1850 can be traced everywhere, and at the center of this impressive development of ideas and initiatives we find a man who knew his limitations and thus was always able to direct his efforts effectively and find his way to the core of an issue.

In 1802, at the young age of 27, he became secretary for the foundation *Ad usus publicos*, the art foundation of the day, which had made a number of contributions in connection with Hans Christian Andersen's education in the 1820s. It would also make possible his travel dreams in the early 1830s. Collin held the position of foundation secretary for thirty years, whereupon the post was handed over to his son, Edvard Collin. During the 1820s and 1840s Jonas Collin also spent long periods as the financial manager of the Royal Theater. His was the deciding vote whenever the other advisers could not agree on the quality of a new Danish play. These two vital posts in Danish cultural life, which Jonas Collin took on at a relatively young age, put him in personal, amicable contact with the greatest Danish artists and intellectuals of the day. The bonds that were created by Jonas Collin between art and finance in the 1820s, under the absolute monarchy, were of inestimable importance for the development of what is known today as the Golden Age in Denmark. It meant that in the 19th century, the city of Copenhagen could muster a long list of geniuses and prominent figures in the arts and sciences. And many of them would achieve a worldwide fame which even today defines Denmark and the Danish mentality. Among them were Søren Kierkegaard and Hans Christian Andersen.[12]

In the 1820s and 1830s, a father figure such as H. C. Ørsted opened his arms to all that was childlike in Andersen's nature; this was the very root of his genius, and Ørsted envisioned bringing it to bloom through constant affirmation and encouragement. Jonas Collin, on the other hand, declared it his goal to bind the young man's character to the earth and daily life. Sober-mindedness and self-control, which included the ability to douse the blood with cold water, were Collin's ultimate contributions to Andersen's education. It was clear that the sensitive young man had need for more than just a pat on the head, and sometimes he even needed a dressing-down from a firm father figure. Collin's reserved manner, in contrast to the groveling admiration exhibited by many others toward Andersen, occasionally made the young man take a much more critical look at himself. The famous Collin reticence certainly did not make Andersen happier, but it challenged and shaped him more than anything else at the beginning of his adult life. It also provoked a flood of literary works—poems, stories, plays, and novels—which behind various disguises, wigs, and thin layers of makeup were often directed at "The Home of Homes," as Andersen called the Collin household.

After parting from Simon Meisling in 1827, Andersen needed both a protector and a new authoritarian counterweight, so that his soul and character could develop. For that reason nothing was more important for him during the early 1830s, when he was dependent on further support from the Collin family, than to show his love, gratitude, and loyalty to the patriarch himself. One of the things this led to was almost thirty years of uninterrupted production of birthday songs for Jonas Collin every January 6. On that occasion all generations of Collins would gather around the head of the family to pay tribute to "the core of our lives together," as Andersen calls Collin in the first verse of his birthday song from 1854, in which all the voices around the table rise up in a sisterly and brotherly choir of jubilation:

> You, whom we from our first years
> Looked to as our leader,
> You, now standing in the home of homes,
> A treasure which we cherish.
> Each day no doubt has its glory,
> And the year has many a feast.
> Hurrah! The sixth of January—
> For us it is simply the best![13]

In addition to these birthday songs, Jonas Collin also received during the 1820s and up until his death in 1861 regular reports and depositions about his new son's diligence and cleverness, sprinkled with lively examples of his steadily increasing popularity both at home and abroad. And it was the latter, in Andersen's opinion, that provided the most splendid proof that the investment of Frederik VI had borne fruit. Like a proud son, Andersen wrote home from Berlin to his "kind-hearted father" in the winter of 1845-46, when he was on a triumphal procession through Germany, a country which, in contrast to the author's own, had long ago embraced the Dane:

"In my thoughts I stand at your side as you read this. I press your hand, my beloved, blessed father . . . You know, of course, that my greatest vanity, or call it rather joy, resides in the knowledge that you consider me worthy of you. I think of you as I receive all this recognition. Yet I am truly loved and appreciated abroad; I am—famous. Yes, you may well smile. But the foremost men fly to meet me, I see myself welcomed into all their families. Princes and the most talented of men pay me the greatest courtesies. You should see how they flock around me in the so-called important circles. Oh, that's not something any of all those people back home think about, they overlook me completely and no doubt they would be happy with a droplet of the tribute I receive. Yet my writings must have greater merit than the Danes give them. Now Heiberg has also been translated, but no one talks about it, and it would be odd if the Danes were the only ones wise enough to judge in this world. You should know, my beloved father, you should realize, that you did not misjudge me when you welcomed me as your son, when you helped and protected me."[14]

Whenever Andersen wrote in this manner—triumphant and with good reason intoxicated by his success—about his encounter with every possible European notable, polishing his medals and mentioning his latest awards, Jonas Collin would give a brief, reserved nod. He never overflowed with praise or pats on the back; instead, he tried to keep Andersen's feet on the ground with remarks such as: "It gives me pleasure to see that you are so comfortable and happy in that sphere. For my part, it seems in the long run to be as little beneficial for the spirit as a diet of nothing but bonbons and marzipan cake would be for the body."[15]

In the deepest sense, all Andersen's declarations of filial love with regard to Jonas Collin over the years had to do with maintaining, fortifying, and expanding his contact with the Collin household. He had made a persistent effort to wedge his way into the family when he returned to Copenhagen in the spring of 1827 and was promptly installed in the garret room at Vingaard-stræde 131, not far from the Collin family's comfortable half-timbered house between Bredgade and Store Strandstræde. Once again Andersen succeeded in playing the few modest cards he possessed in the most resourceful way. By getting Jonas Collin to intercede with Meisling, he had lured his benefactor out of hiding and into a paternal role. By removing Andersen from his teacher only one year before final exams, Jonas Collin had assumed responsibility for his protégé's welfare, which went far beyond the duties of his positions at the Royal Theater and the foundation *Ad usus publicos*. No doubt it had never been part of the plans of a busy man like Jonas Collin. He probably did not expect this to be the consequence of developing Andersen's talent when he sent the boy off to Slagelse and Headmaster Meisling in 1822.

On the other hand, this was precisely what Andersen had dreamed of and hoped for all along. And Andersen had a plan ready when he returned to Copenhagen, but he also knew that he had to tread lightly and adopt a cautious approach. This is evident in his memoirs from 1832, which were written for the Collin family, when Andersen was looking back on the very difficult and decisive phase of his life and work after his return from Helsingør: "I had a real fear of Father [Jonas Collin], even though I loved him with all my soul, but this fear was based on the fact that I considered my life's happiness, yes, my very existence, to depend on him."[16]

His plan was simple. First, it was important to finish his studies and then to publish as much as possible of the poetry he had already written. Immediately after passing his exams, Andersen would publish a real book, and by using the critics' expected approval of his brilliant work, he would then win the favor and goodwill of the Collin family. The sympathy of the children, in particular, was a crucial goal. Edvard Collin, who was Andersen's peer, always seemed so cold and short-tempered whenever Andersen paid a visit. And it would soon become apparent that Edvard— the third-eldest child—was the one who held the key to the Collin household. During 1827-28 the busy Jonas Collin turned over a significant portion of the responsibility for Andersen's education to his son, who was supposed to help the student, so lacking in grammar and spelling skills, with his Latin essays. So it was the confidence of this son that Andersen had to win as quickly as possible, and preferably in the form of a spiritual brotherhood, which he had discussed several years earlier in a school essay:

> "We're all children of one Father, of course. We all live under one roof, God's glorious star-strewn heaven. We all aspire to one goal; why then act cold toward each other?"[17]

The Hebraic Müller

Yet the person who was to have the greatest influence on young Andersen in 1827-28 was not Edvard or Jonas Collin but the young private tutor that Collin had hired to help Andersen complete his studies. His name was Ludvig Christian Müller, but because of his knowledge of Eastern languages and cultures, he always went by the nickname of "The Hebraic Müller." He was a committed, gifted, and deeply religious man who later in life became both a pastor and the head of a college.

Judging by the essays that Andersen wrote in 1827 and 1828, when he would stroll out to see Müller in Christianshavn a couple of times a week, this new teacher, who was about the same age, was the perfect sparring partner, both intellectually and professionally. Müller's concrete comments and corrections, which could be both genial and ironic, in the margins of Andersen's essays may have had a little of the Meisling sting to them when it suddenly said: "Nonsense!" or "Sob!" But they were based on a much more intelligent form of pedagogy, which would turn out to provide the proper counterweight to Andersen's self-absorption and daydreaming. In an essay from 1828, when Andersen falls into his usual elegiac tone and starts to speak in an overblown way about the springtime that will soon pass, Müller notes in one of his typical parentheses:"Then we'll have something to eat!" In another place the private pupil once again verges on narcissistic sentiment when a hopeful youth has to bleed from the executioner's sword and then ravens and crows devour his heart. Müller skewers the melodrama with the words:"Good for them!"[18]

But these teasing remarks were not intended as mere fun and games, as evidenced by the relatively lengthy constructive discussion that was often appended to the brief comments and directed at the aesthetics and ethics of the essay. Especially when it was a matter of religious questions, or of perceptions about humanity or life in a broader, deeper, more moral respect, an urgent tone would enter Müller's corrections. And Andersen undoubtedly listened to and, in certain instances, took note of this. How dynamic the relationship was between the two, and how much Müller respected Andersen, is clear in *The Fairy Tale of My Life*:

> "I expressed myself as a man of nature, and my teacher, who was one of the noblest and most loving of people, but firm about the literal words of the scriptures, would often become anxious on my behalf. We debated, while the same holy flame burned equally pure in our hearts. But it did me enormous good to visit this untainted, talented young man, who had just as remarkable a character as I had."[19]

Müller felt equally inspired by and possessed a great veneration for his unusual private student, as is apparent from his official report to the university after the completion of the exams at the end of 1828, when Andersen graduated with the following precise certificate of reference:

> "During the time that I have studied with him, there has been as little reason to complain about his behavior and diligence as there is to offer any objections to his moral character in general. A high degree of good nature makes him liked by most of those who get to know him well; on the other hand, it cannot be denied that he suffers from a good deal of vanity, which in a strange way clashes with his almost childlike timidity. His memory and intellect, if not extraordinary, are by no means paltry, but if he does not better learn to control his imagination, of which he possesses a great preponderance, in the future it might easily lead him astray."[20]

In spite of his young age, the tutor Müller knew what he was up against. This was apparent from a trick he was forced to use at one point

when his private student with the overactive imagination began to domi-
nate the lessons with endless readings from his own work, which he had
brought along. Andersen no longer had to comply with the Meisling ban
on writing or declaiming poetry, and so he seized every opportunity to air
his Rhyming Demon. None of the families who took turns providing him
with supper in the evening, nor the Hebraic Müller, was able to escape his
readings during 1827-28. The problem, of course, was that these long interruptions, no matter how entertaining they might be, would push the curriculum requirements into the background. So one day Müller decided to
take the floor himself and tell Andersen a short Russian story about a
writer who always insisted on reading his work to others. Andersen fell
silent and listened intently as the story proceeded:

"Eventually all his listeners gave up. Today, as he sits alone in his room
with a new creation, he exclaims in despair: 'If only I had someone to read
to, even if it was the Devil himself!' The words are barely out of his mouth
before the gentleman he has summoned appears, bringing along a contract
for his signature. He agrees to listen to the readings for seven years, whereupon he will be entitled to claim the writer's soul. The contract is signed,
and the readings begin. Eventually the listener grows restless and starts
heading for the door, but the author blocks his way with his manuscript in
hand. The Devil then tries to escape up the chimney, but the writer is alert;
he grabs the fleeing Devil by the tail and keeps on reading!"

And it was here—at the end of the story, when the Devil flees up the
chimney, leaving his tail and the writer behind—that the silently listening
Andersen suddenly covered his face with his hands and said: "Oh, I'm the
one that you mean!"[21]

But Andersen passed his exams with respectable marks; as Edvard
Collin later wrote in his book about the author, it was largely due to
Müller's great efforts that the young, freedom-starved Andersen managed
to gain control of his intellect. And that was certainly no easy task in 1827-
28. "The sudden transition from imprisonment, which the school had been
for him, caused a reaction in Andersen toward a striving for independence,
in retaliation for the long lack of freedom."[22]

The Hebraic Müller allowed Andersen to make room for his skepticism, not just in regard to religion but also in terms of the educational
ideals and school system that Andersen hated so much; during this period
of liberation it found its way, time after time, into his poetry and prose.
"Why kill the flowers of life with calculation?" Andersen asks in the short
lyrical story "The Beautiful Grammatica" in 1830 . In this story, written in

prose form and with a gleeful glint in his eye, he turns Jacob Baden's Latin grammar book into a lyrical poem. And Andersen's instinctive resistance, as a man of nature, to anything that had to do with education was also allowed to surface in the essays he wrote for Müller. A brilliant example is an essay entitled "We have here no permanent place, but seek the future one," which presents a lively picture of the strong, rebellious forces that were at work in the young poet and student in 1828. And with Müller's inserted corrections and comments we have evidence of a few more examples of the inspiring opposition the teacher offered to the budding genius. In the essay Andersen thanks Jonas Collin and Müller for interceding in his life, which meant that the pure, true poetry in the brilliant, child-like artist—"the much too dreamy, happy spirit"—was finally allowed to develop freely instead of being suffocated in a prison of a grammar school:

> "Many of the most glorious years of youth are spent here, closed off from nature, so that the child can learn what the man forgets; so that time can be squandered on things he does not need; time that could have been put to much better use [L. C. Müller comment: *much too wise*]. A school has always seemed to me like a peculiar troll with an eternally youthful face. Year after year it repeats the same things, and the children happily leap from the cold arms of the mother who feeds her children with dead grammars and uses the ferule and rod in her holy rage."[23]

It was this very opposition to the bastions of education that served as the basis in 1828 for large parts of Andersen's debut novel, *Walking Tour*. At one point in this furious and impertinent book, the protagonist—a young man who dreams of becoming an author—is locked up in a bird cage and told that now all his dreaming has to come to an end, because we humans are not summoned to life to moon around with a pack of romantic fools: "Alas! You still have a great deal to learn in school, you'll be plagued and pressured and cut and cropped before you can become a passable worker-bee in the big hive. The first thing that must happen is for you to go within yourself and renounce all writing!"[24]

Andersen found inspiration for the novel on his walks out to Christianshavn to see Müller, and he completed the book back home in his garret room on Vingaardstræde, while he was studying for his final exams in the late summer of 1828. At the same time he became a recruit in the Royal Guards. The very next day after taking his exams in October, he took his oath of allegiance. His uniform, which was an old, used one that Andersen had bought from a secondhand dealer, was not only too short in the sleeves and too tight in the waist, but the coat tails splayed out behind. His shako—the tall, stiff military hat with visor—was much too small and sat too far back on his head, but the proud graduate, poet, and now soldier went in full regalia directly from the drill house to town to show off his attire to friends and acquaintances. On Østergade he actually met Prince Ferdinand and Princess Caroline, who had always been so good to him, offering him sweets and buying him books. The poet promptly presented arms before the royal couple, swept off his shako, and bowed deeply, which certainly made an impression since he was six feet tall. The royal couple started laughing, and Princess Caroline said: "Oh my God, it's Andersen!"[25]

Romantic Walking Tour to Amager

Walking Tour from Holmen's Canal to the Eastern Point of Amager in the Years 1828 and 1829—or simply *Walking Tour*, as Andersen called the book —is a magnificent piece of Romantic literature that deals not only with a soldier's life in tempo but with the emergence of a writer. All in the course of one night, so to speak. The process of development and the book's fourteen chapters take place on New Year's Eve 1828, during the hours just before midnight—when the first-person narrator suddenly discovers that he's going to be a writer—and lasts until dawn, when the cock crows on the shore out at the eastern point of the island of Amager, announcing a new year as well as a new day. The narrative covers a relatively short span of time, but it contains a great inner spaciousness and limitless vistas, which on the human plane deal with a person's obligation to find himself and choose the right path in life.

More than any other work in Hans Christian Andersen's entire oeuvre, *Walking Tour* calls into question the author's claim later in life that from the very beginning of his writing career he was a poor, weak, and eternally tormented person who was completely dependent on the good Lord and the resolute help offered by powerful people. The plot of *Walking Tour*, its defiant style and tone, as well as the deliberate staging of the book's publication on the very day after the last scene in the final chapter supposedly took place—all of these things reflect a self-aware, goal-oriented writer, who, with his first novel, had mobilized all his psychological and physical forces, having taken up the gauntlet thrown down by his headmaster with his parting words: "Go to hell!"

That was precisely what Andersen now did with *Walking Tour*. Through thirteen concentrated chapters, plus a final chapter that contains only dashes and exclamation marks, the reader follows the young narrator and future author on his hunt for material for his first book. The tour goes through the center of Copenhagen from the tower of Nikolai Church to the Stock Exchange, across the bridges to Christianshavn, and through the city gate out into nature on the flat island of Amager. It's a walking tour filled with the most amazing experiences. Along with the author, we float in a bread basket over Copenhagen in the year 2129; we meet a tower that can recite all the monologues in *Hamlet*; we try on St. Peter's magic spectacles and a pair of seven-league boots; we meet a giant from the planet Sirius who is sixty kilometers tall and has learned Latin from Cicero; and toward the end we take a tour of hell, which—as mentioned in the previous chapter—is filled with schoolmasters.

The very style in which the twenty-three-year-old Andersen reports these countless absurd, adventurous, and often quite funny events reveals a writer who is aesthetically fearless, possesses tremendous courage, and has an indomitable will to try out all his literary skills, letting his Rhyming Demon loose in every imaginable—and unimaginable—direction. As B. S. Ingemann wrote in a letter in 1828, in which he remarked on sections of Andersen's roguish novel that had been printed in a journal in advance of publication, this novelistic tour might end anywhere: "It's impossible to comment on the overall idea or presentation until I've read the whole tour in context and seen whether it leads to heaven or to hell or to Amager."[26]

Hans Christian Andersen's debut novel quickly became widely known in the literary circles of Denmark in 1829-30. That is no longer the case today. Over time, many literary scholars have denounced the book, as Andersen himself did, as a "childhood disease," and considered it to be a literary work that is more a curiosity than possessing any real quality. It's true that the novel is intermittently difficult and annoying to read, with its ostentatious displays of literary erudition, in which learned references and philosophical profundities are interwoven with satire, sophomoric nonsense, and parody. But when you come to the last page, it's clear that all along there has been a purpose to the madness, primarily to illustrate that imagination and poetry can never be contained or limited. Especially not in a book. The fact that *Walking Tour* has been ignored by subsequent generations is no doubt because the novel's narrator is a real quick-change artist who is difficult to pin down. The narrative structure is also flighty and ephemeral, and the novel has no ending, aside from a spirited challenge to the reader to create his own in the fourteenth and last chapter, which, as mentioned, consists solely of dashes and exclamation marks.

As a work of art, *Walking Tour* at first glance seems to challenge the educational values of the day, which, taking the novel of education [*Bildungsroman*] such as Goethe's great *Wilhelm Meister's Apprenticeship* as a model, would become the sound and stable backbone of literary history during the 19th century. But under its surface parody, *Walking Tour* is itself a novel of education because it deals with the formation of an artist. At the same time it sneers at all the Romantic didactic stories seeking harmony, in which the hero must always endure terrible trials before returning home as a good and wise person. And there the author would bring the story to a peaceful and orderly end. But Hans Christian Andersen's first novel— which, unlike Goethe's classic work took fifty days to write instead of fifty years—never ends. We leave the hero in the thirteenth chapter as he stands in water up to his knees at the easternmost point of Amager. About to sail over to Saltholm and thus overstep the outer framework of his story, the narrator has been caught in the act by a future critic, disguised as a quivering merman with terrifying spiked hair made of quill pens.

> "At that moment he struck me with his stick right across the nose, so that St. Peter's spectacles flew overboard and vanished in the waves. And with them went the merman. But I stood there, embarrassed and alone, on the desolate shore, feeling myself scarcely qualified to write a beautiful closing chapter."[27]

The young artist has reached the outermost boundary of his work, where he is knocked back into place by a critic with the words: "You've titled your book: *Walking Tour to the Eastern Point of Amager*, and now you dare go farther!"[28] That's why the exhausted author, who by now has exhausted his imagination, asks the reader to finish the book himself in a "fourteenth chapter (containing nothing)," where the future review can be conveniently pasted. If there ever is a review, that is. If not, the narrator says, "then I owe you [the readers] a final chapter, which I will take pleasure in recounting to you in person, if you should honor me with a visit. I'm at home from 8 to 9, but for the ladies I'm home anytime. Live well!"[29]

Oh yes, *Walking Tour* certainly makes fun of the subdued, harmony-seeking novels of early 19th-century Denmark. The Danish critic Georg Brandes fiercely took aim at the same thing in 1891 when he cast a critical eye over the entire past century of Danish literature, with a particular emphasis on the lack of literary daring during Danish Romanticism in the years 1800–30. "It seems to me that what we have failed to cherish enough in literature is boldness; the boldness that is the same as an author's ability to express ruthlessly his particular artistic ideal."[30] Brandes defined "boldness" as an artist's ability to strive fearlessly and unwaveringly for the imaginative. As he dryly remarked, during Romanticism Danish writers never fell and hurt themselves because they always left the task of climbing Mont Blanc to others. In that way they no doubt avoided breaking their neck, but they also never managed to find the rare flowers that grow only on the highest mountain peaks at the edge of the abyss.

It may seem surprising that Georg Brandes, who was an expert on the work of Hans Christian Andersen, should overlook *Walking Tour* in his polemical denunciation of early-19th-century Danish literature. In his prose Andersen never drove his imagination to the demonic heights of E. T. A. Hoffmann, nor did he pose with such recklessness as a Lord Byron or Heinrich Heine in his first three poetry collections. And yet *Walking Tour* was exactly the type of original and bold ascent to "the most daring heights" that Brandes was looking for. Even though the heights were as prosaically flat as Amager.

Consider the novel's pompous title: *Walking Tour from Holmen's Canal to the Eastern Point of Amager in the Years 1828 and 1829*, which sets the basic tone by promising the reader a detailed portrait of an expedition to Amager. The title says that this is a tour on foot that lasted two years, regardless of whether it's actually possible to spend two years exploring the easily circumambulated island of Amager. Just as puzzling were the years cited. How could this book with the realistic title encompass all of 1829 when it was published just thirty-six hours after that same year began? The answer is, as previously mentioned, that the narrative time covers only five or six hours, lasting from New Year's Eve 1828, when the narrator gets up from his desk, until the dawn of January 1, 1829 when he stands on the shore at the eastern point of Amager and finds himself the author of a novel in fourteen chapters. In other words, the mischievous title reveals the entire Romantic aim of the book: to portray the education of a person not by using reason to suppress the emotions, but by releasing them.

Andersen easily and lucidly seizes hold of this educational project right from the start, when the narrator, who is now on his way out to find the material that will make him both an author and a man, leaves his garret room near Nikolai Tower and heads for Amager. Near the Stock Exchange and Christiansborg Castle he is confronted, like all fairy-tale heroes (and Copenhageners), with a body of water (Copenhagen Harbor).

Here he has to make the crucial decision for his journey (and his life): Which bridge should he take to Amager? Which bridge should his life take? Should he cross the citizen's classical, straightforward Knippelsbro? Or should he choose the bohemian's imaginative and unpredictable Langebro? This is the classic choice between reason and emotion, which Andersen had encountered through his own martyred body and soul during his school years. Our hero in *Walking Tour* takes only a few seconds to make up his mind on this New Year's Eve. Instinctively he puts his life in the hands of the female figure who holds the keys to Langebro—the tall, pale, and ethereal Heloïse. Even though the sensible, maternal Amager woman beckons from Knippelsbro, our author-hero refuses to head out into life along the straight road of reason. No, our young hero is going to construct colorful enchanted palaces along the meandering roads of emotion and imagination.

"Romanticism" is the key word here. The education of the narrator in *Walking Tour* is shaped as a type of entrance exam to the private club of Romanticism. The novel builds on a long series of themes, motifs, symbols, stylistic elements, quotes, and references to artists and works of art,[31] which the narrator in his solitude encounters out on "flat Amager, the great, glorious playground of the imagination."[32] The intent is to show that the youth is ready for the adult life of a writer under the strictest and most exacting Romantic guidelines. In the 1820s, these guidelines meant that in his art, a person should dwell on the state of his soul, cultivate dreams, and allow his imagination to develop freely and without limitations. And like young men in primitive cultures and tribal societies, the novel's young protagonist has to survive the rite of his literary coming-of-age out on Amager in utter solitude. In that way he will become conscious of his divine inner drive toward freedom and artistic recognition, while he simultaneously demonstrates the endurance of his imagination. The events that occur in the first six chapters are presented in broad strokes, as the clock strikes twelve and the year begins for the newly fledged student and future author. Desolate Amager is the site and stage for a number of magical encounters with ghosts, giants, and talking animals equipped with supernatural abilities and magic implements connected to the symbolic and mythical world of Romanticism.

It's evident that in his anti-authoritarian first novel, Hans Christian Andersen still obediently and humbly bows before one specific power: Romanticism. He adjusts the thoughts and perceptions of his narrator to this literary tradition, which developed in earnest in Germany during

1800-30. Authors such as Novalis, Friedrich Schlegel, Jean Paul, Heinrich von Kleist, Adelbert von Chamisso, Ludwig Tieck, and E. T. A. Hoffmann wrote poetry and prose in a fantastical and often fragmentary form that was supposed to be a kaleidoscopic expression of the author's own fragmented persona. Nearly all these German writers appear in Andersen's novel, either named directly or quoted. In certain cases their works become part of the very plot, such as E. T. A. Hoffmann's novel *The Elixir of the Devil*, which deals with the Evil One splitting a soul, and Adelbert von Chamisso's novel *The Strange Story of Peter Schlemihl*, in which the main character sells his shadow to the Devil for a well-filled purse. The innumerable living and talking shadows, ghosts, and sleepwalkers in *Walking Tour* all point to the comprehensive pattern of fragmentation underlying the novel at its deepest level. This also has a direct connection with the young narrator-author's split personality, which is under close scrutiny throughout the book. On one hand we get to know the young narrator as a carefree person who often speaks to us directly in a mischievous manner. On the other hand he also turns out to be a lonely and anxious person who—as it says in *Walking Tour*—likes to decorate his pale, unhappy face with a comical mustache and a poetic paper crown. If we lift the lid on this educational cauldron of a first novel, we get a glimpse not only of young Andersen's chaotically jumbled literary workshop in 1828-29, but we also have a touching picture of his contradictory, feverish character, in which "the most painful melancholy is mixed with the shrill jubilation of lunacy," as one of the narrator's many mirror images says in the fourth chapter.

Several years later, on his summer walks at the estate of Hofmansgave, located in the northern part of Fyn, Andersen learned to use a microscope and became deeply fascinated with the tremendous, intense battle for survival that can take place in a single drop of water. In a sense, his first novel offers a sort of microscopic view of all the urgent forces and intentions in the emergence and first stages of a literary career. In any case, it's possible to read the fourteen chapters as a survey of the young man's teeming caprices—such as vanity, melancholy, aggression, inferiority, megalomania, and arrogance—which creep and crawl their way under the narrator's skin and down onto the page. With *Walking Tour* Andersen set off on the long journey inside himself, which over time would result in thirty volumes of literary works, ten volumes of diaries, and countless letters. And they all stemmed from a statement so typical of Andersen: "What a mystery I am to myself!"[33]

★ ★ ★

In this first novel we do not find a weak, tormented writer but a combative and searching artist-soul, who cannot conceal his enormous need to pose and play a role in both a literal and figurative sense. *Walking Tour* was also a very strategic book, in which Andersen meticulously sought to charm all the proper friends in the Romantic movement. At the same time, he trampled on all those who insisted on modesty and "noble groveling" from art and the artist, especially when it was a matter of a first-time novelist. With great vanity and unmatched impudence, Andersen managed to place himself and his *Walking Tour* in an extremely rebellious relationship to all possible competitors in art and criticism. And he did this deliberately. As the young narrator and budding author says in Chapter Seven to the wise giant from Sirius: "Just think, noble sir, this [*Walking Tour*] is my first work, the first big step I'm taking in my life. It can contribute so inexpressibly much to the favorable or unfavorable opinion that people will have of me."[34]

In the years when Andersen was publishing his first novel, poems, and plays, a violent battle was taking place among the literary elite for the top position, which had belonged to the recently deceased Danish author Jens Baggesen. During 1829 and 1830, Hans Christian Andersen promoted himself in accordance with the assertive maxims that the old fox in Chapter Five of *Walking Tour* presents to his son, who is about to go out into the world to seek his fortune: "One other important lesson I want to give you has to do with the social circles you may possibly enter. Never pay any mind to the colorful birds fluttering above your head; beautiful feathers but small minds build nests high up."[35]

In this way Andersen used *Walking Tour* to attain a prominent position; at the same time he created respect for his own feathers, many of which he had borrowed. But the novel also had a price, and over the years he would pay it back tenfold. A first-time author cannot go unpunished after ridiculing certain sectors of the art world and all the critics, the way Andersen did in *Walking Tour*. This ridiculing takes place—in addition to the aforementioned meeting with the merman at Amager Shore in Chapter Thirteen—in the novel's eighth and ninth chapters. Here we visit the Temple of Poetry, a holy place where all sorts of hideous frogs and vile vermin are trying to get in through the porous brick facade. "These beasts, they told me, were the ignorant critics, and they were always likened to *Cerberus*."[36] Then Andersen adds that this comparison to Cerberus—who, in Greek mythology, is the friendly guard to the entrance of Hades, but always casts himself with great ferocity at anyone trying to exit—isn't really valid, since the ancient monster had four legs and three heads, while 19th-century literary critics have two legs and no head at all.

Playwright and Academic

Walking Tour was a magnificent beginning for a Romantic author's career and life, in which all the literary possibilities were immediately dispersed from the start and now pointed in all directions. Most of them pointed away from the bourgeois way of life and a culture of education, which Andersen on the one hand was rebelling against, while on the other hand he was fiercely courting it, especially through his connections with the Collin family.

When *Walking Tour* was published in January 1829, it aroused attention in particular because of the sly launching of the book that was inherent in the final chapter, where the reader had to create his own ending by using his imagination and pen or by taking a scissors and glue pot to the daily newspaper. The critics were very favorably disposed toward the novel's sophisticated play with illusions and all the leaps in the text through time and space. Most also took a broad-minded view of the first-time author's banter and provocations directed at critics in such sentences as: "Never pay any mind to the yapping dogs; they have to stay down on the street while you swing yourself up onto the roof."

The young lion among Danish critics of the day was Johan Ludvig Heiberg. He was enthusiastic about this satirical comedy of a novel. Yet Heiberg would have had to stretch his skills in equal measure to give the readers of *Maanedsskrift for Literatur* a plot summary, and so he settled for writing a great number of philosophical circumlocutions about the book's formal structure and its basic poetic tone. In several places Heiberg's critique leans toward the word "genius." He praises the work's many wild ideas and thought associations, pointing out the novel's lively, constantly changing form—a "musical fantasy," in which the young "fantasy player" surrenders to the inspiration of the moment and dares to be "so little master over it that he allows himself to be carried away by it."[37]

Andersen was, of course, exuberantly happy for himself and for all those who had always believed in his literary vocation, such as the kind Kamma Rahbek out at Bakkehus. He immediately sent her a free copy of *Walking Tour* so the Rahbeks could see how clever "The Little Declaimer" had now become. For several days in January 1829 Andersen waited for Fru Rahbek's verdict, but it never came. Instead, he heard from others that the matriarch of Danish Romanticism lay on her deathbed. And one day when Andersen ran into Commodore Wulff, he learned that Fru Rahbek had died. Andersen's first reaction was: "Oh, I wonder if she managed to read *Walking Tour?*" Wulff flew into a fury and shouted: "Sir! No, that's going too far! Do you think anyone cares about your *Walking Tour* when they're about to meet Our Lord?"

We don't know what Andersen replied, but his grief didn't last long. After the book had been reviewed in a couple of newspapers and journals, the second printing of his novel was barely out before the young author was again in the news. At the end of April 1829, Hans Christian Andersen made his dramatic debut at the Royal Theater with a so-called Heroic Vaudeville in One Act. At long last he achieved success on the stage where, ten years previously, he had attempted to dance, sing, and speak his way to fame.

The play was called *Love at Nikolai Tower, or What Does the Gallery Say?* The peculiar subtitle indirectly refers to a theater phenomenon of the Golden Age and the section of the theater known as the "gallery." The applause and boos during and after the performance of a scene would indicate the popular opinion of the artistry just witnessed. In those days the furor could grow so fierce in the Royal Theater, even becoming an outright ruckus, that for a while a military guard was stationed at the foyer entrance to the seats on the main floor. That way the forces of law and order could immediately intercede if a disturbance occurred in the cheap seats. Of particular concern was the gallery, which was the section on the main floor behind the finer seats reserved for younger courtiers, officers, and government officials. The gallery contained a few benches, but for the most part the audience members preferred to stand. The spectators here consisted of master artisans, tradesmen, and people holding low-level government posts, as well as younger civil servants, students, writers, and other good citizens more or less knowledgeable about art. The distinguished people in the box seats were often too refined to make their opinions known by shouting and clapping, but that was not the case with the gallery. From there came the first important reactions, revealing whether a play would be met with indifference, or whether it would be judged a great success or an utter fiasco.[38]

And what did they think of Andersen's debut on the royal stage in 1829? The audience in the gallery, where the author, well in advance, had positioned a considerable crowd of student and soldier friends, went wild with enthusiasm. At one point they shouted: "Long live the author!" This was more than the author could handle and, according to *The Fairy Tale of My Life*, he rushed out of the theater in tears and went straight across Kongens Nytorv to the Collin family's home. There the mistress of the house tried to console him by saying that even Oehlenschläger and other great writers had once been booed; whereupon the sobbing Andersen replied: "Yes, but they weren't booing at all! . . . They were clapping and shouting long live the author!"[39]

The vaudeville took Andersen a week to write, and the ending, in particular, was inspired by Ludwig Tieck's story "Puss in Boots." It takes place in Copenhagen, where Ellen is waiting for the love of her life, the journeyman tailor Søren Pind, who is on a long sea voyage. Suddenly she gets word that Per Hansen, a watchman at St. Peter's Church, has asked for her hand in marriage. Both Ellen's father, who is a watchman at Nikolai Tower, and her old confidante Maren urge her to say yes. "What is your tailor compared to this diamond? / Nothing but a butterfly compared to an elephant!" Ellen is under a great deal of pressure, but before she gives in and betrays her tailor, he returns home. Their love blossoms at once, becoming stronger than ever before, and together they flee out to Amager. That's where Ellen's father and suitor have to go to bring Ellen home to the tower in the city. After much rhetoric and many pleas, the impasse in the drama and the love story is resolved when Ellen's father puts the decision in the hands of the theater audience. Just before the curtain falls, it's announced from the front of the stage that if the play brings pleasure to the audience, Søren and Ellen will, of course, stay together. But if the play is booed, then she will have to marry Per Hansen. The question is then asked from the stage: "What does the gallery say?" And we have to imagine—as Hans Christian Andersen did, at any rate—that the curtain fell and the audience broke out in spontaneous applause and shouts of "hurrah!" on behalf of Ellen and Søren, the wonderful play, and the wonderful author!

The critics were not quite as enthusiastic about this sophisticated ending as all the good friends and students that Andersen had managed to place among the "shouters" in the gallery. A few days after the premiere, the magazine *Kjøbenhavns-Posten* bluntly called the play "a feeble copy" of Wessel's popular *Love Without Stockings*. The magazine also spoke of a trivial and tedious work "that bears witness to equal amounts boldness and lack of taste," and it more than hinted that the author had overpromoted both himself and his play before the premiere. "For that reason most people had expected much more of this vaudeville which had been talked about and heralded for so long, and even more of the author who at every opportunity seemed to want to draw the public's attention to it, thereby undoubtedly harming his work significantly and weakening the public's interest in it."[40]

In Heiberg's *Maanedsskrift for Literatur*, a finger was also pointed at Andersen's Romantic parodying of national treasures such as Adam Oehlenschläger's plays *Axel and Valborg* and *Hakon Jarl*, which in Andersen's hands were strongly ridiculed in several places.[41] The critique then concluded with the same basic diatribe about the young playwright's rather too clever organization of the gallery for the premiere.

Even though *Walking Tour, Love at Nikolai Tower*, and *Poems* were all written in accordance with modern Romantic ideals, Andersen's actual admittance to the brotherhood of Romanticism had yet to occur. It would take the shape of a pilgrimage to all the Romantic hot spots and landscapes in Germany.

After sailing from Copenhagen to Lübeck, Andersen traveled by various coaches—*Postkutsche, Schnellpost*, and *Eilwagen*—via Hamburg, Braunschweig, Goslar, Halle, and Leipzig to Dresden, which he reached two weeks later. There Andersen discovered that he was neither a stranger nor unknown. As mentioned previously, a doctor in Meissen was taken aback when he heard the Dane's name: "'Are you perhaps related to Andersen, the famous writer?' I then said that no other Danish writer had that name other than me, whereupon he said that he had read several things by me in German, which had pleased him."[42]

Andersen had left Copenhagen in mid-May 1831, suffering from a toothache which in Hamburg compelled him to note in his diary that a person's nerves are actually like fine piano keys on which the air pressure plays: "And that's why it plays in my teeth, first piano, then crescendo, all the melodies of pain according to the changes in the weather."[43] But the pain soon faded at the sight of the magnificent nature of the Harz Mountains. For the first time Andersen was high up and walking on clouds. The young man experienced a tremendous expansion of his view of nature. As he later wrote in the introductory chapter to his travel book: "A new world opened before me in the mountains."[44] The high point of this Romantic pilgrimage, which lasted five weeks, was seeing the famed sandstone cliffs near Bastei in the "Saxon Switzerland." As it says in his diary on June 7, 1831: "Wild mountain gorges, slopes with black spruces over which the bluish gray mist hovered in peculiar shapes . . . the whole thing looked as if it were a painted picture." It was here, in the cliff and forest world of Bastei that Goethe had wandered, and painters such as Philipp Otto Runge and, later, Johan Christian Dahl and Caspar David Friedrich, in the early 19th century, had explored with their paint boxes and easels, following Friedrich's maxim: "The painter should not only paint what he sees before him, but also what he sees within."[45]

It was to this view of nature and art that Hans Christian Andersen was now to be initiated. Also of central importance in his letters and diary from the journey, as well as in his travel book *Shadow Pictures*, which was published only three months after the trip, were his meetings in Dresden with the author Ludwig Tieck. Equally important was his encounter with Raphael's famous painting *Sistine Madonna*. The painting hung in the gallery of the Baroque castle Zwinger in the middle of Dresden, close to the Opera House and the Brühl Terrace near the Elbe River, where people strolled in the evening or floated in gondolas. It was in the gallery, face-to-face with Raphael's inscrutable, beautiful Madonna, whose face Andersen described as "childishly ethereal," that the foremost German Romantic writers such as Schlegel, Tieck, Kleist, and Hoffmann had knelt in the late 1790s.[46] On one of his first days in Dresden, Andersen stood for a long time before Raphael's painting and afterwards wrote in his diary that it was not the paint on the canvas that a person should worship or kneel before. "It's the *spirit* that reveals itself, corporeally before the corporeal eye."[47]

The only disappointment on Andersen's relatively brief and hasty trip in the summer of 1831 was that he did not meet Goethe, whose Sturm-und-Drang writing Andersen had cultivated so intensely during the 1820s. But he had later distanced himself somewhat from Goethe's work, in keeping with his sudden enthusiasm for the younger and more hard-boiled German Romantics such as Hoffmann and Heine. When it wasn't possible for Andersen to make contact with the master himself, Ludwig Tieck was an excellent substitute, since he was regarded by many people in Germany as the "King of Romanticism."[48] The fifty-eight-year-old Tieck had an extensive and varied literary career behind him, which included novels, short stories, plays, and a collection of "Volksmärchen" [folktales] that contained the story "The Fairies," which Hans Christian Andersen often mentioned and made so famous. The German author was quite knowledgeable about

Nordic literature. He was an enthusiastic reader of Holberg's works and a close friend of B. S. Ingemann, who had given Andersen a letter of introduction to take along. For Andersen, his meeting with Ludwig Tieck took on the same glow as Adam Oehlenschläger's meeting with Goethe several decades earlier—especially after Andersen returned home and sat down to write *Shadow Pictures*. Around 1830 the Oehlenschläger-Goethe meeting was also the subject of renewed interest in Denmark, in connection with the publication of Oehlenschläger's memoirs both in Germany and Denmark.[49]

When you read *Shadow Pictures*, you have the impression that the great Ludwig Tieck—"the man who is the master of an entire school of Romantic poetry, the writer who is closest to Goethe in age, stature, and the admiration of his countrymen," as Andersen writes in his travel book[50] —was already deeply familiar with the young Danish writer and his books. The encounter between the two men on June 5, 1831, must have been a peculiar sight: the young, towering, thin Dane who spoke broken German facing an elderly, corpulent German, who spoke a little Danish and whose one shoulder was lower than the other due to rheumatism. Tieck, who also looked pale and sickly because he was afflicted with rheumatism, was a gentle and friendly person. And to Andersen's great surprise, it turned out that the master had already read *Walking Tour*. At any rate, that's what Andersen says in Chapter Ten of *Shadow Pictures*, where he describes his meeting with Tieck, who was then given a few more books, including Andersen's latest poetry collection, *Fantasies and Sketches*. "After I had given him the books and Ingemann's letter, he kindly took my hand and asked whether I was the one who had written *Walking Tour*, and when I answered affirmatively, he said something complimentary, welcomed me heartily to Germany, and asked about Ingemann, of whom he was very fond."[51]

What a feather in his cap! It sounded as if Andersen was already known abroad by great artists such as Ludwig Tieck. Yet the truth was that a year and a half earlier, on February 1, 1829, Hans Christian Andersen had sent a copy of *Walking Tour* to Ludwig Tieck along with a letter containing a lengthy and pithy introduction to the young Danish writer's romantic life story. The letter began with the words:

"Although I have not personally had the honor of making your acquaintance, I cannot resist satisfying the desire I have to send you a copy of my first work . . . So as not to be completely unknown to you, I will here, in all brevity, present a short outline of my own story, which despite my youth does include some variety . . . Now my school life is over. In

October 1828 I graduated, and at the New Year I delivered my first work: *Walking Tour to Amager.* It is arousing more attention than I dreamed of, and after one month I can start thinking about a second printing, since the first is nearly sold out."[52]

This was all a carefully devised plan on Andersen's part, and it turned out to be so effective that he later used it with regard to other foreign artists who might add their approval to his life and work. In his letters, travel accounts, and autobiographies Andersen often made it seem as if these foreign notables in the 1830s had become aware of or acquainted with his books all on their own. That was rarely the case until after Hans Christian Andersen became truly famous in the 1840s. For example, in 1838, Andersen received a letter from the Swedish Romantic writer P. D. A. Atterbom, and he promptly sat down and wrote to his friend Henriette Hanck: "Yesterday I also received a letter that pleased me, from a man whom I've never met, never spoken to, and yet he says that he loves me, that we are kindred spirits and *eternal* friends, that was from the writer Atterbom in Upsala."[53]

This was wishful thinking on Andersen's part. The above-mentioned letter from Atterbom reveals that in 1837 Hans Christian Andersen, who had recently heard that the Swedish Romantic writer had read his novel *The Improvisatore*, sent his *Agnete and the Merman* directly to the Swedish author along with a curriculum vitæ and a request that the established Romanticist in Sweden acknowledge the gift with an assessment of the young Danish writer. Atterbom did so in 1838.[54] During a difficult period, with a great deal of disfavor from the Danish critics at home, it was important for Andersen to acquire some favorable critiques from abroad. He would then immediately—as we see from the letter to Henriette Hanck—put them into circulation as happy travel anecdotes about the steadily growing popularity of Hans Christian Andersen outside of Denmark. This was also the method that Andersen used with regard to Ludwig Tieck in 1829 and in the following year as well with yet another delivery of books abroad. During the summer of 1830, Henriette Wulff was about to travel to Dresden, and so Andersen gave her his *Poems* and a letter to Tieck to take along. He also made use of Edvard Collin's willingness to help him with the wording of the letter, and afterwards—in Collin's own letters to Henriette Wulff in Dresden—to ask Henriette to make sure that Ludwig Tieck had not only received the books but had read them![55]

All of this meant that there were good, logical reasons why Ludwig

Tieck would seem so receptive and well prepared when Andersen, along with the Norwegian painter J. C. Dahl, showed up for an evening of readings at Tieck's home on June 5, 1831. The guests at the salon were to hear samples of the German author's translation of Shakespeare's *Henry IV*. New faces in the crowd—such as Hans Christian Andersen—were always properly introduced to the salon's other guests before the readings began. The audience was thus primed and could be observed and used by the reader as a sort of partner in the performance. Ludwig Tieck had once dreamed of becoming an actor but never got closer to being on stage than assuming the role of dramaturge at the royal theater in Dresden during the 1820s. He now performed entire plays at home in his own parlor. There were works by Sophocles, Aristophanes, Calderón, and Shakespeare that he himself had translated. Tieck would never indicate the individual characters by mentioning their names—which was something that Andersen noticed on that June evening in 1831. Instead, Tieck would act out the different roles, giving each character a specific voice and temperament. Andersen was utterly enchanted, absorbing everything and "forgetting the writer for the man," as he later wrote in his diary. Everything was registered in Andersen's memory and later entered in his diary and travel account.

It's clear to see from *Shadow Pictures* that the high point of his trip to Germany in 1831 was his meeting with Tieck in Dresden. His departure from the city on the Elbe River on June 10 is described as a holy and magical moment, when the Danish writer's enrollment and acceptance into the German brotherhood of Romantics was confirmed with gifts and "the kiss of ordination," as Andersen later, in *The Fairy Tale of My Life*, called Tieck's embrace and letter. Tieck more or less said:

> "Send me now and then a thought from afar. Proceed contentedly and optimistically along the path of poetry, which you have already so beautifully and bravely trod. Do not lose courage if the much too pedestrian criticism should vex you—as it will! Give my greetings to the lovable Ingemann and all my other acquaintances in Denmark, and I hope that one day—preferably soon—you might return to us in Germany, healthy, lively, and richly gifted by the muses. Your true friend, *Ludwig Tieck*."[56]

The Shadow Picture, Riborg Voigt

In the Romantic stage setting of Hans Christian Andersen's first trip abroad, which is what *Shadow Pictures* is, an unhappy love relationship with a woman also plays a role. We never hear the name of the woman, but this is a tremendously important role for Andersen's ordination as a Romantic writer. The love story provides the melancholy undercurrent for the travel book, and the woman is all the unhappiness and pain that the writer is trying to put behind him during his journey, though he is constantly reminded of it and sees shadow pictures of it in nature and the cultures through which he travels. And it quickly becomes apparent that he uses this sense of longing to produce tremendously good writing. We have barely stepped aboard the ship headed for Germany along with the author of the travel book before the first signs of this unhappy love affair wash over the ship like a wave of passion:

> In the rocking boat, on the surging sea,
> I sat with the maiden of my love;
> Captivating desire!
> She placed her head on my breast,
> I wrapped my arms around her,
> Felt her kisses burn,
> Burn my lips and cheek,
> As the sail billowed in the wind;
> And she pressed my hand, and with lips and eyes,
> She gave me fidelity.
> We parted—I saw the tears of her pain.
> I stayed with my rocking boat.
> — God knows if she has forgotten it all?
> How awful that would be![57]

The real woman behind these poetic verses was Riborg Voigt. In his autobiography from 1832, Andersen wrote about the first time he met her in Faaborg in August 1830, describing the encounter as if the whole thing had occurred many, many years earlier: "I was at that time in my twenty-fifth year, had never really been in love. My own personage had given me enough to think about so I had no thoughts for anyone else. There was truly no thought yet of passion."[58]

Riborg was the daughter of the wealthy Fyn shopkeeper and merchant, Laurits Peter Voigt—"the richest man in town," as Andersen calls him in a letter.[59] The young author visited the family because he was in the area on his summer travels, and in Copenhagen he had studied for exams along with Riborg's brother, Christian. Even though Andersen later elevated Riborg to a heavenly beauty with his little poem "Two Brown Eyes,"[60] Riborg Voigt was not, in some people's view, especially beautiful. She was, however, extroverted and charming.[61] And it was precisely the merry, intrepid, and good-natured side of Riborg's character that Andersen fell for. In a letter to Ingemann from January 1831, he calls her "a witty, childish creature."[62]

It was during these years that Hans Christian Andersen was a great fan of Heine's poetry. In *The Fairy Tale of My Life* he describes his admiration, which he shared with his friend Orla Lehmann, with the words: "I had become familiar with a poet who sang from my soul and who reached inside it to seize the most strongly vibrating strings."[63] There are many examples in Andersen's writing from the time that reveal how Heine had infused his blood. In 1831 all three verses from Heine's poem "Ein Jüngling liebt ein Mädchen" ["A Youth Loves a Maiden"] suddenly appeared in Andersen's vaudeville *The Ship*,[64] when the male protagonist asks a young woman whether she is fond of Heine's poetry. Then he instantly launches into a recitation of the poem about the youth who loves a girl who loves another man who is already engaged and marries someone else, whereupon the girl, in defiance, marries the first man to come along. The youth is left with his pain over his unrequited love; no one loves him at all. And Heinrich Heine concludes: "It may well be an old story, / Yet it is eternally new, / And whoever must endure it, / His heart will split in two."[65]

The poem essentially contains the Romantic formula that Andersen uses in *Shadow Pictures* when he presents and describes the first time he fell in love, and that's why he repeats the lines in the fourth chapter of his travel book: "*Es ist eine alte Geschichte / Doch bleibt sie immer neu.*" [It is an old story / Yet it is always new.] In this way Andersen emphasizes his book's Romantic scheme à la Heine.[66]

In the spring of 1831 Riborg Voigt married "the first man to come along," Jakob Bøvring, who was a forestry graduate. She was already engaged to him by the time Andersen arrived in Faaborg in August 1830. And that was exactly one of the reasons why Riborg was so attractive in the writer's eyes. She was unattainable and, as such, the perfect woman on which to cast his romantic gaze. Andersen didn't try to thwart Riborg Voigt's wedding plans; instead, he daydreamed about being part of them, only to withdraw gallantly in the duplicitous letter he sent to her in October 1830. With all its contradictory proclamations of love, the letter was the exact opposite of a proposal. Rather, as it said, it was a warning against the very idea of a relationship between them.[67] This "proposal letter" also shows how Andersen makes reality into poetry by transposing the whole situation into Heinrich Heine's tableau from his poem about the youth who loves the maiden:

> "If you truly love another, then forgive me! Forgive me for having ventured this, which must then be considered presumptuous. I hope you will both be happy! And forget a creature who can never, ever forget you."[68]

Three months later a farewell letter arrives from Andersen, in which he has stepped into the role of Heine's rejected and eternally unhappy youth: "I will never be happy, but that's how it must be! And so forget me! Never give me a thought! You will be happy, and there is nothing more that I wish! Live well! Only once more will I hear from you—then never again! Do not feel sad for me, Riborg! God is good and merciful! Live well! Live well forever!"[69]

By withdrawing from a love relationship—or whatever such an affair might be called that had been limited to three meetings lasting a couple of hours and just as few letters, but a wide-ranging and lively flood of poems—Andersen remained in the role of the chaste lover. And this would prove to be his preferred role on the stage of love throughout his life. It was precisely in the role of the reticent man who cultivates his love from an appropriate distance to flesh and blood that we meet him in *Shadow Pictures*. This is the case in one of the first poems in the book, which has to do with the phenomenon of a "kiss." A sort of commentary to the poem states that only a married man can understand something as intimate and tender as a kiss, but a poet, on the other hand, is allowed to write about it.[70] Throughout *Shadow Pictures* we see all these lyrical enactments of the age-old drama of love between a man and a woman. And between the lines of the twenty poems that are scattered throughout the travel book, we're pulled back—at a symbolic, impersonal distance—to the encounter in Faaborg in August 1830. Then we move onward to the cautious feeding of the flame of love in October 1830 when Riborg Voigt was in Copenhagen and met Andersen, and finally to the predictable separation. Then all that remains are the sweet pains of memories and dreams, and these pains are filled with poetic possibilities. As the traveler says in his first major poem from Hamburg, for him the distance is never great from sorrow to song: "I fly off from town to town, / Oh, if only I could forget the flower! // I grieve—yet sing even more than before . . ."⁷¹

Little development or variation is evident in Andersen's use of his unhappy love story in *Shadow Pictures*. He doesn't try to mend the emotional shards along the way, but they provide an abundance of effects. At regular intervals, symbols and images are presented and repeated in a form that seems more extroverted and coquettish than ardent and painful.

His love for Riborg Voigt was impossible, but not nearly as unhappy as Andersen described it to others. It is not a deeply wounded lover who writes lines of verse such as: "—*Aimer, aimant, aimé*—how many memories can be found in a regular verb like that?"⁷² The poet actually seems rather proud to show off his fashionable infatuation as the book progresses, striking a tone and a theme in keeping with Heine and the zeitgeist: "I found a sweetheart. / My mind and soul I felt burning / for her alone. / She loved me—she was true, / True—therefore we parted, we two."⁷³

In other Heine-inspired poems, Andersen voiced his desire to have at his disposal in his poet's workshop just such a personal pain and unhappiness, which would make him a "real" Romantic poet and could evoke the elegiac conditions that produce dreams and poems. This was true, for example, of "Avis aux Lectrices" from 1830. This self-mocking poem, whose title means "Advice to my Female Readers," is a sort of "personals ad" ("Seeking muse!") that was written several months before Andersen met Riborg Voigt. Although the irony is evident, the poem also tells us quite precisely what it was the impatient poet was searching for and shortly would find in the south of Fyn:

> I'm missing something—shall I speak the name?
> It's not a rare sort of thing;
> I'm missing—well—a tiny little girl —
> Oh, dear God! Now they'll laugh at me!
> Dare I never love, never pine?
> What? Am I not old enough?
> God knows, I do not wish to offend a soul,
> No, to love, that is what I want.
>
> Every poet, even someone very young,
> Has a sweetheart—that must be nice!
> Someone is unhappy, he sighs and moans,
> Oh, I must join in! and it must be soon.
> But I still have no one properly in sight,

So I might be rid of my longing;
God knows, I pine enough for my poems,
But good Lord, for me that's not enough!

No, I must have—what should I say —
A sweetheart, then my heart will doubtless find peace;
A little, just a very little girl,
For I am tall enough for both of us!
Oh, come! Let not sweet hope forsake me;
For love befits folks so well.
But you must praise all my poems,
For I will be off as soon as you forget![74]

Many scattered thoughts and impulses lay behind this search for "a sweetheart." There is no doubt that the man inside the poet, especially in a bourgeois, social sense, was tired of being a child. Andersen, who was no longer so young but was still deeply innocent, could see that all the other men around him who were his peers were one by one getting engaged, married, and starting families. And his personal problems in this area were quite apparent. It was one thing that he did not have an attractive appearance on his side. But it was quite another matter that at the age of twenty-five he was still unable to approach the opposite sex in the manner that young men had always approached women, ever since the days of Adam and Eve. The sensual side of love between a man and a woman was completely alien to his nature, as is evident from his descriptions of Riborg Voigt in letters to B. S. Ingemann, Edvard Collin, and Signe Læssøe. Not once in his presentation of his "sweetheart" from Faaborg—nor in his poetry or prose—does Riborg appear as a grown-up woman with a body; she is always depicted as an ethereal being or a child. Sexually mature women were not only alien to Andersen, they were also terrifying, and at times—whenever the conversation or his thoughts turned to prostitutes—disgusting and vile. In his autobiography from 1832, in connection with a discussion of his friends Carl Bagger and Fritz Petit, who were his own age, Andersen says that he finds the behavior of all young people in this regard excusable, and then adds: "On the other hand, my contempt for women rose to such an extent that it undoubtedly was *that* which continued to preserve me uncorrupted and innocent."[75]

Hans Christian Andersen's Autobiography 1805–1831 was the author's first, big, unified attempt to explain himself and "my own character which was quite inexplicable to me"[76] to his closest acquaintances, whose astonishment was continuing to grow. In 1832 these acquaintances still included only the Collin family. In this first book of memoirs, Andersen was surprisingly open in his depiction of his problematic relationship to the opposite sex. If this autobiography was written, as claimed, specifically for the eighteen- or nineteen-year-old Louise Collin and to be regarded as a form of courtship, then the following passage about the suitor's relationship to the female sex during his boyhood must have been far from delightful reading for a young woman. These are the words of a man who, deep inside, realizes that he will have trouble loving a grown woman, the way that a man and woman love each other in a normal marriage:

> "I only liked being with little girls; I still remember a pretty little one about eight years old who kissed me and said that she would be my sweetheart. That pleased me, and I would always let her kiss me, though I never kissed her myself, nor did I allow anyone but her to kiss me. In general I felt a strange revulsion for older girls, those who were more than twelve years old. They actually made me shudder. And I even used an expression for everything that was unpleasant for me to touch, saying that it was so 'girlish'!"[77]

Andersen's Order of Nuns

In the early 1830s, Hans Christian Andersen's preferred women, outside of poetry, were first and foremost those who either downplayed their sexuality or—because of age, social class, or physical infirmity—pushed it into the background. They included "mothers" and "sisters" such as the aforementioned Signe Læssøe, Henriette Hanck, Henriette Wulff, and her mother, the stern Fru Wulff. And throughout Andersen's life there were many other "epistolary sisters," such as Jette Collin, Mathilde Ørsted, Fru Serres, Fru Melchior, Clara Heincke, Fru Scavenius, Mimi Holstein, and Jonna Stampe. Many of these women, in Andersen's eyes, shared a spiritual similarity with Raphael's Sistine Madonna, before which the Danish writer had so reverently lingered in Dresden's gallery in 1831. They all expressed a serene and exalted calm beyond their gender and body. These mothers and sisters were also divinely unattainable in the sense that they were either much too young, much too old, already married, or—like some of the most loyal, such as Henriette Hanck, Henriette Wulff, and the German, Clara Heincke—hunchbacked or dwarfishly short.

The term "sister," which Andersen never relinquished, had a double meaning. On the one hand, he used it to place himself immediately inside a familial framework as the "brother." At the same time, by using the honorable term "sister," he emphasized the spiritual aspect of the relationship. As a loving but carnally reserved Johanne says to the honest, steadfast Knud in the fairy tale "Under the Willow Tree," as she sets off into the world, leaving behind her childhood sweetheart, who at the hour of parting has proposed to her: "Don't make yourself and me unhappy, Knud! I will always be a good sister to you, that you can rely on! But never anything more!"[78]

The boundaries were firm and clear. The "sisters" formed Andersen's order of nuns, which all his life remained one of his strongest safeguards against being seduced and losing his innocence. And the women loved him for his innocence. Not, as Charlotte Bournonville so delicately expresses it in her memoirs, because he was a *primo amoroso*[79] or handsome in appearance. As the German harpist and pianist Clara Schumann once said without hesitation, the Danish fairy-tale writer was "the ugliest man imaginable"! And yet women, both young and old, thronged around him almost everywhere he went in the world. He possessed a type of magnetism that other men couldn't help noticing. For instance, during a royal banquet, King Frederik VII of Denmark, who was quite a ladies' man, once saw his own Countess Danner disappear into the enthusiastic crowd surrounding Hans Christian Andersen. At one point the king broke through the crowd and asked the author what it was he possessed that the other men at the banquet apparently did not. Andersen, who had to give his king some kind of answer, ended up putting a masculine innuendo in his reply, though it was no doubt unintentional: "It must be hidden attributes, Your Majesty!" "I beg your pardon!" shouted the king, as he looked the writer's lanky body up and down. "I would never have believed it. I can't see it in him!"[80]

Time after time, as a brother and son in relationship to a sister and mother, Andersen succeeded in isolating young, alluring women in a sacrosanct position and in this manner neutralized their sexuality. The phenomenon is exceptionally well illustrated in a later story such as "The Porter's Son" from 1866, in which it says of the general's attractive daughter Emilie: "how charming she was . . . how she floated, how delicate she was! If she were to be drawn, it would have to be as a soap bubble."[81] Riborg Voigt and, soon after her, the young daughter of Jonas Collin, Louise, about whom we shall hear shortly, were the first great soap bubbles in Andersen's adult male life. These two young, sexually mature women were transformed by Andersen into "sisters" and admitted to his order of nuns, which thus canceled their "dangerous" sexuality in relation to Brother Andersen. Like the general's daughter who attends a masked ball in "The Porter's Son," the female bodies of Riborg and Louise become dissolved in hazy, angelic contours when Andersen describes them: "*Psyche*, in gauze and lace. She was like floating swan's down, she had no need for wings, she wore them merely as an emblem of Psyche."[82]

Andersen's infatuation with Riborg Voigt first came seriously to light and under discussion in January 1831 when he published his poetry collection *Fantasies and Sketches*. He immediately sent a copy to Ingemann and his wife, who reacted swiftly, since they had noticed the unhappy tone of several of the poems. They now asked this young friend of the family to ease his heart by confiding in them. That was exactly what Andersen needed and was waiting for. On January 18, 1831, he laid his cards on the table in a letter to his good friends in Sorø:

> "I am no longer the same person I once was. Life, everything has acquired a deeper meaning for me. I have been placed in a position in which I can see the vast whole in all its depth, but realize that I will never be happy! I will conceal nothing from you, because you can feel it, you will feel it with me! No, my poems are not fantasy, something real is at their core; oh, it is so unhappy that it hardly looks like reality at all. All my soul and thoughts cling to one creature, a witty, childish creature, the likes of which I have never seen. She loves me in return, but, oh, it sounds so hideous, I can sense it! She is engaged and will be married next month."[83]

Andersen went on to explain that it was a matter of a very wealthy family, and because Riborg and her fiancé had been childhood sweethearts, it was now her duty to protect her fidelity and marry. "Oh, dear, dear Ingemann! I wish I were dead! Dead!" His writer friend in Sorø replied at once. With a fervent, romantic empathy for Andersen's suffering, he offered a brief lecture in his letter about "the pain of sentencing," from which a higher ardor can often develop:

> "My advice, therefore, is not to forget and dismiss what cannot nor should be forgotten. No, on the contrary—honor and preserve a feeling which seems only for a time to make you unhappy, but which can and must give you infinitely more than it deprives you of, since it will open

for you insight into a heaven that only few people know . . . The more you can manage to elevate this feeling to a great and eternal idea, the easier it will be for you to free yourself from the torture rack and combat the passion."[84]

In reality, what B. S. Ingemann, who was sixteen years older than Andersen, was advising was for him to turn the loss of Riborg into an asset through his imagination and writing. And in April 1831, he followed up his advice in a letter to Andersen, who no longer seemed as gloomy or despairing to his friends. By now, with the help of what Ingemann calls a "self-liberating explosion," he seemed to have written his way out of defeat and banished his bleak thoughts. Ingemann pointed out that with "a resolute will, a disposition resigned to the will of God, and a beautiful and noble goal in view," he could accomplish a great deal. And Ingemann was tremendously pleased with the outcome of Andersen's affair with Riborg Voigt.[85]

At the urging of Ingemann and others, Andersen instead cultivated his love and rejection as a condition in which a writer feels the emotion and through his writing turns the pain of separation into a joy. And this type of masochism was not at all foreign to Andersen. "I love this longing in my breast!" he says on the first page of *Fantasies and Sketches* in January 1831.[86] And in a little verse about "Young Love," which stems from his ballad opera *Little Kirsten* from 1846, Andersen emphasizes the sweetness of longing and loss: "In love no sorrow is too great, / Oh, what does it mean to suffer and long! / What joy it is to be young, / But most joyous of all to embrace one's young bride."[87]

Dear Frøken Louise!

As we will see in the next chapter, there were other objects for Andersen's longing on his journey through Germany. Another one of the images that Andersen carried with him was of a young man back home in Copenhagen who refused to adopt a more intimate form of address with Andersen. His name was Edvard Collin, and he was the older brother of Louise Collin, with whom Andersen carried on a relatively intense and emotional correspondence during 1832-36. This correspondence was carefully monitored by the Collin family, since they were on their guard in terms of the quixotic Andersen. What was he seeking to gain with his letters to eighteen-year-old Louise Collin?

Viewed from the outside, Andersen's emotion-filled letters of 1832–33 might seem to be an attempt to make himself an eligible marriage prospect for "Frøken Louise" [Miss Louise], as he called her. As her husband he would have won admission to the Collin household for all eternity. Yet if we look more closely at the letters—which today include only Andersen's half of the correspondence, since Louise failed to burn them as she did all her own letters—other important motives show up behind Andersen's advances. For instance, he had a strong need to establish a triangle, a close friendship between a sister, a brother, and a writer. This was the same type of configuration that Andersen had created for himself in the Voigt family, when first Riborg and then her brother Christian became the object of his longing. In a letter from May 1831, when the relationship with Riborg is finally over and Andersen is on his way south, he describes Christian Voigt with words such as: "The one that above all others I feel most bound to . . . It is as if he has bewitched me; I don't know why I should be so fond of him!"[88] And while the writer in the travel book dramatizes his unhappy love life, making the reader believe that in his heart he thinks of nothing and no one else but the young girl who has refused him back home in Denmark, Andersen writes in his diary on May 26, after being away from home only ten days: "How strangely my thoughts flit around Riborg, Christian, Eduard, Fru L. [Læssøe] —but there are so many loving people in this world!"[89]

In spite of everything, Riborg did not hold any greater place in his thoughts; apparently many other goals, full of longing, had already appeared on the horizon. Five months earlier, when his love had been at its peak, Andersen wrote to Ingemann that he had only one solace: "I have won over her brother, he knows everything, and feels and suffers along with us, he is so deeply fond of us both."[90] At that time Andersen elevated his relationship to Riborg's brother—under the heading "To My Friend"—to a separate part of the large-scale poem "Life a Dream" that concludes *Fantasies and Sketches*, which was published in January 1831. In three long acts Andersen recalls the first love story of his life and bemoans the loss of the beloved woman, but by way of introduction he begs her brother for loyalty in pain and in desire:

> Your open gaze, your pure childlike heart,
> And she—*our sister*—bound me tight to you;
> Now she is dead—I saw your silent pain,
> While your lips would console me—
> Oh, brother, life's best bubbles burst,
> Oh, may your strong friendship never be lost!

This same configuration of a sister, a brother, and a writer by the name of Andersen is evident in the many letters addressed to Louise Collin in 1832-33, when Riborg has been relegated to the past and Andersen still has yet to experience his decisive breakthrough as a man and an artist. As mentioned before, at first glance the letters to Louise seem like cautious letters of courtship which, under light camouflage, are feeling their way within the four walls of the Collin household. Letter by letter Andersen comes closer, showing a little more of himself, but seemingly courting only the young lady's confidence and sympathy. At least that's how it looked on the surface, but between the lines there was much more going on. Beneath the confidential information about his own character and his distressing loneliness, the letter writer was weaving a larger net that was also intended for Louise's older brother, her father, and the rest of the Collin family.

In the fall of 1832 Andersen stood at a crossroads in terms of both his career and his love life, and a careful examination of his letters to Louise Collin reveals that his attempts to win the young girl's interest were also motivated by his wish to establish close contact with Edvard. At the same time, she might put in a good word for the young author with her father, who in the most literal sense held the key to the national treasury, which would sponsor Andersen's next trip abroad. And if the sympathy he thought he sensed in Frøken Louise should, in addition, result in a platonic love affair, which he could then use in his writing, so much the better for Andersen.

After his summer journey to Jutland and Fyn in 1832 when he had worked intensely on his autobiography, Andersen sent the book to Louise for her to read in the fall, even though it ended quite abruptly, in the middle of quoting a letter from B. S. Ingemann. The author also failed to say more—as he had promised to do—about his apparently very ardent and emotional friendship with a certain Ludvig Müller during the summer of 1832. By all accounts, Andersen never managed to finish the book before he set off for Rome in April 1833.

With its opening remark about "the paternal heart that has always beat for me!" Andersen's *Autobiography* was the ultimate petition for admission to what was in all respects a large and stable family. And the book was also deposited at the Collin house when Andersen left Denmark in 1833 with instructions from the author that if he should die on his way through the great world, his memoirs were to be published posthumously.

Before then, Andersen had stepped up his correspondence with the Collins. Whereas previously Jonas Collin and his son Edvard were the only recipients of his letters, now Louise also began receiving these fervent communiqués in which Andersen asked for permission to be alone with her "spiritual persona." At the same time he enclosed poems and thanked her for all the cordiality and "sisterly sentiment" she had shown him:

> "You cannot know how it lets sunshine into my life. It is so difficult to be a stranger and alone in the world. In the evening, when I sit alone in my room, I feel it so strongly and grievously. Just think if you had no parents, no siblings. That is a loss that you cannot imagine! . . . I suppose that's why I'm also more fond of Edvard than you can know, even though he has often made me sad. Yet since I came home from the country, he has been so loving; that good creature, if only he will continue thus. Won't you speak on my behalf? Make him feel a proper fondness for me. I am, truly, very sensitive in the area of love; a dark look can disturb my peace for a long time. But I suppose this seems to you a strange letter?"[91]

Yes, they were indeed strange letters that Andersen wrote. Wildly divergent feelings and demands fluttered about, seeking a plethora of goals and means. About the poetic and confidential nature of his letters, Andersen explained in a letter to Louise on September 21, 1832: "My whole life seems to me a poetic invention, and you are certainly beginning to play a role in it; yet do not be angry about this. Since I regard Eduard as a brother, it is only natural that you should be—*his* sister."[92]

Louise, the younger and prettier of Jonas Collin's two daughters, was by nature gentle and merry. Within the family she was considered all her life to be the epitome of fairness, and a good and loyal friend to her friends.[93] Andersen painted a beautiful portrait of her in his novel *The Improvisatore*, in which she is disguised as the little abbess, "the good angel of the house," who wishes so dearly to beg forgiveness for the sins others have committed against the main character, Antonio, who is meant to be Andersen himself. As she says to Antonio, his many teachers have their own way of treating him, and they all think their own is the right one. Antonio is grateful to her for understanding this, and he subsequently says that her "sisterly soul" gives him self-confidence and binds him so nicely and securely to her. It was precisely this type of bond that Andersen had tried to establish in the letters he wrote in 1832, three years before he wrote the novel. "You can lead me and control me!" he says in October 1832, and begs furthermore, "Be a sister to me too, I have trust in you, give me courage!" And a month later Andersen's emotional request is given even greater emphasis: " . . . be a little more to me than the others, be a sister to me, be for me the one who shows me the goal, the path to achievement and honor." And all these pleas contained the eternal hope of attaining greater access to the family ranks and a higher place in the social hierarchy—an ever-restless yearning, as Andersen writes to Louise, one day, with time, to feel "affluent enough to buy my entry into the great dance hall."[94]

As was the case with Riborg Voigt, Andersen merely toyed with the idea of a marriage to Louise Collin. And in both instances, we see how he makes a bid for something that in his heart he knows full well he can neither achieve nor live up to in any possible way. But in the case of Louise Collin, there was again no real danger that Andersen might have to marry. First, Louise was being strictly monitored by her married older sister Ingeborg, who read all the correspondence. Second, the young woman's engagement to the judge advocate J. W. Lind was already in the works during the winter of 1832-33.

Was Andersen ever truly in love with Riborg Voigt and Louise Collin? Yes, in the sense that he, with his unstable character and a temperament that was always easily influenced, could fall in love at any time, any place, and with anyone. Andersen, who always wore his heart on his sleeve, learned in the remarks of a Danish critic to his poem "What I Love" from 1831 that a human heart could not possibly contain so many different emotions.[95] But he continued to fall in love in every possible—and impossible—direction during the following years. Yet there was one person, among all the sisters and brothers, with whom he constantly sought contact and who always sparkled in the distance like an unreachable star. His name shows up again and again in the letters to Louise in 1832-33:

"In Edvard I have found the most loving, the best friend, that I know; he will not forsake me."

Chapter Four

Your Only Fault Was Love (1832-1836)

"Mezzo caldo, per favore!" he says to the waiter at the bar, reaching for the cigar box on the counter. He leafs through all the letters but looks in vain for one addressed to "Monsieur H. C. Andersen. Voyageur danois, Caffè Greco, Via Condotti, Rome." Annoyed, the Danish writer turns around, completely forgetting what he ordered, and makes his way through the dense, thick clouds of smoke and the loud voices in the café's cramped center room, which is known as the "Omnibus." Here he manages to rid himself of the worst of his disappointment among the guests and waiters, the shoemakers and tailors who have brought their bills for the foreign artists whom they have a greater chance of meeting here than in front of Raphael's Stanze in the Vatican. In the Omnibus everyone sits packed together, conversing and drinking Falerno wine at small marble tables covered with coffee rings and hasty little sketches or drafts for a masterpiece, drawn on the tabletop and sentenced to imminent obliteration by the waiter's wet rag.[1]

The dark room at the very back of the café that Andersen is struggling to reach is reserved for the slightly older regular guests, grouped around four long tables with white marble tops. Seated at two of them can often be seen Russian and German artists such as Gogol, Reinhart, Koch, and Overbeck. The German painters wear tall, wide-brimmed hats à la van Dyck, and their long pipes rest on their beards unless they're feeling merry and start singing songs about "Knödel und Sauerkraut," as they tap the rhythm on the tables and plates with their forks and knives.[2] A third table belongs to the Englishmen and Americans: Flaxman, Gibson, Turner, Fenimore Cooper, Washington Irving, as well as—not too long ago—Shelley, Keats, and Byron.

At the very back of the room the Scandinavian colony can be found sitting around a long marble table in semidarkness. The group includes writers such as Ludvig Bødtcher and Henrik Hertz, and the philosopher Zeuthen, who flails the air with his big cane and the daily issue of Diario di Roma. *Also present are the sculptor Bissen and painters such as Jerichau, Sonne, Petzholdt, Koop, and Albert Küchler, who has recently been working on a portrait of Andersen.*

Seated at the table is also the Norwegian Thomas Fearnley, who is an expert at painting the rushing flood tides and waterspouts in the Gulf of Naples. Perhaps that's why he also has such a good eye for the natural forces in Hans Christian Andersen. And of course the sculptor Bertel Thorvaldsen is there too, the party's Nestor, who has come straight from his large workshop on the Piazza Barberini. As so often before, he has forgotten his hat, there is still clay under his fingernails, and his coat is daubed with plaster.

Most of the men are smoking clay pipes, conversing quietly, and drinking vino bianco. But suddenly Hertz interrupts when, through the clouds of smoke, he spies the gaunt, pale figure of Andersen, who has finally managed to edge his way through the Omnibus.

"Here comes the big giraffe! Oh, now don't be angry, Andersen! It's such a nice animal!" [3] All conversation at the table ceases, and for a brief moment Andersen smiles, until he remembers all the non-existent letters from Denmark.

"I'm going to jump into the Tiber River if I don't get a letter soon!" he says, sitting down on the sofa as one of the others at the table gently pats his shoulder.

"You do that, Andersen. You're much too tall to drown, anyway!"

When the laughter has subsided, someone asks about Küchler's portrait of Andersen, and the Danish author promptly replies that it's a masterpiece! He's especially happy with the big furry collar, which elevates his face so superbly. Küchler smiles and can't resist telling the others about Andersen's recent encounter with a seventeen-year-old beauty, who cast off her shift in the middle of the studio so the painter could assess her merits as a model. "Holy Andersen," as Küchler calls him, turned deathly pale at the sight and rushed out the door.

"So paint him with a halo above his head, Küchler!" someone suggests, and everyone except Thorvaldsen laughs and shouts: "Hear, hear!"

The sculptor hushes the group and then asks Andersen for an impromptu verse. Andersen immediately pulls a pencil out of his coat pocket, and looks around the room, where the waiters are in the process of setting the big, three-armed oil lamps on the tables. Then he leans over the cold white marble and writes:

Before the spirit of poetry here I kneel,
After all, your only fault was love! [4]

"I'VE LOOKED INTO THE DEPTHS of his soul, and I have not allowed myself to be confused by the excesses of his imagination," wrote Edvard Collin in his book *Hans Christian Andersen and the Collin Family*, which was published in 1882, seven years after Andersen's death. [5] The two men, who were almost the same age, had known each other for nearly fifty years, during which time Andersen was an active member of the Collin family, participating in all the family celebrations: births, engagements, weddings, and funerals. Similarly, the Collins had more or less voluntarily taken part in Andersen's life, seeing to it that he was able to take his first long trips abroad, for example to Italy in 1833-34, which proved to be tremendously important for the young writer's life and work.

Among Jonas Collin's five children, it was Edvard—or "Eduard," as Andersen often spelled his name—who held a special position in relation to Andersen. Quite typical is a statement in a letter from 1832 in which Andersen, after an eventful and joyously boisterous summer spent at the manor houses of Fyn, writes to Christian Voigt: "I have many new acquaintances, yet I long so much for Copenhagen, for all the Collins! Luise is in Jutland, Gottlieb too; the others are out in the country, but the most important, *Eduard*, is at home."[6]

In comparison to what we today think of as a friendship between men, the life-long relationship between Andersen and Edvard Collin belonged to quite a different world and type. "Our friendship is a wondrous creation!" Andersen states in a letter from the 1830s, when the author's relationship to Edvard had grown more demanding than the latter cared for. The author's sorrows and worries, his constant requests for one thing or another, as well as a smugness that occasionally verged on megalomania had become steady ingredients in a friendship which, for Edvard Collin's part, had merely started out as temporary tutoring in Latin in 1827. But for young Andersen it had quickly become a window opening onto the larger and more beautiful world that he longed to conquer. As such, Andersen's wondrous friendship with Edvard Collin also became a lifelong test of strength between two extremely different personalities and temperaments. Opposition bred opposition, and passionate forces surged and poured out, not only in Andersen's literary works but also in the unrivalled correspondence between the two men, consisting of more than five hundred letters. On top of that, we have to add a lavish production of songs that went on for three or four decades, during which the two "brothers" competed to create the best songs and recitations for gatherings at the Collin home. It was a veritable "song war," which we will examine more closely in Chapter Nine. Their long friendship, which lasted from 1827-28 to 1875, was a ceaseless battle for power between the two, in which Edvard Collin, by virtue of his social position and natural status in the family, was always the superior. This is evident from a diary entry in 1865, written by Andersen at the age of sixty: "Dinner at the home of Edvard Collin; finally his position over me is beginning to diminish. I truly seem to him to be an independent individual."[7]

And it was certainly about time, we might think. The passage also says something about how long-lasting, deep, and lively their bond actually was. For his part, Edvard Collin, as he expressed it in his book about Andersen, never wanted under any circumstances to have a "mawkish relationship" with the author.[8] Edvard refused to be yet another one of Andersen's enraptured, uncritical admirers. And for his part, Andersen would bridle every time Edvard came striding in with his bookkeeper demeanor and his whole schoolmaster-like "Besserwissenschaft," as Andersen liked to call his know-it-all attitude. Andersen could be quite sarcastic, even within the walls of the Collin household, and so for a time he called the home of his best and dearest friend "a title-proud office" where his wife and daughter were the only suns in the sky. Andersen felt that Edvard Collin was forever trying to educate him. He was always supposed to become more cultivated, learn to govern himself better, and—as Edvard said—try to acquire a keener sense for what was proper. But all his life Andersen preferred to follow his own nature, even though it could carry him off in the most extreme fashion.

In this way the two men each pulled on his own end of the rope of friendship over half a century. This was largely because there was some-thing in Andersen's character, in spite of all the insensitive rejections he suf-fered through the years from Edvard, that continued to crave and plead for their friendship. Almost nothing was required—a few kind words in a hasty subordinate clause in a letter from his friend—and Andersen would imme-diately feel that all his love was reciprocated, and he would once again view their friendship in an idyllic light. This was true in spite of the fact that Edvard, for forty-three years, refused to address Andersen with the infor-mal "du" instead of the formal "De" used in Danish (comparable to "du" and "Sie" in German or "tu" and "Vous" in French). And yet Edvard per-mitted this form of intimacy to other friends in his social circle who were not nearly as close to him. But for Andersen the old love never became tainted. In the 1860s the aging author writes to Edvard Collin's wife, in a draft of a letter that was never sent, about the life-long companion they shared: "He is still as dear to me as when I saw in him a son of the mighty Collin, and I was the impoverished Andersen whom you all dared to kick and mock."[9]

From the very beginning, the two of them placed quite different val-ues on the friendship. Around 1830, Edvard Collin, who was still a bache-lor, was looking for a comrade; he admits as much in his book about

Andersen. The gentle, effeminate student and writer, on the other hand, put all his emotions on the line in an attempt to establish a friendship that would lift him out of the proletariat and raise him up, both in terms of the social hierarchy and the romantic zeitgeist. For Andersen, it was a matter of love, within the endless depths and mysterious intimations of friendship, which during Romanticism a man was allowed to invest in a relationship with another man.

"It's so strange that people can't see that a whole world can exist— even in a friendship," Andersen writes to Edvard Collin in 1832.[10] By that time he had spent almost three years using letter-writing as a disguised and secretive means of communication, by which, in various tempos and modes, he could entice a dear friend into a more intimate relationship. Andersen had a very romantic—and complex—view of letter-writing, as is apparent in a passage from Chapter Ten in *Walking Tour*, where advice is offered to those who wish to look over the shoulder of the human psyche:

> "Crawl into a mail sack! That's the place where you can study the human heart. No poet could describe the multiplicity of characters there presented. There the passions play in all their colors: love and hate, a zest for life, and despair. There you can look over the shoulder of the hypocrite and uncover the secrets of the lover. Believe me, it's not through life but through a mail sack that you will peer inside the human heart."[11]

It's evident from the correspondence of Hans Christian Andersen and Edvard Collin during 1829-32 that the boundaries of an ordinary, formal friendship were quickly exceeded by the insistent and, in certain respects, very impatient Andersen. Early on he began to gush in a manner that seemed repellent and dangerous to a straightlaced man like Edvard Collin. Even though people during Romanticism, as we shall soon see, had a relatively liberal view of male roles and male friendships, Collin quickly retreated when he felt Andersen's letters take on the guise of an embrace. As Collin tersely and accurately described the dilemma in his book about his famous friend: "He dreamed of finding in me a 'novel-friend'; but I was not at all suited for that."[12]

But what exactly does he mean by a "novel-friend"? Edvard Collin actually allowed the author himself to explain this posthumously, seven years after his death. In a note to his book about Andersen, Edvard refers to an old verbal statement by the author, who had described the friendship between the two men as: "This contrast and yet great harmony, a mystery that does not dare to be analyzed."[13] This was a profound and thought-provoking interpretation that had nothing to do with various superficial disputes or annoyances between the two; it focused on the inner fervor of the friendship and a sensitive manner of interaction that was permitted and cultivated at the beginning of the 19th century. Today, in the 21st century, it would be an unthinkable relationship between two men—unless they could be immediately categorized as "homosexual." Yet for Hans Christian Andersen and a number of other men of his day in the more educated, elite circles of society, these sensitive, Romantic male friendships were a social reality.

The Men of Romanticism

In other words, we should be wary of reading and interpreting Hans Christian Andersen's longings and dreams for a closer, more intimate relationship with Edvard Collin as a sign of the author's homosexuality. By categorizing him in that way, we would see only a small part of the author's erotic constitution, which could feel love for far more than one person and one sex. Andersen was, in this area as well, one of the rare products of nature. In 1838 Søren Kierkegaard chose to describe his older author colleague as a *rana paradoxa*—a rare and paradoxical work of nature—which, according to the philosopher, could be compared to the flowers in which the male and female exist on one stalk. We will return to this characterization of Andersen's eros in the next chapter.

Andersen *was* a rare blend of impulses. By putting him in a box labeled "homosexual," "heterosexual," "bisexual," or "asexual," we fail to see his exuberant nature or the era's more nuanced and expansive perception of what a man's role in life actually could be. During Romanticism men were permitted, to a much greater extent than today, to show their feelings, to flirt with and treat each other in a loving manner. That's also why Andersen's compulsion to fall in love with quite a number of men but few women, and his determination to realize this desire within the framework of a sensitive friendship, should be understood in light of the times in which he lived. It should also be viewed in relation to what, in our day, is the rather unknown concept of *Platonism*, which set its mark on the image of the human being during Romanticism.

In the period 1800-50, men could more or less freely display the feminine side of their character in a larger social context. They could also allow themselves to test the boundaries with regard to sex and love. At the same time, the idea of the sensitive friendship held the possibility that men could differentiate and actually choose between "a love feeling" and the sexual act in relation to other men.[14] The men of Romanticism, if they wished, could draw a moral and ethical line in their love life within the framework of the sensitive friendship. And for a man like Andersen, the platonic aspect—"the metaphysics of love," as Voltaire called it—was preferred. For Andersen the attributes of the soul were more attractive than the purely physical form, which is why, during a large part of his life, he maintained an aesthetic relationship to the carnal side of love. In other male friendships during Romanticism, however, it played a major role. Men could love each other not only on the level of the psyche but with their entire body, without causing the surrounding society to call them to account or burn them at the stake.

Officially, sexual relations between men were forbidden. Earlier in history, especially during the Reformation, men had been decapitated or burned at the stake for what were called "offenses against nature." With the Danish Law of 1683 under King Christian V, these punishments were not mitigated, but neither were they made more severe or specific. The law contained a special paragraph about sodomy that dealt with sexual intercourse with animals and between men, and it forbade—as it said—"the thing inside the thing and the outpouring of seed." In the 18th century the enforcement of the law was left more or less up to the church, where it fell to the lot of eloquent pastors to stifle any rumors of what was going on out in the parish between people and animals. They delivered fire-and-brimstone sermons and threats about God's wrath so all the sin and shame wouldn't spread any further among the congregation or population. The ban against "the thing inside the thing and the outpouring of seed," after centuries of a blatant settling of accounts with the executioner or the blazing flames, had taken on the form of silence. And well into the 19th century the state was still using suppression and silence as the best means of making the phenomenon invisible. Bizarre desires and vices were to be silenced to death.[15]

Both in the provinces and inside Copenhagen, the question of a man's love for other men was thus bound by silence, especially on the part of the authorities. This is apparent in connection with the so-called Dumont case in 1814, when a group of fourteen homosexual men, including several actors from the Royal Theater, was exposed. Afterwards, discussions were carried out on the highest ministerial levels as to whether a lawsuit should be initiated or whether they should opt for silence, letting the gossip die out and handing out punishments in secret.[16] This quiet and discreet administration of the law regarding "offenses against nature" meant that there was a relatively free playing field for male love, as long as the men acted with discretion and refinement.

At the time when the young Hans Christian Andersen sent his first ardent letter of friendship to Edvard Collin in the late 1820s, there was not yet any visible regulation of male or female sexuality in Danish society. The condemnation and prosecution of sodomites or pederasts—as Ludvig Holberg called them in the 18th century, with the term becoming more and more commonly used in the mid-1800s—was virtually nonexistent. For the same reason, there were no clear perceptions of what it meant to be or not be "homosexual." The word simply didn't exist in the Danish language during Hans Christian Andersen's lifetime. We have to look to the years just prior to his death in 1875 before we see the public sector taking action against pederasts. Supported by both medical science and the law, steps were then taken to make love between men an illness and a crime.

A large part of the romance between two men in a sensitive friendship anno 1830 took place in diaries or via a steady stream of confidential letters, like the ones that Hans Christian Andersen sent off to Edvard Collin in the early 1830s. A good, true, and honest letter was, according to an arch-Romantic like Novalis, "a poetic letter" that both revealed and concealed aspects of the sender. And as Johannes the Seducer writes in Kierkegaard's *Either-Or*, in which the epistolary and diary genres romantically merge together, an inanimate letter of the alphabet often has far greater influence than a living word. In an exchange of letters, both the sender and the recipient, no matter how much they may have revealed about themselves in writing, are masters of the situation. They feel no pressure from any external judgmental authority, and they can freely cultivate both their ideals and each other.

And so, during Romanticism, it became an advantage among young men to be able to write sensitive, flirtatious letters in which a person would reveal and conceal all his minor or major infatuations with both sexes.[17] As is evident in the letters remaining today from and to many prominent Scandinavian men in the 19th century—including Orla Lehmann, Knud Lyne Rahbek, Georg Brandes, Lorenz Frölich, Johannes Fibiger, Bjørnstjerne Bjørnson, and Clemens Petersen—these sensitive friendships often developed into psychological laboratories in which men used the confidential form of the letter for little seductive games, but also as mirrors. For instance, in a lengthy correspondence between the Norwegian writer and jurist Conrad Nicolai Schwach and the teacher Maurits Christopher Hansen, we can see how the men sought self-knowledge through each other and began to mature as they continued to write letters.[18]

In this respect, the nearly fifty years of correspondence between Hans Christian Andersen and Edvard Collin represents a moving documentation of the developmental process of a psyche whose paramount theme was Andersen's attempt to realize a love that was in keeping with his true nature. In one of his idealistic homages to the male friendship that Edvard Collin refused to be drawn into or participate in, Andersen wrote in 1835 that "friendship" is an emotional relationship in which everything ought to be thought and nothing understood. And in another letter from the same year, in which Andersen elaborates on his point of view, he couples the freedom of a sensitive male friendship with an even greater and mysterious freedom that places the two friends on an equal footing, merging and elevating them in a divine brotherhood, raised above social and biological bonds:

> "All of my soul I could express to you, even the deepest secrets of my heart, but our friendship is like 'the mysteries,' it cannot be truly analyzed. Oh, if only God might make you very poor and me a rich, distinguished nobleman. Yes, then I would properly initiate you into the mystery. You would come to value me more than you do now. Oh, if there is an eternal life, as surely there must be, there we would properly understand and value each other. There I am no longer poor, in need of interest and friends; there we are equals! All forms fall away!"[19]

Around 1800 Romanticism had brought with it a new view of humanity, in which the emotional life of the individual was highly valued. In the 1780s, as a reaction to the reason and rationalism of the 18th century, Rousseau, with his novels about human naturalness, and the philosopher Kant, with his *Critique of Pure Reason*, had turned attention to the natural state of the individual. By the time Hans Christian Andersen, in the early 1830s, cast his love upon Edvard Collin and other men and women, the Romantic cult of emotions had long ago spread its message throughout Europe. The message was that a human being should become aware of his own nature, especially the dark sides. For the Romantics this sense for the darkness was proof that a human being has a soul. In literature, in particular, they sought words that would give them an under-standing of the vital significance of their feelings and urges. Inspired by the immortal hero of Goethe's novel *The Sorrows of Young Werther*, by Lord Byron's poetry, and by the entire destiny of writers, the sensitive young men of the day turned themselves inside out through close, intimate friendships with other young men.

It's true that male artists and intellectuals, often from relatively wealthy families, would seek out each other's company and friendship during their youth and early adulthood. Men of the lower social classes, on the other hand, were forced to do so right from childhood. In the early part of the century, a man's attitude toward and relationship with other men was not burdened by the anxiety about touching that exists among many men today. Fear, envy, and a sense of competition were not the only emotions at play among men during Romanticism; security, intimacy, and love were also present, nourished in particular by the more or less compulsory shar-ing of beds in those days. Around 1800 the two sexes were strictly separat-ed in terms of their work and free time. The women would gather to do chores around their mothers and sisters, while the men, from a very young age, lived and worked in close proximity. This resulted in close relationships between men, both physical and psychological, at home in the family, out on the farms and in the factories, in orphanages, schools, and boarding schools, on board ship, in the army, in monasteries and ecclesiastical circles, and so on. Whether a boy was an only child, like Hans Christian Andersen, or grew up with a swarm of siblings, he would be accustomed to sharing a bed with other males. "Farm hand with farm hand, and farm hand with boy" was the rule rather than the exception.[20]

As a child, Andersen at first enjoyed the privilege of sharing his sleep-ing bench only with his mother and father on Munkemøllestræde, since his half-sister Karen Marie (born 1799) had been sent to live elsewhere. Furthermore, the boy had his mother all to himself after his father died in 1816 and before she remarried. Only when Anne Marie Andersen went out to the country to help with picking hops or took part in markets did Hans Christian have to share a bed with other children and youngsters. Yet there were certain exceptions, if we're to believe the older Andersen, who never hid the fact that as a child he preferred sleeping with boys, because the opposite sex smelled so unpleasant. When he was ten, his family on Munkemøllestræde once had a visit from a certain Lisbeth, who was a relative from his mother's side of the family.[21] The country girl was sup-posed to sleep with Hans Christian, but he objected to this arrangement in the most strenuous manner, saying: "No, I won't, I *refuse*, because she smells so much like a girl!" Whereupon his parents scolded him and called him a naughty boy. But that did no good, and Lisbeth had to sleep on three chairs that the shoemaker shoved together, and it was not at all comfortable.[22] Later on, both in Slagelse and Helsingør, when Andersen was a pupil at the grammar schools, he would occasionally share a bed with other young men. In Helsingør he was regularly locked out of the house by Fru Meisling and would have to go to the home of one of his classmates. "There I rang the bell and shared a bed with him that night."[23] That's what he had to do and, as previously mentioned, he had also shared a bed with the other lodger in Madame Henneberg's home in Slagelse. This was the boy who was the son of Pastor Fischer from Ringsted. And it was a difficult—and dangerous—acquaintanceship, whenever the pastor's son would once again get drunk and vulgar, and "quite rudely" tumble about in bed, so Andersen had to flee upstairs to his landlady and spend the night on her sofa.[24]

That was how insensitive reality was for the young men of the proletariat and lower middle class in the 19th century. This is what Andersen says or hints at in many places in his memoirs. And presumably he mentions only a fraction of the harsh and often degrading experiences he must have endured during his childhood and youth, when men would badger and mock him because of his peculiar appearance and girlish behavior. In this respect, there was a lengthy and painful trail through all of Andersen's adulthood, having to do with the fact that even his best male friends—such as those Andersen met every day at the Caffè Greco in Rome in the 1830s—had a burning desire to see the virginal author on the lap of a dark and sensual bella donna. But Andersen held his ground, preferring platonic love. And in this regard, it should be remembered that as a platonic lover he was passionate and insistent; a driven seducer who seldom accepted no for an answer.

Brothers in Joy and Pain

Over the years, all possible variations of the sensitive friendship were attempted by Hans Christian Andersen, both in his personal life and in his literary work. This began in earnest in the 1830s, when he ventured to establish platonic love relationships with quite a number of men and a few women. And in his art he began circling around these complicated and not particularly happy emotional ties, although they did offer inspiration. In his art we find one of the most sensitive male friendships in the magic opera *The Raven* from 1832. The opera is about the closely intertwined brothers Millo and Gennaro, whose boundless "fraternal tenderness" is the secret behind their idyllic, joyous reunion.

In the 1830s, Andersen, like Gennaro, was constantly on the lookout for an opportunity to bare his brotherly breast and establish the sort of sensitive, melodramatic friendships that are depicted in *The Raven*. This meant harmonious, strong relationships between men that could contain pure feelings and boundless passion. And on paper there was no limit to Andersen's desire. In August 1833, as he was on his way to Italy after spending merry days in Paris, he sent a letter from Lausanne to Joachim Melchior Grevenkop-Castenskiold, who was an attaché at the embassy in Paris, and whom Andersen had fallen for in the city of cities:

> "Only now that I am parted from you do I feel how dear you have become to me! I am a most peculiar person, the way I can end up loving people. I think a whole nation might benefit from all the love that I possess. That is what makes me suffer and why I am so terribly thin. But seriously, I would be inexpressibly happy if you truly felt any friendship for me. Here is my hand, dear Castenskiold, and let it be for eternity."[25]

In spite of his impulsive attempts to establish sensitive friendships with many different men in the 1830s, Andersen always reserved the role of his greatest passion for Edvard Collin. This friendship was depicted in much of Andersen's literary work during 1830–40, as well as in diary entries and letters. Disguised behind all sorts of names and both sexes, hidden behind beards and uniforms, suits and hats, Andersen's love for Edvard Collin winds its way in and out of his poems, plays, novels, and fairy tales. An extravagant and beautiful example of everything that Andersen invested in the friendship is his novel *O. T.* from 1836. In this book Andersen not only flings open the door to reveal a series of scenes and dialogues from a love relationship between two men, he also presents a precise and detailed picture of what Romanticism's sensitive friendship actually meant. From the very beginning of his friendship with Edvard, Andersen fantasized about taking a journey out into the world with his "brother." He would also hint at and air the idea in small asides, but he never received a response. For that reason, in the same year that *O. T.* was published, Andersen wrote a fantasy letter that was never sent—most likely because he consistently allowed himself to use the informal "du" to address "Eduard," and he also played with the idea of a spiritual love relationship that Edvard Collin had long ago rejected:

> "My dear Eduard! How often I think of you! How open your soul is to me. I wonder if you can comprehend, comprehend the love that I have for you! At this moment I see you, the way blessed spirits no doubt see each other; I could press you to my heart! Is that infatuation, an over-wrought state? No, it is pure noble emotion! There must also be moments when you feel something similar. As all good people must feel. At this moment there is no ice-cold 'De' between us; I say 'du' and your lips meet me with the same sound, which you for the first time in this world will utter. Oh, if only I were rich, we would both fly off to Italy, glorious Italy, which I haven't enjoyed in the slightest! Oh, if only we were there together! If only we were there just one month!—Eduard, I have many young friends, yet none do I love as I love you . . ."[26]

Edvard Collin, who couldn't abide this kind of syrupy letter, always dug his heels firmly into the Danish soil whenever Andersen happened to mention traveling together. That's why the love letter was never sent but stayed in the drawer like a little obsessive dream among all the other papers Edvard many years later would inherit and eventually read. No, Collin had never wanted to venture out into life along with Andersen. For that reason the author had to disguise himself and his dear friend in his novel *O. T.*, and then he could imagine the rest along with the reader. Andersen would be the impoverished Otto from Odense, and Edvard Collin the wealthy Baron Vilhelm, whose sensitive friendship on the journey south grew stronger than ever before:

> "Otto and I were sitting in the compartment. Imagine us wearing white blouses, *Schawlsmützen*, and green satin slippers, because only the Devil travels in boots, they hurt the feet. We both have mustaches! I have beguiled Otto. They suit us devilishly well and give us an impressive air, and that's a good thing now that we're entering the land of scoundrels, where it's important to surprise the robbers. And so, we continued on."[27]

This tender description from the coach depicts two men of about the same age, close friends and fellow students, Otto Thostrup and Baron Vilhelm. The latter is the one who sends this little snapshot from the pair's "sentimental journey" to Italy in a letter home to his sisters and mother at their estate on Fyn. The two closely bound young men are seen in this part of the novel in a sensual, spiritual light. They are still far away from the alarming phase of their lives, when they will have to make several decisive choices with regard to their careers and to love.

Twin Souls

In many respects, the novel *O.T.*, which was written during the summer and fall of 1835, has a central place in Andersen's unceasing, decades-long conflict with Edvard Collin. It depicts the rules and merits of a Romantic male friendship. The plot is filled with secret Romantic invocations and spontaneous, warmhearted outbursts of emotion: "'We will always be friends, loyal friends!' said Vilhelm when they parted. 'Loyal friends!' Otto repeated."

In the novel we also follow the very solemn rituals surrounding the difficult and emotional transition from using the formal means of address ("De") to the informal ("du"), which for men during Romanticism could signify an admission that was almost religious in nature. It was an act on a par with a baptism or a wedding. Andersen himself has drawn a parallel to this way of thinking in the story "A Pact of Friendship," which he wrote after his trip to the Orient in 1841-42. And several years later, in Kierkegaard's *Either-Or*, we also hear about this solemn, symbol-laden transition from "De" to "du," which he describes as a "spiritual disrobing" and a type of rebirth, when men divest themselves of their old personas and afterwards know each other to the depths of their souls.

In *O.T.*, which was written seven years before Kierkegaard described the phenomenology of seduction, there is talk of "dissolving the dissonant *De* of friendship into a harmonious *du*."[28] But whereas Vilhelm immediately signs his letters "Your friend and brother," using the informal possessive form of "du," Otto regards this highly personal matter with much greater seriousness. For him, it concerns more important things than a hasty signature. It has to do with his very soul, which a person doesn't just hand out left and right, the way Vilhelm does at a large student party at the beginning of the novel. He quickly agrees to be on an informal footing with everyone. For Otto Thostrup, it's a matter of a pact of friendship for life. And when he finally sends off an affirmative reply to Vilhelm, and then like a virgin immediately regrets his action, he says: "He is the first one to whom I have given my 'du'!"

In fact, Otto's consecration of male friendships is so pronounced that he fears that by going beyond the formal ("De") means of address he will vulgarize what is poetically sublime about the relationship and curtail the passion that exists in loving and desiring from a distance. On the one hand, Otto longs for the closeness inherent in being able to say "du" to Vilhelm. On the other hand, he wants to continue to use the formal "De" because it promotes and maintains the ideal. The two men should preferably relate to each other in the most pure and innocent manner possible. Then their friendship will reach a divine level where they can be closest to each other, not in body, but in spirit. Then they will be "twin souls." All of this has to be understood in light of the Romantic perception of reality, in which the soul is an entity independent of time and space. And male friends bound together by their souls, such as Otto and Vilhelm— alias Hans Christian Andersen and Edvard Collin—could easily meet on a nonmaterial plane. This was primarily through letters, in which there is the room and freedom to embrace, kiss, and caress without it becoming too carnal. It's a question of exciting only the mind, or, as Andersen describes it in Chapter Eighteen of his novel: "The corner of the page on which *Vilhelm's* name stood he [Otto] pressed to his lips. His heart was utterly filled with noble friendship."[29] Secrets, mysteries, and consecrated looks are thus part of this type of friendship. As Kierkegaard says in *Either-Or*, there is nothing that is so pervaded with seduction or curses as a secret. It contains an unparalleled energy, but only as long as it remains a secret. As Vilhelm says to Otto:

> "There are no doubt secrets of such a delicate nature that one dare not speak of them even to one's dearest friend. As long as we keep our secret, it remains our prisoner, but if we let it fly, we are its prisoner. And yet, Otto! You are so dear to me, I trust you as I do my own heart! It contains a secret that floods me with joie de vivre and delight!"[30]

In *O.T.* we see the difficult, sensitive period between youth and manhood described in detail. An explanation is presented for Otto's and Vilhelm's great difficulty in freeing themselves from the emotional ties to their own gender when marriage and family life are waiting just around the corner. And Otto and Vilhelm use each other, as many young men did in the sensitive friendships of Romanticism, to prepare themselves for this great leap into life. This reciprocal intimacy contained an emotional security, support, and solicitude, which was why a friendship with another man often became a type of initiation into sharing life with another person. At the same time it was a sort of transitional ritual to marriage.

Always lurking in the background of these sensitive relationships between two young men was the danger of a swift dissolution of the friendship. Hans Christian Andersen personally experienced this time after time in his life, when young men would leave him for the women in their lives. Many of these male friends also clearly used their close relationship to the author as a spiritual experiment and an emotional preparation for marriage. For instance, in 1834, one of Andersen's sensitive male friends— the law student Otto Müller—opens all of "his inner rooms" to Andersen. That's what Müller writes in a letter, in which he honestly and candidly shows the author around in the chambers of his heart. Here is room for both men and women, and, as he says, a special place has been reserved for his future bride of the opposite sex:

> "You will find the chambers of my heart partially occupied, both by friends and women; you will notice traces of various charming girls who have now gone, but also plenty of room for '*die Holde, die kommen wird*' [the fair one who will come], because, thank God, I am still free."[31]

But Otto Müller was not the only one who was on the verge of exchanging male friendships for marriage. Practically all the men with whom Andersen attempted to enter into long-lasting sensitive friendship during his life—the brothers Otto and Ludvig Müller, Christian Voigt, and Edvard Collin in the 1830s; Henrik Stampe and Hereditary Grand Duke Carl Alexander in the 1840s; the ballet dancer Harald Scharff and the painter Carl Bloch in the 1860s—all of them backed out of brief, sensitive relationships with Andersen and disappeared into engagements and marriage. Left behind was the bachelor with his bedraggled nightcap:

> "Everyone is getting engaged! Eduard Collin is happy with his Jette; I often visit the Thybergs [Jette's family] and see the happiness of the lovers. It's absurd of me, but I can't help myself; every time I hear that someone has become engaged, I fall into a bad mood! Even though our Lord knows that I'm not the least in love with any of them who have departed."[32]

Say "Du" to Me

How did these two actually become friends? Edvard Collin and this— as Collin remembered him from the 1820s—overgrown boy "with a long, old face, pale eyes and pale hair, and a pair of yellow nankeen trousers that reached only to the middle of his shins."[33]

There was certainly no question of friendliness at first glance. If we read Andersen's early autobiography, it appears that the author didn't care for Edvard Collin at all in the beginning. Coldness and hostility emanated from Jonas Collin's middle son whenever his father's protégé would show up for brief visits at the family home on Store Strandstræde. "Eduard looked so cold, so forbidding, to me that I truly believed he couldn't stand me, that he was arrogant and even my enemy!"[34] But by the time Andersen returned from Helsingør in 1827 to stay in Copenhagen and complete his studies with the help of the Hebraic Müller out in Christianshavn, both had apparently undergone a certain maturation. As Edvard Collin writes in his book about Andersen: "When he once again came to the city, I naturally remembered quite well how he had previously looked, and I noted with astonishment the change for the better that had taken place with regard to his physical development."[35]

In 1828 Jonas Collin gave the new graduate some fatherly praise with the words: "Go now in God's name along the path that you have evidently been meant to follow; that will no doubt be for the best!"[36] At the same time he directed his son, who was studying law and had helped Andersen with his Latin essays, to continue to guide the erratic Andersen. In terms of both writing and the social graces, he needed to learn better manners. Nor was Andersen any genius when it came to spelling. And his Rhyming Demon was now stirring so often inside him and thirsting for freedom that Jonas Collin, who had quite enough to tend to with his various positions, appointed his twenty-year-old son as a sort of guardian and adviser to Andersen. Edvard was supposed to pay particular attention to Andersen's grammatical skills, manners, and financial sense. Hans Christian Andersen would never have come so far in the world during the 1830s and 1840s without this crucial teaming up with Edvard Collin. In 1832 he wrote that he had now started to trust Edvard, who had recently passed his bar exams and was dreaming of a career like his father's. He could hardly have imagined in his wildest dreams that his brief, formal meetings with Andersen regarding his Latin essays would develop so dynamically and prompt a lifelong friendship. The two of them, in Andersen's words, were "much too different" for that.[37]

What seemed at first to be a highly mismatched fraternal relationship, filled with social and psychological differences, quickly developed into respect and mutual fascination. In the summer of 1820 Collin still had misgivings about what was going on inside of Andersen. This is evident in the first letters the two exchanged when Collin paid a visit to Andersen before the author traveled to Fyn for the summer. He apparently seemed so friendly that Andersen, in his letter from Odense, writes: "My heartfelt thanks for the little visit with which you honored me the evening before I left. I must tell you that I also look quite strongly for your support, since you are no doubt one of those who is the most sincere toward me."[38]

With Andersen as the indefatigable *primus motor*, the relationship now began to develop. The two men had found points of interest other than the Latin essays, and an open and merry tone that was occasionally downright flirtatious began to show up in their letters, even from Edvard Collin's side, although with moderation and refinement. And Andersen's first, relatively cautious attempts to win a new friend and brother soon grew into a flood of letters with enclosed poems and emotional undercurrents that startled the young Collin and put him on his guard. This would actually become the pattern and theme to their correspondence for the next forty years. Each time, Collin's reaction was the same: whenever Andersen boiled over with emotion, he would immediately cut back his already modest production of letters and give even terser replies, unless he simply retreated altogether and ignored the letters in which Andersen tried to establish a seductive link between Edvard's life and his own.

In 1830-31 the busy poet began playing in earnest on the whole register of innocence and emotion in relation to his new friend. As a letter-writer Andersen was a driven seducer. In the short run and by using very few letters, he was able to weave a tight net around the object of his longing. Poetry and prose were brilliantly and alluringly interwoven in the author's letters during 1830-31. Many times the young Collin found himself surrounded and seduced by an argument regarding something in which he had already stated that he would not participate. Even though Andersen was quite aware of this, he would plow straight through his friend's reservations, undaunted. As he had done in 1819 when he rang doorbells all over Copenhagen, he now put his foot in the door of correspondence and squeezed his way in to a room of dreams and longings.

It was in the early summer of 1831 that the dramatic part of the story about the friendship between Edvard Collin and Hans Christian Andersen took its first sharp turn. In May the author was to leave on his Romantic educational journey to the Harz, Dresden, and Berlin, and over the past winter he had told his friend about his unhappy love for Riborg Voigt. But in the letters that he now began sending home from his travels through

Germany—letters that started arriving almost as soon as the steamer pulled out of Copenhagen Harbor—the veil was slowly lifted from the love story that Andersen had been using as camouflage and enticement for a much larger catch: a declaration of all his love for Edvard.

Andersen was usually very openhearted, and from the first letters he sent in 1829-30, he was constantly promoting the idea that the two of them should not have a single secret from each other. But now, in the first three long letters from his travels, he employs a tremendously subtle method of reasoning. If you place all the letters next to each other and examine their step-by-step development and complexity, it's possible to conclude that rhetoric is being used for the purpose of sneaking into the other man's thoughts and eliciting specific replies and promises. As Andersen says in one of the last travel letters to his friend back home: "I almost think that each little summer journey brings me closer to you; on paper the heart can better confide, without feeling pushed back by one's physical persona."[39]

In Andersen's first "homing pigeon" letter from his trip, which was sent from Hamburg on May 19, 1831, he very cautiously opened a door to his dream palace. Rhetorically speaking, in this first letter he gave his friend the opportunity—if he so desired—to write himself into the Romantic performance that the author was about to launch. In light of Andersen's letter, Collin could now declare himself and not only acknowledge Andersen's warm feelings but also proclaim his undivided sympathy for the author. As an exercise in how to lay the groundwork for a sensitive, confidential male friendship, the letter from Hamburg is a stroke of genius. As Kierkegaard has his seducer say in *Either-Or*, the whole trick is to use ambiguity so that the one listening understands one thing from what is said, but then suddenly realizes that the words can also be interpreted in another way. What Andersen does in his letter is first to inform his friend that for a long time he has had personal sorrows, although he avoids being more specific about who or what has been tormenting his soul for the past few years. With great care he makes sure not to reveal the deeper causes of his pain but merely states that he has been very depressed, and several times he was on the verge of sharing these exceedingly personal problems with his friend. "But I was frightened away; I feared that you might not want to accept things as they are."[40]

The mystery spreads through the letter, in which the ambiguities have the subtle goal of enticing the recipient—Edvard Collin—to fill in the words for everything that the sender both hints at and conceals. The recipient will be lured into an ambush and then put names and words to the pain, which the sender, through his mystifications, has made encompass more possibilities than the breakup with Riborg Voigt. Between the lines the sender—Andersen—plays with an unidentified love, which, because of the text's consistent omission of details about the actual person and gender, could very well concern a man. This intriguing game with gender roles and objects of love can be seen in many other places in Andersen's texts from this period. For instance, in the poem "She's the One I Mean," a real game of blindman's buff takes place with the personal pronouns.

After this piling up of ambiguities, Andersen finally falls to his knees in the Hamburg letter and dares speak the four words that cannot possibly be misunderstood: "Say du to me!" This imperative, which could never have been uttered face-to-face with the proper and reserved Edvard Collin and therefore had to be staged from a distance across sea and land, was something that Andersen had been building toward through many letters. And the fear and trembling of love shines from the little sentence with the exclamation mark: "Say du to me!" Over the course of that year, Andersen's letters had contained increasingly urgent phrases and advances, so it was truly "with a pounding heart," as Andersen writes, that he now bared his feelings and verbalized his innermost dream:

> "Of all people, you are the one that I in every respect regard as my true friend. Always be that for me, dear Collin. I truly need an open heart, my friend, but the one that I can love as such must also have a spirit. I must be able to respect him in that regard, and it's something fundamentally lacking in the few others that I'm quite fond of. You're the only one of my peers to whom I feel truly bound. I have one more request. You may laugh, but if one day you would like to please me, to give me true proof of your esteem—when I deserve it—then—oh, you mustn't be angry!—Say du to me! I could never ask you this in person, it has to be done now, while I'm away . . . Are you angry? You can't believe how my heart pounds as I write this . . ."[41]

But a new law graduate like Edvard Collin was not easily fooled, and his reaction to Andersen's request was a firm and blunt "no." In his letter of reply dated May 28, 1831, Collin mentions that he has clearly noticed Andersen's pain and even claims to know the source of it. But Collin doesn't allow Andersen's rhetoric to seduce him any further, and he refrains from putting a name to the cause of this purported pain. Only in the matter of Andersen's request that he use the informal "du" is Collin unambiguously candid.

There is not even the slightest hope. It now became eminently apparent that Collin was a man who defended the classical male virtues such as self-control, duty, and courage; he hated sentimental gushing among men. It was made crystal clear, once and for all, that it would be pointless for Andersen to repeat such a proposal:

> "There are aspects of my character that I will truthfully reveal to you here. Only then will it be impossible for you to misunderstand me, which is something I greatly fear. It is my disposition with regard to your request that we say 'du' to each other that I want to explain to you. As I mentioned, Andersen, trust in my vow that I am speaking honestly! ... What purpose would this change in our relationship serve? Is it to give others a sign of our friendly relationship? That would be superficial and mean nothing to either of us. And isn't our relationship quite comfortable and advantageous to both of us? Why then start over under a changed form? A form that in and of itself is something insignificant but for which I, as I said, have an unpleasant feeling ... There could never be any question that I would be angry about your request; I do not misunderstand you. I only hope that neither will you misunderstand me."[42]

Only after receiving this reply, which shouldn't have left any hope of a more emotionally formalized friendship, did Andersen finally reveal the ostensible reason for his pain and sorrow during the past winter and spring. From Berlin, on June 11, 1831, Andersen thanks Collin for his honest reply and at the same time emphasizes that he too wishes to be open and honest with "my true, perhaps most honest of friends." He then, at long last, reveals the gender and social status of the person who has caused him such pain. But the guessing game is still not over, since he doesn't give the person's name:

> "Last summer I became acquainted with a rich, beautiful, witty girl, who feels the same for me as I do for her. She was engaged, and circumstances required that she marry a man who wanted her solely for her fortune. She was married shortly before I left. A few words are all that I have from her, in which she asks me, as a sister, to forget everything. That was why I wanted to go away. Oh, I have wept like a child."[43]

This semi-revelation was hardly of any surprise to a well-informed Copenhagener such as Edvard Collin. In several of his previous letters to Andersen he had demonstrated that he had a keen ear for rumors. And back in the fall of 1830, he had, of course, already heard of Andersen's relationship to the daughter of Voigt, the merchant. This was partly because Riborg, in connection with the illness of a relative, had spent several days during October and November in the capital, where she had met Andersen one evening and listened to him read from his opera *The Raven*.

Hans Christian Andersen brought back home to Denmark his last long letter from his travels in Germany, and it was then sent from Copenhagen, since Edvard Collin was spending the summer holidays in Jutland. It was a letter that ended with eternal optimism and showed that Andersen, in his infatuated state, seemed to have forgotten the blunt rejection and was dreaming more than ever before of a sensitive friendship:

> "Yes, all that is truly in my heart I will always confide to you, and you will always be what you are to me: a brotherly, true friend. If only I could let you read my soul and thereby win you as I wish."[44]

Edvard Collin's Book About Andersen

We don't know what else happened or how the relationship developed during the winter of 1831 or the spring and early summer of 1832. At that time Andersen had also launched a charm-offensive via letters addressed to Edvard's sister, Louise. These letters could also be interpreted as a way of courting the entire Collin family and a form of collusion in honor of her brother. There is a large gap here, extending over a period of eight months, in the otherwise comprehensive and meticulously preserved correspondence with the Collin household. Perhaps an exchange of letters wasn't particularly necessary during this period, since both Andersen and Edvard Collin were in Copenhagen for the most part. And the two friends—judging by a letter from Andersen to Henriette Hanck in November 1831— were closer than they had ever been before. Collin was still insisting on using the formal means of address ("De"); nevertheless, at the beginning of this period he seemed much more amenable toward Andersen, which was immediately noted by the author, interpreted as a good sign, and recorded in his diary in November 1831:

> "I just came home from visiting the Collins. The next-eldest son, a splendid fellow that I love as a brother, treated me with a closeness that melted my soul. We promised each other always to be honest, dear friends, under all circumstances in life."[45]

But entries in diaries and calendars tell us nothing about the development of their friendship up to and including the summer of 1832, when the productive author was channeling all his longing and pain into a great outpouring of literary work. In less than a year Andersen finished *Shadow Pictures* and his poetry collection titled *Vignettes for Danish Poets*. He also wrote the libretto for the ballad opera *The Bride of Lammermoor*, based on Sir Walter Scott's novel, and the vaudeville *The Ship*. The latter is an adaptation of a foreign play in which the main male role is the introverted, well-read merchant Jonathan, who in terms of love calls himself "a dead lump." He is confronted by his old friend, a handsome sea officer by the name of Edvard—a name that was on the mind and lips of Andersen more than ever before.

Letters and occasionally an entire correspondence are missing for certain crucial periods in Andersen's life when he fell in love with men and women. The author is hardly to blame for this, since Andersen, for most of his life, collected and saved all manner of documents and papers. Letters, brief notes with greetings, manuscripts, and newspaper clippings were all placed in bags, boxes, and chests. In his calendar Andersen attempted during periods of his life to keep track of important letters he had sent. Not all letters were registered, but a considerable number were. For the same reason, most of the letters that Andersen received during the years 1830–75 are extant in the enormous collection of documents that Edvard Collin inherited in August 1875 and would subsequently administer. Moritz G. Melchior, who was appointed by Andersen as co-executor, was not given any opportunity, nor was he allowed, to interfere with this portion of the estate. There may have been a good reason for this, since it's quite clear that, regarding one issue, the residuary legatee—Edvard Collin—neglected to follow his friend's last wishes. According to a codicil that was added to Andersen's will a month before his death, it was the author's express wish that "all manuscripts and letters of interest regarding Andersen be delivered to C. St. A. Bille and Nicolai Bøgh for their use, but thereafter should be delivered to Councilor of State Collin as his possession."[46] Before he died, Andersen had given permission for his two good friends—Carl Steen Andersen Bille, who was an editor and member of parliament, and the young author Nicolai Bøgh—to produce a large volume of letters to and from the author of fairy tales. It was published in 1877–78, after a slight tug-of-war with Edvard Collin, who was not at all enthusiastic about the testamentary right of the two men to look through the more personal collection of documents.

As Andersen writes in his last great story, "Auntie Toothache," something often ends up in the bin that shouldn't be there at all. After the author's death, it was Edvard Collin who decided where the bin ought to stand and what should be put in it. He determined what should be returned to the numerous letter-writers and what should be preserved for posterity in the "Collin Autograph Collection." With legal support in the phrase "all manuscripts and letters of interest," Edvard Collin evaluated what was of interest—presumably with the assistance of his son Jonas. And he also decided what Bille and Bøgh would be allowed to see and use in the collection of letters that Andersen had wanted them to produce. Almost immediately Collin informed the two men that they could not, at any rate, use the correspondence between Andersen and the Collin family because he intended to write a book about his friend himself, and he would be using those letters.[47]

Edvard Collin quickly assumed the role of censor, and he knew what he needed to look for in the piles of letters stored in chests and boxes. After sorting through the material during the fall of 1875, Collin wrote to Moritz G. Melchior, whose family had nursed and taken care of Andersen during the last years of his life: "Let this serve as notification to you and your family that I consider it my duty to deliver to all those now living the letters that are to be found written in their hand among Andersen's papers. I look immediately for the signatures and use them to do the sorting, so that everyone can rest assured that the letters are unread."[48] In other words, all those individuals who, over the years, had written letters to the author that were a little too tender or sensitive could now breathe easy. All these indiscretions, many of which had connections through family or friendship to the Collins, would now be returned to the sender instead of being collected, sealed, and preserved for a later generation's research into the life and work of Hans Christian Andersen. As early as the 1830s, Edvard Collin had a feeling that his own correspondence with Andersen, in particular, would over the years become a much-coveted collection of documents. This is apparent in a prophetic letter from the summer of 1836. Edvard, in a rather sarcastic tone, rereads Andersen's latest letter and with a glint in his eye then writes (in German) about a peculiar, vague part of the letter that will be of interest to posterity, "when Andersen's and Collin's correspondence is published."[49]

But in the fall of 1875, the letters were returned to the senders. This was a decision that we might well regret. After the old letters had been thoroughly but very hastily sorted and returned, there were undoubtedly lesser auto-da-fés taking place all over Copenhagen and its surroundings. Especially among many of Hans Christian Andersen's sensitive male friends who, during an age that was becoming homophobic, didn't want inquisitive contemporaries or future generations to disturb the peace of their private lives. For instance, it's likely that the ballet dancer Harald Scharff, with whom Andersen was so smitten in the 1860s and with whom he had carried on a significant correspondence, burned all of Andersen's letters as well as his own pompous epistles from the early 1860s. We will return to this relationship, which also included the actor Lauritz Eckardt, in Chapter Nine.

Presumably Andersen's estate included correspondence that reflected the author's many platonic love affairs with men. This seems indicated by the male names and mention of letters that intermittently recur throughout Hans Christian Andersen's diaries and calendars. In this correspondence with younger men, in particular, the author developed a side of himself that has been more or less repressed in the Andersen research done by established Danish scholars over the past 120 years, even after Wilhelm von Rosen's groundbreaking doctoral dissertation in 1993, which includes a discussion of Andersen's love for his own gender.[50] With reverence and respect, scholars have for generations restricted themselves to the story that has been handed down about Andersen's unhappy love affairs with women such as Riborg Voigt, Louise Collin, and Jenny Lind. But if we take a closer look at these love stories, they start creaking like Little Claus's horse-hide under the farmer's table in the fairy tale "Little Claus and Big Claus." The fact that it was the male gender that occupied Andersen's dreams and thoughts to a much greater extent was something to which Andersen scholars have homophobically given a wide berth ever since 1882 when Edvard Collin published his book *Hans Christian Andersen and the Collin Family*. As many have later pointed out, this book is based on some oddly blurred and contradictory explanations of the author's psyche and the relationship between the two men who were close friends for more than forty years.[51] With this volume the Collin family shielded Andersen's posthumous reputation to such a degree that in 1906 Edvard's son—Jonas Collin—could publish a collection of diary entries titled *Hans Christian Andersen's Last Years* with a foreword in which he states that his father's book about Andersen must be regarded, "in all essential respects, as the definitive characterization of Andersen as a human being."

With the Collin family's instinct for protecting its own, including Hans Christian Andersen, an iron band was immediately placed around the estate's many letters after the author's death in 1875. Only a minimum of information seeped out. And the story about the relationship between Andersen and the Collin family, which especially manifested itself through the tense, lifelong relationship between the two "brothers," was firmly and authoritatively presented by Edvard in his own book. As a work of literary history it would have decisive importance for succeeding generations' access to and interpretation of Andersen's life and work.[52] Collin's unsentimental book is based on a retrospective assessment of the author's life and work. We are at the very source, and we notice right from the first pages that the book was written by a jurist. It is structured almost like a trial, in which documents and explanations are presented by an author who, in regard to his subject, is often more prosecutor than defender. To a certain extent Edvard Collin actually lectures his old friend, switching between individual depositions and solid documentation in the form of letters, anecdotes, and scattered critical assessments of Andersen's art. In this lengthy and ostensibly objective account of a friendly, familial connection to the Collin household for more than four decades, the events from the first half of the 1830s play quite a central role, also for the overall appraisal and pronouncement of sentence. And here it becomes apparent that the defender is occasionally not only biased but also unreliable and downright dishonest in his documentation. His selection and abridgement of the letters from Hans Christian Andersen is extremely subjective and blatantly manipulative.

In the introduction to his book, Edvard Collin explains his method: "I have abridged the enormous amount of correspondence as much as I thought appropriate." And he adds that he has also created his book on the basis of "scraps of paper" that Andersen had occasionally given to him when he came to visit the Collin family. But Collin says nothing about the extent of the correspondence, nor were readers in 1882 given any real explanation for why he decided to publish the book, other than some vague phrases about a noble regard for the author's many friends and acquaintances, "who no doubt might wish to have a deeper insight into his earlier life and a clearer understanding of his personality."

We have to remember that the forty-seven years of correspondence between the two friends was not yet known to the public in 1882. And at that time it was certainly not Collin's intention that the 800 letters should be published *in extenso*—at least not while he and his wife and children were alive. Up until the 1930s the restricted source material stipulated in the codicil as well as its interpretation rested securely in the hands of

Edvard Collin. The story belonged to him, so to speak, for nearly fifty years, just as it had in the late 1870s when he blithely edited, abridged, added, and omitted whatever he liked. When the correspondence could finally be published in full at the beginning of the 1930s, the Danish publishers wrote in their introduction that Edvard Collin's discussion in his book of the enormous wealth of letters was pure sham. This was now quite apparent. There was even talk of Edvard Collin's "list of sins," and sharp words were used, such as "an inexcusable misrepresentation."[53]

Even today it's possible to see the pattern that took shape under Edvard Collin's diligent use of the scissors and glue pot if we sit down with the collected correspondence in four large volumes and compare the letters to Collin's book about Andersen. Most often Collin deleted the sections of letters that were too tender or effusive, passages that might look as if he too had been captivated by Andersen for a while. If he did choose to include these emotional passages, it was usually because he could use the excerpt to illustrate the tremendous difference in the way the two friends behaved as men. For instance, in a letter from the summer of 1836, Andersen denies that his feelings for his friend are mere sentimentality:

> "Oh, Eduard! If only you were here with me! Yet in my mind I look into your loyal eyes. If you laughed at me, called my feeling sentimentality, which it most certainly is not—well, then you were 'a small person'!"[54]

Collin manipulates the letter so the brief but very important clause— "which it most certainly is not"—falls victim to his scissors in 1882. He wanted to use the abridged quote to emphasize that Andersen's basic emotion was merely sentimentality and not a purer, more noble feeling.[55]

Of course there was only room for a small and limited selection of the numerous letters from the 1830s in Edvard Collin's book, but his choices and priorities were still biased. The many omitted documents cover vital aspects of the initial stages of this odd friendship. One such omission was the touching letter from the summer of 1830, in which Andersen for the first time rejoices at the fact that Edvard has signed his letter "friend" and written in such a sincere tone—"letters more sincere than my own." And Andersen feels that there is reason to take another step in this sensitive friendship: "When you offer me sincerity, I ought to show you my trust."[56] Other omissions made by Edvard Collin pertaining to the motives and driving forces early on in their friendship included documents from those myth-shrouded August days in 1830 when Andersen met Riborg Voigt in Faaborg and wrote the poem "Love." Its daring opening lines: "See the sun flare with the red of love, / It rests its head on the lap of the waves," seem to have been written solely with Riborg in mind. In reality, the amorous confession was copied out and enclosed with a letter to his friend back home in Copenhagen. Here was something worth examining. Along with the poem, which has a second verse about two lovers in a boat hidden behind the reeds, Collin also received the following words:

> "Do not be surprised that I repeat what I have said before, that you are the only one I consider my friend and that I cling to you with all my heart. This is something that I may never be able to say to you in person, but rest assured that I weigh every one of your words, and so, do not ever push me away—but I'm being too sentimental. Surely you understand me! May God grant that I always, with all my heart, will dare confide in you! Of poems I have two new ones, which I will copy for you here. What do you think of them?"[57]

Enclosed with a couple of the letters that Edvard Collin chose to print in their entirety or in abridged form, Andersen had included new poems, which he asked his friend to read and evaluate. Most of these lyrical texts wrap lovingly around the reader. Collin chose to include only one, much less effusive poem, entitled "The Moment of Death." At the same time, he neglected to mention anything about the series of love poems Andersen often submitted to him during the 1830s, asking him to be the very first reader and to assess them—not as a literary critic, but as a human being. This was a process in which others such as Louise Collin, Henriette Hanck, Henriette Wulff, and B. S. Ingemann were also involved.

Edvard Collin's own emotional confessions in his letters were, of course, not included in the book. For instance, in 1832 we meet a rare, unrestrained Collin in the role of jealous lover because Andersen has told him in effusive terms about his encounter with the charming young Ludvig Müller, whom Collin also knew. Even though the letter may have been mostly a coquettish playing to the gallery, it did include these words: "I have been a little jealous at hearing about your love for L.M.; you're not about to dismiss me, are you?"[58] This was not something that Edvard wanted to acknowledge in the late 1870s, after he had erased from this male friendship all traces that might be misunderstood and eventually taint the Collin family. Like his father, Edvard Collin was reserved about anything relating to his private life, and at the age of seventy he said: "What I think about my inner life is something that I keep to myself."[59]

Nameless Love

Edvard Collin had good reasons for what he said, wrote, and edited in his book. He feared the growing interest of the public in the dark and most private aspects of human life. He could see that in the wake of medical research and the interest in sexuality and its import, it had become highly fashionable to interpret art by examining the artist's character. In the late 19th century, people began searching through the biographies of great artists for depraved and abnormal aspects of the artists' psychology and love life. And especially suspect were the more or less platonic relationships that a world-famous male artist had to other men.

That was why Collin chose to follow the course he did in his book, which blurred Andersen's odd "sorrows of the heart" and placed the blame and responsibility for the unusual relationship between the two friends on the author's character. Proof was provided by all those carefully chosen scraps of correspondence, which were supposed to document how abnormal, and at times depraved, Hans Christian Andersen actually had been. It might seem surprising that Edvard Collin managed to slip unscathed from the jumbled and often contradictory reasoning presented in *Hans Christian Andersen and the Collin Family*. The basic premise for the book was "If he wasn't a great man, he was at least a famous man."[60] And its intent was to show certain aspects of the author's character that he had kept hidden from the public. For that reason, it can be hard to accept that in the book, after many leaps and detours in various directions, Edvard Collin ultimately gives the reader such a mystifying description of Andersen's love life. This occurs in a letter of reply to his relative Jonna Stampe, who had strongly objected to Collin's portrait of Andersen. In 1878, with great sympathy, Collin had presented his personal thoughts about Andersen for critique and discussion among members of the Collin family who had truly loved and lionized Andersen. And in his reply to Jonna Stampe in March 1878, Edvard starts obscuring the facts:

> "But now that we are discussing his sorrows, you no doubt want to hear about his *sorrows of the heart* as well. I can only confirm *that* he had them, but cannot say *what* they were. I can't draw attention to myself with any information about it. Throughout his life, he never told me *one* word about this matter, but he did show me his sorrow so that I could guess at

its cause. Yet he couldn't quite conceal it from me, as is apparent in one of his letters to me. Nor could he keep the world ignorant of it (writers never could, of course) . . . I am convinced that the ladies have known far more about Andersen's affairs of the heart than I did, because of their incomparable ability to ferret out and invent. For my part, I have the fortunate quality not to be inquisitive. Yet among his papers I did find letters and outbursts of emotion, even names. But of these, the ladies will hear nothing from me . . ."[61]

Quite an impressively vague description, considering that one of Edvard Collin's intentions with his book was to point out some of the truths about Andersen's character, which the author himself had obscured in *The Fairy Tale of My Life*. Collin says, "I can only confirm *that* he had them, but cannot say *what* they were." And with that he slipped into a linguistic gray zone that had to be used at the end of the 19th century for such a delicate and controversial subject as a man's love relations with another man. It was what made Oscar Wilde's lover "Bosie," during the same period, speak in a poem about "The love that dares not speak its name."[62] And so it was one of the most sensitive issues of the day that haunted Edvard Collin when he wrote his book in 1882, filling it with an abundance of ambiguous impressions of the caliber known as "equivocal" in the Collin family—what Collin in his book calls "sickly shoots" of Andersen's imagination.

Certain lines in the portrait jump out from the correspondence cited in Collin's book because of the catchword "sick." They fit hand in glove with one of the new sexual diagnoses of the day: *Psychopathia Sexualis*. This was also the title of a book by the sexual researcher Richard von Krafft-Ebing from 1886, which was published in countless expanded editions over the next decades and was translated into numerous languages. Collin's own diagnosis of what he time and again in his book calls Andersen's "sickness" is given neither a name nor an explanation. Edvard doesn't dare put a name to his friend's love, and toward the end of the book, his assessment of Andersen's character is presented under such diverse labels as "sickly psychological state," "paroxysms," and "a disposition—physical or spiritual or both." At first it sounds as if it has something to do with what we today would call megalomania or schizophrenia or narcissism. But then there is a cautious, reticent searching for a medical label for the condition he calls "nervous love." If readers did not obtain any specific name from Edvard Collin in 1882, they did receive some rather blatant hints via his scattered, diffuse use of words such as "excesses," "disgusting," "repulsive," and "scandalous." And as he said:

> "I cannot deviate from my opinion that Andersen is best served by showing the world how sickly his temperament was so that it is clear to everyone that all that was repellent, all that scandalized the world, was due to this temperament. He was aware of his illness, but had no idea what to do about it, and he was often truly unhappy about it. I have not presented any description, merely a hint of the paroxysms during which he was utterly deranged."[63]

The evaluation of Andersen's psyche and sexuality stayed in the hands of Edvard Collin until well into the 20th century. But rather than believe what it says in Collin's book, we should search for Andersen's true eros in the sections of the enormous correspondence that Edvard omitted from his account of the author's life. We should also look at the flood of literary works that poured out of Andersen during the 1830s and which, word by word, page by page, book by book, brought him closer to the complicated truth about himself.

If we delve into Hans Christian Andersen's literary works from the years 1830-40, we notice a slow, gradual opening inward toward the darker and more uncertain points in both the writing and the writer. The reckless Rhyming Demon inside of Andersen that was constantly sloughing off poetry was now joined by other voices and shadows asking questions and demanding answers. These were forces that it became increasingly necessary to understand and define. As Andersen formulated it in countless variations, it was a matter of "expressing it as it lives inside me." The words stem from the author's urgent foreword to *Agnete and the Merman* from 1834.

It was only after his return from Italy in 1834-35 that Andersen, with his novel *The Improvisatore*, took the first big step into the fragmented and unclarified regions inside himself that had to do with gender. A new path in his writing was thus opened, and it swiftly led to the novels *O. T.* in 1836 and *Only a Fiddler* in 1837. In these books Andersen, in his search for firmer ground under his identity, used his art to plumb the depths of his inner self. In these three great novels, which were all written in less than four years, the author's radical investigation of what it means to be a man and a woman moved slowly toward a shattering of the concepts "man" and "woman." This meant that in 1837, in *Only a Fiddler*, Hans

Christian Andersen could present to the reader an androgynous figure. Her name is Naomi, and in the novel she is compared to Goethe's androgynous heroine Mignon, who appears in *Wilhelm Meister's Apprenticeship*, the great classic *Bildungsroman*. "The androgynous individual" was one of Romanticism's great metaphors, which was supposed to represent the harmonious, universal merging of all things and all ages. In *Only a Fiddler*, there are all sorts of peculiar transformations and gender changes that occur along the way, combined with an exploration of the dualities within and between the protagonists Christian and Naomi. As a result, this novel, like no other in Andersen's oeuvre, expresses the complementary state between the two sexes.

Even in earlier works, Andersen had made great strides in his attempt to describe and explain the ways in which men and women fall in love. For instance, the play *Agnete and the Merman* from 1834 was meant to express "the wondrous longing for a new, a different existence." Another example was *Meeting and Parting*, which appeared in 1835, although the first draft was written four years earlier. In the summer of 1835, Andersen wrote to Edvard Collin from the estate of Lykkesholm on Fyn that he had now completed the first part of Act Two of *Meeting and Parting*. He also mentioned that this meant the play could be submitted before the start of the theater season, and, if he did say so himself, it was a splendid play: "Undeniably the best (and no doubt the only good) drama that I've ever written. Yet I fear that it will not be accepted."[64] In *The Fairy Tale of My Life* Andersen points out that the play was a natural extension of his love for Riborg Voigt and the poetry collection *Fantasies and Sketches*, which testified to all that was oppressing his heart at the time:

> "A rewriting of the story of my own heart emerged in a serious vaudeville: '*Meeting and Parting*,' which was put down on paper with only one change, that here the love was mutual. The play was performed five years later at the royal Danish theater."[65]

We find numerous such rewritings of the stories of the author's heart during the 1830s, but *Meeting and Parting* is particularly interesting because it casts light on Andersen's deeply divided perceptions about gender and love. The play is a vaudeville structured around two strained love stories that extend through several generations. The first act is set in Odense in 1808, when the Spaniards are in town, and the dark-skinned, passionate men set fire to the hearts of the girls of Fyn. Augusta, who is Danish, and Francesco, the Spaniard, first realize the seriousness of their feelings for each other on the very day when Francesco is to leave with his battalion and Augusta is to marry her childhood friend, Ludvig. At that stage you would think that all hope is lost. But love conquers all, even time. Cheerfully and intrepidly, the vaudeville now leaps forward twenty-five years. In the meantime Augusta has become a widow and now lives in Helsingør with her beautiful but impoverished daughter, the seamstress Louise. Francesco has become a wealthy envoy, and his handsome son, Diego, has ended up staying at the home of Augusta's brother, where we find a daughter named Hanne, who is the same age as Louise. Of course the young man from the south falls in love with Louise. But when the envoy arrives in Helsingør, he categorically refuses to give his son permission to betroth and marry a girl so far beneath him in social status. That is, until he discovers that Louise is the daughter of his old flame from Fyn from that idyllic summer when he was a soldier. Then he sings a different tune.

A happy ending, you would think. But before the curtain falls, we're suddenly presented with a particularly soft minor key—and dissonance—that gives the play a most surprising nuance in the last act. As we prepare for the great redemptive fall of the curtain, the play's ultimate loser steps forward to lament her misery. It's the melancholy Hanne who, much to the dismay of her parents, did not win Diego. That's something that she can easily live with. Much worse is the fact that she will never win Louise, whom she has always loved deep in her heart, and much more ardently and passionately than she will ever love a man. Even from the beginning of Act Two, it is evident that Hanne harbors deep and intense feelings for her friend. We see her with Louise as the two girls sit together in comfortable and intimate companionship, sewing a dress for Hanne and discussing Diego as a potential husband and lover. Suddenly Hanne reveals her feelings and her deepest nature. It's not men like Diego that she was meant to love, but a woman like Louise:

> "He's not someone I could ever love! I am much more fond of you! My whole life I would like to spend with you; you satisfy me more than Diego. A woman, a soul created like mine, with the same feelings and ideas, that's what I can merge with, join forces with. But a man—well, you may laugh at me—but he's a different sort of being! I grow truly alarmed whenever I think about being his, belonging to him, imbibing his spirit and ideas! And yet I do not hate men. I've never loved. Have you, Louise?"[66]

I Want to Be Kissed Too

Andersen had never loved either, and in 1832 his feelings for Collin had by no means abated. On the contrary. He resumed his battle to win his friend's complete trust, and in this regard it was of little importance that Edvard Collin had become engaged in April to the eighteen-year-old Henriette Thyberg. Inherent in the supple but strong framework of the sensitive friendship was the idea that brotherly love conquers all. Even a dear brother's marriage to the other side. There would still be no doubt that Andersen, for his part, would express everything that he was thinking and feeling, "even the deepest secrets of my heart." At the same time, he emphasized to his newly engaged friend that their letters should continue to be their secret meeting place:

> "Oh, dear, dear Edvard, how I love you, though I can't properly say what I feel. I most assuredly have too much love! In writing, and this is my last letter from here, I can tell you everything in my heart; when we meet face to face I feel embarrassed to express myself in that manner."[67]

It's important to note that Edvard Collin, in the year following the "De vs. du" controversy, did not distance himself in any clear or significant way from Andersen's flirting, which, after subsiding for a brief period, was once again on the march. In reality, Edvard's passivity gave his wistful friend a microscopic hope of winning, as did greetings in his letters such as this: "It's late and I suppose I should stop now. But first a friend's loving greeting to you, dear Andersen. I know that you too will always think of me with friendship."[68]

It was enough to make the author weak with happiness. The laws of love are such that Andersen read these letters from Edvard as proof that at heart the interest was mutual, even though certain external circumstances—such as Edvard's engagement and his whole career as a civil servant—created several prosaic obstacles. Among the small signs that Andersen eagerly seized upon was an unexpected effusive tone in Edvard's letters during the hot August days of 1832, when Andersen was staying for two weeks at the Nørager estate near Tissø in western Sjælland. There he wrote a great many poems for his next poetry collection, *The Twelve Months of the Year*, including "August." The words of the poem were gathered like a bouquet of roses in two verses and then enclosed in a letter to the author's newly engaged friend, who may well have had other things to think about, but that was no reason for him to forget Andersen. "Why must I go alone; / And my yearning be subdued? / The flowers stand confidently, / They are kissed in the wind, / I want to be kissed too!"[69]

Yes, Andersen wanted to be kissed too, and there were plenty of reasons to pucker up while staying at the pleasant estate where an unrestrained atmosphere reigned among the many young, clever, and handsome people who were visiting during those August days in 1832. The guests included Louise Collin, Edvard's sister; the well-known doctor and phrenologist Carl Otto; and, of particular interest, the young bishop's son Ludvig Müller, who had also been a regular guest of Andersen's private tutor out in Christianshavn in 1828. Andersen could not nor did he want to hide his enthusiasm for this "lovable" Ludvig, who was also one of Edvard Collin's close friends. Here was a trio—Andersen, Edvard, and Ludvig—that was full of poetic possibilities! On the spot, and with the nature of Sjælland as the idyllic framework, Andersen portrayed the three of them in a long poem with seventeen verses, "Summer Escape and Repose." The poem was meant to represent all of "July" in the poetry collection *The Twelve Months of the Year, Sketched with Pen and Ink by Hans Christian Andersen*, which was published right before Christmas that same year. In this dalliance of a poem, in which the center section joyously whirls around the names of Ludvig and Eduard, Andersen presents an idyllic portrait of summer life in the country. After a picturesque visit to a fisherman's family in their little house down by the shore, the poem's narrator wanders through the woods at dusk. There, behind the thick hazel tree boughs, he meets a friend named Ludvig, and his presence, along with thoughts of his other male friend, Eduard, who's waiting in the wings, causes the narrator to "tremble with desire." That was how much love a poet could hold:

> Ludvig, let us together
> Arm in arm stroll the shore,
> See how the clouds change
> Their shape in the night air.
> I put my arm around my friend,
> Heart clings to heart,
> Friendship, my soul sings your praise,
> Every sorrow that burdens the heart,
> Then vanishes in the scent of flowers.

You will know my heart's depth;
Your spirit's rich treasures,
And the innocence God put
In your glance, won my heart.
Brother, let our watchword be:
"Friendship, knowledge, art, and honor,"
The heart's fresh tree will bear
It like blossoms and fruit, my dear!
I thank God I found you!

My thoughts flit through nature,
Fly across rippling waves,
To the linden, lovely by the wall,
Growing in the big city;
There I will visit Eduard;
Happy among his books,
He sits and smokes, content,
Cleverly searching for knowledge;
He is so dear to my heart!
Even with you, I miss him,
My heart embraces you both,
Your dear, dear names
Live, breathe in my breast.
You both initiate my life to action!
Every dismayed voice falls silent.
The eye sees only harmonies.
Childish, pious melodies
Quaking me with desire.[70]

After returning home from the Nørager estate in the fall of 1832, Andersen managed to make room for both of Ludvig's brothers, Adam and Otto, on the periphery of his new dream-trio. When Otto Müller was on a long educational journey through Germany in 1832-33, he carried on a lengthy correspondence with the author, who was back home in Copenhagen. Andersen was able to give his traveling friend a particularly clear picture of what young men such as Edvard, Ludvig—and Otto—meant to him:

"*He* [Ludvig] and Eduard Collin are my closest, most intimate friends; they both have taken a place in my very being. If only I might always keep them! I see them as often as I can, but I hardly dare say how dear they are to me. It's not something that people can comprehend; but mine is also a poet's heart, and that gives me, of course a great deal of feeling."[71]

Yes, it was necessary to show a little discretion, even if it was merely a platonic love affair—"it's not something that people can comprehend," as Andersen writes. But he thought that Otto Müller, down in Germany, *could* comprehend it. And so two months later Müller received another, more detailed letter about the ideas behind the network of male friends that the author—with some difficulty—was in the process of establishing. Ludvig, who had been so amenable at the Nørager estate, had suddenly retreated, and throughout the fall he had in general been extremely reserved about his feelings. Could Otto perhaps convince his older brother to change his attitude?

"It's a veritable kind of love, a pure, spiritual feeling, that makes me cling to them. I wish Ludvig would realize this! And yet it took years before I won Eduard over completely. I'm sure that dear Ludvig will someday understand me too."[72]

There is some reason to doubt how great or genuine Andersen's infatuation with Ludvig Müller actually was. It's possible that the bishop's son was merely a type of bait in letters and poems that would make Edvard attach himself more strongly to Andersen. In any case, the stage-setting of his "love" for Ludvig was both effective and meticulous. His ardor is quite apparent in his autobiography, which was written during the same period and was intended as a documentation of Andersen's life up to the present. It was then put into the hands of the Collin family. In the autobiography, Ludvig Müller is presented as a very special person, "who has since become so inexpressibly dear to me; in an almost magical way he has attracted my heart and my trust, which he deserves, by virtue of his being so lovable."[73] Furthermore, Andersen notes in this passage: "Our friendship became quite intimate and well-founded, and I will give more details later on." In other words, he was promising that later on in his autobiography, he would present the rest of the story about his friendship with the "inexpressibly dear" Ludvig Müller. But that never happened. The book we know today, which was discovered and published in 1926, appears to be an unfinished work that ends in the middle of a letter from B. S. Ingemann regarding Andersen's "love affair" with Riborg Voigt. But Andersen's strategy apparently worked. First, Collin reacted surprisingly quickly to Andersen's lyrical portrait of his double infatuation in August 1832. He immediately replied to the letter containing the poem about the three men. Second, Edvard made his friend extraordinarily happy by confiding to him that the whole family certainly missed him. Edvard himself had started looking forward to the joys they would share in the fall, including "many a good, intimate, sensible chat together."

The fact that Edvard dared respond to such an advance may have been because he was now engaged, which meant that Andersen had to realize how utterly hopeless a sensitive friendship would be. But in this matter he was terribly mistaken. As we will see, neither a Ludvig Müller nor a Henriette Thyberg was any obstacle to Andersen's love for Edvard. On the contrary, these two "new" individuals were further incitements that spoke to Andersen's poetic heart. There was always room for a couple of minor love affairs next to the one and only. On this point too, as previously mentioned, there was a certain similarity between the thought processes of Hans Christian Andersen and those of Søren Kierkegaard. In his *Diary of a Seducer*, Kierkegaard has his shrewd seducer argue that a person can certainly be in love with many individuals at the same time, because he loves each in a different way:

> "To love one is too little; to love all is superficial; to know yourself and to love as many as possible, to allow your soul to conceal all the powers of love inside in such a way that each receives its specific nourishment while consciousness encompasses the whole—that is pleasure, that is living."[74]

Søren Kierkegaard's words, written in the early 1840s, cast a sharp and elucidating light on Hans Christian Andersen's unusual, searching love life in the 1830s, which was directed at both sexes. And, as previously discussed, Andersen often felt most comfortable in constellations of friendship that included both men and women, and preferably a pair of siblings. The more intrigue, the better, in Andersen's eyes. In a letter to Henriette Hanck from 1831[75] and in the middle of a verse in the play *Banquet at Kenilworth* [another Scott adaptation] from 1836, Andersen uses the phrase "friendship is a puzzle-game"[76] as an apt and precise expression for his penchant for complicated emotional ties and platonic games with sex roles in his letters and poems. In Andersen's writings from the early 1830s, it's often evident that the narrator—as in Shakespeare's sonnets—is speaking to a "you" that could be of either gender. A literary example of this type of puzzle-game is the poem "She's the One I Mean," written during the intense fall of 1832 when everyone around Andersen seemed to be forming couples. The lonely author wrote to Otto Müller: "Every time I hear of someone getting engaged, I fall into a bad mood!"[77]

During the fall and winter of 1832-33, the relationship between Andersen and the Collin family was developing rapidly. Every Tuesday Andersen would eat dinner at the old family home, and he would often visit his friend in his rooms. But in a letter from March 1833, it's clear that Andersen had not significantly altered his romantic behavior, and once again it was necessary for Edvard Collin to distance himself from what he considered unmanly behavior and effeminacy. In this letter Andersen writes that he has daily noticed how his friend is distancing himself more and more from him, turning his back at the very moment when he needs someone to be his confidant:

> "I feel there is something imploring, something hideous in my plaguing you for empathy, but my pride collapses beneath my love for you! I am so inexpressibly fond of you, and I am in despair because you cannot, will not be the friend to me that I, if our positions were reversed, would be to you . . . What have I done? What is it about my character that you find so offensive? Tell me! . . . Just tell me, I must accustom myself to losing!"[78]

Two weeks earlier Andersen had written to Henriette Wulff that there were pages of his heart's diary that were so inscrutable that there were "sorrows whose cause I dare not suggest; it dwells in a feeling within me that I cannot properly name!"[79] Nor did he give a name or gender to the object of his longing when he wrote to his other, younger, friend, Henriette Hanck, in January 1833: "Yes, I'm a strange creature! My heart is a diary, in which certain pages have been glued together, but the book itself is open to any man's inspection. Most of the reasons for my actions are on the pages that are pasted together. Certain people may think the paper is so thin that the writing shines through, but, as you know, in that fashion you would be reading it backwards—meaning wrong."[80]

No letters exist from Edvard Collin from the spring of 1833. This was a period when Andersen was in a state of limbo, waiting to hear about a possible travel grant to Italy for which he had applied to the foundation *Ad usus publicos*, where Edvard Collin had recently taken over his father's position as secretary. The author's diary was also on hold, waiting to be taken along on a new journey south. But hope was still alive, invested in a large poetry collection of previously published texts. These *Collected Poems* included a little, hastily improvised verse, which had been used the year before as the dedication in a copy of the libretto to the ballad opera *The Bride of Lammermoor*. The male protagonist bore a slight similarity to Edvard in terms of his name: "Let not our friendship's lovely dreamland / Like Edgar sink dead in shifting sand."[81] Andersen was not just fighting for his Italian trip, which at first seemed unlikely because of the many qualified applicants, but also for his friend. In March 1833, when he thought the financial support for the trip would not be forthcoming, he reacted as if his friendship with the foundation secretary, Edvard Collin, had also been decisively rebuffed:

> "This trip was the dream that embodied all my hopes, perhaps even my life itself. Be completely candid with me, Eduard . . . Do not fear that I might go about offering my sorrow to view. I promise you that I will hide it, squeeze it tight in my heart, and appear quite sensible. But tell me all your objections, everything that I ought to know, but soon, dear friend, as soon as it is possible for you."[82]

Although no clarification resulted regarding his relationship with the new foundation secretary, Andersen's trip to Italy did come through on April 13, 1833, when a royal decree announced that 600 *rigsdaler* annually, for two years, had been awarded to the young author. And that was a small fortune. Edvard Collin was new and green at his post as secretary of the foundation *Ad usus publicos*, but in the background Jonas Collin had made sure that all the right strings were pulled, while his son corrected the spelling mistakes in the application. And, as usual, Andersen himself had a sense for doing the necessary leg work. *The Twelve Months of the Year* was published in late 1832, while his application was being considered. Andersen dedicated the volume to His Majesty, which won him an audience with Frederik VI, and—at the urging of Jonas Collin—he told the absolute monarch about his tremendous desire to go out into the world to further educate himself.[83]

Andersen tried this same tactical offensive four years later, when he once again asked the Collin family for help in connection with his application for royal support of his travels. Edvard Collin recounts in his book that when things didn't go as quickly or smoothly on this occasion as Andersen had hoped, the author decided to play the senior and younger

Collin against H. C. Ørsted. The latter was asked to persuade the king, since no one in the "home of homes" was willing to do so. As Edvard Collin says:

> "His longing to travel argued away all obstacles and caused him to ignore what should have been so obvious for anyone who knew me and my position well. I, as the young secretary of the 'Foundation *Ad usus publicos*,' meaning as a junior official, would merely make myself ridiculous by acting as his protector, since this was a matter of quite an extraordinary favor."[84]

Our Child Agnete

Initially Andersen had to share his travel stipend with the writer Henrik Hertz, and on Saturday, April 20, 1833, he headed south for Italy. During one of the very first stages of his trip—after the voyage from Denmark to Germany—Andersen received an unusually heartfelt letter from Edvard Collin, "full of love," as Andersen triumphantly and optimistically notes in his diary on April 23. The loving tone of his friend's letter went right to the most tender part of Andersen's heart: "I wept like a child, but I had to go into a corner to hide it from others."[85] And when Andersen reached Paris, where he stayed for three months, another letter arrived, full of confidences and with a discussion of the ties of friendship that not even Ludvig Müller could break.

Yet over the course of the summer in 1833, their correspondence began to lapse more and more into familiar patterns. Andersen wrote twelve long letters, full of news, while his friend—with the exception of the above-mentioned missive—replied in three brief, dry, and formal letters. "You almost always write only on the first page; the other three are white paper," complained Andersen. "Twenty lines comprise the usual tariff allotted me!"[86] Edvard Collin used the excuse that he was obligated to write so many letters in his daily work. At the same time, he urged Andersen to tear his thoughts away from all that he had left behind, which was preoccupying his mind far more than was healthy. Danes who happened to meet Andersen in Paris had privately reported to Edvard—who was always so well-informed—that the author was spending more than half of each day writing letters. "Don't keep writing home so much!" admonished his friend.

But Collin was speaking to deaf ears. Inside Andersen an old artistic idea had begun to stir, and a decision began ripening inside him during his stay in Paris. If Edvard Collin's soul would not come to Andersen, then he would come to Collin in the form of a play entitled *Agnete and the Merman*.

Even though Andersen had conceived the idea in January of that year, when it was—as he wrote in a letter to Henriette Hanck—"daily growing in my mind,"[87] it wasn't until he was in Paris in the summer of 1833 that he started work on his dramatic interpretation of an old Danish folktale. What was new about his idea was that the play would also be a shadow picture of Andersen, the human being. And his friend would have a difficult time putting it aside or ignoring it as he had done with certain letters. This was because, right before Andersen's departure, Collin had promised to take a thorough, critical look at everything that Andersen wrote along the way and sent back home. Furthermore, he had agreed to play the role of Andersen's literary agent and send out potential works, both large and small, to Reitzel the publisher, to the Royal Theater, and to various magazines while the author was traveling in the south.

In a letter dated June 11, 1833, Andersen mentions that he has started writing a drama that is very close to his heart. And in his usual ambiguous manner, he lets Edvard understand that *Agnete and the Merman* stems from—and should be viewed as part of—the running dialogue between the two friends regarding their relationship. Andersen almost made it sound as if this play was a shared spiritual project. As Andersen writes from Paris in June: "I'm making progress on *Agnete*; with God's help we will both have some joy from it. You and I, that is."[88] Since he knew how Edvard would probably react to this type of disingenuous statement, Andersen hurried to add that their shared joy also depended on the financial returns from the play, which would enable Andersen to repay some of his debt to the Collin family.

On August 14, 1833, Andersen sent off the first part of *Agnete and the Merman*. It was at this time that he left Paris, traveling by stagecoach and heading southeast. The journey took him to Switzerland. Via Geneva, Lucerne, and Neuchâtel, he traveled to Le Locle to visit the brother-in-law of the Danish watchmaker Urban Jürgensen, whom Andersen had recently met in Paris. His time in Paris had been quite merry. Andersen had lived right next door to Otto Müller—Ludvig's brother—and while the ink was still wet, he read aloud the first couple of scenes from *Agnete and the*

Merman to his friend. Otto had described the work as "a beautiful impression of a beautiful form."[89] That was the sort of critique that Andersen craved. In the letter that he enclosed with the manuscript, which he was now sending to Denmark, Andersen fervently begged his friend "to love me and my Agnete as I love you." As a postscript to the letter he included a so-called "title page that should not be printed." It contained various remarks to all the trusted readers back home in Denmark: Edvard Collin, Henriette Wulff, Ludvig Müller, and Signe Læssøe. At the same time, this title page gave an outline of the plot and explained what the author actually wished to express with this story about the fragmented and restlessly seeking Agnete:

> "It seems to me that in the old ballad about Agnete there is a vivid portrayal of the wondrous striving for something other than what a person possesses, something that is found in everyone. Dissatisfaction and striving for some unknown, new being is what drives Agnete into the waves. She wishes to be back with the merman, and when her wish is fulfilled, she feels doubly unhappy, until death offers peace to her restless soul."[90]

With an improviser's natural preoccupation with what he had just finished or was still creating, Andersen regarded *Agnete and the Merman* as the most significant piece he had ever written. At the same time, he felt that the dramatized folk ballad was a painful part of himself, and in Paris Otto Müller agreed with him, as did many of his readers back home in Copenhagen, including Henriette Hanck, who wrote: "You compare yourself to your Agnete, but you don't seem happy about the similarity that you see between her and yourself."[91]

Andersen's quite lucid and personal attitude toward the main character of his play was also apparent from the title page's final testamentary provision. It said that if he should die before completing the play, the manuscript was to be published along with his autobiography, which had been given to the Collins for safekeeping. Yet it is primarily the fervent way in which Andersen describes *Agnete and the Merman* to Edvard Collin that reveals what an organic part of his soul this work of art was. In his letters from Le Locle in September 1833, he actually describes the play as a living creature, as a newborn child that requires special care and understanding from those closest to it. On September 12, Andersen then sends off the second, final part of the play, which he had completed in a great rush of work. Andersen described packing up the manuscript as feeling like a mother's first, cautious embrace of her naked, delicate infant:

> "I am sending you my Agnete, now finished, but not yet seen by any eyes but my own . . . Please receive with kindness this good child, born among the mountains, but Danish at heart . . . When you see her in her entirety, you will recognize what resides in me . . . Be a father to my Agnete as I fly over the Alps and perhaps dream of a new Agnete rising up from the waves . . . Is there anything else I should tell you about this dear child? I don't think so! . . . Dear, dear friend! How my heart pounds as I pack up Agnete! . . . Oh, send word to me soon, word of Agnete! . . . Let Agnete be as well equipped as possible, divide her into columns and give her a half-title."[92]

But Edvard Collin was not at all proud to be the father of *Agnete*, as Andersen had hoped. During the fall of 1833, four letters reveal his reaction and assessment of the play that his friend "had carried under his heart," as he said. In brief summary form, his evaluation can be described as strong opposition to the first part in August, and restrained joy in September and October over the second part, which on that occasion he found to be intermittently "touching" and "beautiful." Then, suddenly, comes his overall, fierce critique of the play in December, when he rejects *Agnete and the Merman* with a great show of aggression. Although there had been some positive signs in Collin's critique during the fall, he now found the play to be a complete failure, using adjectives such as "misshapen" and "formless." His objections to the work include such things as a "sickly, soft tone" to one of the male roles. And in this regard, Collin had said in his first letter back in August, that he was looking for a more robust, straightforward and objective delineation of character from the author's pen. The entire psychology and unfolding of destiny came straight from Andersen himself, as his friend pointed out:

> "You're playing a part in the lives you depict; you're writing down your feelings, because you're putting yourself body and soul into the situation. But you lack the level-headedness and the firm advantage and power over your thoughts possessed by an author who observes himself standing at some place outside the world that he describes."[93]

In addition, Edvard Collin was infuriated that Andersen had included lines in the dialogue between Agnete and Hemming, her half-brother and suitor, that were taken directly from conversations in the Collin home:

"Yes, I assure you, in expressions that I have often heard you utter to me whenever you, in an undoubtedly sickly and soft mood, thought that I was not fond enough of you."[94] Yet Collin did not mention any examples of the many lines borrowed from the correspondence between the two friends, which were also scattered throughout the play. For instance, this little remark that Andersen puts in the mouth of the play's much too feminine man, Hemming: "The spoken *De* becomes the heart's *du*, / that is the dream of friendship!"

Andersen's reaction to his friend's criticism was surprisingly serene and dignified. He readily admitted his lack of objectivity, but he couldn't deny feeling both relieved by and proud of this dramatic birth. It's easy to see why. It was an amazing accomplishment to have written such a concentrated drama in only two months with long, perfectly formed poems such as "Agnete's Lullaby" and "The Miller's Daughter." But Andersen's satisfaction primarily had to do with the fact that he had finally said everything he wanted to say. It couldn't be taken back. "What I wrote, I wrote!" was his reply to Edvard.[95] And he couldn't help it if his friend was offended because lines from their friendship had been lifted out of the private sphere and were now on public display in *Agnete and the Merman*: "Believe me, dear friend, if you had known Schiller or Byron as you know me, you would have heard them say in the same words a great deal about what their poems express."[96] The very central yet rather vague point in Collin's critique that has to do with a "sickly, soft tone" was not something that Andersen tried to deny or repudiate. Instead, he chose, once again, to show his friend that notes in a minor key were part of his nature and thereby also an inseparable part of his great, never ceasing love for "my heart's dearest friend," as Edvard was called when Andersen finally reached Rome in September.[97]

For the first time in the history of their friendship, after four years of fierce struggle to establish a sensitive friendship with Edvard Collin, Andersen gave a name to his secret and his pain. It happened on his way from Le Locle in Switzerland to Rome, in a long letter that was mailed from Milan on September 24, 1833. It's a letter that is among the strongest and most beautiful that Andersen ever sent. This letter to Edvard, which was written before Andersen received his criticism of *Agnete*, reveals the author's deep insight into himself and his temperament; it also shows a cognitive calm within him, which was a kind of afterbirth from *Agnete*. The person speaking in this letter is certainly not happy, but he is composed and—in particular—relieved:

1. LEFT: Guiseppe Siboni, the Italian-born choirmaster at the Royal Theater, painted in 1829 by J. F. Møller.

2. BELOW: The travel pass for the fourteen-year-old "boy Hans Christian Andersen" was filled out by the head clerk at Odense Police Station on September 4, 1819. A travel pass was required for anyone who wished to cross a domestic Danish channel such as the Great Belt. It was stamped with a visa in Nyborg, Korsør, and Copenhagen.

3. Kongens Nytorv, depicted here ca. 1850 by H. G. F. Holm, was the center of Hans Christian Andersen's Copenhagen. Throughout a fifty-year period a large part of the writer's life in the capital took place within a radius of 500 meters from the square.

4. Andersen had a life-long love for the theater, which shaped his literary writings and paper-cuts. It also led him to create puppet theaters and to cut out small puppets and costumes, as well as little stage sets for children, as illustrated here.

5. Adam Oehlenschläger (1779–1850) was one of the Danish Romantic writers whose works the young Andersen read and imitated. The budding poet made the acquaintance of the older, famed author in 1821–22 during his visits to Bakkehus. In the early 1800s, Oehlenschläger's work signaled the birth of the era known in Denmark as the Golden Age.

6. In 1822, Jonas Collin, who was the financial director of the Royal Theater and who took an active interest in new talent in all areas of life, persuaded King Frederik VI to invest in the young Hans Christian Andersen by providing funds from the foundation *Ad usus publicos*. Collin was one of the most visionary and powerful financiers during Denmark's Golden Age. In addition to his countless philanthropic endeavors, Collin had a great influence on the king's support of artists during the decades following the national bankruptcy in 1813.

7. Many places in Andersen's writings, paper-cuts, and collages, we encounter a river, along with its flora, fauna, and mythology. In this large paper-cut from *Christine Stampe's Picture Book* from 1859, storks, swans, and trees are gathered around an idyllic space, imaginative and dreamlike, such as Andersen describes in the prologue of his first published book. In the middle of this primordial scene Andersen has written: "The stork brings the children / from the water, / the swans sing of / the land of eternity."

8. Simon Meisling, Andersen's headmaster in Slagelse and Helsingør from 1822 until 1827, was a man who was both peculiar and feared. Among his pupils and colleagues he was notorious for his stern demeanor and fiery temperament, but he was also known for his odd appearance and gait, as well as his lack of personal hygiene.

9. Slagelse was a small town with 2,000 citizens in 1822, yet it had its own library, a modern British fire pump, a newspaper, a theater, and a grammar school. The school was located on Bredegade, one of the town's main streets, which also formed part of the road between Copenhagen and Korsør. On this same street, depicted here in 1910, Andersen found lodgings with Fru Erikke Henneberg, the widow of a judge.

10. In C. W. Eckersberg's portrait of the middle-aged and slightly corpulent H. C. Ørsted from 1822, the physicist is shown with some of his favorite instruments. In his hand he holds a resonating plate that was meant to be stroked with the bow on the table. Visible in the background is a galvanic battery with copper vessel, as well as a piezometer, intended for experiments dealing with the compressibility of water. With his epochal discovery of electromagnetism in the same year as Andersen arrived in Copenhagen, H. C. Ørsted contributed to the electrification of the 19th century.

11. In late May 1826, Andersen moved to Helsingør with his headmaster. Kronborg Castle and the view of Sweden, depicted here in 1825 by J. P. Møller, made a strong impression on the budding author, who wrote to Jonas Collin: "As seen from the road, Helsingeur didn't promise me much, but now that I'm inside, it seems to me a little Copenhagen . . . The Sound is studded with ships that float past the shores like seagulls . . . Oh, a person feels compelled to become a poet or a painter at the sight of this lovely nature. Oh, benefactor, thank you, thank you! for every happy moment! How glorious life is!!!"

12. In the spring of 1827, Andersen returned to Copenhagen and, with the help of Jonas Collin, found lodgings on Vingaardstræde and hired a private tutor in Christianshavn. The path was then opened to him to the Collin family's venerable home, which stood between Bredgade and Store Strandstræde, close to Kongens Nytorv and Nyhavn. This was the birthplace and childhood home of Jonas Collin, and the residence he now shared with his wife and five children.

13. The 24-year-old Riborg Voigt was the daughter of a wealthy merchant in Fåborg and the sister of one of Andersen's fellow students. The author met her in the summer of 1830. In his autobiography from 1832, Andersen writes: "I was at that time in my 25th year, had never actually been in love . . . As yet there was actually no thought of passion."

14, 15. Included among his numerous maternal and sisterly women friends were Henriette Wulff (above) and Henriette Hanck (right). About the same age as Andersen, they were his steadfast correspondents during the 1830s and 1840s. With great empathy and responsiveness, they answered every letter from their adored "brother," doing their best to satisfy his thirst for recognition or solace.

16. "Day by day everything around me becomes more and more poetry; my whole life seems to me a lyric poem, and you are beginning to play a proper role in it, yet do not be angered by this. Since I regard Eduard as a brother, it is only natural that you should be . . . his sister." This is what Hans Christian Andersen wrote on September 21, 1832, to Louise Collin, who was the more attractive of Jonas Collin's two daughters—beautiful, cheerful and good-natured but not as bold and bubbling with life as her older sister Ingeborg. In 1833, Louise Collin became engaged to the jurist J. W. Lind. She remained Andersen's good friend until the author's death in 1875.

17. In the summer of 1869 Andersen and Edvard Collin spent three weeks together at the Nørager estate near Tissø. The relationship between the two men then entered a phase which Andersen described in his memoirs from 1832 in this way: "Collin's family displayed greater and greater kindness toward me. I entrusted Eduard with my confidences, and I regarded him as a friend, as my clever, sensible friend, to whom I nevertheless did not quite dare open my heart, meaning tell him everything until I had considered whether it would be sensible, because I possessed no secrets, least of all of the heart."

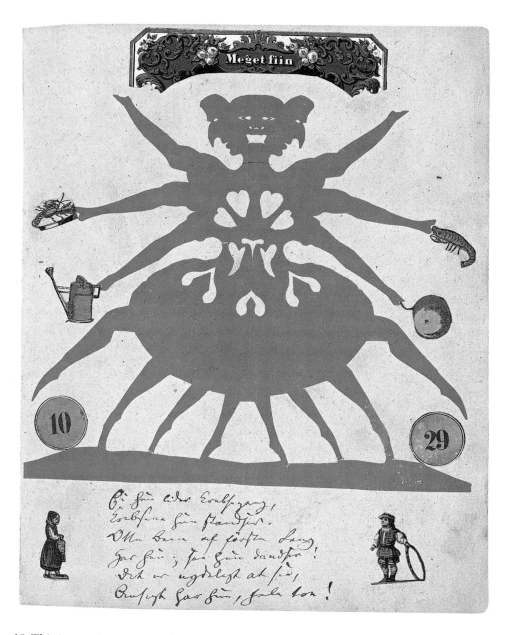

18. This impressive orange crab of a dancer with eight slender legs, six powerful arms, two masks, and one face stems from *Christine's Picture Book* from 1859. Above the figure Andersen has pasted the words "Quite splendid," while below he explains this magnificent hermaphrodite with the words: "No crab's gait does she endure, / crabs are what she stops. / Eight legs of the first order / does she have, how she dances! / So charming it is to see, / the face she has, all three!"

19. At the Danish manor houses and in the salons of Europe Andersen found a loyal audience, which was primarily female. And everyone knew the unwritten rules that applied to his readings. No coughing or scraping of chairs, no sniffling or inquisitive children. The author's joy at reading his own fairy tales was not only famous but notorious, as evident in this sketch from *Corsaren* from 1847. Andersen is reading a story to an English audience with an intensity and tenacity that has robbed most of the listeners of consciousness.

20. Andersen told stories using both his pen and his scissors. Over the years, a great many of his paper-cuts formed complete stories or served as illustrations for an improvised tale. Others were tiny toys that could be blown on at the table or hung up in the window or on the Christmas tree, such as this red man with a ladder reaching up to the mill, or this odd strongman with the whole world on his head.

21. One of the first great European luminaries that Andersen called on during his trip in 1831 was the French-German writer and naturalist Adelbert Chamisso, who knew Danish. He was the author of the novel *Peter Schlemihl*, which prompted Andersen's enthusiasm during the 1820s. This book later inspired his own novel *Walking Tour*, as well as his fairy tale "The Shadow." Chamisso translated several of Andersen's early poems to German, including "The Soldier," which was set to music by Silcher and became something of a German hit in the 1830s.

22. During the Golden Age, Hans Christian Andersen and Søren Kierkegaard were the two Copenhagen citizens who were most often the subject of caricature. For years the magazine *Corsaren* was particularly adept at excoriating the two brilliant and eccentric men who were such odd figures in the city. This image of the stooped Kierkegaard was drawn by Wilhelm Marstrand.

23. All parts of the globe meet in this paper-cut from *Christine's Picture Book* from 1859. The images include troll heads, palm trees, mermaids, and men waving their arms as they perch on a swan's wing, all the while alertly monitored by the hen yard.

24. As critic, editor, and permanent dramatist and adviser at the Royal Theater, Johan Ludvig Heiberg ruled Danish literature around 1840. And Andersen felt that Heiberg often tried to curtail his career with aesthetically and philosophically based critiques. Heiberg, who was fifteen years older than Andersen, had made his breakthrough in the mid–1820s with several successful vaudevilles. The two men first met in 1827-28, and at that time they were favorably disposed toward each other. Heiberg published many of Andersen's early poems in his journal and paved the way for the publication of his novel *Walking Tour* in 1828-29 by printing excerpts and a major review of the book.

25. The critic Christian Molbech was dubbed "the disgruntled beast." In 1835, when Andersen began publishing a series of fairy tales that made Molbech's own fairy-tale books pale in comparison, the critic's tone turned vicious. Molbech and Andersen never ceased hating each other, and in 1839 Andersen wrote in a letter: "Molbech wants to grind me into the dust, but I am going to live on, live on while he is a dead name in an ancient folio."

26. Portraits of Hereditary Grand Duke Carl Alexander von Sachsen-Weimar-Eisenach and his wife, Princess Sophie of the Netherlands, in the 1850s. At that time, Carl Alexander was a handsome and quite boyish man with narrow shoulders and a slender waist. Following in the proud footsteps of his grandfather, he became a patron of the arts and sciences.

27. During a visit to Graasten Castle in 1845, Andersen made this paper-cut, which reveals his life's dream: uniting a lanky author figure with a stout and powerful king. Underneath he wrote in German: "The singer must walk with the king / Both stand at the pinnacle of humanity."

"Our temperaments are quite different; my very softness was enough to bend me to your will! If I had possessed the feeling at home that is now stirring inside me, then your manner would have certainly pushed me away, back when I didn't know you. With all the trust of a child I offered you my brotherly 'du,' and you rejected me! Then I wept and fell silent; this has always remained like an open wound, but my very softness, my semi-womanliness, allowed me to cling to you when I managed to see so many other glorious qualities in you, so I had to love you, remembering that it was merely a small flaw among so much else that was good. Do not misunderstand me, Edvard! Now it is my turn to use that phrase you so often say to me! The two of us must be sincere with each other; my soul lies open to you . . . Since you complain that I write too many letters, I suppose that I ought not send this one to you, but I need to talk to you, because you are night and day in my mind; I share everything spiritually with you! If only you could understand my love."[98]

But Edvard Collin neither could nor would understand. In particular, a phrase such as "my semi-womanliness allowed me to cling to you" must have struck him right in the solar plexus. Even though Edvard Collin, of course, did not consider Andersen to be a sodomite or a pederast—he more likely viewed him as an innocent Tartuffe, as Andersen himself had suggested in a letter from Paris[99]—it was still, under any circumstances, a repugnant exposure and display of a man's "sickly soft" nature. The fact that Andersen had suddenly started to call himself a "semi-woman" may have also worried Edvard Collin on a more legal level. The politician and civil servant Anders Sandøe Ørsted was a close friend of the Collin family, and he was a frequent guest in their home. Edvard Collin clearly must have known that around 1830 Anders Sandøe Ørsted was working to strengthen the threat of punishment that had always been part of the law regarding "conduct against nature between men." Pederasty was no longer something that should be silenced to death and be kept outside the societal reality in Denmark. It was now to be treated in keeping with and within the same common administration of justice as other crimes. So in 1833-34, when Andersen initiates Collin into the secret about his constitutional "softness and semi-womanliness," Denmark is moving toward a different and more visible form of justice regarding pederasts. Sexual relations between men had suddenly become something very real, and this development meant that the role and identity of a "pederast" began to be consolidated over the course of the next decades.[100]

★ ★ ★

Collin's letter, with his definitive critical obliteration of *Agnete and the Merman*, which Andersen received in Rome in early January 1834, also contained other unpleasant news. By way of introduction, he informed Andersen that the author's old mother and last remaining relative had died back home in Odense. But that didn't mean that this was a letter offering any kind of consolation. Keeping in mind Andersen's latest talk about his feminine nature, Collin harshly and methodically proceeded to execute *Agnete*, supported by Just Mathias Thiele, whom he cites in the letter: "I'm sending back the manuscript and washing my hands; you should do the same! We may one day regret that we served as godparents to this child."[101] This long letter—one of the longest Edvard Collin ever wrote to Andersen —contained no wishes for a Merry Christmas or Happy New Year. On the other hand, it did contain an introduction to Edvard's healthiest child in the south, namely "The Danish Library" in Rome. This was an institution that Collin, using his position as secretary of the foundation *Ad usus publicos*, had taken the initiative to establish. The fact that in his letter he so literally claims paternity for a few stacks of bound books was no random joke but pure and simple rhetoric:

> "No doubt you've made frequent visits to my library—I call it mine, since in some sense it is my child; and if so, then it has the honor of being my first-born. I shall never forget it. I will always strive to maintain it by sending the best that Denmark produces in a literary respect."[102]

But Andersen had also now reached a point where it was necessary to retreat and set a limit. In September 1833, when he received the first negative reaction to *Agnete and the Merman*, he noted in his diary that he would no longer put up with such condescending treatment. And when he received Collin's letter with all his criticisms along with news of his mother's death and the death of his own honor, it was the last straw. In despair and rage, Andersen sat down and wrote a letter which, returning in kind, dealt with this unbearable "badgering" and much, much more. The letter was folded up and enclosed in a letter to Jonas Collin, who could then give it to his son if he wished, after having looked at it and drawn his own conclusions. Andersen was giving his friend the cold shoulder, and at the same time ensuring that the patriarch of "the home of homes" would be embroiled in this dispute between sons. Not so that the father would mediate, but so that he would realize how coarse and heartless his biological son truly was. And later that same month, when Andersen wrote to Louise Collin, he made sure to instruct her to give his greetings to everyone in her family and circle of friends—except her brother. If Andersen no longer wrote or spoke directly to his friend, outwardly trying to deny his existence, in his thoughts Edvard was constantly on his mind and in his diary:

> "*Eduard*, the more I think about everything, the more I see your matchless egoism, the monstrous injustice that I am suffering; you have created a breach between us that will doubtless never be mended."[103]

Here we catch a glimpse of the proud, strong, and deeply injured Andersen. Not until the end of February 1834, when he received a letter from Edvard, did he again write directly to his friend. In this manner their friendship survived this crisis too—even though *Agnete* and the Danish Library in Rome did not come to share the same father. A strong line had been drawn on both sides of the friendship front. Especially because old Jonas Collin, with diplomatic finesse, had known how to protect both sons. He burned Andersen's letter at once, and then spoke to his son in private. To the author in Rome he wrote calmly and deliberately:

> "He [Edvard] is at heart extremely fond of you and is, when needed, your warmest spokesman . . . At every opportunity he takes an interest in you, without wishing to draw attention to himself. In that sense he is like Gottlieb [Edvard's older brother] and like his father, who do not wish to have anyone look into their heart. I do not subscribe to his lecturing of you. But my good Andersen, do not hold it against him. Everyone has his weakness, and that is his. We must be tolerant of each other . . . I end with the best wishes for your welfare. Your paternally devoted Collin."[104]

The Androgynous One

To understand Collin's aversion to *Agnete and the Merman*, the play must be viewed as more than a work of dramatic art. It has to be read either as a novel or as part of an ongoing discussion, in writing, between the two friends, during which one of them suddenly projects all his feelings and urges onto a big screen and shouts: "Look at me, this is how I am!"

The old folk ballad about Agnete and the strong, secret forces of nature that ravage human beings was a frequently used myth in the early Romantic period in Denmark. Danish authors such as Johannes Ewald,

Schack Staffeldt, Jens Baggesen, and Adam Oehlenschläger had all made use of it before Andersen. And it was especially Oehlenschläger's interpretation of the folktale that intrigued Andersen. In Oehlenschläger's version, Agnete does not belong either above or below the water; death has to resolve her existential conflict, and in the end her spiritual and corporeal longings all merge. As Andersen writes in the epilogue to the first part of his play: "If you want to see the image of love, / Then seek the foam on the shore!"[105] The story is about Agnete, filled with longing, who chooses the powerful merman instead of the weak fiddler and half-brother who has far too much "maiden's blood" in him. The story appealed to Andersen's imagination. Here was a well-known, Romantic narrative and several folktale figures that he could use in order to write about himself, his moods, and his emotions. So the stage for the drama about the fragmented Agnete was also set inside of Andersen, and that's why *Agnete and the Merman* became such a sensational blend of ancient folk poetry and the introspection, reflection, and daydreams of a modern young writer.

We can find the twenty-eight-year-old Andersen in both Agnete and her half-brother Hemming, who loves and desires his half-sister, repeatedly calling her "half of my being."[106] Hemming is not especially extroverted or energetic, but he does have great insight into his inhibited nature, and at the beginning of the play he acknowledges that he is "too soft as a man."[107] But if Hemming is very conscious of who he is, Agnete, on the other hand, is bewildered by and unaware of the dual roots of her character. Whereas her half-brother is a man with too much woman in him, she is similarly a woman with too much man in her. This is a typical conflict for many of Andersen's protagonists in his plays and novels from the 1830s. As the merman says to Agnete: "Your soul is strong and bold like a whale, / a man's courage and thoughts live inside you."[108] And when Hintze, the rich butcher, shows up at the beginning of the play and proposes to Agnete, she rejects him with these words: "There is a mighty longing inside my soul, / that drives me on, I cannot explain!"[109] Something in her female nature goes beyond her gender, and this restless seeking for something indefinable is a constitutional element in Agnete's character. Like Hemming, she is capable of looking deep within at her divided nature, but she also has to conclude that she can neither understand nor explain her uncontrollable longing: "I am a strange and unfortunate being, / who wishes only for what I myself cannot comprehend!"[110]

Agnete, who would rather be out on the shore with a becalmed sea and a full moon than inside her family's stifling rooms, is an amphibian. She is neither the first nor the last mermaid and toad figure that we will meet in Andersen's works. There is a direct line from the figure of Agnete to the fairy tale "The Little Mermaid," written in 1837, and "The Marsh King's Daughter" from 1858. For that matter, there is also a link to Hans Christian Andersen himself, who all his life loved to romp through the waves among other mermaids and mermen. In fact, throughout his life Andersen was something of a water fanatic and loved to swim. On the shores of Denmark and abroad, he would rediscover his own persona in the sea. In Barcelona, at Basnæs and Skagen, at Copenhagen Harbor, Præstø Fjord, and the tidal flats of Føhr, he loved to throw himself into the waves so he could then rise up again—as he said—with a feeling of being reborn and see the world from a whole different perspective. After one such refreshing visit to Skagen Beach in August 1859, when he made do with paddling in the water and riding in a horse-drawn buggy along the shoreline, Andersen writes in his diary: "It was like an amphibian journey, half in the water, half on land."[111]

In the same way, Agnete is torn between the sea and the earth, and life in the heavy surf is the young girl's inheritance, since she comes into this world at the point where sea and earth meet. Her parents have gone out to fish at low tide when her mother, Gertrud, suddenly goes into labor and has to give birth in a wrecked ship stranded on the sand. And this birth— as her mother hints—has marked the beautiful, good daughter for life. She has the entire raw and wild underwater world in her blood. On the other hand, life on earth, with all its cultivated nature, does not have the same seductive power over her, and soon the elements begin fighting for Agnete's soul. In the first part of the play, a highly colorful and harmonious orchestra consisting of a talking beech forest, flowers, fairies, hunting horns, and church bells—probably some of the most bizarre minor roles ever to be seen on a Danish stage—rallies around Agnete's earthly suitors, Hintze the butcher and Hemming her half-brother, trying to wake her. This takes place during a fierce battle on stage with an even more powerful chorus consisting of waves, storms, and sea birds, all intent on serving the much stronger merman. He has begun to materialize on shore for Agnete in the figure of a handsome knight, and he speaks directly to her desire and dreams of love.

Agnete surrenders to nature, following her instincts, and allows the merman to take her. The day before she is to marry her half-brother, she disappears into the sea, where the energetic merman immediately builds her an enchanted palace, adorned with "diamonds from Bornholm" and pieces of amber filled with insects and blossoms. Two whales with their tails bound together form the entrance to the palace, while the floors of the halls are made of sparkling fish scales. And from Italy and Greece he has brought back silk fabrics and polished marble gods. Oh yes, they know how to celebrate great love down in the sea, and the results are soon forthcoming: Agnete quickly becomes the mother of three children, and she could have lived happily to the end of her days if it weren't for the fact that she is an amphibian. She possesses a deeply split nature that houses two possible forms of existence.

Agnete cannot stop thinking about what she has renounced. She feels a great sense of longing. So when her children start asking about her family and the unknown grandparents on their mother's side, there is no avoiding it. Her longing becomes an ever-growing call; Agnete has to return home, go up on land, and see once again her loved ones and the part of herself that she had abandoned. But it's impossible to build bridges across the deep division inside of Agnete. Like so many other tragic heroes and heroines in the works of Hans Christian Andersen, she is condemned to eternal homelessness. The sea and the land inside her do not share the same space and time. Her seven years at the bottom of the sea are now traded for fifty human years on land. When her somewhat worried merman allows her to spend a single hour in the earthly element of her childhood and youth, it turns out that her mother, Gertrud, is dead, and Hemming has become an ancient and even more pitiable fiddler, who has devoted his whole life to mourning the loss of his beloved half-sister. Now Agnete understands her long-standing blindness to the family and God that she once deserted, and with a broken and contrite heart she asks: "Where does compassion reside?" Can she be forgiven?

No, in Agnete's case there is no mercy, because what she is up against is her own nature. She is the way she is. The woman with the man inside— like her brother with the sister inside—is condemned to live and die in the strong surf where she was born. "Forgive me, Lord Jesus! Receive me, deep sea!" Agnete cries, beside herself, as she tries to go back to the water. But she collapses, lifeless, among the rocks and dies at the boundary where she was born, in the territory of mermaids and mermen, amphibians, hermaphrodites, and other androgynous creatures.

Now, *Agnete and the Merman* is no Shakespeare or Schiller drama, and it does seem both a little too clever and rather awkward that the author moves the second half of the play forward fifty years in time and promptly introduces ten to fifteen new characters on stage. The restless Andersen loves these quantum leaps in time and space, which, from a dramaturgical perspective, are deeply problematic. They also made the directors and actors tear out their hair in desperation. But if the play is read with our eyes today, it is still an extremely lively piece of literature. The play is a portrait of a strong woman, full of longing, who was born with an invisible fish-tail, and whose double nature Andersen would use again several years later in his story "The Little Mermaid." The play has both artistic and deeply psychological stature. In places the play is also astonishingly modern, with the brief inserted calls for women's emancipation, such as: "Even a woman's thoughts are a bound falcon on the hand of a man, trained to do his will." And the play not only discusses a young woman's sexual desire ("the wild fire of the blood"), but it also presents the difficult existential choice between security and freedom. Should a person choose firm ground underfoot, or dare—as Agnete does—to move out into the deep water?

The second half of the play is particularly interesting because Andersen here moves definitively away from the soft, feminine man, Agnete's half-brother Hemming, who not once in his life is capable of satisfying a woman's erotic longings. Instead, after the first scenes, the author shifts his attention and focus to Agnete, whose blood flows in a more brisk and vir-ile manner. This is the same type of shift in point of view—from weak man to strong woman—that is repeated several years later, although in a much more striking, almost schizophrenic way, in the novel *Only a Fiddler*. In the beginning of this book the author also conceals himself in the fiction behind a weak man (Christian). Then, midway through the novel, as in *Agnete and the Merman*, he jumps several decades ahead in time, and strips Christian of the main role, shoving him to the background in favor of the strong woman, Naomi. She, along with the narrator, is prepared to follow her longing beyond all boundaries.

This curious playing with male and female roles, which is so conspic-uous in Andersen's literary works in the 1830s, has to do with the identity of a human being, both physically and in terms of sex. This is strongly emphasized in *Agnete and the Merman* with the inserted story at the begin-ning of the play's second half, when we follow along with the preparations for a wedding on a Fyn estate in the 12th century and hear about two mar-riage-eligible sisters. They are the wild and mannish Maiden Bodil, who wants freedom at any price, and the gentle and femininely shy Maiden Karen, who prefers security to freedom. This story has absolutely nothing to do with the folktale text, but its intent is to make the reader aware of the core problem in Agnete's dual nature: her feeling of having both sexes inside, and thus two different directions in which to develop. This is in addition to her longing to be someone other than she is. As Andersen also wrote in the preface to the play, he wanted to illustrate a human being's singular yearning for something other than what he possesses, this "striving for an unknown, new existence."[112] And by means of the little side story about Maiden Bodil and Maiden Karen in *Agnete and the Merman*, Andersen shows us additional paths into the story about the oddly bisexual nature of certain men and women.

The idea of the bisexual, androgynous individual, who unites essential elements of both sexes—and even in some cases possesses both sex organs and can thus be called hermaphrodite—can be traced all the way back to antiquity. All through the history of civilization this concept of the androgynous person has continued to exist and develop in art—for instance, in the work of Shakespeare and Mozart—as a game with gender and sex roles. In the period 1790–1840 the androgynous person becomes a metaphysically integrated part of the Romantic zeitgeist, which is apparent not only in art but also in science. An example of this is H. C. Ørsted's holistic concept of "the spirit in nature," which was the title of his last great book in 1850 and a strong expression for the entire era's optimistic view and belief that opposites and divisions can meet and unite in an all-encompassing idea or guiding principle.[113] But the androgynous person was also a rhetorical figure in the literature of Romanticism, an emblem of unity and a symbol for the longing to include and merge not only the two genders but also the fragmented universe—from the smallest leaf to animals and humans to the farthest galaxies. It was possible to conceive of and intuit the interconnection of all things during Romanticism, based on the idea of the androgynous person, who possessed not only male and female aspects, but possibly a third sex as well, which was created through the union and dynamism of the two opposites.

The notion of complementarity was a large and important part of the Romantic philosophy of nature. For instance, we see this in the ideas of Friedrich Wilhelm Schelling, who, in his lectures around 1800, pointed out the living coherence in nature and demonstrated the unity of all things that seem to be opposites. The basic principle of nature and its development is polarity, Schelling said, as well as the idea that an original entity divides into two opposites, which then once again strive to unite. This is precisely as we know it from Aristotle's myth about the former cohesion of the sexes, to which Hans Christian Andersen often referred in his works. This is evident, for example, in the play *On Langebro*, in which the main character, Frantz, who loves the young impoverished Meta, says:

> "I once read an old book in which a certain Greek said and wrote of marriage that every person is like half a sphere that went rolling out into the world, rolling and rolling, to find its other half. Many met others that didn't fit properly, but many also met their appropriate halves, and then united to roll off in eternal happiness. My other half is Meta, and I am hers."[114]

This serious game of the sexes during Romanticism, and the whole idea of the androgynous person, can also be traced in Goethe's *Wilhelm Meister's Apprenticeship* (1795-96), in which the figure of Mignon is an image of the divine androgyny. We also catch a glimpse of the androgynous person in the work of Novalis in the 1790s, including the idea of a "divine primordial human." And it is present in Friedrich Schlegel's sophisticated novel *Lucinde* (1799), and later in the novel *The Queen's Diadem* (1834) by the Swedish writer C. J. L. Almquist, as well as in Honoré de Balzac's *Séraphita* (1835), and Théophile Gautier's *Mademoiselle de Maupin* (1836). In these works all possible, diverse, opposing pursuits are united in universal virginal figures such as Mignon, Lucinde, and Almquist's enchanting female figure Tintomara. To this list of androgynous female characters during Romanticism, we might add four of Hans Christian Andersen's figures from the 1830s: Agnete, the mermaid in "The Little Mermaid," Hanne in *Meeting and Parting*, and Naomi in *Only a Fiddler*.

The Improvisatore

In the spring of 1834, when Andersen was on his way home to Denmark, he and Edvard Collin had reconciled, as always happened after a bitter dispute between the two brothers. It was as if each had been given permission to express his fury—and nothing had changed. After Edvard's crass critique of *Agnete and the Merman* and Andersen's stubborn refusal to write any letters to him for two months, thus allowing his friend to taste some of his own medicine, the two had once again put their improprieties and misunderstandings behind them. It's evident in their correspondence from the spring of 1834 that Andersen's nearly year-long trip was coming to an end, and with that a new phase of their friendship was beginning, and neither of them truly knew what this might mean. The author had been far away in the world and deep inside himself. In a letter from Munich at the end of May 1834, he took stock of their friendship—and promised far too much: "Never will I touch on this matter again; it leads to a whimpering that is unworthy of a man."[115]

That sounded too good to be true, but there was something to his promise, as it turned out. During the winter of 1834-35, Andersen moved into third-floor lodgings at Nyhavn 20 in the house of Karen Sophie Larsen, and because he was in acute need of money, he applied for a position at the Royal Library. At that time there was apparently a certain "manly," respectable distance between the two friends. The following summer Andersen was staying at the Lykkesholm estate on Fyn and making a final appraisal of his trip to Italy, which during the winter had resulted in a long novel containing many Italian motifs. At that time Andersen still seemed outwardly composed and levelheaded about his friendship with Edvard Collin. In his first letter from the Fyn estate to his friend in Copenhagen, it seemed as if Andersen, for a brief moment, had stepped outside of their relationship to regard it from a slight distance and to evaluate whether the relationship had actually changed:

> "It's my friend that I'm speaking to, the only one I have, the one who is my friend as completely as he can be, in accordance with the circumstances of his life. I seem cheerful, happy; perhaps I have never felt greater pain than since I returned home. I can't help it. I feel myself a stranger here at home, my thoughts dwell solely in Italy. Oh, Eduard, if you had breathed in that air, seen all that loveliness, you would long as I do. Remember that I have no parents, no family, no bride—never will! I am so exceedingly alone in the world."[116]

In spite of his despondency and pessimism, Andersen actually radiated calm and dignity during this period, which might seem surprising. Even though, judging by his letter, he was treated royally at the Fyn estate and had every reason to rejoice over the birth of a new novel and a couple of small books of fairy tales, his future prospects in terms of love remained dim. "You now have a sweetheart, a loving, almost too beautiful little creature—yet I have one just as loving and even more beautiful: all of Nature. She has the intellect of an entire world, as well as a youth that will never diminish. She sings for me, she kisses me, and it's from her that

I obtain butter, buttermilk, and strawberries, all of them a perennial dowry."[117]

Yet Andersen's most important asset in 1835 was and remained his novel *The Improvisatore*, which was also about to be published in a German translation. It would have great importance for widening the Danish author's reputation in the rest of Europe. After a number of lean years in terms of finances in the wake of his debut in 1829, there were now signs of a fresh start. In April the novel came out in Danish, followed in May by a small book of fairy tales that, over time, would turn serious literature on its head. We will return to these tales in the next chapter.

The Improvisatore is a novel in which the depiction of the friendship between the protagonist Antonio and his friend Bernardo comes very close to the relationship between Andersen and Collin. As was the case with *Agnete and the Merman*, we recognize here characteristic lines taken from the correspondence of the two friends. For instance, Antonio says to Bernardo: "So often do I long for you—in such a way you cannot think of me; that's how it is with our different natures. But how I wish I had you!" This passage is identical, word for word, to a passage in one of Andersen's letters to Edvard in 1831.[118] And so Andersen has chosen to ignore his friend's request not to transfer parts of their private conversations to his art.

In literary history we often see *The Improvisatore* and *Only a Fiddler*, which was published two years later, categorized as artist novels. This means that the former novel is an account of what shaped the artist Antonio, created his works, and—as it says on the back of today's editions of Andersen's breakthrough novel—carried Antonio's life forward to "a happy ending, when he finally finds the woman of his life." We might as well call *The Improvisatore* a gender novel and point to the widely spun but never dropped thread in the plot, which Antonio seizes hold of down in the casemates of Rome as the novel begins. Both in terms of art and sex, this is a fateful thread, which the author uses to follow and explain both the male protagonist's improvisational talent and the nature of his sex, as well as the fact that Antonio is one "of those spiritual amphibians; you can't tell if they actually belong to the corporeal world or the world of dreams!"[119] Is it love he is longing for and seeking at the end of this thread? A woman, a man, both, or none at all?

These big, unresolved questions inside of Antonio—and inside Hans Christian Andersen himself—are further addressed in the thematic connections between *The Improvisatore* and the next two novels, *O. T.* and *Only a Fiddler*, which were published in quick succession. We're talking about three novels totaling a thousand pages, written in less than three years, which are quite close mental extensions of one another, since Andersen did not make any lengthy, disruptive trips abroad in 1835 or 1836. As a consequence, on an internal level, the three novels move along the same track and present the same issues: the development of a youth into a man and—in the case of Antonio and Christian—an artist. For this reason the three novels can be viewed as a trilogy about art, sex, and love, in which Andersen investigates, via a series of increasingly bold images, various forms of love, both earthly and divine. And on this inner journey, various sexual and artist roles are played out.

In *The Improvisatore*, Antonio's friends and benefactors subject the impoverished, orphaned young man to a comprehensive educational process for body and soul. A large part of this process has to do with orienting him toward a normal bourgeois pattern of sex roles, in which he, like the majority of men, will be united with a woman. Among Antonio's friends, including Bernardo, Santa, Federigo, Francesca, Fabiani, and Gennaro, there is an extraordinary amount of interest in Antonio's innocence and at regular intervals they complain about his childish fear of women. Antonio's virtuous nature is simply a thorn in the side of the public and these guards of normality with regard to sex and love. In the admonishing words of Santa: "You are also a man. We must find you some female company, teach you a few things about how to behave!"

This process described in the novel was a direct reflection of Hans Christian Andersen's own reality. It portrayed his repeated experience of always being lured into sexual traps and ambushes. For example, when he was a twenty-eight-year-old virgin in the midst of sensual Italy, he was a constant source of annoyance to the Nordic artists seated around the table in the Caffè Greco. On Christmas Eve in 1833, Andersen wrote a song in praise of innocence for the celebration held at the Villa Borghese. Everyone, of course, was expected to have vine leaves in their hair and, later in the evening, preferably a buxom woman in their arms, even though Andersen had tried to hold on to the pious Christmas mood with lines such as: "Let us, like the child, rejoice, / We are all children at heart, / The only difference from the child's soul / Our happy Christmas Eve!"[120] But the serpents at the Villa Borghese had begun to stir as the evening went on and the wine took effect. Andersen reported the next day in his diary that the Norwegian painter Thomas Fearnley had at one point begun whispering with the Danish sculptor Thorvaldsen about how someone ought to seduce the Danish archangel. Fearnley had talked at length, and in a loud voice, with the sculptor about Andersen's incomparable innocence.[121]

If Fearnley and the other younger artists were a constant threat to Andersen's innocence, then Thorvaldsen was just the opposite. He offered fatherly sympathy and seemed particularly sensitive and understanding toward the author. In January 1834, when a despondent Andersen, upset by letters from home, paid a call on Thorvaldsen, the sculptor was in the midst of his work on an enormous bas-relief. Nevertheless, he allowed himself to be interrupted and put aside his tools to listen to the pale and unhappy young man. The sculptor's hands were covered with clay, and when Andersen had finished talking, Thorvaldsen put his hand on the author's shoulder and told him that the important thing, not just for an artist but for a human being, was to feel and follow your own power. You should not, said Thorvaldsen, be led by the judgment of the masses but instead calmly proceed at your own tempo and in accordance with your own nature.

In *The Improvisatore*, which Andersen—encouraged by Thorvaldsen—started writing in Rome, Antonio is extremely aware throughout most of the novel of how different he is from others, both as an artist and as a sexual being. And what is both fortunate and unfortunate is that Antonio has a burning desire to follow his own nature. As he says to his good friend Bernardo: "I do not judge your view of life by mine; everyone must follow his own nature!"[122] Even as a sixteen-year-old, Antonio senses the otherness of his character. And here the author once again uses the word "dissonance," which appeared in *Shadow Pictures* in 1831 to describe the phenomenon. At the beginning of Chapter Eight he writes: "Resounding in my soul were dissonances that I myself was unable to resolve."[123] These dissonances are closely tied to the young man's shaky sexual identity and entire sexual nature. As the masculine Bernardo reminds Antonio, he is simply "a paltry man," whose hot Italian blood has been diluted with goat's milk. And all the Trappist abstinence hasn't done him any good either.[124] Whereas Bernardo seeks out and establishes carnal relationships with the opposite sex, Antonio settles for giving his friend amorous looks and listening to his reports of these rendezvous, which he then converts to art. Bernardo calls Antonio cowardly. He mockingly refers to his friend's intensive reading of Dante's *Divine Comedy* and the fact that Antonio's eyes easily burn with the same sensual fire and masculinity as Bernardo's. "I've seen it myself!" says Bernardo. And he's right, because Antonio has always been in love with Bernardo, with whom he went to school. He is practically obsessed with his friend, and he has elevated and encapsulated his love into a shrine, which means that he might suddenly say to Bernardo: "I have to enter your magic circle!"[125] His love for Bernardo bursts into flames in earnest at a grand ball in the Villa Borghese in Rome when Antonio, filled with yearning, catches sight of his friend's Adonis figure. On that evening Bernardo looks like a Greek youth carved from marble, clothed in a handsome red, gold-embroidered uniform and tight, chalk-white pants. "Everything fit so ethereally on those lovely forms; he danced with the most beautiful of all; he gave him an intimate and loving smile. How it vexed me that I could not dance."[126]

Antonio, who is waltzing around inside at the sight of Bernardo, comes to a panicked standstill when a woman invites him for a little free exertion on the dance floor. Then he says, firmly and obstinately: "I don't dance, I never dance!" And things get worse when women entice him into embraces that he finds abominable if they are not the motherly or sisterly kind. We hear that from the time he was a child, Antonio has had a terrified aversion to female embraces, in which he risks disappearing in a fragrant suffocation. When the child Antonio is embraced by the lovely Matiuccia, who often models for the painter Federigo, and she presses his head to her breasts and bare shoulder, Antonio tears himself away with the words: "I don't want to have any sweetheart or any wife! . . . I want to be a priest or a Capuchin like Fra Martino!"[127]

Yet *The Improvisatore* ends with Antonio's charmingly normal wedding to a woman who is so ethereal in Andersen's description that we forget about her the instant the book is closed. But this does not mean that Antonio's education has been a success; rather, it's an expression of the author's powerlessness with regard to the unfolding and fulfillment of the deeper themes of his novel: art, sex, and love. Antonio's beloved Bernardo quietly fades away on a waiting sidetrack of the novel, where he is apparently parked as an unattainable ideal. But he will soon return in new disguises in *O. T.* and *Only a Fiddler.*

The same thing occurred in Hans Christian Andersen's own life in 1834–36 when the real Edvard Collin was tentatively set aside in favor of the dream about Edvard. As the author phrases it in a letter six months before the publication of *The Improvisatore*:

> "In the evening I feel sensitive. Last night I again wrote a verse for you that you will not receive. Now don't think this is the old sensitivity; no, as my Neapolitan Signora says, it's as if the heart longs for something

outside, and so I have the idealistic Eduard, a very loving friend. And I stretch out my arms toward him, but it's not you at all; you have far too many flaws, shadow sides, and phantoms for me to dream about you."[128]

Wedding in the Collin Family

In the summer of 1836 it was time for Edvard Collin and Henriette Thyberg to celebrate their wedding, and the bridegroom was apparently taking no chances. "My wedding day has not yet been decided," he casually writes at the end of a rather lengthy letter to Andersen in July. At the time, Andersen was vacationing on Fyn, but he wasn't so far away that he couldn't accept an invitation to the ceremony if the bridal couple wanted him to attend. But they did not. No more doors were going to be left ajar for the profoundly difficult "brother," who had recently tried to squeeze his way in between the bride and groom in the most cunning manner. During the spring and summer of 1836, everyone in the Collin family circle—except for Andersen—seemed to have been regularly kept abreast of where and when the wedding would take place. Andersen had to continually ask about it. Not until July 29 did he receive word that the wedding would most likely take place on Thursday or Friday of the following week, and the news came not from his friend but from Jonas Collin. The site for the wedding was not revealed, and in yet another letter from the elder Collin—written five days later—it was announced that the date for the wedding had finally been set for Wednesday, August 10. Where it would take place was still a secret, and Andersen didn't receive the letter until the day before the wedding. That was why he didn't have time to send the wedding song that he had offered to Edvard Collin back in June. Knowing how excessively ambiguous and embarrassing Andersen could be, the bridal couple was probably not at all disappointed that neither the author nor his song was in attendance. And on August 13, Jonas Collin briefly informed Andersen that the ceremony had taken place in Søllerød, while the wedding banquet was held at the Fortunen Inn.

It might seem like an insult that a close friend of both the groom and his family should be kept away, but it was most likely an arrangement that was absolutely necessary. It may also have been done at Henriette Thyberg's request. Over a long period of time, through his letters, Hans Christian Andersen had finagled his way into the couple's engagement in the most imaginative and scheming ways, trying to interfere by alluding to everything that he and Edvard Collin had shared. Nor did Andersen make any bones about the fact that, for his part, he intended to achieve exactly the same goal in the friendship as a man and woman seek in the intimacy of marriage. In a rhetorical sense the prospective bride had many times been written off onto an emotional sidetrack while at the same time Andersen—in casual little phrases—downplayed the emotional significance of marriage in general ("A very good house is the chief concern in a marriage"[129]). Or else he would actually ask Collin to solicit a kiss from his betrothed, which was supposed to be from Andersen— or from one of the characters in a novel who was haunting the author's consciousness:

> "The sun is warm and I'm talking to my dear, dear Edvard! Ask Jette to tell you so beautifully from me: *'I love you!'* Surely she dares say *'love,'* surely she can use the informal *du*. With a man it sounds like sentimentality, and that is something that I have shaken off my sleeve, just like Bernardo, shaking off his innocence. So instead of this *'I love you!'* let us always say *'I'm teasing you!'* and use the formal means of address. If the intention is good, it shouldn't make any difference."[130]

In this mischievous triangle, which no doubt was more fun for Andersen than for anyone else, the novel *O. T.* from 1836 plays an important role. The book was written during the summer and fall of 1835; as previously mentioned, it deals with yet another fraternally tender friendship between two young men. These two men not only resemble Edvard Collin and Hans Christian Andersen, but in large part they are actually meant to be the two friends. The book was intended as a sort of wedding present, and while Andersen was writing it, he had quietly started to interfere in his friend's betrothal with a poem and his new novel under his arm. The poem was addressed to "My dear Edvard's Jette," with the subtitle "With the promise of a new novel that I am now working on." The poem was sent to Henriette Thyberg on her birthday at the end of October 1835. And in verse Andersen promised her a new novel with the working title "The Two Students." The novel was to be about two young men who had been unable to stay together:

"Consider among today's gifts / my promise of: The Two Students, / a new novel known only to me, / soon will kiss your hands, / I alone cannot give it beauty! / With you it will become the most beautiful."[131]

Andersen had already told his friend many times over the course of the summer in 1835 that Edvard would play a significant and intimate part in his new novel, which eventually was titled *O. T.* The first time Andersen mentions this (on July 27), he assures Edvard that it's nothing more than an innocent story from their school days, to which he will give a nod of recognition. But a month later (on August 28), the whole issue and the material culled from reality for use in the novel have taken an ardent turn. Through his writing, Andersen has clearly revitalized his feelings for his friend—so much so that in his letter he openly calls Edvard "a lovely woman from Calabria with the dark eyes and fiery glance."[132] In the same breath he repeats the old questions he had actually promised never to ask again: Why won't Edvard love him? Why can't they use the informal "du" with each other? And in the same desperate line of thought, Andersen reports that their friendship will be the subject of a thorough examination in his forthcoming novel. There's no way of avoiding this, and so his friend must be prepared to see that significant elements of himself and his relationship with Andersen will soon be made public:

> "In my new novel there is a character for whom I have borrowed many elements from you. You will see how dear you are to me, and with what care I handle this character. But you have flaws, and the character will have more than you. He will have some of your flaws—can you forgive me for this? He wounds the hero of the book in such a way as I once—I imagined a story that I can never forget, unless I became a nobleman and you [were] in a lower position in life than I, and that is an impossibility! I must portray this character this way, although I knew you would not approve. I could give up the novel, even though it would have been my greatest triumph. Our friendship is a wondrous creation! No one has been so much the object of my anger as you! No one have I ever wanted to thrash, no one has brought so many tears to my eyes, and yet no one has ever been so loved by me as you are. I would despair if I lost you. Our friendship is perfectly suited to such a portrayal, and yet—I fear that it must not happen. Perhaps it seems unnatural to show this contrast and yet great harmony!"[133]

We don't know how Edvard Collin reacted to the novel when it was published in April 1836—four months before his wedding. But it's indirectly evident from Andersen's announcement of yet another new novel in the summer of 1836 that *O. T.* could not be ignored and that it had presumably been the subject of a curt and sharp discussion in private. The new novel was to be about a fiddler, and a sarcastic Andersen writes to his friend: "A new novel is haunting my thoughts. Doesn't that make you especially happy? My greetings to your sweetheart!"

When Andersen left for his summer vacation on June 1, 1836—heading for Næstved, Sorø, Slagelse, and Fyn—he knew that his friend's wedding would take place sometime that summer, and he undoubtedly could sense that he would not be welcome. He had bid Collin a nice, polite farewell in Copenhagen and sent him a bottle that did not contain bitters but rather stout, which the author couldn't drink in the heat. And he had also threatened to send Edvard an opera manuscript with the highly apropos title *Renzo's Wedding*. This might have been seen as a provocation, but Andersen merely asked his friend, tactfully and courteously, to read through the manuscript with his usual sharp attention to all the linguistic false notes. By the end of July 1836, Andersen had reached the butter-yellow estate of Lykkesholm on Fyn, where he had worked on *O.T.* during the previous summer in the very same tower room with the vaulted ceiling, round white stove, and view of the moat. This was the room he had used for the setting of a central scene in the novel, in which the two male friends embrace and decide to travel to Italy together. In a letter to Henriette Wulff, Andersen describes the rather bizarre situation with the words:

> "I am here at the estate you find described in *O.T.* where Louise and Sophie lived. I have the room that I had imagined Otto lived in, and this year it seems to me as if I had almost lived the whole story myself."[134]

At first Andersen seemed to be flying high in this surreal mixture of fact and fiction. He was sitting in the stage set for his novel and writing copious, merrily teasing letters to Edvard Collin, who refused to be Andersen's "novel friend" and was soon to be married. Andersen, on the other hand, was like Otto in *O.T.* and had to make do with dreaming about marriage and about his friend. But Andersen's tone grew sharper during July 1836, when he received a letter from Edvard Collin, who called Andersen "my worthy friend." That was the last straw. Worthy! How reserved and impersonal could someone be in a close friendship?

> "Why do you call me your 'worthy friend'? I don't want to be worthy! That is the most insipid, boring word you could use. Any fool can be called worthy! . . . I don't want to be worthy, *refuse to be worthy*, maybe I have hotter blood than you and half of Copenhagen. Eduard, I feel so infuriated by this loathsome weather! I also long for you, to shake you, to

see your hysterical laughter, to be able to walk away, insulted, and not come back home to you for two whole days."[135]

As a sort of demonstration of his own engagement, Andersen enclosed with his letter a poem that was more effusive than any other he had previously written to his friend. And Collin had learned the origins of the poem in a letter sent earlier in the summer, when an unrestrained Andersen told him that he had taken a "provincial rose" to bed one evening, kissing it the way a nun kisses her Infant Jesus, and then placing it under his pillow. In his letter of reply, Edvard Collin had promptly stifled all such nonsense with a nit-picking comment about the syntax of the poem: "What does it mean to kiss the bed?"[136] At the same time, he asked about one of Andersen's previously announced poems, and that gave the author an opportunity to improvise in the provinces an entirely new poem about the rose kiss, addressed to the bridegroom in the capital:

> Rosebud, so firm and round,
> Lovely as a young girl's mouth!
> I kiss you as my bride!
> Ever lovelier, you blossom forth.
> One more kiss my lips will send you,
> Feel how I am burning!
>
> I confess to you, as I should,
> That I have never kissed another.
> No young girl waits for me!
> Rose, I must kiss you.
> Ah, you do not know my longing.
> Feel how I am burning![137]

When Andersen arrived in Svendborg two weeks later, the previously mentioned letter from Jonas Collin was waiting for him, with the news that the date for Edvard's wedding had now been set. Andersen didn't have time—as someone like Henrik Hertz might have done—to write a wedding song. Instead, he chose to write a dual letter to the bridal couple in which Edvard, for his part, was informed in no uncertain terms about the future sensitive friendship with Andersen. Even though Andersen's demands would always be much greater than his friend's, he could make do with the unequal division of emotions, and he concluded: "Give me as much as you can, you are the one I love most."[138]

In the other letter—to "my dear Edvard's Jette!"—he conscientiously delivered a kiss on the hand in addition to a few words of good, solid advice with regard to the friend whom Andersen felt he knew far better than Jette did. Among other things, Andersen said that she shouldn't allow her husband to have all the power. Nor should she allow him to become bad-tempered, or yield to him on every issue. "He must be set to his pace, handled in the proper manner."[139] Finally, Andersen asked the bride to give the groom a loving kiss from the author, and he added that he would soon pay a visit to their little household. He was looking forward with great pleasure to the couple's happiness, and, of course, to resuming his friendship with the man of the house. Edvard had not heard the last of him.

Chapter Five

In Fairy Land (1835-1840)

"Tell us a story, Anser!" says the girl with the red bows, and her older sister nods eagerly.[1] The author puts down his big scissors and unfolds the orange paper-cut as little scraps of paper sprinkle onto the floor. He sets the row of merry men on the table and blows on them gently so they start dancing hand in hand across the tabletop. The girls laugh loudly and then start pestering him again for a story. Anser promised them, after all, because they were so nice about helping him to pull a bad gooseberry thorn out of his thumb and blow on the wound.

The author's big hand slides slowly over his face, from his forehead to his mouth, as he peers at the delicate, round shoulders of one of the girls. She gives him a special confidential smile. Some of the grown-ups say that Anser looks so horrid, but the children know that as soon as he takes his hand away from his mouth, he is no longer a troll with a big nose and small eyes, but a butterfly that will carry them on his wings over land and sea to gentle places out in a forest where the air is always mild and the moss gleams like green fire. They've tried this before, these girls, and they know that there are other worlds than the one to which they awake each morning. Just as there are different kinds of grown-ups. Anser once told them that a person could easily be black on the outside and white as a swan on the inside.

"I wonder if you know the story 'The Fairies' Flowers'?" he asks and then slowly begins to tell them, in verse, about the poor little farmhouse out in the country with grass and house leeks growing on the rooftop. Once upon a time a little girl was sitting outside, drawing on the ground among the dock plants:

> *And as she played, from the forest edge*
> *came two beautiful children in white gowns,*
> *each bore a flower clear as a diamond,*
> *and with a scent like the scent of violets.*
> *They said, "Come! Now you shall see,*

many more are growing in there!"
Then they went into the forest, all three.
And the little girl was never seen again.

Both of the children are staring at Anser's lips, which keep opening and closing. Out come birds, trees, bushes, flowers, sunshine and clouds, and from leaves and blossoms hop tiny, bright figures. They are the flower spirits, dressed in transparent clothes and with wreaths of lilies shimmering like silver on their heads. Leading the way is the Fairy King, searching for the place in the forest where the moon shines brightest. When he finds the spot and touches the ground with his scepter, masses of silver lilies spring up at once, forming a mighty throne. And there the Fairy King sits down with his Queen. Other fairies—many more than the two girls can count—lie down quietly, rocking in the calyxes of the flowers and sipping at the honey dew. Those who are too restless to sit still are sliding down the damp leaves or swinging in the spiderwebs.

In the background Anser's voice can be heard, telling the story of the girl who disappeared into the forest. One day her little brother was also lured away to Fairy Land. Many years passed, but the children never came back. Then their mother died, and the grieving father was left all alone, without children or wife, but with a long and lonely life. He would often go to the churchyard, sit down on the three graves sprinkled with sand, and look up at the clouds. One time, on an autumn evening, he saw some strange clouds off in the distance:

> *Then a swarm of children came down from the forest,*
> *floating with flowers beyond compare,*
> *and two walked hand in hand, he knew them,*
> *they were his own little boy and girl.*
> *They were headed for church; the others*
> *raced lightly across the field, like doves in the air.*
> *He saw them go to their mother's grave,*
> *they brought flowers, he smelled the scent.*
> *"My children!" exclaimed the father joyfully,*
> *and ran inside to the churchyard graves.*
> *In the moonlight he could see each leaf,*
> *there was a scent like in a flower garden,*
> *but the children, the whole fairy host,*
> *had disappeared. But over the graves stood*
> *an abundance of flowers, mostly roses,*
> *beautiful as they grow only in Fairy Land.[2]*

They don't manage to hear any more verses of the story. A door in the huge house slams, followed by the sound of quick footsteps on the stairs, and a woman's voice, loud and authoritative, calling the two children. Gone are the fairies, gone are the girls, and gone is the smile on the author's face.

*T*HERE ARE TWO DIFFERENT PATHS that have to be taken to enter the fairy-tale world of Hans Christian Andersen. Along the way it's possible to see how and under what conditions many of his tales came into being or passed muster. On one of the paths—we can call it the *salon*—the author was always among adults and had to behave as a grown-up himself, meaning as a serious and relatively sensible "Artist," written with an impressive and aesthetically elaborate capital "A." But on the other path, the *children's room*, he was the "Child"—a playful person driven by emotions and imagination, surrounded by like-minded individuals.

When he was among the adults in the salon, he preferred to position himself in front of an audience seated in a semicircle or horseshoe shape. This was the arrangement he had seen and sketched in his diary in 1831 at the home of one of his Romantic mentors, Ludwig Tieck, in Dresden. That's the way Andersen also liked to give readings later in his life. And preferably with no one seated either behind him or too close on either side, and with a door nearby so he could quickly slip away. In the salon he would read directly from a manuscript or book, in which the fairy tale had been given its final form, after the tiniest linguistic detail had been carefully considered. And here, in the salon, Andersen's art would be presented in a manner that demanded concentration, calm, and the utmost attention from his audience. This type of scene has been abundantly documented. The readings would last an hour or more, in front of a crowd of adults and one or two children, who had to be quiet as mice while Andersen read from his tales. Ida Thiele, who is the model for the girl in "Little Ida's Flowers," grew up to marry Captain Alexander Wilde. And in Captain Wilde's memoirs, he provides detailed descriptions of Andersen's readings in the salon, which always proceeded according to a definite, ritualistic pattern. When the audience had all taken their seats and Andersen had practically fallen onto his chair, laboriously placing one long leg over the other, he would give everyone in the crowd a friendly glance, hold the manuscript in his right hand, and let his left hand slide slowly over his face:

> "While his hand hid his expressive eyes, he seemed to be resting or gathering his forces. And when he once again removed his hand, what a change would have taken place in the face of that peculiar man! A hazy veil would be covering his entire countenance. The look he had given us in greeting as he sat down would now be turned inward, away from his

surroundings. Quietly and without elaborate flourishes, the work of literature would emerge. A mother could not handle her firstborn with greater
care or tenderness than our author handled this creation of his mind. His
movements, which were usually so awkward and ungoverned, became
well-balanced and in total harmony with every word he spoke. If he
stretched out an arm, raised a hand, or lifted a finger, it was done with perfect grace. And even though his voice was not in itself especially beautiful, his readings sounded like muted music."[3]

Like Captain Wilde, many adult listeners fell under the hallucinatory
spell of Andersen's reading, and only after the tale was over did they realize how far they had followed the author into his flight of fancy. In the
1840s, one of Andersen's foreign friends, the German composer Felix
Mendelssohn-Bartholdy, attended a reading the author gave in Germany.
Afterwards, the composer recounted that he was so elated and excited by
the experience that he couldn't wait to thank Andersen, but instead "jubilantly flew" at him and said: "But you are a marvelous reader; no one reads
fairy tales like you!"[4]

Rather more reserved was the English author and critic Edmund
Gosse. During a visit to Denmark in the 1870s, he sought out the old,
world-famous author at "Rolighed," the country estate belonging to the
Melchior family which was located just outside Copenhagen near
Svanemøllen. Gosse expected to find a handsome old man and not, as he
said, a gorilla with excessively long, loose-jointed arms, giant hands, and a
hideous face. But Gosse too witnessed the transformation that took place
as soon as Andersen began to speak. A beautiful music and an inner refinement promptly poured forth from the aging author. "As soon as he spoke,
yes, if he merely smiled, his genius was evident," writes Gosse.[5] Hans
Christian Andersen showed his guest the wonderful view of the sound, and
then, quite slowly and in a low voice, he began reading a fairy tale that he
had just written. "And as he read, everything I was looking at—the daz-
zling sails, the sea, the coast of Sweden, and the bright sky—was set ablaze
as the sun went down. It was as if nature itself were blushing with delight
at the sound of Hans Christian Andersen's voice."[6]

There was clearly a certain amount of seduction in Andersen's readings, which carried the listener toward other moments in time and space.
There was something original about the way he performed his readings
that other readers lacked.[7] And his audience didn't truly come back
down to their chairs in the salon until he had stopped reading and swiftly

disappeared into a neighboring room, either alone or with the evening's host. People were allowed to applaud, but there was never any question of permitting any kind of debate or discussion about what had just been read. According to August Bournonville, the purpose of these readings was not for the members of the audience to give the fairy-tale writer advice, suggestions, or guidance. Rather, the point was for the author to give voice to his passion and hold a sort of dress rehearsal for a new tale.[8] Since this was the case, the communication was purely one-sided. The attentiveness, concentration, laughter, and, in particular, the vigor and duration of the applause, were the barometers by which Hans Christian Andersen measured himself and his fairy tales. Afterwards he would go home, evaluate all his impressions, and, if the story in question had not yet been published, he would do the final editing and fine-tuning. One day in January 1864, Andersen dropped by the Collin home to eat a typical Danish meal of *øllebrød* (a sort of soup made from rye bread and weak beer), and he took the opportunity to read aloud for Edvard and his wife. In his diary entry for that day, he discussed the method he used for editing his work: "By reading a piece aloud more often, the language improves; I read and change things according to a natural way of speaking, and then when I come home I make the corrections."[9]

Andersen loved to perform, and during his childhood and youth he was called both the nightingale from Fyn and "*der kleine Deklamator*" [the little declaimer]. He loved to hear his own voice and try out the newly written words in their spoken context. There was something almost tyrannical about Andersen's way of using and abusing the patience of his regular audience members. As one of the author's young friends said several years after Andersen's death: "I think the circles in which he was a regular participant had practically memorized most of his fairy tales. There was something tyrannical about this. The ladies had to put down their needlework, the gentlemen had to leave their conversations and cigars to listen to him read what they had all heard hundreds of times before."[10]

For instance, Andersen managed to read aloud the tale "The Most Incredible Thing" from April 1870 no less than seven times in only a few days. The readings began one evening at the home of the Koch family. That was the very day on which the author had finished writing the story. Then over the next few days he visited by turns the homes of the Hartmann family, the Collins, Thieles, Høedts, Ørsteds, and Melchiors. And the day after making a final copy of the tales "The Comet" and "Sunshine Stories," both of which were written in January 1868, Andersen took the tales with him as he called on seven or eight groups of friends, including the Bloch and Bournonville families as well as the families mentioned above. He wanted to know which of the two stories people liked the best. There are numerous instances throughout Andersen's life and work of this sort of audiovisual method, which involved listening to and observing the reactions of the audience. And the most important guideline in the salon was always the applause. The louder it was and the longer it lasted, the fewer corrections he would make—which meant that the story would have a shorter and quicker route to his publisher, C. A. Reitzel, or to various magazine editors.

Things proceeded very differently along the other path—the *children's room*—which also leads to Andersen's fairy-tale world. But on this path it is much easier to see than in the *salon* how and under what conditions a story was created. In the children's room Andersen used the papers he brought along only to make paper-cuts, and as a storyteller he almost never read from his work but improvised instead. He was an oral story-teller of tales both big and small, whatever happened to strike the fancy of his heart. And he would allow himself to be carried away in the small, private groups that were exclusively comprised of children. Preferably no more than two or three, best of all if there was only one child. Then Andersen could be like the old grandfather in the story "In the Children's Room" from 1865, who, in a deeply intimate partnership with the child— a kind of world outside the world—creates one illusion after another and is able to stage quite a long play with the help of a pipe bowl, a glove, an old vest, and any other odds and ends that lay jumbled together in some random desk drawer.

The children's room gave the fairy tales free rein, much more so than in the salon, where "art poetry" was cultivated. In contrast to the reverent silence that Andersen required from the politely listening adults and children in the salon, in the children's room all sorts of prattle and foolishness were allowed. The childish everyday language was elevated in the author's ears to "natural poetry," and he too participated in the chatter and laughter. As one person said, he could "tune his voice to a specific tone," and he had a remarkable ability to bring to life the sounds of nature in his tales. For instance, when he read "'Hoo-ooh! Pass on!' said the wind," this created an illusion that couldn't help but make a strong impression on a child.[11] Christian Christoph, son of the Count of Holsteinborg, remembered in particular how entertaining Andersen could be. Of course, he also recalled the author's enormous mouth in the ever-mobile face:

"How we laughed time after time as he read—but that didn't offend him in the least. He doubtless had no idea that the laughter was often mixed with our amusement at him, with those extraordinarily big and exceedingly pliable lips (which, as a matter of fact, reminded me a little of Pierrot's)."[12]

In 1866, Emilie Horn was a fourteen-year-old servant at the Holsteinborg estate in charge of looking after the count's children, and at the time she also became friendly with Andersen. This meant that they would run races together in the manor garden and reassure each other during thunderstorms. Once a week Countess Mimmi Holstein would gather all the servants on the estate in the garden room so they could hear stories told by the author himself. Emilie Horn never forgot that experience:

"He didn't read, he narrated . . . Andersen was completely inside the atmosphere of the story. He was the figures he told us about: Clumsy Hans, the princess, the witch in 'The Tinderbox,' and the animals whose droll movements and funny sounds he could imitate perfectly, although he never exaggerated. It was the atmosphere he wanted to portray, and just by looking at him you felt carried away to another, strange world."[13]

Many of Hans Christian Andersen's fairy tales arose not only on trips or hikes in nature, but also via intense interaction with human nature, at its source and in all its liveliness inside the children's rooms. He found inspiration while bending over puppet theaters, making paper-cuts, fashioning flower bouquets, or from toys, songs, and games. Quite often scattered ideas and little, spontaneous oral tales would be later developed further at the desk of the grown-up author. For that matter, it's inside the children's room that we find the fundamental prerequisite for all of his 156 published tales. Here was an intimacy between the storyteller and an audience that had all its senses alert instead of sleeping like a log, the way the adults did—as portrayed in satirical drawings from several of Andersen's readings in manor-house salons and music rooms.

In a beautiful passage in his book about Andersen from 1882, Edvard Collin talks about these gatherings of various children's groups in the homes of families that Andersen visited regularly. The author would tell the youngest children stories that he either improvised or borrowed from little tales and folklore that he had heard during his own childhood. Here he felt utterly secure, at the very roots of the language, and his narrative style was completely his own:

> "The story continued unceasingly, richly furnished with idiomatic phrases that were familiar to the children, and with appropriate gestures. He brought life to even the driest sentence. He wouldn't say: 'The children got into the carriage and drove off.' Rather: 'Then they got into the carriage, goodbye Father, goodbye Mother, the whip cracked, snip, snap, and off they went, yee-ha, get moving!' Those who have later heard him read his fairy tales could have only a faint idea of the extraordinary liveliness of his delivery in the children's circles."[14]

Here in the children's room Andersen's imagination was always so strong and richly outfitted, and he immediately shaped everything into images and more images. Here, throughout his whole life, the author discovered and gave expression to so many scenes, characters, and conflicts, which, in the form of fairy tales, reached far beyond the physical confines of the room. If Andersen started talking about the little field mouse in "Thumbelina," before long he had also created a mouse hole out of thin air and then—along with the listening children—he would crawl inside to visit the field mouse, try out her bed of straw with comforters made out of mint leaves, greet the mole dressed in his velvet coat, and look at the four spiders who spin and weave night and day. That's how agile Andersen's imagination was in the children's room. In there he had direct access to his creative powers and to all the childish illusions and moods that a Romantic writer of fairy tales could possibly wish for. And in 1864 he rejoiced over this fact in a note from his diary, after he had spent some deeply inspirational time with little Mathilde at the home of the Koch family. He proclaimed her a highly promising child, full of "nature and will."[15]

Hans Christian Andersen's fairy tales are practically overflowing with promising children who sprang from the children's room as little improvisers, full of nature and will. Take, for instance, the supremely pampered, wild black princess in "The Flea and the Professor" from 1870, who is described in this manner: "She had seized power from Father and Mother because she had a will and was so marvelously charming and naughty."[16] With her own house in which the walls are made of sugar cane, and with an anti-authoritarian relationship, to put it mildly, with her powerful black chieftain father, this Pippi Longstocking figure anticipates all of modern child psychology and pedagogy as it would blossom in the wake of Romanticism and Andersen's fairy tales. And this wild black princess is far from an isolated case in the works of Hans Christian Andersen. His stories are swarming with wild, natural, free children whose manner of speech as well as their thoughts, games, sense perceptions, and dreams Andersen might have remembered from his own childhood. Or, with his special ability to understand the brilliant reach of childish and naïve remarks, he might also have gleaned them from his journeys through all manner of children's rooms, where life was lived with swan wings on your back, seven-league boots on your feet, magic ear trumpets, and eyeglasses harnessed to the senses.

In the 1920s Else Bruun de Neergaard—the second eldest daughter at the Holsteinborg estate—objected to the rumor that had spread after Andersen's death that he actually couldn't stand children. She remembered that he had held her on his lap and told her stories, and he often illustrated his stories as he told them with little paper-cuts. He also cut out silhouettes, and even though he was generally a nice person, he didn't refrain from scolding the pampered, impertinent little Else if she happened to start kicking when she grew too eager. "Sit still, little madame," Andersen commanded. That was his nickname for her because one morning at the breakfast table, when the author said, "Good morning, Madam," she had turned to her governess and triumphantly said: "It's pronounced *Madame!*"[17] (giving the title the proper French pronunciation).

Else's older brother, Christian Christoph, who later became count and a politician under the name C. C. Holstein-Holsteinborg, didn't remember that Andersen was particularly child-friendly in the sense that he was always surrounded by merry groups of children. When Andersen spent time in his rooms or wandered through the estate's garden, where fairy tales were often born in his imagination, he preferred to be left in peace. During these strolls the author would pick all sorts of flowers, both delicate and wild, and bind together weeds and cultivated plants into artful bouquets. If a child happened to meet him out walking, Andersen might call to the child and right on the spot tell him a story about all these strange and wildly different plants that had been put in the same plot of ground. And then they would all promptly turn into princes and princesses, poor folks, horrid trolls, and stalwart knights in the author's imagination. These chance encounters might produce a nature story in several dimensions. At Holsteinborg the children were always in a festive mood whenever Andersen arrived. Then he would take his place at the table in the summertime dining room and start telling them about his experiences and travels. That's when he was in his element. The dinner table was, after all, a wonderful blend of the "salon" and the "children's room." There Andersen could both read aloud and improvise. There it was possible to debate, persuade, and play. And there the author's little bouquets of wild flowers, water lilies, sheaves of grain, and roses would be displayed. A servant might have actually distributed these bouquets to the ladies before everyone took their seats at the table because Andersen always made the flower bouquets with a specific purpose in mind, and each had its own little story, reference, or symbolism. In short, they represented small nods from the child inside the author to the children inside the grown-ups.

One winter, when Andersen was spending both Christmas and New Year's at Holsteinborg, it was decided that New Year's Eve would be celebrated with some merriment at the dinner table. On the verge of a new year, it was traditional to tell fortunes about the future. So pens, paper, and scissors were brought out, and Andersen was asked to improvise. This soon materialized in the form of a big, oval paper-cut, with a notched border clipped all the way around the edge. On each little flap Andersen then wrote a hasty fortune in verse and folded it over so no one could read what it said. Each little flap was given a number. Then each guest chose a number, and the fortunes were read, one after the other, by the author, who was having a splendid time. On similar festive evenings they might also put on an amateur play in which both the adults and children participated. Or Andersen might decide to perform solo with his marvelous and vastly entertaining ability to improvise on the spot a lengthy poem that was tied together with ten or twelve suggested pairs of rhymes and a theme chosen by the guests. This demanding art form was called *Bouts rimés*, and Andersen was a true master who could produce a poem—as Edvard Collin says in his book—with "almost incomprehensible haste."[18]

Yet best of all was when Andersen, with great humor and originality, would pull out all the stops and recount his experiences from his latest travels. Funny scenes from streets and alleyways, theaters, trains, and coaches would be turned into pure fiction. "That's a lie, the Devil take me, that's a lie. That sort of thing would never happen to any of us!" Commadore Wulff once said when Andersen had entertained the guests with a droll scene.[19] At Holsteinborg Andersen also liked to tell his travel stories. For instance, he reported on his memorable trip to Spain with the younger Jonas Collin in 1862, when the author climbed onto the back of a donkey. Only after a couple of good raps with a solid stick did the animal start moving, and then it took off so fast that Andersen began squealing and shrieking like a stuck pig: "'I'm going to fall off, I'm going to fall off,' but

I didn't fall off, because it ended with the donkey dashing right through my long legs, and I was left standing on the ground."[20]

The First Fairy Tales

Hans Christian Andersen could never stop himself from telling fairy tales. They were a completely natural part of his childhood and youth. At first this penchant was restricted to the spoken word, but very quickly a pen and scissors came into the picture, and it's likely that when he set off in 1819 for Copenhagen, he carried both of these items among his scanty belongings. During his student days in the 1820s, he would write and cut out paper images whenever he found the time and opportunity. But it wasn't until 1830 that he tried out his skills in earnest as a writer of fairy tales, when he included at the end of his first poetry collection, *Poems*, a folk story from Fyn called "The Ghost." And he added a message to his readers, saying that if they liked this type of literature, it was very possible that the author had more of the same in a drawer at home.

> "As a child it was my greatest joy to listen to fairy tales; a great many of them are still quite vivid in my memory, and some of them are very little known or not at all. I have here retold one of them, and if I see that it meets with approval, I will make use of more of them, and one day deliver a series of Danish folktales."[21]

But this news did not prompt any jubilant cry of enthusiasm. On the contrary. At least one strongly dissatisfied reader spoke out in *Maanedsskrift for Literatur*; this was the ill-tempered Christian Molbech, who had gradually begun to take a critical stance toward Andersen after giving a relatively positive reception to most of the author's debut poems. But as for "The Ghost," the critic—who had himself attempted to publish and retell fairy tales—had no doubt that the young and slightly too lively Andersen had utterly "failed to capture the epic tone, in which such fairy tales must be told." The story about Johannes, who ventures out into the world with his blue eyes, was much too subjective and at the same time overly embellished with too much "misplaced elegance of expression," as Molbech wrote. What in the name of a harmonious heaven was a sentence such as "both her legs beat time like drumsticks" doing in the world of literature? And to think anyone would perceive of a delightful summer evening torn apart by childish linguistic yelps such as: "The gnats performed their quadrilles, and the frogs sat like damp fiddlers, croaking a merry chorus in their deep orchestra." And with that, Andersen's desire to write fairy tales was dead and buried for a while.

But the drawer holding the tales was once again coaxed open in early 1835. A new, irresistible force was at work in Andersen's writing, which at first he thought was due as much to need as to desire. And that's why he turned to all manner of literary genres that might produce some income. Hans Christian Andersen's financial situation was very precarious during the winter of 1834–35 after he returned home from Italy. He had moved into lodgings on the third floor of Nyhavn 20, where his monthly rent was eight *rigsdaler*. But the author hadn't brought home any finished works that might earn him money. All he had was an abundance of experiences, adventurous impressions, stacks of drawings, and copious diary notes that had to be turned into art as quickly as possible.

At the same time, in November 1834, Andersen's application for a position at the Royal Library was rejected, so hardship was truly standing at the door during the first months of 1835. This is evident in a letter to Jonas Collin, in which the desperate Andersen describes his financial situation. He has no money for new clothes, boots, linens, or rent. And he now asks for a loan of 100 *rigsdaler*, in addition to the 100 that he already owes the Collin family:

> "I am poor and feel my poverty much worse than the most wretched beggar; it is cowing my spirit and my courage. I am much too familiar with the reality of life to dream about better times. I am facing an unhappy future, which I hardly have the courage to confront. A time will come when I will have to apply for a poor teaching position out in the country or a job on the coast of Guinea. If you should die, then I would have no one to take an interest in me, and my talent is nothing except under favorable circumstances."[22]

Collin answered this cry for help on the very same day and, as always, his reply was ultra-brief—and enormously levelheaded: "Stay calm tonight and sleep well! Tomorrow we will have a talk and think about resources. Your C."[23] Andersen borrowed twenty *rigsdaler*, twenty more in June, and another thirty in August; then once again, around September 1 and October 1, he had to ask Collin for fifteen *rigsdaler* each time. More of Andersen's plays, such as *Little Kirsten*, had been accepted by the Royal Theater, but they had not yet been performed. And until that happened, a playwright would not receive royalties, which varied from 100 to 200 *rigsdaler*, depending on the number of acts in the play.

It may seem surprising that Andersen could be so poor in the spring of 1835, when he had two book publications in the wings: *The Improvisatore* and *Fairy Tales, Told for Children*. But his publisher, C. A. Reitzel, would only pay the 200 *rigsdaler* royalty that Andersen had demanded if the author himself secured a hundred definite buyers for the book. He was not successful in 1835, when he could round up only eighteen subscribers. This meant that the publication of *The Improvisatore* was delayed—as was payment of the royalty. For his first two small books of fairy tales, which came out the same year, Hans Christian Andersen received from Reitzel the sum of thirty *rigsdaler* per book, which would pay for less than four months' rent, or two pairs of trousers, while a new coat cost about forty *rigsdaler*, and a round-trip ticket to Fyn, for instance, cost approximately fifty *rigsdaler*.[24] Yet by the following year—in August 1836—the author was on his feet again financially. This is evident from a letter to Jonas Collin.[25] Andersen had just received 180 *rigsdaler* from his publisher for the second printing of *The Improvisatore*, and he had actually started putting money aside in the Savings Bank. This was something he would continue to do for the rest of his life, and it would eventually make him a millionaire, calculated in today's currency. In other words, over the course of ten very productive and golden months the thirty-year-old Andersen had managed to turn poverty into an almost stable income, to reduce his debts to the Collin family by a couple of hundred *rigsdaler*, and even to establish a bank account.

It was the staging of plays such as *The Banquet at Kenilworth* and *Meeting and Parting*, as well as the publication of his novel *O. T.* in the spring of 1836, that brought in some money and laid the foundation for the author's private housekeeping. And this was something he had never before tried. For *O. T.* alone, which came out in a print run of 500 copies and sold out two months later, Andersen received 300 *rigsdaler*. Reitzel had gradually realized that he had a golden goose in his possession. He demonstrated this when he bought a portrait of the author holding a manuscript in his hand that had been painted by C. A. Benzon. Reitzel quickly arranged for a steel etching to be made of the portrait, and he then distributed the picture to booksellers so they could introduce a new, exciting author of the day in their display cases.[26]

One of Andersen's many literary projects in the spring of 1835 was a handful of tales "told for children," as he added to the title page. In May 1835, Andersen still had no idea that this would soon become the strongest playing card of both his life and work; he was thinking more about the money he might earn from these little stories. Yet he was excited about his new attempts in this literary genre. Andersen wrote to Henriette Hanck in January 1835 that he would soon be ready to publish several children's fairy tales: "I'm going to see about winning over the coming generations, let me tell you!"[27] And a month later it was B. S. Ingemann who was informed about his plans for these stories. Andersen's optimism was enormous: "Next, I've started on several 'fairy tales *told* for children,' and I think I've made them a success. I've presented a couple of the tales that I myself liked as a child, but which I don't think are known. I've written them exactly as I would tell them to a *child*."[28] Even beyond the Danish borders, Andersen had announced this shift in his literary career. In April 1835, his friend and fellow writer in Berlin, Adalbert von Chamisso, was informed that the Dane's fairy tales had now reached the printer, and that there was every reason to expect a great deal from these texts. As Andersen concluded: "I believe that in these stories I have managed quite remarkably to express what is childlike."[29]

In other words, Andersen was eager to hear the reaction, but at the same time—as the latter remark indicates—he was conscious that he had done something radically different in the fairy-tale genre with his small handful of stories about a bold soldier with an enchanted tinderbox; two headstrong brothers; a very refined and sensitive princess; and a little girl and her half-grown friend, the student, who can tell stories and cut them out of another world. Deep inside, Andersen was of course aware that these fairy tales would meet opposition from the established literary elite. Molbech's critique of "The Ghost" had more than intimated this. And deep inside, the Romantic avant-garde artist in Andersen would have also been rather disappointed if he hadn't encountered the sort of criticism that the student in "Little Ida's Flowers" experiences, when the boring councilor interrupts the story that is unfolding between little Ida and the imaginative young man and calls it nonsense!

In the 1830s children were not taken seriously, and very few adults respected the child for his own nature or for the emotional and imaginative life that Andersen allows to blossom in the story about little Ida. From the very first sentence in his fairy-tale production, Andersen also uses a child's way of speaking as the strong, lively foundation of each text. Yet from the beginning, the way children spoke was regarded as an uncultivated, wild, primitive language that had nothing to do with the finer art forms, unless it could be perceived from an appropriate distance, through the monocles and opera glasses of the grown-ups. But here came Andersen with plenty of prattle, nonsense, and unaesthetic words like "baa" and "boo" in his pockets. What an assault was about to commence on the royal palaces of art! The very first sentences in Andersen's collected production of fairy tales say it all: "A soldier came marching along the road: left, right! left, right! He had his knapsack on his back and a sword at his side . . ."[30]

The author was armed and ready for battle, and he had strategically placed himself in the middle of every single one of his first four fairy tales in May 1835. He was not only dressed up as the resourceful soldier with a sword and magic tinderbox, he was also the spirited and creative Little Claus, and the hypersensitive princess who could feel the pea through twenty mattresses and twenty eiderdown quilts. And last but not least, he was also the mighty rebel of the children's room—the student in "Little Ida's Flowers"—who was fabulously skilled at cutting out figures with his scissors and who could tell a whole different type of story. In the spring of 1835, it was this skill at improvisation—the student's ungovernable pen and scissors—that sprang out of the author's desk drawer, revolutionized world literature, and freed the child from centuries of confinement in adult art. With his captivating way of speaking, directly addressed to children and to the child within the adult, Andersen was able to paint unknown worlds and nighttime scenes before the eyes of little Ida so that she would never forget them. The flowers in the vases and pots that hung their heads during the day because they had been out dancing in the night were so alive in the story, in contrast to the councilor. He was the sallow, ill-tempered representative of all the dullards of reason who had tried to thwart the fabulous conversation between the student and little Ida by intervening in the narrative: "Is that any way to pull the child's leg! It's a foolish fantasy!"[31]

With his first four fairy tales Hans Christian Andersen immediately discovered a literary genre in which he could allow little girls and boys, armed to their baby teeth with imagination and the ability to fantasize, to make an appearance and speak in a rebellion directed at all manner of educational philistines and parents. And of course the critics didn't allow the anarchical tone that seeps out of the four stories in the first book of tales to go unchallenged. Molbech had set the course in 1830, but Andersen received an even clearer message during 1835 when the first book of *Fairy Tales, Told for Children* was published in May. The second appeared already in December, with the hope that many copies containing "Thumbelina," "The Naughty Boy," and "The Traveling Companion" would end up under the Christmas trees. But that did not happen. The critical headwind was still too great. Even a childish, naïve soul like B. S. Ingemann had certain reservations about Andersen's first fairy-tale books, and he advised the author not to write any more of that type of story. Yet it becomes clear from the correspondence between the two at the end of the year that Ingemann had nevertheless given in to this new style of fairy-tale literature with the publication of the second small book, which included the story "Thumbelina," who was a heroine after Ingemann's own heart.[32]

The reaction to Andersen's fairy tales in 1835 was so strong that he waited a whole year before publishing the third small book, which contained two magnificent tales: "The Little Mermaid" and "The Emperor's New Clothes." It also included a foreword addressed "To the Older Readers," in which the author replied to the Danish criticism of his first stories. Andersen pointed out that none of his literary works had ever been given such varied critiques as the seven fairy tales he had written so far. And in an odd blend of pathos and irony, he threatened the older readers of his tales with the possibility that these might very well be the last:

> "While certain men, on whose judgment I place great value, praised them as the best of what I have written, others felt that these fairy tales were utterly insignificant and advised me not to write more. Such wildly different verdicts and the apparent silence with which the official critics ignored them, weakened my desire to produce more of this type of literature. That is the reason why a year has passed before this third little book follows the previous two ... In a small country, the writer is always a poor man. Honor is thus the golden ring that he must reach for. We will see whether I manage to grab it by telling fairy tales."[33]

It's true that in the beginning, Hans Christian Andersen's first two books of fairy tales were ignored in "apparent silence." Of the four reviews that materialized in public in the period up to and including 1837, only one appeared in May 1835; the other three showed up in 1836-37. On the other hand, all four reviewers presented a passionate discussion of the mature author's use of the fairy-tale genre and his view of children and their upbringing. If the absent or heavily delayed critique was an expression of a pronounced inertia, the three reviews of *Fairy Tales, Told for Children* could not be accused of being indifferent or apathetic. Resounding from the pages were words such as "pernicious," "inconsiderate," "harmful," "indefensible," and "indelicate." Andersen's fairy tales not only toppled a number of literary dogmas of the day—including the pious, instructive tradition of fairy tales—but they also strongly contradicted the view from previous eras about the natural stature of children. These new tales were thought to be too unrestrained, in both an aesthetic and moral sense. And a couple of them were considered directly harmful for literature, as well as for children and their parents.

In the newspaper *Dansk Literatur-Tidende*, Andersen's tales were reviewed along with a collection of fairy tales titled *Christmas Gift for Children in 1835*, by the critic and author Christian Molbech. As previously mentioned, Molbech was one of the big fairy-tale producers of his day. He published nursery stories and anthologies with retellings of Danish and foreign fairy tales at Christmastime. In a quite tasteless foreword to his Christmas book for 1835, he whispers into the ears of his young readers that if they like these stories, they should by all means remind Father and Mother that another collection of tales will undoubtedly be published for the next Christmas season. This was precisely the sort of patronizing view of children that Hans Christian Andersen's fairy tales were rebelling against. It was also why they at first received such a hammering from the critics. During Christmas 1835, the two fairy-tale books were specifically compared, and Molbech's calm and simple narrative style was found to be much more appropriate and beneficial than Hans Christian Andersen's "striving to enter into the livelier and less orderly discourse of the oral narrative."[34]

If we compare the four reviews from the period 1835–37, we see that the criticism was based on a specific series of dogmas.[35] The first said that literary texts were not allowed to be oral narratives. And before these new stories for children were even presented to the reader, one critic maintained with heavy-handed resolve that it was not acceptable, in published literature, to "express oneself in the same disorderly way in print as is perfectly acceptable when expressing oneself in verbal discourse."[36] In the 1830s, to write the way people talked was regarded as a means of undermining the true and beautiful values of literature. It was unheard of to replace the standard written language with the free language of thoughts— to grumble, hum, sob, and plainly speak your mind as Andersen did in these tales intended for children.

The second dogma with which the tales collided was the view of childhood. Andersen consistently gave his children characters active, independent roles, as in "Little Ida's Flowers." In the opinion of the critics, this story moved too far from the traditional form of the fairy tale and into the ill-mannered world of the child. This meant that the reader wasn't even spared from hearing about how Ida and her two Norwegian cousins, equipped with dangerous bows and arrows, pretend to hold a funeral and shoot the arrows over the grave "because they didn't have guns or cannons." That was how an Andersen tale was allowed to end, without a single adult stepping in to instruct the children about right and wrong. The critics said that depicting the world of children and animals so realistically was not only unaesthetic, it was also dangerous. Andersen's much too lively and straight-forward use of language overstepped the bounds of an utterly necessary and pedagogical distance between adults and children, whose self-image could be severely damaged by a storyteller who was such a congenial equal with children. The fairy tale was supposed to be a link in a child's education and to enforce power, as pointed out in *Dansk Literatur-Tidende*:

> "As mentioned, children must not be given occasion, in their per-
> ceptions, to get up on a high horse or become critical. What is afforded
> them always ought to stand above them, and it is also such things that they
> most wish to hear."[37]

The third dogma that Andersen challenged was the necessity of a vis-ible message or moral in a fairy tale. In the magazine *Dannora*, the critic stated that, for his part, he didn't dare vouch for the harmlessness of these tales. And he polemically asked his adult readers whether the books their children read, even in their free time, should be merely for pleasure: "Surely the person who wants to give children something to read ought to have a higher purpose, at least privately, than a mere wish to entertain them."[38] The critic in *Dannora* also felt that "The Princess on the Pea" was not only indelicate but also morally indefensible, "to the extent that the child may absorb from it the false perception that such a noble lady must always have dreadfully tender skin."

That was how Andersen's fairy tales were received and judged in 1835-36. One critic concluded with the hope, which Andersen's good friend B. S. Ingemann had also expressed, that the otherwise very talented Hans Christian Andersen in the future "will no longer waste his time on writ-ing fairy tales for children."[39] Oh yes, Andersen's view of children, as well as his view of childhood as an independent and inherently significant and valuable period in a person's life, was considered heretical. These ideas had been buried by many people in distant memories of Jean-Jacques Rousseau. In the midst of an age that sought conventionality, comfort, and decorum—and later came to be known as Biedermeier—it was cer-tainly not appreciated when children behaved so freely and intrepidly in Andersen's tales.

The Cult of Childhood

Refusing to listen to the most negative voices of Danish literary criticism in the mid-1830s, Andersen quietly and calmly continued to produce fairy tales, even though he still had no clear notion that it was in this literary genre that his future lay. A certain amount of caution and doubt characterize his publications up until 1840, since the fairy tale was still just one artistic option for him alongside the novel, the poem, and the drama. Before Hans Christian Andersen's journey to the Near East in 1840-41, he wrote seventeen independent tales. This was a modest number compared to the following decades, when his tales found their ultimate form, turned their backs on the petty Danish criticism, and made their way beyond the ramparts of Copenhagen and the borders of Denmark to central Europe. There people seemed to have a greater understanding for—and genuine interest in—the improvisations of the young Dane, who wrote poems, novels, travel books, plays, and fairy tales marked by a Romantic view of humanity. In addition, he had a noble life story to tell, which in 1843 was canonized in the fairy tale "The Ugly Duckling." Immediately after publication, when it was translated to German and English, this story became Andersen's calling card, gaining him admittance to the top echelons and royal courts all over Europe. Out in the world people understood much faster than in Denmark what was so groundbreaking about Andersen's fairy tales. They realized and acknowledged that his texts represented a renewal of literature in terms of both form and content. And they recognized that no previous Romantic author had made use of the child in such a radical way in his art as Hans Christian Andersen was now doing. In reality, this traceable line in his work had been under way and in development for nearly ten years. During this time Andersen had animatedly experimented in his literary works with giving the child and childhood more space and bigger stages on which to perform. In his debut novel, *Walking Tour*, as well as in his first two poetry collections, *Poems* and *Fantasies and Sketches*, we are introduced to several different forms of childhood and childishness in the texts. For instance, in the poem "Phantasus," the poet-narrator very clearly says that his art is based on a deeply childish and playful nature, and the poet more than hints that he would rather live his life in the children's room than in the salons:

A child myself, I would rather play with the young,
They are best able to know my magic world;
In huts and in castles they understand me,
I bring with me such marvelous treasures.
We do not know the struggles or sorrows of life,
For us, the corner of the hut becomes a knight's castle,
Even the stick is a brave and noble steed,
The little swallow the castle's master-singer.[40]

By "playing with the young" and materializing his own magical world in fairy tales, Andersen brought a number of new, essential impulses not only to art but also to science during the 19th century. Romanticism had placed the child on the elevated pedestal of the poetic muse and used the child's nature as an incorruptible ideal and unquenchable source of inspiration. Then Andersen stepped onto the world stage in 1835, lifting the underaged child down from the pedestal and putting him into literature on his own natural terms. He then allowed children of all ages and of both sexes—"the voices of the innocent"—to speak in the magnificent dialogues and lines that turn everything upside down and see right through the essential lies of the adults. "But he doesn't have anything on!" as the little child says among utterly mute adults when the naked emperor comes past in his new clothes, and then the whole crowd shouts in unison after the child: "But he doesn't have anything on!"[41] As mentioned before, we witness this revolutionary shift in voice and point of view from the adult to the child in Andersen's poem "The Dying Child" from 1826. The young person, who was previously a passive object in world literature, becomes in the art of Hans Christian Andersen an active subject who thinks, talks, feels, and especially imagines. In this way the child points to the fund of creative assets that every person possesses. And these psychological values, if they are not repressed or even obliterated as the child grows up, can then have great importance later in life.

The idea of childhood as a specific phase in life did not exist until the end of the 17th century when John Locke, the English philosopher and pedagogue, and Jean-Jacques Rousseau in the following century, began taking an interest in child-rearing. For this reason, Dante Alighieri's literary work around the year 1300 is typical for the times. In his work, all children are left in Limbo, and no *infanti* are sent to Hell, Purgatory, or Paradise because Dante's great epic poem, *The Divine Comedy*, only has room for and takes into account fully developed, adult human souls.[42] The high infant mortality rate in the Middle Ages was not the only reason for marginalizing the little citizens in the eyes of the adults. Half of the male and female children born in Europe died before the age of five, while those who made it through the diseases and perils of early childhood were quickly drawn into a much-too-adult life. Children had to find their place and survive by taking part in the work of grown-ups and their way of life. Both at work and in their free time, children were regarded as "little adults." This is apparent in the paintings of Pieter Brueghel from the 16th century, in which children are depicted in more or less merry situations, but it's not always easy to distinguish between what are games and what are assaults. Among the peasants, children were hardy slaves who were exploited both socially and sexually.

After the Renaissance, a new view of the child and childhood arose. Writers and thinkers such as Rabelais, Montaigne, Locke, Swift, and Defoe saw "The Child" and "The Savage" as the sole remaining remnants of the natural human being in modern times. And in the 18th century during the Enlightenment the child became, especially in the ideas and writings of Jean-Jacques Rousseau, a paradigm for the ideal human being. Yet the voices of children are never heard during the Enlightenment, and we seldom see them develop into whole people in pre-Romantic literature. The exception was the work of Rousseau, who laid the foundation for elevating childhood and making it visible; around the year 1800 childhood began to find its way into art via the whole Romantic movement. This occurred first and foremost in Germany and England, where the preoccupation of writers and painters with the child and childhood is a vital part of a broadly based and general interest in human consciousness and education.

Rousseau was inspired in turn by John Locke, who in the 1690s had advanced the theory that a child's character should be developed by disciplining the body and soul, and sound judgment should be given higher priority than book learning. These were the ideas that Rousseau drew upon in the 1760s when he designated childhood as a period in a person's life that is of independent and especially great value because it's the time when every individual is closest to the natural state. "The human being is by nature good," said Rousseau. "For this reason, give the child the greatest possible freedom so that all talents endowed in him by nature can be developed. Allow the child to see and touch everything!" This type of child becomes the focus in 1762 in *Émile*, which is both a novel and a pedagogical text. In this book Rousseau ventures the claim that the most crucial concern in all education should be for the child's own individual nature and identity—what makes him unique—instead of following the norms of the adults. Previously, it was considered very important for a child's clothing to match that of an adult as much as possible. Rousseau, on the other hand, tears the constricting shoes from Émile's feet and lets the lad run around barefoot. And every progressive educator in the late 18th century followed the rule that a person's first teachers in philosophy are his feet, hands, and eyes. The novel about the rich man's son Émile, who is left in the hands of a broad-minded educator with an entire manor house at his disposal for his pedagogical experiments, aroused enormous attention and scandal in France. And because of the text's religious escapades in particular, Rousseau's novel was banned and burned on a pyre by the executioner in Paris three weeks after it was published. On the same occasion, a warrant was issued for the author's arrest, and he had to flee into exile.

In spite of a gap of more than seventy years between *Émile* and *Fairy Tales, Told for Children*, there is significant philosophical solidarity between Rousseau and Andersen. In his preface to *Émile*, Rousseau writes that he wished a man of intelligence and discernment might one day give people a primer on how to observe children, because such a text would be of great importance for the education of humanity. Such a "primer" is what Hans Christian Andersen by and large would write with his more than 150 fairy tales during the years 1835-72. Andersen is the first author after Rousseau who consistently takes children seriously, and time after time he presents the child in terms of his natural state, while sharply proclaiming childhood as a phase in life with independent value and importance.

There seems to be a dogma in the history of world literature that has also been repeated in the scholarly investigations of the child in Romantic literature over the past few decades. This dogma says that active children who behave and speak independently were missing from literature after Rousseau and almost a hundred years forward in time. We have to assume that this is why many international dissertations about "The Romantic Child" in world literature have neglected Hans Christian Andersen, whose literary works before 1850 are teeming with children.[43] If we look at his first fifteen fairy tales, written during 1835-40, we find exceedingly active and lively boys and girls in "Little Ida's Flowers," "Thumbelina," "The

Naughty Boy," "The Emperor's New Clothes," "The Chamomile," "The Garden of Eden," and "The Wild Swans." And in the 1840s even more children appear, differing widely in flesh and blood, voice and will, longings and desires. Each has his own personality, individuality, and, in particular, name: Claus, Ida, Ib, Christine, Georg, Emilie, Marie, Kai, Gerda, Johannes, Elisa, and many more. These are children with individual dispositions and temperaments ranging from the relatively cautious, well-bred models of virtue such as Hjalmar in "The Sandman" to the uninhibited little robber girl in "The Snow Queen." She is described as being so wild, ill-mannered, and odious a child that she instinctively bites her own robber hag of a mother on the ear.

Of course, Hans Christian Andersen was not the only one to write about children and childhood after Rousseau did so in the 1760s. Both before and after the year 1800, we find a great interest in the child among Romantic writers, including Blake, Herder, Goethe, Schiller, Novalis, Jean Paul, Wordsworth, Coleridge, Hugo, Tieck, Hoffmann, and Dickens. This interest often takes such adoring and myth-shrouded forms that we can speak of "the cult of childhood."[44] From this infatuation emerged a type of writing that was more concerned with the dreamlike moods of a child and the idyllic character of a child's life than with the physiological nature of children and their social circumstances. In the works of Friedrich Schiller, for instance, we find this almost heroic cultivation of the child in the German author's preoccupation with the concept of "the naïve." The child and childhood become the universal measuring stick for true art and the true artist. This is apparent in Schiller's classic work *On Naïve and Sentimental Writing*, in which he pushes to extremes the relationship between artistic genius and a child's nature in statements such as: "True genius must be naïve, or it is not genius."[45] In Goethe's work we find fifty different descriptions of children, but they are mostly of an ideal or philosophical type. The portraits seem superficial or stereotyped, in that the child is primarily used to put the writer and the scientist on the track of the dualistic spirit in nature, which was the great guiding principle of Goethe's work.[46] Symptomatic of the child's generally anonymous and abstract role in the writings of Goethe and Schiller is the latter's poem "Der spielende Knabe" [The Playing Boy], in which the child is never allowed to express himself even though the theme of the poem is the energetically playing child. Instead, throughout the poem the child must settle for being an object for study and a muse for the sentimental poet who, with his adult suffering and longing, celebrates the childish innocence that will soon be lost: "*Spiele, liebliche Unschuld! Noch ist Arkadien um dich . . .*" [Play, dear innocence! Arcadia surrounds you yet].

If we turn our attention to England during High Romanticism, it is in the works of Wordsworth, Coleridge, and Blake that we find the strongest traces of the worship of childhood. For William Wordsworth, the child became the basis for an entire philosophy of human nature, and large parts of his writings can be read as an apotheosis of the child, gathered up and concentrated in the famous maxim: "The Child is the Father of the Man." With his comprehensive sense for the relationship between the child and nature, as well as the importance of childhood in relation to the adult, Wordsworth is a central figure in Romanticism's cult of the child. Yet in his writing we see how the child is chiefly used in a process of liberation addressed to the adult and not to the child himself. The child remains an idealized figure in whom everything that is lost in life is at once mourned and glorified: "Our childhood sits / Our simple childhood sits upon a throne / That hath more power than all the elements . . ."[47]

Aside from Rousseau, William Blake is the Romantic author who seems closest to Hans Christian Andersen in terms of how each viewed a child's nature. Blake's interest in the child was not accidental, temporary, or abstract, which was the case among most of the other Romantic writers in England and Germany around 1800. The child and childhood had a much more concrete and often religious significance for Blake. In keeping with his belief in the revolutionary possibilities latent in childhood, he sporadically allows the voices of children to speak in *Songs of Innocence* (1789) and *Songs of Experience* (1794). In these works Blake is concerned with the eternal, universal loss of all the innate strengths and potentials of a person's life, and he writes with an intense rebellious impulse that is quite reminiscent of the young Andersen's constant battle against the tyranny of reason. William Blake also wrote adamantly against pedagogical and educational systems of Rationalism, and he gave his favorite opposition—innocence vs. experience—marvelous names such as "Man of Imagination" and "The Idiot Reasoner." This opposition is practically identical to "Phantasus" and his spoilsport older brother "Reason," which Andersen uses in the previously discussed student essay from 1825, when he was asked to write about the relationship between emotion and reason.

There are other interesting parallels between Hans Christian Andersen and William Blake, especially regarding the English author's utopia, a society filled with people who have a clear awareness of their own original innocence and innate prescience, which they are condemned to lose through a systematic and often insensitive socialization process. Andersen could almost have written Blake's poem "The Schoolboy," while Blake in turn might have composed the fairy tale about "The Nightingale." They were both familiar, ad nauseam, with the story of the human bird who was born to sing but was forced into a cage with clipped wings, making him unable to utter a sound.

The Manifesto of the Fantastic

Fairy Tales, Told for Children, published in 1835, represented both a cultural and an artistic revolution. Andersen was the leader of the rebellion, which drew boys and girls of all ages out of anonymity and into his fairy-tale universe. There they not only had a voice and a name, but they were also allowed to set their onomatopoetic stamp on the language. An early example is little Ida's doll, Sophie. At the end of the first fairy-tale book, Sophie becomes a wallflower during the flowers' ball at night, and so she has to draw attention to herself with discreet but impatient sounds: "So she sat in the drawer and thought that surely one of the flowers would come and ask her to dance, yet no one came. So she coughed, hm, hm, hm! but still no one came."[48]

Over time, more and more examples of stronger and stronger onomatopoeia appeared in Andersen's fairy tales. This quickly became one of the trademarks of an Andersen tale. This emphasis on the spoken language was something quite new in the more refined, written fairy-tale literature, although it had always been present in the living, oral folk language of ordinary people and children, who would spontaneously imitate the nature and culture surrounding them. Even today children and childlike souls use onomatopoeia to indicate the personality of an animal or a certain object. This is also the case in Andersen's fairy tales. "Cairn! Cairn!" screech the black scavenger ravens and crows in the lesser known tale "The Folksong's Bird" from 1864. "Quick now! Quick now!" we hear from the ducks in "The Sandman." And in "The Will-o'-the-Wisps Are in Town," it says, "Whoosh! They were gone!" about the young will-o'-the-wisps. In "The Flying Trunk" it says of the fireworks, "Whoosh, how they flared!" and in "The Little Match Girl" the magical but quickly extinguished matches say "Scritch!" Even something as soundless as a hot iron says to a collar "scrap!," while silent tallow candles sputter their "fut, foy." And a heavy rammer (called a "maiden" in Danish) that is used to pave streets can utter plenty of sounds when it strikes the cobblestones, crying out its "maid–!" in "Two Maidens" from 1853. It seems as if the orgy of sounds never ends in Andersen's fairy tales. The watchdog in "The Snowman" snarls his "Sweeeeeeeeet-hearts!," and in "The Elf and the Mistress," the elf blows on the cooking pot so it boils over with a "surra-rurra-rup!" because the mistress would rather moon over the teacher trainee than cook the porridge. And in 1848, in the tale about "The Drop of Water," we hear the mysterious sound "baf!," which is supposed to indicate the sound of a leg being kicked away during a scuffle.

Nature is allowed to speak in these imitative sounds that often have their roots in Andersen's own childhood and its shifting landscapes. When the lapwing in "Chicken-Grethe's Family" scolds and screeches: "You thief! You thief!" we are deep in the south of Fyn, where the farm people all knew that a lapwing always cries "Teevi! Teevi . . . veef!" if anyone got too close to its nest and eggs.[49] Similarly, in the old days the inhabitants of Fyn had an equally folksy onomatopoeia they used to mimic the chattering of geese in the stubble fields. People would mutter quickly and softly: "If you take it, then I'll take it! If you take it, then I'll take it!" This onomatopoeia seems to have been handed down to Clumsy Hans as, "If she takes me, then she'll take me! And if she doesn't take me, then I'll take her all the same!"

Over the years there is a definite development in the way Andersen uses onomatopoeia in his tales. He starts out in the 1830s with brief little isolated sounds such as: hum, uh, plop, ho, and hee-ya! But with time, the sounds become more and more bold, acquiring greater power and exuberance. For instance, in the tale about "Peiter, Peter, and Peer" from 1868, the nightingale sings "Kluk! Kluk! Zi! Lo, lo, li!" And the big fire drum in "The Golden Treasure" from 1865 makes the tale vibrate with decibels: "Dum, dum, dum! Dummelum! Bam, bam, bam! Bamalam! Come, come! Trammerim, trammerim, it's him! Tummelum, tummelum, tummelumsk." This increasingly comprehensive and sophisticated use of onomatopoeia in his tales made Andersen something of a modernist even in the other genres in which he wrote. From the fairy tale, these sound experiments slid over into his plays and poems.

This was a new type of poetry, expressed in a childish yet anything but "sugar-coated" language that Andersen wanted to create with his tales. And among the solid, natural building blocks and materials in his author's workshop we find children's names rich in vowels (Elisa), rhymes, and jingles ("snip-snap-snurra-bassalurra"), as well as made-up words and concepts that were created in the children's room. For instance, in "The Shepherdess and the Chimneysweep," Andersen surely presents the most splendid military title in all of world literature: "Billygoat-Leg-Field-Marshal-Brigadier-General-Commander-Sergeant."

In Hans Christian Andersen's author persona, children found for the first time a grown-up who not only respected their nature but also listened to and understood their language. And in his fairy-tale world he raised the everyday life of children up to the same level as that of adults. Andersen had a unique sense for the reality of the psyche of boys and girls. Throughout his works there are many acute and profound observations of the nature of children, glittering like gold. For instance:

> "The deep sorrow in a child's soul is as great as the greatest sorrow a grown-up knows. In his pain, the child has no hope; reason cannot stretch out a helping hand to the child; at that moment he has nothing but his sorrow to cling to."[50]

These words stem from *Only a Fiddler* from 1837. In many places in this novel, the adult narrator, with the child as his guide, attempts to plumb the unconscious, which during Romanticism was still untouched, virgin territory that was waiting to be mapped out by Sigmund Freud. And this brief portrait of a child's type of sorrow reveals that Andersen was capable of entering and describing a child's reality from the inside. Andersen had a deeply rooted belief that heaven belongs only to children because no one can reach the highest of the high without naïveté and innocence. And with his fairy tales, written during the period 1835 to 1872-73, Andersen opened the door not only to the modern breakthrough in art, but also to modern child psychology and pedagogy in the next century. And it would be the 20th century—as Ellen Key, the Swedish reform-pedagogue, predicted in 1899—that would belong to the child.[51]

Yet, as previously mentioned, Hans Christian Andersen was not the only author in the history of world literature who was writing about children in the 1830s. Charles Dickens, for example, was also preoccupied with the social and psychological world of children in his big-city novels such as *Oliver Twist* and *Nicholas Nickleby*, which both came out in the late 1830s. But we have to leap ahead to Lewis Carroll's *Alice in Wonderland* in the 1860s and after that to the literary modernists in the early 20th century before we find artists who dared depict children in such an uncompromising manner—

not merely as a gilt-edged motif but by using the thoughts, language, and imagination of children as a driving force in the creation of art. Led by Andersen fans such as the Swede August Strindberg, the Dane Johannes V. Jensen, the Russian Wassily Kandinsky, the German-Swiss Paul Klee, and the Frenchman Jean Cocteau, all that is "childlike" became the well from which modernism, to a great extent in all art forms, would pour out in the early 20th century. And as such, the fairy tales of Hans Christian Andersen served as one of the most important foundations for modernism.[52] With his insistence on the rights and potential of children, Andersen anticipated not only the psychoanalysis of Sigmund Freud but also the surrealist manifestos of the 1920s. André Breton stated that artists live only fleetingly in the emotional world—which is largely created during their childhood—when it rises up in brief, isolated moments, such as in dreams. That was something that Andersen and the surrealists shared: a sense for leading the human mind back to a childlike center—and the courage to do so. And it is solely from this place that the psyche can emanate. It was the land of the unconscious—this secret territory inside a person that shows up so strong and colorful when we, as children, dream and see visions—that was such a mainstay and decisive force in the life and work of Hans Christian Andersen, just as it was for many modern artists seventy years later.

Where Did the Fairy Tale Come From?

"All literature begins with folk poetry," Andersen wrote in 1868.[53] And with this statement, he was emphasizing his great respect for the marvelous world that lies hidden in the stories, legends, myths, and traditions handed down by the peasantry and urban poor—stories often associated with various kinds of superstitions. Here we find the nourishing roots for a large part of the fairy tales and stories that Andersen wrote for forty years. There was a particular spirit and voice in nature that a person could always seek if he had the sense to listen for it, along with enough patience. In the tale "What a Person Can Think Up" the wise old woman tells the busy young man from the city, who is studying to be a writer and wants to be done by Easter, that poetry happens to come from nature itself—if a person has a sense for it: "Here is an abundance, in every respect, of things you can write and recount, if you're able to recount. You can pull it free from

the plants and crops of the earth, pour it out from the running and stagnant waters, but you must understand it, understand how to catch a beam
of sunlight."[54]

This was more or less the same thing the aging Andersen once said,
while visiting the Glorup estate, to a young admirer who asked "Professor
Andersen": "Where in the world do you get all your ideas from?" The
author then answered, "Oh, my dear, if one fine day you should happen to
go out and sit down under a flowering hawthorn bush, you would have
exactly the same thoughts; the only difference is that you keep your
thoughts to yourself, while I write mine down."[55]

Andersen had imbibed the old folktales and myths with his mother's
milk. And in rather large doses, at that. Early on, the shoemaker father
read aloud from *A Thousand and One Nights* to his son at home on
Munkemøllestræde. And the imaginative boy would go with his mother
out to the farms of Fyn, which were frequented by the great storytellers of
Fyn during harvest time. The women and children would gather in the
barn in the evening, and Hans Christian learned what it meant to tell a
story so that fifty people of all ages would hang on every word. In the
foreword to his third book of *Fairy Tales, Told for Children* from 1837,
Andersen writes that all these folktales lived on in his adult imagination,
and now that he had become a storyteller himself, they were becoming
more insistent. "I have told them in my own way, permitting myself any
change that I found suitable, letting my imagination liven up the faded colors of the images."

All his life Andersen paid very little attention to literary proprietary
rights, and he seldom worried about whether the main idea for a poem, a
dramatic scene, or the source of a tale actually stemmed from some other
author. As a child, Andersen had "borrowed" entire scenes from his books
when he wanted to put on a play. And as a young writer in Copenhagen
in 1821-22, Andersen had turned to the works of popular Danish authors
such as Adam Oehlenschläger, Jens Baggesen, and B. S. Ingemann, and
expanded on their literary ideas. This was a common practice among the
artists of Romanticism. Andersen's debut novel, *Walking Tour*, makes use of
large parts of German Romantic literature to build the scaffolding for its
fragmented narrative. Similarly, two out of three of Andersen's ballad operas
and plays in the early 1830s were retellings of stories by Scribe, Mazares,
Gozzi, and Bayard, among others. Andersen continued on in this fashion
for the rest of his life, piecing together stories and "peeling" passages away
from foreign novels, short stories, and plays that had inspired his own writing.

And he didn't always think it was worth the trouble to assign credit on the title page or in a footnote.

This was not considered a crime. For one thing, copyright laws didn't exist at the beginning of the 19th century. And besides, no one knew better than the Romantic writer Hans Christian Andersen that art always depends on other art and that all literature, consciously or unconsciously, is written under the influence of or in opposition to other literature. This was especially true of the fairy-tale genre, which has its origins and existential foundation in the oral retellings of stories and legends by primitive peoples. These stories then wandered from culture to culture, in a nomadic fashion, and gradually became changed and renewed through retellings and rewritings. In the oral storyteller tradition, no one could be said to "own" a work of literature. It was collectively accessible, much the way authors in all eras have also used and been inspired by each other. As Georg Brandes formulated it in his essay on the fairy-tale art of Hans Christian Andersen in 1870: "The naked idea, of course, can't write; but without the idea and without the context it sets in motion, the author can't write either."[56]

And Andersen certainly knew how to make use of all the good ideas he happened to come across in the voracious reading that he did at all the manor houses with their excellent libraries. He also used everything he saw and heard in the theaters when he traveled around Europe. With his responsive imagination, Andersen would clip and copy, cut and paste, using passages from all the literature that was in circulation at the time. He would constantly borrow literary elements from near and far, tucking them into his own art, where they frequently took on a metapoetic function and—especially in his novels—appeared as direct or concealed quotes, referring to the art of the day. Andersen was well aware that not only his own work but also the "classics" of world literature were based on powerful inspiration from other authors' books, sometimes even shamelessly exploiting them. This is evident in Andersen's first novel, *Walking Tour*, when the young narrator and author, who steals from right and left to be able to scrape together a whole book, has a bloody vision and sees all the classics of the world scattered on the ground like disfigured corpses. He watches three hearses move past, filled with wounded men of letters with no legs or arms or eyes:

> "They are partly old classics, partly little-known texts, from which minor authors of the day steal an arm or a leg; here an eye, there a hero's arm, and in this manner they patch together for themselves a reasonably tolerable hero or heroine whom they can present as their own. And since

this kind of picking apart is being done, what will be left of the carcasses? God knows, we patch together enough from them."[57]

As an author of fairy tales, Andersen was always open to the many possibilities of the present, and this included the art of all eras. It wasn't because Andersen couldn't have thought up the ideas himself. We can see his formidable inventiveness and his ability to master his material in ever new forms and variations, especially in the wide range of voices and disguises he made use of when he was going to tell a fairy tale. Then he would transform himself into objects, animals, and humanlike creatures, such as the Sandman, Mother Elder Tree, or the wonderful Stork Father in the story "The Marsh King's Daughter" from 1858. This Andersen tale, more than any other, illustrates how stories and literature will always wander through time and space via voices and "beaks" from new eras. "The Marsh King's Daughter" is an astonishingly ambitious tale in which we shuttle back and forth from pyramids and mummies on the waters of the Nile to a Viking stronghold in northern Jutland. An Egyptian princess dressed in a swan skin has been given the task of bringing back a life-giving water lily for her deathly ill father. But as fate will have it, she sinks into Wild Bog, where the filthy Marsh King takes her by force. She then gives birth to Helga, who grows up among the Danish Vikings and endures terrible trials in her deeply divided life. In the daytime she is a beautiful young woman with an evil and wild temperament, but after the sun sets she becomes a hideous toad with a beautiful and calm disposition. It's Stork Father who tells us this amazing tale, and he manages at all times to keep his eyes open and his tongue straight in his beak while he recounts the story in which he plays an important supporting role. And he wants very badly to make the moral of the story comprehensible to his youngsters at home in the nest and to his eternally impatient, petit-bourgeois wife, who merely wants to be entertained. At one point Stork Father says to two strange birds: "Let's have a talk . . . now that we can understand each other's language, even though the beak may be cut differently on one bird than on the other."[58] And that's precisely the way it is with stories from one era that are told in a different time. They have to be communicated with a new beak if they're going to find an audience. As the author suggests, the trick is to find the basic tone that gathers the old and the new and ties the past to the present.

This is part of the very nature of fairy tales, as we learn in many of Hans Christian Andersen's stories, for example in "The Buckwheat" from 1841. "I, who am telling this story, heard it from the sparrows! They told it to me one evening when I asked them for a fairy tale."[59] In Andersen's fairy-tale universe, stories come not only from the speech of humans but also from the peeping of sparrows and the clacking of the storks' beaks. Fairy tales are brought by the moon, the wind, a ray of sunlight; by bees, fairies, snails, roses, and thistles that stretch, full of longing, over the parapet to the manor-house garden and pass on their words to a tulip. Fairy tales are always waiting to leap out of nature, hiding behind the smallest leaves, in scattered straw, in willow trees and old headstones. Fairy tales move like a current and a pulse through all of nature's forms and figures, stirring like the surface of the sea in "The Wild Swans": "The water rose faintly, like the breast of a sleeping child."[60]

In other words, the fairy tale is a medium for "the spirit in nature." The Romantic scientist H. C. Ørsted dearly wanted Hans Christian Andersen to write an academic treatise about his fairy-tale aesthetics and by so doing, shape this "spirit in nature" into a conscious foundation for his work. But this sort of theoretical, written synthesis of art and science was, after all, too much to ask of Andersen, who had endured more than enough academic training in the 1820s. Yet he expresses it even more beautifully and with greater pride in his heart—for example, in "The Will-o'-the-Wisps Are in Town." In this story, the man who is looking for the fairy tale is on his way into the woods from the open shore when he suddenly exclaims: "The earth sensed it, every little blade of grass that sprouted would have told about it. Tales never die!"[61]

If you systematically set out to trace the sources on which Andersen built his literary works, you might be surprised to see how many of his novels, plays, poems, and fairy tales rest solidly—and often quite directly—on the stories of other authors. Andersen lifted their motifs, characters, and stage sets and put them in his works, giving them his *own* artistic treatment and deeply original finish. As a Romantic author he drew not only from tradition but, as mentioned, also from contemporary literature, and "borrowed the subject" as he says about his play *The Mulatto* in 1840. If we restrict ourselves to his fairy tales, there are countless examples of the way in which Andersen found inspiration in both classical and modern or contemporary world literature. In the tale "The Flea and the Professor" from the early 1870s, which displays a fascination with hot-air balloons, Andersen takes his material from various novels by Jules Verne, whose works he had read and admired.[62] Early fairy tales such as "The Rose

Fairy" and "The Naughty Boy" were created on the basis of a Boccaccio story and a poem from antiquity by Anacreon. And even a story like "The Emperor's New Clothes," which is so lively and beloved in our culture— one of the most "Danish" stories that we can show to foreigners—took its basic setting and plot from an old Spanish fairy-tale collection from the Middle Ages titled *Patronio's Fifty Stories*. Andersen found this story in a German fairy-tale collection and immediately saw its possibilities.

The Spanish fairy tale is about a king and three swindlers who call themselves the world's best weavers and tailors. Now, on their lucrative way through the world, they propose to sew clothes for the king of Castile. The cloth is so fine that only the man who is the flesh-and-blood son of his father can see it. On the other hand, anyone who claims to be his father's son but is not will be unable to see the cloth. For this reason, all the courtiers and ministers who fear that they might not be their father's son praise the invisible cloth. But in the end, the trickery is exposed. Not by a sweet and bold little child, as it is in Hans Christian Andersen's tale, but by an African Moor who rubs his eyes and then steps right up to the king's procession and says:

> "Your Majesty, I have never had the honor of knowing my father, and I have absolutely no interest in knowing who he was. That is why I dare tell you right to your face that you are riding through the capital completely naked."[63]

Andersen didn't want to venture using the paternity trickery in his narrative, and so he softened the vulgar and wild part of the original Spanish tale. For reasons of decorum, he instead put his own trademark of innocence on his retelling of the story. This is apparent in other Andersen fairy tales as well. For instance, "The Swineherd" from 1842 contained, in its original fairy-tale form, vulgarities that the author stripped away. In later comments about his fairy tales, he rationalized his choices: "'The Swineherd' has a couple of elements from an old Danish folktale, which, as it was told to me as a child, could not be decently repeated."

It was especially in old Danish folktales and legends, fables, parables, and proverbs that Andersen constantly found material for his own fairy tales. Many of his retellings demonstrate how brilliantly he made use of not only the foreign fairy-tale tradition but also the wealth of folk literature from his own country, which was still very much alive in the 19th century.[64] Andersen revitalized the folktale genre by giving these gruesome and crude stories a little more innocence, as well as a refined psychology, a little philosophy, and, in particular, a linguistic artistry that completely exploded the bounds of the original, primitive narratives. Like no Danish author either before or since, he managed to fill the old and often stereotyped stories with all manner of lively little details. By injecting his characters with a life that was deeper and much more individual than in the classic, one-dimensional folktales, Andersen was able to make all his readers experience and share the timeless sorrows and joys of his fairy-tale figures.

Each generation tells fairy tales with its own beak, as Stork Father and Stork Mother say in "The Marsh King's Daughter." And even though Hans Christian Andersen did so in the 1830s in an utterly new and radically different way, it's important to remember that he did not invent the fairy tale. In the 1820s he found himself in the midst of the literature of Romanticism, which cultivated the fairy tale in contemporary art. There was a tremendous interest in the fairy tale everywhere in Europe at the beginning of the 19th century. People enthusiastically embraced old, half-forgotten folktales and legends, which were collected from the peasantry and brought to the fine salons. In Denmark the genre became very fashionable in the 1830s and 1840s. Initially this was not because of Andersen but because more and more fairy-tale anthologies based on old Danish traditions and newer German and French collections were seeing the light of day in Denmark. They were regarded as a form of *exotica* and were read aloud to elite gatherings by celebrated actors such as Fru Heiberg, Madame Nielsen, Rosenkilde, and the popular Ludvig Phister. Later on Andersen's works became part of the repertoire, and for a number of years Phister's biggest hit was his reading of "The Emperor's New Clothes."

The breakthrough of Romanticism also awakened a sense for folk culture in its primitive forms, along with an interest in folklore. The theory of the German writer and philosopher Herder was that old folktales reflect the soul of a people, and this idea now became popular. Supernatural and heathen notions, the kind that had existed for centuries and had been passed down among the peasantry by oral storytelling, were suddenly acceptable for the drawing rooms. Fairy tales became extremely fashionable among the upper echelons. There it was not only claimed that the soul of the peasants had been found to have metamorphosed in fairy tales, myths, traditions, and legends, but that these same primitive peasants were a basic cornerstone of an entire culture. The Brothers Grimm in Germany aroused a great deal of attention by collecting and publishing folktales, recounting them in the guileless narrative form of the peasants. At the same time, writers in Denmark such as B. S. Ingemann and Adam Oehlen-schläger published retellings of folktales. The latter produced a two-volume work in 1816 titled *Tales by Various Writers* that contained an enlightening foreword in which Oehlenschläger spoke in favor of the genre and defended the basic Romantic principle that "it is only the imagination that is able to comprehend beauty."

A couple of years later Hans Christian Andersen's good friend Just Mathias Thiele began collecting Danish folk legends, which were published in four volumes from 1818 to 1823. These books became an almost inexhaustible source of material for young Andersen in the 1820s, when he was itching to write. Some of Andersen's first attempts in literature—the play *The Robbers of Vissenberg* and the historical account "Apparition at Palnatoke's Grave"—were inspired by Thiele's books. During the same decade Andersen also buried his nose deep in Mathias Winther's collection *Danish Folktales* from 1823. A number of the stories in the book were presented in a form that was fairly close to how they must have sounded on long winter evenings next to the hearth in a farmhouse, when the farmers and old matrons rambled on.

In the period 1820-30 a great surge of fairy tales from abroad washed over Denmark, with translations of *Fairy Tales* by the Brothers Grimm, Charles Perrault's *Mother Goose Stories*, and many tales by Johann Karl August Musäus from his *Volksmärchen der Deutschen* [Folktales of the Germans]. A discerning soul such as the Danish author and critic Poul Martin Møller looked on this surge with skepticism. In the mid-1830s he warned that the excessive reading of fairy tales would lure children into a fairy world that would take up a disproportionate amount of space in their consciousness. This would enchant and confuse them more than was healthy in terms of the real world in which they were growing up. "With this type of poetic gluttony they will become accustomed to regard what is told to them as so vague that their minds will become a poetic junk room, filled with fragments of all the nation's favorite stories."[65]

Into this open and colorful fairy-tale landscape stepped Hans Christian Andersen in 1835-36, with his very own fairy-tale style. His stories exploded all boundaries of what writers at the time were allowed to do with a fairy tale, including how they spoke *about* children and *to* children. No fairy-tale author in the whole world had ever before rambled so freely in writing. At the same time, he invoked the human right to use the fairy tale and, through the retelling, to refine it. As Andersen so beautifully formulated it in the beginning of a tale that he remembered from his childhood, though he didn't write it down until he was an old man: "Now I'm going to tell you a story that I heard when I was little, and every time I've thought about it since then, it seems to be even more beautiful."[66]

Kierkegaard and Andersen

The fairy tale, with all its diverse religious, philosophical, scientific, and artistic ideas and ambitions, reflects the zeitgeist like no other literary activity during the first half of the 19th century. The truth of this statement is reinforced when we hear that Søren Kierkegaard was something of a fairy-tale fanatic. Like many of his pseudonymous alter egos that appear throughout his works, he could spend entire days reading fairy tales from all eras and regions of the world—even though he, unlike Hans Christian Andersen, had not been brought up with fairy tales at home.[67]

In his journals from 1837, the twenty-two-year-old theology student wrote that whenever he was "weary of everything and sated with life," fairy tales would always provide a rejuvenating bath and a mental tonic that made it possible for him to find joy, even in sorrow.[68] At the same time that Andersen was in the process of establishing himself as a writer of fairy tales, the young Kierkegaard was trying to free himself from that very genre, whose influence on his philosophical studies was becoming a bit too powerful. Yet his interest in fairy tales, and the joy they gave him, ran like a red thread through both his life and work.[69] This came to light in April 1856, after Kierkegaard's death, when his large book collection was put up for auction, and the catalogue revealed nearly a hundred volumes of the people's form of literature. They included Greco-Roman legends and tales from Romania, Holland, Hungary, Ireland, and Germany. There was a copy of *A Thousand and One Nights*, books by Grimm and Æsop, Danish folk ballads, and a number of books about fairy-tale and myth-shrouded figures such as Don Juan, Faust, Ahasuerus, and Till Eulenspiegel—a mysterious wanderer and storyteller from the 14th century who was immortalized in a German folk book filled with stories and anecdotes. Kierkegaard's large collection of fairy-tale books was not something he had inherited, but rather works that he had acquired in the 1830s and 1840s. The collection included several volumes of Hans Christian Andersen's *Fairy Tales, Told for Children*, although the philosopher was never a great fan of them. In fact, he was so dissatisfied with Andersen and his way of telling fairy tales that in the 1840s he once stated in a sudden fit of rage that Andersen had no idea what a fairy tale actually was: "Why does he bother with poetry? He has a good heart, that's sufficient . . . It's very innocent, but fairy tales!?"[70]

These words were uttered in Frederiksberg Gardens in Copenhagen as Kierkegaard was taking a walk with the philologist Israel Levin, who at that time was the philosopher's secretary. To further support his opinion of Andersen's much too sentimental fairy tales, Kierkegaard retold on this walk a few indecent and demonic tales, including one titled "Attic Nights," a story about carnal love between men. Another story was about an ascetic hermit whose sole purpose in life was to stifle the call of the flesh. Levin reports that there was no stopping Kierkegaard, and finally the philosopher emphasized that it was this kind of daring, both in form and content, that good fairy tales should always strive for. And the philosopher played his trump card in this intellectual diatribe with the words: "Poetry is not for children with a pacifier in their mouth or for half-grown girls, but for mature individuals."[71]

Measured against such a powerful ideal regarding fairy tales and authors, it's no surprise that Andersen and his stories for children and childish souls would fall short. But it's interesting that Kierkegaard would display such vehemence in this debate with himself about the nature and purpose of fairy tales. Kierkegaard indisputably possessed a great deal of knowledge about the genre, and he shared with Andersen a Romantic's interest in the importance of the child and childhood. So it would seem that Kierkegaard should have had a keen eye for the radical nature of *Fairy Tales, Told for Children*. Yet Kierkegaard never expressed any appreciation for Andersen's fairy tales. But why was it so necessary to take such a deliberate and strong stand against everything that was naïve about Andersen's writing, as Kierkegaard did in his debut book in 1838? He summed it all up under the precise label: "sniveling." Was it simply a matter of differing views of what a fairy tale is and what a writer of fairy tales should do? Or was Kierkegaard's criticism also an expression of the hidden rivalry that had always existed between the two men and that continued through the 1840s?

We have to go back to the mid-1830s to answer these questions. Back to the time when the tall, lanky author had written his first fairy tales, and the short, stooped theology student with the great ambitions, strong will, and handsome face had not yet published his first book. The paths of the two men would occasionally cross at the Students' Association or the Music Association, in cafés, at the theater, on Østergade, or at the home of the

Heibergs in Christianshavn. Yet they never made any show of enthusiasm for one another, nor did they ever come close to using the informal "du" to address each other. They were much too different for that, although they did share some essential emotions: loneliness, a fear of women, enthusiasm over fairy tales, an interest in the importance of childhood, and a desire to figure out other people.

From their very first encounter, these two observers of God's grace had scowled a bit at each other. And each had found his counterpart to be comical, not to mention ridiculous. It's highly likely that in 1835 Hans Christian Andersen, through various indirect means, had learned of the young Kierkegaard's opinion of his literary *enfant terrible*, *Agnete and the Merman*. This was the play that had prompted such disapproval from Edvard Collin and others in Copenhagen in 1834, primarily because of Agnete's half-brother, Hemming. In the words of the play, he was "too soft for a man." Many of Andersen's male friends who read the play in the winter of 1833-34 called Hemming an "unmanly, sniveling, pitiful lover."[72] The opinion of twenty-year-old Søren Kierkegaard about the strange amphibian, Agnete, and her worm of a brother was equally harsh. Sitting at his desk in 1835, Kierkegaard wrote a note stating that *Agnete and the Merman* was a wretched work because the siblings Agnete and Hemming were so obviously Hans Christian Andersen himself. In Kierkegaard's words:

> "There are authors who, like beggars seeking to arouse sympathy by exposing the flaws and deformities of their body, strive to reveal the tattered state of their heart to attract attention."[73]

So we see that in 1835 Kierkegaard had already set out on the path of criticizing Andersen. This was the path he would follow in the coming years, largely with the intention of portraying the fairy-tale writer as a sniveling genius who clung to the skirts of women. Between the lines of his note from 1835, which was addressed to his mentor Poul Martin Møller, Kierkegaard is looking for an ethically stronger author persona who will take responsibility for himself and his life, for example by separating the writing from the writer to a much greater extent. In Andersen's case, this criticism was not entirely wide of the mark, even though the same could easily be said of Kierkegaard, who loved the sound of his own voice and the scratch of his pen across the page.

Is it possible that Andersen may have had similar thoughts when a little bird told him about Kierkegaard's criticism in 1835? At any rate, it looks as if he decided to reply in a couple of minor amateur performances at the

Students' Association in the mid-1830s, in which he made fun of cogitating and loudly boasting young students with a penchant for Heiberg and Hegel. Here Andersen was aiming at an intellectual type of man who closely resembled Kierkegaard and all his colleagues.[74] At that time Andersen was beginning to distance himself from the group surrounding Heiberg, who swore by the conservative direction of the Hegelian school of thought and who dominated Denmark's literary and theater criticism of the day. Heiberg had previously been favorably disposed toward Andersen, but he was now making greater and greater demands on the aesthetics of new works. Andersen presumably saw in Kierkegaard—the young, rambunctious theology student—the archetypal critic, whom he lumped together as "form-cutters" and "pavers of the garden of poetry." Kierkegaard had a burning desire, as did Andersen deep in his heart, to become part of the Heiberg clique. As we will soon see, Kierkegaard's debut work from 1838 was shaped as a literary execution of the novelist Hans Christian Andersen. Kierkegaard also used this book to appeal for a vacant spot in the city's leading literary club by drawing Heiberg's old mother, Fru Thomasine Gyllembourg, into the text and extravagantly praising her literary works.

But before things reached that state in the fall of 1838, Andersen had managed to incense the young Kierkegaard further. This was due to the fairy tale "The Galoshes of Fortune," which came out in May 1838. At that time Kierkegaard's announced article about Andersen's latest novel, *Only a Fiddler*, had not yet gone to press for Heiberg's publication *Perseus*, to which all the weighty arbiters of taste in Copenhagen subscribed.[75] To all appearances Andersen's tale takes aim at Kierkegaard partway through the story, in the section about "the transformation of the copyist." Here the reader is introduced to an exotic bird who philosophically babbles on, constantly shaking his head and sending ripples through his birdlike coiffure and crooked nose. It was almost as if Andersen had placed a miniature portrait of a well-known Copenhagen magpie and chatterbox in his story. And many people in the city nodded with recognition at this bird who was so good at "making a quip, quip, quip" and lavishly scattering philosophical remarks, such as: "Now, let's be sensible people!"[76] With his unflagging sense for the striking similarities between animals and people, the fairy-tale author—on paper—had an easy time with a Heiberg parrot such as young Søren Kierkegaard. It was said that the theology student's "dialectical" tongue never stopped wagging when he was among educated people. As Andersen wrote in his story: "Everything else it screeched was just as incomprehensible as the chirping of a canary."[77]

Andersen should never have done this. Kierkegaard now had most of the summer in 1838 to tighten his own critical portrait of Hans Christian Andersen as a novelist. Instead of being an incisive analysis, the article became more of an execution of the author. This change in approach may have been too much for the editor J. L. Heiberg. In any case, Kierkegaard's text was never published in *Perseus*, and the first-time author had to look around for a new editor and publisher. C. A. Reitzel, who was also Andersen's publisher, had no compunctions about printing the critical work as long as the young man could cover any deficits resulting from his small book. The matter was settled, and Kierkegaard's revenge was sweet.

Kierkegaard's eighty-page book, *From the Papers of One Still Alive*, was published on September 7, 1838. Taking a few words from Andersen's tale "The Door Key," the book seems at first glance "pyramidal malice." But there were many different layers to Kierkegaard's critique, as evidenced by the mysterious title. Who was this half-dead person and what were these papers? Were they the treatise itself or its subject—meaning Andersen's novel? Or did the title actually refer to Søren Kierkegaard, who in 1837–38 had been hard hit by deaths among those closest to him? Or was it also possible that the title was a joke for the benefit of a small, exclusive group of insiders who knew about a diverting notebook that Kierkegaard had once heard mentioned in the home of the Hebraic Müller out in Christianshavn? On many occasions Müller would talk about what an oddly naïve and stubborn fellow Andersen was; the author always carried a little collection of handwritten poems with him, bearing the peculiar title: *Poems by Hans Christian Andersen. Deceased 1828.*[78] In 1838, Kierkegaard was looking for an effective title for his treatise about this Andersen who couldn't write proper plays, novels, or fairy tales, and yet at the Students' Association he dared make fun of intelligent people. Kierkegaard didn't have to look far to find a way to retaliate. The title he chose had already been conceived in the notes for a philosophical farce that Kierkegaard had once started but never completed, which was to have the subtitle: "From the Papers of One Still Alive."[79]

But what was the actual basis for Kierkegaard's critique? And why couldn't he stand *Only a Fiddler* or the novel's author? This Andersen, whose pen spread not only ink blots but gossip—as the first-time writer said of the established author. Here we should pause for a moment to think about what Andersen had achieved with his three novels published in

1835, 1836, and 1837. Each in its own way, but with a shared context and rising intensity, dealt on some level of the text with the problematic presence of two genders in one person. As mentioned in the previous chapter, readers of *The Improvisatore*, *O.T.*, and *Only a Fiddler* witness a rather formidable battle between the two sexes in three different, yet in some ways similar, male protagonists, who all bear a resemblance to the author. It was a battle of the sexes which, to use a few incisive terms from Kierkegaard's critique of *Only a Fiddler*, ended with "a broken masculinity" giving way to a "sustained femininity." Young Søren Kierkegaard had a keen eye for the whole question of androgyny that Andersen dealt with in his three educational novels of 1835–37, especially in *Only a Fiddler*. And this was one of the reasons why he "thoroughly declined Andersen through the various grammatical cases of life," as he writes.

Kierkegaard had uncovered the female soul in Andersen's character. This is made clear in several sections of his furiously well-written treatise, in which the reader has to proceed through various complex linguistic labyrinths and run the gauntlet between parentheses and notes to reach those places where the patterns of his critique are quite comprehensible. In fact, even Hans Christian Andersen—who, as Edvard Collin so aptly expressed it, was no thinker, much less a brooder—could follow Kierkegaard's delicate and not so delicate insinuations.

In large part, his critique of *Only a Fiddler* is a haughty, patronizing screed about Andersen's impotence, both in his life and his work. "The Bachelor Class," brays Kierkegaard when he embarks on a biographical portrait of Andersen, who is eight years his senior. And the term was painfully true, even though the same could be said of the younger bachelor Kierkegaard. But Andersen was always an easy target for other men— they could always so easily shift their own masculine troubles onto his shoulders. And Kierkegaard had early on taken note of this and written comments in his journals: "Andersen isn't so dangerous; based on what I've seen, his followers consist of an auxiliary choir of volunteer undertakers and several roving aesthetes, who are perpetually asserting their integrity."[80]

The aesthetic and ethical points of Kierkegaard's critique come together in a challenge to the novelist not to allow his life to "burn out," as so undeniably happens with the life of Andersen's male protagonist Christian in *Only a Fiddler*. Christian's pessimistic and passive view of the world was comparable to everything that Kierkegaard, several years before, had criticized in another soft man in Andersen's writing, Hemming in *Agnete and the Merman*. Kierkegaard could not accept such an unmanly perception of genius as Andersen now repeated in his literary work. Nor was this perception contradicted by Andersen's own spineless persona. According to Kierkegaard a genius should not be indulged but should instead pull himself together through his own force of will: "A genius is not a tiny flame that goes out in a breeze, but a conflagration that a storm merely stokes." And Kierkegaard made it clear how this should be done as he launched in the same breath a veritable hurricane of criticism against Andersen, both as a writer and a human being.

One interesting and overlooked item in Kierkegaard's critical broadside is that he was the first one to point out that the lax and weak aspects of Andersen's writing were due to the author's sexual confusion. Kierkegaard wrote that the author found himself in a "middle ground," deeply divided between what was innate and what was determined by environment. Andersen's problems with love and sex had gradually become so apparent that the root of these problems was now visible high up on the stalk. At any rate, this is the message that was concealed in one of the most dramatic notes in world literature, in which Søren Kierkegaard perceives Hans Christian Andersen as a hermaphrodite plant: "Andersen's primary power should instead be compared to those flowers in which the male and female reside on one stalk."[81]

The question of androgyny in Andersen's life and work is mentioned in many other places in Kierkegaard's text. For instance, in the very first note, the reader is introduced to a different image and concept of the plant and animal kingdoms, which is supposed to explain and point out the dual gender of Andersen the writer. Kierkegaard pulls a tadpole onto the stage, a so-called *rana paradoxa*—a creature that, in the old days, was thought to undergo a reverse process from a frog, so that in the end it became a little tadpole. Kierkegaard uses this amphibian with frog legs and a salamander tail as an image of how far it's possible to stray from the legitimate and main development of an animal and—metaphorically speaking—a human being. Kierkegaard's use of this zoological phenomenon is no doubt connected with his reading of *Agnete and the Merman* in 1835. As mentioned, he was not the least receptive to Andersen's paradoxical frog by the name of Agnete, who also lived a double life, half in water and half on land. Kierkegaard's zoological metaphor was not taken out of thin air, as he emphasized several years later in *The Concept of Dread*, in which the *rana paradoxa* is again used to indicate something that goes against the natural order, although this time he is talking about corrupted and degenerate children.[82]

Eternal Rivals

This was not only Søren Kierkegaard's first book, it was also the first work that was solely devoted to Andersen's writing. And no one had ever previously undressed Hans Christian Andersen the human being so thoroughly in public. Andersen was of course deeply shocked when he learned of the critique on September 6. During a brief, chance conversation with Kierkegaard on Østergade several months earlier, Andersen had gotten the clear impression that it would be a relatively positive review. But he realized that the situation might be quite different as the day of publication approached. A note in his calendar on August 30, 1838—a week before the book was to be published—demonstrates that Andersen's anxiety had begun to grow: "Felt pangs of the heart about Kierkegaard's not yet published critique."[83]

As previously mentioned, the criticisms contained in *From the Papers of One Still Alive* and Kierkegaard's aversion to Hans Christian Andersen's fairy tales may seem surprising. How could the fundamentally sound sense of judgment in such a well-read and sensitive person as Kierkegaard fail him in certain areas, apparently swallowed up by narrow-mindedness and envy? At any rate, the rivalry between the two men became a fact the moment Kierkegaard threw down the gauntlet in 1838. And during the following years, insults were regularly exchanged between the author and the philosopher. These two men, better than any of their contemporaries, were able to illuminate and describe "the Romantic individual," but neither of them could see or was willing to admit how much they had in common. They shared not only a joy in fairy tales and a desire to be a seducer on paper, but also a belief in individualism and an awareness that each person must take responsibility for his own life. Each read the other's work more often than he would admit. Over the years, little notes in Andersen's diaries, even after Kierkegaard's death, reveal that the philosopher's books were frequently taken out and read, though almost secretly. There was no room for grand, enthusiastic gestures. Only a brief, terse comment, almost like an epitaph, although that's not what it was at all: "Have read Kierkegaard."[84]

The first time that Hans Christian Andersen seriously responded in kind to Kierkegaard was in 1840 with the entertaining one-act play *A Comedy in the Open*, which was performed at the Royal Theater on May 13.

The play's subtitle is "Vaudeville in One Act, Based on the Old Comedy: *Actor Against His Will.*" And here Andersen saw his chance to take direct aim at the sophomoric subtitle of Kierkegaard's critique of Andersen from 1838, which was "Published Against His Will by S. Kierkegaard." The play is about a traveling theater manager who disguises himself in various male roles. The cast includes an intellectual, misanthropic fool of a haircutter who introduces himself with the words: "As an individual depressed by the world but at bottom guided by a philosophy for the existence of my tranquility! I am the theater hairdresser!"[85]

Both visible and audible is the fact that Andersen had placed an echo of Kierkegaard's critique of *Only a Fiddler* from two years earlier in the mouth of this philosophical hairdresser. Various phrases from the reasoning in *From the Papers of One Still Alive* were transferred directly to Andersen's comedy. For example: "I am a hairdresser! These few words will give you a concept, which thoroughly declined through the various grammatical cases of life, will tell you how unhappy I must be. Our art has been declined!"[86]

With exquisite pleasure, Andersen then confronts the theater hairdresser, who thinks that the art of the day is nothing but dregs, with the farm foreman Frantz, who naturally doesn't understand a word of the convoluted speech. "Won't you simply tell me what you think?" asks the bewildered farmer, who still can't make out a thing, even though the theater hairdresser tries to reassure him with the information that it's merely the way in which the words are presented that is "chaos-ing" him. "Just tell me what you want of me," pleads the farmer at last, only to receive another round of admonishments:

> "What I want? It's one thing to want, another to be able to! Will is often a phenomenon in the most respectable of figures, the way it appears in Hegel's great attempt at starting with nothing."[87]

It was the worst mumbo-jumbo, and for a while it took the wind out of Søren Kierkegaard's sails on the finest stage in the land. Andersen's counterattack was launched a few weeks before he was to embark on his long trip to the Near East. Kierkegaard responded swiftly, even though his furious reaction never got any farther than his own desk. He then put it away, among all sorts of other papers, but even today the words still tremble with rage.

"Wait a Moment, Herr Andersen" was the title that Kierkegaard gave to his reply, in which the fairy-tale author was thoroughly ridiculed, using easily accessible language that was quite unusual for the philosopher. Only in the following tirade did Kierkegaard's language become slightly more complicated: "Andersen the author, who is the monopolizing negative proprietor of all philosophy and all higher scholarly configuration."[88] Regarding his own original attack on Andersen in 1838, Kierkegaard revealed:

> "In keeping with my abilities, I strove to capture the tangled and motley Andersenian writer-existence in all its windings, curvings, turnings, squirmings, and twistings."

Kierkegaard chose not to make public this sharp retort to "Andersen, famous in Europe, who will soon set off on his triumphal procession without affecting my own insignificant personage." Instead, his reply was allowed to remain in a drawer until one day—presumably in 1843—when the philosopher suddenly received Hans Christian Andersen's *New Fairy Tales.* The volume contained an inscription offered as a peace pipe that was also an elegant and deep obeisance to Kierkegaard's masterpiece *Either-Or*, which Andersen had read and apparently understood, seeing more of himself reflected in it than he would ever admit. The inscription read: "*Either* you approve of my things, *or* you do not approve of them, yet you come without *fear and trembling*, and that at least is something." Søren Kierkegaard did not thank Andersen for this unexpected gesture until years later, in 1849, when he sent a copy of *Either-Or* to Andersen, who clearly had not thought this type of brotherly connection was possible between the two of them. And so he instantly replied:

> "Dear Herr Kierkegaard! You have given me great pleasure by sending me your *Either-Or*! I was very surprised, as I'm sure you may realize; I had no idea that you would think kindly of me, and yet here I see that you do! God bless you for that! Thank you, thank you! With heartfelt devotion, yours sincerely, Hans Christian Andersen."[89]

No deeper form of reconciliation ever took place between the two, even though Andersen, in Chapter Seven of *The Fairy Tale of My Life*, obscured both their natural adversarial relationship and their rivalry. In fact, he almost managed to make Kierkegaard's character assassination of 1838 seem pleasant:

> "People also joked that only Kierkegaard and Andersen ever read the whole book; that is, *From the Papers of One Still Alive*. Back then I under-

stood it to say that I was not a writer but a poetic figure who had escaped from my group, and that it was the job of a future writer to put me back inside it, or to use me as a figure in a piece of writing in which he created my supplement! Later I better understood this author, who over the years has met me with kindness and judiciousness."[90]

But inwardly Kierkegaard was never given absolution for his merciless critique of 1838. After the philosopher's death in 1855, Andersen always made sure to place his criticism of Kierkegaard in someone else's mouth, such as Esther in the novel *To Be or Not to Be* in 1857, who "admired the gifted person, but grew tired of climbing over the pavement of language to the temple of ideas; for her the road was long, and the green that she found was not newly sprouted."[91]

Yet all their lives, both Hans Christian Andersen and Søren Kierkegaard possessed a love for fairy tales and an interest in children and in the importance of childhood in human life. In this sense the two were not as far apart as it may have seemed from their rivalry and their mutual desire to cut each other down to size. It has often been pointed out, as it was for the first time by B. S. Ingemann during those emotional fall days of 1838, that Kierkegaard actually thought more highly of Andersen than he showed. And in the conclusion of his first book, in a convoluted rhetorical manner, the philosopher admitted that as a reader he evaluated Andersen in a different way than he did as a critic.[92] In the words of Ingemann:

> "Presumably he [Kierkegaard] thinks much more highly of you than he has acknowledged. I believe the conclusion hints at this kind of friendly, though oddly repressed, tone. But it is narrow-minded and unfair to voice one's censure aloud while whispering praise and recognition in the ear, to express one's disapproval with printer's ink and write one's thanks and approval with invisible ink. I wish that he would realize this and make amends by means of an equally detailed elaboration of what he back then could only whisper in your ear and by holding the proper light to the invisible ink himself. He owes this to your readers and his own, as much as to you and himself."[93]

What Ingemann was asking for between the lines of his wise and consoling missive to Andersen was for Kierkegaard to correct the "missing half of his observation," for instance by taking a closer look at *Fairy Tales, Told for Children*. Kierkegaard never did so. But to finish off the story of the eternally tense relationship between the author in the galoshes of fortune and the philosopher in his small, tight shoes, we need to look at Kierkegaard's rough draft of a treatise on the art of telling stories to children, which he wrote in 1837. This was after nine of Andersen's fairy tales had been published.[94] Kierkegaard wrote this literary monograph, which was never completed, partially in opposition to his mentor Poul Martin Møller and his essay on the consequences of the excessive reading of fairy tales. On behalf of children, Kierkegaard demands "mythology and good fairy tales" instead of "poetic wash-water." And he asks the crucial question that Hans Christian Andersen's fairy-tale universe would take up and treat in a way that the world had never seen before: "Does childhood have any independent merit?"

In contrast to Møller, who had warned against filling children with fantastical stories so that they would go astray in a boundless fairy-tale world, Kierkegaard maintained that children ought to be stuffed full of fairy tales and legends. Although, of course, they should be fairy tales of the type that in a Socratic manner would awaken the child's desire to ask questions. "What is important is to position the poetic in all ways in relationship to their lives, to exercise a magical power," Kierkegaard wrote. He emphasized that people should not refrain from telling fairy tales, because that would make room for a child's natural, innate fear, which is summoned and nourished by the child's own lively imagination. Kierkegaard thought that fairy tales have a psychological, cleansing effect. And at a certain stage of development, children need the horror and tension of fairy tales to work through and release their fear, which is an unavoidable human condition. Kierkegaard's prescription was clear: "Mythology and good fairy tales are what the child needs!"

With this therapeutic view of the fairy tale, Søren Kierkegaard anticipated the whole school within modern child psychology, for which Bruno Bettelheim, among others, became the spokesman many years later. This school maintains that the fairy tale not only educates and supports, but it also contains the redemptive words that can liberate children's emotions.[95] In Kierkegaard's opinion, it was important that the era's fairy tales for children were neither toothless nor overly sweet. And the storytellers should not be nice, old uncles who, instead of stimulating the children's "anxious" curiosity and desire to ask questions, would lull them to sleep with idyllic nonsense about the eternally happy world of childhood which they would soon be leaving. And with that, the children were well on their way to being traumatized, as Kierkegaard pointed out.

In Kierkegaard's eyes, Andersen's fairy tales were too naïve and senti-mental. In the draft of his treatise on fairy tales from 1837, we see Kierkegaard's nightmare of a fairy-tale writer: "those tall pups who are so innocent and so naïve, who would give almost anything to ensure that their whiskers never grew so much that they had to be shaved off, so they might always be downy-cheeked, bare-necked youths." Kierkegaard writes that these storytellers, instead of leaving childhood behind in a harmonious manner, desperately play at being children. They not only ceaselessly talk about children, but they have adopted the speech patterns of children, and they would much prefer it if all adults would immediately start speaking and writing like children. There can be no doubt that the fairy-tale writer Hans Christian Andersen was one of the storytellers that Søren Kierke-gaard had in mind. "It's a tragi-comic sight to see these tall, childlike jump-ing jacks leaping around the floor and playing hobbyhorse with the sweet little children, and listen to their listless stories about 'innocent and happy childhood.'"

Yet Andersen was not seriously affected by all these polemics in writ-ing and in the various corners of the upper echelons. In the fall of 1838 he published a new book of fairy tales that opened with the words: "Now let me tell you!" His voice was undiminished, and completely ready for fairy tales such as "The Chamomile," "The Steadfast Tin Soldier," and "The Wild Swans"—three texts that in no sense elevated children to angels. Instead, they put a knife into the hands of a few of them and showed how brutal, short-sighted, and egotistical in temperament children can be. Kierkegaard and other Danish critics who doubted Andersen's stature and courage as a writer of fairy tales were thoroughly put to shame with this fourth volume of *Fairy Tales, Told for Children*.

The following year Andersen published *A Picture Book Without Pictures*, which was a group of little stories with the moon in the role of a heavenly Scheherazade who every evening—if the clouds permit—peers down at the impoverished, lonely artist in his garret room, which has a view of fac-tory chimneys and of nature off in the distance, which he once abandoned and now misses. The moon consoles the lad with little stories about every-thing he experiences on his nightly voyages across the sky, "above the waters of the deluge down on earth." But through the power of words and poetry, the moon will prompt a new and beautiful world to blossom. And the primordial force of humanity that will carry the new epoch is introduced by the moon—and Hans Christian Andersen—to the readers in the very last epistle, "The Thirty-third Evening," which was added in the 1840s. Here the moon starts off by saying that he is so infinitely fond of children because they are fun and spontaneous. He also tells the young artist that he loves to sit up in the heavens and look at children when they have to go to bed at night: "First the little, naked, round shoulder comes out of the dress, then an arm slips out, or I see a stocking pulled off, and a charming little leg, so white and firm, emerges; it's a foot worth kissing, and I kiss it!"

On this very last evening the moon has chosen the child who will personify the hope for future life on earth. The curtains have not been closed in the home of the large family with many children, including a little girl, four years old, who knows her prayers so well. Her mother sits near the bed and listens to the girl rattling off the words while the other children are making a ruckus in the background with chairs and toys. Suddenly the mother gives a start and asks the girl to repeat what she adds every time she says "Give us this day our daily bread!" The girl glances up at her mother in embarrassment and says that she mustn't be angry at the fact that she has just rounded off her prayer with the pious hope: "and with plenty of butter on it!"[96]

By this time Hans Christian Andersen himself had begun to have plenty of butter on his daily bread. In 1838 he was awarded a permanent annual stipend, granted by King Frederik VI. But before this happened, he had worked in the wings, as always, to persuade the proper potentates to speak on his behalf to the king. Andersen wrote a lengthy letter in December 1837 to the prime minister, Count Conrad Rantzau-Breitenburg, who was an enthusiast of poetry and Italy. He had previously taken a great interest in the author of *The Improvisatore* and visited him in Nyhavn. Andersen now attempted to convince this powerful man to support his cause:

"The happiness of my whole life, all the undertakings of my future do I place in your hands; simply tell the king what I know you have so fondly said to others about me! Do not refuse my plea! If you believe that there is anything stirring inside me, then speak my case. Only this one time will I beg for your kindness. You will win distinction through me, with God's help, you will! . . . The happiness of my life is at stake. Deliver to the king my application, and with God's help, you will not be shamed by me! . . . Respectfully, Hans Christian Andersen."[97]

The good count could not and would not refuse Andersen, who many years later in *The Fairy Tale of My Life* remembered the noble deed of Count Rantzau–Breitenburg in 1838. But in Andersen's memoirs there is no mention of his letter; he says only that the prime minister visited him in his lodgings on the Charlottenborg side of Nyhavn and on the spot promised to be a loyal friend and energetic supporter in the future. And he was. In May 1938, Frederik VI granted to Andersen a permanent annual sum of 400 *rigsdaler*. As Andersen concludes in Chapter Seven of *The Fairy Tale of My Life*, with a single stroke he was suddenly far less dependent on the people he knew in Copenhagen. He could once again take out his seven-league boots and his flying trunk and polish them for departure. A grand and adventurous chapter of his life was about to begin, even though a year earlier Andersen—thinking of the prospect of a per-manent author's stipend from the national treasury—had written to Henriette Hanck that people shouldn't expect that this meant he was about to enter the ranks of adults:

> "I must have 1000 a year before I dare fall in love, and 1500 before I dare marry, and before even half of this happens, the young girl will be gone, captured by someone else, and I'll be an old, wizened bachelor. Those are sorry prospects . . . No. I will never be rich, never satisfied and never—fall in love!"[98]

Chapter Six

Distant Shores (1840-1846)

"Allah is great!" whispers the author in the middle of the dark, foaming Sea of Marmara, on his way to Constantinople in May 1841. Under the steamship's flag with the crescent are veiled women dressed in silk, velvet, and Morocco leather, and reclining men smoking water pipes and wearing fezzes and turbans. Among them, the tall, thin stranger looks like one of the lanky birds with red legs and enormous beaks that every autumn arrive from the north and then in early spring once again leave the shores of the Cyclades and the waters of the Nile.

He has settled down in the middle of the deck with all his belongings grouped close around his big, clumsy wings: valises, hat boxes, and a big, spiral walking stick.

He's dressed in an uncomfortable, tight-fitting suit, with the trouser cuffs snugly tucked into a pair of enormous boots. He constantly removes his top hat as he greets people all around him in a language which, to the ears of people who speak Turkish, Arabic, and Persian, sounds like the clacking of a stork's beak or some other remote form of gibberish. Everyone responds loudly and cordially; they've never seen anyone like him.

The stranger can't sit still. He rummages through his pockets and suddenly produces a piece of paper covered with handwritten poems to show to a handsome young Persian, who twists and turns the paper with the peculiar letters and then shrugs his shoulders.

Only when a little Near Eastern girl, full of curiosity, makes her way over and tries to decipher the odd symbols does the author finally find someone with whom he can talk. The girl's dark, gleaming hair hangs over her shoulders in two long braids interwoven with jingling gold coins. On her head she wears a little golden cap that glows like a sunrise.

Her name is Zuleika, and the author instantly forgets all about the towering gray waves of the Sea of Marmara, the rolling motion, and his fear of shipwreck. He summons a waiter and orders the sweetest jam the ship has to offer. It arrives in a glass *bowl, and the daughter of Asia swiftly and meticulously eats all the jam, licks her lips, and then vanishes. But barely a moment later she reappears with her dearest possession in her hand: a little Turkish drinking vessel, shaped like a horse with a bird behind each ear.*

Who else but this fairy-tale author from the land far north would have appreciated the splendor of this fabulous animal?

If he could have spoken Turkish, Arabic, or Persian, he would have promptly told Zuleika a story about the toad with the gemstone on its head. But under foreign flags and crescents he has no other fairy tale to tell than what is right before his eyes and can be seen and felt. He looks at the girl and starts to speak:

> *"The head is such a singular globe! The outermost and largest promontory is called the nose, and it's very steep on one side. Here we also find two deep holes, where we often notice very odd phenomena. They're no doubt volcanoes that are not yet extinct. Close by is a long throat and an abyss called the mouth. It has lovely red coral shores, and if we climb over them we find the most charming ivory cliffs that extend in two long chains, forming the outermost boundary. On each side of the nose and mouth lie two lovely stretches of land that are somewhat rolling and covered with roses. If we climb higher, we find two peculiar, cool lakes with salt water. They are constantly in motion, possessing a wondrous power, and they can make you feel quite strange if you stare into them! It feels as if you're looking at an entire spirit world. You can sense a bliss that cannot be expressed! High above the lakes looms a mountain, and inside, the mighty fairies are building Imagination and Reason. A spirit world stirs inside: here memory has hung all its mighty images, and here—in the elegant magic mirrors—all of human life is reflected. All the dreams of the heart rise up like tiny winged creatures, and here God and reason have their holy altar. If we leave the mountain and continue our wandering, we come to a huge forest, but no geographer dares to enter, for fear of getting lost in this huge, densely overgrown tract."*[1]

The author looks down at the silently listening Zuleika. "And now you will give me your mouth and eyes!" He makes a gesture with his hand, as if to pluck them away. She shakes her black braids, laughs, and points out to sea. The steamer has entered calm waters, and the coast of Asia can be glimpsed in the distance.

*H*ANS CHRISTIAN ANDERSEN'S long journey to the "Orient" in 1840–41 took him via various land and sea routes through Europe to Rome and Naples, where the author made a lengthy stay. He then continued on by ship through the Strait of Messina and past the mythological rocks of Scylla and Charybdis, known from *The Odyssey*. Shrouded in fog and with fangs and whirlpools, they devour everything that comes near. But Andersen mercifully slipped past and headed across the Mediterranean toward Greece. After a brief stay in Athens, he sailed through the Dardanelles and the Sea of Marmara for Constantinople. There the author once again allowed his indomitable sense of curiosity and his desire to see new horizons conquer his fear. He continued his Homeric journey alone, traveling through the Black Sea to the Romanian coast near Constantia. From there he set off overland by closed mail coach, then by river boat along the Danube, which even back then meandered through countries involved in almost constant civil wars. Traveling by various river boats through Romania, Bulgaria, Serbia, and Hungary, Andersen once again reached Central Europe, and after brief sojourns in Vienna, Prague, Dresden, and Hamburg he was finally ready—more or less—to return home to Denmark.

By the standards of the day, it was an overwhelmingly long and perilous trip that covered thousands of kilometers. No Dane had ever before made this journey. Like the writing process which, after the author's return home, would transform his ample and detailed diary into a travel book, the journey lasted "nine cycles of the moon," as it says in a little fairy-tale sketch about Muhammad in one of the travel book's chapters about Constantinople. The account is from May 1841, when Andersen roamed the bazaars of the city as the Prophet's birthday was celebrated.

There are a great many metaphors of birth and death in *A Poet's Bazaar*, as the travel book came to be known. This epic travel account, nearly 400 pages long, is structured around a series of birthlike tableaux in which the traveling and narrating author is forced through narrow passages and strong currents at the Strait of Messina, the Dardanelles, the Bosporus, and the Iron Gate between Orsova and Drencova during the Serbian stage of his Danube voyage. There are places where it's possible to use the old Latin proverb: "He who wishes to avoid Charybdis often falls to Scylla." The sites mentioned above, which are all associated with water, are described in the book as ritual crossings in which the traveling author is in danger of losing his life, but each time—as the "sensitive traveler of the age" that he is—he chooses to take the risk.

More than any other of Andersen's travel books, *A Poet's Bazaar* takes place on seas, lakes, and rivers. It can be read as a creation story about a Nordic artist who fled south and was reborn in the East, but on his way home he panicked at the thought that his native land was once again so close:

"Endless sparse forests lay before us! The air in the early morning heavy and hot; it did not shine as over the Mediterranean and Bosporus. I seemed to be home on an oppressively warm summer day! My journey was now over. Dejection weighed on my heart, a premonition of something quite terrible! In little Denmark each talent stands so close to the other that they push and shove, since they all want to have room. As for me, people only have eyes for my faults! My path at home passes through heavy seas! I know that many more swells will crash over my head before I reach harbor!"[2]

One of the destinations on this long journey, which Andersen had been anticipating with great excitement and yearning, was Constantinople. According to his diary for 1841, his sojourn in the fabled city lasted from April 25 to May 4. Yet in the travel book, the author's stay became tinged with fiction of such a sensual and mythological power that those ten days grew into something resembling a thousand and one days. Constantinople became the fabulous focal point of the travel book. From this Aladdin's cave of a city, with its long underground roots beneath the Bosporus stretching toward both Europe and Asia, Andersen extracted a treasure without realizing its full value or extent. It wasn't until a couple of years after his return to Copenhagen that the contents of the treasure chest became apparent: a string of pearls composed of fairy tales such as "The Sandman," "The Rose Fairy," "The Swineherd," "The Buckwheat," "The Angel," "The Nightingale," "The Sweethearts," "The Ugly Duckling," "The Fir Tree," and "The Snow Queen." These stories were all written during the years following Andersen's return from his trip to the Near East. Not until 1843 did Hans Christian Andersen realize that a decisive shift had occurred in his life and work. In a long letter to B. S. Ingemann, he acknowledges this realization and announces that he has finally found his *own* authorial voice:

"I think it will please me if I'm right in deciding to write fairy tales! The first ones I produced were, of course, mostly old ones that I had heard as a child and which I, in my own style and fashion, retold and rewrote. Yet the ones I created myself—for example 'The Little Mermaid,' 'The Storks,' 'The Chamomile'—won the most acclaim, and that has allowed me to take flight! Now I tell stories from my own heart, seize an idea for the grown-up—and then tell them for the children while I keep in mind that Father and Mother are often listening, and they have to be given a little to think about! I have a great deal of material, more than for any other type of writing. It often seems to me as if every fence, every little flower is saying: 'Look at me, then you will absorb my story,' and if I wish, then I'll have a story!"[3]

For Andersen, his journey to the Near East was like coming home to some of the best moments in his childhood, when his shoemaker father on long winter evenings on Munkemøllestræde would read aloud from *A Thousand and One Nights*. Back then the talented boy devoured all the stories about the Roc, Ali Baba, Aladdin, and Scheherezade. But Andersen's nine-month-long trip in 1840-41 was also important in terms of other Gordian knots in his life and work. This is partly evident in the many observations about himself in the diary and letters he wrote both to and from the Near East. It's also apparent in the reflections that spread like a foaming wake in connection with the writing of *A Poet's Bazaar* during the winter of 1841-42. And in *The True Story of My Life* from 1847, it's quite clear that along the way Andersen had explored some boundaries within himself. In particular, the chapters dealing with Naples and the voyage from Italy and Malta to Greece and Turkey are presented as a turning point, both geographically and existentially. After traveling due south, the poet-ship turned eastward and set course for "the Orient":

> "It was as if a new life were about to open for me, and that was truly what happened. If this can't be read in my later writings, it animates my views of life, all of my inner development. I no longer felt sickly. As I watched my European home, if I might call it that, vanish behind me, it was as if a current of forgetfulness passed over all bitter and sickly memories. I felt health in my blood, health in my mind; robustly and bravely I once again raised my head."[4]

Oh yes, there were a great many things to flee from when Hans Christian Andersen sailed away from Copenhagen on October 31, 1840, aboard the steamship *Christian VIII*. He arrived in Kiel, terribly seasick, on the following day. In a letter to B. S. Ingemann, Andersen had said farewell to "deadly Denmark." He felt persecuted by the Copenhagen intelligentsia—by J. L. Heiberg, Christian Molbech, Søren Kierkegaard, and other "ink men" who, unlike Andersen, preferred to live their lives behind their Copenhagen desks and seldom went beyond the city ramparts. The restless, romantic Andersen needed a much larger world, and he was now searching for a type of writing that would be based not only on nature and himself but also on a new era and all its marvels.

Critical Headwinds

In the legendary dispute between Hans Christian Andersen and his numerous Danish critics, the lines were sharply drawn in 1840. This involved many Danish artists of the day and also several different art forms, since it was just as much a clash between various attitudes and temperaments as it was a cultural and political clash between various "schools" and "-isms." In 1847, in his rather belated but enormously positive review of *A Poet's Bazaar*, the critic P. L. Møller discussed the whole unfortunate polarization in Danish literature around 1840. He also used the opportunity to side with Andersen and his view of art:

> "In our day, when every other author seems almost diligently to stifle what is naïve and youthful in the imagination and emotions in order to display an old, faded, and wrinkled physiognomy of reason, it is utterly refreshing to encounter a text such as this one, in which nature and life step forward to greet us with what is natural and alive, glorified in the concave mirror of a poet's sensibility."[5]

Laurel wreath or crown of thorns—that was how sharply the literary front lines were drawn in Denmark in 1840. Søren Kierkegaard's attack on *Only a Fiddler* in 1838 was merely a fresh outbreak of a battle that started in 1830 when the author Henrik Hertz took aim at the young Andersen in his *Ghost Letters*. Hertz made fun of "Holy Andersen," who had come riding in from Slagelse on "the muse's newborn foal," with a moth-eaten saddlebag filled with incoherent literary works, grammatical errors, and other "crude blunders." Nor could the writer Carsten Hauch resist pointing a finger at the thoroughly ridiculous figure and physiognomy of the first-time novelist, primarily because Andersen had teased him in his book *Walking Tour*. In his satirical comedy *The Babylonian Tower in Miniature* from 1830, Hauch portrayed the young author, traveling on foot, as a tragicomic Pierrot and his overrated *Walking Tour* as one huge "madhouse." As we will see in this chapter, Carsten Hauch revived his view of Hans Christian Andersen as a lunatic in his novel *Castle on the Rhine* in 1845. He portrayed the author as a megalomaniac, unmanly writer, and at the end of the book Andersen goes stark raving mad and has to be locked up.

But it was especially Søren Kierkegaard's extremely insensitive exposé of Andersen's disjointed life and work that laid the last great cornerstone for the broad critical assault against the author around 1840. And this was an assault, incidentally, in which Kierkegaard again did not actively participate. Instead, he left it to Johan Ludvig Heiberg and his whole clique of loyal artists and critics, whom Andersen incisively dubbed the 'Form Cutters Guild." It was an aesthetic fraternity, inspired by the German philosopher Hegel and led by Heiberg, the writer, dramatist, and critic. The emphasis was on rational, cogent thinking and against the type of Romanticism, in particular, that was too improvisational and casual in its treatment of the sacred aspects of art. And that was why Andersen, with his unshakable faith in the importance of emotion and instinct for the beauty of a work of art, became the epitome of everything the Form Cutters Guild turned against and sought to defeat.

Whereas Heiberg's group was first and foremost interested in the form of art, Andersen always gave priority to the content. He underscored this in *O.T.* in 1836, when Otto Thostrup says that the same holds true for poetry as for the tree that God allows to grow: "The inner force expresses itself in the form; both become equally important, but I regard what is inside as more sacred." In other words, it was the emotional filling that Andersen sought, and his work method was that of the phenomenologist. He would rather create art on the basis of all that unpredictably and chaotically confronts the improviser from the outside, filling his soul with material and inspiration, and quickly is turned into literature. The "form cutters," on the other hand, wanted art to have a plan and a meaning, or as Andersen mischievously writes in his play *Ahasuerus* in 1847: "Ding dong! Ding dong! / Same song, same song!"

No matter what part of the life and work of Hans Christian Andersen you happen to look at around 1840, it's tempting to wrap him in a cloak of sympathy because it seems as if for long periods of time a regular witch hunt was waged against him. But if we take a closer look and go a little beyond the spectacular diatribes, we see that Andersen was not entirely without blame. At times he even sought out these confrontations with the Form Cutters Guild. As previously mentioned, Andersen was tremendously aware that a Romantic genius does not come crawling, and especially not with regard to the critics. As the naturalist and philosopher Henrich Steffens said in his philosophical lectures in Copenhagen at the beginning of the century, "the genius breaks through all the rules to which others wish to subject him, blazing for himself, and for his entire era, his *own* trail."[6]

As such, Andersen felt a need to sharpen his image even more during the years after Kierkegaard's attack and to draw even greater attention to himself and his marginalized, underdog position. Yet, in spite of everything, the Danish critics around 1840 were not as negative or oppressive as Andersen portrays them in *The Fairy Tale of My Life*. The author actually received more positive reviews than he wants to admit in his memoirs. In a letter to Henriette Wulff from May 1840, Andersen clearly shows how he—for both ideological and psychological reasons—constantly strives to maintain an adversarial relationship between art and the critics. Outwardly the unremitting Romantic wants to be understood and defined as an "outcast," as the artist who is both chosen and ostracized, pervaded by a rare power, instinct, and his own will. While the form cutters represented the predictable masses, Andersen saw himself as original and unique, the one who possessed—as he writes in his letter to Henriette Wulff in 1840—"this naïve, brilliant, self-centered, and yet semi-frivolous way of arranging his thoughts."[7]

The critical headwinds were necessary for Andersen, both in terms of his Romantic author's role and his poetic nature. It was also a matter of an essential stimulus in the creative process. Andersen may not have been aware of this, but it meant that every time he was subjected to serious critical pressure from the outside, his strength of will, his courage, and his poetic imaginative powers would merge into a higher, creative unity. We see this in works such as *A Picture Book Without Pictures* and the fairy tale "The Flying Trunk." Both were written during a period in the late 1830s when Andersen had seriously gotten his fingers caught in the aesthetic machinery of the Form Cutters Guild. Yet, as so often before and later on, he knew how to draw on an inner strength and continued to demonstrate his overwhelming self-confidence, stubbornness—and audacity. This was especially true of the inflammatory passages in "The Flying Trunk" in which Andersen portrays the Danish critics of the day as fiery little matches that impetuously flare up but go out almost as soon as they're lit. Originally this section of "The Flying Trunk" was meant to be a separate satirical story called "The Matches," written for Fru Heiberg and her family circle. Her mother-in-law Fru Gyllembourg played the role of the storytelling stoneware pot, her husband J. L. Heiberg was the old iron pot that always stands nice and clean on the shelf, Fru Heiberg was the sparking tinderbox, the critic Christian Molbech was the old quill pen over on the windowsill, while Andersen was, of course, the nightingale in the cage outside the window.[8]

★ ★ ★

"Yes, there's something childish about me—but neither am I lacking in gall,"[9] says Hans Christian Andersen in April 1839 in connection with the traumatic discussion of his play *The Mulatto* and its acceptance by the Royal Theater, which we will return to shortly. A determined Andersen launched a counterattack against the Form Cutters Guild and seemed to surprise himself with the courage and strength of will that he mobilized:

> "My friends say that they have never seen me so incensed, so resolute and filled with vengeance ... but it must come out! It must be performed! All it takes is resolve!"[10]

Over the years so many people have mistaken this inner strength in the artist for vanity and smugness, while others have called it sheer megalomania. Yet at no other time in Andersen's life or work was it so clearly laid bare as during the period from 1840 to 1850. With inflammatory but also understandable pride in himself, Andersen spread out his glorious tail like some kind of peacock. In this way he set the petty, provincial view of himself and his art at home in Denmark in sharp contrast to his popularity and fame abroad, which was on the rise in the early 1840s. This meant that even in Weimar, he would show up dressed to the nines, with a dress sword and three-cornered hat whenever he was invited to court or a royal banquet. And of course he would then have to write home to the Collins in Copenhagen about these triumphs, but in the "home of homes" his letters were always met with restraint and skepticism.

It was only natural that the pronounced split between the enthusiasm abroad and the silence in Denmark wounded Andersen. Whenever he was traveling and got wind of a "critical cackling" back home or heard that his latest triumphs abroad were not being reported, he would vent his bitterness in furious and despairing letters that were filled with curses against the Form Cutters Guild back home. "Those who are the spokesmen in my native land renounce me ... Few love Denmark more than I; but those who do the writing and speaking spit on the worm because it shines. My worst hours come from home, God forgive!"[11]

But the critics in Denmark were never able to put a halt to Andersen's literary expansion. He realized all the grand plans for conquest that had been germinating inside him ever since he arrived in Copenhagen in 1819 and discovered that he was going to be a writer. No one could have kept Andersen down during the 1820s and 1830s—not a couple of stern benefactors, a tyrannical headmaster, a private tutor well-versed in the Bible, a highly respected civil servant's family like the Collins, or ten wild critics all with the same goal in mind. And during the first days of 1839, when Andersen's fairy tales and novels were about to be published in Sweden, the author, like a Napoleon of poetry, took stock and evaluated his plans for possible conquests during the coming years:

> "I have won recognition, infinitely vast recognition. Germany and Sweden are being conquered; in the long run little Denmark will be proud of this and say: 'What a devil of a fellow!' and then I'll have Denmark in the bag too . . . Today Rantzau-Breitenburg has honored me with a visit; he was also pleased with my German conquests, but how will I acquire France and England? I must have those two great powers; until then I cannot rest! To have them is to have all of Europe, along with the fuse."[12]

Dining with the Form Cutters Guild

At one time the leader and fulcrum of the Form Cutters Guild—Johan Ludvig Heiberg—was favorably inclined toward Andersen. That was during the period when the young author published his first novel, *Walking Tour*, in 1829. Back then Heiberg's positive attitude toward Andersen had great importance for his breakthrough as a writer. But the increasingly peculiar Romantic direction of Andersen's work in the 1830s and his frequent ridiculing of philosophical, aesthetic author types in his literary creations slowly caused the two men to drift apart.

Andersen noticed the new and exceedingly powerful headwinds in Denmark at a grand banquet in August 1838, hosted by the Heibergs at Søkvæsthus in Christianshavn, at which the guests had consumed a great deal of food and vintage wines. It was presumably on this occasion that Andersen first heard the rumors of Kierkegaard's negative critique of *Only a Fiddler*, which was soon to be published. In the days following the festivities at the Heibergs' home, the prospects of this imminent storm in his life and work prompted Andersen to complain to and seek comfort from various women with whom he corresponded. He reported, in particular, the conspiracy about which he had gotten wind during the course of the evening at the Heibergs' home. He sensed that something was in the works: "I know that the giants of criticism here at home are working in silence to storm my Olympus."[13]

On Andersen's side stood P. L. Møller, backed by weathered Romantics such as B. S. Ingemann, Adam Oehlenschläger, and H. C. Ørsted. On the other side could be found J. L. Heiberg, Henrik Hertz, Carsten Hauch, Christian Molbech, and, at first, Søren Kierkegaard. And the antagonism of the Form Cutters Guild toward Andersen was no less diminished when the members saw in 1839 the eagerly awaited monograph on Nordic literature, *Histoire de la Littérature en Danemark et en Suède*, written by the Frenchman Xavier Marmier. The monograph presented Hans Christian Andersen with great pomp and circumstance. This was an international reference work, and in one section titled "New Literature" in Denmark, Marmier had swept all other younger Danish authors together into ten lines in order to make room for sixteen pages devoted solely to the thirty-four-year-old Hans Christian Andersen.

Marmier lived in Denmark from 1837 until 1838. During this time he not only became the sweetheart of Oehlenschläger's daughter, Maria, he also became very good friends with Andersen. During the following years the Frenchman's book on the literary history of Scandinavia became widely known throughout Europe, and thus set the agenda for the entire world's view of Danish literature around 1840.[14] Marmier's essay on Andersen in 1839 was largely identical to his laudatory article in the periodical *Revue de Paris* from two years earlier, and Andersen himself had submitted most of the wording in terms of the biographical material. But one significant difference between the two publications was that Marmier's book, because it was a work of literary history, would contribute to shaping the view of newer Danish literature outside of Denmark for decades. And his work was virtually single-minded in its focus on the sole Danish author who was apparently worth considering: Hans Christian Andersen.

The fact that Marmier's original portrait of Andersen in *Revue de Paris* in 1837 was based on Andersen's own interpretation of his literary life is apparent from the introduction to a French translation of the Dane's fairy tales, *Contes d'Andersen*, which was subsequently translated back to Danish in 1861. It included the following statement about Marmier's "collaboration" with Andersen in the late 1830s:

> "One day while I was staying in Copenhagen, a tall man entered my room. His awkward manners and his rather common deportment would have displeased a refined lady; but his kind eyes and his open, honest face immediately aroused sympathy. It was Andersen. I had a volume of his works on my desk. We introduced ourselves at once. After he had spent several hours with me in one of those poetic conversations that open the heart

and evoke mutual confidence, Andersen told me about the hardships he
had endured. And when I asked him to tell me about his life, he gave me
the following depiction: 'I was born in Odense in the year 1805 . . .'"[15]

After one of these conversations, which took place in the fall of 1837,
Marmier rather mischievously asked Andersen whether all of Europe now
might know everything he had recounted, whereupon the Danish author
replied: "I belong to the world! Let them all know what I think and feel!"[16]
And that's what happened. In 1839-40 Marmier's little Andersen portrait
in *Revue de Paris* had spread so far through Europe that even Lord Byron's
widow sent the Danish author an appreciative greeting via the French
ambassador to Denmark. On the other hand, Johan Ludvig Heiberg was
very tired of Andersen's self-promotion at the expense of all other Danish
writers, and one day in 1839-40, when he met Andersen on the street,
Heiberg caustically said:

> "I see that you're being translated in the south and praised in German
> newspapers. I suppose you know how it's done? It's your publisher who is
> paying for it." "Oh, is that so?" replied Andersen. "I suppose you know that
> we have the same publisher, so it's odd that he hasn't arranged to have *your*
> books praised." "Yes," exclaimed Heiberg, "it's odd, isn't it, that he won't
> spend a couple of *rigsdaler* on me too?"[17]

On his trip to Skåne in southern Sweden in 1839, Andersen was actually accompanied by Molbech on the way there, while on the way home
he was hailed as grandly as a king by the students in Lund. Immediately
afterwards Heiberg was ready with the following ironic salute to Andersen
upon his arrival home: "When I travel to Sweden, you must come with
me so that I too might experience such a tribute!" Andersen countered
elegantly: "Go over there with your wife, and you will win it much
faster!"[18]

But the leader of the Form Cutters Guild refused to accept Marmier's
disavowal of the broad scope of contemporary Danish literature. In 1840,
in *Jahrbuch für wissenschaftliche Kritik*, he objected to the Frenchman's single-minded book. Modern Danish and Nordic literature was, after all,
much more than the marvelous Andersen. Heiberg had already encountered the consequences of Marmier's superficial work during a trip to
Germany in 1839, when he was met with a flood of questions that all had
to do with Hans Christian Andersen. When Marmier heard about Heiberg's
imminent opposition in the scholarly literary journal, he supposedly said,
according to Andersen: "If he writes against me for a hundred, I'll write

against him for 3,000! Heiberg is a poet who is fashionable among the Danes but is insignificant for Europe; they're interested in Oehlenschläger and . . . Monsieur Andersen!"[19]

This was sweet music to Andersen's ears, and it was no lie. But it was also true that Marmier's book was too one-sided and superficial. Even Monsieur Andersen had to admit as much in a letter to Henriette Hanck in December 1839: "He's very fond of me, that dear Marmier, but unfortunately his book is quite weak!"[20]

Heiberg's trusty squire in the showdown with Hans Christian Andersen around 1840 was Christian Molbech, who as early as 1830 had sneered at the young writer's use of language in the fairy tale "The Ghost." In the winter of 1833-34, this learned man—who was a historian, philologist, man of letters, critic, and adviser at the Royal Theater—reviewed two of Andersen's poetry collections in "The Monthly Scream," as the venerable *Maanedsskrift for Literatur* was called. And Andersen's literary work took another beating.

Molbech's critical ill-will toward Andersen increased as the volumes of *Fairy Tales, Told for Children* began to appear. It might be regarded as sheer envy except that Molbech's analytical arguments never budged an inch from his first and actual opinion of Andersen's writing. This was presented in a letter to Andersen in 1830, and it had to do with "this light, careless play with form," which, in Molbech's view, ignored the gravity of art, the importance of form, and thereby "ruined the very poetry."[21]

Molbech was a permanent adviser at the Royal Theater, although he seldom made an appearance and was barely familiar with the actors or repertoire. But during the crucial years of 1839-40, when opinions were divided regarding Andersen's dramas *The Mulatto* and *The Moorish Girl*, Molbech held a powerful weapon in his hands, and he used it. Even such a coherent and—at first glance—well-conceived play by Andersen as *The Mulatto* was roundly rejected by Molbech. He offered arguments whose primary goal was to put a stop to the career of this sniveling and smug Romantic.

For this reason *The Mulatto* had to go through a barrage of trials before it was finally accepted for performance at the Royal Theater. Molbech's criticism of the play, which was delivered to the theater management in March 1839, was unrelentingly negative. "Tasteless, tactless, bereft of ideas, trivial, and affected" were the words of his scathing condemnation. And in his evaluation of the leading male role, Molbech wrote that Andersen hadn't understood how to make his mulatto into a truly interesting and exalted figure: "He is, like all the others, merely a sentimental phrase-monger."[22]

"I'm being trampled by a tyrant!" Andersen wrote to Edvard Collin on Easter morning in 1839, complaining that his last three or four submissions to the theater had been rejected. That's why Andersen now decided to give as good as he got: "My play must be performed, otherwise I have played out my role! I cannot and will not endure this injustice. My friends must either come to my defense or give up on me!"[23]

And so they did. Andersen was heard, and after a fierce battle among the members of the theater management, *The Mulatto* was accepted. This occurred primarily because Frederik von Holstein, who was head of the theater, found the slave scene in the last act extremely spectacular and remarkable. He told the playwright that such a spirited trade in human beings under the equatorial sun would make even a pampered Copenhagen audience sit up in their seats. "Slave markets, we don't have enough of them! Oh yes, that's certainly something! I must be honest with you. That slave market is to my liking!"

Success at the Royal Theater

The premiere of *The Mulatto* coincided with the death of Frederik VI and the proclamation of Christian VIII as King of Denmark in December 1839. By then there had already been plenty of problems with the staging of the play, and the date for the premiere in late November had been postponed several days. From his windows at the Hotel du Nord, Andersen had a view of both Kongens Nytorv and Holmens Canal, and he could just catch a glimpse of Øresund beyond the big chimney of a smithy. From there he surveyed with interest the traffic to and from the theater's stage entrance, where stage hands and set workers hauled inside huge palm trees and grass huts. And then, on the very day of the premiere, when people had stood in line from early morning to buy a ticket to *The Mulatto*, Frederik VI died—and the premiere had to be postponed once again. In this sorrowful hour for his country, Andersen's thoughts turned not to the dowager queen, the rest of the royal house, or to his fellow Danes, but to himself—the poor writer whose play had been shelved. How long would the theater remain closed? Was it possible, as some claimed, that the mourning period would extend well into the new year?

But in January 1840 the theater placards were once more posted on the streets and lanes. And on February 3, the Royal Theater came to life again with *The Mulatto*, which, before a sold-out and expectant hall, marked the beginning of a new royal reign. That alone ensured the success of the play, since who would dare jeer at a new play on the first evening that the new king made an appearance at his theater?

Christian VIII and Queen Caroline Amalie were well acquainted not only with Andersen but with his play *The Mulatto*. They had met the author in August 1839 at Gisselfeldt, where Andersen entertained them with songs and paper-cuts. It was particularly the paper-cut of a sun with little rhymed verses on the numerous sunbeams that had impressed Princess Caroline Amalie. And subsequently she had invited Andersen to the royal residence in Copenhagen to read aloud from his new play. But it was one thing to impress the royal couple and quite another to please the people. Would *The Mulatto* also win acclaim from them? The author sat on pins and needles all evening during the premiere, with his attention shifting constantly from Fru Heiberg, Madame Nielsen, Dr. Ryge, and the other actors on stage to the audience on the main floor and up in the box seats. Andersen thought that during the first acts they were all terribly quiet, and even the best scenes seemed to go over the heads of the silent, introverted audience. Did they feel no enthusiasm for what they were watching?

They did indeed. Seldom had the pampered Copenhagen theater-goers—just as theater manager Holstein had predicted—seen anything to match this play. And so it was a greatly relieved Hans Christian Andersen who, several days later, described in detail the premiere evening to Henriette Hanck:

> "During the fourth act a little southerly blood seeped into the veins, and during the fifth, the whole crowd had finally turned tropical, and then the curtain fell! What jubilation! Today the king requested that I appear for an audience; he wanted to see me. He was very gracious and said that he was pleased by the success the play had enjoyed."[24]

As B. S. Ingemann so vividly expressed it, *The Mulatto* was "a transatlantic painting in strong, glowing tropical colors, with a true and glorious palette."[25] That was not wide of the mark. And it's not difficult to see why even Andersen's older friend, the hot-blooded merchant's widow,

Catharina Bügel, who was infatuated with the author in the 1830s, was extremely enthusiastic about this play about slavery, dominance, raw love, and noble birth—a play whose social moral is: "No one will fall to slavery if his soul has nobility."

The play is one of the best that Andersen ever wrote. "If the reins are held taut, anything can happen!" as it says in Act Five. This line is not only a good expression for the master-slave issue, but also for the dramaturgical formula itself. In very few other plays that Andersen wrote during his life-time did he manage, as he did in *The Mulatto*, to keep the roles, lines, action, and themes all in check throughout the five acts. The explanation for this may be simply that Andersen didn't have to struggle to invent the play; he borrowed the plot, all the roles, and even a good share of the themes from a recent French short story by Madame Charles Reybard that was published in the periodical *Revue de Paris* in 1838. This was the same jour-nal in which Andersen had appeared in Marmier's biographical article the year before. Andersen either chose to overlook this fact, or he merely for-got to cite the story as his source when he delivered his play to the theater. And this omission was repeated when *The Mulatto* was later published in book form, still carrying the subtitle: "Original Romantic Drama in Five Acts." A truth with qualifications, you might say, just as it's quite an under-statement when Andersen, in letters to Henriette Hanck in both 1840 and 1843, mentions Reybard's story as "the little tale from which I borrowed the subject" and "the little story that gave me the material for *The Mulatto*."[26] It was much more than that.

Yet *The Mulatto* cannot be dismissed as a play, and this has to do with the fact that Andersen's dramatization gave the French short story a sub-stantial and original dimension via the play's daring focus on the slavery question, also in relation to the spiritual and erotic desires of the individ-ual person. And this intriguing theme—a drama within the drama—was completely Andersen's own invention. It kept the pot boiling through five whole acts, all the way to the redemptive moment when the chalk-white, innocent noblewoman Cecilie (in the enchantingly lovely figure of Fru Heiberg) is united in a lovely embrace with the attractive mulatto, whose freedom she and another woman have just paid for at the slave market.

The play is about power and about being enslaved to the urges of both other people and of oneself. The animal aspects of the human being had begun to interest Andersen more and more during the 1830s, and they play an important role in *The Mulatto*. It was these same demonic urges that Andersen had let loose two years earlier in Chapter Ten of *Only a Fiddler*, with words such as: "The wild animal resides inside of every person; in one it's a ferocious wolf, in another a snake that knows how to crawl on its belly and lick the dust. The animal has been given to us; now it's a matter of whether we or the animal possess the greater strength."[27]

This exploration of "the wildness in the blood," as Andersen also called it, had become an increasingly clear part of the themes of his three novels in the 1830s. Andersen further loosened the restraints around human urges and passions in *The Mulatto*. In the play, the animal instincts of the human being are no longer regarded as a form of madness that should be feared and fought—as they were defined in the depiction of Christian's godfather in *Only a Fiddler*. Instead, it seemed that in *The Mulatto*, Andersen now allowed the animal within the human being to come into its natural right. He proceeded to examine desire as a force that is not only evil and devouring but also possibly a creative and rejuvenating element in sex, love—and art. In November 1838, when Andersen was writing *The Mulatto* in his lodgings at the Hotel du Nord in Copenhagen, he merrily confided to Henriette Hanck that it was quite inspiring to have a black servant to wait on him, but then he suddenly turned serious and cast a far from humorous glance at his work, which was becoming more and more like a mirror:

> "There is no theater finery whatsoever; it's all human emotions, my 'evil blood,' and my 'nobler self,' which I'm learning to present in supple verse. This play will determine whether I will work for the stage or merely as a novel writer."[28]

Five of the eleven performances of *The Mulatto* in the short winter season of 1839-40 were sold out, and the rest also had remarkably large audiences. Yet Molbech did not put in an appearance at a single one of the performances. As Andersen concluded in a letter to Henriette Hanck: "That's certainly consistent!"[29] When the news of Andersen's success reached Odense, the newspaper *Fyens Avis* could report that the Copenhagen public had shown an enthusiasm that had not been seen or heard in a long time and surely must be highly flattering to the author. Andersen gleaned even more honors from the reviews, which almost unanimously gave a standing ovation to *The Mulatto*. The one expression of disapproval in the jubilant choir came from an anonymous piece in a magazine, which strongly hinted that Andersen had stolen the plot from a French story that was in the process of being translated and published in the periodical

Portefeuillen.[30] Andersen received this complaint with astonishing composure. In his defense he could say, for instance, that J. L. Heiberg had solidly based his own play *The Fairies* on Ludwig Tieck's German fairy tales, and that Oehlenschläger had not invented Aladdin when he created the most popular Danish play of the Golden Age.

But this little anonymous objection was drowned out by all the acclaim. In relative peace and quiet, Andersen could enjoy the nice royalty of 1,000 *rigsdaler*, along with various gifts from friends and acquaintances. These gifts included a diamond brooch from Christian VIII, as well as the long-awaited admission pass to the royal boxes, where Oehlenschläger, Thorvaldsen, Hertz, and all the others had numbered seats and could consort with royal courtiers, diplomats, and the country's foremost government officials. Finally he no longer had to prostitute himself with random owners of loge seats, including the demanding Widow Bügel, who always wanted to have Andersen all to herself; now he no longer needed her. "Welcome to our picnic!" Thorvaldsen was supposed to have said when Andersen surveyed his new seat. Commodore Wulff was more crude and sly in his response: "What a damned lot of authors we're getting in here! There sits Andersen in His Excellency-so-and-so's seat—who the hell is giving them all these seats?" But Andersen knew Wulff and replied: "There are two gentlemen who are giving them out; Your Excellencies have been given yours by His Majesty the King; I have been given mine by Our Lord."[31] And on the same occasion he showed off his new royal brooch with nineteen diamonds—"of which one is big, four are quite beautiful, the rest are small!" The author had been given the brooch at a royal audience, during which J. L. Heiberg and the composer J. P. E. Hartmann had also received gemstone gifts.[32]

But Andersen had no time to rest on all these sudden laurels. The volume of his work during January and February 1840 gives us the impression of literary mass production by an author who was much too vain and avaricious to say no. And for this reason, in letters to friends and acquaintances, he had to apologize for his "letter-debts," which eventually became the only tangible debts that Hans Christian Andersen carried in his life. It's easy to understand that he had begun to feel burdened with work. In January 1840, Andersen contributed several works to the Students' Association's memorial celebration honoring the late Frederik VI, including a cantata about the king's battle to liberate the serfs. Several weeks later, when the same association asked Andersen to write a comedy for their Shrovetide celebration, he was just about to decline. At the same time he was also supposed to deliver a poem for H. P. Holst's evening entertainment, an epilogue for the actress Anna Nielsen, and a vaudeville monologue for the actor Ludvig Phister. For this reason he settled for drafting an outline for the Shrovetide play for the Students' Association, which was titled *Nothing*. In all haste he then wrote several scenes with a little dialogue, and the students could then fill in the rest![33] In addition to these daily trifles, Andersen was deeply involved in plans for his next big drama with the working title "The Spanish Girl." And he was hoping it would be his next great success at the Royal Theater:

> "*The Mulatto* has lifted me up on its shoulders, but now I have to see about going a step higher! Forward, forward, or die, in order to fly off on another star, that is my constant thought. You know that I have decided not to travel abroad, with the exception of Sweden, until after the coronation; I think I can amuse myself very nicely here at home, and besides, the money from *The Mulatto* isn't enough to travel; *The Spanish Girl* will have to give me that. I am enjoying writing the play. In my mind I have so often seen the sturdy women of Spain, heard the jets of water splashing in the Alhambra's halls; I see a whole romance in the customs of the Moors, am often torn apart by the great dissonances of life; surely I must be able to present an image of what is now stirring inside me."[34]

What was now stirring most strongly inside the author at the beginning of 1840 was, in other words, a depiction of his own divided emotional life, as well as the promising thought that the theater would soon open its cashbox with the large bills so that Andersen might set off on a long journey. With Fru Heiberg in the role as the enchanting Spanish girl, the big breakthrough that would bring Andersen eternal riches and fame was just around the corner. But it would not prove to be so easy.

Fru Heiberg

It was Johanne Luise Heiberg—the wife of Johan Ludvig Heiberg and the uncontested first lady of Danish theater—who was given the task of spokesperson in the summer of 1840 when Hans Christian Andersen had to be told a few truths about his dramatic art. Her sober-minded husband preferred to hide behind his writing, and so it was only after Andersen had left Denmark in December 1840 and found himself in Munich that Johan Ludvig Heiberg dared to tell Andersen and his art to go to hell! This occurs in Heiberg's *New Poems*, in the poem "A Soul After Death," in which Mephistopheles tells "the soul" what hell is like. He reports, among other things, that in a theater down there *The Mulatto* is read to the sultan's wives and *The Moorish Girl* is read to all those who are scheduled to be strangled.

Andersen's play about the "Spanish Girl" had ended up with the title *The Moorish Girl*, with the lead role written for Fru Heiberg. The play had its premiere and was published in book form shortly before Christmas in 1840, as Andersen was on his way to the Near East. The play included a Prologue, composed in a weak moment of self-pity a few days before his departure; it was laced with what Andersen later called "my sickly disposition." He wisely removed these introductory explanatory remarks from later versions of the play, and yet he certainly meant every word of sentences such as:

> "As I depart, my prayer to God is that I may return to my home with greater strength in my soul and prepared to deliver the works that will cause my foes to become my friends."[35]

The four or five months prior to his departure had been filled with a series of controversies between Andersen and Fru Heiberg. As strategists and tacticians, Johan Ludvig Heiberg and Andersen were virtual equals, but Heiberg could control himself and his emotions to a much higher degree than was possible for Andersen, who was often like an open book. And last but not least, Heiberg often operated surreptitiously, via an extensive network of connections in and around the theaters and periodicals. Even so, *The Moorish Girl* is an example of the fact that Heiberg didn't always get his way, even though he exerted all his powers to force through his will. In August 1840, in fierce defiance of his advisers Molbech and Heiberg, the theater manager Jonas Collin accepted Andersen's play for performance at the Royal Theater within the next few months. But Heiberg had not yet had his final say in the matter. When rehearsals began in September and Heiberg, as usual, was to supervise the first complete read-through of the play along with the actors, he immediately complained about the angular penmanship of the handwritten script and demanded a completely new copy of *The Moorish Girl*. It was the first time, but far from the last, that the play was delayed.[36]

But this type of malice was nothing compared to the humiliation Andersen experienced when Fru Heiberg refused to play the lead role, which had been written specifically for her. In fact, she refused to participate in the play altogether. She could no longer take Andersen's dramatic art seriously, and she says in her memoirs that even in *The Mulatto* she had played her role as Cecilie with a certain ironic distance, although no one seemed to have noticed.

"If you want to get ahead in the world, then bow!" This had always been one of Andersen's guiding principles on his way to the top echelons. And in the summer of 1840, when *The Moorish Girl* was to be steered toward success before Andersen set off southward for the Near East, there was no getting around the Heibergs of Christianshavn. And so on Saturday, September 29, Andersen went out to pay a call on *die berühmte Frau* [the famous lady], as one of his female correspondents called Fru Heiberg. He went to see her partly to read through the entire play one more time, and partly to ensure the prima donna's participation in the staging of the drama. But Fru Heiberg was not in an amenable frame of mind. In the spring, during another of Andersen's visits at Søkvæsthus, she had already urged him to change the female lead from a quiet, introverted girl to a lively young woman. Andersen thought that he had done just that, but Fru Heiberg now called the part of Raphaella in *The Moorish Girl* a "man's role," and she labeled the play itself "a tumor." Andersen was shaken and unhappy; he wept and pleaded, but his wailing was in vain. Fru Heiberg refused to budge.

Andersen never forgot this humiliating incident. Like Edvard Collin's refusal to agree to Andersen's request to adopt the informal "du" as a means of address back in 1831, this afternoon at the Heiberg home belonged to the author's most bitter memories. When Hans Christian Andersen, at an advanced age, told his young friend Nicolai Bøgh about the clash with Fru Heiberg, he could almost remember word for word their fierce quarrel:

> "'Fru Heiberg, you make me desperate! I've built all my hopes around the idea that you would play the role. If you refuse, the play will fail, and I won't receive the money that I need. There is so much lacking in my education; I must acquire it by going out and traveling. I *must* go to Greece, to Constantinople, I *must* have the money for that. You can obtain it for me, and that's why I *beg* you to play the role; just play it five times. I beseech you to do it.' 'I *cannot* and I *will not!*' she replied. 'Oh, Fru Heiberg, how should I plead with you, how should I speak to you? Tell me how I can beg my way into your heart to convince you to do it! If you do not agree, I may be lost.' She replied: 'Yes, but I don't *want* to do it; I've told you that.' Then he persisted: 'How far down should I stoop? I can sense how unworthy I am; but tell me: how far down should I stoop

for you to honor my request?' She replied, 'How shameless! You say you must stoop far down to implore me!' 'Yes, that's what I'm *saying!*' he shouted. 'I'm ashamed at the way I'm behaving here; but this is a vital matter for me. And that's why I prostrate myself before you and implore you with all my heart: play the role!' Then she answered: 'I don't play *men's roles!*' Now Andersen grew furious and shouted: 'Oh, Fru Heiberg, how can you insult me like this! You have no heart! You are not a good person! But let me tell you this: Right now *you* are standing cold and proud at the top of the wheel of fortune. But beware! You could end up at the very bottom, and *I* could end up sitting at the very top, and then I will crush you!' At the sight of his menacing posture and the diabolical look on his face, she retreated a step and then backed her way out the door as she said: 'Get away from me, you demented person! You're evil, you're vicious!' He shouted after her: 'Yes, I am, and you're the one who made me that way, because I'm not like this by nature.'"[37]

The Heibergs can't be blamed for digging in their heels. *The Moorish Girl*—which takes place in the mountainous region of Córdoba and Granada in the 13th century when the Moors and Christians were battling—was nowhere near the quality of *The Mulatto*, which possessed solid dramaturgy and far more developed roles and dialogue. And the critics hammered the play when it was finally performed on stage in December 1840.

When Andersen left Denmark at the end of October 1840, he wrote a brief letter to Fru Heiberg, in which he told her how distressed he was by her refusal. At the same time, he predicted that when the two of them happened to meet in the future, she would extend her hand to him, as he was now doing with this letter. That is Hans Christian Andersen, the human being, in a nutshell. Very cunning and at the same time profoundly sincere. And mostly the latter. In reality, the author was almost always ready to make peace with his worst enemies. Many years later, Fru Heiberg commented on this well-formulated attempt at reconciliation in her memoirs. She said that she had once found it comical that Andersen had urged her to extend her hand in reconciliation, since she was the one, and not he, who should feel genuinely insulted.[38]

After J. L. Heiberg and Andersen were both dead and could spend their time glaring at each other in Elysium, Fru Heiberg had one more comment about the power struggle between the two. On the occasion of the publication of Edvard Collin's book about Andersen in 1882, she sent Collin a letter in which she praised the polemical book about the famous author's relationship to the Collin family. Then she offered her own opinion:

> "I am convinced that most people will realize why Heiberg could not sympathize with such a tentative and unmanly temperament as Andersen possessed, and not fault Heiberg for something that he so utterly lacked. His criticism was not written out of envy at Andersen's good fortune and fame abroad—something that Heiberg had never desired to achieve."[39]

This view of the connection between Andersen's unmanly nature and his artistic abilities, primarily with regard to the theater, was further discussed in Fru Heiberg's memoirs in 1891-92, in which she wrote:"Andersen could never become an author of dramas; his nature was too feminine for that."[40] To all this Edvard Collin replied that he had a great deal of proof that Andersen could not have done without Heiberg, and the author had been quite aware of Heiberg's importance to and position in Danish literature. In Collin's opinion, it was particularly during the 1830s that Andersen looked up to Heiberg. But he also emphasized that this relationship changed completely in the 1840s when Andersen became recognized and famous abroad:

> "This fame was his measuring stick for the worth of a writer; achieving it was, for him, the task of a writer. This *good fortune* confused his imagination; he placed himself next to, perhaps even above the greatest Danish authors, who happened to be less well-known outside of Denmark. This was his affliction."[41]

"The Show-Off"

Every time Andersen returned home during the 1840s from a long trip abroad, both the Form Cutters Guild and the Collin family would treat him like Jean de France in the Holberg play and call him "the show-off" or "Europe." His childishly enthusiastic reports of his success were ignored, ridiculed, and regarded as boastful caprices or megalomania. But in his day, Andersen was not alone in possessing this type of lunacy. As George Sand wrote in her diaries in the 1860s, as she looked back on Romanticism and its zeitgeist, it was extremely fashionable back then to be "great."

It's debatable whether Andersen became a victim of his own vanity in the 1840s, as Edvard Collin hints in his book. But it's true that the Danish author enjoyed every second of what he saw in the mirrors on the walls all around him in Europe's salons, royal houses, and princely estates during the 1840s. In letters and conversations with friends and acquaintances, he was a font of pride whenever he talked about himself in Germany, France, or England. During the period 1843-47, Andersen spent just as much time abroad as he did at home in Denmark. And during his travels in 1845-46, he was away for nearly twelve months, during which time he met such luminaries as Alexandre Dumas, Honoré de Balzac, Victor Hugo, Heinrich Heine, Jacob and Wilhelm Grimm, Carl Maria von Weber, Robert and Clara Schumann, Franz Liszt, Felix Mendelssohn-Bartholdy, Alexander von Humboldt, F. W. J. Schelling, Benjamin Disraeli, Charles Dickens, and various kings, princes, grand dukes, counts, and barons—most of whom wanted to establish a firmer connection between their courts and the Danish author or even to become his patron.

Hans Christian Andersen, of course, relished his success. A good example of this strong impulse in the author, which he never made any attempt to mute or repress during his lifetime, can be found in an account of the coronation festivities at Frederiksborg Castle in July 1840 when Christian VIII was to be installed in his new position as king. Andersen had been given a distinguished seat in the great hall with a few select individuals and an excellent view of the procession as it entered the castle. During the long ceremony, the author began to feel bored. Then he suddenly realized that the fresh jasmine blossom in his buttonhole, if viewed from one of the other castle windows or from down in the courtyard, must look very much like a big, beautiful badge of chivalry. What a sweet thought! Happiness was being a Knight of the Jasmine![42]

All emblems of honor, both great and small, were enjoyed in this way, like the scent of jasmine. All the details of his proud triumphal success during the 1840s were recorded in his diaries and letters. If these life-affirming signs of success happened to be omitted, Andersen was never hesitant to summon them forth. He carried on a self-indulgent bookkeeping, which involved recording every indication that his name—so ordinary in Denmark—was becoming widely recognized and that his literary work commanded fame and respect abroad. A little example of this was evident during Andersen's trip to the Near East in 1840-41, after he had arrived in Vienna.

In one of the city's great shopping streets, he passes a bookstore's display case, which holds a collection of *"Ausländische Klassiker"* [Foreign Classics]. And there, in between volumes by Florian and Tegnér stands a book by Hans Christian Andersen! The Danish author immediately enters the bookstore to inquire about any other books by this Andersen that might be on the shelves. The bookseller can find only *The Improvisatore*, which he promptly hands across the counter, but it turns out to contain only the first part of the novel, as Andersen points out. The bookseller, mildly insulted, assures his customer that this volume *is* the entire novel. And even though the obstinate customer continues to protest in his foreign tongue, the bookseller insists that he is right and finally proclaims loudly in German: "I've read it myself!" Whereupon the customer smartly replies in the same language: "And I wrote it myself!" Only then does the Austrian bookseller fall silent and bow to the "foreign classic," made manifest in this tall, lanky figure.[43]

This "chasing after applause," as an envious Henrik Hertz called the phenomenon, was viewed by many prominent Danes during the 1840s as a sickly flaw in Andersen's character. And during that period it was elevated many times to a theme in Danish literature. In 1844, for instance, we find an analysis of Andersen's personality and psyche in Carsten Hauch's novel *Castle on the Rhine*. In quite a sensational minor role, we encounter a Danish author by the name of Eginhard who loves Germany. He has settled down near the Rhine because he's so obsessed with old German legends, and he's always on the lookout for new stories and spectacular locations for his prolific literary career, which keeps pouring out books. Hauch describes Eginhard as a very sensitive and self-absorbed man who acknowledges that he suffers from a craving for rank and titles, coveting fame and admiration. He also admits that he has paid dearly for his laurel wreath, and in the midst of all the honors showered on him, he feels lonely and forsaken—without wife, lover, children, or a permanent residence.

When Andersen read the novel in 1845, he recognized himself at once in this portrait, which compiled and magnified all of his known weaknesses —vanity, childishness, restlessness, negligence, narcissism, fear of women, and a fondness for young men. And he had no doubt that this fictional portrait ("my vile image") possessed a documentary value and was strikingly true in its depiction of certain weaknesses. An admirably composed Andersen wrote to B. S. Ingemann that the most shocking thing about reading the novel was the portrayal of Eginhard's psychological disintegration and burgeoning insanity. In many ways, it felt as if he were opening doors to his own psyche:

> "Oh yes, they have a right to say: this is Andersen. Here all of my weaknesses have been gathered. I hope and believe that I have moved beyond this period, but everything the poet says and does is what I could have said and done. I felt uncomfortably seized by this glaring portrait, which showed me in all my misery . . . What has shaken me, what at certain moments burns in my mind, is the poet's fate . . . the disintegration in *this man*, who is *my* image. I have a feverish feeling at the thought of what I have read here, at this touching on one of the deepest chords of my heart . . . The most bitter part about it is that I, slightly wiser than my glaring portrait, must henceforth strive to be less open, but that might also be good and wise."[44]

Yet Hans Christian Andersen did not reproach Carsten Hauch in the slightest. This sense of forbearance may have to do with the difference in social standing between the two writers, as well as with Hauch's roots in the whole Sorø milieu surrounding the loyal B. S. Ingemann. Whereas Andersen was a proletarian, Hauch was an aristocrat—a nobleman among the writers of Denmark's Golden Age. And perhaps this was one reason why Andersen tolerated Hauch's plebeian treatment of a colleague in a novel that ends with Eginhard being transported to the madhouse, sitting in a cart with his old laurel wreath on his head and various medals and decorations, cut out of shiny paper, dangling from his chest and stomach. A pitiful but also laughable sight. And the cheering crowds accompany Eginhard through the city streets, just as it was foretold in Andersen's childhood that he would one day be escorted through his hometown, which would be lit up in his honor. In the cart the megalomaniac Eginhard talks to himself nonstop about the Queen of the Sandwich Islands, who wants his autograph and picture, and about booksellers in distant exotic lands who have ordered several thousand copies of his *Collected Works*. Suddenly he shouts to everyone standing around him that he has to set off for darkest Africa at once because there are so many people in those parts who are longing to see him.

It says something about Andersen's ability to tolerate and fend off even the most severe attacks against him that in the above-mentioned letter to B. S. Ingemann, in September 1845, he wrote that Carsten Hauch couldn't possibly have meant to subject him to mockery and ridicule:

"Hauch is so noble, so big-hearted. I know he appreciates whatever good I may possess within me; I still have the greatest faith in and affection for him and will continue to do so."[45]

If Andersen's treatment of Hauch in 1845 was worthy of a man of the world, there wasn't quite as much magnanimity to be found in his rejection of Thorvaldsen's daughter, Elisa Paulsen, who had recently been widowed and left on her own with a young son. In the fall of 1843 she had asked the Collin family if they could persuade Andersen to accompany her on a journey through Europe and act as her son's teacher. In a letter to Jonas Collin, Andersen replied honestly that this was completely out of the question, since his reputation at the present time could not be tainted by this type of traveling party:

"To the Germans I am the best-known and most respected writer that the Danes now have; whether I am truly entitled to this position is not something to be discussed here, but to the Germans it would look rather pitiful if I trudged through their country as the teacher of a little boy."[46]

By Railroad Through Europe

On his four great journeys through Europe in the mid-1840s, which were all fashioned as triumphal processions, Andersen definitively freed himself from the oppressive and petty conditions in Denmark and made an irresistibly thunderous appearance on the European cultural scene. Andersen's international breakthrough coincided with the explosive impetus of modern technology in Europe in the 1840s, when all manner of mechanical forces were let loose with steam and electricity, and the faith in progress was still so innocent and optimistic—as Andersen depicted it in his fairy tale "The Muse of the New Century" in 1861. The inventions and modernizations of the day in terms of traffic—especially the operation of railroads—were revolutionary liberations of time and space. And for a traveling egoist and Romantic like Andersen, they were greater advances than the political revolutions occurring in the same period. In 1833-34, the Danish author had traveled through Italy by means of mail coach, stagecoach, and Italian *vetturina*, when it took twelve hours to cover 50 to 100 kilometers, with long rest stops so that both the horses and the passengers could gather their strength for the next stage of the journey. Now the "fiery dragon," as the author had promptly dubbed this rocket of a new-fangled train, meant that in the same number of hours he could travel at least 400 kilometers farther out into the world. And do so in comfort. Andersen traveled from Magdeburg to Leipzig via Halle, which was the first railroad on the continent, in November 1840. On this route he covered 120 kilometers in under four hours, and this experience of speed—almost 30 kilometers an hour!—was practically hallucinatory:

> "Now I have an impression of the earth turning; close to me moved grass and fields like twirling spinning-wheels; only the objects farthest away seemed to retain their usual calm. Now I can imagine the flight of migratory birds; this is how they must leave the cities behind them. It was as if one city lay very close to the other. There is something quite magical about it. I felt as if I were a magician who had harnessed my dragon to my wagon and was now rushing past the poor mortals that I saw creeping along in their carts on the side roads like snails. When the steam is released, it sounds like a demon gasping. The whistling signal is abominable; it's like listening to a pig shriek when a knife is jabbed into its belly."[47]

The latest technology developed at a wild pace—as did Andersen's career. His way was paved with the first translations of his novels and fairy tales into German, English, and French, which in the 1840s were widely distributed in the world by means of the modern printing technology and a rapidly expanding book industry. This meant that by the time Andersen started off on his literary campaign in 1840, rumors of the romantic life and biography of the Danish writer had begun to reach the German upper echelons. And during the following year Andersen's *A Picture Book Without Pictures* became a huge hit in the German-speaking regions of Europe. The fairy-tale book, in various abridged and shortened versions, found its way into academic journals as well as the more popular magazines, the so-called "*Volkskalender*" [Folk Almanacs]. This meant that Andersen had reached most German families with both an avant-garde and a more cozy type of offering to readers.[48]

All four of his European journeys in the mid-1840s took him through Germany. And during his long sojourns in Munich, Dresden, Weimar, and Berlin, Hans Christian Andersen did a superb job of promoting himself by giving readings and constantly retelling the romantic fairy tale of his own life. This occurred at banquets in the palaces of princes and kings, as well as at salons and soirées where the era's influential representatives of art and finance in Europe were always in attendance. Andersen acquired a large and robust network of friends, colleagues, and business connections in Germany. These were people who were always available to him, artistically, commercially, and as friends. This in itself represented a tremendous expansion of his own world view—rather like traveling by train, where one town (and good friend) seemed to be very close to the other; the cities (and the houses in which Andersen was invited to stay) were moving closer and closer together.

On his first long trip of the decade, his journey to the Near East in 1840-41, he had already met with luminaries such as Franz Liszt and Mendelssohn-Bartholdy. As he continued traveling southward, Andersen would meet a modern, enterprising bookseller like Friedrich Campe on one day, and on the next he might see daguerreotype pictures for the first time. Then on the third day he would become friends with Gustav Kolb, who was the publisher of the newspaper *Allgemeine Zeitung*. In Munich he could comfortably manage to see comedies, tragedies, the Gallerie Noble, the Panoptikon, and make daily visits to the painters Stielers, Peter von Cornelius, Kaulbach, and the philosopher F. W. J. Schelling. The Danish author made contacts everywhere along the way and created a number of amicable and collegial bridgeheads in the largest German cities. In the long run, this meant that—in addition to room and board, and comfortable theater box seats that were at his disposal in Munich, Dresden, and Berlin—he always had a translator and publisher within easy reach. Similarly, he entered into agreements with various illustrators or painters such as Wilhelm Kaulbach, whose illustration of Andersen's fairy tale "The Angel" became one of the era's most widely distributed reproductions. Anyone from Stavanger to San Sebastián could now obtain one of Hans Christian Andersen's fairy tales as a lithographic poster.

In other European metropolises such as Paris, Vienna, and London, Andersen also made personal contacts and created small or large networks that would serve him well for the rest of his life. This can be ascertained by casting a glance at Andersen's big *Album*, which is a scrapbook measuring half a meter high and weighing three kilos. Andersen pasted into this book various written greetings, pictures, and other souvenirs from all of his trips.[49] Through this documentation we are witness to forty years of ceaseless traveling and socializing, a true train-station throng of European luminaries (nearly 500 of them). With autographs, poems, letters, portraits made with steel engravings, sheets of music, and dried flowers they sent greetings to the Danish author from the European settings he had inhabited with such ease or passed through from 1830 to 1870. It's a collection of diverse handshakes, embraces, and kisses. And, as such, it's proof of the Danish author's status and international acclaim in 19th-century Europe. Andersen had great access to the cultural elite, and his big album is also a cultural map of Europe over four decades in which the kings and princes, painters, writers, composers, and actors—both male and female—step forth. They included, for instance, the French actress Rachel, who captivated Andersen with her art in Paris in 1843. Surrounded by admirers in her dressing room, she took the time to write a note to Andersen with delicately penned letters: "*L'art c'est le vrai*" (art is truth). No motto is more perfect for this vast guestbook, which reflects Andersen's artistic and social ambitions as well as the idealistic, formative idea of his prodigious travels. Andersen sought truth through art, but of course also through the artists themselves—face-to-face and hand in hand—on the thirty long trips abroad that took up nearly ten years of the author's life.

The Collin family, as mentioned, had very little understanding of or interest in this cosmopolitan aspect of Andersen's travel activities. From Paris in 1843, he tried to explain to them this accumulation of famous new friends and highly interesting acquaintances with the words: "These numerous dear friends who have all treated me like a spiritual relative."[50]

Andersen often made good use of his stubbornness on his travels in the 1840s. In some countries it seemed that artists were less enthusiastic about meeting Andersen than he was about meeting them. Or maybe they just slept later than he was accustomed to back home. During his stay in Paris in 1843, at any rate, Andersen had to do a good deal of knocking on doors before he was able to meet writers such as Heine, Balzac, Dumas, Kalkbrenner, Hugo, Lamartine, Vigny, the sculptor David, and the actress Rachel.

Heinrich Heine, who had inspired the Dane to write his sensitive, lyrical travel account *Shadow Pictures* in 1831, was high on Andersen's wish list in 1843. He had actually called on the German author ten years earlier in Paris, but at that time each man had brought certain reservations to the meeting. Now, when they saw each other again, Andersen quickly discovered that Heine, who had lived in exile in Paris since 1830, had become much more of a Francophile. As he told the Danish author: "French pleasures, French sorrows, a French wife!" Of Andersen's works, Heine had read *The Improvisatore*, which he found to be "well-formed." In a diary entry in March 1843, Andersen quotes Heine as saying these solemn words: "You are a true poet!"[51] Several years after the Dane's visit to Paris, Heine was more critical toward Andersen, who during his last visit had looked like a tailor:

> "He is a lean man with a hollow, fallen-in face whose outward appearance betrays an anxious, submissive personality that princes appreciate. That is also why Andersen has been received so resplendently by all princes. He perfectly represents writers as princes wish them to be. When he visited me, he was sporting a big stickpin; I asked him what it was he was wearing. He replied with an unusually unctuous demeanor: 'It's a gift that the Electress of Hessen was gracious enough to bestow on me.' Otherwise Andersen's character is most respectable."[52]

Andersen's interest in Heine's literature remained undiminished throughout his life. As late as 1865, during a visit to the Basnæs estate, the sixty-year-old Andersen set out to read all twenty volumes of Heine's works that were part of the manor-house library, in a paperback edition that Andersen would have liked to own. He confided this to Edvard Collin in a letter, to which he added: "I find that there are very few volumes that could be read to ladies." Andersen started his summer reading with prose works such as *Elementary Spirits* and *Gods in Exile*, as he recounts in another letter home to the Collin family in Copenhagen. In these works he detected a certain hesitation in the German writer's "fluttering, unchristian caprice," but after five days of intensive reading, there was no longer any doubt in Andersen's mind:

> "Heine is like glittering fireworks that are extinguished, and you are left in the black night. He is a witty gossip, ungodly and frivolous and yet a real poet. His books are elf-maidens dressed in gauze and silk that are crawling with vermin, so you can't let them run freely in the room with properly dressed people."[53]

In Paris in 1843 Andersen also paid calls on Honoré de Balzac, Alexandre Dumas, and Victor Hugo. The meeting with Balzac took place in a very deep velvet sofa. On one side of the Dane sat a flirtatious courtesan who called herself a baroness and wore a coal-black gown with jewels. On the other side sat an extremely well-dressed Balzac, who in the Dane's diary was described as "a little, broad-shouldered clod" with chalk-white teeth behind red lips.[54] The baroness and Balzac were splendidly entertained by Andersen, and several times they asserted that the Dane spoke a very "original" albeit incomprehensible French. About his quite modest linguistic abilities in French, Andersen himself said during that same year:

"Sometimes I talk my way into a standstill, but then I say '*voila c'est tout!*' and then I let the other person take the floor."[55]

Those were lively and merry spring days. At least that's how Andersen made it sound whenever he wrote home from the city of cities in 1843. "I thought it would be so difficult to gain admittance to Parisian salons, but nothing is easier!" was his modest claim in April in a letter to his female correspondents back home.[56] And in another series of letters to people with contact to the European province far to the north, Andersen made it sound as if he were seeing Heine, Balzac, Dumas, and Hugo on a daily basis. But that wasn't true. Andersen usually spent most of his time with other Danes in Paris, such as Frederik Læssøe, Theodor Collin, Andreas Buntzen, Johan Bornemann, and Frederik Schiern. Or he was content to sit in the Café de Danemark and read Danish newspapers.

Andersen allowed his French friend and biographer, Xavier Marmier, to arrange, via well-phrased letters of introduction, his visits with the French luminaries, with whom he had trouble carrying on lengthy conversations because of the language barrier. Yet the French authors were rarely home, and Andersen tried in vain several times to call on Balzac, Victor Hugo, and, in particular, Alexandre Dumas. But the third time that Andersen knocked on the door belonging to "Wooly Head," as he dubbed Dumas, he met with success. This was primarily because, after sending his letter of introduction to Dumas, Andersen stood at the front door and waited for the man to show up. A short time later a servant came out and invited Andersen to follow him to Monsieur Dumas's bedchamber. It was very beautifully furnished, but in terrible disarray. In the midst of the clutter and featherbeds, Dumas had installed himself, wearing a blue-striped nightshirt, with pen, paper, and ink. He nodded kindly to the Dane and said: "I live like a regular *garçon*, but you'll simply have to take me as I am!" Dumas scattered the pages covered with his beautiful upright penmanship on the floor as he was done with them. Time passed, and Andersen stood on his toes, afraid of treading on the pages. The Frenchman was talking to himself the whole time, and suddenly he shouted aloud: "Viva! Now the third act is done!" Whereupon he rolled his enormous body out of bed, wrapped the blanket around himself like a toga, and marched straight toward Andersen as he declaimed like a madman from his old play *Caligula*. A terrified Andersen started retreating backwards toward the door, but Dumas was too quick for him and blocked his way, seizing Andersen by the lapels: "Isn't it grand and worthy of a Racine?" Andersen had to agree. "And this is my new play," explained Dumas, pointing at the floor. "I like to write one act or more before lunch!"[57]

After the meal, Dumas obtained free tickets to a play with the promising title *Les Petits Mystères de Paris*. And a couple of days later he introduced the Danish author to the twenty-two-year-old mega-star of French theater life, Rachel, who was playing Phædra at the time. Andersen managed to see her on stage four times and was also granted an audience in her private quarters where the diva—dressed in black and sparkling with beauty, as Andersen writes—received a bevy of admiring men at the stroke of eight against the backdrop of a glowing hearth, red velvet draperies, and a red carpet. Dumas also enticed Andersen out to the green room of the Théâtre-St Martin, which was teeming with sparsely clad ballet nymphs, who during the intermissions were pawed and grabbed between the legs by the male stagehands, as the Danish author remarked. Dumas and a pale, embarrassed Andersen quickly became the focal point of a small throng of agile young ladies wearing leotards and tulle skirts. When Andersen attempted to slip away, Dumas seized hold of his arm, pulling Andersen back into the circle of female dancers, and introduced him to two who had been particularly chosen: "No shirking, my good friend! Come over here and be pleasant to the ladies."

At the home of Victor Hugo at Place Royale Andersen met another Frenchman who enjoyed life. The Dane clearly remembered his first visit in 1833, when the great man and author of one of Andersen's favorite novels, *The Hunchback of Notre Dame*, received him warmly, wearing his dressing gown and "elegant house slippers," as it says in *The Fairy Tale of My Life*. Ten years later, Hugo was still in his dressing gown, but this time he invited Andersen to stay for dinner at his beautiful home, the walls of which were papered with cupids of every shape and color. Later Hugo wrote a beautiful verse for the Dane's scrapbook, which indicated why Hugo was almost always home and in his dressing gown in the daytime:

> Happy is the one who loves! And who in the black of night
> While he seeks faith, can find love.
> He has at least a lantern while he awaits the day.
> Blessed is his heart! To love, that is half a faith.[58]

Lovers' Go-Between

After Andersen returned home from his long European trip in 1843, during which he spent two months in Paris and met all the great French authors, he became tremendously enamored of Henrik Stampe, the twenty-two-year-old eldest son of Baron Hendrik Stampe and Baroness Christine Stampe (née Dalgas). Stampe was also the heir to the barony of Stampenborg, which had its seat at Nysø, near Præstø Fjord. Andersen had visited the estate in previous years, and that was how he became acquainted with Henrik. Like Thorvaldsen—who had visited so frequently that he had been given his own studio, called "Vølund's Workshop," in the estate's garden —Andersen was a regular guest at Nysø around 1840. In the summertime he took great pleasure in the blue waters of the Baltic, which lay right outside the windows of the manor house.

Andersen's winter of 1843-44 ended up being completely dominated by the young baron. The Swedish soprano Jenny Lind, to whom we will return later in this chapter, had been in Copenhagen earlier in the fall and bewitched Andersen for ten days with her extraordinarily beautiful voice and tremendous radiance on stage. But Jenny, who found Andersen "childish," was now out of the picture and thus out of the author's impressionable mind.[59] For a time the stage belonged solely to Henrik Stampe. In October 1843, the young man, who was studying in Copenhagen, began paying regular calls on Andersen. The author found himself in a restless period, working frantically but marked by sadness. One day he would be writing sinful poems, while the next his mood barometer would point to pious fairy tales like "The Angel." And then Henrik Stampe appeared on the horizon. The two men already knew each other from Nysø, but their first brief meetings, beyond the realm of letters, took place in October 1843. An entry in the private notes of the author's diary soon indicated that Henrik had come "to tea," which was a relatively rare invitation for Andersen to extend. He had never been a very enthusiastic host; he preferred instead to visit others or to receive guests who called on him briefly, and this happened quite frequently. On his thirty-ninth birthday in 1844, after looking through the usual collection of marvelous gifts, the author ascertained that there were "21 calling cards in my door. Not in the mood tonight."[60]

Yet he *was* in the mood whenever Henrik Stampe knocked on his door in the winter of 1843-44. It was during Andersen's stay at Nysø in November 1843, when Thorvaldsen's birthday was being celebrated, that a significant change had occurred in the relationship between the two men. On December 4, 1843, Andersen notes in his calendar: "Hendrik exceedingly lovable." And later in the month he received many long letters from his young friend, in reply to several letters that he had sent. Henrik Stampe recounts that never before in his life had he "opened my *whole, undivided* heart to anyone, as I have to you." And he asks one thing of his older friend: "Have absolute faith in me, and *always* take my part."[61] Over the next four or five months it's possible to follow—point by point in the few extant letters and brief little notes and entries in Andersen's calendar from December 1843 to May 1844—the development of a sensitive, platonic friendship between the two men. And no sexual connotation should be perceived in a word such as "pampered":

15 Dec 1843:	Hendrik lovable
17 Dec:	H. trusting
27 Dec:	letter from my beloved Henrik
4 Jan 1844:	Spoke sensibly with H., who promised me everything
6 Jan:	Dinner at H.'s; happy!
8 Jan:	Visit from H. this evening
13 Jan:	Henrik pampered me
16 Jan:	Every day at Henrik's
7 Feb:	Wrote for Henrik, who came home and was loving and kind
4 Mar:	Visited H., then he came to see me, he pampered me
11 Mar:	Henrik was here tonight, loving and kind
18 Mar:	Henrik suffering from jealousy
30 Apr:	Henrik indifferent to me
2 May:	Have not seen Henrik for two days, that's not kind of him
6 May:	Went to see him ... He was not as he was before; is love over!
13 May:	Henrik sensitive and warm toward me yesterday
23 May:	Departed at 7 in the evening ... Henrik saw me out[62]

Along with the strong yearnings 'and visible signs of joy in Andersen's calendar whenever he and Henrik saw each other in January and February 1844, it's possible to see how the sensitive relationship day by day was accompanied by jealousy, melancholy, and a sinful guilt having to do with masturbation. Yet it could not conquer his desire, and Andersen's little x's and crosses in his calendar increased in February 1844. A type of eczema and rash also began spreading over the author's body in March and April, about which he writes: "penis tender," "penis hurts," "penis sick," "penis very bad." In May Andersen's skin was raw in many places and he had to seek medical treatment and vaccination against his psychosomatic afflictions from Emil Hornemann, who was his doctor for most of his adult life. Hornemann examined the author many times during that spring, a sensitive time in every sense of the word.

Neither his internal nor external suffering ceased until Andersen set off southward in May 1844. Over the course of a lovely long summer in Germany, he was able to distance himself from Henrik Stampe. And during his travels he became infatuated with a different young man, who turned out to be none other than the Hereditary Grand Duke of Sachsen-Weimar-Eisenach. In the meantime, back home in Denmark, Henrik Stampe became engaged to a girl who was quite young. This was a love relationship that Andersen—at the same time as he was in love with Henrik Stampe—had empathized with and written himself into, with his always alert sense for the poetic possibilities of an emotional triangle.

The girl's name was Jonna, and she was the daughter of Ingeborg Collin (Edvard Collin's sister) and Adolph Drewsen. She and her younger brother ("Little Viggo") were favorites of Andersen among the Collin family members in the 1830s. And with that knowledge in the back of his mind, Henrik Stampe had apparently initiated a sensitive relationship with Andersen, knowing full well that the author held the key to the beautiful, unreachable maiden Jonna.

This was at least what Andersen more or less implied many years later in a letter to Henriette Collin, sent from Montreux in 1862. He intimated that he had been used as a *postilion d'amour*, a lovers' go-between, by the young law student and baron. Andersen had nevertheless felt neither jilted nor offended; rather, he had felt enriched by having participated in a sensitive friendship that had room for jealousy, flirting, and falling in love. In Andersen's platonic love life, there was always room for one more. And especially for the exchange of letters, which he called "perfume for the soul."

Andersen did not hesitate around the turn of the year in 1843-44 when Henrik Stampe asked him whether he could arrange a meeting with the sixteen-year-old Jonna Drewsen, on whom the young baron had long had his eye from his seat on the main floor of the Royal Theater. Quick as lightning, Andersen became so deeply and intensely involved in the stolen glances and secret greetings of the young couple that he couldn't help falling a bit in love with Jonna himself. He had known her since she was very young. She was now sixteen and no longer a child but a grown-up and beautiful young woman. Naturally, Andersen could see the many possibilities of a spiritual and physical union between the beautiful young girl of the Collin family and the handsome baron from Nysø, who would one day inherit a great deal of land and property.

And so, at the end of January 1844, Andersen was prepared to convey a number of letters to Jonna, who was visiting her cousin, Fanny Beutner, out at Springforbi. The two girls were the same age, and Fanny had also been drawn into the intrigue of the sensitive, flirtatious correspondence by Andersen.[63] It was a virtual space in which all four were present as potential letter-writers and recipients, since none had as yet made any binding agreements. For that reason they could participate in good conscience in the piquant game of emotions and reflections of body and spirit. As Andersen formulated it in a letter about the relationship between the two young women and himself: "How marvelously I see her image in your soul!"[64] That was how they viewed each other and themselves via letters, preferably filled with "perfume for the soul," as Andersen wrote. And he, of course, was the most eager of all. In January 1844, when his calendar was filled with longing for Henrik, he wrote in a letter to Jonna:

> "My dear blessed Jonna! You cannot comprehend how much you fill my thoughts, how favorably disposed I am toward you, how close you are to my heart! You must always trust in me, as if I were your elder, loyal brother!"

Rather more down-to-earth were the references to an "H. S.," whom Andersen cannot be accused of overselling to Jonna, even though he had promised the young baron to put in a good, heartfelt word on his behalf. Rather, Andersen made Jonna understand that Henrik also belonged to him. He did this through little phrases, full of intimations:

> "On Sunday evening I'll be in the company of Henrik Stampe at the home of the Hartmanns. H. S. sends his greetings to you and Fanny—I dine with his mother and see him daily!"

As we have previously seen, Andersen was quite compulsive in this game of emotions in writing. He not only conveyed duplicitous greetings from one to the other, but he also participated in a Kierkegaardian fashion in the shaping of the correspondence, since he acted out several roles and stages at once. He wrote his way into the love between a young man and woman under pseudonyms such as "Your loyal *eldest brother*" and "Your poet."[65] And Jonna's cousin Fanny was also drawn into this sophisticated parlor game. All of this, oddly enough, took place several months after the publication of Søren Kierkegaard's book about the forms of seduction, *Either-Or*, in which a pitched game of emotions is carried out behind masks and the psychology of love is examined.

There are quite a few parallels between Kierkegaard's novel and Andersen's secret romantic intrigue in 1843-44. In the philosopher's book we see how one of the main characters (Johannes) coldly and cynically stages the phases of falling in love with the help of letters. And for a brief moment, he considers—merely for the sake of intrigue and the excitement of the experiment—whether he should let the young girl (Cordelia), whom he has caught in his web of words, become engaged to his best friend (Edvard). Andersen assigned himself the same role in his romantic "setup" in writing. In the flood of letters between the young couple, he could picture himself as the young Henrik, while at the same time playing the older, infatuated writer who desired Jonna and flirted a little, second- or third-hand, with her cousin Fanny. The crowning glory of the work were several sly letters in early 1844, in which Andersen slowly—both deliberately and against his will—led a young man and woman together while he, for whom the whole situation was poetry, stood back in the perfume-for-the-soul space of the writing as the doubly unhappy lover.

"If I don't see you or him at once, see those *I love*, you and those I love are nevertheless always in my thoughts and will remain there until my dying hour," Andersen wrote to Jonna (and Henrik) in early May 1844. This was after his job as a romantic go-between had borne fruit, and he was now on his way south toward new Romantic adventures.[66]

There is hardly any doubt that Andersen's love for Henrik Stampe was stronger than his love for Jonna Drewsen. But the author, as always, preferred to dream and fantasize about love, to cultivate it in spirit, instead of living it with his body. As it says in a letter to Jonna that Andersen wrote on his way to Weimar in June 1844:

> "Give my beloved Henrik thousands and thousands of greetings; I see his gentle eyes and yours smiling at me! Oh yes, all three of us are loyally fond of each other! A bit more strongly between the two of you, but I have not been forgotten!"[67]

Yet he did feel the sting when, on his journey through Germany in the summer of 1844, he learned that Henrik and Jonna had become secretly engaged back home in Denmark. His emotions played a trick on him, and his jealousy suddenly burst into flame. A feeling of being excluded was difficult to suppress. In a curt, bittersweet entry in his diary he wrote: "Engagement declared last week. It's a lie."[68]

The Hereditary Grand Duke Carl Alexander

A month after Andersen left Henrik and Jonna behind in Copenhagen, he stood for the first time in Weimar. His visit to the hometown of Goethe and Schiller would be a brief but intense encounter with the small ducal residence and its young hereditary grand duke, Carl Alexander. Andersen arrived at dawn on Monday, June 24, 1844, and was delivered to his hotel. His first excursion had been planned for many years, and its destination was Goethe's house. There, a rather disappointed Andersen was allowed to view only the stairs and garden. He was annoyed at being turned away, and by the whole museumlike atmosphere that had already descended over the place. The house was occupied by Goethe's daughter-in-law, Ottilie von Poswisch, whom Andersen had met several years earlier at the home of Felix Mendelssohn-Bartholdy as he was making the long journey back to Denmark from the Near East. But now Frau Poswisch was "utter marble" toward the Danish author, as Andersen wrote in his diary.[69] And his first day in Weimar would have been sheer disaster if Andersen hadn't managed to visit Schiller's house on his way home from the theater, where the opera *The King and the Tenant Farmer* was being performed, in honor of the birthday of the young hereditary grand duke.

But Andersen would shortly meet the entire ducal family out at Belvedere, the sun-yellow palace with a view of Weimar and the surrounding region. Grand Duke Carl Friedrich, who was said to be an expert on German legends and sagas, also turned out to be familiar with *A Picture Book Without Pictures*, from which Andersen had chosen to read aloud at the banquet. The talkative Grand Duchess Maria Pavlovna showed Andersen the rare American trees in the garden, although in the imaginative eyes of the Danish author, they looked more like asparagus tips. But the two had a good long talk in the beautiful garden, and the Grand Duchess spoke warmly of Copenhagen while at the same time complaining that Oehlenschläger had never felt properly at home in Weimar.

The following day's excursion took Andersen to Ettersburg Castle, which stood in a beautiful location on a forest-covered mountain slope northwest of Weimar. In 1844 the hereditary grand duke had begun to revive the castle's tradition of hunts, literary soirées, and an intellectual salon life. And for the next four years, Ettersburg would serve as the framework for some of Andersen's happiest periods spent in Germany. Beneath the resplendent chandeliers and the rows of antlers the Danish author met the young Hereditary Grand Duke Carl Alexander von Sachsen-Weimar-Eisenach. Andersen had caught a glimpse of him and his beautiful young wife, the twenty-year-old Princess Sophie of the Netherlands, at the theater on his first evening in Weimar. Now the young nobleman suddenly appeared in his slender, fairylike figure, and it was, according to Andersen's diary, a sight for the gods: "A young twenty-six-year-old man with a handsome figure. I didn't know him. No one told me who he was, but I could guess. He said a few kind words to me, about how pleased he was to make my acquaintance!"[70]

For Andersen, this was his big chance to establish a friendship of aristocratic caliber at the heart of German culture. And for the very culture-oriented hereditary grand duke, a friendship with one of the day's hottest authors in Europe meant an opportunity to link yet another modern artist to Weimar, which was now about to draw upon the inheritance of Goethe and Schiller and enter into a new and great era.

On a June day in 1844, when Andersen for the first time threw open the windows to his new private chambers at Ettersburg, situated high in the mountains, he didn't have time to lose himself in the view of the Thüringen Forest. All of Ettersburg was already busily preparing for the *Volksfest* and the celebration of both Midsummer and the twenty-sixth birthday of Hereditary Grand Duke Carl Alexander. Tall poles had been erected with fluttering ribbons and a prize at the top for the farmer who could climb up most quickly to claim it. At dinnertime the merry sound of violins was heard beneath the flowering linden trees in the castle's courtyard. The Danish author looked on with admiration as Carl Alexander and his merry cavaliers swung the local peasant girls in a dance. The hereditary grand duke's greatest passions were hunting, books, and social gatherings with artists. This would all reach a synthesis out at Ettersburg, where Carl Alexander, on his hunting expeditions, would bring along a volume of poetry, which at regular intervals replaced his shotgun and was used for meditation. The elegiac poetry of August von Platen-Hallermünde was especially close to Carl Alexander's heart.[71] This poet, who is less well-known outside of Germany, was renowned in the 19th century for his love of other men. Consequently, Heinrich Heine had tried to crush von Platen's poetry with harsh, condescending criticism, which included describing the count and his circle as "a clique that is rumpishly inclined."[72] Even though the hereditary grand duke was newly married in 1844 and was soon to become a father, he continued all his life to read von Platen's praise of the friendship between men, which included such phrases as: "I accustom myself to honor women more than I love them, to love men more than I honor them."[73]

On a walk around Ettersburg, Carl Alexander discussed the big plans that he had for the castle and Weimar. In cultural harmony with neighboring metropolises such as Dresden, Leipzig, and Berlin, the city would once again—as in Goethe's day—become part of the zeitgeist. This goal would be achieved with the help of a new generation of celebrities such as Hans Christian Andersen, Jenny Lind, Berthold Auerbach, Ferdinand Freiligrath, Richard Wagner, and, in particular, the charismatic Franz Liszt, who had already given his first concerts in Weimar. He would soon be appointed the court *Kapellmeister*, with a private residence and a permanent, substantial monthly salary, financed by the town and the duchy. Hans Christian Andersen was certainly quite interested in this type of sponsorship, and in early July 1844, he forwarded these grand plans to Edvard Collin with the words:

> "God's ways are strange! I couldn't leave Denmark entirely, but I do want to live for periods in Weimar, live with the dear Carl Alexander; I truly love him!"[74]

Andersen had quickly assessed his opportunities. This sort of arrangement would have a crucial advantage. As a "commuter" between the great cities and cultural centers of Europe, and with Copenhagen and Weimar as his permanent bases, he would not only have princely living quarters but also sensitive friendships at many different places in Europe. "It would be like a beautiful dream for me to be able to imagine the possibility of living partly in Copenhagen, partly in Weimar, and there see my Danish friends, my Eduard and Henrik [Stampe], dear Theodor [Collin]—but surely I'm dreaming!"[75]

The rest of Andersen's weeklong stay in Weimar in 1844 was veiled in a fairy-tale glow. Andersen attended a banquet hosted by Carl Alexander's father at Belvedere Castle, where the Dane, perspiring heavily, sat between a learned lady-in-waiting, who adored the author's fairy tales, and a Francophile princess. Across from him sat the grand duke himself, entertaining Andersen with his personal interpretation of *Hamlet*. And seated next to the grand duke was the grand duchess, who regularly opined that the Danish author had already become quite dear to her beloved son, who had such great plans for Ettersburg. Andersen was, as the grand duchess whispered to him in confidence, a significant part of her son's plans to revitalize Weimar's cultural life. "Remember that here you have *true* friends!"[76]

On June 28, 1844, they paid one last visit to Ettersburg for the summer. In Andersen's honor, Carl Alexander had arranged one of his literary soirées. These soirées had been started as a new tradition that same year, and from the very beginning they followed specific guidelines. Everyone gathered at six o'clock at the tea table, as poetry and prose pieces were read aloud. Later on, supper was served, followed by conversations that lasted until close to midnight, when the carriages would roll up to take the guests back to Weimar. These evenings at Ettersburg became an institution during the period 1844-52, attracting many celebrities from both Germany and abroad. They were also called "journal evenings," since a secretary was employed for the express purpose of keeping a meticulous journal or record of all the meetings. Afterwards the contributions that had been read aloud were collected in a specially designed album, which—in the opinion of critical observers—ended up containing mostly "*literarische Wassersupper*" [literary dishwater].[77]

A remarkably diverse group of learned individuals and musical people gathered for these soirées. In addition to Carl Alexander and his wife, Baron Beaulieu-Marconnay, Chancelor Friedrich von Müller, and Goethe's former secretary, Johann Peter Eckermann, the Ettersburg circle included a number of authors, composers, painters, classical philologists, doctors, and jurists. And of course there were dozens of cultivated countesses and eccentric widows who made a point of closing in around the dandies and rakes, such as Franz von Schober and the well-known landscape architect and globetrotter Prince Pückler-Muskau. Among the numerous female personalities in the Ettersburg Circle, as the salon also became known, was the author Amalie Winter, whom Andersen saw a great deal during his visits to Weimar in 1844, 1846, and 1847. She was married, the mother of four, and the provocatively blatant lover of her cousin's husband. Amalie Winter described the free and fruitful intellectual life at the hereditary grand duke's castle with these words: "Ettersburg is an enchanted palace where you can eat strawberries all year long, and there are no rules of etiquette."[78] Andersen slurped up words along with the tea and the crisp baked meringue that tasted of vanilla and roses. And the Danish author made contacts with mature, older women wherever he went during those years. In addition to Amalie Winter in Weimar, there was Bettina von Arnim in Berlin, Ida Hahn-Hahn and Frau Serre in Dresden, Lady Blessington in London, and many others. They were clever, strong-willed women who could do more than just ride around in a coach, as Andersen writes of the queen in "The Tinderbox." They often took the lead in the soirée debates, and by virtue of their courage and experience, they frequently liked to discuss delicate matters of sex and love. In short, they were the precursors of the women's movement, and they enjoyed a great deal of sympathy from Hans Christian Andersen.

In one of the stories that Amalie Winter read aloud at Ettersburg, she called marriage without love "a form of prostitution blessed by law."[79] Andersen couldn't have agreed more, and in his eyes the intellectual matrons such as Amalie Winter were the heroines of the day. With their odd and strongly individual temperaments, they were roaming thorns in the eye of normality. And in all their *Eigentümlichkeit* [distinctiveness]—this positively loaded word that both Hans Christian Andersen and Hereditary Grand Duke Carl Alexander often used in their emotionally charged correspondence—these weathered women resembled Andersen himself. As he writes in his novel *The Two Baronesses*, which was composed in the same period of the 1840s: "The eccentrics must not die out; they have the same effect in the world as full dress uniforms at the theater." And Amalie Winter never forgot her encounter with Andersen, who in the summer of 1844 seemed to her like "a cross between a Newfoundland dog and a child,"[80] primarily because the Danish author with the big dog eyes had trotted around at the heels of Hereditary Grand Duke Carl Alexander.

For the literary soirée on the eve of Andersen's departure on July 1, the hereditary grand duke had decided to read aloud his short story "Waldeinsamkeit" [Forest Loneliness]. But Andersen, who by now was exhausted after many days of feasting and speaking foreign languages, suddenly felt unwell and was about to vomit. He managed to bring his body under control by taking the floor and reading one fairy tale after another: "The Princess on the Pea," "The Emperor's New Clothes," and "Little Ida's

Flowers." Andersen struggled through his repertoire and afterwards mobilized his forces enough to tell the stories of "The Swineherd" and "The Nightingale" without a script and in faltering German. It apparently went quite well, or as Andersen says in his memoirs, "like a brilliant dream."

At the hour of departure, Carl Alexander said many times that Andersen must write to him soon, and he in turn would send the author several copper engravings with portraits of himself and of Hereditary Grand Duchess Sophie. Carl Alexander held on to Andersen's hand firmly and for a long time, attempting to make him stay, saying that he was the Danish author's friend. He gave Andersen a twig from the linden tree in the castle garden as a farewell gift.[81] The twig became a talisman blossom that Andersen kept, and it was in his thoughts when he was back in Denmark and finished his idyllic Romantic comedy *The Flower of Happiness*. With choreography by Bournonville and the emotional music of Henrik Rung, the play was accepted in October 1844 for performance at the Royal Theater. The lead characters in the comedy were named Henrik and Johanna, and their resemblance to Henrik Stampe and Jonna Drewsen was not limited to their names. In the first act of the play, the symbol for the strong love of the couple is introduced. It's a flowering branch that is produced as fertile proof that the primary source of happiness comes from believing in it. That was largely what Andersen himself had done, as a go-between for the young couple and as the sensitive friend of Carl Alexander. "Happiness can be found wherever people, rejoicing in life, love and are loved in return."

This new sensitive friendship resulted not only in a series of unforgettable visits to Weimar during the 1840s and 1850s, but also in a lengthy correspondence, which Andersen initiated on August 29, 1844, with these words, written in German:

> "My dear Duke! After my departure from Weimar, my thoughts have—daily, I dare say—flown to the place where I felt so merry and so happy."[82]

With small, involuntary interruptions caused by the political disturbances around 1848 and 1864, their correspondence continued all the way up until 1874 and included at least 170 letters, beginning less than a month after Andersen's return home from Germany. How moved Andersen was by his first encounter with Weimar and Carl Alexander is clearly apparent in his letters to his foreign friends and acquaintances during the months following his visit in 1844. The first report of his new German friend was actually sent from Altenburg on July 2—only one day after Andersen, "filled with tears and melancholy," had left Weimar. And the letter was, of course, addressed to Edvard Collin. A handsome and witty prince with his own castle, his own princess, and a view of the entire realm was in every respect a feather in the author's cap. And in the rapture of his writing, he immediately revived his old dream of establishing more intimate terms with Edvard. Andersen now approached his friend back home in Copenhagen in a much more fervent and loving manner than he had dared in many years:

> "My beloved Eduard! The person whom I address as 'De'; that is fundamentally an affected relationship, quite contrary to my feelings—but enough of that. You do want to be eccentric! I have now left Weimar, my beloved Weimar, the place on earth where I have felt so happy for days! Oh, dear Eduard, I have been so happy, so satisfied with Goethe's and Schiller's city, felt properly that from God I must possess something that deserves to be appreciated at home."[83]

The Danish author received two long letters from Hereditary Grand Duke Carl Alexander during the fall of 1844, and now the friendship began—on paper—to develop into a flirtation between two male souls, becoming a medium for spirit and poetry. As it would later turn out, the young hereditary grand duke had an idealized picture of the sensitive male friendship as a sort of Hindu ascension, in which one man relinquished part of his own soul to make room for the other's. As Carl Alexander writes to Andersen: "You should enter into my soul, like a deceased soul in India."[84] In the spiritual correspondence between the two men, Carl Alexander appears in the role of the tempter who continually tries to entice Andersen with this "Nirvana" of a castle at Ettersburg. There the two of them would wander arm in arm through the surrounding forest, where Carl Alexander had recently—as he reports in one of his letters—sat to read the Danish author's lovely letters, which had been brought in his hunting bag along with ammunition and von Platen's poems.

In a ritualized and ceremonial world like that of Carl Alexander, there existed under the official masks a great need for "true friendships," which he sought and found through correspondence with men such as Walther von Goethe, Franz von Schober, Ludwig II of Bavaria, Archduke Stephan of Austria, and Hans Christian Andersen. These voluminous exchanges of letters have since been labeled "Carl Alexander's cult of friendship and love."[85] The label arose, in particular, because of the grand duke's forty-year-long platonic love affair with a contemporary adjutant, Count Leo Henckel von Donnersmarck, or "The amiable Count Henckel," as Andersen called him during one of his visits to the city in the 1850s. Fearing that his favorite adjutant would move away from Weimar, the hereditary grand duke bound his friend to the ducal city by providing him with free lodging and a yearly appanage. In this way the two could continue to cultivate their sensitive friendship until Leo's death in 1895.[86]

Falling in Love with Jenny Lind

In 1844-45 Andersen's international reputation was solidified, even at home in Denmark. The author was invited for a bathing holiday on the island of Føhr in the North Sea by the Danish royal couple, and his good relationship with Christian VIII became even closer. By the time Andersen turned forty, many editions of his work had been published in German, English, Swedish, and Russian. A new collection of fairy tales was also published, containing wonderful stories such as "The Elf Mound," "The Red Shoes," "The Jumpers," and "The Shepherdess and the Chimney Sweep." The first printing of the volume was 2,000 copies, which at the time was a very large number. With all of these accomplishments behind him, Andersen went to King Christian and asked for a raise in his stipend. It was granted at once, and the fairy-tale author was now earning 600 *rigsdaler* a year from his permanent author stipend financed by the kingdom of Denmark. At the same time German publishers and translators had begun vying to publish the Danish author's collected works in Germany. The name of "Andersen" was hot, and Danish painters and lithographers stood in line to produce his portrait. Andersen was now planning another grand tour of Europe in 1845, but his preparations for this trip were dramatically interrupted when the Swedish singer Jenny Lind suddenly appeared in Copenhagen again. She stayed nearly all of October, busily occupied giving concerts and singing the leading roles in Bellini's *Norma* and Donizetti's *The Daughter of the Regiment*. She also celebrated her twenty-fifth birthday in Copenhagen, and Andersen clung to her like a shadow—happy, naïvely hopeful, terribly vulnerable, and at times, as he wrote in his diary, "sick at heart." Yet there was no romantic emotion in the way Jenny Lind behaved toward the Danish author. In fact, she made great efforts to seem both boring and reserved whenever he was near. And even an enraptured Andersen couldn't help noticing this after a few weeks. "She drank a toast to me as if I were her brother," is the curt entry in his calendar for October 21. The occasion was a farewell party for Jenny Lind at the home of the Bournonvilles. In his speech the host declared that from now on all Danish men would be Jenny Lind's brothers. That was a splendid opening for the Swedish songbird, who promptly replied: "That's far too many for me! I would rather choose one of them as my brother." Whereupon she turned to the hopeful Andersen and added, "Will you be my brother?" This sly rhetoric felled a considerable number of Danish suitors with one blow and at the same time skewered Andersen. He may have been the chosen one, but he was also relegated to a fairly anonymous brother-sister relationship. Many years later, Andersen himself illustrated this situation in an anecdote from Copenhagen in the fall of either 1843 or 1845 when Jenny Lind was in town. Late one night after a large dinner party, Andersen and Lind were accompanying August Bournounville and his wife home. In the moonlight the author and the songbird had dropped back a little, and Andersen was, of course, feeling romantically inclined under such favorable weather conditions. He was just about to declare his undying love for the Swedish songbird when Jenny Lind, quite insensitively and unromantically, exclaimed: "Well, Andersen! Move those long shanks of yours! The others have already reached home!"[87]

All of these little but clear indications made Andersen flail helplessly. Inwardly he was, as it says in his calendar during the days before Jenny's departure, "dejected," "sick at heart," and "sickly." But outwardly he could still shower her with superlatives whenever the conversation turned to "*die liebenswürdige*" [the lovable] Jenny, as she was also called in Germany. And in spite of Jenny Lind's unequivocal discounting of Andersen as a suitor and as a man, he loyally continued to praise her to the skies. He did so, for instance, in a letter to Hereditary Grand Duke Carl Alexander on October 30, 1845, in which the Danish author also announced his imminent arrival in Weimar with a number of new fairy tales. But first he would travel via Berlin.

On paper it had seemed extremely promising. Jenny Lind was going to spend Christmas and New Year's in Berlin, where Andersen always felt at home. In 1831 he had made the acquaintance of the German writer Adelbert von Chamisso, and since then he had made several visits to the lively city. On one occasion Andersen had been seduced by a young Frenchman, who lured the Dane to a "*rue de plaisir*," and another time—at the prospect of returning again soon—he wrote in his diary: "Now I'm headed for the German Sodom—Berlin!"[88]

But his love life did not turn out to be nearly as exciting during

Christmas and New Year's in 1845. Instead, during his stay, Andersen realized that his love for Jenny Lind was just as transparent and "literary" in nature as his affair with Riborg had once been. Even before the Christmas holidays arrived, the author felt betrayed and affronted by Jenny, but time after time he used his pain and ostracism as a poetic motif in his letters to friends back in Denmark. And he wrote in his diary: "I don't love her as one should, I can sense that."[89] On the same evening he wrote these words, Andersen arrived in Berlin to find moonlight and frosty weather. He had a lovely hotel room on Unter den Linden, and he was in time to hear Jenny Lind's spellbinding singing at one of the city's theaters. Afterwards he envisioned himself in her performance on stage and wrote in his diary:

> "She sings German the way I no doubt read my fairy tales; something familiar shines through, but, as they say of me, that's exactly what makes it interesting."[90]

And Andersen did come closer to the Swedish singer during the days around Christmas and New Year's, but there was never any question of a breakthrough in terms of love. Jenny Lind was reserved and distant, like the female main character in "The Snow Queen," one of the fairy tales that Andersen was reading aloud to great acclaim at the time. Equally aloof and reserved was the Christmas present she gave her Danish brother: a bar of soap that reminded Andersen of a piece of cheese! In a letter to the Collins from January 1846, a desperate and affronted Hans Christian Andersen discusses all his unsuccessful attempts to come in closer contact with the songbird in Berlin. The only result was an hour spent conversing on a sofa, during which they talked mostly about the Collin family back in Copenhagen. And even on Christmas Eve Andersen had sat waiting in vain. At least that was what he usually told his friends, even though his diary revealed quite a different story, since the author had protected himself against Jenny's possible failure to appear by making tentative plans elsewhere in town.[91] Jenny Lind never did show up, and Andersen grieved in his diary, although mostly over his own fate:

> "She has filled my breast—I don't love her anymore! In Berlin she has cut out the sick flesh with a cold knife! I wonder what thoughts occupy her since she takes so little notice of me? I came to Berlin mostly for her sake."[92]

Yet the visit to Berlin was productive. There was very little time for loneliness in the steady stream of coffee and tea parties, dinners, royal banquets, and meetings with prominent individuals. Among the more bizarre experiences was Andersen's reunion with Goethe's old friend, the quick-witted author Bettina von Arnim, and her daughter, whom the Danish author had met the year before in Berlin. On that occasion the clever woman had said of the Dane's fairy tales that they were now being read by all of Europe's kings and princes, who in this way were learning life's beautiful truths.[93] Frau von Arnim had not grown any more attractive in appearance, although Hans Christian Andersen had—or so she said. This was immediately recorded by the Dane, along with the unforgettable picture of the frumpy but unbelievably energetic and sharp-tongued Berlin salon hostess: "Suddenly the door opened and she waddled in, dowdy, peculiar! 'You look better this year than last!' she said. 'Move away,' she told her daughter. 'You haven't gotten any prettier, but he has!'"[94]

There was also a gathering at the so-called "*Kaffèter-Gesellschaft*" in Berlin. This was another of the city's many literary salons, organized by women who categorized themselves as "coffee-ologists." The membership was composed of relatively well-to-do spinsters who wished to create a feminist forum and counterpart to the male-dominated salons of Berlin. Wilhelmine Bardua, or "Mine" as she was called, was the recordkeeper and editor of the coffee society's little newsletter. The illustrations and cover designs were done by her older sister, Caroline, who, as a young and talented portrait painter and pianist, had lived with Goethe's family in Weimar. Shortly after the association was founded in March 1843, the delicate question was raised of whether men could become members. Mine Bardua had misgivings about the issue, as did most of the women. She suggested that they should settle for making the Danish author Hans Christian Andersen an honorary member under the name "Anderlein." The proposal was accepted and, according to Mine Bardua's diary, the expectations of the coffee sisters reached astronomical heights when they heard in December 1845 that their honorary member was in town to celebrate Christmas and the New Year. "The presence of the author Andersen is stirring up all of society, from the court and downward—he's the lion of the day. Everyone is talking a good deal about his vanity."[95] Naturally, the sought-after bachelor received an invitation to the *Kaffèter-Gesellschaft*, which he accepted, enchanting all of them, even though—according to Mine Bardua's diary—he was a bit short-tempered. He kept looking at his watch and said that he was going to the theater and afterwards had several other visits to make. A deeply fascinated Mine Bardua also noted that there was no trace of vanity in Hans Christian Andersen, other than "the pure childish nature of a writer who doesn't allow himself to be eclipsed by the clouds of incense of kings or the great world." And during the dinner, the forty-eight-year-old Mine fell utterly in love with the peculiar bachelor from the North:

"He looks quite good, and I estimate him to be forty years old. There is something guileless about his whole being, guileless is also the way in which he speaks about his fairy tales and the rest of his literary production. It may be that in the company of men he talks a little too much about himself . . . He is so preoccupied with his own world of the mind that he takes only scant interest in anything else, but one doesn't dare construe this as pure and simple vanity. Vanity always seeks in some way to conceal itself, although it can somehow be caught. In Andersen there is nothing to catch; he is so open-hearted, so guileless and happy in the awareness of his poetic gifts."[96]

Yet Andersen was preoccupied, first and foremost, with his repeated encounters with the Prussian royal house in Berlin and Potsdam, culminating in banquets hosted by Friedrich Wilhelm IV, and the awarding of the Order of the Red Eagle to the Danish author. His fame in Berlin was just as great as Jenny Lind's. This was especially true because Andersen fully understood how to present himself in the halls with the polished, patterned floors made of Italian marble and wood from linden and cedar trees. Over the course of two weeks, he was invited six or seven times out to Potsdam and to the palace located in Berlin itself to read aloud for the king and queen, for Alexander von Humboldt, and for princes and princesses, who also had their books signed with inscriptions such as "*Gott segne die edlen Herzen!*" [God bless the noble hearts]. The Collins back in Denmark had to settle for an account of Andersen's whole Berlin sojourn in a long, detailed letter in January 1846. Andersen dwelled in particular on the aspect of his trip that had to do with the fact that their "son" had now become just as great a European draw as Jenny Lind. "Oh! I'm practically dead! I can't stand it any longer! I'm a lion, I'm a Berlin lion, I've become a male Jenny Lind, I'm in fashion!"[97]

This casual remark—"I've become a male Jenny Lind"—contains, in a sense, the key to understanding Andersen's strange idolization of the Swedish singer. His adoration never completely diminished but continued to burn faintly for the rest of his life. This was apparent in the apartment he had in Nyhavn as an old man, where the bust of the author in one corner of the parlor was joined by a bust of Jenny Lind in the other corner. Even though late in life he no longer had any contact with her, he still paid homage to his memory of her, just as he regularly praised her in phrases such as: "I treasure her with all the soul of a brother."

Among Andersen scholars, there never seems to have been any doubt that Jenny Lind was Hans Christian Andersen's great, unrequited love, also in an erotic sense. Yet this traditional presentation of Andersen's relationship to the Swedish singer can certainly be debated, because there are so many indications that Andersen's fascination with Jenny Lind was more of a spiritual than a sexual nature. Andersen's adoration was primarily platonic and similar to the way in which he usually approached younger women and men in that particular phase of his life. In that regard, it's indisputable that he fell in love with Jenny Lind as soon as she was within sight and within reach in 1843 and 1845-46. This is evident in 1845 when she once again appears in Copenhagen, and Andersen immediately becomes obsessed with the petite, slender woman with the large voice and radiance, who on a stage—like Andersen himself—was transformed into a noble improviser. "A pure vessel in which the sacred draught is offered to us," as he writes. "A new revelation in the realm of art."[98]

Jenny Lind was in all respects an illusion. It was in the theater and the concert hall that her power to fascinate and affect the author was culminated and dispersed. For Andersen, she was the chaste, virginal muse who would lead him into "the genuine sphere of sentimentality . . . through the fairy tale's childish games to life's merry and serious truth," as Henriette von Schwendler of Weimar, another of Andersen's European sisters in the 1840s, expressed it during the winter of 1845-46 in the Danish author's album.[99] Jenny Lind raised Andersen up toward a world of ideas; she didn't bring him down toward the world of the senses, the way that Santa and the harlots, for example, entice Antonio in *The Improvisatore*. Jenny Lind was, instead, a living personification of the Lara figure in the same novel: brilliant, beautiful, and romantic. She was like the shepherdess or the sylph, which was a popular figure in ballets of the day and at the same time one of the most loyal and recurring figures in Andersen's world of paper-cuts.

Hans Christian Andersen shared these views of Jenny Lind's radiance with the Swedish author Fredrika Bremer. Or at least he made strong use of Frøken Bremer's opinions in a letter to Fru Collin in November 1843. At that time Andersen had not yet found the proper words for his own ingratiating admiration for the songbird, and so he turned to Bremer, who at the time was as spiritually in love with Jenny Lind as Andersen was. In this letter the Danish author allows his Swedish colleague to describe the songbird as beautiful, innocent, and indefinable, also in a sexual sense. Bremer pointed out an androgynous aspect in Jenny Lind's "power to enchant," and Andersen quoted the Swedish author as remarking:

> "Moreover, she captivates as many women as men, and she does so with her shy, naturally fresh, pleasant manner . . . Her entire face and being radiate the beauty of joy and inspiration."[100]

The fact that Jenny Lind was for Andersen more spirit than body can be seen especially in the brief, intense periods in 1843 and 1845-46 when she visited Copenhagen and the Danish author toyed with the idea of marrying this phantom woman. His utterly disembodied way of describing her in his letters, diaries, and literary works never approached the type of sensuality that was often at play in Andersen's texts when younger representatives of his own gender—either in tight-fitting uniforms, leotards, or bare-chested—were within sight. For instance, in 1831 when Andersen arrived in Berlin for the first time on his way home from Dresden, he learned there a little about the sinful side of life in Europe's big cities. In his diary, he recounts a difficult encounter with a Frenchman who took him along to a brothel. Andersen managed to extricate himself, but he had seen enough on that day and evening to write a fitting ode to Berlin and the male body:

> Winding streets, palace after palace,
> How tiring it is to walk and look.
> Handsome soldiers—the first one I saw,
> I felt pass right through my heart.
> And I exclaimed: "What a body, what legs!
> My God, what a charming one is he!"[101]

It was not Jenny Lind's body or legs that Andersen desired in the 1840s, but rather her soul and spirit. She hovered above earthly desires like an angel, her sex effaced and apotheosized. In Andersen's eyes, the two of them had so much in common, including their fame, that on one of the first days he spent in Berlin in 1846, he wrote home to the Collins in Copenhagen that he was "a male Jenny Lind."

Andersen had said something similar in his Romantic one-act play *The King Dreams*, which he wrote shortly after his first real encounter with Jenny Lind in September 1843. The following year he submitted the play anonymously to the Royal Theater. The play is about the legendary love in the early 16th century between Christian II and his mistress Dyveke, whom Andersen presents as one more of the restless young king's many dreams of love. Dyveke explains why this dreamer of a king has not once in his life been able to realize his eros: "A man like Christjern loves only himself."[102] Winning a queen is merely a formality for a king, Dyveke points out; it's part of a well-ordered royal household that a man and woman should sit beautifully on the throne, hand in hand. "But do they love each other?" The fact that Christian never marries a woman out of genuine, true love is because deep in his heart he is only capable of loving himself. And furthermore, the king confirms this. In the king's insight into himself, we may have the answer to the question about Andersen's strange adoration of Jenny Lind: "But when he / loves her, then she becomes half of him, / and then in her he loves himself! I know that, Dyveke! I certainly know that."[103]

Reunion with Weimar

After the lively Christmas and New Year's days in 1845-46, Andersen set off for Weimar. The journey seemed to take a terribly long time, since Andersen was so eager to see the hereditary grand duke again. A fellow traveler in the coach, who kept on wanting to regale everyone with bawdy stories about all his young girls, soured the trip for Andersen. Things got even worse when two filthy men wearing shabby fur coats that stank of cheese squeezed their way into the cramped space. But Andersen's reunion with Carl Alexander was worth all the suffering. Yet both men had to restrain themselves when they met in the evening at a grand ball. Carl Alexander apologized for acting in such a formal and official manner when he welcomed Andersen, saying in a subdued voice: "I cannot receive you here as I would at home."[104] The close embraces— and visible signs of what Carl Alexander in one of his letters to Andersen had described as, "When two souls are so close to one another, each always has a right to the other"[105]—would have to wait until the next morning at ten o'clock, when Andersen called upon Carl Alexander in his magnificent rooms:

> "He came toward me, pressed me to his breast, kissed me several times, thanking me for my love for him. Arm in arm we went to his rooms and

sat there for a long time, talking, until he was summoned to the Council of State. Then we went together, arm in arm, to the front door!"[106]

This was followed by two happy weeks in Weimar and at Ettersburg. Because the hereditary grand duke and duchess lived quite separate lives, Andersen and Carl Alexander could cultivate their sensitive friendship undisturbed. At a party given by Amalie Winter in January 1845, Andersen read three fairy tales, including "The Bell," which was a great success, and the hereditary grand duke told Andersen that the story most certainly must be alluding to him. Andersen nodded, and Carl Alexander added that he, like the king's son in the story, "will strive for the noblest and greatest goal," whereupon everyone toasted the author.[107]

Hereditary Grand Duchess Sophie is conspicuous in her complete absence from the Danish author's fairy tale about the poor boy and the handsome prince who, lured by the ringing of a mysterious bell, meet in a happy embrace in the midst of the sunset at the top of a slope in the forest. In Andersen's story the sound of the bell is only for men. If we compare his diary entries from 1846 with those from his first visit to Weimar in 1843, something similar happened in his diaries. In 1846 Sophie disappears entirely from the scene in Andersen's diaries and suddenly becomes a "gentle and blessed" observer in the background as her husband makes many attempts to establish sensitive friendships and revive Weimar as the cultural hub of Europe. In Andersen's case, these two projects were closely intertwined, and Carl Alexander used every opportunity to encourage Andersen to stay as long as possible, or, even better, to settle permanently in Weimar and become German, since the Danes failed to appreciate Andersen's genius:

> "'But we Germans think more highly of you than the Danes! So now you alternate between us; give me your hand!' He held it so firmly in his own! Said that he loved me, and pressed his cheek to mine!"[108]

They embraced, held hands, and walked arm in arm during those January days of 1846. And this went on to such an extent that in spite of the liberal attitude of the day toward friendships between men, Andersen and Carl Alexander had to keep their feelings for one another under the table. At a banquet hosted by the old grand duke, Andersen was seated next to Carl Alexander, who gave the author's hand an intimate squeeze under the table. And afterwards—Andersen recounts in his diary—they went out to a little gazebo together, where Carl Alexander was "so loving and kind." But this twosome fell apart when Jenny Lind showed up in Weimar on

January 22, 1846. She drew everyone's attention with such intensity that for several days—also according to Andersen's diary—there was room only for the songbird. These diary entries at the end of January 1846 reveal a clash of emotions, impulses, and urges in Andersen. His longings for both a man and a woman collide in the light of jealousy because Carl Alexander also seemed unusually fond of Jenny Lind. He had immediately eyed the possibility of linking her to his corps of artists who would lead Weimar into a new period of grandeur.

This sudden confusion of emotions, provoked by a woman between two closely bound men, was a theme that Andersen had already used several years earlier in the fairy tale "The Pact of Friendship," which he wrote on his journey to the Near East in 1840-41. The story is about the ancient, unwritten laws for noble, emotional relationships between men, which include the notion that a female maiden should always be present to bless the most admirable form of masculine intimacy. The fairy tale was based on a Greek myth and tradition, with roots in Hellas, which Andersen learned about in April 1841 in a church in Smyrna, although he didn't outline it in his diary until two months later, after arriving in Vienna:

> "In the midst of the perfidy that exists between Greeks, their blood brotherhood is so splendid. When two men are truly fond of each other, they become blood brothers. They select a pure virgin, and with her they go to church. She stands before the altar and encircles their necks with a scarf as they swear eternal loyalty to each other, in life and in death. The priest then gives his blessing. In misfortunes, they stand by each other, they make sacrifices for each other, and they meet death together."[109]

In the fairy tale "The Pact of Friendship," problems arise when one of the sworn brothers, in spite of his strong love for the other man, harbors an inner, unconscious longing for the opposite sex. This is what threatens the pact of love that is otherwise so natural. And this was also the situation in Weimar in January 1846, when Jenny Lind suddenly appeared. Instead of blessing the love of the two men, she caused it to falter. All the conflict-laden adoration and jealousy surrounding Jenny and Carl Alexander made Andersen "annoyed, uncomfortable, and sick." Fortunately, there were others ready to offer solace and consoling kisses during this difficult time. On his way home from a dinner on January 27, Andersen was accompanied by the bachelor Baron Carl Olivier von Beaulieu-Marconnay, with whom he had stayed when he was in Weimar in 1844. The baron now attempted to comfort the unhappy Dane by suggesting that they take turns baring their souls to each other:

> "Beaulieu told me that I was in the process of falling in love with Jenny! I told him that wasn't true. He told me the story of his heart; I thought of my own and wept."[110]

The German baron made a great effort to play the role of spiritual adviser and therapist, but the best cure was when Jenny Lind left Weimar. Andersen's calendar for January 28, with its staccato rhythm, speaks for itself: "Frost. With Jenny to the library. Visited Countess Redern with Jenny and the hereditary grand duke. Concert tonight at Jenny's; serenade. Farewell!"

Finally Andersen could once again concentrate all his efforts on Carl Alexander, the tea dances, and the royal balls. On the latter occasions the Dane would be presented like some kind of emperor in a throng of uniforms and ladies dressed in gowns with long trains. On the grand duke's birthday, he was even lifted up by pages and carried in to the banquet in a sedan chair, whereupon many whispered in Andersen's ear that he would soon be appointed "Knight of the White Falcon." When Andersen left Weimar on February 7, 1846, his departure was feverish and charged with emotion. He paid a call on the hereditary grand duke at eight in the morning to say a proper farewell, and Carl Alexander received him "dressed only in a shirt, with a cloak over him," as it says in Andersen's diary. He was not embarrassed, nor did he feel compelled to apologize. "We know each other!" as he said to the Danish author, and then he embraced him, kissed him, and added: "Think of this hour as if it were yesterday; we are friends for life." But that still did not enable them to put the farewell behind them. In the days that followed, both men were filled with longing, and, as Andersen wrote in his diary:

> "When parted from one another, I feel in the absence how great is my love; in my thoughts I recall every little memory."[111]

And the ink in Andersen's diary was barely dry before Carl Alexander showed up in Jena in person with a letter he wanted the Danish author to take with him to Austria. The hereditary grand duke couldn't resist seizing the opportunity to see Andersen one last time, and the Dane was, of course, overflowing with happiness:

> "I ran out into the snow and slush; there he was, threw his arms around me, we kissed each other . . . That dear man! . . . We went together

to the castle, where we once again embraced. He asked me to come in the summer, not to go to Italy, to stay! We embraced and kissed; this time I did not weep. That beloved man!"[112]

He Is Not a She

Back home in Copenhagen, the Collin family was not the least bit enthusiastic about all the hysteria that had enveloped Andersen when he was in Weimar. In January 1846, when he reported that he had been given a ring in Oldenburg, a medal in Prussia, and now in Weimar "a full heart," and with that a love that outweighed all else,[113] Edvard Collin tried with all his might to bring his infatuated friend back down to earth and teach him the proper decorum among real men:

> "You are well liked in Germany; in Weimar they spoil you. You are kissed and hugged by all the distinguished people there. We who are your friends here at home and who, once and for all, do not like to see men kissing each other, we did not melt with emotion over this. But in our hearts we are pleased by the story that is at the core, meaning that you are a success, that you are acquiring friends, who, for the time being, I will assume are genuine."[114]

The author's reply came a month later, not in the form of a letter but a comedy with the title *Herr Rasmussen*. It was a play that, after some disagreement among the management, had been accepted by the Royal Theater, but only one performance was staged. After that the play was removed from the roster and hidden away in the theater's archives. Later it was also excluded from Hans Christian Andersen's *Collected Works*, even though the comedy has certain witty passages and is no worse than other dramatic works in Andersen's oeuvre that were published as part of his collected works in 1854-79.

Nowhere else in Andersen's work do we find such an unvarnished and daring depiction of the type of platonic love for his own gender with which the author was involved most of his adult life. *Herr Rasmussen*, which was submitted anonymously to the Royal Theater in August 1845, had its premiere on March 19, 1846. After his monthlong stay in Weimar with Hereditary Grand Duke Carl Alexander and shorter stays in Leipzig, Dresden, and Prague, Andersen was then on his way from Vienna to Trieste.

From there he was to travel on by ship to Ancona and then overland to Rome and Naples.

The play, whose author on paper was anonymous, was a tremendous flop. Many members of the Collin family cringed during both acts. Edvard decided he'd had enough after the first act and left during the intermission. In the in-house journal of the Royal Theater, it was noted immediately after the curtain fell: "The performance began at six o'clock and was over at nine o'clock. Everything proceeded in the proper manner. The play was royally booed."

Andersen had chosen to submit the play anonymously because of the massive flood of criticism that had been directed at both his art and his person at the end of the 1830s. Among the elite in Copenhagen it had become fashionable to create an ironic and condescending distance from the phenomenon of Hans Christian Andersen. And three actors had even refused—as Fru Heiberg had done with *The Moorish Girl* in 1840—to perform in *Herr Rasmussen*; they gave up their roles after the very first rehearsal. Andersen was furious when he heard by letter of this demonstration against his art, and he immediately wrote from Berlin to Edvard Collin in December 1845:

> "Which roles are they? Tell me that. Which ones have turned down the roles assigned to them? I suppose it's Madame Nielsen, Nielsen, Herr Phister, Fru Heiberg? . . . These people at the theaters are the masters, to whom the management and writer must bow, these few of the 47 million actors and actresses, who each year are the foremost in the world! I'm furious!"[115]

It cannot be said that *Herr Rasmussen* is a great or perfect play. Yet it did make its way onto the royal stage, no doubt helped along the way by the elder Jonas Collin. But then it was roundly booed. There was nothing sensational about women dressing up as men or vice versa on the royal stage. This had been seen many times before during the golden age of vaudeville. But for tall, burly men to court each other so openly—even in a vaudeville or comedy—was nevertheless a rarity. One of the Collins who was present that evening, Ingeborg Drewsen, thought the play was not only awful but embarrassing, and she wrote to Andersen after the scandalous premiere: "As Edvard doubtless has told you, *Herr Rasmussen* was far from successful. I was embarrassed to a degree that I have never experienced from a comedy. Louise [Lind] and I would have left in the middle but it would have caused a stir. I felt so terrible that I told Louise I was about to die! It was unfortunately not the least bit amusing to watch . . ."[116]

Ingeborg Drewsen also pointed out, and quite rightfully so, that the plot of the play was much too disjointed and filled with long monologues with no discernible inner logic. During the first act, the play moves from its initial daring focus on men's love of both men and women to the more diffuse question of identity: "Whose children are we actually?" This was no trifling question; like a menacing shadow it had begun to spread over Hans Christian Andersen's life and work in the 1840s. It had picked up steam when the Danish author was asked in 1846 by his new German publisher, Carl B. Lorck in Dresden, to write his first comprehensive autobiography. Andersen was then forced to consider the first shadowy chapters of the fairy tale of his life. We will take a closer look at this process of writing and remembering in the next chapter.

Johan Ludvig Heiberg was one of the advisers at the Royal Theater when *Herr Rasmussen* was being considered. It was his opinion that even though there were occasional amusing or lively sections of dialogue, the play was much too burdened by speeches and phrases "that seem to borrow from colloquial expressions belonging to quite private circles, which will consequently not be comprehensible to the audience."[117] Heiberg did not specify further which circles in Copenhagen he was alluding to in his report, which also contained statements such as: "Verges on the sordid." Theater adviser Heiberg and his actress wife were in complete agreement. Fru Heiberg had immediately extricated herself from taking any role in this pitiful play. Her brief message to her good friend, theater director Jonas Collin, said:

> "My kind good, dear, sweet, pious, sensible, loyal Privy Councilor! Please leave me out of *Herr Rasmussen*. I have hundreds of reasons why I would rather not have anything to do with that person, but I will spare you from enumerating them."[118]

Her request was honored, while Herr Heiberg's strongly negative evaluation was ignored by Jonas Collin. And that was why the theater director's own son, who refused to address Herr Andersen in the informal manner, ended up having to suffer the humiliation of watching *Herr Rasmussen* from his orchestra seat on March 19, 1846. As previously mentioned, Edvard decided he'd had enough during the first act, and in the intermission he hurried to the cloakroom and vanished out into the fresh air of Kongens Nytorv.

The main character in the play is the orphaned Per Emil Rasmussen, who has always dreamed of a career as a solo dancer, but he has now been fired as a dance pupil from the Royal Theater. For this reason, he has to put aside his dreams and settle for a job as a private tutor for several ill-mannered and spoiled children of a count on a Fyn estate. In the opening scene, Rasmussen is out taking a walk through the fields of the estate, and there he meets his old friend, the painter Julius Kryger. Rasmussen lived with the painter's family for a time in his childhood; he was raised by them and still feels strong ties to them. Kryger tells Rasmussen that he has just leased the forester's cottage because he has discovered the motif for his life here. Her name is Grethe, and all of Kryger's inner canvas smolders with love for the local beauty, who at the moment is in great danger of being married off to Svaneberg, the landowner. But Julius Kryger is not the only bachelor in love in that summer landscape on Fyn. Per Emil Rasmussen has also found love, and he can't help opening his heart to his childhood friend. Soon Kryger becomes initiated into Rasmussen's great secret, which, whispered from the edge of the stage on that March evening at the Royal Theater, must have sent an embarrassing shock through the many "real" men in the audience, especially Edvard Collin, whose own father had pressed to have this play performed:

> *Rasmussen*: Here on Fyn I've found one of the most noble, one of the most deeply feeling temperaments! I've never known anyone like this before! I've seen most of the comedies, participated in all of our ballets, but such a personality has never been portrayed. Oh, how happy I am! . . . I have strong feelings; now I have found what I needed!
>
> *Kryger*: Congratulations! Is she pretty?
>
> *Rasmussen*: He is not a she; he's a teacher trainee![119]

And so Per Emil Rasmussen's "beloved" is not a woman but a man. On the very day when he happens to meet his old friend and half brother, Julius Kryger, Rasmussen and his male friend have arranged a rendezvous. At a specific time they will stand approximately thirty kilometers apart, each in his own spot at the side of the road, to celebrate the happy day and the happy place where the two once met. Here the dance pupil Rasmussen and the teacher trainee Larsen, at a distance and by virtue of their thoughts and emotions, toast each other and switch to the informal "du." As Rasmussen says in a emotional voice: "Raise our glasses, think of each other, and say *du, du*!"

When *Herr Rasmussen* was removed from the roster in 1846, the Danish author was in Rome. On his birthday, April 2, he wrote home to Louise Collin that the hereditary grand duke of Weimar, with whom he had recently parted, was waiting for him on his return from the south. He now had grand plans of installing both Andersen and Jenny Lind as permanent residents of the city. As for his own personal relationship to the Swedish soprano, Andersen had finally realized that his idea of marrying Jenny—or any other woman, for that matter—was a dream with no basis in reality, and that was what it would remain:

> "In Jenny I have a *sister*, a loyal soul, *nothing more*. She most likely does not want to marry, if I have perceived and understood everything. I know a great deal about her decision, but have no right to speak of that! As for myself, I have thus realized that I can resign; I will construct no dream castles but accept what God allows to happen to me . . . God knows whether I, as a married man, would be any happier, whether I could make anyone happy. So whatever is best will happen!"[120]

This was followed by two strenuous months in southern Italy, when new records for high temperatures were set daily. The traveling proved to be physically quite taxing on the author, and in July 1846, in that insufferable summer heat, Andersen had to give up yet another dream: the idea of making his first journey to Spain. Instead, he set a course for Weimar and the hereditary grand duke's beloved castle of Ettersburg. He stayed there for three weeks, enjoying the luxurious life in the great halls with the elaborate Rococo furnishings and the footmen who called the Danish author "*Gnädiger Herr!*" [gracious Sir].[121]

From his windows Andersen could savor the enchanting view and observe the final work on the magnificent gardens, which had been designed by Europe's leading landscape architect, Prince Pückler-Muskau. The gardens included hundreds of different kinds of roses and a great many rare rhododendrons from the slopes of the Himalayas. The Danish author's favorite walk took him through the "Pücklerscher Schlag," which was a cleared section of meadow in the midst of the thick forest below the castle. According to the daring, adventurous visions of the landscape gardener, the entire forest, garden, meadow, yes even the entire cosmos, should be gathered in the senses of the observer. In the midst of this German paradise, Andersen rested and recouped his strength after his traumatic passage through southern Europe. This journey—as we will see in the next chapter—was also a journey into himself, directed at his past and childhood.

The material poverty of his childhood was in sharp contrast to the milieux that Andersen now frequented in the 1840s, in which people generously welcomed him with open arms. In the midst of this Biedermeier period, when the tea urns simmered and people read aloud at the round tables in their parlor, the world apparently couldn't get enough of the charming and romantically edifying story about how an ugly duckling from Fyn once became an enormously beautiful swan of an author.

What Andersen had never mentioned in his basic recounting of his childhood were all these "rips in the beautiful picture book," as he calls certain things[122] he had experienced, such as bestial poverty, prostitution, criminality, drunken mothers and fathers, and children born out of wedlock. This was a part of his life story that he had found it necessary to suppress. Now, as he began work on his first full autobiography during his journey through southern Europe in the summer of 1846, he was forced to recall this aspect of his past and reevaluate it. At its core, this story of his life was rather like the secret that the main character in *Herr Rasmussen* had also revealed, which had offended many of the author's friends and acquaintances in Copenhagen. It laid bare the sensitive aspects of Hans Christian Andersen's mysterious nature and possibly also pointed to a future, about which the author had never told anyone. As it says in a scene from *Herr Rasmussen*:

> "Like a pup I was cast out into the world, and she—my mother—cared nothing for me! I was left completely on my own! There I stood in the foyer of the theater at the barre, raising my leg in the air, and the master looked at my leg and my kneecap and he said: 'You will never be a solo dancer, Peter Emil.' Yet I have danced solo and am still dancing that way all my life. Blows and shoves have I endured, and now—I am an old pup."[123]

Chapter Seven

The Water of Life (1846-1850)

"We need to use the body too!" cries the author to the king and leaps into the waves. It's a warm day in late summer, and King Christian VIII and Queen Caroline Amalie have invited the thirty-nine-year-old Andersen to the island of Føhr in the tidal flats off the west coast of Jutland. He was initially hesitant to accept the invitation because the long and difficult trip would eat into his already strained travel budget. But how could he say no to his king and queen when he is the son of impoverished parents, loves to swim, and has been offered a banquet on the shore, with Viennese waltzes beneath a full moon, and with his own bathing house on wheels, side by side with His Majesty?

The European railroad has not yet reached as far as Denmark, so the journey is both slow and uncomfortable, as he travels by mail coach, sailing ship, and stagecoach via Assens, Aarøsund, Haderslev, Aabenraa, and Flensborg, which is the last stop in civilization. Next comes a long, damp stretch across the marshlands with a scattering of wretched inns and dour, filthy farmers. Everything seems muddy in these parts, thinks Andersen. And to top it all off, the little ferry at Dagebüll is crammed with stinking cattle and sheep. But the crossing makes an impression on the author. The sky above the brownish-yellow wading sea grows bright, and space acquires greater depth the farther they move away from the continent. From a distance Føhr looks downright nice and clean, Andersen decides. He has barely come ashore at Wyk, where Danish flags are flying all along the waterfront and the long white sandy beach, before he is met by lively young female voices: "Mother, here's Andersen!"

With hearty shrieks, the three charming daughters of the Duke and Duchess of Augustenborg welcome the fairy-tale author. He is terribly distressed that they have to see him in his traveling clothes, weary and worn out. Yet he's also flattered, and the spontaneous joy of the girls is the overture to a particularly beneficial sojourn on the island in the tidal flats, where Andersen many times has the honor of swimming with the king. This takes place in so-called bathtubs—little changing rooms on big wheels that are pulled by horses far out in the shallow water. There the swimmer is left to himself, alone in nature. Only when he signals by putting a red flag on the roof of the bathtub is he brought back to shore by a horse and rider.

Andersen is a real health fanatic during the two weeks of his stay there. Not even dark skies or thunder rumbling in the distance can keep him away from the glorious amphibious life of the shallow sea, and Edvard, back home in Copenhagen, receives an enthusiastic report: "I have been swimming every day, and I must say that this is the most marvelous water I have ever been in! It's so salty that tears run from your eyes when you come up! The blood is set in motion most wonderfully; you burn all day long, like fire."[1]

After a week Christian VIII has also softened up, particularly with regard to the author's many hints about his financial situation. One hundred rigsdaler are paid out on the spot, as a travel allowance, along with gracious promises of a raise in his annual author's stipend. The queen is also feeling generous; she gives Andersen a valuable ring and puts a boat and crew at his disposal so that the author can explore the unusual archipelago and see how the forces of nature have shaped the landscape and marked the islanders. While the king goes rabbit hunting on the neighboring island of Amrum, the crew vigorously rows Andersen around. The author is also carried on the powerful shoulders of handsome sailors whenever it's necessary to wade ashore to all the little islands that form a protective reef around the lush green island of Føhr.

"Alas, these beautiful days are already over!" say the king and the author as they dispatch one last rabbit after two weeks of swimming, taking excursions, dancing, and banqueting. Before this, Andersen had been invited by the duchess to visit Augustenborg on Als, but he's not eager to do so. There are too many political tensions in the area, and besides, he neither can nor wants to leave as big a tip for the servants as the emperor of Russia did during his visit. Yet Andersen does visit Augustenborg on his way home, staying for two weeks and then returning the following year. On that occasion, during a dinner party, the daughters entice the author with five pairs of rhymes. Can he come up with an impromptu verse in ten minutes that has to do with the beautiful amphibious life of the wading sea? Of course he can:

> *I tell everyone, both woman and man,*
> *To travel to Føhr, and as fast as they can.*
> *Black as a chimney sweep, it doesn't matter,*
> *You'll twist and you'll turn so fine in the water.*
> *So do travel to Føhr, that is my advice.*
> *It's no terrible deed, it's actually quite nice.*
> *No torments will you taste on the marshy track,*
> *But don't look forward and don't look back.*
> *So merry and brave go to pleasure's country,*
> *It swims in what my poem is: namely, the sea!*[2]

ONE OF HANS CHRISTIAN ANDERSEN'S greatest roles throughout his life was that of guest. This was the case both at home in Copenhagen, where he took turns dining with various friends and acquaintances, and throughout Europe, where he visited kings, princes, and dukes. He was often a long-term guest at the Danish manor houses as well, both when the sun was shining, warm and gentle; or when the frost creaked outside, and indoors the fireplaces were lit and everyone danced around the Christmas tree. But Andersen was most fond of setting off around Midsummer, when the sun was high in the sky, the witches were gathering on top of Bloksbjerg, and the flowers, plants, and sacred springs acquired a curative power. He would head for his favorite bases in southern Sjælland and Fyn: the estates of Holsteinborg, Basnæs, Bregentved, Gisselfeld, and Glorup. Here the author's own rooms always stood ready, and here he could settle in for lengthy periods to concentrate on reading and writing. At the same time he would make the rounds of other distinguished estates and farms of the region whenever restlessness suddenly overcame him. In the 1840s these visits to manor houses became an inseparable part of Andersen's extremely active traveling and writing life. In the middle of the year, when everything reached a turning point and the migratory birds settled into their Danish nests after making the long trip from the south, Andersen would also settle down to take stock; finish projects, both large and small, that had languished in the city; conceive new ideas; and make plans for a late-summer or winter trip to the south.

Andersen would always stay at the Danish estates free of charge. Almost everywhere he was provided with services that included everything from transportation to the laundering and pressing of his clothes and barbering. There was also a large servant staff, who—as they did at Gisselfeld—would wish the author each evening "a humble good night!" But Andersen did pay a price for "living like a count" in the Danish summer landscape. Oranges didn't just fall into the author's turban, nor did roasted pigeons fly straight into his mouth of their own accord. The author had to work for his elegant room and board. His hosts expected that Andersen, aside from drawing a crowd, would also provide a good deal of the entertainment at the dinner table and in the evening hours. The guests looked forward to hearing the author read, and they also expected him to have a couple of polite surprises up his sleeve. At the very least, he was supposed to provide several festive bouquets and unusual table decorations, such as a big cornucopia made from rushes. He could also present various improvisations or parlor games using words and end-rhymes—the so-called *bouts rimés*—or flower lotto, paper-cuts, songs, and amateur comedies.

As long as Andersen was the focal point and object of admiration in these familiar settings, he fulfilled and performed his dual role as guest and entertainer almost to perfection. He was charming, amusing, inventive—and very different. No one could spark life in a stagnant conversation at a gathering the way Andersen could. In one of his fairy tales he gives a very concise description of his role at the manor houses as "the word and the spirit at the table." Similarly, he mentions in *Only a Fiddler* that wherever the wealthy and regal meet, that's where the artists and luminaries of the land also gather, those "whose humor and wit are often regarded in such circles as a type of public fountain; they are invited so as to make it spout for the other guests."[3]

Yet Andersen could also be a terribly difficult guest, who occasionally behaved as capriciously as the Danish summer weather. But this was something that his many hosts accepted, as long as he simply lent a luster to the manor house with his presence. For his part, Andersen submitted to this exploitation of his name and reputation, even though at times it did feel like a sort of intellectual prostitution. He willingly improvised for the distinguished guests in the evening, as long as he had the rest of the time to himself. And he did. The daytime hours spent at the peaceful Danish estates, protected by the venerable gardens and parks and surrounded by lakes and forests, were balm for his soul. For more than forty years, they had an inestimable importance for Andersen and the development of his art. He describes it so beautifully himself in *The Fairy Tale of My Life*:

> "Near the quiet lakes inside the forests, in the grassy green fields where the wild game leaped past and the stork walked on his red legs, I heard no politics or polemics, heard no speeches or *Hegel*; nature around me and inside me preached to me my mission."[4]

Between 1830 and 1870 the Danish estates provided a constant, secure, and inspirational frame around the creative processes, both large and small, of Andersen's literary work. In the summer of 1842, when he was writing "The Ugly Duckling," Andersen began thinking about the significant role that the manor houses had played in his artistic life. After several days at Gisselfeld, the author went over to nearby Bregentved, where the Moltke family lived. During his stay there, it occurred to him that a Danish manor house was actually like the Blue Grotto on Capri. A person found himself in a luminous fairy world, cut off from normal, drab reality, which appeared only as light ripples on the water at the entrance to the cave. Andersen found himself in just such an idyllic space in that fruitful summer of 1842, when he shuttled back and forth between Gisselfeld and Bregentved, which were located less than an hour's drive from each other in southern Sjælland. Both estates were—as Andersen writes in his diary—a "fairy cave, in which only the criticism of the magazines reaches me like a breeze and reminds me of the restless sea outside."[5]

He was surrounded by nothing but friendly and obliging adult faces, happy children, and extremely lively animals, including a stork family up on the roof, which tossed one of the fledglings out of the nest, and a couple of new-baked and very irritable swan parents down in the moat. At Gisselfeld in early July 1842, Andersen conceived the idea for what he immediately named "The Story of a Duck."[6] The idea percolated inside of him for the rest of the month, while the days constantly offered new sights and faces: "What variations in nature: the green oats, the yellow grain, the hay in stacks, the storks in the bogs." He visited Holmegaard Glassworks, where the peasant boys ran around with glowing flasks on iron rods, "as if they contained glowing champagne." Another excursion took him to Vemmetofte Cloister, where Andersen saw himself in the old spinsters of the place. In his diary he remarks optimistically that the eldest was ninety and the youngest, called "the child," was about sixty. He also paid a visit to Vallø, took part in a large duck hunt, and attended various balls. One day, south of Køge, he suddenly passed a barrow with two ancient hawthorn trees on it; people in the region called it the "Elf Mound." Andersen stored the sight away in his memory, and a couple of years later he lifted the barrow out on a glowing rod in his enchanting fairy tale "The Elf Mound," which teems with primordial Danish elves and a couple of tough old Norwegian trolls from Dovrefjeld.

But "The Story of a Duck" was the text that preoccupied Andersen most during that lovely summer of 1842. At the end of July, when he was once again back at his "fairy grotto" at Bregentved, he began composing in earnest this story, which, more than any previous tale, would be about himself. He now gave it the working title "The Cygnet."[7] We don't know how much of the story Andersen wrote before he continued on his summer tour and then returned to Copenhagen, where he went into hibernation, gathering his forces and stocking up provisions for his grand tour to Germany and France during the coming year. In fact, it's astonishing how little is known about the creation of this key fairy tale, which is so brilliantly told. The story would become part of the national heritage practically from the day it was printed in November 1843, and it would accompany the author like a loyal squire wherever he went and was asked to read—especially on his travels abroad.

Everyone who knows of Hans Christian Andersen also knows of the trials of the ugly duckling, but to date—unlike so many other fairy tales written by Andersen—not a scrap of the original manuscript has been found of "The Ugly Duckling," which was the title given to the story at the very last minute. We do know, however, that autumn had arrived in 1843 before the story was finished and published. On October 7, the entry in Andersen's calendar reads: "Finished the story 'The Cygnet.'" A month later "The Ugly Duckling" was published along with "The Angel," "The Nightingale," and "The Sweethearts." The reception of this particular book of fairy tales in November 1843 was historic, in the sense that all the Danish critics took a positive view of Andersen's new work. Not even a trace of irony or perfidy could be found in the reviews. This was a completely new situation for an ugly and scorned duckling like Andersen, and he actually found it rather difficult to receive so suddenly the jabbering acclaim of the entire duck yard. Andersen, with his enmity toward critics, felt in a way disarmed in his role as artist. It's possible to sense in several of the author's letters from the time that in the midst of this sudden praise, which he had always sought, he could foresee future disagreements between himself and all his critics. In December 1843, for instance, he writes to Henriette Wulff in Lisbon:

> "I'm being acknowledged as the foremost teller of fairy tales—in brief, this time I have reason to be very satisfied with the public! That pleases me; it's good to have a little esteem in reserve, because no doubt the occasion will arise when I end up in heavy seas again, so at least I'll have a board to hold on to."[8]

Both in Denmark and throughout Europe, "The Ugly Duckling" instantly became Andersen's most popular tale. This was partly because he immediately began including it in his repertoire whenever he gave readings. He also took the story along on his subsequent travels through Europe in 1843-47, where it met with great success. The universal story of a persecuted, misunderstood creature who has to endure such terrible hardships before he can realize his own hidden greatness was an instant hit all over Europe. Anyone, regardless of gender, age, rank, or birth, could see himself

in both the sophisticated psychology of the duck yard and the easily understood story about an "ascent." Another reason for the fairy tale's enormous
popularity was its clear connection to Andersen's own life, in which he had
apparently encountered a good deal of adversity. But with the help of his
unusual talents and the guiding hand of the good Lord, he had managed
to fulfill his destiny. And Andersen had no complaints about the fact that
so many people read and interpreted the tale as a story about him, equat-
ing the duckling with its author. On the contrary, he strengthened the
growing interest in his life and work in Europe with "The Ugly Duckling,"
which became part of a larger cycle of biographical texts about the Danish
author that also saw the light of day in the 1840s. His myth had been
steadily growing since the late 1830s, and with this story about a duck, the
stage-setting of Andersen's life and persona received a huge push. At the
same time, this tale about a poor, ugly bird who is constantly bitten,
grabbed, pushed, shoved, and ridiculed played into the myth of sympathy
that Andersen shaped in his first full book of memoirs in 1847, *The True
Story of My Life*, and repeated in 1855 in *The Fairy Tale of My Life*.

The story about the duckling's struggle for life and his right to assert
his own nature and personality acquires along the way an oddly grating
defense in the form of all the tenderness and sympathy that develops in the
text on behalf of the poor duckling. This is especially true of the sentimental *kleinmaleri* or tableau at the end of the story, where the contrast
between the duckling's strength and weakness becomes clear. The persecuted and eternally struggling young bird withstands all the humiliations
with such an indomitable and proud spirit, only to end up so weak and
obedient on the last pages of the story. He now eats from the hands of the
children and their parents, who stand around on the shore. This bourgeois
group applauds just as enthusiastically and rhythmically as Andersen's great
audience did everywhere he appeared, reading from his art during the
1840s. And they exclaimed, just as they did in the fairy tale: "The new one
is the most beautiful of all! So young and so lovely!"

The German Autobiography

A direct line can be drawn from "The Ugly Duckling" in 1843 to
Andersen's first big autobiography in 1847, which was first published in
German and began with the words: "My life is a lovely fairy tale, so rich
and happy." But this line also has its roots in the very first international

biographical portraits of Andersen from the late 1830s, which had already been circulating for a long time. Of equally great importance as Xavier Marmier's portraits of Andersen's life and work in the years 1837-40 was the forty-page-long *Biographische Skizze* [Biographical Sketch] in the German edition of *Only a Fiddler* from 1838. This biographical introduction to the German translation was signed "Copenhagen, May 1838," followed by the name of the translator, "C. F. V. Jessen." Once again, it was the author himself who had played a role in shaping the text. This is evident not only in the linguistic tone of the brief biography but also in contemporary letters to friends, both male and female, in which Andersen quite prophetically foresaw that the little biographical sketch would become one of the cardinal points of his European breakthrough. The year was 1838, and Søren Kierkegaard's frontal attack still lay ahead, but an optimistic Andersen was looking forward to his international fame, which was now within his grasp:

> "Day by day I experience more and more how much I am recognized. In Germany it seems as if my name will soon be as known as it is here at home. Yesterday I completed my biographical *Skizze* which will be inserted in the front of *Nur ein Geiger* [*Only a Fiddler*]. I venture to say that it will be printed in many German magazines and will have much influence on how I am judged. My childhood is quite extensively described, including my grandfather's insanity, my sojourn at the Hersfeld Factory, and my father's enlistment as a soldier. Touched upon most lightly are the affairs of the heart, although it will be understood that the author has twice been in love."[9]

The German and the two French biographical portraits of Andersen at the end of the 1830s were all cut from the same cloth. The main points and the supporting details of his picturesque life story included the idealized poverty in snug little Odense, along with the time of trials in Copenhagen, when the son of nature proved his God-given worth and broke through with "a very original character," as it said in a German book about Scandinavian culture from 1845.[10] Both "The Ugly Duckling" and the German autobiography in 1847 further solidified the basic mythical story. The borderline between Andersen's life and work had gradually vanished so thoroughly in his literary production that it was no longer possible to distinguish between fact and fiction. This was especially true of his own descriptions of his life; Andersen withdrew deeper and deeper into his fairy-tale world. Many of his letters from the 1840s reveal that he repeatedly speaks of his recently completed visit to Weimar as "a chapter in the fairy tale of my life."[11] And it was especially in his work on the German autobiography in 1846 that Andersen descended into the blue fairy grotto that he had spoken of at the Danish manor houses in the summer of 1842—a realm in which dream and reality flowed together in a rich and beautiful eternal state, in which Andersen was at the same time the main character.

The German autobiography, *Das Märchen meines Lebens ohne Dichtung*, was written as Andersen traveled through southern Europe in the summer of 1846, and the intent was for the book to be published in Germany during the fall. (It was later published in English as *The True Story of My Life*.) Andersen's memoirs would function as a great prelude and appetizer for the German translation of his *Collected Works*, published in thirty small volumes. The autobiography came out in January 1847, and that same year it even reached England, where it was published while Andersen was there on an official visit. Denmark had to wait another eight years for the first full biography written by the author himself.

At the end of February 1846, after fierce negotiations with several German booksellers and publishers, in which Andersen was aided and advised by his friends in Weimar and Berlin, the author secured a lucrative contract in Leipzig with the Danish-born publisher Carl B. Lorck. The agreement was for the publication of Andersen's collected works. And before he set off southward for warmer latitudes, where he intended to work intently on his autobiography, Andersen managed to persuade Edvard Collin to be a reader and editor of the book, which, according to a verbal agreement with Lorck, was supposed to be finished in May 1846.

The agreement with Collin became in many ways Andersen's salvation, because the work on this first full autobiography in book form quickly proved to be much more problematic than he had imagined. Andersen the improviser was suddenly not able to be as free with his material as was his custom. At the same time, it was difficult to create a natural flow in the writing process when he was traveling and constantly had to depart, settle in, and then depart again. The manuscript swelled up, heading off in all directions, which made a tight editing and revision process necessary, even after the first chapters of the book were done. Andersen didn't want to be involved in this tedious part of the creative work, and so he put the responsibility for the final shaping of his memoirs in the hands of his "critical tailor" back home in Copenhagen. The division of labor between him and Collin was crystal clear. On the day after signing the contract with Lorck in Leipzig, Andersen informed his adviser back in Copenhagen:

> "I've promised to deliver a biography which he [publisher Lorck] is to receive in May, but with the condition that it be sent to you with postage, and you are to be allowed to delete from it whatever you like. I can't just write something about myself and my circumstances, flowing right from pen and onto the press. I have to have a proven friend who knows all the circumstances, who weighs my words; won't you do it? I write without embarrassment and trust that you, before the court of your own conscience, will vouch for what is printed. From you the biography will go straight to the printer."[12]

It was—as Andersen knew full well—quite a task that Edvard Collin now undertook. He agreed not only to be a filter between the author and reality, but he consented to make a clean copy of his friend's manuscript with all its scribblings and countless crossed-out passages and additions so that the translator would be able to read it. Collin's assistance was enormous throughout the whole process, which Andersen also acknowledged with a warm thank-you letter in August 1846 when his part of the job was finally completed and he was resting up while visiting Hereditary Grand Duke Carl Alexander in Weimar. "Thank you, thank you!—I will never forget this example of your brotherly temperament; it is an embrace, it is a kiss—it is a toast to 'du'—I'm sure you know what I mean. Thank you!"[13]

As usual, Collin declined Andersen's kisses and embraces. Instead he replied in a curt and reserved fashion that he hadn't done this to appeal to Andersen's emotions but simply because his editorial eye couldn't stand to see a manuscript that was written to such an extent with a flowing pen and nowhere showed any "trace of paring."[14] The Collin family had once again resolved a huge problem for its demanding son. Yet scholars who have compared Andersen's original manuscript with the final version of the autobiography, which was published in 1847, have shown that Edvard Collin exacted a payment along the way. He went far beyond the authorized powers of his role as editor and adviser. He used this unique opportunity—far removed from Andersen himself but very close to his manuscript—to edit the life story of his friend. With a strange mixture of pedantic linguistic precision, envy, irritation, and a sense of protectiveness with regard to Andersen, Collin weeded out parts from the original manuscript, which had arrived from the south by mail, chapter by chapter, in the summer of 1846.[15]

Particularly affected were Andersen's bad habits that Edvard hated most: his sniveling and his vanity. He also pared down and edited so much of Andersen's unique style and tone that in the German translation, which was now going out to a large audience, we find a much less biting and dangerous Romantic than Andersen, the Rhyming Demon. And so, in *Das Märchen meines Lebens ohne Dichtung*, we often hear only an echo of his special rhythm and diction, in which the sentences and words swirl around each other like arabesques. Edvard Collin didn't care for this sort of circumlocutions in prose, and he seized upon this welcome opportunity to shorten or omit whatever he liked. He did discuss various major changes with Andersen, but most of the corrections—for instance, cutting sentences or even entire sections—Edvard undertook on his own initiative, just as he generously scattered periods through every chapter. The pattern and method in this "puritanical extermination campaign against all superfluities and ornamentation"[16] are quite indicative of the approach that Edvard Collin would use many years later in his treatment of his famous friend's letters in his book *Hans Christian Andersen and the Collin Family*. But in a legal sense, he did restrict himself to what Andersen had asked of him: to correct and produce a clean copy of the manuscript about the story of the author's extraordinary life.

Andersen, on the other hand, was unable to keep his part of the agreement. It quickly became clear that the autobiography could not possibly be completed by May 1846. At that time Andersen had just arrived in Naples, but after a good deal of socializing in Prague, Vienna, and Rome—not to mention the strenuous journey across the Adriatic and through the Appenines—he had not made it any farther than to the introductory chapter about his childhood in Odense in 1805-19. This was a story that he could usually rattle off by heart, but he was now having trouble with it, and he needed help and inspiration from outside. For instance, he chose to use a couple of long passages from the two lengthy biographical sketches that he had in his suitcase. He drew upon his own old introduction to the German edition of *Only a Fiddler* from 1838, as well as a quite new biographical essay by the critic P. L. Møller, which was printed in *Dansk Pantheon* in 1845. This documentary material was supplied with other excerpts from articles and letters, including Carsten Hauch's accolades to Andersen, published in *Dansk Ugeskrift* in January 1846. In this article, Hauch heartily praised Andersen, offering a form of compensation for his excoriation of the fairy-tale author in his novel *Castle on the Rhine* in 1845. Hauch's essay arrived in Vienna by mail in March, and Andersen at first complained about it in a letter to Edvard Collin. He nevertheless decided to clip out the most favorable passages and paste them directly into his autobiography, as yet another acknowledgement of his genius. And suddenly Hauch was even "one of the noblest characters that I know,"[17] as it said in Andersen's autobiography in 1847.

It was not until reaching Naples that Andersen truly began to make progress on *Das Märchen meines Lebens ohne Dichtung*. In less than six weeks in the sweltering heat of the city beneath the volcano, Andersen made a great deal of headway, producing in a virtual ecstasy of writing nearly a hundred pages, which form the most interesting and solidly written chapters of the autobiography. This section deals with the author's arrival in Copenhagen in 1819; his relationship with Edvard Collin in the 1830s; and his encounters with Riborg Voigt, Jenny Lind, and Hereditary Grand Duke Carl Alexander. His reunion with all of these beloved friends on the page was a means of reconnecting with them. Andersen was able to establish a closeness with them through his writing, in the midst of his loneliness and longing in the south. The dear women and men represented a kind of Fata Morgana. Andersen briefly reflects on this phenomenon in his autobiography and writes: "When a person distances himself from the mountains, that's when he can first properly focus on their whole contour."

That's also how it was with all the other images in Andersen's memory. When the autobiography was finally finished and at the end of the year he could look back on the hard work of writing it, the whole process seemed like a distant, hazy mountain. It had been a nerve-wracking, startling, and exacting process beneath the glaring sun of the south. "It was all spawned in one piece," Andersen wrote in a letter to Edvard Collin in the early summer. Several months later, when the final period was in place and he was once again philosophizing about how strenuous the writing process had been, he says:

> "Let me tell you that it has not been an easy task to gather everything together in my mind, to compress it onto paper, and to do it in a single effort of writing it down. I am also certain that this work has affected my whole nervous system as much as the heat has."[18]

His Childhood Home

Authors can be extremely forgetful when they talk about their own life. Hans Christian Andersen also displays a surprisingly poor memory, in places even muzzling himself and reining in his tongue, in his charming reconstruction of his childhood in Odense, both in his autobiography from 1847 and eight years later in *The Fairy Tale of My Life*. The black holes in his past are both numerous and large, if we look at the wealth of details and sharpness of depth that characterize the childhood stories that Andersen chose to tell and included in his autobiography.

Even the very beginning of the autobiography shows a lack of credibility. Here the reader is presented with a happy and harmonious couple, Anne Marie Andersdatter and Hans Andersen, and their little newborn son in a poor but immensely comfortable and tidy home in 1805. And we're told a touching anecdote about the bridal and birthing bed, which stands in the center of the home. The boy's skillful shoemaker father had cobbled it together from the catafalque under the coffin belonging to Count Trampe. Yet we have to leap ahead to 1807 before a count by that name dies on the island of Fyn.[19] And Hans Christian Andersen makes little effort to expand on the idyllic opening scene of the autobiography, in which the parents are described as a man and woman who "were so infinitely fond of each other." Instead, during the rest of the chapter his parents are depicted as two people who did live under the same roof for several years, but with an emotional and spiritual distance between them, since there was such a difference in temperament, manner, and age.

When Andersen says in the first chapter of his memoirs that his mother was "several years older" than his father, it must be added that this meant a full ten years. Born around 1773, Anne Marie Andersdatter was thirty-one or thirty-two, while Hans Andersen (born 1782) was twenty-two when the two married in 1805. Hans Christian once heard his father teasing his mother with the label "old mother," and he annoyed her with remarks about her "always wanting to have a young fellow," and "you would rather have had the potter's assistant."[20] Here the shoemaker was most likely thinking of the man (Daniel Jørgensen Rosenvinge) who was assumed to be the father of Hans Christian Andersen's half sister, Karen Marie (born 1799), whom the author meticulously avoids mentioning in any of his autobiographies. The author's mother was also significantly older than her second husband, the shoemaker Niels Jørgensen Gundersøn, whom she married in 1818 after Hans Christian's father died. At the time, she was around forty-five, while he was thirty-one years old. Yet in those days it was quite common for younger men to marry women who were much older. A man "took on a matron," as it was called, and in this way escaped having a partner who would undergo childbirth every other year and foist upon him a whole flock of little children, giving him numerous mouths to feed.[21]

There are many indications that the author's parents, right from the beginning in 1805, didn't share much beyond the legal formalities of their marriage, their clever son, and the annual excursion when the beech trees bloomed in the woods near Odense River. In a period of Danish history when promiscuity was rampant, the country was swarming with illegitimate children. Single mothers made up their own social caste, and they often ended up in prison because they had given birth to three children outside of wedlock. This being the case, it's not unlikely that the marriage to shoemaker Hans Andersen was a necessary and thus, in its own way, "happy" arrangement for Anne Marie Andersdatter. At any rate, the couple was married sometime in early 1805, when the very pregnant bride, wearing a myrtle wreath and veil, must have had a great deal of trouble kneeling down because of her large belly. They showed up in church two months before the birth but did not move in together until almost a year after Hans Christian was born. It can be ascertained, without a doubt, that Hans Christian Andersen's parents were homeless in 1805, and had not, as he says in his autobiography, rented "a poor little house," in which his father had "hammered together his workshop." As mentioned, they didn't move in together as husband and wife until early 1806. They then lived in several different places in Odense until May 1807, when they rented part of a house on Munkemøllestræde, which became the frame for Andersen's childhood.

What we know today as "Hans Christian Andersen's house"—the low yellow, corner building which we visit in the belief that it was here he was born and lived—is one of the many myths about the fairy-tale author's life that, over time, has been stage-set and maintained, although not by Andersen himself[22] It was not here that the author crawled around the floor as a child, took his first steps, cut and sewed, or wrote his first clumsy attempts at plays with the help of his neighbors. In fact, we don't know for sure where in Odense the author was born on April 2, 1805. It might well have been in the little house at the corner of Hans Jensens Stræde and Bangs Boder, which has been designated a museum since 1908. But it's also possible, just like in the fairy tale "The Tinderbox," to draw a cross on the doors of many other houses in Odense, where Hans Christian Andersen might have come into this world. Upon celebrating his seventieth birthday in 1875, Andersen snorted at the assumption that his birthplace was on Hans Jensens Stræde, saying that it definitely was not "in that hovel."[23] Andersen had given an equally sharp retort a couple of years earlier when his American publisher, Horace E. Scudder, wanted to confirm the rumor that an admirer of the author had supposedly purchased the little corner house in Odense where he was born and had then turned over the house to Andersen. Was this fabulous story true? Scudder wanted to know. Andersen replied at once, and his message was quite clear. No one had bought or given him the corner house on the narrow, impoverished lane—fortunately. As he wrote in English: "There is no suspicion of anyone having bought and presented me with my birthplace in Odense, nor do I entertain any such desire."[24]

In other words, Hans Christian Andersen, late in his life, was thoroughly fed up with all the rumors that he had supposedly been born in a less than flattering part of Odense. It's true that his maternal grandparents had lived in the corner house on Hans Jensens Stræde from January 1802 until the end of 1804. And, by all accounts, they had taken care of Andersen's four-year-old half sister when his mother lived and worked as a maid in the home of the merchant Birkerod in another part of town. But when Hans Christian announced his arrival in the world in April 1805, the corner house was no longer occupied by his grandparents but by poor folks with numerous children who were apparently related to Hans Christian Andersen's father.[25]

There were many reasons why the aging, world-famous Andersen hated the idea of being born in a rented house located in the section of St. Hans Parish where approximately one-third of the children were born out of wedlock and were received with anything but joy and delight.[26] Even in 1867, when Andersen was made an honorary citizen of his hometown, he declared loudly and clearly that he didn't know the exact place of his birth, but that he assumed it was on Skulkenborg or Ramsherred—both of which are located near the corner house on Hans Jensens Stræde.[27]

But if Hans Christian Andersen gives us in his memoirs only a few specially selected and quite idyllic postcards of his family history and upbringing on the island of Fyn in 1805-19, where should we look for the truth about his childhood? Where should we seek all the memories that, as he writes, "made a dark impression on him"?

One place we can look is in the literature that Andersen created before the 1840s, when he cemented the Romantic myth about the path of the beautiful swan through the filthy duck yard of life. There are striking differences between the glowing images that Andersen presented to his readers in his autobiography and the far more evil and cruel world that we see in the rest of his works, especially before 1840. It's even possible to say that in his fiction—epic, lyric, and dramatic—Andersen was much closer to reality in terms of his childhood story than in his purportedly factual memoirs, in which it is his imagination and dreams that guide his pen and everyday life must never be dreary, sad, or evil again.

As previously mentioned, *Das Märchen meines Lebens ohne Dichtung* was supposed to live up to the Romantic era's dream about the pure and untainted person who, like the child, was filled with impulsive spirit and nature. This was one of the reasons why the German autobiography in 1847, and later *The Fairy Tale of My Life* in 1855, were sanitized of anything in the depiction of the author's life that might seem dirty or unsavory, split or unharmonious. The autobiographies were meant to express a positive story about the divine in human beings. This was why the bestial traces, which by all accounts were a part of Hans Christian Andersen's childhood story, were instead channeled into the author's diaries, letters, and literary works.

In Andersen's work there is an abyss of contradictions between all the pleasant, orderly relationships between the father, mother, and child in his autobiographies, and the chaotic, shattered, and traumatizing family patterns that we find in his fairy tales, novels, and plays. On occasion it's a matter of fictions that open up like Pandora's box, and out pour evil stepfathers and unnatural mothers, rapes, incest, and—in particular—children who are lost or gone astray, who have no knowledge of their biological origins. In other words, there is a social reality in Andersen's work that has been kept out of his autobiographies but appears in his novels, fairy tales, and plays. The world was a cruel place around 1800. It was filled with fatherless and motherless children, conceived in adultery, born in secret, and killed after birth or abandoned; in the best of circumstances the children might find a foster family. It's especially in Andersen's early works that we encounter all of these lonely, unhappy creatures from the lowest levels of society who seldom know who their real father might be.

It's apparent from little, scattered remarks in his literary works that Andersen, as a boy, saw and heard rough and cruel things, and on his way through the streets of Odense he experienced various types of human degradation. As it says in *Only a Fiddler*, "A person can forget the fresh, clear water he receives as a refreshing drink, but he never forgets the muddy or the bitter!" And as an extension of the swamp symbolism that permeates his work, Andersen mentions in the fairy tale "Peiter, Peter, and Peer" that a little mud and duckweed from the millpond always clings to a person's life story.

For his own part, the author didn't start telling a little of his own muddy childhood story until he was an old man, and then it was almost always in conversations with various young men whom he trusted and with whom he traveled. This included, for instance, Edvard Collin's son, Jonas, who wrote down some of these very personal and intimate stories, which have been preserved for posterity but have never been published. Andersen once told Jonas about an experience he had at a market in Odense. He was then a little boy, and at the colorful, lively market there was a fortune-teller with a strange peep-box, which, for a fee, would allow a look into your future. On this occasion the author's mother wanted to know what would become of her unusual, talented son. The fortune-teller looked deep into the box and then handed her a fortune that was printed in little verses. And the aging Andersen could recite one of them for Jonas Collin: "He may become a whoremonger—but never a thief!" His mother had to settle for that, and turning to the women standing all around, she promptly declared: "Oh well, good Lord, at least he won't be stealing from anyone else!"[28] We don't find any little stories like this in Andersen's auto-biographies, but they do appear in his early literary works, such as the three novels from the 1830s: *The Improvisatore*, *O.T.*, and *Only a Fiddler*. These novels use the author's own biography as a powerful sounding board to portray the difficult development of a boy as he becomes a man and seeks answers to the question: "Who am I?"

In terms of their connection to Andersen's own life story, the three novels have in common a peculiar mixture of openness and camouflage regarding his life story, which was already known to many readers in Denmark in 1835-37. On the one hand, all three books are practically overflowing with recognizable sources from the author's own past and present. On the other hand, the narrator quite often conceals and distances himself from certain specific associations and relations so they won't be directly connected to or mistaken for the author himself. Instead, the text is heavily veiled. A good example of this occurs in *Only a Fiddler*, which was written in one long improvisational rush in 1836. It was almost a process that resembled automatic writing, in which Andersen, from the very beginning, had no set plan for how the novel would proceed. Instead, he allowed his pen to dance freely across the page, so that both the characters and the plot more or less did the steering. Almost intentionally the forces of Andersen's subconscious were released during the creative process, and this had a personal, redemptive effect on the author, bringing him to an understanding and overview that he discusses in a letter to Ingemann in February 1837:

"As far as my mood goes, it's the best I can remember for many years. I've arrived at a clear perception of the world and myself. I feel more than ever before what Our Lord has given me and done for me; it would be ungrateful not to be happy, and thus I want to look at everything from the brightest side, and that actually comes easy to me. If dark whims ever arise, I will conduct myself like the Icelandic skald: I will sing out my sorrow. All sorrows, all bitternesses—go into the novel. It's going to be a peculiar book, let me tell you! It is, like most of what I write, a mirror of myself. In *O.T.* I had a specific plan before I wrote down a single word; but this time I am letting Our Lord take care of everything . . . this time I'm not writing a single word unless it is *given*, almost forced upon me."[29]

The Swamp in *Only a Fiddler*

It cannot be confirmed with any certainty whether this clear perception of himself and the world, which Andersen had achieved through his writing, was shaped by a particular recognition of the fluid boundaries of gender within himself. It's also possible that it had to do with the fact that suddenly, by putting his feelings about his past into words, he had illuminated some of the dark and concealed aspects of his childhood. Presumably it was a combination of the two. But one thing is certain: the novel *Only a Fiddler* is continually seeking words and images that are redemptive. This is a force that we also find in the author's later novels, including *The Two Baronesses* from 1847, in which it says that as a human being, you must be prepared sometime in life to plumb the bottom of your miry insides to study the fat water snakes there and the spiders as big as plates. This graphic imagery appears in a specific chapter of *The Two Baronesses*, which repeatedly uses catchwords such as "unconscious" and "dream." At one point the narrator also points out that even a swamp has its lilies, in whose filaments "the invisible heavenly thread" resides.[30]

We find similar invisible heavenly threads in the very long fairy tale entitled "The Marsh King's Daughter" from 1858. The turning point in Helga's story is the young woman's attempt to emerge, on her own, from a tragically divided and amphibian self. She has to return to Wild Bog and dive below the surface of the swamp, which has been the determining factor in her cursed life. Helga is the tragic offspring of the brutal Marsh King's rape of the divinely beautiful Egyptian princess. She had come to Denmark wearing a swan skin, in search of a curative remedy for her ill father who lives on the banks of the Nile. And there, in the middle of the swamp, Helga was conceived. She now has to return to the very same place and see her reflection in order to come to an understanding and recognition of everything that caused her divided and unhappy life. As the Christian priest and spiritual adviser says to the almost grown-up Helga: you have to "shatter the watery shield over the deep quagmire, pull out the living root of your life and your cradle."

This was half a century before Sigmund Freud presented his concepts of the super ego and the id. Yet Andersen used his Helga figure in the fairy tale "The Marsh King's Daughter" to create an image of how inner opposing forces, conditioned by heredity and environment, can cause a person to split. And these forces will either emerge into the sunlight or remain down in the depths of the mud. In February 1854, in a letter to Hereditary Grand Duke Carl Alexander, Andersen made it clear that he—as Freud would do—associated all this swamp symbolism with human sexual drives. In this letter Andersen speaks of the discomfort he had experienced— along with many other Danes—upon reading a new novel, *Minona*. As soon as it was published, this book became the subject of much indignation and discussion because of its candid depictions of a sexual love relationship between a brother and sister. The author of this controversial novel was Clara Raphael, which was the pseudonym of Mathilde Fibiger, one of Andersen's good friends. In his letter to Carl Alexander, Andersen compares his reading experience to holding "a stinking, poisonous, and slimy water plant" in his hands. Nevertheless, he had made his way through the entire book. And for this reason he could analyze and explain his loathing for a novel that did not express the love of a soul but was exclusively preoccupied with a love prompted by blood.[31] In a letter sent to B. S. Ingemann around the same time, Andersen once again took up the question of the swamp symbolism, wanting someone who shared his views to be equally indignant.

"Have you read the book? She must be sick, that author! I wish for her sake and for the sake of literature that it had never been written. I feel as if I had seized hold of a foul-smelling, poisonous water plant and now that I have the whole thing in my hand, it disintegrates, slimy and disgusting! How is it possible for a young girl to get lost in such ideas? Or if, in the service of purity, she has wandered off toward a swamp in order to hover above it and point out the power of the marsh, then she has ended up stuck in it."[32]

★ ★ ★

Considering all the swamp and marsh images that can be found in Andersen's writing and that often contain more or less hidden references to the author's own life, it's worth taking a closer look at a few specific sections of the novel *Only a Fiddler*. These are the passages that reveal much about the prostitute Steffen Karreet. In an epistolary discussion of the novel, Andersen called her "one of the capital's unhappy marsh-images."[33] In five extremely concentrated and mysterious pages at the beginning of the second part of the novel, the author circles around human moral depravity both close up and at a distance. This occurs through words and phrases such as "cesspool," "marsh," "the grave's poisonous stench," "the heavy earth of sin," and "big hideous toads with slimy bodies." And at a deeper layer of the narrative about Steffen Karreet's sad fate, the swamp symbolism has roots in the author's own life, which, in a suggestive manner, becomes intertwined with the plot and turns a strangely compelling chapter into a mixture of art and self-knowledge, difficult to distinguish.

That was how Andersen's Swedish friend, the author Fredrika Bremer, described this chapter at any rate, after she had read his novel. In the summer of 1837 she met Andersen on a steamship in Sweden. There, during a moment of confidences at the railing, he had sketched out what was for him a crucial, central chapter in his new novel, which he sent to Bremer when it was published in November 1837. She replied several months later with a lengthy letter that reflected how moved and touched she was by the above-mentioned chapter's description of "depravity at its lowest level," as Andersen called it. Bremer was deeply fascinated by Andersen's character and personality, and so she had read the novel in light of unhappy events in the author's own life, events that Andersen had hinted were the basis for the fiction.

> "In your *Fiddler*, I enjoyed very much reading a scene that was unforgettable for me, after an evening aboard the steamship when you gave me a hasty sketch of it (the one between Steffen Karreet and the sailor). What a strange and mighty alchemist art is! From life's most unpleasant events, from topics that are raw and vile and in real life arouse only our disgust, the artist creates in his refiner's fire the purest gold, and we are entranced by what would have otherwise made us shudder."[34]

In the chapter in question, the boy Christian, who is trying to find a foothold in Copenhagen, lands in the human swamp of the big city. The chapter begins with a quote from a poem by Victor Hugo, which is both an homage to and a warning against all the errant women of the day "who sell the sweet name of love." This sets the tone and direction: the reader is about to sink down into the mire! And it's true that we are pulled down beneath the surface of the sea along with Christian, who has sought shelter and a bed in a dark low-ceilinged cabin on board a ship berthed at Nyhavn. He has recently met the aging, maternal Steffen Karreet, and in his loneliness has attached himself to her. Now she shows up at the ship in Nyhavn, late at night, along with one of her steady customers, Sailor Søren. The boy is sleeping heavily and at first doesn't hear anything. He's dreaming about a good, loving woman with the exceedingly strange name of "Steffen Karreet." It should be noted that at the time, and for men who were older than Christian, this name was a clear indication of the world's oldest profession. In Danish "karreet" means "the cart." A prostitute was commonly called "beggar box," "the crooked hearse," and "wooden ass."[35] In the boy's dream, his maternal friend—this good, gentle angel—takes him by the hand and leads him from a barren and desertlike landscape to a garden of paradise that is filled with flowers, music, and joy. Within this little creation-narrative of a dream, Steffen suddenly gives Christian a violin made of silver. And as soon as he slides the bow across the strings, the instrument sounds more powerful and beautiful than thousands of other instruments put together. Then Christian awakes at the sound of voices, and in his half-dreaming, half-alert state, he listens to the muted conversation of the adults. Among other things, he hears that Steffen is pleading with Sailor Søren for help because she is pregnant. She's willing to pay the man everything she owns if he will simply marry her. In that way she will escape shame and punishment in the form of public condemnation, prison, and fines, along with further degradation and ostracism in a society which around 1800, both in the countryside and in the cities, was filled with single, roaming women with fatherless children. Christian is no longer asleep; he is listening to her plead with Sailor Søren:

> "It all depends on you," she said, "whether a body and a soul will sink down into the eternal cesspool."
>
> "Have you become one of the pietists?" asked the sailor, laughing.
>
> "I must tell you everything that is in my heart!" she said in a strangely broken voice. Christian was listening, because no doubt she was going to talk about him . . .
>
> "Save me! . . . I'm in the mire!" she said. "No one respects me. I don't either. Save me, Søren! I have honestly shared my money with you. I still

have forty *rigsdaler* left. Marry me! Take me away from this misery, carry me off to a place where no one knows me, where you won't be ashamed of me. I will slave for you so the blood springs from my fingernails! Oh, take me with you! In a year it will be too late."

"I should take the likes of you to see my old parents?" said the sailor.

"I will kiss their feet. They can beat me, and I will patiently endure every blow! I'm already old, I know that; soon I'll be twenty-eight, but this is an act of mercy that I'm begging of you. If you don't do this, no one will, and then I'll have to drink until my head bursts so that I can forget how miserable I have made myself!" She clung to the grimy sailor.

"Is that the important news that you wanted to tell me?" And he pushed her away.

These tears, these sighs, combined with the desperate words, pierced Christian's heart. A dream image was extinguished, and he saw the shadow side of reality.

Once again he was alone.[36]

Was it possible that in this chapter of *Only a Fiddler*—which, according to Fredrika Bremer and other female correspondents, held great existential significance for the author—Andersen was presenting a scrap of truth about his own family and ancestors? Could it also be touching on the circumstances of his own birth, which he couldn't tell the world in the romantic version of the fairy tale of his life?

The narrator of the novel is constantly at work in this surrealistic chapter. He keeps intervening, almost nervously, to give us information that isn't really relevant to the plot. Even in the middle of Christian's dream, which doesn't need to be justified because it's a dream, after all, the narrator interrupts and starts explaining why we as readers should be witnesses to such a degrading, unpleasant, and private conversation between a man and a woman. This is a scene, the narrator says in apology, that will arouse both loathing and sympathy, but it's necessary to recount it. And then comes what we, as readers, find truly astonishing about the narrator's quite heavy-handed intervention: Without any further explanation, an entirely new female character is introduced in the chapter. She's a woman who at first glance seems to be a mirror-image and parallel to Steffen Karreet. But upon closer examination and comparison (especially with regard to the age of the women), she appears to be a woman from an entirely different era, even an entirely different space from what is presented in the novel. Maybe she's from reality. She's the one the narrator speaks of when he addresses the reader, ignoring Steffen and Sailor Søren and Christian:

> "If eighteen years ago you had seen the slender, fourteen-year-old girl with the pure joy of life in her eyes, then you would have thought of *Semele*—yes, *Semele* waited for *Jupiter* in all his majesty. And her lover did come, not as the sun that warms, but as fire that burns, and she turned to dust in his arms, as the myth tells us. Dust, earth became the image of beauty."[37]

This almost ostentatiously precise pronouncement of the dream woman's age might be a reference to Hans Christian Andersen's maternal aunt, Christiane. Exactly eighteen years before the publication of this novel— in 1819—she opened her home and brothel to the innocent fourteen-year-old Hans Christian. He had just arrived from Odense, and when he sought out his aunt, he found "depravity at its lowest level," as it says in *Only a Fiddler*. It took some time before the boy discovered what sort of business his aunt was conducting in her lodgings, which were presumably located somewhere near Holmensgade, in those days a street swarming with "loose women."[38] It's important to clarify that the narrator of *Only a Fiddler*, by speaking directly to the reader ("I am showing her to you. Don't turn away.") is attempting to understand this woman and wants to explain that she is, in the deepest sense, a victim of heredity and environment. No matter how confused and unhappy her life may have turned out, the narrator envelops her with a certain tenderness and understanding that, in the midst of the swamp, is put in perspective. "Happy are you if you found a home where modesty did not desert you. She did not. What poison can a man's sweet words drip into a woman's soul, initiating her into disgrace?"

Is it his aunt's fate that he's referring to here, and lamenting? Is Hans Christian Andersen in the same breath drawing a cautious connection to all his relatives on his mother's side, whom he not once in his adult life wanted to come near in his autobiographies? At any rate, he tried to erase all trace of such a connection. He did so primarily because Anne Marie Andersdatter came from a family in which immorality and loose living among the women seems to have been the norm rather than the exception.

Andersen's maternal grandmother, Anne Sørensdatter (1743-1825), had three children by three different men. All the children were born out of wedlock, which in 1773 landed her in the prisoners' cellar beneath Odense Courthouse, where she was sentenced to bread and water for a week.[39] This was the punishment for "committing fornication." And it can't be denied that Andersen's grandmother was at times involved in a type of prostitution and ran a brothel. This was quite common and often provided a means of survival for the wandering female proletariat, to whom Anne Sørensdatter apparently belonged in the late 1700s. At any rate, it's not known who Andersen's maternal grandfather was, but he may have been one of the many soldiers from the large cavalry regiment that was garrisoned on Fyn at the time[40]

We know that one of the three daughters born to Hans Christian's grandmother, the previously mentioned Aunt Christiane Jansen (1778-1830), took part in organized prostitution in Copenhagen. In Andersen's autobiographical work from 1832, which wasn't published until many years after the author's death, he recounts with great poise and without revealing too much that in the difficult autumn of 1819 he sought out his aunt in the big city. He also describes an encounter between his mother and aunt in Odense when he was a child. Anne Marie Andersdatter had reproached her half sister for her "fondness for finery," which among the general public at the time was regarded as a sign that a woman was a harlot.[41] Andersen's mother was the big sister, after all, and she was now respectably and legally married. No doubt she felt compelled to give her younger sister a moral lecture, which presumably made Christiane quite angry. In 1819, when Hans Christian turned up at her Copenhagen address, unannounced and as destitute as any other beggar, she said—within earshot of the boy—to some of the girls in her brothel: "Well, look at that, after treating me so badly, now she's saddling me with her child! And a boy, at that; if only it were a girl!"[42]

Yes, if only the lanky, ugly lad had been a pretty and lively girl from Fyn, someone his aunt could have instantly enrolled in her Copenhagen company of young maidens! Andersen ends his little story about his brothel-aunt from 1832 by saying that it was because of Fru Thorgesen—his landlady on Holmensgade—that he one day finally figured out what his aunt and all her finery-mad ladies were actually up to whenever they withdrew to a room with a male guest. At the same time, Andersen hastens to emphasize that after this discovery he immediately said farewell to that part of town, and he never saw his aunt again. "I never saw her after that—I suppose she's dead; or neither of us would recognize the other."

In Andersen's later autobiographies from 1847 and 1855, Christiane Jansen has been deleted. Any connection between this woman, who in the 1832 autobiography was called "a sort of aunt," and the now famous author of fairy tales was permanently excised. And the sporadic references to her profitable enterprise were shifted to the shoulders of others who were not as recognizably associated with his family, under labels such as "the woman" and "the captain's widow." But Andersen never forgot Christiane Jansen and the whole milieu surrounding her whorehouse on Holmensgade. There is no doubt that his brothel-aunt, in some form, is present in the very lively and atmospheric descriptions of Steffen Karreet in *Only a Fiddler*. Here we find traces of a close relative who, at her death in February 1830, left behind two girls who were not her own biological children but products of an "accident" by her employees on the job.[43]

Immoral Fyn

Hans Christian Andersen chose to delete various biographical facts about his family and ancestors from *Das Märchen meines Leben ohne Dichtung* in 1847 and from *The Fairy Tale of My Life* in 1855. These facts reflect a reality on Fyn that was anything but idyllic or pleasant during the years 1790–1820. Andersen was once part of this reality, though he later chose to flee from it, and he had good reasons for doing so.

Much of the secretiveness that Andersen displays in terms of his childhood has to do with male children having one mother but several possible fathers. This is a pattern that recurs throughout his works. His poems, plays, fairy tales, and novels are filled with children who demand to know from their mother who their biological father is. Or we hear about children who are either put to death or sent away after being born under clandestine circumstances. If we take a look at life in Odense and all over Fyn around 1800, we see many women in the towns and surrounding regions who, like Andersen's mother and grandmother, were burdened with children born out of wedlock. And we quickly stumble on a human swamp of considerable size and depth. In order to survive at all, many of these lower-class, destitute mothers with children in tow were forced into various forms of prostitution in the cities, on the farms, and in the fields and markets all over Fyn. We find the same desperate pattern everywhere in Denmark around 1800, but historical accounts of the moral conditions in Denmark at that time maintain that the poor people of the Fyn countryside and towns were especially immoral and known for their loose ways.[44] For as far back as such conditions have been investigated, Fyn has actually been the region of the country that could boast the largest number of births out of wedlock per capita.

In a book from 1888 the prison pastor S. M. Hafström conducted a survey of the morals among the Danish peasantry and poor folks. He began his small but statistically well-documented pamphlet by stating that each year in the kingdom of Denmark, "6,000 children were born out of wedlock," which was comparable to ten percent of all childbirths at the time. In his study, Hafström reported that very young girls among the poor on Fyn would return home to their parents a short time after being confirmed at the age of thirteen or fourteen in order to give birth. Similarly, young men who were practically still boys were regularly alleged to be fathers. Loose living was also seen among many women, who had one illegitimate child after another—three, four, five, or six in all. The prison pastor's conclusion regarding the moral conditions on Fyn in the 19th century was this:

> "In all of Europe it is possible to find only a couple of areas where the immorality might resemble that on Fyn . . . Why do the farmers of Holsten, who live in equally fertile areas and who have just as much natural liveliness, have far higher morals than those who live on Fyn? On Fyn we find disgraceful examples of parishes with 20 or 30 percent illegitimate children; yes, even parishes where the majority of the women have had illegitimate children."[45]

The poor people of Fyn, where there was more sexual intercourse outside of marriage than in any other region of Denmark during the 19th century, had a relatively casual attitude toward women who became pregnant and gave birth to children out of wedlock. And it was about such forgotten children that Andersen, in his fairy tale "Anne Lisbeth," uses the phrase "never loved."

This is not what we normally think of when the conversation turns to Fyn and Odense, in connection with the author's fairy-tale childhood. Usually the discussion is more about all the glory that the governor and Prince Frits—who later became King Frederik VII—cast upon the city. And people talk about the distinguished middle class of civil servants, important military personnel in stately uniforms, and all of Fyn's nobility who in the winter came from their estates out in the country to the cozy capital of the island and settled into their part of town, which was known as "Little Copenhagen."[46] Then we also hear about the life in the clubs, about concerts and theater performances, balls and masquerades, which drew signet engravers, portrait painters, silhouette artists, and other vendors to the city. Now and then they also made room for local luminaries and budding geniuses such as the strange boy from Munkemøllestræde, who could rattle off entire plays by heart, dance ballets, and sing like a nightingale. Oh yes, Fyn was a fine place!

But what about the small craftsmen, day laborers, beggars, and all the orphaned children who roamed the streets of Odense around 1800? What about all the misery, the filth, and the swamp beneath the shiny surface? What about all of Odense's women, who for decades frequented "Skøgestræde" [Whore Lane], one of the little side streets of Vindegade? Along with other women of easy virtue or impoverished single mothers, they again and again committed fornication in the hopes of finding a husband. But they had to settle for the usual penalty of six *rigsdaler*, which was comparable to the price of a horse or a year's rent for lodgings, or else they were sentenced to a flogging at Fisketorvet and then thrown out of town.[47] No, we seldom hear about all these other minor characters when the conversation turns to Odense in the years 1805 to 1819, in connection with the life of Hans Christian Andersen. Nor do we read about them in the author's own memoirs about his birthplace.

Beyond the elegant white palace, Odense was an unsavory place, both in terms of the environment and the morals within the city gates. In an area of relatively few acres of land, 5,000 people and 500 large animals lived in close proximity. Children and adults were crammed into tiny lodgings, with two to four people sleeping in each bed. This meant that not only physical but also sexual hygiene was close to that of the livestock. In the Odense where Hans Christian Andersen was born in 1805, there was no proper water supply, sewage system, or any type of publicly organized garbage removal.[48] Pollution flowed from garbage heaps, along the gutters, and from open "privies." This widespread filth could also be read in the way people lived, in the way they talked, and in their sexual morals. The men, in particular, were quite blatant about their urges. If you leaf through the records and court archives for the city of Odense from that period, you'll find dozens of corporals and privates from the Fyn regiment's light dragoons, along with potters' and shoemakers' apprentices, glovemakers, hatmakers, and saddlemakers all named as fathers and sentenced to pay a fornication fine of twelve *rigsdaler*, which was double the woman's fine. This ignominy was suffered by the potter and grenadier Daniel

Rosenvinge in January 1800, when he was named the father of Hans Christian Andersen's half sister, Karen Marie. Along with Andersen's mother, Rosenvinge had to take the shameful path to Odense Courthouse and there was fined for "having bedded" Anne Marie Andersdatter. Daniel Rosenvinge, like so many other men of the day, was completely unreliable in terms of the opposite sex and any eventual obligations for providing support. At any rate, that same year he was also named as father of a little girl born to a Karen Ulrica Hansdatter. And in 1797, he had been caught up for the first time in the authorities' web when a Christine Sophie Nielsdatter named the potter as the father of her child.[49]

By looking at a specific date in the old church records for St. Hans Parish, it's possible to find a broader masculine selection of such representatives of Odense's love life around 1800, which was anything but romantic. On April 15, 1805, as part of the records for the day after Easter, a small group of godparents is mentioned. They had gathered for the baptism of the little son of Anne Marie Andersdatter and Hans Andersen, who was to be named Hans Christian. All four godparents present at the baptism— Dorch the hatmaker, Valtersdorff the master shoemaker, Jørgensen the journeyman carpenter, and Gomard the porter—had been named as the alleged father of an illegitimate child during 1805. And for several of these gentlemen, this was not the first or the last time. The vigorous Nicolas Gomard, who was the porter at Graabrødre Hospital, was born in France but ended up in Odense after a career as a Danish mercenary, language teacher, and barber. He became a very good friend of Anne Marie Andersdatter, and he was a kind and considerate godfather. Hans Christian came to know Gomard by visiting his house and the hospital where he worked, which was also where the boy's paternal grandmother helped out in the little garden.[50] When Andersen was baptized in the church, the Frenchman had to comfort his mother because the pastor exclaimed in annoyance: "That child howls like a cat!" Gomard whispered to the unhappy Anne Marie Andersdatter that the louder the lad screamed, the more beautifully he would sing as an adult. The virile Gomard managed to father eleven legitimate children before he was alleged—in 1808 at the age of sixty-seven— to have bedded a young, retarded servant girl of his acquaintance, who in April of that year gave birth to a son.[51]

As previously mentioned, the many single women and mothers who begged or sold their bodies to the highest bidder constituted a separate social class in Odense during that time. They could be found in the cramped, close lodgings in the area around Sortebrødre Torv, just a stone's throw from Hans Christian Andersen's presumed birthplace, whether it was on Hans Jensens Stræde, Skulkenborg, or Ramsherred. These women made up a mobile working class. During the summer, they would move around, grateful for any short-term employment as maids, nursemaids, and harvest workers. In the winter they had to settle for the most wretched of conditions within the gates of the larger towns, such as Odense. Under the best of circumstances they would support themselves by spinning, sewing, or doing laundry for other people. But most of these women, in order to survive, had to be willing to undertake work of a more demeaning type, such as prostitution.[52]

Hans Christian Andersen gives a heartrending portrait of the average woman belonging to this class, which included both young and old, in his fairy tale "She Was No Good" from 1852. Here we meet a single mother and washerwoman who is a tremendously realistic representative for this wandering female proletariat who possessed no human rights other than a daily half pint of liquor. Andersen's story about the impoverished, drunken mother who stands in the ice-cold water of the river, working at her washboard with her skirts tucked up is the closest we can come to a photographic portrait of his mother, Anne Marie Andersdatter. At the same time, the fairy tale is a peephole to the author's childhood. Quite a few things in the story verge on reality, including the various dates and times that are mentioned regarding the hastily arranged marriage that the washerwoman has to "settle for" when she can't have the judge's handsome brother, who once gave her a ring. We're told that the pastor reads the banns for the wedding of the washerwoman and Erik Hanskemager on Candlemas, February 2, which was the very same day on which Hans Christian Andersen's parents were married in 1805. In the story, it's the stouthearted and pragmatic washerwoman who proposes to the workman, for whom she has no real feelings. But if she can't have the one she loves, she can try to love the one she marries: "Do you want a girl who respects and esteems you, but doesn't love you, though that may come!" says the washerwoman. "It will come!" replies the glovemaker, whereupon they take each other's hands.

As the inquisitive and in many ways shrewd observer that Andersen was early on, he can hardly have been ignorant or starry-eyed about the various ways of love, as he often claims in his memoirs. From a young age he had experience with both the nice sides and the seamy sides of life. And on at least one occasion, the sexual complications between a man and a woman encroached on his childhood home and became the topic for a loud debate between his father and mother. We know this from a verbal account that the aging Andersen gave to his young friend Nicolai Bøgh in the 1870s. One day Andersen told him about a brazen offer once made to his mother, from which she had escaped. Both the infamous offer and the son's memory of it many years later reflect our conjecture that Andersen's mother was "an older, voluptuous woman with a distinctly erotic disposition."[53]

It so happened that for several years Anne Marie Andersdatter—like the mother in "She Was No Good"—washed laundry for the well-to-do middle class in Odense. One day when she brought the clothes back to the home of a distinguished family, she was accosted by the young man of the house. He had just returned home from Copenhagen with his distinguished university degree. The sight of the voluptuous washerwoman was so tempting that the young man reached for his coin purse and expressed his desire to lie with Anne Marie Andersdatter. All of this she later breathlessly told her husband at home on Munkemøllestræde. He immediately wanted to know what she said and did. "I ran away as fast as I could, the Lord Jesus knows that's what I did, I ran right home to you!" And a little later Andersen's mother added, "Even though it certainly was a lot of money!" Andersen's father, frothing with rage, clenched his fist and shouted, "And a rogue like that is going to be a pastor—a pastor!"[54]

Was He the Son of a King?

Among the papers that Hans Christian Andersen left behind in 1875 was a notebook containing a number of quotes, proverbs, and aphorisms, along with notes out of context. Several statements at the end of this little book have to do with Odense and his childhood. And placed right in the middle of what Andersen calls "a story that I heard as a child" and one of his father's aphorisms, we find two Hebrew adages: each in its own way touches on something painful that Andersen may have carried with him all his life. The first proverb says: "Your secret is your prisoner; if you let him escape, you become his." This little rule to live by has to do with the fact that there are some things that are best kept close, and if they come to the attention of others, there may be fateful consequences. The second Hebrew proverb is directed at family and what is said both within its fold and about it: "The world is not as your mother says, but as your neighbors say."[55]

Gossip in a small provincial town like Odense in 1800–1820 was, like prostitution and begging, such a widespread phenomenon that citizens were actually punished for starting serious rumors. In his first autobiography from 1832, Andersen himself speaks of women who had to "carry the stocks" and wander around on Klingenberg near St. Knud's Church, subjected to public scorn and ridicule. This punishment, which was reserved for women for offenses such as domestic disturbances and the spreading of gossip, was not abolished in Odense until 1811. It involved making the culprit who had spread gossip through the city wear a yoke (stocks) with a big iron loop above her head from which hung bells and a foxtail. Outfitted in this manner, women who were considered to have tongues that were too filthy or too lax had to parade up and down the square for an hour, to the great amusement of the rest of the town. The street urchins were especially entertained, along with all the other gossipmongers who not only were lucky enough to escape the same fate but who now had even more to talk about.[56] This muted buzzing of voices can also be heard in Andersen's novel *O.T.*, when a couple of washerwomen down at the river are talking over the wet clothes and washboards about an acquaintance who was sentenced to wander around with the stocks. "Better to have a little with honor than a great deal with dishonor," one of the washerwomen says to the other as she finishes delivering her news. And the other then replies, "Oh, dear Jesus, does Johanne Marie have to wear the stocks? That pretty girl who looked so proper and dressed so nicely? After the sweet scratching comes the bitter sting!"

Whispering can be heard everywhere in Hans Christian Andersen's works, especially about illegitimate family relationships. One example among many occurs in the sixth scene of *A Picture Book Without Pictures* from 1839, when the moon talks about a singer up on the mountain: "He emptied his mead horn with the wide silver ring and whispered a name, asking the wind not to give it away; but I [the moon] heard the name, I recognized it, the coronet of a count sparkles above it, and that's why he did not say it aloud."[57] We find similar examples of secrecy in Andersen's novels, plays, and fairy tales, in which a great deal of time and space is devoted to describing mysterious tattoos on a human body, or messages hidden inside secret dresser drawers, chests, bottles, and lockets, as well as erased or corrected entries in parish records. They are all secret signs that, under Andersen's direction, often have to do with the true facts about a person's real identity and origin, which he may be carrying around or suddenly acquire. It may be tattoos in the form of branded initials, such as we find on the shoulder of Otto Thostrup in the novel *O.T.*—a stigma concealing both his name and the specific location, "Odense Tugthus" [prison].

And in the old days this might contain the entire story of a person's destiny.[58] Andersen's works are teeming with hidden genealogical signs and latent wishes about discovering the truth about a person's life. As it says in *Only a Fiddler*: "Who should I love as my father?" And in the poem "The Boy and the Mother on the Heath" from 1831, this same desire is expressed quite clearly in the son's questions to his mother:

> Oh tell me please, dear Mother, what you have never said,
> When will I see my father? Has he been laid in the ground?
> Yet never before would you tell me who my father was,
> That is why I often have such strange dreams at night!
> Wasn't my father a king?—I often think about that!
> And why must we eternally walk this heath?[59]

A red thread runs through all of his works, right from the beginning, spun by women who carry the secret of who the father of their children really is. We see it in Andersen's earliest works, such as *The Forest Chapel* and "The Apparition at Palnatoke's Grave." And around 1830 we find it in *Christian II's Dwarf* and later in *O.T.*, *Only a Fiddler*, as well as in later fairy tales and plays, such as *He Was Not Born*. Many of Hans Christian Andersen's texts are small forums for guessing identity in which men—such as the main character in the comedy *Herr Rasmussen* in 1846—were once long ago thrown out of the nest without knowing whether they were ravens or crows. That's why they have to spend their lonely adult lives hunting for their biological origin in secret drawers, hidden chests, and old church records.

The question then arises: Was Hans Christian Andersen himself a "bastard child" who was given by an unknown mother to a young and impoverished shoemaker family in Odense? Was he even delivered by noble or royal hands along with a correspondingly large sack of money and promises of future support?

One of the many myths about Hans Christian Andersen has appeared in recent times and has to do with the idea that King Christian VIII and his noble mistress, Elise Ahlefeldt-Laurvig, might have been the author's real parents.[60] Yet this intriguing idea has long since been refuted by showing that Christian VIII wasn't even in Denmark at the time when Andersen was conceived. In addition, on the evening of April 2, 1805—the day on which Andersen came into the world—the young countess appeared with her father at a concert in Odense.[61] The notion that Hans Christian Andersen may have been of royal birth rests on the tremendous number of references to royal inheritance that are scattered throughout the author's writings. For instance, Andersen's friend Henriette Wulff writes to him in 1848: "You've discovered that you are the prince-child we talked about recently."[62] Might this indicate that the author had royal blood in his veins?

Taken out of context from the letter and the rest of the correspondence, it seems to be a dramatic disclosure. Yet upon closer examination, as with other similar instances, it seems that this discussion of a king's son was meant in a metaphorical sense. The idea that Andersen and others thought of him as a prince-child has to be understood, first and foremost, with regard to the Romantic view of the genius, which the Danish author and other like-minded individuals believed in and cultivated. It was the idea that an artist was particularly chosen, and this perception won enormous support throughout Europe in the 1840s, when Andersen was received and treated like a king. And that was also how he viewed himself—in the world of art, that is. It's in this metaphorical sense that we should read Henriette Wulff's words, as well as a similar statement from Andersen's good friend in southern Germany, the painter Wilhelm von Kaulbach. During one of Andersen's many visits to Munich, von Kaulbach once gave a toast to the author and all the kings of the fairy tale who, according to the painter, were "the true kings, by the grace of God"![63]

Andersen's notion, along with the view of some of his contemporaries, that he was a king's child was more likely a Romantic metaphor and a symbolic picture of his artistic status, spiritual ancestry, and magnanimity. And he had always thought of himself as specially chosen. This is apparent in the first chapter of *The Fairy Tale of My Life*. Here the author says that, in order to impress a pretty little Jewish girl at Fedder Carsten's School in Odense, he drew a beautiful castle and offered the girl a job there. At the same time, he assured her that he himself was a changeling and of very high birth. And God's angels regularly came down to talk to him. The girl regarded him with growing astonishment and finally turned to the other children and said, "He's just as mad as his grandfather."[64]

But Hans Christian Andersen was not mad, nor was he the son of a king. He was the son of a proletarian. There should be no doubt about that. What remains is some uncertainty about the true identity of his impoverished father. Was it Hans Andersen? Or was he possibly just one of several men in 1805 who might have been alleged to be the real father, even though he agreed to marry the pregnant Anne Marie Andersdatter? We can't know for sure. *Mater semper certa, pater semper incertus est*, as an old Latin saying goes. "The mother is always certain, the father always uncertain."

The mystery about Hans Christian Andersen's birth and paternity was already being discussed during his lifetime. In 1867, when he was celebrated as an honorary citizen in his hometown, the newspaper *Fyens Avis* gave the event a great deal of coverage. For four days in a row the front page was devoted almost exclusively to the famous townsman. The first article—on December 4, 1867—dealt with the author's unknown birthplace, and the paper spent a great deal of time wondering why the author, at his baptism in 1805, was not given a last name. Later the author received a name that did not unequivocally tie the bond of blood between him and Hans Andersen, but instead bound him closer to his mother. By all rights, according to *Fyens Avis*, the author—as son of a man named Hans—ought to have the surname Hansen, just as the shoemaker in his day—as the son of Anders—was given the surname Andersen. It's clear that the newspaper had set its sights on a juicy story about the city's famous son right before the big celebration, when Andersen was to be awarded a certificate, bound in red velvet, decorated with gold ornamentation, and furnished with the great seal of the city of Odense in a gilded silver capsule. The implied question was: Was it possible that Hans Christian Andersen was named Andersen and not Hansen because Hans Andersen was not the boy's real father? Was the boy given his mother's surname because, as the author described in such cruel detail in the fairy tale "Anne Lisbeth," a male child after birth might be sent out to the ditchdigger's wife with a sack of coins? "He was the ditchdigger's boy; in the church book it said he was Anne Lisbeth's." Could the same be said of Hans Christian Andersen? "He was the shoemaker's boy; in the church book he was Anne Marie's"? At any rate, *Fyens Avis* wondered about this, but so much research was done, seeking out sextons and old church records, that in the end a plausible explanation could be presented for the author's surname. And with that, peace descended over the city's big celebration in honor of the fairy-tale author:

"The sexton at St. Hans Church has kindly informed us of the following word-for-word entry from the St. Hans Church book: 1805, Tuesday morning, at one o'clock on April 2, Hans Andersen, shoemaker's journeyman, and wife Anne Marie Andersdatter gave birth to a son, the same day baptized at home by the acting curate Herr Ramsing and called HANS CHRISTIAN . . . It can be seen from this baptismal certificate that the author was not baptized Andersen. Before 1814 it was not customary to give the child a surname upon baptism. This was later given to or chosen by the child, usually the father's first name; the author would have thus been called Hans Christian Hansen. It was usually the school that gave the child a surname, and it was often pure chance that determined whether the child in question would use his father's first name or surname."[65]

And so we are led to understand that the author was given his father's surname. If there are still any doubts as to whether the shoemaker was Hans Christian Andersen's biological father, it's important to remember that various written documents exist, and there can be no doubt about their authenticity. Of course the old church records were not infallible, but it says in black and white in the church book for St. Hans parish from 1805 and in various written records and legal archives in the following years that Hans Andersen has been entered as the legal father of the fairy-tale author.

Those scholars and others knowledgeable about Andersen's work who refuse to believe that the shoemaker might not have been the author's biological father usually point to one other document. It's a little crumpled note that was written by the eleven-year-old Hans Christian immediately following his father's death in April 1816. Hans Andersen left behind very little except for an account book from his military service and a pile of old clothes, so it was crucial for his son to hold on to something of his intangible inheritance. With the image of his gentle, well-read shoemaker father in mind, Hans Christian—who, unlike his mother, had learned to read and write—created in the days after his father's death the briefest imaginable biography. It filled one small piece of paper that could be folded into a tiny booklet, badly spelled and with the title "The Life and Death of H. Andersen's Life." Inside the son had meticulously and with almost exaggerated precision entered all the dates of his father's brief life. The calculation of his father's age is wrong, but the dates are all correct:

> "H:Andersen free shoemaker was born on December 14, 1782 and died on Friday at 8 o'clock in the evening on April 26, 1816 and was buried on April 30 at an age of 33 years and 3 months and 3 weeks and 5 days."[66]

That's the full extent of the biography, and it would be impossible to find any stronger proof of a son's love for his father, according to those who protect and defend the idea of a biological relationship between the author and the poor shoemaker. They may well be right, but it should also be kept in mind that this little memory on paper, aside from establishing several important dates and reflecting a boy's sudden longing for his father, might also have been a sort of guarantee and proof. If the rest of the world should have doubts and the air was suddenly thick with gossip, this paper could be pulled out of the poor boy's pocket and, side by side with the church book, it could document Hans Christian's "legitimacy." It could vouch for the fact that he had certainly had a real, living father and was not—like his half sister Karen Marie—a bastard child. It was important to be able to prove this in Denmark during the absolute monarchy. And it was a nice thing to remember if one day a person should start to have his own doubts.

Free Shoemaker and Free Thinker

The sign that hung outside the little yellow house on Munkemølle-stræde said: "Andersen—Free Shoemaker." The boy knew quite well, as he later recounted, that this was not a very fine title; in fact, it was downright "shoddy."[67] It could just as well have said: "Andersen—Free Thinker" on the sign.

Hans Andersen, who was born in 1782 in Rørup parish outside of Odense, was an intelligent person whose situation in life never measured up to his numerous talents. This was a fact that Hans Christian pointed out many times in his memoirs, especially late in his life when he acknowledged his family origins and thanked his father for all he had meant to him. On the same occasion, the author called himself "a shoemaker child,"[68] and remarked that the disappointments his father had suffered in his short life would have certainly turned to pride if he had lived until 1867 and could have witnessed the appointment of his son as an honorary citizen:

> "Oh, if only he had seen the great celebration in my honor in Odense, he would have died of joy! Then he would have been able to accept his own life, if he saw how things had developed for me. He would have understood what was inherently spiritual about it; my mother, on the other hand, never would have grasped it."[69]

Hans Andersen, who lived only to the age of thirty-three, was a short, fair-haired man with a round face. Barely five feet five inches tall, he would have been practically dwarfed by his grown-up son with the long face, pro-nounced features, and dark hair. Even as a child, his son shot up quickly, and with time he reached a height of six feet, which was relatively rare for a man in those days. Hans Andersen was often taciturn, preferring to sit quietly with his own thoughts. He was a well-read and knowledgeable person, and every day around noon he would interrupt his tedious cobbling work for an hour or two and read every word of the local newspaper. He also distinguished himself from the other tradesmen in the streets of Odense by declaring his opposition to liquor and gambling. In 1811, when the whole city was talking about the comet that was a portent of the coming of Judgment Day, Hans Andersen promptly saw a parallel to a couple of other doomsday omens and said: "The two worst comets that I know are liquor and the lottery!"

In his days as a journeyman shoemaker around 1800, Hans Andersen himself had not exhibited much self-restraint. An entry in the Odense police reports from the year 1802 indicates that the author's father was a lively young man who wasn't averse to enjoying a merry time with the other thirsty, skirt-chasing journeymen shoemakers. One October evening in 1802, trouble started and a fight was imminent when seven spirited journeymen shoemakers, including the twenty-year-old Hans Andersen, assaulted the brothers Jørgen and Rasmus Buch in Peder Huus' Inn down by the mill bridge on the Odense River. On that occasion Hans Andersen didn't run off, but he was not in the front ranks when the blows began falling. This was stated in the police investigation, and it meant that he escaped any further charges.[70]

In spite of poverty and many shattered illusions, Hans Christian Andersen's father remained a wise and proud man all his life. One of the son's favorite stories from his childhood, which was included in all his autobiographies, although its authenticity has been questioned, had to do with an incident in 1810 when Hans Andersen applied for a job as shoemaker at Trankær Castle. A skilled shoemaker was needed who would agree to move to Langeland and take up residence in a workshop and house designated for him close to the castle, with its own garden and a pasture for a cow. It sounded absolutely fabulous, and Hans Andersen did his utmost with the application, which consisted of stitching a pair of exquisite dancing shoes for the lady of the castle. The shoemaker from Munkemøllestræde had silk for the upper part of the shoes delivered directly from Trankær, but he had to provide his own leather for the soles of this most important test of his life. There was great excitement and solemnity in the little home when Hans Andersen finally finished the shoes, wrapped them in a handkerchief, and set off to deliver his application. The lady, who was a tall and critical person, received them herself, but, alas, she didn't even try on the dancing shoes. She gave them a fleeting glance, wrinkled her elegant nose, and complained that they were a waste of expensive silk. Indignation and pride welled up inside Hans Andersen, as his son recounts in *The Fairy Tale of My Life*, and with a trembling voice he replied: "If you've wasted your silk, then I can stand to waste my leather!" And he resolutely pulled out his sheath knife, separated the soles from the silk, and went home with his part of the dancing shoes.

Whenever Hans Andersen sat in the dim light and pounded on the last to make the damp leather soft, the sound and the rhythm would cause him to get lost in his own thoughts. Then he looked like a magician to his son. This was particularly true because, as darkness fell, Hans Andersen would keep moving around a big glass ball containing water that stood near the window and candle; it was used to magnify and spread the scanty light far-ther into the cramped, dim room. There is every reason to believe that it was his wise and meditative shoemaker father that Hans Christian Andersen was thinking of, perhaps even directly quoting him, when he wrote a series of aphorisms for a Copenhagen magazine in 1830 under the headline "Thoughts about a few worn-out old shoes." At any rate, the words came straight from the philosophical heart of his father: "It's better to give to the shoemaker than to the apothecary" and "Even if the shoes are crooked, the heart is still straight."[71]

It must be presumed that the same strong memories of a silent, wise, but also restless shoemaker father formed the basis for Andersen's great dra-matic effort of 1847, *Ahasuerus*. In the beginning of the play, we hear of the destitute shoemaker Ahasuerus in Jerusalem. And yet he possesses a great wealth because he is a divinely gifted storyteller. As a child Ahasuerus had, as it says, "imbibed these old chronicles that give the courage to endure." And so, as an adult, he has a very special gift for "soothing everyone with his words." Like Hans Andersen the shoemaker, Ahasuerus also dreams of a different and greater existence based on distant horizons:

> There are times when I think myself suited
> To something better than cobbling shoes,
> Each time the Levites' song reaches my ear,
> I have a desire to sit among them
> And raise my strong voice with theirs!
> Each time I hear the scholars speak
> It pains me that I did not have their learning.[72]

From Andersen's descriptions of his childhood, we have the distinct impression that his father was the parent who had the most desire and time to play with and talk to his son. Hans Andersen had something of a quiet but remarkable pedagogue hidden deep inside, yet the communication between father and son, and the time they spent together, was often of the wordless, reflective sort. On their walks in the woods on Sundays, the shoemaker would let his son entertain himself and play with the materials out in nature—sticks, leaves, rushes, chestnuts, grass, and stones. In the meantime, the father would sit quite still, brooding and watching his son. It was actually only when the two of them sat together with a book that Hans Christian would see his father smile. It was in books that all of the shoemaker's dreams would be realized, while in the tedium and toil of his life as a tradesman, he felt oppressed and unhappy.

Hans Christian Andersen writes that his father had "a superb mind." But instead of being allowed to develop his bookish talents, Hans Andersen, like his father, Anders "Traes" Hansen, was apprenticed to the shoemaker profession at the age of twelve. At the end of the 18th century, shoemaking was by far the largest trade in Odense, numbering nearly eighty shoemakers. That was double the number of grocers and tailors and more than three times the number of carpenters. Only the glovemakers, whose products had made Odense quite famous all over Europe, composed almost as large a group. And then there were, of course, the distillers, whose numbers couldn't be counted in Odense, that den of iniquity where nearly every other man distilled his own liquor.[73] Hans Andersen never got over his bitterness at being forced into a life as a simple "boot pegger," which was something that anybody could learn. Nor did he ever forgive his father for refusing to allow him to attend grammar school. Hans Christian Andersen recounts in his memoirs that one day they were visited by a pupil from the city's grammar school, which was located at the end of Munkemøllestræde. The pupil wanted to order a new pair of boots from Andersen, and while he waited, he showed his books to the shoemaker and his odd son. He also told them about everything he had learned up at the school. Afterwards Hans Andersen looked at his son for a long time, then kissed him and said, "That's the path I should have taken too!"

This great disappointment of his life was no doubt the reason why Hans Andersen, right from the beginning, was as involved in his son's upbringing as he seemed to be. During the first six or seven years of his son's life, the father clearly took pride in nurturing and developing a spiritual and intellectual relationship between the two of them—something in which Hans Christian's less gifted mother could not take part. It was an intense relationship that lasted through some of the most important and character-building years of the young boy's life. But it came to an end in 1812 when his father joined the military under the banners of Napoleon and didn't return home until 1814, a disillusioned and burned-out man. Yet before that happened, he had managed to make an impression on his son that would last a lifetime, if we're to believe the fervent third verse of the poem "Odense," which Andersen wrote five months before his own death in 1875:

> Here I ran about in clogs
> And went to the charity school,
> But the whole world lay before me
> As if I wore the clothing of a count!
> No, I was not a poor lad,
> Nor was my father,
> He read fairy tales to me
> And I myself became a storyteller.[74]

Hans Andersen was a musical person who was also good with his hands. In addition to heading up the third company of the Odense Civic Guards, for which he played drums and flute during the years 1808-12, the shoemaker could also write poems and make paper-cuts. He was especially a master of the little affectionate notes that were a forerunner of the valentines we know today. Around 1800, these affectionate notes were extremely popular in Denmark among the nobility, the townspeople, and farmers. They could take the form of a friendly joke, or a suitor's or sweetheart's letter containing a little gift. The letters were written in merry, rhymed verse, inserted in imaginative cutouts and colored with complicated patterns or calligraphic inscriptions on shiny paper.[75] As a boy, Hans Andersen had loved to whittle, plane, hammer, and chop wood, and so he possessed both the carpentry and artistic skills that were necessary to make toys for his son, who took special care of his little theater and diorama in which the images could be changed by pulling on a string. Various nodding dolls were also created for little Hans Christian, as well as a so-called stamping mill, which could make the miller dance endlessly once it was set in motion.

A Rousseau-inspired pedagogy can be seen in all of these sensitive and imaginative objects given to his son—a type of pedagogy that Hans Andersen made use of and on many occasions formulated so clearly for Hans Christian that as an adult he still remembered what was said almost word for word. In many places in his memoirs, Andersen presents little samples of his father's pedagogical creeds. For instance, in his German autobiography from 1847, Andersen writes: "My father let me have my way with everything; I possessed all his love! He lived for me." And in his autobiography from 1832, the twenty-seven-year-old Andersen refers to one of his father's frequently repeated comments: "I was never to be forced to do anything; even if I wanted to be the most unreasonable thing of all, I was to have my way."[76]

Hans Andersen had a relatively progressive, modern view of the human being. This view had to do with concepts such as "nature" and "will," inspired as he was by the French Revolution and by the high ideals of the Enlightenment regarding an individual's freedom and the development of the whole person. These ideas had come to Denmark at the end of the 18th century, but they had not yet been generally accepted by the broad, lower class of the population. In this sense, the shoemaker had something in common with the two other father figures in Hans Christian Andersen's life: Jonas Collin and H. C. Ørsted. Like them, the poor shoemaker on Munkemøllestræde was also convinced that children would benefit from fresh air, loose clothing, and good hygiene—as well as being allowed to develop and follow their own inner nature. This pedagogy, with its deep respect for the unique character of the individual, seeps into various literary father figures and educators many places in Andersen's writing. For instance, in the play *Herr Rasmussen*, we suddenly hear a squire exclaim, "My blessed father, the Lord Chamberlain, always said, 'Let human nature fend for itself!'" Hans Andersen couldn't have said it better.

The Odd Father and Son

A particularly important book that held a central and elevated place in Andersen's childhood home was a novel with the title *Der Sonderling* [*Odd Enough, To Be Sure!*], written by the German author August H. J. Lafontaine in 1799. The book was translated into English and Danish in 1802. It begins with the words of the translator: "Read, judge, and utilize!" And shoemaker Andersen must have taken this challenge to heart during the years 1805–16. Quite a few of the modern principles regarding child-rearing, which he managed to put into practice with his own odd son, seem to have stemmed from Lafontaine's novel. The book is about the impulsive and enormously rich Ludvig Burchard and his carefully planned and executed upbringing of his son, Ludvig Johan. In the novel, this sensitive schooling is carried out in accordance with a reasonably exact "Educational Plan," which is based on what the father has learned on his countless travels around the world—for instance, "That human beings are human beings everywhere"—and on the ideas of Jean-Jacques Rousseau regarding a child's free will. In the universe of the novel, this means that the infant Ludvig Johan does not wear diapers, nor is he dressed in tight-fitting clothes. And the first five years of the boy's life are devoted to play-ing—playing and more playing, dressed in loose-flowing attire and going barefoot out in nature, where the lad reaps his own experiences according to the slogan: "No apron strings! First crawl, then walk!" This is a type of pedagogical practice that circumvented the mother and thus made a child's upbringing an endeavor between father and son. With his little newborn son in his arms, Burchard explains this with the words: "I will teach him to enjoy happiness!"

It can be imagined that this was exactly what Andersen's father, at an early stage of his son's life, had conceived as his ideal for instilling in Hans Christian. It's fair to ask then whether Hans Andersen, with this type of upbringing that was actually very goal-oriented, contributed to isolating the boy and strengthening the feelings of loneliness in an inherently intro-verted child. Hans Andersen's child-rearing was clearly not meant to make his odd son fit in with society or the times. By all accounts, no limitations were put on his personal development or imagination, nor was any attempt made to quell his peculiar character or sensitivity, which early on in his childhood had already aroused attention in Odense. Hans Christian was allowed to keep playing with his flowers and leaves, his theater sets, pieces of fabric, and his costumed puppets, just as his imagination was allowed free rein in his recitations, dancing, playing, drawing, writing, sewing, and cut-ting shapes from paper.

Playing with other children was another story entirely in Andersen's childhood. As long as there wasn't a whole group of them, he would some-times play with girls, but he seldom played with boys. This fact is often repeated in the author's childhood memoirs. And in one of his first lyrical texts, from his debut book in 1822, the seventeen-year-old Andersen describes himself as "a boy of nine, playing / Not with the other hale and lively boys, / But weaving lovely flower wreaths."[77] Twenty-five years later, this is repeated in *Das Märchen meines Lebens ohne Dichtung*, in which it says: "I almost never spent time with the other boys; even in school I didn't take part in their games, but stayed inside." And in *The Fairy Tale of My Life* in 1855, it says of the intolerable school life when he was forced to confront a wall of boys' faces: "I was afraid of the poor boys who had ridiculed me." His fear is understandable, since it was largely due to the fact that he was so different. But in a certain sense it's paradoxical because at the same time, all his life, Andersen loved to stand alone on the stage and perform for others. The theater was in his blood, and it gave him the courage both to act and to observe. We find a striking example of this in the anecdote about the tall, lanky Hans Christian who ran through the streets of Odense with a huge calf's head that he had picked up from a butcher shop. "Do you want to see something strange for two *skillings*?" he asked everyone he met, lifting up a corner of the scarf that covered most of the animal's head. If the answer was yes, the person was granted a look at the calf's muzzle, but only after paying the two *skillings!*[78]

Very early in his life, Hans Christian Andersen was aware of his odd disposition. This is evident in his memoirs and in his previously discussed autobiographical sketch in his debut book, *Youthful Attempts*, in which Andersen introduces himself as a boy on the banks of the Odense River. There he sits, all alone, weaving an author's crown and launching little reed boats out into the waters of life, while the other boys are climbing trees, fighting, and playing wild games nearby. And in his autobiography from 1832, Andersen explains and shows how the little Hans Christian time after time had to retreat from large groups of boys who were playing. He did this not only out of fear but also because he felt completely alienated by the violent masculine behavior in the boys' ritual games. The young Andersen repeats this episode in a lengthy letter to Jonas Collin in 1825, in which he wants to tell his benefactor something more about himself on the occasion of his twentieth birthday. Here he places particular emphasis on describing his childhood isolation, based on both gender and class: "I never spent any time with the other boys; I was always alone."[79] And in his 1832 autobiography Andersen once again points out the quiet, isolated boy who, all things considered, was always happy in his solitude and never missed playing with the other boys:

> "I only found it amusing to spend time with little girls; I still remember one beautiful little one, eight years old, who kissed me and said that she wanted to be my sweetheart. That pleased me, and I always let her kiss me, although I never kissed her back, nor did I ever let anyone else kiss me except her."[80]

This oddness, which the shoemaker encouraged and shielded via his child-rearing methods, was something that young Andersen noticed in earnest at puberty, after his father was dead and he was left even more vulnerable and alone in the world. We can only guess how far things actually went with the various humiliations that the adult Andersen alludes to in his memoirs. But they did occur in the author's childhood and youth. We know this from his autobiographies, which in small but vivid glimpses show us a boy who had to endure being tormented and ridiculed both because of his special talents and his peculiar physical appearance. This happened, for instance, at the textile mill in Odense where he was supposed to work with other children and youths. The boy quickly showed himself to be "tremendously soft." As the adult Hans Christian Andersen writes, he was not at all "suited to be among those wild boys and girls."[81] Things went wrong after only a couple of days at the textile mill, where Hans Christian was enticed to sing for the crude workers. He did so with joy, and he also recited from Holberg. Then the workers sang their own vulgar songs, which made Andersen blush and whimper:

> "First they laughed at me, said I was a girl, and began a very vulgar amusement, *hoc exquirendo*, so that in tears I begged my mother to let me stay away from there."[82]

In all three of his autobiographies, the adult Andersen describes in terse sentences what this "vulgar" entertainment consisted of, and how he, as a boy at a most sensitive and shy age, on several occasions was undressed and subjected to various types of examination of his genitals.

In his memoirs, Hans Christian Andersen says that his mother was also fond of Lafontaine's *Der Sonderling* and much preferred to hear that novel read aloud rather than stories by Ludvig Holberg. She always had a difficult time seeing the comedic side of Holberg's work. "How can you laugh so much at that?" Anne Marie Andersdatter one day asked her husband, who replied: "But can't you hear how funny it is? Just listen to what Henrik is saying!" And then he read the whole thing aloud again.

His son, on the other hand, devoured everything the shoemaker read to him. A little poem from 1822 with the pretentious title "My Life," begins with the words: "Tears trickle when I recall, / you, my childhood, with all your joy." In this way the seventeen-year-old Andersen was trying to describe some of the strongest literary experiences of his childhood. They included Aladdin, Shakespeare's vile witches and magicians, and the world of Holberg, in which human nature and whims were "examined" and an individual had to learn to "investigate" and "find out" on his own. On one of the first days of Hans Christian's life, his father sat next to his wife's bed and read aloud from Holberg while the infant screamed louder and louder. Then Hans Andersen supposedly joked: "Do you want to sleep, or do you want to listen calmly!"

In his first autobiography Andersen mentions that his father "was not without education and had a splendid mind; in my mother, everything was of the heart." In this precise appraisal of his parents' very different temperaments, his father appears as the clear-sighted and rational person, in contrast to the religious and superstitious mother. She undoubtedly felt a close connection to Our Lord, but at the same time she took great heed of oracles, witches, and quack doctors. It was regarding life's religious questions that Andersen's father and mother had their greatest quarrels. All their disagreements, along with the differences in their character, attitudes, and intellect, combined to form two diametrically opposed points of view. One time the shoemaker decided that they should read aloud from the Bible; a short time later he closed the book and began telling his wife and son that he didn't have the same faith as the mother, the son, and all the other devout spirits in Odense. "Christ was a human being like us, but an extraordinary, glorious human being!" announced Hans Andersen with an emphasis and intonation that made a deep impression on his son. His father also called himself a "free thinker," and said that the Bible couldn't possibly have been written by God. And he said that there was no hell, other than what existed in an individual's imagination. When the pious Anne Marie Andersdatter heard this ungodly talk, which the adult Hans Christian Andersen judges in his memoirs to be "sensible," she immediately made the sign of the cross and then took the boy out to the peat shed behind the house. There she threw her apron over his head and whispered: "That was the Devil speaking in our house, Hans Christian, it wasn't your father, and you must for-get what he said, because he didn't mean it!"[83] But his father stood firmly and stubbornly by his views. And he challenged his wife's authority even further one day when, in his son's presence, he repeated that there was no devil other than the one that we all have in our own heart.

God or Napoleon

The closest Hans Andersen came to a personal oracle was Napoleon. It was as if all the shoemaker's dreams of a different and better world, along with a new and more heroic life, came together in the figure of the French commander as a charismatic warrior and conqueror. The gifted, courageous

Napoleon and his proud, vigorous attempts at defending all the social results of the revolution seemed to the shoemaker to be "the most beautiful example worth imitating." In Odense in 1808, the sight of the Frenchman's dark-complexioned army, which had been sent to Denmark to help the Danes attack Sweden, released all of Hans Andersen's yearnings for distant horizons and greater achievements. He was now going to put an end to this eternal repairing of everyone's worn-out, foul-smelling shoes. And just as Christian's tailor-father in *Only a Fiddler* is enticed by a sergeant with stories about the romantic soldier life, in which the troops march off singing and always fall with honor, Hans Andersen now heard an inner voice whispering. It told him that he, with his bright, intelligent mind, was created for something other than working with an awl and pegging hammer. These are the enticing tones that the son allows to echo through the first chapter of his novel about the fiddler: "You live by traveling and marching. The field is the proper life for you. Forward, march! A badge of honor on your chest! Before the year is out, you'll be a commanding sergeant."

These dreams were not something that Anne Marie Andersdatter shared with her husband, by any means. She had no fondness for "the military," as her son writes in his first autobiography. When his father read aloud from the daily paper the articles dealing with the war news from Germany and he came to the high point of the day, it always had to do with Napoleon's latest daring maneuvers and victories in the field. And then Anne Marie Andersdatter would say: "*There* he sits, reading all this time about that *Napoleon*; I can never understand what enjoyment there is in reading about someone who kills and destroys everybody!"[84]

The shoemaker's restlessness and dissatisfaction increased as the war progressed, as Napoleon advanced, and—in particular—as the lack of work and money grew worse in Denmark. Odense, like the rest of the country in 1810-14, was plagued by rising inflation, a drop in real wages, and sharp increases in the price of food, which caused the standard of living to sink even lower among the poor. Those were especially hard times for Odense's shoemakers. In 1809 a pair of boots cost eight to ten *rigsdaler*, but in 1814 the price rose to between 20 and 30 *rigsdaler*, due to the cost of leather. No one bought new shoes anymore, and the shoemakers had to work hard to make even a meager weekly income. At the same time, there were two or three shoemakers on every street in Odense.[85] This prompted Hans Andersen to make a decision. It was time to "lace up his knapsack" and seek his fortune in new surroundings and with new work, for instance in the military. There he would have not only guaranteed food and a steady salary, but also the opportunity for adventure and even more money if he volunteered to accept a bribe to take the place of a soldier who had been called up for service. After toying with the idea for several years, Hans Andersen joined up in the summer of 1812. And it should be noted that he took the place of another man who had been officially called up. Because Hans Andersen lived with his family within the city gates, he was exempt from normal military service. Instead, he assumed the military service of a rich farmer's son from out in the country who didn't want to participate and who had long ago seen through a dreamer such as Napoleon. And so it was a well-to-do farmer's son from Viby who, in the summer of 1813, paid Hans Andersen an unknown sum of *rigsdaler* to take his position when the King's 5th Regiment, 3rd Battalion, after having been garrisoned on Fyn for nine months, finally headed south.[86]

The little family back home on Munkemøllestræde, now reduced to mother and son, badly needed every *skilling* during the period 1813-14, when Denmark went bankrupt and the crisis was felt everywhere in society. Apparently the bonus that Hans Andersen received for taking the place of the wealthy farmer's son in the regiment was not enough to fill the gap in the family's hopeless financial situation. At any rate, in 1813 we find "the wife and son of free shoemaker and musketeer Hans Andersen" on the list of more than fifty-five individuals and families in Odense who received assistance from the public sector in the form of rye bread, pork, grain, butter, and peat.

The shoemaker himself was happier than he had ever been when he departed for Holsten in September 1813. His son remembers that on that day, when the drums finally sounded and the company left Odense, he sang and talked more merrily than he ever had. The drums and pipes of the Civic Guards had been exchanged for the effective musket, which along with the fine red uniform was a sign that Hans Andersen was now part of his native land's right arm, wielding the sword. The constant longings and disappointments of his life were now replaced with pride and hope. The plan was for the Danish corps of 10,000 men, led by Prince Frederik of Hessen, to join forces in Holsten with the French army under the command of Marshal Davoud. The enemy was the northern German army, which, along with the Swedish auxiliary troops of Bernadotte, was threatening Denmark's southern border. Andersen more than implies in *Only a Fiddler* that his father, who was otherwise so intelligent, displayed an infatuation with Napoleon's war machine that was based on a deeply naïve patriotism. In the novel, Andersen says of little Denmark's efforts in connection with the great Frenchman: "A loyal, enthusiastic heart, but the strength did not match the will."

The shoemaker's military career was tragically brief and not very heroic. He too met his Waterloo, although without ever fighting a battle under the fluttering eagles of the French banners. Hans Andersen didn't manage to fire a single shot in the war. By the time the regiment finally reached Holsten in 1814, where according to the plan they were supposed to meet up with the French troops, the war was actually over. After a few skirmishes and an endless number of long marches, Hans Andersen returned home to Munkemøllestræde in 1814, both physically and psychologically marked by his fruitless, passive days in the field. Once again, he had failed to achieve anything great—other than managing not to die from an enemy bullet. His account book for his military service ends on March 8, 1815, with the modest payment of four *rigsdaler* and forty-six *skillings*.

Hans Andersen quickly took up his old position next to the window where his hammer, pliers, awl, and cobbler's thread were waiting for him like a collective reminder that a shoemaker ought to stay by his last. For a brief time he seemed to flourish and regain some of his old spiritual strength. He told his son about all his soldier experiences, about the constant singing and the choir of stomping boots on the way to the front: "*Reise zu Fuss, reise zu Fuss! / Da verstehst du Menschengruss! / Reise zu Fuss!*" All this talk about heading out along the highway of life strongly appealed to the lively imagination of his ten-year-old son. In his autobiography from 1847, the adult Andersen recounts how he, for example, picked up a few of his father's broken German phrases and used them. When his father heard this, he said to his son, half in jest but half seriously: "It would do you good to travel! God knows if you would get very far, but you must! Keep that in mind, Hans Christian!"[87]

His father was not able to recover, either physically or psychologically, from the failed campaign. "His health was ruined," was the touchingly brief and precise assessment that his son included in his memoirs. One harsh winter day in 1815, when all the windows facing Munkemøllestræde were frosted over, the exhausted father propped himself up on his elbows and said: "Look, there you can see the Ice Maiden on the windowpane; she's coming now to get me." And illness tightened its grip on Hans Andersen, who grew thinner and thinner; he was plagued by fever and often delirious. He frequently hallucinated about Napoleon's campaign, and one day he threw out his arms toward his horrified son, mistaking him for a French soldier: "What, boy, don't you see my emperor! Make way for him! Cap off, you whelp, when the Emperor is riding past!"[88]

During the last weeks of his life, Hans Andersen lay in bed—pale and sallow, nothing but skin and bones—looking like the father of Johannes in the fairy tale "The Traveling Companion." As if the sight of his deathly ill father wasn't enough, Andersen was sent off by his mother on an April evening in 1816 to seek help from Mette Mogensdatter, the wise woman of Ejby. It never occurred to Anne Marie Andersdatter to summon a member of the modern medical profession. This was partly due to the fact that it cost money that they didn't have, partly because she preferred the magical form of medical treatment. In *The Fairy Tale of My Life*, Andersen described his encounter with the wise woman, who measured the boy's arms with a piece of woolen yarn, drew strange signs above his head, and then placed a green bough on his chest, claiming that it came from the same kind of tree that was once used to crucify Christ. Finally she said: "Go home along the river! If your father is going to die this time, you'll meet his ghost!" The boy shook like a leaf the whole way home, but he didn't meet his father's ghost. The shoemaker died two days later, after the boy had pestered his mother in vain to summon a doctor instead of any more wise women. Anne Marie Andersdatter's personal grief was undoubtedly possible to bear in 1816. But for her son, the loss was enormous, even though his father had been more or less absent from daily life for the past couple of years. As Andersen, many years later, wrote in his novel *To Be or Not to Be* about a young boy's experience of a parent's death, it was a matter of his first great loss in this world: "The first breach in the beautiful picture book of life . . . half of the world was gone."[89]

At the funeral in St. Knud's Church on April 30, 1816, Hans Christian —like Johannes in "The Traveling Companion"— walked right behind the coffin, wearing long black mourning crepe on his hat. Maybe it was at the very moment that the pastor cast earth onto his father's coffin that Hans Christian made up his mind to journey out into the world as soon as he was confirmed. He had already taken possession of his father's account book from his military service. It contained the last remnants of a dear but weak father who had taught his son so much. This book was now—day by day, month after month, in 1816, 1817, and 1818—filled with the son's wild ideas. It was here that he secretly recorded all the possible titles of the great plays that he would one day write, perform, and which would bring him fame in the future. As far as dreaming and longing for a bigger world, his kinship was unmistakable. Both Hans Andersen and his son wore shoes that wouldn't stop moving.

Anne Marie Andersdatter

In his descriptions of his family, Andersen often makes it sound as if they did not live under straitened circumstances in his home. His daily life, as well as his general environment, seems stable, secure, and quite idyllic during the first eight years of the author's life. We have to look beyond his autobiographies and turn instead to Andersen's other writings to find phrases such as: "My cradle stood beside the bare wall of penury."[90] In his diaries we also encounter descriptions of poverty that seem to spring from an instinctive recognition and a type of déjà vu. In the summer of 1840, Andersen was at Nysø to be honored by the king for his play *The Mulatto*, and to spend the summer days with Baron and Baroness Stampe, Thorvaldsen, and other distinguished guests. One day he went to the market at Præstø and was disgusted by the sights and smells of everything from cheap yarn and gingerbread to the people of the peasantry. "Oh, how impoverished it all is. Common yarn, disgusting gingerbread, phlegmatic people staring at a few colored ribbons in a booth and holding each other's warm hands."[91]

Armod is an old Danish word (the closest English equivalent is "penury") that is no longer used, but it often shows up in Andersen's literary texts. It cannot be translated simply as "poverty" or "destitution" but, according to the *Dictionary of the Danish Language*, must be further defined as "a high degree of poverty and complete impecuniosity."[92] Andersen did not use the word in his autobiographies, but we often encounter it in his poems, plays, and novels. For instance, in the poem "New Year's Night" from 1827, one of the verses says: "In penury and in pain / my mother gave birth to me." We also find it repeatedly appearing in the three novels from the 1830s. In *Only a Fiddler*, for example, Christian is called several times "the child of penury." And in later dramas, such as *The Mulatto* from 1840, we find such phrases as "Behind the garb of penury oft beats the heart of a king."

It's quite a different matter with Hans Christian Andersen's three autobiographies. Here, the concept of poverty that lies behind the word *armod* and can hardly be imagined today in the industrialized part of the world, has been made invisible.

Does this mean that Hans Andersen and Anne Marie Andersdatter were not poor? They certainly were, but in his memoirs the author has managed to make the poverty of his childhood home shine with great purity and comfort, order and decency. This is in sharp contrast to the way things are described in the probate records' sober appraisal of the contents of the home and its appearance following the death of Hans Andersen in 1816, and later, after the death of the author's stepfather Niels Jørgensen Gundersøn in 1822. In his autobiographies, Andersen says that "greenery and pictures decorated our little home." This home on Munkemøllestræde consisted of a large combined living room and bedroom that was barely eighteen square meters within whitewashed, cross-timbered walls, with beams in the low ceiling, and small windows facing the street. It was next to the windows that the shoemaker had his bench and work tools. In his books of memoirs, Andersen fills the room with chests of drawers, a bed, charming curtains, and a shiny stove with copper pipes. As he writes in 1847, this is "our little home, which Mother kept clean and tidy; her pride and joy was that the sheets and curtains were so white." And in *The Fairy Tale of My Life* from 1855 his childhood curtains appear slightly shorter, but on the other hand, they are "snow white." He repeats this image twenty years later with the phrase "snow-white summer curtains in the sunshine," which is from the poem "My Childhood Home." This poem was published on the author's last birthday, April 2, 1875.

The curtains that the representatives of Odense Probate Court, along with witnesses and trustees, saw when they entered the small, empty home on Munkemøllestræde in April 1816 were certainly not little white summer curtains. And the tiny kitchen in the passageway out to the back courtyard, which Andersen in his memoirs describes as a place full of shiny plates and pots, is nowhere to be found in the probate report. All the contents of the estate were examined "most meticulously," and it was determined that there was nothing to inherit. The estate was—as the records show—"barely sufficient to satisfy the creditors." It was thus decided to turn over to the widow and her eleven-year-old son, who were also present, the insignificant possessions of the estate, although only if the widow agreed to be responsible for the estate's debts and paid the probate costs. Finally, Anne Marie Andersdatter duly signed "with wielded pen" as it says in the records under her signature, since she was illiterate and could neither read nor write. [93]

It has so often been said of Hans Christian Andersen's parents that from his father he acquired his love of the imagination, while from his mother he inherited his stature. His intellect from his father, his physical appearance from his mother. Yet this notion does not hold up when we examine Andersen's biological inheritance, even though the differences were certainly apparent between the short, fair-haired father and the tall mother with the powerful arms and brown eyes. Standing in the middle of their small, low-ceilinged home, his mother must have seemed quite a giant in comparison with the stooped, introverted father over by the window.

By all accounts, the voluptuous Anne Marie Andersdatter was quite an attractive woman with a certain radiance that made an impression on the opposite sex. She dressed the way all women of the lower class did at the time, which included wearing a cap. And according to her son's memoirs, she always looked her most beautiful around Whitsuntide when the family would go on an excursion to the woods. That was when she would put on her brown, flowered cotton dress, which she otherwise wore only if she planned to take communion.

In *The Fairy Tale of My Life* Andersen mentions that in his two early novels, *The Improvisatore* and *Only a Fiddler*—both of which were written after Anne Marie Andersdatter's death—he depicts various ages and aspects of his mother's character. She is partially disguised in *Only a Fiddler* as the practical, down-to-earth figure of Maria, who was the same age as the author's mother. She is also partly the model for the older, more loving and talkative Domenica in *The Improvisatore*. As a young woman, Maria was said to have a voluptuous figure, as well as big brown eyes that were capable of summoning a man's heart back from the south. This Maria is both loving and strict toward her son, and at times she can also be harsh and temperamental, as is evident in lines from the novel such as: "Now, keep quiet, or I'll give you something to cry about!" In other remarks from Maria to Christian, there are traces of a reproach directed at the boy's daydreamer of a father, who in Maria's opinion doesn't always have a good influence on the lad. For instance, she says that the boy is "a sissy" and "exactly like his father." Maria becomes a truly fierce mother in phrases such as: "That boy is a whiner! He gets it from his father! But no one can say that I spoil him."

We know very little about Anne Marie Andersdatter's childhood and upbringing at the end of the 18th century. It's not clear who her father was, or exactly when or where she was born. Various items of information taken from the census in Odense indicate that her year of birth was somewhere between 1773 and 1775. And in one of the few bits of information specifically related to his mother's family, which Andersen included in his memoirs, it's mentioned that she was born in the town of Bogense. But neither the church books nor the census records can confirm this. In view of this dearth of information, as well as the nomadic patterns that can be sensed in his maternal grandmother's roaming life during the period 1770-83, we have to assume that Anne Sørensdatter, when she gave birth to Hans Christian Andersen's mother in the 1770s, was part of the wandering proletarian group of single women who—in a social sense—were in an extremely bad position. They roamed the countryside, taking servant posts and doing the harvesting work in the summer half of the year; in the winter they would head for Odense. A scholarly investigation of the moral conditions of the whole Danish lower class in the 18th century points out that "some of the women who constantly showed up with illegitimate children—especially if they were already in dire straits financially—would occasionally enter the realm of prostitution."[94] It cannot be determined with certainty whether Hans Christian Andersen's maternal grandmother regularly participated in prostitution. Yet this does seem likely because of the author's almost complete silence regarding his mother's family in his memoirs, as well as his grandmother's documented childbirths out of wedlock—three children with three different men. Anne Sørensdatter, like many women back then, was a negligent mother who left her eldest daughter to fend for herself, although at times she was sent off with a large group of beggar children. As in "The Little Match Girl," they were sent out in all sorts of weather to beg.

Large groups of beggars of all ages descended upon Fyn in the 1790s, but it was especially bad in Odense and the surrounding area. In the morning these crowds of children and older folks with walking stick in hand and a bundle over their shoulder could be seen heading out the town gates, as if they were off to a normal day's work. Late in the day they would return home with small or large loads of grain, bread, and other provisions. Once inside the city, these items would be quickly exchanged for liquor, coffee, and other more important necessities. At any rate, this was how the phenomenon was described around 1800 by a very indignant Odense citizen, the newspaper publisher and book printer Søren Hempel. Like other good and socially well-situated townspeople, he was tired of the growing swarm of beggars. In his opinion, it was more a question of laziness than real need.[95] Hans Christian Andersen himself confirms in his memoirs that his mother at one time belonged to this great crowd of beggar children. Yet he doesn't speak of this fact in such a horrifyingly realistic way as he does in the fairy tale about the beggar girl who freezes to death with the burned-out matches in her hands and the warm sight of the Christmas feast in the merchant's home still in her eyes. In Andersen's memoirs, he says instead that as a child his mother couldn't figure out how to beg properly, and so one day she sat down to cry under a bridge over Odense River. Her career as a beggar was ostensibly over before it even began.

Yet this story doesn't hold up, even though Andersen may have heard his mother tell it this way. Reality for the ten-year-old Anne Marie Andersdatter in the early 1780s was much more harsh and chaotic. Like so many other rootless and roaming children of the day, she endured her childhood without any familial moorings. She had no father, only a younger half sister and a mother, who in 1783 gave birth to her third daughter out of wedlock and was then subject to punishment for repeated fornication.

"Foolishness" is the rather tame term that Andersen uses in his fairy tale "She Was No Good" regarding the tragic consequences of contemporary erotic norms among the lower class, imbued with cynicism and heartlessness. Any man who was alleged to be the father had to pay a fine of twelve *rigsdaler*. After that he could continue to fornicate relatively freely; in the worst case he would simply receive additional fines. But loose women were punished with a flogging and were then thrown out the city gates. Things weren't quite that bad for the barely forty-year-old Anne Sørensdatter in 1781-82. She managed to steer clear of the long arm of the law for almost a year, since consideration was given to the fact that she was nursing her child. But in the spring of 1783 the hammer fell, and Andersen's maternal grandmother was sentenced to a week's arrest on a diet of bread and water in the jail beneath Odense Courthouse. As soon as she was out, she immediately got married—for the first time, it should be noted—to a man who had also just been released from jail. While she came from the dark cellar of the courthouse, he came from Odense Prison.[96]

At that time only the eldest daughter (Andersen's mother) could take care of herself. The girl, who was then thirteen or fourteen, was registered for the first time in the census for 1787. She is listed as a maid in the employ of the distiller and innkeeper Rasmus Ibsen on Gråbrødrestræde. Around 1800 we find her working for the grocer Bircherod on Nørregade. After that, it's impossible to ascertain her whereabouts during the years leading up to—and immediately following—the birth of Hans Christian. She may have taken work as a servant and nursemaid in central Odense.

And we don't know whether her own little boy came into the world in April 1805 on Nørregade, Skulkenborg, or at the corner of Hans Jensens Stræde and Bangs Boder, in the present-day "Hans Christian Andersen House." There is a touch of a nomadic existence even surrounding the fairy-tale author's own birth.

A Woman with Second Sight from Fyn

Anne Marie Andersdatter's strong tendency to superstition attests to the fact that she was also a person full of imagination and fantasies. To use a quote from the fairy tale "Anne Lisbeth," it might be said that her superstitions were constantly "running hot and cold in her blood." She took a lively interest in the numerous signs and omens occurring both night and day, such as the great comet of 1811, about which her son later wrote an entire story:

> "And the comet appeared, gleaming with its fiery core and threatening with its tail. It was observed from the rich palace, from the impoverished home, by crowds in the street and by the solitary person walking across the trackless heath. Each had his own thoughts about it. 'Come and see the sign from Heaven! Come and see the magnificent sight!' people said, and everyone rushed to look. But inside the house the little boy and his mother stayed where they were. The flame of the tallow candle flared to a point and then curled. She thought this meant that the little boy would soon die. The wood shaving had turned toward him, after all. It was an old superstition, and she believed it."[97]

And Anne Marie Andersdatter believed it too. She threw her heart and soul into the religious gatherings of the annual midsummer market at St. Regisse Spring in Frørup in southeastern Fyn. There, beneath the midsummer moon, ill people would seek a cure in the curative waters of the spring, which on that particular night possessed a special power. In the hours leading up to the occult moment, their relatives would hang various gifts in the tall trees surrounding the magical spring. This spring, which still exists today, is located a few kilometers from two of the Fyn estates that Hans Christian Andersen loved most in his life: Glorup and Lykkesholm.

Among the spiritualists and mediums that his mother visited most often was Mette Mogensdatter from Ejby, who was known for her remedies made from herbs, oils, and plasters. She was also able to look into a person's future by reading the lines of his palm or deciphering patterns in coffee grounds. The author's mother believed in these wise women, who were capable of more than just reciting the Lord's Prayer. Some of them could cure ailments with turpentine oils, formic alcohol, herbal baths, and rubber plasters. Others would advise those who were ill to seek out places of execution and there obtain and drink the warm blood of the criminal only minutes after the executioner had severed the condemned man's head from his body. And certain wise women were especially good at "putting on the pot for someone." This was an art that consisted of brewing a magical concoction made from the pages of a hymnal, a little moss, some houseleeks, fresh cock's comb, and certain engagement rings. In the proper combinations and conditions this brew would have a magnetic, suggestive effect across sea and land on a sweetheart who was traveling somewhere out in the world but was now strongly missed back home on Fyn. We hear more about this powerful witch's brew in Andersen's fairy tale "What Old Johanne Told." In this story, at the specific moment when the moon is in its first quarter, the brew is cooked so vigorously that a man who has been much missed and long-awaited is awakened in the far reaches of the world and immediately summoned home, "where the pot is boiling and his sweetheart awaits him."

Mette Mogensdatter cured both humans and animals and was particularly skilled at closing up open and bleeding wounds. She had twenty-five years of healing behind her by the time she received her first sentence for quackery in 1813, but she quickly resumed her practice. And in 1816 she was the one who sent Anne Marie Andersdatter's lanky son home with the admonition that if he met the ghost of his ill father on his way home along the river, then his father would die very soon.[98]

Ghosts were very much part of reality in Denmark around 1800. After night fell, you might encounter them anywhere out in the country or in the towns. In Odense, especially in St. Knud's Cemetery, where Andersen's father was buried in April 1816, there was a lively traffic of ethereal beings. In the dark hours of evening or night, men might run the risk of being hailed by wild women who sat on their graves, about to give birth to a child, begging someone to give them a piece of linen in which to wrap the newborn. This would terrify most men, who would turn on their heel and rush out of the cemetery, while behind them they could hear how the woman's loud laments would sink deeper and deeper into the earth until the lid of a coffin slammed shut. These sorts of stories about hauntings, omens, and signs were quite prevalent among the poor people of Denmark well into the 1800s. Almost a thousand years after Ansgar had introduced Christianity to Denmark, people still firmly believed that a woman who died in pregnancy would give birth to her child, but only when the time was right. That's why people used to place baby clothes in the coffin of the deceased pregnant woman. And men who were braver than those who tended to run away from the female ghosts in St. Knud's Cemetery would promptly tear strips of fabric from their shirts so as to deliver the dead mother in the grave.[99]

"I grew up pious and superstitious," recounts Andersen in his memoirs. And behind these words we find Anne Marie Andersdatter and her down-to-earth personality. She was also very much a resident of Fyn, and she possessed second sight. From her emanated what Andersen later in life called "the pious feeling of faith without comprehension."[100] It was especially through his mother's superstitions that Hans Christian, in his childhood, became bound to his region of Fyn; it was an anchor that he never lost. Both as a boy and as a grown man, he felt himself strongly and genuinely attached to the common people, with everything this entailed, including a primitive poetic sense and a belief in Jesus, as well as in the Nordic gods Thor and Odin. Both as a boy and as a grown man, Andersen possessed an uneasy, always restless current and force within him that was deep and turbulent like the Odense River, which he loved. In spite of his enthusiasm for the marvelous progress in technology and science in modern times, Andersen never let go of his belief in the old, heathen peasant culture. This is particularly noticeable in his sensual retellings in his autobiographies of various occult incidents from his childhood. He depicts superstition as the very basis for the thoughts and actions of the common people. As Andersen says in *The Fairy Tale of My Life* about the period when he too lived under the childish power of the imagination: "I listened to everything that superstition said around me; for me it ranked with the holiest of faiths." In many ways this meant an animistic view of life, which has always had a strong influence on primitive peoples and formed the core of their religion, whether they were of Nordic, Indian, Inuit, or Aboriginal extraction.

The belief in everything that lives and breathes and is in some way animate was handed down to Andersen in rich portions by his mother, who could neither read nor write. Yet this gave her even greater incentive to describe all her fantastical ideas about the powers of darkness in her conversations with her son. She introduced him to a world filled with beings and objects that had to be either conquered or animated, which meant shaping them in his own image. From his father Hans Christian absorbed a more enlightened and modern upbringing that made him see the spirit in nature as a positive force. But time after time, in the company of his mother and all her women friends with second sight, he learned to respect—and fear—the countless spirits of nature, harnessing them via oral narratives. According to Anne Marie Andersdatter, these spirits existed in such great numbers and possessed such powerfully negative charges, that at home on Munkemøllestræde they had to keep birch branches hanging in the corner by the stove, livelong plants up on the ceiling beams, and horse-shoes above the door in order to ward off werewolves, ghosts, and other apparitions. Very early in his life, the shoemaker's son was well aware of the terrible sights and sounds of the night. He knew about the existence of subterranean creatures in burial mounds; he had heard about the ghost horse and knew about the presence of elf girls, vampire ravens, sea cattle, dragons, nymphs, basilisks, and will-o'-the-wisps. And he was particularly aware that water sprites lived in the Odense River and Munke Bog, which was why, after nightfall, you could see steam from the bog woman's brewing vat and hear the cries of owls and ravens. Hans Christian could see and hear all of these secret powers that ruled and operated in nature but seldom revealed their presence, unless you were one of the initiated. And for this reason the strangely wise and sensitive boy who knew about so many things was much in demand. For instance, the old women at Graabrødre Hospital were very impressed by the boy's knowledge and loved to watch him sketch and listen to him tell stories. "Heart, lungs, and intestines!" he might suddenly shout as an introduction during a visit to the hospital, and then he would grab a piece of chalk and proceed to draw all over the door. "There you see! That's what we look like inside!" And then all the wrinkled old ladies would peer at each other, nod, and say: "He'll die young, a wise child like that!"[101]

One of the creatures that the author felt closest to as a boy was the river man. Several times each day Hans Christian would cross the Odense River and rest on the banks during his solitary forays through nature along the river. Or he would explore the water mill that stood at the end of his childhood street, less than a hundred yards from his home. The river, which is associated with so many popular legends on Fyn, became without a doubt the happiest place for Hans Christian during the years 1805-19.

It was here at the river in 1822 that the seventeen-year-old budding author chose to place himself in the figure of a nine-year-old boy on the very first page of his literary debut. The boy is weaving from green reeds a poet's ship, which rocks on the surface of the river and sets course for much bigger worlds than the flimsy little paper boats he used to sail in the water basin outside the house on Munkemøllestræde. That was what the river meant for this boy, filled with yearning; it was the path that he himself would one day travel out into the wide world. Against the current, if need be. Whenever big changes occurred in Hans Christian's life—his father died, a new stepfather appeared, and the whole family suddenly had to move to a different house—the river stayed right where it was, in its familiar place. It was a steadfast and enchanting world of reeds, water lilies, fish, dragonflies, weeping willows, dock plants, snails, and butterflies that spoke to him all day long, no matter whether he followed the current of the river to the east or to the west, or sat near Munkemølle and watched the water rushing over the three huge wheels of the old mill. He enjoyed the music from the cascading rhythm of the millwheels, he watched the uncovering of the river bottom as the sluice was opened and it was finally possible—in the seaweed—to catch sight of a couple of wriggling fish or a fat water rat that had scurried out from a hole in the mill's foundation.

Stories and storytellers were everywhere in Hans Christian Andersen's boyhood during the years 1805-19. This was especially true out in the country, in the fields and the hops gardens, where mother and son would go in September to join the other harvest workers. After the sun set they would settle down in the barns to pinch off the stalks of the yellow hops catkins, and while they worked, people would tell stories. As Andersen writes, that was when "the lantern of superstition would cast its picture light." For hours on end stories would be exchanged about portents, ghosts, hops, and the mystique of brewing beer. The gathered and plucked hops plants were to be used to brew beer, and back then no other place in Denmark had such plentiful or such good hops plants as Fyn. The older harvest workers would talk about the old days when people would still do anything for the sake of good flavor. And there was nothing better for the beer's fermenting process and taste than the fresh, bloody finger of a thief. But, of course, it had to come from a person who had just been hanged. So in the gloom and dark of night the brewer would slip out and cut off a finger from a corpse that was still dangling on the gallows. Then the bloody finger stump would be lowered into the beer barrel through the bunghole. Those were the days! That was the kind of tale that circulated around the hops vat and kneading trough as the piles of plucked vines grew. Once Hans Christian heard an old man at the hops vat say that God knew everything that was going to happen. The grown-up Andersen recounts in his autobiography from 1847 that he was so overwhelmed by this idea that he decided to test the validity of the theory that very evening. He sneaked over to the village pond and stood on a large rock right above the deepest spot in the water, intending to challenge his belief in a long and happy life. If he jumped into the water and drowned, then it would be God's will, and the old man at the vat would be right. Should he or shouldn't he? He thought so hard that his mind groaned, and suddenly a third and better compromise occurred to him: "It's the Devil who wants control of me!" And the boy uttered a shriek and dashed home as if he were being chased by all the elves, trolls, and will-o'-the-wisps on Fyn. Then he threw himself into his mother's arms. Like all the other women in the barn, Anne Marie Andersdatter was convinced that the inconsolable lad had seen a ghost.

Young Andersen also heard strange stories in the passageways of Graabrødre Hospital, which he visited occasionally, listening to the speeches and songs of the inmates. Or the tales would come from the poorhouse on Overgade or from Odense Prison, which stood adjacent to the back of his childhood home on Munkemøllestræde. Here gossip and wisdom flowed in an uninterrupted stream as the spindles twirled between the hands of the young girls and old matrons. Many of these women were locked up for theft, prostitution, or unpaid fornication fines. Although they may not have possessed any of the king's coins, they did have a wealth of good stories, especially the oldest of them who, as Andersen said in one of his fairy tales, were like "a book of chronicles, with recipes and old memories."[102]

But some of the strangest tales from the peasantry to whom Andersen belonged came from his mentally disturbed paternal grandfather, Anders "Traes" Hansen, or "Traes from Killerup," as he was also popularly known on Fyn. His grandfather was one of Odense's eccentrics who liked to adorn his head with beech branches and flower wreaths whenever he came to town from the country. He would wander the streets with his basket filled with strange, carved wooden figures that were supposed to depict humans with animal heads and extremely odd beasts with wings from quite a different world than the one occupied by normal people. As we will see in Chapter Ten, it wasn't very far from the primitive carvings of the lunatic grandfather to large parts of the genius grandson's paper-cuts, drawings, and his entire fairy-tale universe. In Andersen's story "Holger Danske" from 1845, we have what might seem to be an idealized glimpse of his grandfather. In the story, he is portrayed as almost normal as he carves big, strange pictures out of wood and at the same time tells his grandson the story of Holger Danske and his beard that grew to become part of the table. The story takes place in the grandfather's work-shop and is about how a tale can leap out of a block of wood as the old man carves it. The story makes such an impression on the grandson that after he is tucked into bed he can't sleep and keeps pressing his chin into the quilt as if it were a long white beard that had become part of the bed. In Andersen's memoirs we learn that as a child he was afraid of his grand-father, who at times was so demented that he couldn't distinguish Hans Christian from the sons in the Bible. Singing at the top of his lungs and with flowers hanging in his face, he would march through the city with a swarm of jeering boys following behind. Once when Hans Christian was lying on the ground and playing with some stick men in the water under the gutter plank, his grandfather suddenly appeared above him. He looked down at the boy for a long time and then solemnly asked: "Aren't you the son of the holy Lazarus?"[103]

When he was an old man with no teeth, Hans Christian Andersen thought that he looked like his grandfather. Proof that the author actually did consider shoemaker Hans Andersen to be his biological father was his fear that he might someday lose his mind like the men in his father's fam-ily. In a letter to B. S. Ingemann in 1845, in which Andersen expressed out-rage that Carsten Hauch had portrayed him as a raving lunatic author, he practically shouts his fear from the page: "My own grandfather was insane; as was my father before he died!" In the same manner, Andersen recounts in *The Fairy Tale of My Life* how he was also pursued through the streets of Odense, and he always felt an icy chill pass through his body whenever anyone in the rushing mob of boys behind him would shout: "He's mad, just like his grandfather!"

Yet his grandfather's sad fate was not something that particularly con-cerned Andersen in the 1820s when Anders "Traes" was locked up in Graabrødre Hospital's section for the mentally disturbed, also called the "Madhouse." On the other hand, the author's mother continued to have contact with her parents-in-law after the shoemaker's death in 1816. This was perhaps because Andersen's grandparents owned a little house on Pogestræde, in which she took lodgings. There was rarely any room for sentimentality in the milieu in which Hans Christian Andersen grew up.

His Mother's Imploring Letters
and Her Death

In his book about Hans Christian Andersen, Edvard Collin says that the author was always very reserved about discussing his mother. At the same time, it was his impression that her relationship with Hans Christian was much on the son's mind.[104] If this was true, then the author's relatively minimal interest in his mother's sad fate during the 1820s seems surprising. This was in sharp contrast to a number of his poems from the same period that are addressed in a tender and compassionate manner to a mother figure. During the last years of his mother's life, from 1829-33, Hans Christian made his debut as a novelist, poet, and playwright and at times even had a little money (although he was still dependent on support from others). And so it seems that he turned his back on his impoverished mother in Odense who was increasingly suffering from alcoholism, while in his literary works he regularly falls on his knees before the Virgin Mary. We see Otto Thostrup do just that in the novel *O.T.* in 1836, in which there is talk of "in a Roman Catholic manner putting the mother above the son."

In many places in Andersen's writings we encounter these declarations of love for a mother on high. Even in a poem with a title as personal as "To My Mother" from 1823, it's clear that the mother is more of an idealized figure in a spotless and idyllic childhood than a real, biological mother. If the son, in this poem, is directing phrases such as "I owe all my happiness to you" toward Anne Marie Andersdatter, we have to wonder why it wasn't more difficult for him to leave behind his childhood home in 1819. And he apparently never suffered from the least bit of homesickness during the days and months after his arrival in Copenhagen, or for the rest of his life. It seems as if Andersen, after his confirmation, had to escape Odense as fast as possible, not only to be taken on at the Royal Theater but also to create a new life for himself—"his own noble birth and genealogical tree," as it says in *O.T.* From his very first day in the capital, this determined and ambitious boy seems to have set an existential goal for himself: to make a fresh start in an entirely new circle of family members and friends, which meant that his family tree had to be wiped clean.

In the long and dreary last chapter of his mother's life, which extended from the death of her second husband in 1822 until her own death at the poorhouse called Doctors Boder in the fall of 1833, the son could hardly have made her life any easier, in a financial sense, than he did during the years 1820-25. Even though he was studying for his exams in Slagelse and received support from the state treasury, nearly all his funds went directly into the pocket of Headmaster Meisling. In answer to his mother's imploring letters to her learned son, Hans Christian would occasionally send her a nominal sum for shoes and clothing. He also turned over one-fourth of his inheritance from his paternal grandfather (15 *rigsdaler*) to his mother in 1824. But after 1825, Andersen cannot be called any sort of "spirited solace and support for a needy mother," as he writes in an early poem.[105] There were evidently lengthy gaps between letters to his mother, and in that sense Andersen hardly lived up to the ideals he had promoted in a school essay about "the duties of children toward their parents" in the mid-1820s: "No one, other than those who are utterly depraved, can forget the sacred duties owed to those who gave him life."[106]

If we look at the twenty-five letters still extant which Anne Marie Andersdatter sent to her son during 1822-33, and which she, being illiterate, had to ask others to write for her, we gain a clear impression of the type of emotions and interactions between the two. *He* is the one with book-learning, the well-read son out in the wide world. *She* is the illiterate one, the poor old mother back home in the small world; she constantly has to remind the boy of her existence and beg him for a little money. There is never any sense of an intimate, confiding conversation—and that wasn't even possible since the mother couldn't write in her own voice but instead, over the years, had to make use of five to ten different letter writers.

It was also at Graabrødre Hospital—in the section for destitute old women, which was called Doctors Boder and was situated on the top floor, right under the roof, with just enough room for sixteen beds—that Andersen's mother was taken in as a pauper during the spring of 1825. No one had any further use for her as a washerwoman. Her increasing alcohol abuse had long portended the end of a wretched life during an era of Danish history to which her son was in the process of bringing glory.

The last time the two saw each other was in the summer of 1832, when Andersen spent a month on Fyn. He socialized with "the foremost families,"[107] living comfortably at the home of Lieutenant Colonel Høegh-

Guldberg or out at the Fyn estates of Bramstrup, Hofmansgave, Sanderumgaard, and Lykkesholm Castle, where he was properly pampered and fed. In a letter home to Edvard Collin, he writes on August 3: "At Lykkesholm they almost did too much for me, stuffing me with everything I desired; they enticed every little wish out of me."[108] While Anne Marie Andersdatter was dragging out her life in the poorhouse in Odense, her son was performing Holberg in the Hofmansgave garden, learning waltz steps at Bramstrup, and being luxuriously conveyed from one estate to the other in a coach-and-four, accompanied by the landed gentry. He had no desire to spend time in Odense, and in a letter to Edvard in which he asks for ten *rigsdaler* for his further travels, he describes his encounter with his hometown. He does not mention his mother.

> "All my childhood memories, every spot seems dark to me. For me, it seems as if I were dead and have now returned to a place where, in quite a different form, I lived and romped. I feel an uneasiness, a longing for Sjælland—I can't explain it myself."[109]

His mother died a year later, in October 1833. In her last letter to her son, sent in February, she thanked him for "sending 1 *rigsdaler*," which she described as "a welcome help to me during these times."[110] Two weeks later, on March 13, 1833, the promising young writer received a travel grant from the foundation *Ad usus publicos* to the tune of 600 rigsdaler over two years. This was an enormous sum of money, and he immediately started making plans for a grand cultural tour to Italy. There is no indication that Andersen, before his departure in April, sent his mother any additional help. The irregular stream of imploring letters from mother to son had ended. In December 1833, Andersen received word in Rome of his mother's death in Odense. His grief cannot be labeled either great or long-lasting if we look at how it is reflected in his diary and letters from that period. He is moved, of course, by the news he receives in a letter from Jonas Collin on December 16, but in the same breath he almost seems more concerned with his sudden status as a man without family. On the same day that he hears the news about his mother, he writes home to Henriette Wulff:

> "Her situation was a harsh one, and there was almost nothing I could do for her; this has often grieved me back home. But I could never speak of this! Now Our Lord has taken her, and as a son I am thankful for that; but it has affected me deeply, now I am truly alone—no one is bound by nature to love me."[111]

The emotional aloofness of his letters and diary in 1833–34 with regard to his mother and her "harsh situation" and fate is in sharp contrast to the sympathetic way he depicts her twenty years later in *The Fairy Tale of My Life*. In his autobiography Andersen looks back on the news of his mother's death in December 1833, describing the experience as "my endlessly bitter anguish." He also writes:

> "Collin sent me the news, and my first exclamation was: 'Thank you, God! Now her suffering, which I could not ease, is over!' I wept but could not accustom myself to the idea that now I have not a single person in the world who, by blood and nature, must love me. This new impression brought tears; I cried my heart out and had a feeling that the best had happened for her. I would never have been able to make her last days bright and free of sorrow. She died with a joyous faith in my happiness, that I *was* somebody."[112]

Andersen was obviously grateful that his mother's sufferings were over, but he was also personally relieved. In terms of family and relatives, he was now all alone in the world and thus—more than ever before—ready to create a new family life for himself. "You have to climb upward!" is the motto of the nimble and ambitious Rudy on his way toward the heights in the fairy tale "The Ice Maiden." And Andersen had long ago realized that the first steps on his own path to the top were via the distinguished and respected Collin family. Here was a sound and well-functioning family with no loose women, fatherless children, dreamers, lunatics, or beggars. The first book Andersen published after his return from Italy in 1834 was the novel *The Improvisatore*, which he dedicated not to his deceased mother but instead to his new, very much alive family on Bredgade with the words:

> "To Privy Councilor Collin and his noble wife, in whom I found parents, to his children, in whom I found siblings, to the home of homes, I here present the best that I own."

Andersen also spares his readers the details of his mother's death in his autobiographies of 1847 and 1855. But the details can be found in the church records of Graabrødre Hospital, where all paupers were cared for in Doctors Boder on the top floor of the building. The brief and concise entry in the church records says of Anne Marie Andersdatter:

> "On October 7, 1833, Marie Jørgensen, resident of Doctors Boder, widow of shoemaker Hans Andersen, died at the age of 66. Cause of death: Delirium tremens."[113]

In one of his confidential conversations in the 1870s with his young traveling companion Nicolai Bøgh, the aging Andersen revealed the fact that his mother had drunk herself to death and toward the end of her life was deranged due to liquor. On this occasion the author said that his mother back in Odense "began deteriorating more and more." Young Bøgh then adds in his document twenty years later that:"According to various concordant testimonies from her contemporaries in Odense, she spent her last days in a constant intoxication that made her very maudlin."[114] So her son had good reason to be a little tightfisted about offering his mother financial help in the 1820s when the pattern of Anne Marie Andersdatter's life was taking shape, as her son writes in one of his fairy tales:"One dram was good, but two were better." Early on he had emphasized his own position, which resembled that of his father, with repeated admonitions in his letters. The aging Hans Christian Andersen makes this clear when he recalls that in a now-lost letter he had reminded his mother to refrain from too often "taking the cork out of the bottle that's in the cupboard. It will sincerely grieve me to hear from my friends and acquaintances in Odense that my dear old mother is being ridiculed."[115]

Yet it's impossible to ignore that behind all these well-intended words there is a hint of fear from the upward-striving son. He worried that in the better circles of the capital he might be confronted with embarrassing gossip and loose rumors from the swamp of Odense that would cast shame over the romantic reputation he was in the process of building in Copenhagen.

Sister Karen

From everything around us grow the most wonderful stories, as it says so beautifully in the fairy tale "Mother Elder Tree" from 1845. In this story, a lovely elder tree suddenly springs from a teapot and sprouts branches as the old man tells stories to the boy who is lying in bed with a cold and fever. From the daily life of the author's childhood also sprang a couple of tales, although of the more cruel sort, which with time came knocking on the door of reality. One example was the large-as-life half sister named Karen Marie, whom Hans Christian had done his utmost to banish from his mind. As a grown man he always used any means possible to keep her existence a secret.

Her full name was Karen Marie Rosenvinge, and in 1842 she suddenly appeared out of nowhere and knocked on the author's door. She was roughly six years older than Andersen and now called herself Ane Kaufmann. The author's mother had given birth to her out of wedlock in 1799, and she presented a serious threat to the romantic image of the author's childhood on which Andersen, from his very first day in the capital in 1819, had based his new identity.

So it was no surprise that Andersen was furious when his half sister suddenly reappeared. He had felt the same anger back in 1824–25 when, in his new life as a pupil with royal funding at Slagelse Grammar School, he suddenly felt his half sister breathing down his neck. Sitting in his lodgings at the home of Madame Henneberg, he became obsessed with the idea that Karen Marie might well be the new maid at the headmaster's house: "The Meislings have hired a new maid from Copenhagen; I suspect that it's my sister, and they say that her name is Maria." But the next day he could breathe a sigh of relief in his diary: "This time my suspicions deceived me; I don't know this maid at all."[116] In 1833 thoughts of his sister's fate once again sparked great nervousness and anxiety in Andersen. In a letter to his mother he asked whether she knew where Karen was living and what she might be doing. Her reply reassured Andersen: "As to where Karen is or how she is doing, I can tell you nothing since I don't know where she lives."[117]

Then on February 8, 1842, she drops into Hans Christian Andersen's life like a shadow. She had sent him a letter that was actually more a little note than a lengthy or formal sort of letter. We don't know the contents, since the letter is one of the relatively few among all those Andersen received during his lifetime that he did not save. But it's clear that this sign of life from Karen gave him a shock, as evidenced by the wording in his calendar entry that same evening:

> "When I came home I found a letter from my mother's daughter; I experienced what I had described in *O.T.* Feverish; a terrible night; emotions and despair scornfully filled my mind."[118]

A completely uncontrollable fear and anxiety spread through the author, and the image of his half sister rode him like a succubus. But why all this despair and panic? And what had he once written in *O.T.* that had now come true?

As for the latter, the main character Otto Thostrup carries a stigmatized memory of his childhood, which was anything but beautiful or innocent. Etched into his flesh are his initials, and these two letters also stand

for the terrible truth—Odense Tugthus [Prison]—which reveals that Otto
is an illegitimate child, born in prison. Yet the grown-up Otto has always
used every means he could to conceal this fact, especially among the finer
circles in the capital, where with his unique bookish talents he is headed
for a great future. But one day his past suddenly intervenes in the form of
the conjuror Heinrich, who seeks out Otto several times in order to threat-
en him and pressure him for money. Otherwise he will divulge Otto's true
background and various disreputable relations.

The fact that Andersen did not just grab this theme out of thin air is
evident from a letter to Henriette Hanck in 1836 in which he discusses the
title of the novel. In this connection, Andersen writes that it's "a title that
is not in the least contrived but the most natural thing in the world." And
the natural truth, which the novel's Otto Thostrup wants to conceal at all
costs and which is a reflection of the real Hans Christian Andersen, was
that he had a half sister who had far from lived up to the ideal of a sister
in body and soul. Both the protagonist and the author wish their sister to
be like the lovely, chaste Eva in *O. T.* And in the novel's happy ending, contrary to all expectation and logic, she turns out to be Otto's real, flesh-and-
blood sister. But before this dream is fulfilled, we meet the brother's nightmare of a sister in the person of the loathsome and demented Sidsel, who
frequents the bottom of life's swamp and is described as more animal than
human. During the course of the novel, Otto, like Andersen during the
1820s, repeatedly has fearful, obsessive thoughts about when she might
appear from her filthy darkness and cast the true shadow of his family over
his bright and pure future. And yet, in the midst of his anxiety about his
terrible sister and everything she brings with her, Otto suddenly expresses
a tenderness for her and a distaste for his own fleeing from his familial
responsibility:

> "My sister! My poor, neglected sister, who has the same right to
> develop her mind as I have. How I fear that meeting! It will be bitter. I
> must get away. I will get away. Life is suffocating here! I have means, after
> all. I will travel. Lively France will chase off these whims and . . . then I'll
> be away, far from home. Next spring I'll be a stranger, out among
> strangers."[119]

During the days following February 8, 1842, which was when
Andersen received the letter from his sister, he couldn't get her out of his

mind. On February 11, he sends her a note which the next day results in a visit from Karen's husband. He looked "honest and decent," Andersen notes in his calendar. He told the author about the couple's hardships, whereupon Andersen gave him four *rigsdaler*. "He was very happy, as was I."[120] This visit was repeated a month later, although his sister's husband only managed to cadge two *rigsdaler*. And as far as we know, he showed up again in September, when Andersen reduced the alms to one *rigsdaler*. Only then— at the prospect of not receiving anything more—did the forty-three-year-old sister appear on the scene to visit her half brother. On September 30, Andersen writes in his calendar: "This morning visit from Karen; she looked quite well-dressed and young; I gave her 1 *rigsdaler*."[121]

His sister's visit prompted Andersen, the very next morning, to go to the Collin family and ask Edvard for advice and assistance with this awkward matter. He had to put his foot down with Karen, once and for all. After his sister's first appeal in February 1842, Andersen had already enlisted the help of Adolph Drewsen who, in his position as Assistant Chief Constable and with his daily presence at the Copenhagen police court, was just the person to investigate whether Karen Marie and the laborer Peder Kaufmann were engaged in an "illicit cohabitation."[122] Was the couple living in sin? And was there any basis for suspecting that she was one of the countless girls from the provinces who had come to seek her fortune in the capital but had ended up in a brothel or walked the streets on her own, protected and exploited by a pimp?[123]

After the second visit in February, Andersen noted in his calendar: "Early this morning went to see Collin and confided everything to him; through Drewsen he will find out who her husband is."[124] We can only guess what this little but capacious word "everything" might mean, but apparently it had to do with "my mother's daughter" and the associated painful truths about loose relationships and illegitimate children among his maternal relatives. For the first and last time in his life, Andersen lifted the veil and revealed to the Collin family a less innocent side of his childhood story. He knew that within that family, with its abundance of jurists and government officials, he could count on complete discretion, and "Karen" would continue to be a well-guarded secret. There was no room for her in Andersen's life story. And after October 30, 1843, when Karen showed up at his door, Andersen never mentioned her or their sibling relationship again in his calendars or diaries. Not even in his most personal and confidential correspondence do we find a single word after this date that explains what was meant by "everything."

Yet what Andersen could never change with his lies was the fact that Karen had once rested under the same maternal heart as he had. And it seems just as certain that during specific periods of the author's childhood Karen was physically present and presumably shared a bed with him for varying lengths of time. In November 1805, when shoemaker journeyman Hans Andersen applied to become an independent shoemaker in Odense, it says in his royal application: "Wherefore my wife and two children can hardly be fed, even less can all of us be housed, clothed, or retain anything for firewood."[125] Reference is made to two children, which ought to be kept in mind when considering the wording much later of the mother's letters to her son in Copenhagen and Slagelse, in which Karen very clearly is referred to as "your sister." There is much to indicate that Hans Christian Andersen was not at all the only child in the family the way he, in his memoirs, subsequently depicted himself.

So what happened to his sister? Presumably at the age of eight, as was the custom for girls of the proletariat, Karen was sent out as a servant in Odense and the surrounding area. For this reason, after 1807-08, contact with Andersen's half sister was more sporadic, and the two probably only met a few times and on special occasions, such as for Karen's confirmation at St. Knud's Church in Odense in October 1814. At that time she was listed in the church books as Karen Marie Rosenvinge; the records also say "illegitimate child." In the same entry she is also described as having good religious knowledge, having conducted herself in a virtuous manner, and even survived smallpox, which all in all, and despite her poverty, indicated a healthy and innocent girl. We know nothing about her actions during the following decades until she suddenly—four years before her death —seeks out her famous half brother in the hope of receiving a larger sum of money.

In November 1846, Karen Marie was found dead in the garret room of the back building on Borgergade 20, in the center of Copenhagen's red-light district. This was the area frequented by a particular faction of the city's prostitutes, meaning those who were slightly older and more worn-out. Here they serviced their customers in the corners of the back courtyards, in the stairwells, and in miserable little rooms where the girls' pimps would show up to oversee the source of their income. In 1848 there were thirty-seven separate brothels on Borgergade alone. In the past, the street had a reputation as belonging to a respectable part of town, but in the 1840s, with the tremendous growth in population, these streets quickly became a slum district, filled with old, dilapidated buildings, which in many cases were transformed into rented lodgings with back buildings and extra stories.[126] In the Trinitatis Church records, Andersen's half sister is listed in November 1846 as "Laborer Kaufmann's wife." The cause of death is given as "consumption," which, in addition to venereal diseases, was the most widespread ailment among the city's poor, who led unstable and unhealthy lives under terribly filthy and unhygienic conditions. Karen's deathbed in the garret of the back building was situated less than one kilometer from her brother's comfortable lodgings on Kongens Nytorv. He was not at home the day she died in the fall of 1846. He was dining with H. C. Ørsted, where he was asked to tell the entire dinner party about his recently completed travels through Europe. Once again Andersen had been royally received wherever he went. He had even signed a lucrative contract with a Danish-German publisher who wanted to publish Andersen's collected works in German; as an introduction, the Danish author would write his first full-length autobiography.

Karen Marie didn't live long enough to read her famous brother's memoirs. At the age of forty-seven, she was buried on November 22, 1846, in Assistens Cemetery, in a pauper's grave, row 9, number 125. On that day Hans Christian Andersen was again among fine company at the home of the Collins on Amaliegade, that "home of homes," which was always so filled with brothers and sisters, mothers and fathers. As mentioned, Andersen never again said a word about Karen in his writings. Nor did she leave behind any trace worth mentioning. Only the landlord put in an appearance for the settling of her estate in the garret of the back building on Borgergade 20. The so-called Herr Kaufmann had long ago vanished from the scene, and probate was handled quickly since Karen—like her mother, maternal grandmother, and the two deceased stepfathers back home in Odense—owned nothing of any value.[127]

Swinging London 1847

After what was for Andersen a very distressing year, he set off in May 1847 on another grand European journey, his fifth in seven years. Now the fruits were to be harvested from the hard work he had undertaken the previous summer in the south when he had finished his autobiography in record time in spite of the extreme heat he had to endure and all the mental exertion demanded by the writing process. Andersen had managed to write two hundred pages in three months during a period in which the desertlike temperatures in the south had taken their toll on his health. After returning home, he had written to B. S. Ingemann that he was still feeling poorly:

> "The summer heat of the south has, if I might say so, peeled the bark off me so that I'm nothing but nerves; and it's terrible to be a virtual barometer in all my limbs."[128]

But as the spring of 1847 approached, Andersen again felt a prickling in his wings. This time his journey would take a circular route through Holland, England, and Weimar, where he would visit his beloved Hereditary Grand Duke who, like all his other German friends, had read or heard about the Dane's new work, *Das Märchen meines Lebens ohne Dichtung.* The first wave of German reviews in March and April 1847 were overwhelmingly positive and favorable. They were filled with long quotes and references, comparing Andersen's book to Jean-Jacques Rousseau's *Confessions* from 1765-70. This was a work that, in its day, had sprung from the French author's desire to examine himself through his writing. "I want to show people a human being in the full truth of nature, and that human being is me," as Rousseau wrote.[129]

The common element in all the positive parts of the critique referred to the Danish author's touching, simple, and naïve depiction of his childhood, which nearly all the critics in Germany, even the most cautious, agreed was the most successful section of the autobiography. One critic even praised Andersen for his courage to speak so openly and honestly about his impoverished childhood. In these times when so many are without parents, the critic pointed out, few dare to acknowledge their original social status.[130] This first wave of positive reviews in the spring of 1847 unleashed a new stream of publicity with special focus on Andersen's life and work. The presses were whirring, and Andersen's autobiography was in demand. But more critical reviews soon followed, and for the first time in the evaluation of Andersen's work during the 1830s and 1840s, some critics began to contest the Danish fairy-tale writer's mythologizing of his own life. Exactly how remarkable or mysterious was his distinctive character? Was he as original and brilliant as he himself suggested? The criticism was prompted by the weakest section of the autobiography, which carried the narrative forward to the summer of 1846. Many German writers were in agreement about labeling this particular section as "a tiring and morbid enumeration of attacks from critics and those who are envious."[131] In other words, for the first time a more negative critique could be traced regarding the phenomenon of Hans Christian Andersen abroad. After almost ten years of being constantly in favor and enjoying a rising value on the literary stock exchange in Germany, Andersen and his art were no longer beyond reproach.

Yet in other parts of Europe Andersen was still a new and sparkling star in the firmament of art. This was true in London, for example, where publishers, booksellers, and all the literary salons of the city waited excitedly in the early summer of 1847 when rumors began circulating about the Danish fairy-tale author's imminent visit to England. And in this connection, nothing was to be left to chance. Consequently, Andersen's visit was synchronized with the publication of *The True Story of My Life—A Sketch*, Mary Howitt's title for her translation of the autobiography, which had been published in Germany earlier in the year. On the title page of the English edition, the words "Story of My Life" were deliberately emphasized and magnified, so that the German title's elegant play on the title of Goethe's canonized autobiography *Dichtung und Wahrheit* was considerably subdued.

In this way the clear, concise English title promised much more than it could offer, but that didn't bother Andersen, who was focused on the profits that his works promised to produce in the British Isles. His three novels from the 1830s had already been translated into English, along with the travel book *A Poet's Bazaar* and quite a number of collections of fairy tales. In the year preceding Andersen's visit to England, three translated books of fairy tales had been published, including *Wonderful Stories for Children*. The publisher of this volume was just as busy and market-oriented as the Danish author, whose name appears misspelled on the jacket as "Anderson." The road to applause and fame had once again been paved for the Nordic Andersen, whose greatest wish was to meet another of the great international names of the day: Charles Dickens, or "Boz," as he was called, after the title of his first book. In December 1846, the Danish author wrote to the English author and critic William Jerdan, who was the editor of the *Literary Gazette*. Jerdan had originally introduced Andersen's work to England, and he had many times during the past ten years tried to entice the travel-happy Dane across the Channel.

> "How dearly I wish to shake the Boz's hand! When I read his books, I often think: I've experienced that myself, I could write that! . . . I love England because of its writers! I have long and often felt a yearning to go there."[132]

And Charles Dickens felt the same desire to meet Andersen. Like many Englishmen, he had heard about and read many of the Dane's works: *The Improvisatore*, *A Poet's Bazaar*, and fairy tales such as "The Little Mermaid." He felt a great curiosity to meet a man who like himself was a daydreamer, a man who loved children, the theater, Christmas Eve, traveling, journalism, and reading aloud—as well as big mirrors that stretched from floor to ceiling. "I musch see Andersen!" was what Dickens supposedly said, according to Andersen, who was not very good at speaking or writing the English language.[133] As it turned out, Dickens was not alone with this wish. Andersen had barely registered at his hotel on Leicester Square, which H. C. Ørsted had recommended, before publishers, translators, ministers, diplomats, bankers, newspaper editors, and members of the nobility began flocking to the place and competing for the Dane's attention. Everyone wanted to set up an appointment for the author to make an appearance at their respective social groups. As Dickens mentions in a letter to a friend at that time, it was important to warn the Danish author at once about all the bloodthirsty "Nimrods of London" who would otherwise suffocate the thin and frail writer with etiquette and festivities.[134]

Andersen was in truth the great attraction of the season in London. This was very similar to his previous experiences in Berlin, Weimar, Vienna, and Paris. "One of the Most Remarkable and Interesting Men of His Day," as it said in the city's newspapers, and Andersen instantly reported home to the Collin family: "It's no jest! I am extraordinarily happy! I can't understand it. I am truly famous, more than I myself or Denmark realize."[135]

Foreign Minister Palmerston, Lord Mahon, the duchess of this and the baron of that, along with a steady, jostling stream of upper-class ladies dressed in satin gowns with lace trim and glittering diamonds, surrounded Andersen, twittering their enthusiasm for "The Ugly Duckling," "The Sweethearts," and *The Improvisatore*. For a brief time Andersen was quite dizzy from all the recognition and honors, although it wasn't arrogance but weariness that would eventually make him feel indisposed from joy, as he assured Edvard Collin in a letter sent home to Copenhagen. He had gradually learned how to conduct himself on the polished floors of high society.[136] And during his first week in London, the deeply moved Danish author repeatedly had to offer his thanks for the overwhelming reception and at the same time apologize for his rusty and primitive English: "I can not speake Englisch, bat I hope I scal in a neuw Worck give the Sentiments of my Heart! I thank you!"[137]

Andersen's English must have sounded quite odd, but it looked equally odd when an elderly and extremely rich hostess took the author's hand and kissed it with the words: "I must kiss this precious hand! It has written comfort and joy for so many!" Andersen, who hated to be embraced by mature women, was terror-stricken and confused; he grabbed the woman's free hand and swiftly kissed it eight or ten times. "What was I supposed to do?" as he writes in a letter to Henriette Wulff.[138] On another evening when he had dearly hoped to meet Dickens he was once again confronted with a long line of fawning and fatuous celebrities at a social gathering. The hostess, Lady Duff-Gordon, introduced herself as the daughter of the solicitor John Austin, but Andersen was convinced that she had actually called herself the daughter of Jane Austen.

Charles Dickens quickly heard about all these slightly awkward episodes, the peculiar traits and repeated linguistic errors, as well as the confusing of people and their names. But it only made him all the more eager to meet this Andersen. It was just such an eccentric personality that was needed in the formal and boring salon life of London, according to Dickens and others. Two authors, William Allingham and Leigh Hunt, had paid a call on Andersen at his hotel. Afterwards they touchingly agreed that the Dane, with his long, radiantly innocent face, looked and acted most like an angel. The two young men thought that the Dane's friendliness, intelligence, and naïveté had far outshone all other persons of rank in the hotel lobby.[139] The Scottish author Elizabeth Rigby also had a strong first impression of Andersen: "A tall, gaunt, fleshless man who twisted and bent his body like a lizard with a hollow-cheeked, cadaverous face." She was especially taken with the Dane's innocent radiance and noted in her diary that it wasn't so strange that Andersen found everyone to be friendly: "Any sort of formality rolls right off him, since he quite clearly has a childish disposition."[140]

The will-o'-the-wisp from Denmark had truly arrived in London!

Dickens and Andersen met for the first time on July 16, 1847, at the home of the controversial Lady Blessington. In the 1840s she was well-known, notorious for her exclusive gatherings at Gore House, located in Kensington between Hyde Park Corner and Palace Gate, where the Royal Albert Hall stands today.

Marguerite Blessington had such a tainted reputation among London's fine ladies that it was largely men who attended her celebrated salon, which went under the name of "The Gore House Circle." No British upper-class woman with any respect for herself, her country, and Queen Victoria could justify being caught at that scandal-ridden house where the lady lived in sin with her son-in-law, the handsome Count d'Orsay. Quite unprepared, Andersen had encountered the collective female condemnation of Lady Blessington in London when, a few weeks earlier during a dinner at the home of Lord Stanley, he had spoken with enthusiasm about the visit he had paid that very day to Lady Blessington. She was one of many diligent female novelists of the day, and in literary terms she was most known for her travel book *Conversations with Byron*, which had appeared ten years earlier, in 1834. The book was about her meeting with the great Romantic icon in Genoa in 1823, when Lady Blessington had actually found Lord Byron much less heroic than his myth and reputation would indicate. In fact, she found an extroverted and natural person like Andersen to be far more interesting; it was much easier to exchange literary ideas with him. During an inspection of the various pets of the house, which included several exotic birds, Lady Blessington had lavishly praised *A Poet's Bazaar*, calling it "a treasure of poetry," beyond anything that could be found in many books put together. Oh yes, Andersen liked her, and when Lord Stanley's young sister, who sat next to the Danish author at dinner, heard him speak of the scandalous woman in such exuberant terms, she pursed her lips and gasped: "You visited her?!"

Even though Lady Blessington's name was unwelcome in the finer female circles, intelligent and eloquent celebrities such as Charles Dickens, Bulwer-Lytton, and the poet and politician Benjamin Disraeli were regular guests at Gore House. Others included the leading actors of the day, as well as painters, scientists, and politicians from both England and abroad. And as the grateful Disraeli later wrote about "The Gore House Circle," it was liberating that invitations to Lady Blessington's salons were not issued on the basis of a person's fame or noble standing. Intelligence and talent weighed more heavily. This was also the case on the summer evening in 1847 when the Danish author was the honored guest. At first he was entertained by the stout but elegantly dressed Lady Blessington, who wore sparkling rings on all her fingers and who, in Andersen's opinion, spoke marvelous—and slowly enunciated—English. Then they were joined by her son-in-law and lover, the foppish Count d'Orsay.[141] Shadows of disintegration and exodus were hovering over Gore House when Andersen visited in 1847. There were rumors that Lady Blessington could no longer pay her bills, which had piled up after many years of extravagant entertaining. Rumors of her ladyship's impending financial ruin caused even more old, unpaid bills to pour into Gore House, particularly from the tailor shops on Regent Street, where Count d'Orsay—"The Dandy of Dandies," as he was called—had shopped like a sultan for years. It's not surprising that Andersen, during his stay in London, came up with the idea for a fairy tale about high social rank, with the working title "It Has to Be Grand." Without fully realizing how bad the situation was, Andersen noted that at Lady Blessington's Gore House everyone was so distinguished and French that all the servants powdered their hair. Special lighting had also been arranged around a life-sized portrait of Napoleon, who almost looked as if he were hanging inside a halo.

In *The Fairy Tale of My Life*, Andersen describes the occasion as an unforgettable moment when he and Dickens finally met at the home of Lady Blessington on that summer evening in 1847. Like Count d'Orsay, Andersen was dressed in his finest dandy attire: light-colored trousers and a frock coat, a tall silk hat on his curled and pomaded hair. Charles Dickens wore a black velvet jacket, and in honor of the occasion he had brushed his mop of hair forward over his temples. Oh yes, the two authors and "Fashionables" were certainly the center of the gathering. Both had a penchant for ostentatious silk scarves with diamond stick-pins and gold watch chains with all kinds of fobs, as well as gloves cut in the latest Parisian fashion. At dinner, the Dane was flanked by London's post-master and a woman he thought to be Lady Blessington's stepdaughter. Across from Andersen sat a son of the Duke of Wellington. The Danish author was just writing a few eloquent words in *The True Story of My Life* for his hostess when Charles Dickens came in. Andersen recorded the entire situation and mood in his diary when he came home after his visit to Gore House:

> "We shook hands, looked each other in the eye, spoke, understood one another, and out on the veranda tears came to my eyes as we talked. At the dinner table Count Dorsai proposed that Dickens and I join him in a toast, along with Wellington. After dinner Dickens suggested that we meet at his house on August 1."[142]

Yet Andersen and Dickens never managed to get to know each other very well in 1847. They were both much too busy for that. The restless Dickens rushed between his various residences in London and outside the city, devoting himself to his diverse author and publisher activities and his many social and political engagements. For this reason, the meeting he had arranged with Andersen on August 1 had to be canceled. For his part,

Andersen was also very busy, and he described his overbooked calendar in a letter to the Collin family back home in Copenhagen:

> "I have invitations for today and for the next two weeks; dinner from 8 o'clock to 11, and from 11:30 into the early morning hours; I can't endure it! I'm about to drown; people inundate me with invitations and requests for my autograph."[143]

At the same time Andersen was sitting for several painters and sculptors including Joseph Durham, who in Andersen's opinion had created an "incomparably handsome" bust of him. His later plans for his sojourn in Great Britain included an excursion to Scotland with the Danish-born banker Joseph Hambro, whose son had invited Andersen to stay at his home in Edinburgh. All in all, there was no time for the Danish author and Dickens to meet, but as a sort of compensation, the English writer sent a large package to the Hotel Sablonière in London. It contained twelve marvelously bound volumes of stories by Dickens, with the even more marvelous dedication: "To Hans Christian Andersen from his Friend and Admirer, Charles Dickens." The Danish author was in seventh heaven and hastily wrote a thank-you letter to Dickens, which was repeated when he returned from Scotland at the end of August with the idea that on his way home to the Continent he might drop by to visit the Dickens family. They had a summer residence in Broadstairs, which was on the way to Ramsgate and the steamship to Ostende. There was just one problem, however, and that was the letter to Dickens in which Andersen wanted to invite himself. The confounded English language once again caused him problems, but determination can conquer anything, and the letter was duly sent off:

> "My dear dear Dickens! to morrow I shall kome to Ramsgate, I hope you will giw yours Adresse in the Royal Oak Hotel, where I shall remane till the next morning, when I shall go by the stamboat to Ostende. I must see you and thank you; that is the last flower for me in dear England!"[144]

Andersen's trip to England in the summer of 1847 was extremely successful. As he wrote to Edvard Collin, he was now such a famous author that even the British aristocracy, which normally didn't socialize with writers, had welcomed him. They even found the Dane's terrible English "charming." At least for the most part. At one of the big dinner parties an English lady had thrown herself at the enchanting "Anderson," but quickly had to switch over to elementary Italian in the hope of understanding what the Dane was saying.

She knew that he had been to Italy and even written a novel about the country where lemons grow. But it ended up being a brief conversation since the elegant lady couldn't understand Andersen's Italian any better than his English.

Andersen went astray not only in the language but also in the big city, if we're to believe a good story that came from the Collin family. Having gotten lost before, the Danish author one day approached an English constable to ask how to find his way back to the hotel on "Laster Square," as he called Leicester Square. Andersen showed the policeman a little note on which was written the name of a major street near the hotel that he had copied from a sign on the wall of the building. Unfortunately, it wasn't a street sign that Andersen had focused on but a warning not to put placards on the wall: "Post no bills!" The constable took the peculiar stranger along to the station and wouldn't let him go until the Danish Consul appeared and assured him that the man was quite sane.[145]

But the traveling author couldn't be anyone other than himself, whether in writing or in the spoken language. Andersen never became the sort of linguist who looked up words in the dictionary before daring to speak. He made only modest and superficial linguistic preparations for his new, great journeys through different cultures. Andersen had neither the time nor the patience to sit down and spend a month or two during the winter learning vocabulary or grammar. The language, like everything else on his travels, would just have to develop as he went. Consequently, Andersen's use of the spoken language in the various cultures he visited was both spontaneous and impulsive. In a sense, he was like the little child who always manages to chatter and play with his peers and like-minded children from entirely different linguistic regions. Gestures and mimicking were the main ingredients in the Danish author's international communication. Confronted with even the most unfamiliar and difficult of languages, Andersen was always ready to make his way by improvising. Like poetry, language had more to do with emotion than with reason, and that was why, as he said, it was guided to a higher degree by "the embraces of Aphrodite than the raised finger of Else Schoolmistress." Andersen had particularly learned this during his travels to England and Scotland in 1847, and that's what his standard greeting dealt with in various English guestbooks and albums:

> When the door of language sometimes told me: "Stop!"
> Your eye was the key that opened it up.
>
> In a foreign tongue the song may flee,
> But hear in the heartbeat its melody.[146]

For Andersen it was the very cadence and rhythm of the language that was much more important than any polished, cautious precision. And in a letter to the Collin family from London he said: "I now speak quite a brisk English, utterly wrong, of course, but they understand me and even praise my pronunciation!"[147] What the kind and courteous English were actually thinking behind their cultivated facades when the Danish author rolled out his bizarre, childish mixture of English, German, French, and Danish didn't become fully evident until Andersen's second visit to London ten years later. We'll return to this in the next chapter.

At the end of August 1847, at the home of the hospitable Dickens family, which was swarming with children, everything was still quite idyllic, and no one made faces at the guest's extraordinary language. The family was staying at a small summer residence down by the shore. From the dining room they had a view of the Channel, and here, in the comfortable Dickens home, Andersen ended his English adventure. Father, mother, and children were all sitting at the table when he arrived, and they immediately invited him into their circle. The Dickens family was an exemplary model, and something of an ideal of the Victorian age. All the children kissed the Danish author except for the youngest boy, who preferred to kiss his own hand. The patriarch's dynamic, masculine presence bewitched Andersen, who described him as "youthful, handsome, with a wise and kind expression and beautiful thick hair." The two authors shook hands and agreed to correspond in the future. Dickens was so interested in his Nordic connection that he now wanted to start learning German and, with time, even Danish. When Andersen departed from England early the next morning, Dickens accompanied him to the wharf at Ramsgate, dressed in a green kilt and multicolored shirt—"quite posh," as a gushing Andersen writes in his diary on August 31, 1847:

> "As the ship slipped out of the harbor, I saw Dickens at the outermost point; I thought he had long since gone. He swung his hat and finally raised one hand up toward the sky; I wonder if that meant: we won't see each other again until up there?"[148]

This first brief meeting of the two authors resulted in a sporadic but heartfelt correspondence over the next ten years, in which they took turns showering each other with compliments and loving words. Dickens conveyed to Andersen how beloved he was among his children, and he urged the Dane to return to England soon, inviting him to stay for a longer period as a guest in the bosom of his family. Yet, as mentioned, ten years would pass before Andersen accepted the offer, and by then much had changed.

Distant Political Clouds

When Hans Christian Andersen returned home in September 1847 after having spent a short but intense week among his male friends in Weimar, he received a strangely cold welcome in Copenhagen. While he was traveling, the writers of the publication *Corsaren* had mocked their famous compatriot's latest conquests and fine new friends in Europe. Under the headline "Andersen the Lion," the journal had printed a drawing of a ridiculous-looking author wearing a laurel wreath and a badge of chivalry in the midst of a swarm of admiring women. But others were also quick to offer comments that were meant to remind Andersen that the author—as he himself identified the core of this scorn and criticism—was only "a third-rate writer after Herz the classic, and Heiberg the infallible!"[149] And more of the same followed as soon as he arrived back home. Andersen had barely unpacked on one of the first days after his return when he saw from his window facing Kongens Nytorv that two well-dressed gentlemen down on the street had stopped and were pointing up at his windows, shouting: "Will you look at that—there stands our world-famous orangutan!"

As the year waned, Andersen suffered even more blows. *Corsaren* followed up its September article with another satirical broadside when Andersen published in December a so-called world drama under the title *Ahasuerus*. In the author's own words, the drama was about "the human race, which repudiates the divine and yet moves toward perfection and awareness." Andersen received a stream of negative reactions to the play from all those who were usually quite kindly disposed toward his work. But it's true that this "world drama" was a monstrosity of an evolutionary story that hadn't been terribly accessible even in the handwritten manuscript. Andersen had been wrestling with it for several years, and he had once again convinced Edvard Collin to make a clean copy of it in the eleventh hour. Yet Edvard couldn't refrain from stating, with wry humor, that although the play might be immortal, it could hardly be read by any mortals but himself. One problem was the jumbled contents, which made the figure of Ahasuerus look like a custodian in a museum, said Edvard; quite another matter was the form of the play and the countless failed rhymes and meters: "These four-verse rhymes of two syllables are among the least aesthetic I've ever encountered."[150]

Even a literary giant such as Adam Oehlenschläger rushed to his inkwell in December 1847 when he read *Ahasuerus*, which made an "unpleasant and confusing" impression on this Nestor of Romanticism in Denmark. For someone who had made a thorough and faithful study of world history and not merely skated over its top, there was no pleasure in seeing the great figures of history appear as elves, swallows, nightingales and mermaids. Oehlenschläger's condemnation was crystal clear: "Too much pretension and too little achievement in this work." This was a harsh and bitter critique in the midst of the Christmas peace on earth, which not even the usually so kind and gentle B. S. Ingemann could sweeten, since in his Christmas letter he delivered his own negative opinion of *Ahasuerus*.

And as 1848 began, Andersen had to come to the somber conclusion that life in Denmark was still not a bit pleasant; his seven lucrative years abroad looked as if they would be followed by seven lean ones. This year that Andersen would later call "the volcano year" had barely begun before Christian VIII died, the February Revolution broke out in Paris, the Republic was proclaimed, the French king was forced to abdicate, and the popular rebellion spread like wildfire to Austria and Germany and all of the duchies. The fraternal, harmonious world order that reigned within Andersen became dangerously threatened when the disturbances reached Copenhagen in March. The absolute monarchy was abolished on March 21 after a peaceful revolution in Copenhagen, during which the new King Frederik VII had wisely dismissed his ministers. And to the jubilation of the populace, several days later he also rejected the demands of Slesvig-Holsten for a free constitution and Slesvig's absorption into the German federation. The feeling of nationalism could not be quelled and was strongly voiced in the streets of Copenhagen.

But Andersen was not very happy about all these new liberal, nationalistic ideas, and particularly not about the threat of war. A month earlier he had received the Swedish-Norwegian "Order of the North Star" from King Oscar I, and an equally distinguished honor from the Grand Duke in Weimar. But neither of these awards could subdue the smoldering sense of anxiety and uneasiness that the author was feeling. What good was a king's surrender of his sovereignty? And why did the people so readily want to relinquish something as reassuring as a strong paternal monarch? The nation's violent behavior did not fit with a belief in all that was good and healthy in the human being, as Andersen had just depicted it in *Ahasuerus*. It was one thing for a citizen of Fyn or Copenhagen to have difficulty understanding a snobbish Englishman, but it was quite a different matter and far more serious when entire nations no longer understood each other and now took up arms. "All strife is an estrangement from God," Andersen wrote in a letter to Henriette Wulff in September 1848, adding: "How blessed it is for nations to understand each other; I don't mean in terms of language but in terms of temperament . . . Yet when will we all understand each other? . . . This past year has been remarkably instructive."[151]

While his other male friends—Henrik Stampe, Vilhelm Pedersen, Valdemar Drewsen, Theodor Collin, and the brothers Christian and Peter Wulff—took up arms and headed for the front in southern Jutland, Andersen settled for taking up his pen, diary, and hatbox and heading for Fyn. At the Glorup estate, he was a comfortably strategic distance from the war. From sufficient safety it was possible to hear the distant thunder of cannons from the front and enjoy the sight of the handsome Swedish soldiers who had set up camp on the estate grounds. Large numbers of fresh reserve troops had thrown themselves on short notice into the battle on the Danish side against the more than 20,000 Prussians and residents of Slesvig-Holsten, who had crossed the border into Jutland in early May. Beyond the din of war—out in nature—everything was the same as usual. The elder tree bloomed, fresh and beautiful, the stork clacked from its nest, and the forest birds sang as if nothing had happened. To Henriette Wulff, whose brothers were at the front, Andersen wrote:

> "If I were cut from a different cloth than I am, I would join in, but I'm not suited to all that. You smile! But I assure you, I would not run from the enemy, though I would be afraid, terribly afraid, but keep in mind that to be afraid is not cowardice; the former you cannot control, the latter depends on our will!"[152]

As proof of this, in April 1848 Andersen threw himself into a very courageous peace mission, which on paper would illustrate the author's words that great deeds in a time of war do not reside solely in the stroke of the sword. His letter to the rest of Europe was not only a defense of Denmark's cause but also a brave attempt to use ordinary common sense and a neighborly spirit to press for peace and understanding all across Europe. Andersen's peace dove, as he recounts in his memoirs, came about at the request of "one of our fine government officials." Men with great political influence who were close to the Danish king felt that it would be beneficial if an internationally respected Dane, who was also the epitome of innocence and pacifism, should speak on behalf of the country. The fairy-tale author, who had been much discussed and cultivated in large parts of the Continent during the 1840s, was perfect for this mission. Hans Christian Andersen both understood and accepted the diplomatic challenge, even though political programs and watchwords had never been nor ever would be of particular interest to him. "I'll stick to my Creator and not to politics!" as it was blatantly expressed in the comedy *Herr Rasmussen* in 1846. These words also applied to Andersen.

His peace letter began with the words "Dear Friend," since it was originally formulated as a personal letter to the editor of the *Literary Gazette*, William Jerdan, whom Andersen had met the year before in London. And the wording was sufficiently general, without losing the galvanizing nature of its rallying cry, that it could easily be dispatched to a number of magazines and newspapers throughout Europe. The letter was certainly patriotic, but the tone was remarkably controlled and pragmatic. And in closing his letter, Andersen demonstrated a rhetorical stroke of genius by stepping away from the Danish flag and transforming himself into a European with a capital "E." In this manner he also acknowledged his unshakable faith in the intercultural community of the Continent. The way to achieve the goal was—as Andersen the peace activist so admirably showed—to call the enemy to order in a gentle, unwarlike manner:

> "'To the nationalities their rights, to the clever and good all success!' This is and must be Europe's solution, and with this I see hope for progress. The Germans are an honest, truth-loving people; they will come to understand the conditions up here, and their bitterness will and must be transformed to deep respect and friendship; if only this idea will occur soon! May God allow His face to shine over the countries!"[153]

As soon as the letter was sent off, Andersen went to Glorup, where, as at so many other Danish estates, he felt "so marvelously liberated from the pressures of Copenhagen." A week later he writes in a letter to Henriette Wulff: "I've been here a week now and have once again settled into myself."[154] All his life Andersen had the remarkable ability to seek deep inside himself, to shut out the rest of the world, and to forget even the greatest revolutions and social upheavals on the planet to focus instead on things close at hand. B. S. Ingemann often envied this ability of his to repress all manner of misfortunes and worries and instead concentrate on threads and grains of sand in his own mind. Ingemann called Andersen a very happy person who was capable of "dwelling in the peace of writing in the midst of this time of struggle and rebellion, while the tension of the moment tightens every nerve and sharpens every thought to bayonets and spears!"[155]

In the summer of 1848 Glorup was practically the perfect residence for Andersen, with its blessed peace and quiet of the early morning hours and then the frenzied military atmosphere during the course of the day, when there was plenty to see and hear. For example, Andersen's attention was caught by "a particularly handsome lieutenant colonel," as well as by many dramatic accounts of death and wounding at the front. Even on his way to Fyn, the author had met in the coach a bookseller who had fled Slesvig and could report on "piles of corpses" that lay naked and plundered along the Dannevirke, the ancient earthworks protecting southern Jutland. Andersen diligently made note of everything he heard of this kind. He had put behind him the political aspects of war with his peace letter. What interested him now was the physical depiction of the pain and suffering of war. The author of "Thumbelina" wanted to know all the details of such things as what it looked like when a man was shot in the groin and with "a convulsively contorted expression lay with the grass clenched in his teeth." And he noted in his diary how it smelled at the field hospitals, how the soldiers with huge wounds in the lower part of their body had to let the excrement run out of their sides. About the painter Johan Thomas Lundbye, who had fallen at the front, Andersen heard during his stay at Glorup that most of his head had been shattered by German bullets. The painter was promptly immortalized in the author's diary with the words:

> "We heard the shot and saw Lumby plunge to the ground, shot through the jaw from below, his mouth split apart and a piece of bearded flesh shot off. He uttered a couple of faint sighs; was wrapped in the Dannebrog flag and placed in the earth."[156]

In the midst of this desire to experience the bestiality of war at close quarters as depicted in Andersen's diary from the summer of 1848, we also find the author's childish heroic deeds amid the daily life on the grounds of the estate. He notes on May 23 that today he had "rescued an earthworm that had been caught by a beetle." That's how different the human beings on Mother Earth are. And that's how the middle-aged author could, at any time, become a boy again on the island of his childhood, where even the most evil day in his life might be given an optimistic glow:

"I live in nature, which I examine in every detail; riding and walking with the Swedes and perceiving these souls; this is—in addition to the pleasures of good food and drink—my only occupation, but it's not a question of idling, I give myself good days, just as the man gave his sow bacon, and they [good times] will come again!"[157]

Chapter Eight

The Path from Nature to God (1850-1860)

"And after we eat, Andersen will no doubt read for us!" says the ailing H. C. Ørsted with a cough. As always on Wednesday, Hans Christian Andersen has been invited to supper and a social gathering at the professor's home on Studiestræde. And for once they don't serve him fruit soup. Fru Ørsted seems to think this is the author's favorite dish, even though the warm, syrupy soup makes him terribly anxious and later in the evening, after the theater lets out, he always has to have a plate of open-faced sandwiches to calm his nerves.

But today Andersen's uneasiness is solely due to Ørsted's condition. The old man is sitting up in bed. His toupee looks worn, his face is no longer full, and his eyes squint more than ever. But there's nothing wrong with the spirit of this "professor extraordinarius." Even the greatest misanthrope has to give in and believe in human beings and eternal life when he meets the seventy-three-year-old man who thinks that the vexing inflammation in his lung is merely something that has to be endured. Then the physicist will get back to all his numerous projects between heaven and earth. First and foremost, he wants to move all his furniture, collections, and instruments out to the honorary royal residence "Fasangaarden" in Frederiksberg Gardens, which he has recently taken over from the author Adam Oehlenschläger. It was a family birthday celebration on the preceding Saturday that forced Ørsted to take to his bed. Early on Sunday morning after the party, with insufficient sleep but filled with great ideas, he sat down in his ice-cold work room to continue writing his new book, The Path from Nature to God. Later that day he grew feverish, and in the evening Dr. Fenger arrived and immediately ordered the professor to bed. When Andersen hastily says his goodbyes on Wednesday evening to rush off to his reserved seat at the theater, Ørsted whispers that he has decided to get out of bed on Sunday, at the latest.

But on Sunday, March 9, 1851, H. C. Ørsted is unable to get up for anyone but God. Andersen is hastily summoned to the deathbed early in the morning. The moon is still hovering, big and full, above the slumbering city when he dashes down Østergade and Nørregade to Studiestræde, where Ørsted's wife Birgitte and a couple of the children have gathered in the dimly lit sickroom around the "beloved and glorious Ørsted," as Andersen calls this paternal mentor in his life. Just as little children believe that their parents will remain forever young and immortal, Andersen has never imagined that Ørsted would die—and certainly not before he did. That's why he has to be alone with his grief after he ascertains that Ørsted's body is just resting, and his spirit is not yet ready to depart. Instead of going downstairs to join the other friends of the family who have gathered on the second floor of the professor's home, he locks himself into the next-door rooms. He tiptoes around in the cold, empty apartment, where he has so often read aloud, discussed, made paper-cuts, sung, and decorated the Christmas tree with Ørsted. Now the human sounds have ceased, yet it's said that wherever a great man has lived and worked, that place becomes a part of him. The same must be true of Ørsted. If the memory of him and his home is shattered, the smallest piece of him will still, like a magnet, possess the strength of the whole. Above the sofa and coffee table in the center of one wall hangs Eckersberg's old portrait of the middle-aged, slightly stout physicist in white tie and tails. Yet the distinct harmony of the portrait cannot soothe Andersen's uneasiness and anxiety. He has to get out of these death-consecrated rooms, out to the open spaces of the city and walk off his fear.

His brisk promenade through the city soon takes him in the direction of Amaliegade, where Edvard and old Jonas Collin, thank God, happen to be at home. Here Andersen calms down a bit, and by dinnertime he feels so composed that he can once again return to the university building on Studiestræde. At Kongens Nytorv he runs into Carl Holten, who is doctor of mathematics at the Polytechnical Institute and one of Ørsted's research assistants. The polite author, as usual, doesn't make do with merely tipping his top hat, but takes it off with a sweeping, festive flourish. The mathematician is more reserved. With a curt and swift movement, he presses his hat to his chest and reports that Ørsted is dead.

THE PROFESSOR'S RESIDENCE on Studiestræde was not the only place in the city where death came knocking in early March 1851. Less than twenty-four hours after attending his last Wednesday supper at the home of H. C. Ørsted, another close friend of Andersen's passed away. The wife of the composer J. P. E. Hartmann had died, and during the course of that Thursday, Andersen made several visits to their home, partly to offer his condolences, partly to have one last look at the composer's wife. For a week the author, dressed in mourning attire, took turns visiting the Hartmann and Ørsted households. And as if this demonstration of the conditions of life wasn't enough, Hartmann's five-year-old daughter died of meningitis on the very day that her mother was to be buried. Once again Andersen had to offer his condolences, view the deceased one last time, and try to understand this unfair deprivation of life at such a young age. Andersen thought that in spite of the waxen face, the thin arms, the purplish breast, and the hands with the tiny black fingernails, little Maria still looked like an angel in her coffin. Every detail of her cold, stiff body was precisely fixed in the author's mind and then meticulously and unsentimentally entered into his diary, where Andersen also reported on the double gravesite:

> "Today little Maria was buried at 12 o'clock; shortly before that I went over to the open grave; it was close to her mother's and one whole side of her coffin was put inside there; one of the wreaths hung so fresh inside the child's grave."[1]

The despair was evident in Andersen's diary and letters during this period, and it became concentrated in terse, desperate exclamations such as: "They're all going away—All of them! All of them!" For a couple of weeks he was paralyzed, living in a daze, while coffins, hearses, condolences, black attire, mourning crepe, hymns, graveside ceremonies, and flower wreaths streamed through his mind along with all the dear memories and the great processions of mourners, who were not all equally considerate. H. C. Ørsted's magnificent funeral was held at Vor Frue Kirke [Church of Our Lady] on March 18, 1851, after the university students and polytechnical teachers had carried his coffin through the city, followed by members of the royal family and the government. An elderly county manager, whom Andersen knew from his visits to the estates of southern Jutland, stopped the author to point out that he had now lost a father. Only old Jonas Collin was left, said the man. This simple summing up hadn't yet occurred to Andersen. With Ørsted's death he had not only lost a loyal and trustworthy father figure, but also a source of spiritual inspiration, a man who was filled with deep and genuine respect for the author. This was something that he had never experienced to any comparable degree with the Collin family, who often preferred instead to sow doubt about everything in which Andersen believed. At Ørsted's home, Andersen's visits were almost always festive occasions, during which they all allowed themselves to be carried away with enthusiasm, without reservation or skepticism.

Even though Andersen, during the 1850s and 1860s, adjusted and varied his poetics with regard to Ørsted's ideas about "the spirit in nature," as we shall see at the end of this chapter, the author still never deviated

from his view of what the Romantic scientist had meant for the development of his life and work. And his memory of Ørsted never became
obscured by the pathos and sentimentality to which Andersen was so
prone whenever his elegant and distinguished circle of friends was to be
smartened up and presented in his autobiographies, alongside all of his
awards. Without any sort of evasion, H. C. Ørsted is portrayed in
Andersen's memoirs as "the friend who, in the struggles and trials of my
spirit, most supported me." This was an exemplary and clear statement,
and when Andersen was himself an old and wise man, he further emphasized the importance of their relationship: "Ørsted is undoubtedly the
man whom I have loved most."[2]

Not even Jonas Collin, who died ten years later, in 1861, held such an
elevated position in Andersen's consciousness as Ørsted did. And of all the
many important men the fairy-tale author knew and over time became
indebted to, the physicist was the only one with whom Andersen, in his
own teasing manner, was on a familiar first-name basis. He liked to call the
two of them "Little Hans Christian" and "Big Hans Christian." But he
never let there be any doubt about who was the "Big Hans Christian" in
this role-playing. It was Ørsted.

In short, the spring of 1851 was a sorrowful time. Andersen, like other
people, should actually have been celebrating the peace after the three-
year-war had finally ended and the country had gained a new, democratic
constitution. The "Constitution of June 5, 1849" laid the broad foundation
for the development of a new society, built on the participatory right of
the populace, in which free competition and the forces of the marketplace
were to serve as the basis for trade and production. In 1848 the old view
of society had been shaken everywhere in Europe, and class consciousness
had been given a new and stronger voice. The old faith in authority, which
had kept the people oppressed for centuries, was on the verge of collapsing.
Andersen looked on with growing uneasiness and fear from his bourgeois
side of the barricades, deciding to focus his attention on rediscovering the
spiritual dimension that was necessary for him to complete the many literary projects he had under way in 1851. First and foremost was a book
about his three-month journey through Sweden in the summer of 1849,
which had taken longer than expected and wasn't finished until after H. C.
Ørsted's death. The book, which was titled *In Sweden*, became to a large
extent an homage to H. C. Ørsted.

At regular intervals during the 1840s, Ørsted had urged Andersen to write a treatise on fairy tales, which the author now attempted to insert into one of the most bombastic chapters of this travel book. It was given the title "A Sermon in Nature." Yet it had certainly not been created while Andersen sat on his Scottish blanket out in Swedish nature; rather, he wrote it at a desk in the warmth of his rooms at the Glorup estate and in the Nyhavn district of Copenhagen, where he had now moved. Here the author had dreamed of what he calls "The California of Poetry," meaning a gold mine of writing in the midst of nature and in the present moment. To be precise, it dealt with using the many scientific discoveries of the era in a poetic sense. It meant seeing the universal and timeless beauty in the shiny, turning wheels of machinery, in steam power, in the hovering hot-air balloons, and in the silent humming of the telegraph cables down at the bottom of the world's oceans. Andersen's literary manifesto in the year 1851 was utterly devoid of political slogans; on the other hand, it showed the very strong influence of H. C. Ørsted's great work *The Spirit in Nature*, which was published in 1849-50. The old physicist's book was an attempt to penetrate the meaning behind everything—the "universal reason," as he called it. And so, after many minor attempts, Andersen finally, during the last years of Ørsted's life, threw himself into the fierce debate over the relationship between faith and knowledge, as Ørsted's book had expressed it.

The Spirit in Nature was H. C. Ørsted's scientific testament. For Hans Christian Andersen, who, ever since his early childhood days back in Odense, had teetered between faith and knowledge, Ørsted's work was no less than a bible. This was documented in the author's profoundly grateful letter to the scientist sent in August 1850 when Andersen was at Glorup and scribbling away on his book *In Sweden*. He would take long breaks at the quiet estate to read *The Spirit in Nature*. Certain sections of the book seemed like a mirror in which time after time he caught sight of new truths about himself, his writing, and the relationship between art and nature:

> "It's like one rich stream; and what especially pleases me is that here I seem to see only my own idea, the one that I previously didn't fully see myself. It's my faith, my conviction that is presented to me in clear words . . . I am pleased by your book, pleased with myself too, and it's so easy to read that it almost seems to me to be the result of my own thinking. While reading it, I feel as if I could say: 'Yes, that's what I would have said!' The truth in it has entered into me and become part of myself."[3]

The close relationship between Ørsted and Andersen, which lasted more than thirty years, had its roots in the scientist's first encounters with the very young author, who came knocking on the doors of the Copenhagen bourgeoisie around 1820. The forty-two-year-old physicist, who had recently become world-famous for his discovery of electromagnetism, immediately won the ear of young Andersen. With his great knowledge and sense of curiosity, not only for the sciences but also for art, philosophy, and questions of morality and ethics, Ørsted was an intellectual powerhouse who was uniquely qualified to see the valuable naïveté in the talented, uneducated boy who kept showing up to receive a meal, a *skilling* or two, and to borrow books from the professor's well-stocked library. Ørsted's inquisitive, wide-ranging desire to approach the incomprehensible had led him to the discovery of electromagnetism. And it was this same curiosity and desire that prompted the physicist in the 1820s to let Andersen know that he was always welcome and could count on assistance and support from his family. The relationship between the two men began to develop in earnest after Andersen returned to the capital, finished his exams, and suddenly was faced with deciding whether to choose the path of a writer or an academic.

The Modern Breakthrough During the Golden Age

H. C. Ørsted's view of science and his teachings about "the spirit in nature" were based largely on the belief that there is a correspondence between the natural laws of existence and the thoughts of human beings. Here we find the basis for Ørsted's unflagging interest in Hans Christian Andersen, who became the physicist's ambassador in the world of literature. Quite simply, Ørsted envisioned that Andersen's fairy tales would contribute to creating a popular bridge between art and science, between faith and knowledge. Andersen's novel *To Be or Not to Be*, published six years after his mentor's death in 1857, is structured as a gentle rebellion against Ørsted's teachings. In this book, remnants and echoes can be heard of the old scientist's doctrines:

> "I am convinced that in our time, under the whirring of the turning wheels of machinery, the roar of steam, and the whole tumult, a new hero of literature will step forward, and in the very spirit of science."

28. It was in the summer of 1842 that Andersen began writing a fairy tale with the working title "The Cygnet" while staying in southern Sjælland at the Gisselfeld and Bregentved estates (the latter depicted here). The author regarded Bregentved as a fairy grotto where he could find peace from outside criticism, a refuge where he could take walks, pick flowers, and create flower arrangements.

29, 30. At left is the low, yellow house in Odense at the corner of Hans Jensens Stræde and Bangs Boder, which has been known as "Hans Christian Andersen's House" for the past century. By all accounts, the author was born in this house, although he never lived there during his childhood. The house we hear so much about in the author's childhood memoirs stands on Munkemøllestræde (*below*), on the slope leading down to the Odense River and Munke Mill. The small, low-ceilinged building housed three families with numerous children in three one-room apartments. Shoemaker Andersen, his wife, and son lived in the room on the right. Today the house is a museum.

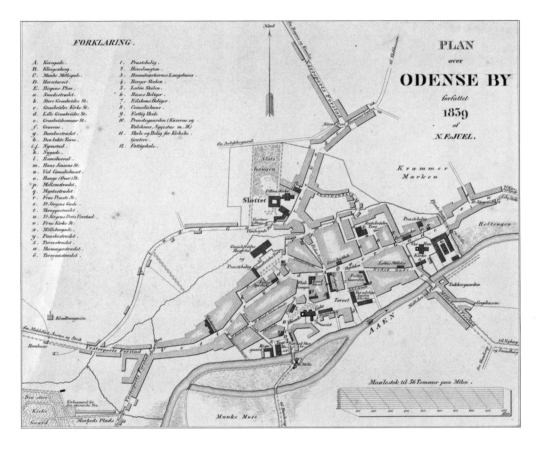

31. In 1805, the year of Andersen's birth, Odense was the second largest city in Denmark. It was a provincial town with six town gates; six market squares; three churches; 40 streets of varying size; 1,100 farms and houses; and approximately 6,000 citizens, half of whom belonged to the lower class, while one-tenth were without any means of support. The castle and its grounds formed the northern boundary of the city; the river was to the south. Visible at the bottom of the map is the mill, and directly across from it is Munkemøllestræde. The river followed a different course and was more powerful than it is today.

32. When the fourteen-year-old Hans Christian Andersen went out into the world in 1819, a fortuneteller predicted that Odense would one day be "lit up" in his honor. On December 6, 1867, the author was awarded a certificate, depicted here, making him an honorary citizen of Odense. And in the evening he was celebrated with an enormous torchlight procession that made its way through the city streets to the courthouse, where the prodigal son stood at the open windows on the second floor to witness the city's tribute.

33. The Ørsted family, gathered in 1849 on the occasion of Fru Birgitte Ørsted's 60th birthday. H. C. Ørsted and his wife are seated in front, flanked by their daughter Sophie—with whom Andersen had been slightly infatuated in the late 1830s—and Ørsted's brother, Anders Sandøe Ørsted. Behind are Ørsted's sons, sons-in-law, and daughter Karen.

34. At the Maxen estate in Dresden, Hans Christian Andersen found a second home during the 1850s with the hospitable and generous Serre family. The large estate included a number of factories and workshops, as well as a marble quarry, which was the owner's major source of income. In the upper right corner of the illustration is the mosque that the Javanese prince was allowed to build, and below is the tree that Andersen planted on the grounds.

35. Franz Liszt was one of the great musical innovators of the 19th century. From 1850 until 1860 Andersen repeatedly visited Weimar and spent time with Liszt and his mistress Princess Wittgenstein. During that decade the popular concert pianist created some of his most important works. The illustration shows a music autograph from Liszt which Andersen had pasted into his large album.

Nemorino.

Una furtiva lagrima
Negli occhi suoi spuntò.
Quelle festose giovani
Invidiar sembrò
Che poi cercando io vo.
M'ama? sì m'ama, lo spero.
Un solo istante i palpiti
Del suo bel cuor sentir,
I miei sospir confondere
Per poco co' suoi sospir.
Cielo! si può morir—di più non chiedo.

36. Andersen's interest in the psychological studies of his day is revealed in this collage from *Agnete Lind's Picture Book* from the 1850s. A man with two pairs of spectacles is studying a profile that resembles Andersen's own. The throat is furnished as a writing room for a scribe. And the pattern of the brain is a paper-cut with 32 tiny faces, corresponding to the total number of points on contemporary phrenology charts.

37. Wilhelm von Kaulbach's painting based on Andersen's fairy tale "The Angel" became enormously popular in the 19th century. The painting was often back-ordered at Kaulbach's studio in Munich; lithographic and photographic reproductions were also made. Andersen had few greater joys than encountering "The Angel" in some remote corner of Europe. "That painting has become for me 'the red thread' for my fame as a writer," he wrote in a letter.

38. ABOVE: Gads Hill in Highham near Rochester, the home of Charles Dickens. Andersen stayed with the family during June and July in 1857, and ended up being a most unwelcome guest.

39. LEFT: Charles Dickens, reading aloud to his two daughters, Mammie (Mary) and Katie (Kate), who lived with their father after their mother, Catherine Dickens, left the family and Gads Hill in 1857. It was Katie who called Andersen "a bony bore," after he finally departed.

40. Two odd characters on their way home from Spain in 1862, photographed here in Bordeaux. Andersen was annoyed at both the cost of the trip and Jonas Collin's caustic nature.

41, 42. Harald Scharff (at left in both photos) and Lauritz Eckardt were both regulars in the Copenhagen theater world, performing as a ballet dancer and actor, respectively. They were often seen walking arm in arm down the street, and here, for the photographer, they assumed the poses of an engaged couple.

43. Hans Christian Andersen's travels were also forays through various languages. In 1860, when Andersen was staying at Madame Orchard's pension in Geneva, an alert boy by the name of Frederick P. Henry sat at the dinner table every day. He never forgot the sociable Dane, and as an old man he recounted how Andersen would lead, or rather monopolize, the conversation at the table, though none of the guests objected. The author's speech was a peculiar mixture of English, French, and German, with a touch of Danish thrown in now and then. Yet he illustrated everything with expressive gestures so that no one had any trouble understanding him. One day Andersen announced that he would be away for a short time, and when someone asked when he would return, he replied: "*Ich reviendrai torsdag!*"

44, 45. Andersen posed
for these photographs in
March 1866, on his way
to Portugal. He was very
pleased with the pictures
and wrote home to
Edvard Collin that there
was something about his
profile that was reminiscent
of Schiller's portrait.

46, 47. Four panels
of the folding screen
on which Andersen
created a collage of
his life. The panels
depict "Childhood,"
"The Theater, "
"England," and
"The Orient."

CHILDHOOD   THE THEATER

ENGLAND   THE ORIENT

48. "Andersen, he's a genius. / It comes out in his paper-cuts!" he once wrote to a young friend. This is especially evident in this large paper-cut given to Fru Melchior in 1874. Here we find a wide selection of the author's characteristic figures, motifs, and symbols.

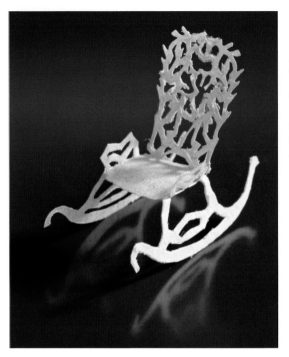

49. With a relatively big pair of scissors Andersen was able to cut out tiny paper sculptures, like this inviting rocking chair, which is small enough to fit in a matchbox.

50. Holsteinborg near Skælskør was one of Andersen's favorite Danish estates. Here he spent many summers during the last twenty years of his life, writing fairy tales and collecting rare snails for Jonas Collin, his young zoologist friend in Copenhagen.

51. "I sit like a condemned prisoner who expects any day to be taken out to his execution," wrote Hans Christian Andersen in his diary in September 1873. To the young Nicolai Bøgh, who that same year was the author's last traveling companion, he boasted that all the seasons of the year were represented on his windowsills at Nyhavn 18: "So I sit down next to whatever season I'm in the mood for, and that's amusing."

52, 53. During the last decade of his life, Andersen spent more time with the Melchior family than with the Collins. The wholesaler Moritz G. Melchior and his wife, Fru Dorothea, generously opened their wealthy home to the author. In the winter he would join the family for dinner on a specific day each week at their apartment on Højbro Plads in Copenhagen. In the summer the family moved out to their estate, called "Rolighed," near Svanemøllen, where Andersen had his own rooms.

54. ABOVE: The Mechiors' summer residence, "Rolighed," stood on Gl. Kalkbrænderivej in Østerbro, with a view of the waters of Øresund. In the late 1860s the estate was bustling with life in the summertime.

55. LEFT: The artist for *Illustreret Tidende* was on hand along with all of Copenhagen when Hans Christian Andersen was laid to rest on August 11, 1875.

Early on—and earlier than any Danish critic of the arts—Ørsted was aware of Andersen's artistic caliber, and his modernity. His prediction is famous. In March 1835, as the first collection of fairy tales was being print-ed, the physicist took Andersen aside after a lecture one evening and said that although his new novel *The Improvisatore* might lead to his fame, the fairy tales would make him immortal![4] Similarly, Ørsted was also the first to see anything significant in the many little sketches and drawings that Andersen had made during his travels in Italy in 1833-34. He remarked that the author could have become a great painter if he hadn't decided to become a writer.

This constant interest and enormous faith in Andersen and his work were of major importance at the beginning of the author's writing career. Unlike so many others in the petty literary milieu of Copenhagen in the 1830s and 1840s, in which everyone jealously kept an eye on each other, Ørsted refused to be annoyed, shocked, or disturbed into altering his fun-damental view of Andersen's work. In the eyes of the physicist, Andersen personified the pure and unspoiled genius who with his naïveté and intu-ition could impart analogies between nature and the human spirit. Here was a son of nature who understood how to write, paint, play, recite, and cut out images of the eternal spirit that pulses through human beings, glows in the platinum filaments, and slumbers in rocks and plants. The year before his death, as Ørsted was in the process of putting the final touches on *The Spirit in Nature*, he urged his protégé once again to write a treatise on his literary career, a sort of *Poetics*:

> "On the other hand, I think you might do well one day to write a treatise on the aesthetics of fairy tales. In such a work you could seriously and calmly point out misunderstandings that had caused an unfair appraisal of your writing; however, I would advise you to keep away as much as possible from the work of others and to refrain from all polemics. Finally, I would never propose such a project for you if it would to any significant degree keep you from your real literary work; no, on the contrary, I would then advise against it."[5]

Under any circumstance, Andersen must continue to travel, Ørsted said, so that he would always be gathering new impressions of nature. The sorcerer's apprentice had early on followed this good advice and often used it in his many applications to the various kings, requesting funds for more extended trips abroad. In 1836, we see how he practices the proper regal tone in a letter to Edvard Collin and then makes use of wording about the school of life which came straight from Ørsted: "Your Majesty! Allow me to travel, for only one year, to Sicily or to Greece! I will show even greater fruit. This path is the school for my education!"[6]

In Andersen's story "The Puppeteer" the traveler feels that the entire top of his skull is lifted off from listening to the clever speech of a poly-technical graduate. Similarly, Andersen, through his friendship with Ørsted, came in contact with all the physics and metaphysics that lay behind the science of the Romantic period and the era's multitude of discoveries and inventions. First and foremost was the epochal experiment that H. C. Ørsted himself had carried out in the spring of 1820, the results of which meant that he was the first in the world to present proof that electric current had a magnetic effect.

With quite a modest collection of instruments, funded by the king, Ørsted at that time held the position of professor of physics in a department that he had fought hard to establish. Like so many others in the arts and sciences during that period, Ørsted was interested in the polarity of nature, and especially in the interplay between electrical and magnetic forces. It was presumably here that the key to the explanation of the true, beautiful unity of nature would be found. And as early as 1806—when, despite great opposition, he was granted his professorship in physics—Ørsted proposed his theory that all phenomena in nature spring from one unifying principle which simply appears in very different and often inscrutable forms. Yet H. C. Ørsted was far from being the first or the last in the field of electromagnetism, which during Romanticism attracted the great dreams of many scientists looking for proof that nature is God and God is nature. "*Die Natur ist der sichtbare Geist*" ["Nature is the visible spirit"], as the natural philosopher Schelling expressed it in the early 19th century. At that time Ørsted was on a study trip with his homemade galvanized battery under his arm. In Jena he attended Professor Schelling's legendary lectures on the innermost essence of nature. "Nature must be the visible spirit, and the spirit the invisible Nature," was the basic Romantic formula that Ørsted adhered to and passed on to his pupil in the world of art, Hans Christian Andersen. Many years later the author repeated this dogma word for word in *The Fairy Tale of My Life*.

"Electromagnetism" was what H. C. Ørsted called his discovery in 1820 in a four-page treatise written in Latin, which was immediately translated into Danish, Dutch, English, French, German, and Italian, because it signaled nothing less than the introduction of a new age. Human thought could now be expected to "acquire iron limbs," as Andersen later expressed it. And a Europe that was soon enveloped in smoke, steam, and speed would reverberate with the heavy, efficient blows of the hammer. Imaginative inventors and enterprising merchants willing to take risks were not particularly interested in the spiritual values of Ørsted's ground-breaking discovery. But they quickly developed an interest in the technical and industrial potential for development, as well as the type of profits which, according to Andersen's Swedish travel book from 1851, primarily says, "Bingo, bingo, and bingo again":

> "I looked with a sort of pride at my era, with the whirring wheels, the heavy hammer blows, the shears that can cut so smoothly through metal plates, the thick iron bars that can be snapped like a stick of sealing wax, and the music in which the hammer strokes say: 'Bingo, bingo, a hundred thousand times bingo!' and everything with steam—with *spirit* and spirit."[7]

The discovery of electromagnetism swiftly led to Michael Faraday's invention of the dynamo, and then the path was open for the use of generators, electric motors, telegraphs, telephones, and electric lights. If we look at the type and number of technological conquests over the course of the thirty years between Hans Christian Andersen's arrival in Copenhagen in 1819, with the discovery of electromagnetism the following year, and H. C. Ørsted's death in 1851, it's easy to understand that the norms and values of the previous eras had to be reconsidered. This included, for instance, the human concept of "speed" and "power." For centuries humans had made their way on water and on land with the help of wind and horses, but by 1830 there were steamboats and steam-driven trains, whose abilities far surpassed the flight of birds, the galloping of horses, and anything else that had been previously used as a measuring stick for the power and ability of nature. At about the same time that Ørsted in Copenhagen proved the existence of electromagnetism, people in England had figured out how to roll steel rails. In the mid-1820s, the world's first railway line was opened in England, and by 1830 the first steam engines were introduced in the stretch between Liverpool and Manchester. On the Continent it would take another five years before traveling could be done by rail, but by the time Hans Christian Andersen was traveling all over Europe in the 1840s, railroad lines had appeared everywhere. There was no longer any excuse for not going out into the world. In April 1846, from Rome, Andersen urges

Ørsted and his wife back home in Copenhagen to pack their suitcases at once, so that "the old folks" in the professorial residence on Studiestræde might see for themselves how much bigger the world had become in recent years:

> "In two years all the railways will be completed, and you and your wife could fly from Copenhagen to Naples in seven days; yet that's nothing. How rich life is becoming with inventions! A person can see and experience in years and days what previously took people a whole lifetime. I find that our era is the most poetic imaginable; reason is producing flower after flower, and yet they belong to poetry; for truth is a part of this triad. In this regard I'm thinking about what you once wrote in my album: 'Reason in reason is truth, reason in will is goodness, reason in imagination is beauty.'"[8]

Lovely Dresden

After an interval of five years, in the summer of 1851, Andersen was back at the Brühl Terrace in Dresden, where, along with the city's foremost citizens, he strolled through the elegant districts along the Elbe River. Having consulted Edvard Collin, Andersen planned his route to avoid Weimar, because of a not particularly hospitable letter from the usually so gracious Lord Beaulieu-Marconnay, who had now become Lord Chamberlain. Much had changed in the wake of 1848. For that reason, Andersen had written to inquire whether, after the war between Denmark and Germany, he would be just as welcome in Weimar as in the past. It was there, after all, that he had always been so royally fêted. But after reading the Lord Chamberlain's reply, Collin concluded that the letter was a great insult and his advice to Andersen was, "I hope you will decline the honor of being able to promenade unchallenged among the noblemen of Weimar, as '*ein lieber, braver Poet, mit dem man eben nicht von Politik spricht*' [a beloved, worthy poet, with whom politics will never be discussed]."[9]

Instead, Andersen chose to promenade among the noblemen and women in Dresden. As a traveling companion Andersen took along the twenty-one-year-old "Little Viggo," who was the son of Ingeborg Collin and A. L. Drewsen. Viggo was no longer a child, to be placed on the laps of grown-ups to ride horsey; he was now a tall student with a self-confident demeanor. Andersen brought along on the trip a review, hot off the press and unequivocally positive, of his travel book *In Sweden*. Even the magazine *Corsaren*, which over the years had castigated Andersen at every opportunity, said in its review that it was now time for the Danish critics to start turning toward all the sunny parts of Andersen's writings instead of hovering in the shadows and firing off arrows that were "honed with malice." These were new times, new attitudes, and so it wasn't surprising that Andersen enjoyed stretching his legs along the Elbe and receiving the recognition of his Central European readers. Another equally cherished reunion took place with the art collections at the Zwinger, where Andersen, ever since his first time in Dresden in 1831, had always started and ended his visit to the city with a pilgrimage to Raphael's painting of the Madonna.

During his many visits to Dresden in the 1850s, Andersen stayed either at the Hotel Stadt Rom or the Hotel Bellevue on Köpckestrasse, where there was a majestic view of the Elbe and across to Kronen Bridge, the Stadtschloss, and the Cathedral. Yet he spent most of his time outside the city at the Maxen estate, which was located two hours away by hansom cab in a beautifully rolling landscape close to "the Saxon Switzerland" and the Bohemian border. Andersen visited Maxen for the first time in July 1844, and he wrote in his diary that the estate "looks like one of our manor houses and has a large rectangular tower; from the garden a view down to a ravine." Seven years later, in August 1851, his first impulse on seeing again the little town surrounding the estate was to say that it needed only a couple of minarets for it to look exactly like a Turkish town. Andersen had apparently caught a scent of an Oriental story in the northern latitudes, and soon he would also discover a sultan and sultaness in the lord of the manor and his lady, Lord Friedrich Serre and Lady Friedrike Serre. In the 1850s the couple attracted a large court of European luminaries to Maxen. Including Hans Christian Andersen.

The Serres had acquired the large estate south of Dresden in 1819. Lady Friedrike was the daughter of an extremely wealthy merchant, and Lord Friedrich was a jurist and officer. Both were intelligent, liberal-minded people who fully lived up to the motto on their coat of arms: "Honor God and love humanity." As an extension of this noble sentiment, they had spent a large share of their fortune on improving the operations of the estate, which had proved most beneficial to the village of Maxen and its seven hundred inhabitants. Part of the money went to scientific purposes, art, and social assistance, which resided mostly in the hands of Lady Serre, who was interested in humanitarian matters. In 1831, for instance, an orphanage was opened on the grounds of the estate, next to a brewery, a sugar beet refinery, a distillery, and various small industries producing copper salts and chromium salts. The economic basis for the estate's extensive operations was provided by one of Saxony's richest shale and marble quarries, which was located on the Maxen grounds. Participating in the excavation of this "Maxen marble" were many miners who brought the precious stone blocks up to the light of day from the wet, dark mine shafts fifty meters below the earth's surface.[10]

As mentioned, Lord and Lady Serre also collected precious resources that existed up in the daylight, walked on two legs, and called themselves artists. These artists were summoned from the local area and from abroad, conveyed in the estate's always newly polished and well-groomed coach-and-four, to lively salons and soirées during the 1840s and 1850s. The guests of the estate included the leading writers, painters, and musicians of the day. In 1841, for instance, Bertel Thorvaldsen spent two weeks at the estate, where he created a large bas-relief with a motif from Amor and Psyche; this work was still there when Andersen visited ten years later. Other guests included composers and musicians such as Felix Mendelssohn-Bartholdy, Carl Maria von Weber, Adolph Henselt, Franz Liszt, Giacomo Meyerbeer, and the couple Clara and Robert Schumann, who stayed at Maxen for extended periods. In gratitude, they dedicated their "Arabesque opus 18" to Lady Serre. Among the painters who visited were J. C. Dahl and Vogel von Vogelstein, while the writers included Berthold Auerbach, Ludwig Tieck, Karl Gutzkow, Julius Hammer, and Hans Christian Andersen. The guests also included a great many well-known figures in European society, such as Ottilie von Goethe, Prince Raden Sherif Saleh from Java, and Prince Aquasie Boachi from Africa.

In winter the fashionable banquets took place in the Serres' sumptuous city residence on Amalienstrasse in Dresden. These social gatherings usually numbered a couple of hundred guests, and the host and hostess could easily provide beds for sixty to seventy guests in Dresden and out at Maxen. The estate, with its calm and scenically beautiful surroundings, was the ideal backdrop for the more sedate part of the salon activities, which Lady Serre handled. The estate's large coach, which could comfortably seat twenty, became a familiar icon of the social life during the summer months. On certain days the grooms would constantly drive back and forth between Dresden and Maxen with guests who were arriving and guests who were departing. And almost every single summer in the 1850s, Hans Christian Andersen would be among those in the carriage.

The old overflowing guestbooks from the Maxen estate indicate that at the Serre gatherings it was possible to meet artists and critics, aristocrats and revolutionary democrats. The guests would debate, read aloud, sing, play music, or stage amateur productions in the theater furnished for the purpose. And the natural setting around the estate, with its rolling green hills and steep ravines, was the daily scene for excursions, walks, and more or less unrestrained entertainments. In May 1854, while Andersen was staying at Maxen for a week, the guests played the telepathic game "Spirit in the Bottle," which involved a key on the table that was supposed to answer a number of enigmatic questions. When it was Andersen's turn, he could hardly hold on to the wildly erratic key, which several times whispered his name. And when the others asked the key what was distinctive about the Danish author's books, the answer came at once: "Magnanimity!"[11]

Various other forms of current popular science and conjuring tricks also appeared on the table at the Maxen estate. One of the big attractions among the guests was the painter and royal physician Carl Gustav Carus, who had been a close friend of Goethe and Caspar David Friedrich; he also belonged to the artist circle of Ludwig Tieck. In addition to being responsible for the good health of King Johan of Saxony, Dr. Carus was one of the most important representatives of Romantic landscape painting. He was also an author, professor of gynecology, and a phrenologist. In his book *Grundzüge einer neueren und wissenschaftlich begründeten Cranioskopie* [Fundamentals of Modern Scientific Cranioscopy] from 1841, Dr. Carus had taken a deep look into the personality of Schiller, based on measurements and examinations of the author's skull.[12] Whenever Dr. Carus visited Maxen, he would spend a great deal of time using his craniometer on the guests of the estate, and then present an evaluation of their true persona. When it was Andersen's turn in 1855, Dr. Carus determined that the Danish author's head was among the smaller kind, and his brain was not particularly large. On the other hand, Dr. Carus said that Andersen's center of imagination and emotion was so well-developed that he presumably would have gone mad long ago if God had not also given him a great deal of will and energy along with the psychological baggage.[13]

Lady Serre's stated goal in life was to win a place for Maxen on the cultural map of the world by attracting to the estate the great personalities of the day—people such as a Danish author, a Javanese prince, and an African chieftain's son. She fussed over this trio, who represented the contradictory signs of Romanticism, as if they were her own children. As Andersen said after another summer during which he was waited on and accompanied to the very door of the theater, to salons and dinner parties: "She is an incomparably solicitous and loving soul toward me."[14] The Javanese Prince Raden Sherif Saleh was allowed to build his own little mosque, measuring five square meters with a gleaming brass roof, in the midst of the lonely German hills a kilometer from the estate; the mosque is still there today. Andersen also left permanent traces on the place. During a walk through the woods of the estate in the summer of 1844, he and Lady Serre came upon a beautiful larch sapling that had been snapped in half by a storm. The Danish author promptly planted a new larch tree on the same ridge of rocks, whereupon Lady Serre resolutely christened it "Andersen's Tree." During the following years she did everything to care for the tree, tending to it from its roots to its crown, even putting in a pathway to the landmark. Ten years later another monument to the Danish author was established in another corner of the estate's grounds. During an outing to the woods, Andersen had once again, in female company, read aloud from "The Swan's Nest" and was then crowned with a laurel wreath. Lady Serre felt quite moved by both the scene and the atmosphere. The next day she commissioned a stone carver to chisel the words "Dem dänischen Schwan [To the Danish swan], 11 July 1855" into a tall granite boulder that was put at the site in the woods where the symposium had taken place. Andersen couldn't resist such an overwhelming declaration of love, and together with Lady Serre he watched the stone carver immortalize his signature in the granite, whereupon he planted woodruff and St. John's wort at the base of his own monument.[15]

Yet not everything was completely idyllic at Maxen. Andersen's magic circle surrounding himself and all his monuments could be broken whenever new guests made an appearance. Male colleagues who were writers could, in particular, cause Andersen problems. This was the case with the author and journalist Karl Gutzkow, who was properly annoyed when he witnessed the almost hysterical adoration that was directed at Andersen. In the summer of 1856 he decided to tackle the Danish author, both verbally and spiritually, and give him a good kick in the rear. Andersen was already feeling quite sore in that part of his body because Lola—one of the many dogs that ran loose on the estate—had taken a solid bite of his rear, which had to be carefully bathed in salted aquavit. Karl Gutzkow, who was also a dramaturge at the Royal Theater in Dresden, was considered one of the leading young writers in Germany. But he was also known for criticizing everyone and everything, and he had previously been sentenced to a three-month prison term in Berlin for a scandalous and slanderous novel. Nor did he mince words when, at the dinner table for two evenings in a row, he challenged the popular Danish author, who had to endure the insulting claim: "You who have almost become part of Germany know so little about its literature!"[16] It was quite true that Andersen, who was an avid reader, never wasted his time reading the books of all sorts of minor local authors, but he was quite familiar with German literature, both contemporary and older works. So of course he was "affected" by this flagrant accusation. But things got even worse when Gutzkow began attacking Andersen's own life and work. First he declared that a fairy tale such as "Under the Willow Tree," which the Danish author had read aloud earlier in the day to hysterical enthusiasm from all the ladies, was sentimental, affected, and confused in its view of humanity. All in all, it was utterly "idiotic," as Gutzkow said. Furthermore, he pointed out that Andersen had no understanding of children! As if this wasn't enough, the German provocateur also began taking potshots at the author's personal life and sexual tendencies. It's not known what Andersen replied, but in his diary he replayed the whole scene and the very personal accusations:

> "He [Gutzkow] was tactless enough to inquire whether I had ever been in love; this wasn't apparent in my books. There love descended like a fairy; I myself was a sort of half man!"[17]

Such blunt talk made the refined facades at Maxen crack. Lady Serre wept as if whipped, and one by one the guests disappeared to their rooms. Like so many times before and since, whenever he suffered a wounding blow, Andersen sought shelter in his diary, where he was almost always able to recover his courage and force of will. But even in his most private space, he held his cards close to his chest and chose not to take a stand against Gutzkow's crass attack. Nevertheless, calm was restored to the estate, and a couple of days later the entire party headed for the place in the woods where, in honor of the day, a wreath was placed on the monument with the inscription "Dem dänischen Schwan." Karl Gutzkow was part of the lunch group, which also included an organ grinder. And Lady Serre coaxed the two fighting cocks to reconcile by composing a poem for the occasion that spoke to the honor of both men by designating Andersen the "swan" and Gutzkow the "eagle." In addition to Lady Serre, the party in the woods included Karoline von Zöllner and Julie Burow Pfannenschmidt. Frau Zöllner was one of Andersen's old friends from the Dresden salons. She was an author who became so inspired by her encounters with Andersen at the Maxen estate that she later published a book entitled *Christian Wohlgemüt*, about which Andersen said: "It's my entire life and story that she has presented."[18] Andersen had a more difficult time with Julie Burow Pfannenschmidt. He had tried to read her stories but found them pompous—just as she was. Once, after Andersen had given a reading of his fairy tales at Maxen, the affected Frau Pfannenschmidt had nearly strangled the Danish author as she tried to give him a heartfelt kiss. For the next few days she followed him everywhere and only loosened her grip on the Dane when they went out into the magnificent nature, about which she had written so many stories. But she was too fat to do any hiking or climbing. With barely concealed glee Andersen notes in his diary that Frau Pfannenschmidt became quite dizzy and had to be led and guided, and she turned back to sit calmly after having tried to follow the party on their trek through the hills. And three days later in his diary she receives one last scathing jab:

> "Thunder yesterday evening, and a hailstorm in Dresden. This morning gray skies and rain. Frau Pfannenschimdt sat outside in the rain: 'Heavenly! What divine nature!' How affected she is! Tired of this affectation and her running after me, such as yesterday when I was sitting in the toilet and she absolutely insisted on knowing where I was."[19]

Yes, not even in the bathroom could Andersen find peace from the Dresden ladies in the 1850s. As he wrote to the Collins back home in November 1860, there were about 365 women writers in the city—one for each day of the year: "I've seen a fog cloud of them; they buzz like flies in and out of the house here. Oh, how empty their buzzing is and their compliments; I've used up my pens writing in albums. 'Just one drop from your inkwell!' an old Sappho sighed yesterday."[20]

But the German-Danish friendship at Maxen was drawing to an end around 1860. A new war between Germany and Denmark was threatening on the horizon, and when Friedrich Serre died in 1863, Lady Friedrike was suddenly left all alone with responsibility for the huge estate. Not until October 1869 did Andersen return to Maxen, and by then much had changed. And yet the estate, as the author wrote, stood there in its "old, ponderous, clumsy form, but with the same warmth inside." By then many of the familiar faces were gone, and Lady Serre herself was so old and stooped that she fainted when she tried to embrace "the Danish swan." But she could tell Andersen that his larch tree out in the woods still stood as straight and beautiful as ever, and much taller than before.

Wagner and Liszt

From Dresden and Maxen it was only a day's journey to Leipzig or Weimar. And so the golden triangle of Dresden-Leipzig-Weimar was a central stage for Andersen's forty-year career as a traveler and artist, as well as for his relationship with Europe, which was changing so dramatically in the 19th century. Not many of Andersen's thirty lengthy trips abroad during the years 1831-73 bypassed this important corner of Germany, which often functioned as a sort of transit area for Andersen. It was here that he began or ended most of his longer journeys, either on his way from Denmark or when he was headed home. And from here he could continue on by land or river to Prague, Munich, Vienna, Paris, London, Berlin, Hamburg, Kiel, and Copenhagen. Within a reasonable distance could be found railways, omnibuses, coaches, and steamships. Nor was there any lack of options for spending the night with wealthy and eccentric friends. Andersen's Danish-German publisher, Carl B. Lorck, lived in Leipzig. In Dresden the Serre family had both an estate and a house in the city. And in Weimar, it was first and foremost the Hereditary Grand Duke Carl Alexander who opened new rooms for the Danish author.

Andersen's visits to Dresden, Leipzig, and Weimar in the 1850s also led to a series of encounters with the rich European music culture of the day. And he formed close friendships with composers such as Mendelssohn-Bartholdy, Schumann, and Franz Liszt, whom the Danish author met in Weimar. There the piano virtuoso was the city's musical director, and he introduced Andersen to Richard Wagner and his music. No other European city in the 1850s could boast such a multifaceted and modern musical life, and Liszt was the magnet that attracted great masters as well as young talents.

Music was of great importance to the author all his life. Even in his childhood home in Odense, dancing and singing were among the favored art forms of the gifted boy. Many, many years later—in 1874, when he was suffering from a liver ailment and bad nerves, when he was plagued by rheumatism, was short of breath, and had not been able to go to the theater for a long time—he wrote in a letter: "I'm not hearing music; this is a time of trial."[21]

Both at home in Denmark, where Andersen was a member of the Copenhagen "Music Association," and during his long trips, a great deal of his time was devoted to music and to meetings with singers, composers, and piano and violin virtuosos. His travel accounts and diaries are teeming with notes about the operas, musical comedies, and plays that he had seen, as well as the names of musicians he had met or would soon meet on those occasions. A wealth of documentation regarding this musical network in Andersen's literary life can be found in the big *Album*, in which the author—who was a great collector of encounters and experiences—archived all the written souvenirs of his travels. This included personal greetings and music autographs from the era's leading composers, who, on scraps of sheet music attached to portraits or dried flowers, had sent their signatures along with sincere or fond greetings to the Danish author. In addition to Danish musicians such as Weyse, Hartmann, Rung, and Gade, the great contemporary European names in music also appear in the scrapbook: Franz Liszt, Giacomo Meyerbeer, Felix Mendelssohn-Bartholdy, Sigismund Thalberg, Clara and Robert Schumann, Friedrich Kalkbrenner, Adolf Henselt, and many others. They sent their greetings to the author in the most remarkable fashion. For example, the autograph of the piano virtuoso Bernhard Courländer from 1833 is a sly rebus drawn on a piece of music paper, forming the virtuoso's name out of meticulously shaped letters and musical notes.[22]

Andersen did not play any instrument. At most he might tap on a drum a bit, as he did back in 1819 when he paid a call on Madame Schall and used his hat as a tambourine while he danced in his stocking feet for the first lady of the ballet. On the other hand, Andersen loved to sing, and as a child his beautiful, high-pitched voice had won him the nickname "The Nightingale from Fyn." In the story "Lucky Peer" we gain some idea of how Andersen, as a child, often made use of the splendor of his voice. It says about Peer: "He sang loudly and deeply, with words and without words, there was no coherence to it. It was like an entire opera. Yet the strangest thing of all was his lovely bell-like voice."[23] As mentioned earlier, his singing voice vanished in the midst of his desperate attempts, at the age of fifteen, to promote himself to the Royal Theater. But no one could ever take away Andersen's desire to sing. In more familial settings, at the estates, at the home of the Collins or the Ørsteds in Copenhagen, or while visiting the Ingemann family in Sorø, Andersen's "songbird-heart" could often be heard. And occasionally the author, especially in his later years, might lift up his voice for the guests. This occurred on one particularly lively summer evening at the Basnæs estate in 1856, when Jerichau-Baumann and his wife, both of whom were artists, danced the *saltarello* while Andersen sang in the voice of an Italian tenor.[24]

In this connection, it should not be forgotten that in many of Andersen's plays, comedies, and vaudevilles music was a tremendously important part of the performance and not just something that was pasted onto a plot at the last minute. As is evident in many of Andersen's dramatic scripts, scraps of contemporary melodies wind their way like an arabesque around various scenes, dialogues, and lines. Andersen, the diligent writer of ballads and songs, often sat and hummed bits of melodies as he wrote his musical comedies, cantatas, and other lyrical texts for different festive occasions. It was always a matter of a specific rhythmic creative process, which is explained quite concisely in the novel *Lucky Peer*:

> "The notes rose up in a melody which at times bore words; they could not be separated from the song. In this way numerous little poems were created, rhythmic, evocative. They were sung in a muted voice; shy and fearful of being sensed, they seemed to float along in solitude."[25]

By following the path of music through Andersen's life, we can conclude that as an adult he listened to or thought about music nearly every single day. His love for music found an outlet, in particular, whenever he made a pilgrimage to the theater, either at home in Copenhagen or while he was traveling. There he was often able to obtain a free subscriber's seat, or he would borrow box seats. In the semi-darkness of the theater, where everyone watches and in turn is watched, a type of imagery and body language exists with which Andersen was on very intimate terms. This was a world of illusion in which words, gestures, and music flowed together and conjured up a different reality for the audience—a reality in which Andersen believed, more than most of his contemporaries. It was often not so much the orchestration that captivated Andersen when he was sitting in the theater or concert hall, but rather the artistic element in the music that allowed its mysterious, magical powers to speak through the performing artists who on stage were transformed into what Andersen called "storm spirits." This sort of keyboard for a different and higher reality was to be found, in particular, in the era's great musical idol, Franz Liszt, whom Andersen first heard in Hamburg during his trip to the Near East in 1840-41. As the notes of "Liebestraum" slowly died away, Liszt leaned back and stared straight up in the air, as if he were looking for an invisible bridge of colors, tones, and thoughts, like the one Andersen had described in his *Shadow Pictures* ten years earlier:

> "Yet the tones are the iris bridge that connects heaven to what is earthly. Color, tone, and thought are, after all, the great trinity of *the all.* What is earthly is expressed in the potency of various colors, which are revealed in turn in the mighty tones that hide the key to the deepest recesses of the heart! Tones alone have the power to release the deep mysteries of thought that are often awakened in our soul."[26]

This quote also contains an essential part of the explanation for Andersen's fascination and periodic obsession with Jenny Lind. Throughout his life, Andersen repeatedly let the world know that it was not until he witnessed her on stage that he understood the "sacredness of art," and became aware of the deepest facets of his own art. Yet Jenny Lind was only one of the many inspiring musicians who captivated Andersen over the years and led him into the sphere of genuine sentiment. The others include violinists such as Paganini and Ole Bull; piano virtuosos such as Thalberg and his archrival Franz Liszt, who always performed his pieces with a force and fragility that had an electrifying effect on his audience and carried the pianist himself through a whole range of torments and joys.

Andersen did not possess any great intellectual understanding of music. In *The Fairy Tale of My Life,* he calls his own measuring stick for the qualities of a musical piece "a plain, natural emotion." In other words, it was instinctive and unanalytical; it felt, if we're to believe *Lucky Peer,* like "a fiery kiss down the spine and into all the nerves." Associating too much mental activity with music was, to Andersen's eyes and ears, a modern practice about which he was very critical. Many times during the 1850s and 1860s, he accused Liszt and especially Wagner of being too intellectual and contrived in their artistic expression. Andersen was in complete agreement with the Danish composer J. P. E. Hartmann, who said that Richard Wagner was music's answer to Søren Kierkegaard. His music spoke too much to the mind and too little to the imagination. Yet Andersen could never quite clarify his relationship to Wagner's music, since he also felt drawn to the modern sounds. This split can actually be traced in *Lucky Peer,* in which the young protagonist is a sworn adherent of Wagner, while the old choirmaster is extremely skeptical. Using Wagner's operas as the basis for his argument, he says, "the speculative is not material for music"; it is what is filled with emotion that "becomes elevated to a poem in tones."

What Andersen preferred to listen to were sounds from the unconscious layer in the human mind. So he thought that music should, to a
larger extent, draw what is beautiful and innocent out of a person, while
toning down what was much too demonically grimacing. Yet he couldn't
help being fascinated by Wagner's great works, even though they took
such a toll on his strength. The first time Andersen heard the overture to
Tannhäuser, he was the only person in the whole theater in Leipzig who
applauded. And in 1852 Andersen can certainly not be called unmoved
when he attended the premiere of *Lohengrin* in Weimar with Franz Liszt.
Immediately after the curtain went down, Liszt, breathless with enthusiasm, came rushing into the box seats where the Danish author was sitting.
As the royal musical director, Liszt was responsible for the performance of
this controversial opera. He thought that such an arch-Romantic story
about a young knight clad in silver armor battling for his beautiful maid-
en and sailing in a boat pulled by swans would strongly appeal to the
Danish fairy-tale author. "What do you think, Andersen?" Liszt asked with
anticipation. And Andersen, who felt utterly trampled after this long opera,
replied, "I'm half dead!"

Yet the greatest musical challenge to Andersen during the 1850s was
Franz Liszt. He heard him play for the first time in Hamburg in 1840, and
he shaped this encounter into a sort of overture in *A Poet's Bazaar*, in
which the traveling first-person narrator of the book sets off on a long
journey with undertones of death and rebirth. At that time it was difficult
for Andersen to determine whether it was Liszt who was master of the
piano or the piano that had mastered him. In any case, his performance was
full of vitality and power: "His fingers are nothing but railways and steam
engines," wrote Andersen later in his travel book. With his long hair and
dark tailcoat, the pronounced and beautiful features of his face, and his
unnaturally long, thin fingers, Liszt and the whole staging of his persona
made an indelible impression on Andersen:

> "I saw Liszt face to face! How much great men resemble mountains;
> they're best seen at a distance; that's when they still have an atmospheric
> aura about them. He looked as if he'd been admitted to the orthopedic
> institute and had been pulled straight; there was something so spiderlike,
> so demonic about him. And as he sat there at the piano, pale and with a
> face filled with great passions, he seemed to me a devil who was going to

play his soul free! Every tone streamed from his blood and soul, he seemed to me to be suffering torture . . . Yet when he played his face came alive; it was as if the divine soul emerged from the demonic. The tones sounded like ringing drops of water. The ladies' eyes sparkled. At the end of the concert wreaths were tossed to him; the bathing attendant at the hotel brought most of them and asked that they be tossed to him."[27]

Later Andersen had many opportunities to hear Franz Liszt play, for instance in Vienna in 1846, where he was even more wary of the "show." Nor was he particularly enthusiastic about the intense shift in tone from minor to major keys. During the concert one piano string broke after the other. At the same time, it was terribly hot in the hall, with a fierce draft, so Andersen couldn't gather his thoughts properly. He wrote in his diary: "He is a storm spirit who plays with the tones. A tone juggler. I am amazed but do not melt."[28]

Yet Andersen did melt in the summer of 1852 in Weimar when he was introduced to Liszt and his companion, Princess Caroline von Sayn-Wittgenstein. It was said that the princess had run off from her marriage to a nobleman in Russia, bringing her fifteen-year-old daughter with her. She now lived in sin with Liszt in Weimar, where he had been the city's royal musical director and composer since 1842, appointed by the Hereditary Grand Duke himself. With his so-called future music and his faith in spiritual enclaves and hothouses where talent and genius could blossom freely but at the same time produce a gracious result with regard to their patrons, Franz Liszt was the great triumph who was to give Carl Alexander the winning hand in his dream for a Weimar that would rank with the Golden Age of Goethe's and Schiller's era. When Andersen returned to Weimar in the 1850s after his involuntary three-year absence from Germany, the myth surrounding Franz Liszt was at its height. The countless stories about the piano virtuoso fed primarily on the rumors about his scandalous relationship with the princess, who was Catholic, Russian, and smoked big cigars. But the creation of the myth also had to do with the erotic spell that had always existed between Liszt and his over-whelmingly female audience.

The appreciation was mutual. Franz Liszt also admired the women and set great store by the steady stream of aristocratic ladies who called on him in private. Princess Wittgenstein was quite aware of this, and she even announced that a man like Liszt needed "women of all sorts, just as an orchestra requires various instruments."[29] She truly understood how to pamper her man, and she used to strew the floors of their house with long-stemmed red roses whenever Liszt returned home from his long tours.[30] In short, she was a princess in the grand style. Even though Andersen was accustomed to feeling comfortable in the company of emancipated women, this couple was a bit too liberated and dangerous in his eyes:

> "He and the princess seem to me like fiery spirits that blaze, flare up; they can instantly warm you, but you can't get close or you'll be burned.—It's quite a sight to see these two fiery beings and know their story . . ."[31]

During a dinner at the couple's house on Jenaer Strasse in May 1852, Andersen was asked to read aloud at the table. As usual, when he was with a new, larger group outside of Denmark, Andersen chose to read "The Nightingale" and "The Ugly Duckling," which always brought his life and work into center focus, no matter in what language. The guests took their coffee in the drawing room. Here stood Liszt's concert piano along with an enormous music library, filled with handwritten scores by Bach, Haydn, Mozart, Beethoven, and Wagner. On the walls hung portraits of Berlioz, Wagner, and Schumann. Hanging in solitary majesty above the piano was Beethoven's death mask, and near the door was a merry drawing that Bettina von Arnim had once made. It depicted cupids juggling sheets of music, and it was dedicated to "Der Alf [the elf]—Franz Liszt!"[32] Over coffee Andersen happened to sit next to Princess Wittgenstein, who was wearing a green monstrosity of a gown and smoking a big black cigar as she entertained Andersen with a rather brisk philosophical discussion about the Talmud, Fichte, and Hegel.

They didn't see each other again until 1855 and 1856, when Liszt expressed his great enthusiasm for Andersen's *Kleine Karin*, as *Little Kirsten* was called in German. But by then Andersen had become even more wary of Liszt and his princess. This was because Schubert had told the Danish author about the princess's daughter, who had apparently washed her hands of her mother. And there were now rumors that Liszt had been fraternizing with Richard Wagner's wife. Andersen absorbed the gossip and wrote down all the ugly rumors in his diary. At the same time, he had begun to feel that he'd had enough of the dissolute musician life in Weimar. During his visit in 1857, he finally turned his back on the two "effect composers," as he called Liszt and Wagner, and left the anniversary celebrations in the city without having used his exclusive free ticket to the gala performance of *Tannhäuser*. The one Liszt concert that the Danish author managed to attend during his brief visit was more than enough:

"It was wild, melodious, and vague. Several times the cymbals crashed; when I first heard it, I thought that a plate had fallen. I went home tired; what damned music."[33]

Kaulbach and King Max

During the 1850s, Andersen often traveled from Weimar on to Munich, where he—like Bertel Thorvaldsen in his day—was a *persona grata* with free admission to all the theaters in the city. And just as in Dresden he consulted the royal physician Dr. Carus, in Munich the Dane made use of Dr. Gietl, who was both a privy councilor and royal physician to the king of Bavaria. Munich was always one of Andersen's favorite European cities. Here, in the 1840s, he established a warm friendship with the painter Wilhelm von Kaulbach. His private home and large, exciting studio, teeming with scantily clad models and artist colleagues playing guitars, was located near the English Garden. The fairy-tale author was a frequent visitor. As Kaulbach's daughter said in her memoirs, the Dane appeared as regularly as the swallows.[34]

In 1860 the hospitable Kaulbach painted his very popular interpretation of Andersen's fairy tale "The Angel," which for a number of years became a prime indicator for the author whenever he wanted to measure his fame. In many places where he traveled during the 1860s—even in distant foreign countries such as Spain and Portugal—he would see reproductions and small photograph cards of Kaulbach's angel displayed in shop windows. Andersen's name did not, of course, appear on the picture, but as he wrote in a letter to the Henriques family, it felt as if "my thoughts, my writing were saying hello." And when Andersen visited Kaulbach during the summer of 1860, the painter could tell him that the art dealer in Vienna who owned the actual copper etching that was used to print so many copies of "The Angel" had become a tremendously wealthy man because of his reproductions. And Kaulbach was constantly getting new orders for oil-painted angels. He always kept two or three pieces on hand at his studio, ready to be sold.

Andersen loved the relaxed atmosphere and familial gatherings at the Kaulbach home on Obergartenstrasse. In the early years he was always greeted at the door by the little Kaulbach children—three girls and one boy—who would shout excitedly into the house: "Der liebe Andersen ist da!" ["Dear Andersen is here!"] The painter's daughter, Josefa, later recalled these memorable times when the Danish fairy-tale writer would visit their home, enchanting children and adults alike with his readings from his fairy tales in broken and halting German.[35] Josefa's nieces never forgot the Danish author either. During a dinner at the Kaulbach home in the 1860s, when all the children were almost grown up, Andersen suddenly withdrew to the parlor with all the ladies and asked for scissors and paper. He then set about cutting the paper as he talked about his fairy-tale life. His words, the rustling of the paper, and the tiny rhythmic snipping sounds gradually carried the group far away from the solid ground of reality and into a fairy-tale land. The niece also recalled another incident, which happens to contradict the rumor that Hans Christian Andersen didn't care for children. On this occasion she had brought her little daughter with her to the Kaulbach home, and with great trust the girl had handed the strange, towering man her very best jumping jack. He thanked her and promptly made the jumping jack leap and dance around in the grass, entertaining both of them for a long time. When the girl's mother thought it was high time to rejoin the others, she told the two playing children to hurry along. But Andersen first had to find his way back to himself. And in order not to frighten the little girl unnecessarily, he settled for giving the jumping jack a farewell kiss. Turning to the mother, he said, "Someday when she's older, old enough to read my fairy tales, and I'm long dead, tell her about me and about how wonderfully we played together. Tell her also that I kissed this toy, and that you . . ." he said, addressing the jumping jack, "you've kept the kiss until then and are now giving it back to her, do you hear me?"[36]

During his trips to Munich in the 1850s when Andersen went to see Kaulbach, he also visited the royal family in Bavaria. In 1852 he received his first official invitation to a banquet hosted by King Maximilian. It was to be held at the royal hunting castle on the Starnberger See, southwest of Munich in the direction of the snowcapped Bavarian Alps. Andersen could glimpse the mountains in the distance as he rode along at a great clip in a lively coach-and-four.

King Max was a learned man who had studied in Berlin and Göttingen and traveled a good deal in Italy and Greece. He was extremely interested in science and quite knowledgeable about Denmark and Danish culture. During their first meeting in June 1852, the king confided to the Danish author that he had long had a desire to go to Copenhagen to try out the modern salt-water baths in the harbor, which were a frequent topic of conversation in Europe at the time. And even though King Max was not as passionately interested in art as his father, the bon vivant Ludwig I, he was quite familiar with Andersen's writings and had read *The Improvisatore* and fairy tales such as "The Little Mermaid" and "The Garden of Eden," which had made a big impression on him.

All this the talkative king told Andersen on the atmospheric sailing trip out to the romantic isle of Roseninsel in the Starnberger See, where King Max had built a villa surrounded by an exquisite rose garden. Along the way Andersen read aloud "The Ugly Duckling," and the king thanked him with a particularly beautiful branch from one of the island's flowering elder trees. Yet another of the distinguished, sensitive friendships, which in Andersen's eyes abolished the division between royal and common birth, was now blossoming:

> "I sat alone on a bench with the king. He talked about everything that God had given to me, about the fate of humanity, and I said that I wouldn't want to be king, it was such a big responsibility that I wouldn't be equal to the task. He said that God had to provide strength, and a person did what he could. We had a warm and confidential conversation, and as we sailed home I read 'The Story of a Mother,' 'The Flax,' and 'The Darning Needle.' The lake was utterly calm, the mountains were blue with snow and sunlight, it was like a fairy tale when we stepped ashore, the fountain leaped, and the king bid me a gracious farewell. I saw both of the young princes and kissed them."[37]

Seven-year-old Prince Ludwig and four-year-old Prince Otto would later have ample opportunity to listen to the Danish author tell stories about swans and storks. Crown Prince Ludwig, in particular, paid close attention. He would become the famous and notorious Ludwig II, who came to power at the age of eighteen in 1865. It was this young, eccentric Ludwig who—until his untimely and mysterious death in the Starnberger See in 1886—became known as Richard Wagner's generous patron. He was also a dreamy and ambitious builder who drained the state treasury of funds in order to erect a number of extravagant fairy-tale castles in southern Bavaria. And romantic swan and stork motifs ended up playing a major role in the kitschy décor and furnishings. The best known of all these fantastical castles was the towering Schloss Neuschwanstein south of Munich near the Austrian border. Ludwig II had it built on such a grand and elevated site in the alpine landscape that in height, size, and décor it far outshone his father's yellow castle located five hundred meters away.

It was the smaller castle—Hohenschwangau, where Ludwig II was born and grew up—that Hans Christian Andersen visited in June 1854. There he spent three glorious days in the intelligent company of King Max and his queen, Maria Hedewig (formerly Princess of Prussia), along with their two young princes, Ludwig and Otto. Andersen had almost decided to stay in Munich. He was suffering from a sore throat and a boil on his cheek, which for several days had forced him to go around wearing a warm poultice, plasters, and a big scarf—even when he went to the theater. But Andersen rarely said no to a king. After a strenuous train ride to Augsburg, he continued on by coach to Füssen, where the royal carriage, after a slight delay, was ready to convey the Danish author the last scenic kilometers up to the castle. Then at last he rolled into the courtyard at Hohenschwangau, where he was shown to his rooms by his own footman. Immediately after his arrival, Andersen was taken by King Max on a drive through the Austrian Tyrol, where they resumed their conversation about Andersen's life and writing. In the meantime, the king had read the Dane's German autobiography from 1847. He was filled with admiration, primarily because Andersen was apparently such a pure and unspoiled son of the people who had overcome many obstacles and over time had won great renown. And this was all due—said King Max solemnly—to the Danish author's unshakable faith in Providence. Andersen didn't contradict him, and he enjoyed the drive immensely. Another unforgettable chapter of his life was in the process of unfolding. Before the footman put out the light in the summer house where Andersen was staying, the Dane took out his diary to record his last impressions of the day:

> "It was a mild, quiet summer evening. A mosquito stung me again on the cheek; the king swatted it off. In the evening at tea, I read *Unter dem Weidenbaum* ['Under the Willow Tree'] and *Es ist ganz gewiss!* ['It's Perfectly True']. The king had retired early; the queen stayed, gave the ladies a rhododendron corsage and presented me with an alpine flower. At dinner we feasted on wild game that the king had shot and a pike the queen had caught. She's beautiful, has a wise face; she spoke a great deal to me, and kindly. I saw the 2 little princes. It was almost 12 by the time I went to bed, quite tired and worn out."[38]

Andersen brought back from the last day's long trek a bouquet of wild-flowers, which he wrapped up in a holder made from one of his paper-cuts that depicted a host of swans. He presented the bouquet to Queen Maria. Andersen not only promised to come back the following year, but he said that for Christmas he would write a long fairy tale about this marvelous swan's nest of a royal castle in Bavaria. He never did write such a tale, but he kept in contact with the royal couple and saw them again on many occasions. The two princes often talked about Andersen after his visit in 1854, when he had told them fairy tales and cut out amusing soldiers and elegant dancers standing on one leg. Crown Prince Ludwig was especially taken with Andersen's stories. He became so absorbed in "The Steadfast Tin Soldier" and the main character's amputated relationship to life that he subsequently became greatly distressed when he found three of his best toy soldiers missing their heads. "Three brave tin soldiers are dead! I wonder what Andersen will say when he hears about it."[39]

Prince Ludwig didn't need to worry; Andersen never heard a thing. The last time the Danish author saw the Bavarian royal family—at a theater performance in Munich in 1860—he caught only a brief glimpse of the princes, who by then had grown up quite a bit. But until his death, Andersen continued to have a privileged relationship to Bavaria. In November 1859, the extraordinarily distinguished honor of the "Maximilian Order for Science and Art" was bestowed on him—an award that was usually given only to native Germans. Once again Denmark and the Danes discovered that the Germans were always ready to make an exception for Hans Christian Andersen.

Rebelling Against Ørsted

After returning from his fifth long trip to Germany in less than six years, Andersen set about completing his novel *To Be or Not to Be* in August 1856. At the time, he was staying at the estates of Glorup, Basnæs, and Holsteinborg, where he also read books on philosophy and theology, such as Friedrich Fabri's *Briefe gegen den Materialismus* [Letters Against Materialism]. Andersen praised the cognitive value of this book by saying: "They [the letters] have enlightened much for me, but have not clearly erased every materialistic assertion. I have more experience, equally wise about spirit and matter, but what is invisible in me seeks the invisible."[40] Undoubtedly. During the periods when Andersen was working most intensely on *To Be or Not to Be* in 1856-57, he was awakened by ghosts that made the estate's tower clock chime. Visions poured out in the gloom and darkness of night. One minute the slumbering Andersen would find himself in Constantinople or Japan, and the next he would feel himself choking on greasy playing cards that tasted horribly bitter. And on one night the author dreamed that he was sitting and writing when the letters suddenly set the paper on fire.

Is "what exists" more solid and real than "what doesn't exist"? And what does it mean "to be"? These are the questions that the young, orphaned Niels Bryde has to wrestle with in *To Be or Not to Be*, which was published in May 1857. In the wake of these philosophical questions there is also a revision of the very positive, almost auspicious view of modern science and its relationship to art, which Andersen, at the start of the decade and with a nod to H. C. Ørsted, had introduced in his travel book *In Sweden*. In the book's concluding paean to "The California of Poetry," it says:

> "The sunlight of science will penetrate the writer; with clear eyes he will perceive truth and harmony in the small and the infinitely large. This will purify and enrich his intellect and his imagination, show him new forms that will more than invigorate the word. Even individual discoveries will engender this sort of new flight. What a fairy-tale world will unfold beneath the microscope when we transfer our human world there; electromagnetism can become a life-thread in new comedies and novels, and how many humorous stories will sprout as we, from our small, grain-of-sand earth, with its tiny, arrogant humans, gaze out at the infinite universe from Milky Way to Milky Way."[41]

During the years after Ørsted's death in 1851, Andersen traveled a great deal, and he devoted long periods of time to thinking much more than to writing. Gradually he began to take a more critical view of Ørsted and his book *The Spirit in Nature*. God was once again making His presence felt. On the one hand, as Andersen wrote in letters to Henriette Wulff and B. S. Ingemann, Our Lord could easily stand to be viewed and evaluated with the common sense with which He had blessed us. On the other hand, it would be difficult to do without God as support. When it came right down to it, Andersen had no doubts: "Faith is given, it's not something you can acquire by thinking!" as he writes at the end of *To Be or Not to Be*.[42] This is the book that contains the most keys to the metaphysics of Hans Christian Andersen's writing.

Like the majority of the author's longer prose works, the novel is not a perfect work in terms of aesthetics; instead, it's more of a mixed bag of beliefs and doubts. An unfathomable number of philosophical and religious balls are tossed into the air at one time, but many relevant questions about existence are asked, and quite a few substantial answers are given. Fifteen years before the critic Georg Brandes sought some form of social involvement from Danish authors that would reach out beyond themselves, Hans Christian Andersen wrote just such a novel in *To Be or Not to Be.* This was a work that not only stirred up debate, it also brought the modern human being under discussion.

What is the relationship between faith and knowledge? Is there an eternal life, or is the soul's ember extinguished along with the body? These are the kinds of questions that *To Be or Not to Be* dares to ask. These are the questions that the protagonist, Niels Bryde, and his Jewish sweetheart, Esther, grapple with until the Three Year War and a cholera epidemic seriously intervene in their lives. We meet Niels Bryde as the impoverished son of the guard at the Round Tower in Copenhagen. One day the boy is suddenly orphaned and left all alone in the world. Pastor Japetus Mollerup becomes the guardian of the talented, sensitive boy, taking him home to his family in Silkeborg. The pastor's daughter, Bodil, quickly develops a great closeness with her new half brother. It soon turns out that the naturally pious and inquisitive Niels wants to be a pastor like his stepfather, but his theological studies in Copenhagen bring him into contact with the irreligious ideas of a new era. Niels swiftly loses himself in a study of the individual cell, with no sense for higher ideas. Modern science, which casts a new, radical light on the nature and existence of humans, transforms Niels and his view of life and the world. Like Holberg's character Erasmus Montanus, Niels returns home to his faithfully waiting foster family in dark Jutland, where they regard the son as something of a heretic. This is especially true when he confesses that he no longer wants to be a pastor but rather a doctor. And the old religious world order collapses completely when Niels becomes engaged to Esther, who is Jewish. Like Niels, she is a very thoughtful young person, but unlike her sweetheart, she believes wholeheartedly in the immortality of the soul. All of these religious considerations acquire even greater importance when Niels Bryde comes close to dying during the war. Shortly after he returns home and regains his health, Esther falls incurably ill. At her deathbed, Niels reverts to the strong, ardent faith in God and eternal life that marked his childhood. In an orthodox Christian sense, this is a "happy end" to a tragic love story, but it's not at all easy for the reader to swallow. Niels's conversion seems out of proportion to the preceding one hundred and fifty pages of the novel, in which we follow Niels Bryde's development toward mature and modern viewpoints such as:

"Believe me, we are no more masters over ourselves and our minds than we are masters over the material parts that separate us from our bodies. Our moods appear as our blood circulates, and that's why, I venture to believe and say, we are no more possessed of soundness of mind than the trained animal."[43]

The conclusion that Andersen chose to give the reader in 1857—six years after Ørsted's death—seemed like a direct renunciation of a view of life that was based more on the natural sciences than on religion. But if we take a good look between the lines of the novel's all-too-hasty final chapters, we find that it's more a matter of a host of contradictory forces within Niels. And the final scene should probably be understood as showing that faith and knowledge are no longer battling inside him because they have joined in a recognition of both God's abstract presence in nature and the concrete facts of the natural sciences. Faith that is torn away from the reality of its time is blind! as Niels concludes. He has learned this from his deceased sweetheart, Esther. At her deathbed he sees the light and understands that the objective interpretation of human beings, as presented by the natural sciences, is dry and impoverished. As the verbose Niels says about the isolated knowledge of the modern human being, it's "an endless fumbling, a falling out of step, and the only support is God; the equation can't be solved without Him."[44]

This was precisely the same viewpoint that Andersen had expressed in a letter to Henriette Wulff in late December 1855. On the verge of a new year—with fog and icy temperatures outside—he talked about the studies of "materialism" that he had undertaken for his new novel. The author was not at all in agreement with the adherents of this sterile view of life:

"The whole artificial machinery is explained to the utmost, yet it remains only machinery, and then it seems to me an existence of despair. The human being then becomes merely a cog in a whole array of creation; immortality—even God—disappears; how terrible! It can't be like that! . . . For me, science illuminates the divine revelation; I go with open, seeing eyes toward the goal which the others seek blindly. Our Lord can easily tolerate being viewed with the common sense he gave us. Peace and reconciliation between nature and the Bible is what I want!"[45]

In the late 1850s, Andersen—like Niels Bryde at the end of his novel, and to a much higher degree than H. C. Ørsted had ever done—wanted to call the unknown guiding force in nature "God" and not just "the spirit in nature." In this sense God made a more personal appearance in Andersen's life during a period when his father figures had begun to fall away. Ørsted died in 1851, and over the course of the decade, it became clear that the sand in the hourglass was also about to run out for loyal and paternal supporters such as Jonas Collin and B. S. Ingemann. So we might say that Andersen was bracing himself. Out of his own doubt in the 1850s emerged—as it did for Niels Bryde—not a renunciation of faith or science but an embracing of both. This meant a more solid, dual anchoring in the old-fashioned beliefs and in modern rationalism, respectively, which he had experienced as a child in the figures of his mother and father. In many ways, this was an eternally productive dichotomy in the adult writer, although he had not been allowed to pour out as much art during the 1850s as he had previously done in his literary career. But the situation was now remedied with the deft ending of *To Be or Not to Be*. Niels Bryde, alias Hans Christian Andersen, creates for himself a new, pragmatic view of life, by which he can both live and die.

With his new novel in three different editions—Danish, German, and English—in his luggage, Andersen once again set off on a lengthy European trip in the summer of 1857. Except for Munich, all of his favorite big cities were again included in his itinerary, along with the new and unfamiliar destination of Brussels. Part of the impetus for this "grand tour" was a letter that the Danish author had received in the summer of 1856 which began with the marvelous words: "My dear and worthy Hans!"

"Hans"—hardly anyone had called him that since he was a little boy. And Andersen promptly informed Edvard and all the rest of the Collin family about this surprising intimacy that turned out to come from Charles Dickens himself:

> "In his native country it's customary to address your closest friends by their first name; as a boy I was always called Hans-Christian, but never just Hans, and he writes 'Dear and worthy Hans!' How that salutation struck me!"[46]

The unexpected letter from Charles Dickens, whom Andersen had not heard from very often since his first visit to England in 1847, contained an apology because Dickens had not made time to meet with a Dane in London who had a letter of introduction from Hans Christian Andersen. Dickens expressed his regrets. He had spent the summer of 1856 in France, and it was from here that he was sending his explanation. At the same time, he enclosed a warm invitation to Andersen:

"And *you*, my friend—when are *you* coming again? Nine years (as you say) have flown away since you were among us. In these nine years you have not faded out of the hearts of the English people, but have become even better known and more beloved than when you saw them for the first time . . . You ought to come to me, for example, and stay in my house. We would all do our best to make you happy . . . I assure you that I love and esteem you more than I could tell you on as much paper as would pave the whole road from here to Copenhagen."[47]

It was now the right time, and in April 1857 Dickens repeated his invitation. On behalf of his entire family—his seven sons, two daughters, and Mrs. Catherine—he invited Andersen to his newly acquired residence Gads Hill, which was located in Kent on the road between London and Dover. In his invitation to Andersen, Dickens also offered to put his London home, Tavistock House in Bloomsbury, at the author's disposal if he wanted to stay overnight in the city. The ever-busy Dickens also said that he would be a much more relaxed and available host in June and July, because by then he would be done with his serialized novel *Little Dorrit*. He was already looking forward to relaxing hours playing cricket and other outdoor games that might amuse the childlike guest from Denmark. It sounded like a truly delightful summer in the bosom of the family:

"The two little girls you saw at Broadstairs when you left England are young women now, and my eldest boy is more than 20 years old. But we have children of all sizes, and they all love you. You will find yourself in a house full of admiring and affectionate friends, varying from three feet high to five feet nine. Mind! You must not think any more of going to Switzerland. You must come to us."[48]

For Andersen, this plan suited him like a glove. With newly printed editions of *To Be or Not to Be* in Danish, English, and German in his suitcase, he was once again well prepared to travel through Europe to meet new people and introduce both himself and his work.

Falling-Out with Charles Dickens

Perhaps Andersen ought to have suspected what awaited him when he had to cope with terrible seasickness on the passage from Calais to Dover. When Andersen once again had solid ground under his feet and had reached Higham Station in Kent, he discovered that even though ten years before Charles Dickens had gone out much earlier in the morning to wave farewell to the Danish author in person, this time he hadn't even sent a carriage for his guest—yet another bad omen that Andersen didn't heed. Instead, he persuaded the signalman to carry his suitcase, night case, and hatbox, and together they strolled off toward Gads Hill. It was also a bad sign when, on the following morning, no one came to pick up the guest's dirty traveling clothes. Dickens's eldest son also refused to shave the newly arrived guest. The cup overflowed when the youngest member of the family—five-year-old Edward, also called "Plorn"—bluntly told the stranger: "I'll put you out of the window!"

In many ways Andersen had arrived at an inopportune time. The day before his arrival, the author Douglas Jerrold had died, and Dickens had promised his close friend and colleague on his deathbed to help his wife and children. Dickens immediately took the initiative to arrange several theater performances in which he and various artist friends, as well as his daughters Mamie and Katie, would participate. The performance consisted of a romantic drama, *The Frozen Deep*, which was set on the ice cap, and a small farce, which amused the distinguished audience at the premiere in early July. In addition to the Danish guest, the audience included the English royal family, the Prince of Prussia, and the King of Belgium. Dickens himself played the role of the unhappy lover, and he did it so well, in Andersen's opinion, that he reminded the Danish author of the enchanting Michael Wiehe back home in Denmark. But no one—especially not the Danish author in the first row—had any idea that this double performance, which was in many ways innocent and improvised, would completely change Charles Dickens' personal life when the plays were repeated a month later in Manchester.

The Dickens family had always represented something of a Victorian ideal that became known around the world along with the English author's enormously popular novels. Now the shadow of animosity and slight annoyance that hovered over Gads Hill during the first days of Andersen's summer visit began to spread. "He was a bony bore, and stayed on and on!" one of the daughters later said. And after Andersen had finally departed, Charles Dickens himself made a little sign that was set on the mantle above the fireplace in the guest room: "Hans Andersen slept in this room for five weeks—which seemed to the family AGES!"[49]

Yet the tense relationship between Andersen and his host family was not entirely his fault; Dickens was also to blame. Beneath the happy, idyllic surface at the stately Gads Hill—where a beautiful, big carved wooden clock with heart-shaped hands stood out in the hall, swiftly and confidently striking each quarter hour—a bitter family dispute was brewing. Andersen didn't notice the little dissonances and first learned of the situation a year after he stayed with the Dickens family, when the rumors about the English author's dramatic divorce reached Sorø. During a dinner at the home of B. S. Ingemann and his wife Lucie, Andersen was confronted with the current rumors about Charles Dickens. Ingemann teased him by saying that perhaps it was the celebrated bachelor from Denmark who had swung his nightcap a bit too wildly and disturbed the night's peace at Gads Hill.

> "Well, I suppose I ought not say this, but Dickens and his wife lived together just fine until Andersen came to visit; then things promptly went wrong, and now she's run off from him. Andersen is supposed to be so harmless, yet he's quite awful; he's caused thousands of troubles with women, and whenever he stays here, I fear for Lucie; it will end with her running off with him. Come here, Lucie, let me hold on to you!"[50]

In the summer of 1857, Hans Christian Andersen never managed to register what was happening. Nor did he realize that several years later he would come to play such an active minor role in the formation of rumors about the divorce between Dickens and his wife that it would cost him his friendship with the English author. Aside from a single letter sent later in 1857, Dickens never said another word to Andersen. Sometime in 1858 or 1859, the Englishman must have made the decision not to answer the Danish author's letters. He neither read nor returned the letters and fairy-tale books, which contained such heartwarming dedications. Andersen was quite simply frozen out, and this both grieved and surprised him. Had he truly been such a difficult guest in 1857? Or was it the many Danish visitors with copies of letters of introduction from Andersen that had once again annoyed Dickens?

"Difficult" was certainly the appropriate word for the Danish author during his visit in the summer of 1857. It was one thing that he expected to have his clothes cleaned and to be shaved by the eldest son. It was another matter, and in the long run a most taxing one, that the Danish author was apparently even worse at speaking English than he had been in 1847. As Dickens wrote to his friend William Jerdan:

"His unintelligible vocabulary was marvellous. In French or Italian, he was Peter the Wild Boy; in English, the Deaf and Dumb Asylum. My eldest boy swears that the ear of man cannot recognize his German, and his translatress declares to Bentley that he can't speak Danish!"[51]

There had also been a melodramatic incident on the lawn where, it was said, a sobbing Hans Christian Andersen had thrown himself to the ground upon reading a critical review of *To Be or Not to Be* in an English magazine. On top of that came the news of even worse reviews back home in Denmark. In *Fædrelandet* Clemens Petersen had called the novel's metaphysical discussions "plaster filling" and the main character, Niels Bryde, a "spiritual coward."[52] Andersen was inconsolable, worse than a child, and his reactions were not the least bit charming.

Slightly more amusing was the Dane's behavior during a brief visit to one of England's wealthiest women, Miss Burdett-Coutts. He hadn't dared ask her elegant servants to put more pillows on his bed; instead, he asked the baroness herself. And thoroughly entertaining—according to Dickens, who constantly retold the anecdote—was the Danish author's fear of being robbed, which meant that he hid his money, watches, pocket knives, scissors, and train schedule in his boots.

Andersen was a very strange and difficult guest. Even the children grew tired of him, with his paper-cuttings and flower bouquets, which, after a festive gathering at Gads Hill, once even ended up on the top hat of the author Wilkie Collins. The English writer didn't discover the wreath of daisies until the end of a lengthy walk. In 1863, he offered his thanks by writing a short story about a famous German writer, "Herr von Müffe," who during a very long visit at the home of his English colleague, "Sir John," is installed in The Bachelor Bedroom. And during his entire stay, he behaves in a most eccentric and odd manner. Even Andersen's bad habits became part of Collins's story. For instance, Herr von Müffe is portrayed as a sentimental cadger, a glutton, and an "unhappy foreign bachelor." All in all, it was a merry and malicious caricature of Hans Christian Andersen, whose relationship with his English host was summarized with the words:

> "There was no harm—upon my word, there was no harm in Herr von Müffe . . . As for poor Sir John, he suffered more than any of us; for Herr von Müffe was always trying to kiss him."[53]

One of the few members of the Dickens family who seemed to enjoy the Danish author's kisses that summer was five-year-old Edward "Plorn"

Dickens. As mentioned, when Andersen arrived he immediately threatened to toss the stranger out the window. Yet the two playmates were soon on the best of terms with each other, and over the course of five weeks at Gads Hill, they developed their own private language and means of conduct. No one could disarm Andersen as Plorn could whenever he suddenly took the tall thin man by the hand and pulled him down to the grass to listen to him speak in his peculiar language. Every time a single Danish word sounded like an English word, the boy would cheer: "I understand Danish, it's so close!" And one day when Andersen ventured to ask the boy whether he liked him, Plorn nodded and said with a big smile that now he would shove Andersen *in* the window![54]

But eventually the opposite occurred, as Plorn's father firmly locked Andersen out of his life. This happened because, in the fall of 1860, the English magazines and newspapers quite unexpectedly printed some excerpts from a brand-new Andersen book that had been published in Germany. It was called *Aus Herz und Welt* [From the Heart and the World], and it included a travel account titled "A Visit with Charles Dickens." In Denmark this section of the book had been published only as a serialized article in the newspaper *Berlingske Tidende*.[55] As so often before when Andersen set off on one of his European journeys, *Aus Herz und Welt* carefully followed the author's itinerary and route so that at destinations along the way he could use the new book for readings, gifts, and to further introduce and promote his life and work. This was the case, for instance, on June 22, 1860, when the Queen of Bavaria was presented with a hot-off-the-press copy of what Andersen in his diary calls "my new book *Aus Herz und Welt*." And a couple of weeks later the King of Bavaria was also given a copy of the account about the happy Danish author's happy visit with the happy Dickens family in happy London.

The publication did not worry Andersen in the least. At no time did he consider sending a letter to Dickens to inform him of the impending travel sketch that presented such an intimate portrait of him and his family during the time when things were falling apart in 1857. And so this naïve, sentimental portrait of his visit with Charles Dickens thundered through all of Europe at the same time as rumors were still circulating among the elite that the English author, immediately after the Danish author's visit, had fallen in love with a young actress.

Andersen had undoubtedly heard the rumors of infidelity and separation, for example from the Ingemanns in Sorø. And both his letters and his diary entries reveal that Andersen also must have known that Dickens had received moral chiding from all sides. For instance, Andersen's English publisher mentions in a letter to the Danish author that the great English writer, with his immoral conduct, had "degraded himself."[56]

At the same time, it says something about Andersen's lack of judgment that it never occurred to him that he was to blame for the breach in their friendship. The temptation to show off his friendship with one of the day's foremost artists in his personal album seems to have brushed aside all consideration for anyone but himself. And this was in spite of the fact that he was quite aware of the private, intimate aspect of the matter. In fact, after his return from England in 1857, he indicated in a letter to Edvard and Jette Collin that "I have much to tell you and your wife about Dickens and his family life. I don't care to put what is wholly private on paper; you never know what might be printed over the course of time."[57]

Also completely forgotten were other wise words to Edvard Collin, even though they were expressed many years earlier. They put a personal emphasis on the necessity of always using discretion when discussing someone's travel life and visits with strangers, so that they wouldn't be offended: "You will see that on this point my wisdom is greater than my vanity." [58]

Charles Dickens, who all his life was known to be a great burner of letters and a very consistent man when it came to the unwanted interference of others in his private life, showed no mercy to Andersen. He had also cut ties with other previously close friends, including the author Thackeray, who in Dickens' eyes had shown disloyalty by publicly denouncing Dickens and speaking on behalf of Mrs. Dickens. For this reason, Andersen's rosy portrait of the family life at Gads Hill during the summer of 1857 could only be interpreted, from Dickens' point of view, as indecent meddling in the affairs of a family and household. Andersen had taken advantage of their hospitality, and now, to top it all off, he had offended them with his misplaced favorable portrait. The Danish author displayed a pompous enthusiasm for Mrs. Dickens, with her "big gentle eyes" and "good-natured smile." He also repeatedly compared the lady of the house with the most beautiful and honest women in her husband's novels, such as Agnes in *David Copperfield*. This could only be interpreted as partisanship, since Dickens' primary arguments for requesting a divorce had to do with his wife being gravely inadequate as a mother to their nine children.

For the inquisitive public in Queen Victoria's England, Andersen's book fell like manna from heaven. Quick as lightning, it was put out on the market in the August issue of the magazine *Bentley's Miscellany* along with an editorial that condemned both Dickens and Andersen. In the eyes of the Englishman, the Danish author had breached the sanctity of private life with his portrait of the happy Dickens family in the happy sunset at Gads Hill: "The whole thing was a lovely midsummer night's dream in the land of *Shakespeare*, yet even more than that, it was reality."[59]

Of course, that wasn't true. Andersen's infatuated depictions of a biblically happy family with father, mother, and children had been dealt a death blow a few weeks after the Dane left in July 1857. Charles Dickens fell deeply in love with a young, unknown actress who was roughly the same age as Dickens' own daughters. Her name was Nelly Ternan, and she came to Tavistock House in London in July and August 1857, at just about the same time that Andersen left England. The young woman was supposed to take over the role played by one of Dickens' daughters in the charity performance of *The Frozen Deep*. Andersen had attended the premiere of the play with great enthusiasm in early July.

Nelly Ternan remained Dickens' great passion for the rest of his life.[60] Hans Christian Andersen never met her. Nor did he see Dickens again. His warm bond with the century's great English author was instead severed, though Andersen never fully understood why. When Dickens died in July 1870, Andersen wrote in his diary: "On the evening of the 9th Charles Dickens died, as I read in tonight's newspaper. So we will never meet again on this earth, nor speak to each other. I won't receive an explanation from him as to why he never answered my later letters."[61]

Feeling depressed, torn, and godless like Niels Bryde in *To Be or Not to Be*, Andersen returned home from his five-month trip to Switzerland and Germany in November 1860. During his travels he had discussed and read from "A Visit with Charles Dickens," to great applause everywhere. But it felt as if his joy at flitting around in the world—the fundamental sense of an eternally youthful restlessness, which was part of Andersen's nature and drove him onward, both in spirit and in reality—had now been stifled. The question of "to be or not to be" was becoming more and more insistent.

"I am dejected, wish to die and yet to live, have no desire to be here at home and yet I know that I don't feel happy anywhere else. What is in store for me? Why have I turned back? On this journey I feel as if I had thrown myself into the sea and let the waves carry me; once again they have carried me back to my own shores; why?"[62]

Andersen spent Christmas 1860 at the Basnæs estate, where the hostess, Henriette Scavenius, for the third year in a row was hard pressed to conceal her melancholy in the midst of the Christmas joy. This did not make Andersen's feeling of loneliness any easier to bear. As so often before, he buried himself in his work between Christmas and New Year's, translating Meyerbeer's opera *Le Pardon de Ploermel*, dashing off several dozen letters, and drafting three new fairy tales: "Twelve by Mail," "The Dung Beetle," and "The Snowman." Just like the snowman on the page, the author was filled with stove-longing, and he could feel the stove poker inside his flesh. Andersen's ability to mobilize humor in the midst of his Christmas depression and loathing for his own weakness and shortcomings was an art unto itself, which he mastered whenever things seemed most bleak. He had the ability to hold all the conflicting thoughts in a productive tension, which at the same time was a balancing act between being and not being. Yet during the Christmas holidays he could not let go of the idea of imprisonment and a slow death. Like the snowman and dung beetle, Andersen longed for the lovely, all-consuming heat. From his windows he could see the powdered trees and the frozen shore. To the south lay the open water, like a very narrow stripe. At night he dreamed about horrible prisons, stinking privies, and cats that clawed and flayed. In the daytime he would take stock in his diary: "My mind is no longer young and fresh; toads and bats have animated my flowers. I'm starting to become a withered stalk."[63]

Chapter Nine

Among Brothers (1860-1870)

"Seize the joy while you can!"[1] *he once wrote in a novel. The words now run through his mind on this festive evening as songs and lights stream from the windows at the home of Edvard Collin. Passersby down on Dronningens Tværgade can see the chandelier in the parlor with its abundance of prisms, which cast flickering shadows across the walls. Champagne corks pop, toasts are raised, songs sung. The entire Collin family, including the Drewsen and Wanscher relatives, has been invited to a birthday celebration and farewell banquet in honor of the author Hans Christian Andersen. Today he turns 56, and soon he'll set off for Rome along with the young gentleman of the house, Jonas Collin. But Andersen is not enjoying the festivities at all. He is feeling quite indisposed and wishes that he were sitting contentedly alone is his regular seat at the theater. Scraps of quotations from a distant past, when he turned himself and his yearnings inside out in literature, are haunting him. Words that are normally connected to the old printed texts seem so strangely alive tonight: "It's better to have enjoyed life too much than later, in solitude, have to sigh over the fact that you didn't enjoy it while you could!"*[2] *Andersen uses only one hand to eat as he massages his burning midriff with the other. Glasses are clinking again. Everyone is rustling pieces of paper and a tune starts up:*

> *Now Andersen leaves his Danish home*
> *To wander among strangers in the south,*
> *He barely heard: Italy is enchanting,*
> *Before his suitcase appeared at the sound.*
> *He says: "I'm off!" and no sooner said than done,*
> *And with a haste we must admire*
> *He packs his suit, vest, and all his shirts,*
> *Except presumably the one he is wearing.*[3]

He looks around at the guests. Many are smiling roguishly. This is intolerable; Edvard has once again written a family song that is better received than Andersen's. As usual, Andersen is to be the whipping boy and the object of the sharp Collin wit, even though he has many times tried to tell his friend that they might know him well here at home, but they wouldn't recognize him when he's out in the world. For nearly three decades the two friends have crossed swords in front of this regular audience, which once again is applauding Edvard's song tonight. To the melody of "Bertrand's Farewell Song," he has shaken six sparkling verses from his sleeve. The suppressed laughter around the Collin table, which Andersen hates because it fre-quently makes him feel powerless and afraid, starts to spread while the friend of the family is reproached in stinging rhymes because he not only writes too much, but he also allows it to be published. Next comes a thorough examination of his personal-ity. The author is portrayed as an odd citizen of the world with long wading legs who likes to fill his travel bag with a gala uniform, his will and testament, and shiny pol-ished medals. Everyone keeps a straight face and peeks at Andersen, who has begun to grimace:

> *He puts aside the other possessions,*
> *Most reminders of the people that he's known.*
> *A pile of princely letters and jewels,*
> *Five knighthood medals and his will,*
> *Sealed as tightly as secret missives;*
> *After he's dead it will doubtless be printed;*
> *Late may that happen, long may he live*
> *And speak about "the Old Testament."*[4]

THE CELEBRATION ON APRIL 2, 1861, was a milepost. For the last time everything was as it always had been in the Collin household. By the time Andersen and the younger Jonas Collin returned home later that year from their trip to Rome, old Collin was on his deathbed. The two had barely unpacked before the patriarch passed away on August 28, 1861. And with that, another chapter in Andersen's life was over. In his poem "The Father," which was printed in *Dagbladet* a couple of days later, he wrote: "A mighty will and a heart large / And warm for all that's grand and just ... / In the home hearth the fire burned out: / Now sorrow dwells in con-cord's parlor."[5]

"Concord" was probably going a bit far. The secluded, unassuming house behind the iron gate on Amaliegade, across from the Casino Theater, had been the home of eighty-five-year-old Jonas Collin for several decades.

There he had lived with his son, Theodor, and his eldest daughter, Inge-borg, along with her husband A. L. Drewsen. The house was now quickly put up for sale, and the close family life at the home of Edvard and Henriette Collin on Dronningens Tværgade became more scattered and sporadic. The natural gathering place had disappeared, and with it the basis for the traditional birthday celebrations on January 6, as well as the ritual-ized coffee hours on weekdays and weekends. In the 1830s, these gather-ings over coffee took place either in the garden room or outside the old half-timbered shop building with its galleries between Bredgade and Stor Strandstræde, where Jonas Collin was born and grew up in the 18th cen-tury. In its heyday, the Collin family tree had included old Collin, his wife Henriette, their five children, four sons- and daughters-in-law, and fifteen grandchildren—as well as Fru Collin's two daughters from her first mar-riage and their children, grandchildren, uncles, and aunts who belonged to the Hornemann, Bindesbøll, and Wanscher families. Now, with the death of Jonas Collin in 1861, the family tree had lost its strongest root. For decade after decade, he had held the large family together with his "sover-eign talent," as his great-granddaughter Rigmor Stampe called it. He had brought them all together with his liberal, benevolent spirit. None of his children seemed to have inherited the most significant traits of the family patriarch: his social and philanthropic talents. Yet most of them did inherit his magnanimity, his honesty and integrity, his lack of snobbishness, and his bright spirits.[6]

The Collin family, both inwardly and outwardly, changed character after the death of Jonas Collin in 1861. This is especially evident from Edvard Collin's comments to his private song collection, which contained 125 songs, all written during the golden age of the family when Hans Christian Andersen was a daily visitor at the house. The big leather-bound work in two volumes has been in the family's possession for more than a hundred years, and Edvard Collin updated it throughout most of his life. It is a documentation and accounting of his production of song lyrics for celebrations and gatherings in the Collin family during the years 1832-76. The book is also peppered with small observations and memories from the evenings when the songs were sung.[7] This song book has never before been used in its entirety for a historical examination of Hans Christian Andersen's relationship to the Collin family. It represents an entire family chronicle in verse that is particularly interesting because of Edvard's occa-sional notes to his 125 songs. These remarks deal not only with the "suc-cess" of the lyrics on specific evenings, when they were put to the test within the closed circle of family and relatives; they are also intensely focused on the fierce "song war" that raged between Edvard Collin and Hans Christian Andersen for thirty years.[8] On the surface, this dispute certainly had to do with who was the better creator of poems for specific occasions. Yet on a deeper level of the texts, and in the explanations by the two friends included in the commentary to the songs, an existential problem is revealed with regard to old Jonas Collin, the Collin family, and the friendship between Andersen and Edvard Collin. Their relationship was always a strained one.

If there were strangers visiting the Collin family on a celebratory evening, the songs were kept under wraps, since they were solely intended for and addressed to family members. As Collin writes in a song from the later 1850s: "We have so often sung of family members, / Each of us has been judged, accompanied with music, / All about each person's bad manners, quirks, and gestures / And whole life story, fate, and character."[9] The songs were intended as an expression of, but also a symbol for, what it meant to be "a Collin." The fact that this was something special is evident from the concluding lines of a wedding song from 1876, when the family celebrated the welcoming of a new member into its exclusive circle: "Let us all take part in the day's homage, and so in haste / We will drink a toast, to each other nod / *Vivat the Collin Clique!*"[10]

They sang about and in honor of the Collin clique. And this regular buttressing of family sentiment was an ongoing project, as shown by another of Edvard Collin's songs, this one from 1855: "The family will tolerate no pause; / About everything they have to sing, otherwise they are mute. // They always find occasion to write a song, / And they never have qualms about writing several."[11] The Collins sang so often and so willingly that it wasn't until the marriage of the younger Jonas Collin in 1876 that his father Edvard, who had now stepped into the role of family patriarch, finally held a regular speech for the exclusive gathering instead of saying everything in a song or two.

Beneath the festive and entertaining veneer of many of the songs it's possible to trace Edvard Collin's annoyance with his author friend. He harbored a sense of irritation that he sometimes had difficulty restraining in his brief, formal letters to Andersen, and thus he gave it free rein in his often original and good-naturedly impertinent songs. The songs provided a safety valve, allowing Edvard—who at the age of twenty had been directed to help and assist Andersen—to air his frustrations.

For his part, Hans Christian Andersen wrote at least as many songs and poems as his friend did for the celebrations of the Collin family, although they were not recorded in Edvard Collin's song book. Instead, they can be found scattered throughout the author's own publications, in the papers he left after his death, or in song books created by other family members, primarily Adolph Drewsen.[12]

Even though the relationship between the two old friends and "brothers" became cooler and more reserved after the death of Jonas Collin in 1861, the old ember merely needed a little spark for Andersen to flare up and declare his steadfast love for his friend. When Edvard Collin was recuperating from a serious cancer operation in February 1872, which involved the removal of part of his jaw, Andersen suddenly felt that his old friend became "so marvelously youthful and soft, in a good sense," as he says in a letter from 1873. For this reason he promptly prayed to Our Lord to allow Edvard to outlive him. And more than a year before his own death, Andersen writes to Edvard Collin from his summer exile at the Bregentved estate: "We don't have many years to spend together; and so in these brief days, be the same loyal friend as always! I could not stand to lose you!"[13]

This was quite true, especially in an economic sense. For forty-five years Edvard Collin was Andersen's financial adviser, always taking good care of the author's ever-growing fortune. And Edvard always remembered to pay the interest on the many thousands of *rigsdaler* that he borrowed from his wealthy and frugal friend. In the annual accounting in his New Year's letter, Andersen would first ask about Edvard's health and then his finances. His friend would then send his reserved reply, written in his best and most arrogant civil servant style. This became a set ritual. And in the Savings Bank for Copenhagen and the surrounding area, which old Jonas Collin had helped to found in 1820, and where Edvard was now the head, Hans Christian Andersen kept not only all his money but also his numerous distinguished medals. In the summer of 1871, when he suddenly wanted to take all of them out of the safe-deposit box to bring on his trip to Sweden and Norway, he was informed by a bank officer that "Herr Councilor Collin" had taken the key with him on his summer vacation to northern Sjælland. Andersen rushed to his inkwell to ask Edvard Collin up in northern Sjælland about his key. Edvard had to put down his wheelbarrow and pick up pen and paper. In an ice-cold and superior tone, he replied: "Yes, that's quite right. Do you think I would take charge of someone's valuables and leave the key sitting in the door?"[14]

Although we see that Collin, as a result of his cancer in 1872, did thaw out a bit with regard to Andersen and wrote longer and more personal letters, the relationship between the two men remained tense, due to their very different personalities and temperaments. It's possible to talk about a "correspondence choreography" that never truly changed during the forty years that they wrote letters and songs to each other. Whenever Andersen persisted with his demanding emotions, Edvard Collin would reply in a manner that might well be cheerful and quick-witted, and yet he was holding his friend at arm's length. This is apparent in 1869, when Andersen happily reports that he is thinking of dedicating his new collection of fairy tales to his friend. Can he accept this, even though it's only a matter of a small handful of stories—and one of them is about a thistle? Edvard's reply was:

> "The dedication is accepted, despite the fact that the book is so thin; a person knows what he has but not what he may get. When the thick book is finished, it might happen at a time when you're angry with me, and then you would regret your promise."[15]

For Andersen, Edvard Collin continued to be through the 1860s and into the 1870s "the unreachable." He was the one that Andersen always dreamed of reaching, yet for the most part he saw only his rigid and resolute back. This is evident from a tremendously symbolic dream that the author had on one of the last days of 1864. Several days earlier, at Basnæs, Andersen had received a Christmas and New Year's letter which, like so many times in the past, was terribly dry and businesslike. Andersen hadn't found much pleasure in the Christmas holiday spent at the estate. On New Year's Eve he and the other guests followed the standard tradition of cracking open an egg and putting the egg white in a glass, which was then allowed to stand overnight. The next day they would read the future in the hardened patterns of the egg whites. Before midnight the weary and dejected author had gone to bed, but he had a restless night filled with the strangest dreams that seemed to be about everything. On the evening of the following day he wrote on a new, blank page in his diary:

> "Dreamed last night that I kept on following Edvard Collin until he finally disappeared behind a door; then dreamed about Meisling, whose school I didn't want to attend any longer. And then the dream shifted to a trip with Scharff and Eckardt. When I came downstairs and looked at the egg white in the glass, the water was murky in my glass and there was a lump like a frog or some shapeless protozoan."[16]

What did this say about Andersen's future? Would the author again grow closer to the actor Lauritz Eckardt and the ballet dancer Harald Scharff? For a couple of years Andersen had been greatly taken with Scharff, and he had also had good reason to feel much admired in return. Would Scharff's interest be rekindled in the coming year? Or did the patterns in the egg white signify that the author's strained relationship to Edvard Collin's son—Jonas Collin the younger, who in 1861-63 had accompanied Andersen on his travels to Italy and Spain—would develop in a more amiable direction?

Traveling as a Means of Rejuvenation

The younger Jonas Collin bore a very striking resemblance to his father, especially the younger, handsome version of Edvard Collin back in 1831-32, when Andersen had attempted to establish a close, sensitive friendship with him. Father and son now merged in Andersen's imagination to become a dream image among many masculine dream images in the 1860s; this is especially apparent in the author's diary from the spring of 1864. After a dinner with the Collin family, when Jonas was also present, Andersen wrote in his diary that both father and son were bureaucrats and impertinent devils; at the same time, he gave them an affectionate kiss by using the word "him" for both of them, making father and son finally meld into one figure:

> "Eduard is rather narrow-minded, from the time of Frederik VI, a bureaucrat; toward me he is more affectionate, more polite than in the old days, yet scraps of old judgments still cling to him. It now annoys me to see Jonas, whom I loved; I possess, I think, hatred for that impudent devil, and yet I sometimes feel a rush of my old fiery feeling for him, who has never felt warmth for me."[17]

As we will soon see, after a rough and hot-tempered start to his friendship with Andersen, the younger Jonas Collin ended up taking his father's place in the perpetually sensitive relationship between the author and the men of the Collin family. When old Jonas Collin died in 1861, and Edvard Collin seized the opportunity to distance himself even further from Andersen over the following years, there was then room for the young Jonas. His primary role was that of traveling companion, and in a sense he fulfilled Andersen's old dreams of going out into the world with Edvard.

The son now went along on these journeys—and the third time is the charm, as it would turn out. We'll return to this later.

Jonas Collin was not the first or only young man to accompany Andersen on his travels through Europe during the 1850s and 1860s. In fact, from 1851 to 1862, Andersen made seven long trips abroad and invited five different young men, who all had connections to the Collin family, to come along. These were extended trips to southern Europe, heading for classical cultural destinations about which Andersen knew everything, giving the journeys an educational character. Andersen was the one who paid, and he largely pictured himself as using a youth who traveled with him as a sort of bodyguard and valet who could protect, entertain, and console him, as well as lift an awkward and heavy suitcase. Yet it was also a matter of indulgence on the part of the author. With these generous invitations Andersen wished to pay back some of his debt to the Collin family, which had to do with more than just money. Andersen was fully aware that without the constant help and support of the elder Jonas Collin during the 1820s and 1830s, he would have gone under as both a person and an artist.

These young men played yet another important role in the author's ceaseless travel plans. They were supposed to be themselves, in all their youthful vitality. Jonas, Harald, Edgar, Einar, and Viggo were the aging author's *aquae vitae* in the 1850s and 1860s. To travel was to live, after all, and for Andersen it also meant "to become rejuvenated." In 1866 he sent a New Year's greeting to Edvard and Henriette Collin from Holsteinborg, where he was acclimating himself after his lengthy, warm trip to Portugal. He was already starting to get travel fever after seeing Edvard's encouraging yearly accounts of his income and expenses:

> "And so if I have health and youth, I can fly off again, a little during the spring or in the summer. Just knowing that: that I can fly off, is to know the way to 'the fountain of youth.'"[18]

The young traveling companions' natural thirst for life could rub off on the experienced and by now rather blasé globetrotter, who had already seen so much of southern Europe. In other words, the young men provided a guarantee for the constant, lively pulse that was so essential for a sensitive traveler like Andersen. In a letter from 1857, addressed to Mathilde Ørsted, the author emphasizes that for him, as a traveler, the most important thing is "to have all the flight of youth in traveling." Andersen repeated this point of view in a little introductory vignette to

Robert Watt's travel book *Through Europe*, which was published in December 1865:

> On the fresh rose petal of youth
> Traveling is written with sunshine;
> For the old man it is a spiritual bath,
> A moment of his spring relived;
> The young man sees at once his ordinary life
> Proceed in the loveliest glow and glory.[19]

Andersen preferred the young men to be between the ages of eighteen and twenty-two, and unmarried, of course. In the early 1860s the fifty-five-year-old Andersen was beginning to sense the division between youth and old age within himself. And as he repeats in his diary in March 1864, he had "the feeling of being admitted to the ranks of the old, and yet inside was young . . . I must be renewed or I will sink into misery. Today I brought home from Bramsen my new teeth in a box. Another admittance to the role of old man, and with my youthful feelings, a ridiculous personage."[20]

With all the intimacy that a trip for two involved, even in those days, the aging author hoped to establish a closer and more personal relationship with the young men. In their company, Andersen was allowed to act out his own childishness, to be young with the young, and to play innocently with the idea of platonic love between men. As Andersen the bachelor wrote in a play in 1865, love had enough wormwood in it, yet at the same time, "it assuages us with inner youth and takes the bitterness from the old virgin."[21] No man of Andersen's age would allow this type of wistful, playful camaraderie. Instead, most of the author's male friends and acquaintances regarded this desire as a sickly, immature trait in Andersen, which is painfully revealed in what he confides to his diary. In February 1864, for instance:

> "A person crumbles bit by bit; that's what the instrument case says; inside I'm still sixteen years old, but don't dare act it, according to what others say."[22]

It was this urge not to be like all the other ordinary people that occasionally cropped up. In that sense he had a stubborn, strong-willed little girl inside him—like Hermania in the play *When the Spaniards Were Here* (1865) or Naomi in *Only a Fiddler*. As Naomi says to Christian at the moment in the novel when the two still have a real chance of reuniting in the higher world: "No one becomes anything remarkable in the world taking the ordinary, calm path . . . Travel! Then I can love you!" To travel meant not only living, but loving. And Andersen had to take abroad with him an effervescent desire to be eternally young in his soul and as close as possible to love. Like the stork, each year he had to fly across rolling waves, far away from the stagnant, muddy, and brackish waters of the village pond that was Denmark. We can follow quite precisely his strong impulses and desires in the entries detailing the days' events in his diaries whenever Andersen was out traveling with a young man. In his diary he would preen his feathers and appraise his relationship with his traveling companion.

Hans Christian Andersen's manner of speech and entire form of reasoning in this regard bear a striking resemblance to the way of thinking and speaking that is familiar from the ancient Greeks' cultivation of young men in "platonic-Socratic" love relationships. Older, single men of high birth—worthy citizens in ancient Hellas—were very susceptible to the beauty and innocence of young men. But they didn't necessarily seek a sexual relationship with the youths. In many cases, it was a higher and more spiritual dimension to love that certain older Greek men emphasized in this philosophy of friendship, which also had to do with stimulating and educating the handsome, bright youth. For the Greeks, the male was most beautiful, and there are many Greek traits in Andersen's manner of seeking out and associating with other, younger, unmarried men. First and foremost, there is the selection process, in which the older, spiritual man—the "teacher"—first chooses a boy or young man, with whom he will then maintain an instructive and solicitous relationship, patiently educating the boy in accordance with specific virtues. Again it should be emphasized that this love for a youth, in its idealistic form, depended on sensual pleasure at the sight of the young man's physical beauty, and thus it was not meant to provoke sexual desire between the youth and the older man.

Andersen's Socratic appreciation of handsome young men, who appear like Greek statues and sculptures throughout his diaries, is also apparent many places in his writings. We often notice—to use an expression from *Only a Fiddler*—that there was a loathing in the author's blood about being "a woman's man."[23] That's how clearly it's stated in this book where the two sexes cross swords both within and around an individual. It's filled with longing glances at other men, such as the splendid Ladislaus, whose tight yellow leather pants cling to his muscular body, which also looks good in red:

"Ladislaus appeared, dressed like a Greek, in rich, dark red satin. His high-crowned cap suited his proud face splendidly. His coal-black eyes sparkled beneath long dark lashes; over his classically-shaped lips played the scornful smile that was his special trademark. No gladiator in an arena possessed greater male beauty."[24]

And Andersen's joy at looking at younger men was given free rein in the play *Ahasuerus*, which culminates in an intoxicating description of blood, sweat, and tears on the stage of the Coliseum: "What a sight! Hundreds of naked lads / So powerful and brown, every muscle swelling, / The chest is high, the eyes coal-black / They step forward, they take a powerful grip."[25] This is followed by a description of the aging but Herculean Ahasuerus, who kills one man after another, until he suddenly faces a much younger, more inviting opponent: the handsome young Trojan prince, Ganymede. According to the myth, Zeus fell in love with Ganymede and carried him off to Mount Olympus, where the youth remained for all eternity as the clever and lovely cup-bearer for the gods. In Andersen's version, Ganymede is also as handsome and lithe as a tiger, "each muscle swells so marvelously in his limbs," and the older man's battle with the youth soon turns into a stimulating dance for two. Yet the young man's strength must fall to the experienced sword of the older man in Andersen's story. And after the people have hailed Ahasuerus, a Roman spectator speaks, urging him to celebrate his victory with Falerno wine and a delightful new cup-bearer: "If you want a good Falerno, come with me, / A lovely boy will accompany you to the baths / And hand you the goblet on the divan."[26]

Andersen was a platonic-Socratic type of lover in his relationship with the young men who accompanied him on his travels in the 1850s and 1860s. He drank from the goblet of youth and regarded these sensitive, intimate travel friendships as a heavenly ladder reaching from simple, earthly sensuality all the way up to the beauty and wisdom that for moments at a time could fill his romantic soul with happiness and more happiness. In this Greek view of things, the journey as well as the companionship was perceived as a complete spiritual movement away from the fleeting world of the senses up toward a more lasting world, from which the soul originated and to which it in due course would return. Andersen did not seek any sort of sexual pleasure with these young men. This is evident from his diaries and from their letters and travel diaries, which were later published.[27] Certainly Andersen displayed a form of infatuation for his traveling companions, but he was equally respectful, attentive, and considerate. At the same time, for young men such as Viggo, Einar, and Harald Drewsen, as well as Edgar and Jonas Collin, Andersen seemed a demanding travel guide, who was prepared to censure the youths if, during the journey, they were unable to live up to the older man's demands for trust, respect, and loyalty.

With Jonas Collin in Spain, 1862-1863

Not until it was the turn of Edvard Collin's son, Jonas, did the author feel struck by cupid's arrow. Yet this was far from evident during the first two trips to Italy and Spain in 1861-63, which were marked by several serious clashes between the traveling companions, reminiscent of the heated, hot-tempered confrontations Andersen had experienced in the 1830s with Jonas's father. Back then, it had led Edvard Collin to forbid Andersen ever to use the informal "du" when addressing him. Perhaps there was a deeper reason why Andersen, in the 1860s, threw his love so directly at Edvard's son and did everything he could to make sure that *he* would learn to say "du" to the author. And Andersen did become very fond of Jonas. This is evident in his long letters to the young man, which occasionally contained poems and lines of verse under the heading "To Jonas Collin":

> We are like two streams of opposing course,
> And yet we were swaddled in the same clothes;
> I was born first, you next, that cheers you a bit;
> So often you speak of the difference in age;
> What does it matter? My heart does merge with yours!
> I believe in your spirit's power; it is not small;
> Our Lord will allow it to grow over time!
> And when you catch up with me in age and years,
> You will be as young as I now stand before you![28]

This beautiful declaration of love—"My heart does merge with yours!"—is repeated in later letters. It became a general, yearning refrain in Andersen's correspondence with Jonas during the years 1860-75. He also used the distinctive wording in other works of the same period, for instance in *On Langebro* from 1864. In this play a young man proposes to a young woman, but her mother expresses doubts that the two are suited for each other. Then the young man resolutely replies: "It was my conviction and belief from the first time I saw her. She has merged with my heart."[29]

Andersen's "wooing" of Jonas during the 1860s, especially when they were traveling together, had its roots in the concession that the young man had granted the older author on their way home from Rome in 1861. Almost exactly thirty years after Edvard had stubbornly said no to the insistent Andersen, Jonas Collin, in a hotel room in Hamburg, had said yes. And this was, of course, a triumph for Andersen, the adopted son of the Collin family, who had been so sorely tested over the years:

> "In the evening I undertook what I had all along determined to do, suggested that he say 'du' to me; he was surprised but said in a firm voice yes! and thanked me. Later, after I had gone to bed, he came to my room before retiring, took my hand, and repeated again such a heartfelt thank-you that tears came to my eyes. He pressed a kiss to my forehead, and I felt so happy."[30]

Jonas Collin did not write his own version of what was for Andersen a sacred moment until many years later; and it undeniably sounds quite different. In Jonas's telling of the story, Andersen—clad in his night shirt—came rushing into his room and began embracing, kissing, and imploring the youth to agree to use the informal "du." At first Jonas had refused, because from childhood he was accustomed to addressing Andersen with the formal "De." But the author continued to insist, using words and phrases such as: "You mustn't say no . . . Your father once refused, and that was distressing to me." In the foreword to the selected diary excerpts from Hans Christian Andersen's last years, which Jonas Collin edited and published in 1906, it says: "I knew nothing about this, and so we decided to address each other as "'du.'"[31] But what Jonas doesn't mention in his foreword is that the following morning, as they continued on to Flensborg, Andersen wrote a little poem which he—presumably without Jonas's knowledge—hid in a place where the young man would soon find it: in his passport.

> You are so young and all you encompass
> So young, rich, and good; increase your treasure.
> See this verse I have put in your passport,
> A better one you will find in my heart.
> Your H. C. Andersen, Hamburg 22 August 61.[32]

In this way, using his literary hallmark that broke down so many barriers, Andersen thanked the young Collin for his consent. And shortly after setting foot on Danish soil again, Andersen, after saying farewell to Jonas at

Korsør and arriving at the Basnæs estate, sent off a letter to Edvard that explained how close he and Jonas had now become:

> "I was distressed to tears at parting from him; for over four and a half months we have been together, night and day, getting to know each other, both weaknesses and strengths. I think that Jonas has developed fond feelings for me, and I have come to love him as a son, not to mention a brother."[33]

It was this last phrase, in particular—"love him as a son, not to mention a brother"—which represented a utopia that Andersen held on to for the rest of the decade. Then in the summer of 1870 he used the same, definitive phrase in a letter that was now addressed to Jonas himself: "You are as dear to me as a son, or rather, I would prefer to call you a younger brother."[34]

We don't know what Edvard Collin had to say to this sudden, strong wedge inserted into the relationship between himself and his son in August 1861, after Andersen and Jonas had traveled together for the first time. Edvard apparently never replied to the triumphant letter Andersen had sent him from Basnæs. Collin had more than enough to tend to that summer, when his old father lay on his deathbed. Yet it's likely that at first pass it must have been a déjà-vu experience to read Andersen's letter, which was so overwhelmingly reminiscent of his own youth and the difficult time he had always had with the author in the early 1830s. Andersen had clearly set his sights on Jonas, in a platonic sense, with precisely the same phrases and cunning form of argumentation that he had once used with the young man's unapproachable father.

Andersen's long trip to Spain in 1862-63—more than any other journey abroad that he had undertaken with other young men—became an attempt to get closer to Jonas and to make his way into the young man's soul. Armed with the "du," which had been agreed upon during their first trip, Andersen tried to take a step closer to Jonas's spiritual enclaves. The trip lasted eight months, which was the longest amount of time that Andersen, as an adult, ever spent with another person. He never came closer, in a more concentrated way, to any other man—or for that matter, any other person—in his adult life. The two quickly slipped into a way of life and frame of mind in which all prudishness—as Andersen describes it in a poem from Seville—"melted away," along with their Nordic piety

and all facades: "It flares up, it cracks, it bursts into flame."[35] In spite
of its considerable breadth and spaciousness, the Iberian peninsula was a
haven of fleshly temptations, and the innocent Andersen was not in the
least blind to the numerous opportunities: "If a person were not an ice-
man, / he would promptly become a Spaniard."[36] In Barcelona, Andersen
witnessed the first passionate dances between a man and a woman, and he
also seized the opportunity to don his "Spanish bathing costume" and go
swimming with Jonas in the Mediterranean. Sensuality began to over-
whelm him. In his diary for September 12 and 13, 1862, Andersen takes
his pulse with some concern and concludes that his blood has now found
its own frenzied rhythm: "My blood in wild movement, a Spanish quick-
ness of temper! . . . My blood dreadfully searing . . . my blood roiling
inside me."[37]

A lyrical vein, of a type and force never seen before or since in
Andersen's writing, surged up in Spain. After the traveling companions had
visited Barcelona, Murcia, and Cartagena on the slightly cooler and duller
eastern coast, they headed for Andalusia, where this vein of blood, sex, and
writing opened up. In the following months, the two men went all the way
south to Tangiers and together under the African moon relieved themselves
in the holes designated for the purpose in the desert sand. Everything, both
inside and around Andersen, turned to poetry.[38] In a series of hotel rooms
with the loveliest views, the Danish author sat down to write an extensive
cycle of poems, an ode to "the lovely women of Spain," which in certain
passages can also be read as a declaration of love for Jonas Collin. On the
surface, Andersen's poems with Spanish themes were directed at the female
sex: "Where is my passport! where is my muse! / Protect me / from Spain's
Medusa! / The Inquisition has me."[39] But beneath the demonstrative adoration of Spain's women lurked the author's fascination and love for his
young traveling companion. In various imaginative love scenes and Spanish
tableaux, the author played with the idea of being captured by Spain's
"dangerous" women, whose shifting masks also hid various Collin faces.
"In love my heart sings out," writes Andersen in one of his many poems
directed at the charmingly lovely Spanish women. But between the lines
there is always room—as we will soon see—for a young friend and traveling companion of the male sex.

When the poems from Spain were published in 1863, there was great
surprise among Andersen's loyal readers. Their indignation was equally
great, especially among the author's circle of friends in Copenhagen.
Ørsted's widow even spoke bluntly of "a dreadfully ardent" book, which,

unlike the author's previous books, could not be given to just anyone.[40] Adolph Drewsen—father of Viggo, Einar, and Harald—also raised his eyebrows, albeit partially in jest, at a large familial gathering at the home of the Collin family. He addressed the poetic persona behind these daring poems from the south when he asked whether in future it would be wise to allow the family's young, inexperienced men to have a ticket to accompany Andersen, since they might risk being lured into female depravity. Andersen took the question quite seriously, and in his diary that evening he reacted with remarkable force to Drewsen's good-natured teasing: "I had to laugh inside at what people think. *Jonas*—and me!—how little they know!—I laughed inside, the sons did too."[41] The shared laughter that Andersen here emphasizes has to do with the young men's deep-rooted knowledge of the author's sexual innocence and his at times comical terror of ending up in the embrace of some hot-blooded woman in the south. And it was this intimate knowledge on which the friendship between the older man and the youth was built during their sensitive journey through Europe.

What captivated Andersen so much in Spain and gave birth to some of the best poems he ever wrote was the daily erotic interplay that he and Jonas saw everywhere in the streets, as they moved through a crossfire of flirtatious glances and blatantly displayed bodies. Andersen found the most concentrated expression for the erotically charged moods of the south in the flamenco dance—this whirl of sex, in which male and female bodies writhed in arabesques around each other. The two sexes—like the whirling dervishes the author had seen in Constantinople—merged, subordinating themselves to a far greater, unifying force of spirit and nature:

> They dance with castanets,
> There is no other music;
> They look in each other's eyes,
> It is an intoxicating drink.
>
> They whirl round like maenads,
> All in the strictest tempo;
> Yet what infinite beauty
> Resides in a human being![42]

Time after time in Spain, Andersen would turn to the flamenco, perceiving it as an allegory and a symbol of human eros. "Emotional fireworks" he calls the clacking of the castanets, and for the Danish author it had a carnal sound to it. The metaphor comes from Andersen's first great poem from the trip, when the two traveling companions reach Murcia and the erotic dimension starts up for the first time with full orchestration. In the final lines the author, with great daring, nudges his secret hopes for a long and sensitive friendship with Jonas into the fiery rhythm and pulse of the flamenco. Like most of the other poems from this trip, this poem has to do with Spain's lovely women, but once again it should be noted how, beneath the surface and between the lines, room is made for another person behind the words: "my friend," "you," "our," and "we."

> Pomegranate, lemon trees—yes, so noble,
> They were the roots of the castanets,
> Which took on the sound of the wood that was carved,
> And the sound of the heat that is in our blood;
> From the blood in the heart out to each finger
> It flows, each pulse can be heard in it;
> From the castanet so mighty it resounds;
> Can you grasp these fireworks of feeling?
> Do you understand the words they are sounding,
> They say what the heart tells you, my friend:
> "The pomegranate blossom may flare and glow,
> Lemon tree, I ignite you, blaze again!
> We embrace, we flare up in blissful meeting,
> And then—you are ashes and I have gone!"[43]

Never before or since did Andersen write such erotically charged poems as he did on that trip to Spain, when he put everything into winning Jonas's complete confidence and at the same time began to dream more and more about his father Edvard. After three months of traveling, Andersen suddenly writes in his diary in December 1862: "It's strange how here in Toledo I dream each night, and mostly about Edvard."[44]

Yet things didn't go nearly as well with Jonas as Andersen had hoped as they traveled around Spain in the fall of 1862. The author had been given a forewarning in Montreux back in August when the entire Collin family had gathered for two weeks, and the usual coolness from Edvard Collin had wounded Andersen on several occasions. It happened one evening when the Danish author was to read aloud for everyone at the pension where they were staying. After the food was removed from the table and Andersen began to speak, the whole Collin family swiftly got up and left the room. On another evening, the mischievous Jonas placed a chair on the railing of his balcony and threatened to sit there the rest of the evening. The whole intention was merely to "frighten Andersen," as Jonas said.[45] Edvard, Henriette, and Louise Collin then left for Rome while Andersen and Jonas set off for the Iberian peninsula. A month later, in October 1862, they reached Granada and commenced their first major and bitter fight, which went through several stages during their two-week sojourn in the beautiful city at the foot of the Sierra Nevada. It was almost as if the showdown that had been smoldering now burst into flames and took on the form of the flamenco. We see in Andersen's diary how the two men each assumed a proud and stubborn stance, circling around each other in a defiant and challenging manner, only to retreat suddenly with the ominous stomp of their boots. After the first fierce altercation, Andersen grabbed his diary and wrote: "My blood at home was surging strongly, I wrote a couple of poems in the lovely moonlight."

The fight between Andersen and Jonas in Granada took a long time to fade away. Andersen was annoyed and wounded by Jonas, that "contrary devil," who was so filled with Kierkegaardian impertinence and rebukes, which sounded like echoes of his father. In Valencia they had already had a discussion in which Jonas was harsh, and the author did not fail to record his reaction in his diary: "I felt testy, but kept quiet for the sake of domestic peace. He displays remarkably little consideration for me; if only I can preserve my composure. It's difficult since I have the urge to love him like a brother."[46] The constant friction along the way made Andersen call Jonas selfish, a coward, and a Tartuffe, who, for the sake of his own comfort, refused to sacrifice even a shred of himself. Nevertheless, the old author continued to have warm feelings for his young traveling companion. After five months of "Spanish" companionship, the two men parted in Hamburg in late March 1863. Andersen continued on alone, heading overland through Holsten and Slesvig toward Jutland, while Jonas took the steamship from Kiel to Copenhagen. In a violent storm Andersen arrived in Flensborg on March 27, and the next morning he wrote in his diary: "Every time I awoke last night, I thought about Jonas, who was now on the rolling sea."[47]

Two Strange Birds

The whole strained and unresolved situation between Hans Christian Andersen and Jonas Collin remained more or less status quo for the next seven years. Their friendship was virtually put on hold, much to Andersen's sorrow. The two men had reached a kind of cease-fire after yet another loud confrontation in Copenhagen in December 1863, when Jonas had looked back on their travels in Spain and in vehement terms reproached Andersen for his boundless selfishness and vanity. The author was shocked by Jonas's cruelty and harshness. As a sensitive friend, he felt himself not only rejected but also betrayed by a youth and traveling companion for whom he had financed such a long and expensive trip.

> "It's strange how Jonas still burns deep in my heart, the way the earth burns when a large edifice has fallen prey to flames. I don't sense bitterness in my feelings, but in my mind. He has disappointed me terribly and rewarded me vilely."[48]

It might be difficult for others to understand Andersen's stubborn devotion to the intermittently unapproachable Jonas. The young man was very preoccupied with his zoology studies in the 1860s. In April 1866, he finished his masters degree, with a focus on Danish land and freshwater mollusks—thanks, in part, to help from Andersen. Starting in 1862, the author had eagerly and faithfully gathered and delivered strange snails for Jonas's large collections, which eventually proved to be quite valuable. This was especially true of his collection of Danish mollusks, which was purchased by the Zoological Museum in the 1880s. It's rather touching to follow Andersen's interest in Jonas and his career via various letters that accompanied large boxes of insects, snails, earthworms, bird eggs, shells, and aquatic animals from the Danish waters and manor-house gardens the author had visited. Andersen also collected items while abroad. For instance, in 1866, the author found in Portugal several little baby rats, which he immediately preserved in alcohol for his young friend back home.[49]

Even within the walls of the Collin home, everyone was surprised at Andersen's unflagging interest in Jonas. Fru Collin, as Andersen notes in his diary, had quite a sharp and alert eye for the faults of her son. Before the

Rome trip in 1861, even Edvard Collin had thanked Andersen for his great sacrifice and warned him about his self-confident son with his exhausting youthfulness—his whole "dilettantism," which so often drew him in directions where Andersen would unlikely be able to follow.[50] And Jonas's outspoken uncle, the theater physician Theodor Collin, said bluntly that he couldn't understand at all the devotion that Andersen displayed, because the author would never be able to conquer Jonas's hard and obstinate temperament. On this score Theodor would be proved wrong, although it would take a long time.

In fact, it wasn't until 1870 that the friendship between Andersen and Jonas began to develop in a mutually positive direction. Around Christmas of that year, Andersen—quite spontaneously and abruptly—had invited Jonas to Nice, where he was staying. The temperature was freezing, and after three months of traveling alone, the author longed for Danish company. "Never have I felt, as I do now, so alone and oddly depressed in spirit . . . My hair has turned quite gray all of a sudden, and the few teeth I have left have all come loose, so one fine day I'm going to lose them. This is not a very enjoyable trip."[51]

Hans Christian Andersen felt so old and lonely that he was willing, on the spot, to spend over 500 *rigsdaler* to redeem his failed trip. If only Jonas would come to see him as quickly as possible. Behind this generous invitation was also an old desire, once and for all, to erase the animosity that had existed between them during their travels in 1861 and 1862. As Andersen now wrote to Jonas, in an attempt to entice him south: "You were ungovernably young, and I—nervous."[52] And time had apparently healed the worst of the wounds, because Jonas was genuinely pleased to receive the invitation, which he promptly accepted, saying:

> "Have no fear of my youth. During the last two years I've grown ten years older—and I was already perhaps far too old rather than too young. I'll see you soon. My thanks again! Your friend, Jonas."[53]

This lovely final comment about their age difference referred to an old Christmas letter from 1863, in which Andersen had analyzed the enmity between them and found a plausible explanation:

> "The two of us are polar opposites in many ways, but in spite of this and our differing ages, we could be good friends. You are too old for your age; I am perhaps too young for mine."[54]

It would take Jonas seven years to see the truth of this, but on January 18, 1870, the old traveling companions were happily reunited in Nice. And it turned out that a purity and nobility had come over their friendship, which had been forced to endure so much during their first trips together in the early 1860s. Andersen now emphasized the essential respect and tolerance that both men had to show each other, and he paved the way by telling Jonas, upon his arrival in Nice: "You're welcome to tell me to shut up, and you're welcome to yell at me, but promise me that that you won't call me a fool."[55] This journey in 1870 ended up lasting two months. The French portion extended from Nice and Monaco, where Jonas lost at roulette, on to Cannes, Arles, Lyon, and Paris. There the two men stayed for sixteen days, going to the theater, the Louvre, and the zoo. Jonas was still in a warm and convivial, almost merry, mood. One day he gave Andersen a beautiful pipe, and the old author was so touched that he promptly replied with a poem: "Never Is the Time of Youth Past!" Andersen fussed over Jonas like a mother, even giving him castor oil for his bowel movements, or "opening," as the author calls it in his diary. First there was the joy of their reunion in Nice; then the quiet, strong peace of reconciliation in Paris. A sense of the idyllic had descended on their once so troubled friendship. In Cologne, on their way back to Denmark, Andersen took stock of their companionship in a letter he wrote to Henriette Collin back home: "We are both very amiable people; we deserve a Traveling Medal for 'Unity and Attentiveness.'"[56]

Andersen always confided a good deal in the young men who traveled with him. But with Jonas, there was almost no limit to what the author communicated during and after their successful trip in 1870, which in his letters and diary entries is given a dreamlike glow. Jonas remained a loyal friend for the rest of Andersen's life, even though for long periods of time they were far away from each other. This was especially true when the young zoologist was appointed as consultant to the Ministry of Agriculture, working with the Limfjord oyster fisheries in northern Jutland. For this reason, Andersen had to take other young men along on his last two lengthy trips abroad in 1872 and 1873, even though both times he would have preferred to take Jonas with him. That was also Andersen's wish in 1875, when—in spite of serious illness and weakness—he was still dreaming of taking one last trip to the south. The planned route would take him to idyllic Montreux, where Andersen, on his way to Spain in

1861, had spent a whole month with both Edvard Collin and Jonas. And this time Jonas was willing to come along, as we see from his last letter to the author, dated July 22, 1875—barely two weeks before Andersen's death. In his letter, Jonas asks if the author has decided whether they should take a servant along on the trip.

Right up until the end, Jonas Collin remained Andersen's good friend and traveling companion, even though he was almost as formal and reserved as his father and grandfather—or at least as reluctant to write informative letters. Andersen was always the one who wrote the most letters, and the longest ones, to the men of the Collin family; and he was constantly asking for more satisfactory replies. For instance, in the fall of 1871, when he was longing for some sign of life from Jonas:

> "I never hear from you; no one tells me how you are or what you're up to! Are you hatching oysters or catching mermaids to preserve in alcohol? Write me a few words or send a frog who can at least give me a 'croak' from you."[57]

Unlike so many of the author's other young male friends, Jonas never let his older friend down by getting married. Not until a year after Andersen was dead and buried did Jonas Collin, by then thirty-six years old, marry Benedicte Knutzon. All his life, Andersen the bachelor had learned the risk of entering into sensitive friendships with other men who would suddenly turn their back on him and wall themselves up in a marriage which had no room for a troublemaker like Andersen. That's why he was holding his breath in the 1860s with regard to Jonas. The young man certainly had his share of female sweethearts, and Andersen knew this, but at the same time, at regular intervals, the author was made aware of something much worse. It was the constant threat of marriage that hovered over Jonas—as a young, well-to-do, well-educated man from a respected family. In 1868, for instance, Andersen warns him against what he calls "the epidemic of engagements," and in the same letter he urges Jonas to remain unattached and free, because only in that way will he and their shared world remain young:

> "Every letter I receive is drip-dripping with engaged couples! Even Fritz Hartmann has surrendered. Dear Jonas, the two of us should wait a bit; you're only young once, and when the pastor says 'Amen,' then you're suddenly forever a patriarch, and for you that would be an injustice to frogs and snails."[58]

As long as Jonas remained in the role of the skeptical zoologist in terms of women and love, as in the fairy tale "Peiter, Peter, and Peer," which was also written in 1868, he was available to Andersen and his imaginative emotional life. The fact that Jonas was unmarried meant that his spiritual innocence was intact and his soul was still in development. He still had to "go through youth's whole, warm blood and psychological struggles," as a satisfied Andersen remarks in a letter from June 1870, in which he thanks Jonas for their recently completed journey home from Nice—the trip that had promised so much for their continued friendship.[59] Finally the old author and platonic-Socratic lover had something to look forward to, as well as something to work on. His door was always open for Amor in the form of a young and handsome man. "You're only young once," as Andersen repeatedly wrote to Jonas.

The Swarm of Confidants

"As amiable, young, and splendid as I could wish to be."[60] This was how Hans Christian Andersen, in 1867, characterized one of the young men with whom he spent time and in whom he saw a reflection of himself during that period. The young man personified the author's hope of holding on to life, which was fleeting. This was a personal struggle, and many traces of it can be found in Andersen's art during the 1860s, as he refuses to let go of his youth and innocence, often describing sensitive friendships and male fellowships. For example, in the first act of the play *On Langebro*, which was performed in March 1864, we meet six young men sitting around a table with wine in their glasses, singing about themselves: "Raise your voices in a chorus! / To the brim the glass is filled. / Every one of us is young, / For us the whole world is gilded."[61] But as the play's main character has to realize, after he has suddenly squandered his inheritance and is deserted by his closest and most intimate male friends, fortune can take a strange turn now and then. No one knows his own fate, everything changes and disappears, which is why a person has to seize the day and enjoy it while it lasts. This theme—*carpe diem*—permeates Andersen's writing for the last ten to fifteen years of his life, crystallizing in the marvelously beautiful poem "Never Come Again." The third and last verse is: "All has vanished—vanished, / Youth, your hope and your friend, / It all disappears like the wind / And will never come again!" Andersen wrote the poem in 1868 and allowed it to be published in the magazine *Figaro*. In 1870 he also included it in the novel *Lucky Peer*.

In Paris, during the summer of 1857, Andersen happened upon one of the most alluring male fellowships of his life. There the fairy-tale writer met the Danish actor Lauritz Eckardt and the ballet dancer Harald Scharff, who were then twenty-eight and twenty-one, respectively. Yet it was only a year later that Andersen truly entered the lives of these two men, whose relationship he envied. During the 1860s he tried to become a part of it. In Andersen's eyes, the pairing of two young men was perfect; they were a sort of Castor and Pollux, and thereby brothers for all eternity. In Munich in the summer of 1860, Andersen mooned around the two men for ten days, laying the groundwork for a future correspondence by letter. Among other things, the author coquettishly announced that in the lottery game in which all three men had participated on one of Andersen's last nights in Munich, he had won Scharff, the ballet dancer, away from Eckardt, the actor.

The couple was well known back in Copenhagen, also by the younger Jonas Collin. In various letters to Andersen in the early 1860s, he expressed his own loathing and disgust for the circle of young, unmarried men associated with the Royal Theater; Scharff and Eckardt were among them. The "Swarm of Confidants" is what Jonas condescendingly calls this masculine group in April 1863. This ironic distancing of himself was resolute and also intended as a territorial marking for Andersen, who should know that Jonas wished to maintain the proper distance from this pair, who had now become good friends with the author.[62] One of Jonas's letters to Andersen, dated December 1861, indicates that Lauritz Eckardt had tried, on several occasions, to enlist Jonas in the Swarm of Confidants, but that Jonas, under no circumstances, wanted to join this emotional freemasonry. He had found it necessary to react quite strongly toward all these invitations and attempts at conversion on the part of Eckardt, whom Jonas in a letter labels "crazy":

> "The fact that [Eckardt] is trying to get closer and closer to me is obvious, and it distresses me. If he knew me, he wouldn't do it, but I don't want him to know me, and I clearly realize that a more intimate relationship between us is an impossibility and that any attempt to establish such will only lead to greater distance. Neither of us can be anything to the other; if only he would understand that!"[63]

Yet Jonas Collin was extremely well informed about what went on among the Swarm of Confidants, and in his letters to Andersen he would often report minor but interesting things about Scharff and Eckardt. This was information that the author eagerly received, because he was particularly taken with Harald Scharff, and he thought the feeling was mutual. In 1861, after spending Christmas and New Year's at the Holsteinborg estate, Hans Christian Andersen returned home to Copenhagen at the start of the new year, 1862. And there his new friend stood, if we're to believe the author's diary, ready to receive him with open arms: "*Scharff* jubilantly received me, threw his arms around my neck, and kissed me!"[64] Things proceeded rapidly during the following months, as Scharff and Andersen spent time together nearly every day. Occasionally Eckardt would join them; at other times the two would be alone at Andersen's apartment, or they would meet in town for dinner, at the theater, or at the salons.

In Andersen's diary it's possible to follow quite closely the development of their relationship during these months. According to the author's enthusiastic notes, the men's feelings for each other began to grow, vacillating between "confidential and pleasant" to "warm and loving." Scharff truly opens up to his older friend, who on January 21 and 23 states that he is "very fond" of his young friend and that Scharff seems "trusting and deeply devoted to me." During this same period Andersen seizes every opportunity to see Scharff on stage at the Royal Theater. At the time, he was the leading solo dancer—often paired with Juliette Price—and was often used by August Bournonville in such works as *Styrian Dance* and *Pas de deux*. The leading theater and ballet critics described Scharff as "a handsome, youthful figure."[65] In early February 1862, Andersen notes in his diary that Scharff is "more and more amiable and trusting." And by the middle of the month he says that Scharff "spoke of a great many things with the most open intimacy."[66]

During this period there was the same torrential undercurrent to Andersen's falling in love as there had been thirty years earlier in his love for the young Edvard Collin, who had refused to reciprocate. And so it was not at all surprising that it should be the Collins who were the first to express sharp reactions to the aging author's infatuation for the young ballet dancer, thirty years his junior. It was Theodor Collin who, on February 17, 1862, informed Andersen that he was advertising his feelings for Scharff much too openly. Even the world outside the Collin family had noticed how smitten he was, Theodor said. He added that many people found the author's behavior both improper and ridiculous. Andersen made note of all this in his diary.[67] The fact that the author had overstepped yet another boundary in the Collin family and that his conduct was unacceptable was confirmed several years later when he was traveling abroad and heard rumors about Scharff that he wanted to have confirmed. In a letter sent back home to Edvard and Henriette Collin, Andersen asks his friends if they would find out—for instance, through the always well-informed Theodor Collin, who as the physician at the Royal Theater found himself in close proximity to the Swarm of Confidants—whether the story was true that Scharff's engagement to a woman had been broken off. "Why? And who broke it off?" Andersen eagerly asks in his letter to the Collin family in November 1869.[68] But in spite of a relatively frequent exchange of letters during the following months when Andersen was in Switzerland and France, Edvard Collin was as silent as the grave, having clearly chosen to ignore the question about Scharff's love life in order to stifle once and for all the embarrassing relationship.

Andersen was wounded by the Collin family's attempts to intervene in his personal life, but in 1862 he had actually tried to heed their criticism, and for a time he had restrained himself with regard to Scharff. But not for long. By early March 1862, after Andersen had also drawn close to young Einar Drewsen, telling him about his "erotic period," as he calls the subject in his diary,[69] the irresistible Scharff was once again dancing solo in Andersen's dreams and fantasies. At home in his own apartment, and especially in his most private writing space—his diary—the author and ballet dancer could meet freely and unhindered. His pen was allowed free rein to say what filled his heart: "Very weak and nervous, stormy weather. Visit from Scharff, who visits me almost every day and confides in me all his little heart-secrets; I long for him daily."[70]

To Andersen's great regret, the relationship came to an end during the fall of 1863. Scharff withdrew more and more, as he concentrated on preserving and tending to his sensitive friendship with Eckardt who, in the meantime, had married the actress Josephine Thorberg. She would soon become known under her esteemed stage name of "Fru Eckardt." At the end of August 1863, when Andersen was back in Copenhagen after a number of summertime visits to Christinelund at Præstø, and to the estates of Basnæs, Holsteinborg, Glorup, and Frijsenborg, he was invited to dinner at the home of the newly married Eckardt. The evening did not proceed in Andersen's favor, however. He could clearly sense that Scharff was no longer interested in him as an older, sensitive, intimate friend. When Andersen later sought solace in his diary, he emphasized that all his life these eternally shifting and fleeting relationships with other men had been of invaluable importance, even though he was usually the one who was left behind, disappointed and wounded:

> "Dinner at the Eckardts. Scharff's infatuation with me has now passed, 'now another object has captured the hero's eye.' I'm not dejected about it, as I have been previously at similar disappointments."[71]

Yet they did continue to see each other during the next few years, especially at the Royal Theater, where Andersen closely followed his protégé's triumphs in Bournonville ballets such as *Flower Festival in Genzano*. The young solo dancer performed the *saltorello* and *tarantella* so it was a joy to behold. But their relationship never reached the same infatuated heights as it had in 1862, even though Andersen, on several later occasions, tried to reel Scharff closer in, as he had done in his friendship with Jonas Collin. For instance, in the summer of 1864, he invited Scharff to spend a few days in Helsingør. There the two men stayed at the baths of Marielyst and took several excursions to Kronborg Castle and Hellebæk. When they were supposed to return home to Copenhagen but were forced to stay overnight at a hotel in Helsingør, Andersen reserved a double room for the two of them, but Scharff insisted on having his own room.[72]

All traces of the author's friendship with Harald Scharff, including their many letters from the years 1860-75, seem to have been destroyed. Yet there are more than 300 references to Scharff in the index of names in the back of the ten volumes of Andersen's diary, and that speaks for itself. The young ballet dancer meant something special to the author, and he also managed to set his mark on Andersen's works during the 1860s. If we look at his total output during that decade, it's surprising that after a complete break of ten to twelve years, Andersen should suddenly turn to writing drama again. In 1864-65 he wrote all of four new plays for the Copenhagen theaters. Why this sudden blossoming in a genre that Andersen, after so many futile attempts, had more or less given up? The answer is, among other things, Harald Scharff. In any case, drama was one possible way for Andersen to find a common platform and stage in order to continue the sensitive friendship with Scharff. In 1864-65, via plays such as *On Langebro*, *He Was Not Born*, *When the Spaniards Were Here*, and especially the fairy-tale opera *The Raven*, Andersen could again come close to the royal stage where Scharff, night after night, leaped and danced. And if we look at the themes of the plays that Andersen wrote in the 1860s, three of them are about brotherly love and deep feelings between men. In widely differing contexts, these feelings are sorely tested with regard to the ideal promoted by the choir in *The Raven* at the sight of the two lead male characters: "See, how splendid! Loyal, loving, they both rest, breast to breast!" In its original form, *The Raven* had been performed as early as 1832, as a ballad opera in three acts with dialogue. It's quite significant that Andersen now took up this play again, after giving it a musical "brush-up" with the help of the composer J. P. E. Hartmann. It was still about two men being loyal to each other, and displaying a brotherly tenderness. But Andersen changed the dialogue to recitatives and also made changes to a specific scene in the third act, in which two vampires are let loose in a bedchamber to drink a man's blood. The cast for the premiere on April 23, 1865, shows that one of the vampires, who "in a rushing whirl and buzzing dance" sucks out the man's blood on his wedding night, was played by Harald Scharff. Yet the play did nothing to unite Andersen and Scharff beyond the stage. And there is no longer any question of a deep friendship between the two after 1865, even though Andersen continued to follow his young friend's career. And, quite unintentionally, he became involved in Harald Scharff's finale as a solo dancer.

It happened in 1871, when Bournonville had written a three-act ballet based on several different fairy tales by Hans Christian Andersen, including "The Steadfast Tin Soldier." The ballet was called *A Fairy Tale in Pictures*. Harald Scharff had been Bournonville's preferred male dancer ever since the 1850s, when the ballet master had returned home from Vienna to take charge of the royal ballet. Scharff was now chosen to play the lead male role in the new ballet.[73] Andersen heard rumors about it and wrote to Jonas Collin: "Bournonville is composing a new ballet based on the motif from my fairy tale: The Steadfast Tin Soldier. Scharff will be the tin soldier. Frøken Scholl will play the dancer, but the setting is not Denmark; it has been set in Scotland and the tin soldier has both his legs to dance with."[74] But things did not go quite that smoothly. During the rehearsal of the gypsy dance in *The Troubadour* in November 1871, Scharff took a bad fall on stage, chipping his kneecap. He had to give up not only the leading role in Bournonville's ballet based on Andersen's fairy tale, but also his career as a solo dancer. And with that Scharff was banished from the footlights of dreams and stripped of his own life's passion: dance. For a brief time he tried acting, first at the Royal Theater, later at Folketeatret, but at the end of the 1875–76 season, he retired for good at the age of thirty-nine. Hans Christian Andersen followed Harald Scharff's sad decline, and in his diary in 1873, he quotes Bournonville's disloyal remarks about the

steadfast dancer's limited talent as an actor. As a ballet dancer, it was
Scharff's youthful radiance that was the foremost factor, said Bournonville,
"but now his youth has vanished. How sad! Sad!"[75] Several years later
Elvilda Møller, the prima ballerina of Scharff's life—whom he had married in 1874, to Andersen's great regret—also disappeared. Harald Scharff
spent the last years of his life in the St. Hans insane asylum, where he died
in 1912.

The Trembling Eyeglasses
of the Traveling Life

No young men accompanied Hans Christian Andersen on his extended trip to Portugal, which he began in 1866. This was after a long period
of impatient waiting until he could once more set off for Europe after
Denmark's war with Germany in 1864-65. Again he headed south, but to
an entirely new destination at the very edge of the continent. It was his
eternal longing to go abroad—filled with a sense of escape and a yearning
for the unknown—that usually reappeared at the end of a long winter in
Denmark and got him moving in May or June. In a letter from the 1840s,
in which he tried to evaluate himself as a traveler, Andersen wrote: "I can
find no peace, I feel as if I have to page through a quarter of the great book
of the world before Our Lord puts me in a higher class, where I will study
the heavens!"[76] At the end of winter in 1856, when the great world was
again calling to the author, he wrote to Henriette Scavenius at Basnæs:

> "Homesickness is a feeling that many know and suffer from; I on the
> other hand feel a pain far less known, and its name is 'Out-sickness.' When
> the snow melts, the stork arrives, and the first steamships race off, then I
> feel this painful travel unrest."[77]

It was especially as a traveler that Hans Christian Andersen dared much
more than most of his contemporaries in Danish literature. Adam
Oehlenschläger had also traveled at the beginning of the century, but he
wasn't fond of any journeys that took six months to a year. Christian
Winther also preferred to stay home within the ramparts of Copenhagen.
Henrik Hertz and H. P. Holst did go out into the world, as Andersen did,
but with time and as they got older, they too stayed home in the duck
pond. J. L. Heiberg loved his Christianshavn, B. S. Ingemann preferred his

Sorø, Søren Kierkegaard his desk, Grundtvig his pulpit, and Christian Molbech the bookshelves of the Royal Library. But Andersen went out traveling. He started at the age of twenty-five, continued until he was sixty-eight, and, as previously mentioned, he was planning his last trip to Montreux with Jonas Collin during the last months of his life in 1875. Whereas previous Danish authors who traveled, such as Ludvig Holberg and Jens Baggesen, had once set their course for central Europe, Andersen wanted to venture farther. He wasn't satisfied with the traditional travel routes through Germany, France, Switzerland, and Italy. He also wanted to go where no other Danish writer during the Romantic period had previously set foot: to the Black Sea, the Balkans, to Scotland, Tangiers, and Portugal. Like an explorer, Andersen's sights were attracted to the distant, unknown latitudes and longitudes. The fact that he never made it to America was for him a deep regret, but his fear of drowning, which was how his good friend Henriette Wulff had died, was too great.

Of all Danish writers, it was also Hans Christian Andersen who truly discovered Sweden as a travel destination, filled with primeval nature, poetry, and modern industrial marvels. He was also among the first to travel extensively through his own country, and he wrote about Amager, Skagen, Føhr, and Falster. He personally tried out the sea all around Denmark, including the waters near the Corselitze estate on the island of Falster: "Open strand at Corselitze! / Out there my heart yearns to be, / Light as Berliners' wits / The waves around us surge. / We can swim, paddle, '*sitze*,' / Rise up as if born anew! / Open strand at Corselitze / In the Danish beech trees' lee."[78]

It was always a great and immediate relief to set off and put on "the trembling eyeglasses of the traveling life"[79] after a long and dark Danish winter filled with self-examination, when he had "like a pelican, fed off his own blood." Yet most of the author's trips were planned well in advance. In many ways, like the stork who lifts off the farmer's roof and sets off for Egypt, Andersen had both an external plan and several internal goals for his many trips abroad over a period of forty years. Almost every time, Andersen would draw up a travel route at home in the shape of a drop, with the starting and ending point in Denmark. And if we place all of these drop-shaped travel routes on a map of Europe, we discover that Andersen's collective travels extended greedily in all directions. Thousands of kilometers, filled with sights and sensory experiences, landscapes and people, to the east, west, south, and north. Such an ambitious and life-long travel scheme, which meant that the road home was almost never the same as the outbound route, was not based on purely improvised whims or chance, even though Andersen savored the sight of Fata Morgana: "The magical land that constantly moves whenever a person comes near," as he so beautifully describes it in his first travel book, *Shadow Pictures*, in 1832. Common sense also went along as the more levelheaded traveling companion, as evidenced by numerous letters and diary entries, as well as many statements from Andersen's various fellow travelers and good friends in Copenhagen. For instance, Edvard Collin says in his book about Andersen that every time a new journey was in the works, the author liked to make a careful plan of which destinations he would visit, when he would arrive, and how long he would stay. Yet this rather bookkeeper-like planning would also allow for improvisation. The liberation of feelings beneath foreign skies, which a trip always entailed, was at the same time a freeing of "the poetry of the moment." A journey held the seed for all future poems, plays, novels, and especially fairy tales.

As far as inspiration was concerned, southern Europe—Italy, France, Spain, and, in 1866, also Portugal—was always ripe with possibilities for a Nordic artist like Andersen. From his very first trip to Italy in 1833-34, he was supremely aware of the unique richness these countries held for a traveling, freezing artist from the far north. We can picture the author, clad in two coats and two capes, on a December day in 1840, stranded at the Brenner Pass and passing the time in the mail coach by writing in his diary. There is no wind, but the coach windows are frosted over, and a groom keeps handing in hay to the travelers to keep them warm; before long they're sitting on a haystack. In the far corner we find Andersen, so sensitive to the cold. He's rubbing his hands together, longing to cross the border and exchange the gaunt cows of Farao for the fat cattle of Italy: "I said a prayer to God and asked for truth, good ideas, and happiness!"[80]

Hans Christian Andersen never deviated from the spiritual travel ideal that at the age of thirty-one he had outlined in a letter to H. C. Ørsted, in which he once more asked for help for an extended trip abroad. In the letter, as a way of taking stock, he looked back on everything that his very first trip to Italy, in 1833-34, had given him. Andersen called this type of traveling "a spiritual school year," and he stated that it was not a longing for a varied, masculine traveling life that made him set off. Instead, it was a "pure striving for development and maturity, which I can acquire only in the world, among people."[81] For Hans Christian Andersen, to travel meant not only "to live" or "to love." To travel also meant "to learn." And more clearly than many other traveling writers of 19th-century world literature, Andersen expressed this idea time after time in his diaries and letters home to Denmark, which are often peppered with the overwhelming kind of learning to be found in immediate sensory and nature experiences, as well as in a shrewd observation of life. It's true that many passages, both long and short, in the author's writings have to do with his own health and well-being. There are also a great many complaints and whimpers about yet another painful tooth, boils on his body, a poor meal, or a shameless coachman. After all, there were so many things that could poison the moment for a sensitive writer out in the world. But every time he directed his pen at the painful spots, and his body and soul had been given the attention they deserved, Andersen would almost always manage to lift his face to the horizon, which was filled with prospects and insights. His life-long urge to travel was aimed at investigating where the boundaries of nature actually lie—within the human being and in the surroundings, both near and far. His desire to travel was, as he described it, "filled with a striving to secure for myself more knowledge of nature and of human life." That's what he wrote in *The Fairy Tale of My Life*, and even on his first long trip to Italy, he acquired a good sense of what a productive trip could mean. In early December 1833, he wrote a long, grateful Christmas letter to H. C. Ørsted: "Each day out here I learn how little I know, what an infinite amount there is to learn during this brief human life!"[82]

Andersen was a tolerant traveler, and it was strangely easy for him to traverse borders and cultures, religious creeds and political systems without fear of the foreign. In more recent times Denmark and the Danes have often approached the rest of Europe and foreign peoples and religious creeds with a great deal of reservation. But Hans Christian Andersen, time after time and without hesitation, bridged the gap between "us" and "them." In this respect as well, he lived up to his great Romantic mentor and ideal, H. C. Ørsted, who felt that national self-knowledge should always serve to develop the common human traits that go beyond the individual and thus also serve to bring nations closer together. Traveling was a distinct feature of Romanticism and the Danish Golden Age during the period 1800-50. A good many Danish artists, scientists, politicians, and businessmen of the day—from Jens Baggesen, Thorvaldsen, and Ørsted to Marstrand, Gade, Lehmann, brewer Jacobsen, and Tietgen—possessed both the courage and the will to go out in the world and expose themselves to foreign ways of life. They set off, dispersed, gathered impressions, and then returned home. It was a time when, instead of forcing a person's knowledge and skills into a few select niches, the niches were torn down and an attempt was made to create the broadest possible unity of spirit and nature. Human life and human spirit were to be united and reconciled; direct communication would be established with nature itself—that was the goal. This was rather like what happens at the bottom of the sea in Andersen's fairy tale from 1871, "The Great Sea Serpent." In this story, an enormous, endless telegraph cable suddenly plops down into the sea between Europe and America, and all the fish in the ocean, after millions of years of linguistic confusion, get together and learn to live with each other, as well as with the new silent inhabitant on the sea floor. "It's no good!" say most of the sea creatures at first about the mysterious sea serpent on the bottom, but one tiny little fish has his own opinion of this foreign entity: "This tremendously long, thin serpent may be the most marvelous fish in the sea. I have a feeling it is."

And that's how all people should treat each other: without a paralyzing fear of everything that looks different. That's actually what we learn right from the beginning in Andersen's travel books, such as *Shadow Pictures* in 1831 and *A Poet's Bazaar* in 1842. Both are based on and written from a naïve and idyllic yet at the same time scintillatingly beautiful view of the world's original unity. They are travel accounts from a time before the world lost its innocence in meaningless revolutions, and before wars between neighbors ravaged Europe. In these first travel books, we find a concentrated and clear impression of the cosmopolitan Hans Christian Andersen; with his unshakable faith in a unifying spirit in nature, he dreams of a harmonious Europe based more on cultural and linguistic communities than on nationalistic demands for borders and narrow, regional political interests.

This utopian goal for his travels became a guiding principle for Andersen. When he was quite young, he listened to and followed a particular calling, which he introduces in *The Improvisatore* in 1835, when an older, more experienced man warns young Antonio against becoming solely preoccupied with his own ego. Instead, the wise man says, you should "go more beyond yourself and let the radii of the spirit slice the great circle of the world." For Andersen, "traveling" was not merely a cure for melancholy or a sudden, refreshing break from the endless daily routines; it was part of a universal rhythm and higher idea: life as a journey of discovery. And Andersen's travels should also be viewed and understood in this context—as an expression of God's great, coherent plan for humanity, created as we are for constant movement in body and soul. Never lose the desire to go, if only you keep on going, then things will go fine! said Søren Kierkegaard. And Andersen added: Go traveling in order to live, love, and learn. Off you go! Everything in nature is in constant movement. That's what the sun, moon, stars, and planets show us, as well as the ebbing and flowing of the tides—and the air, which is constantly tossed back and forth. As Andersen formulates it in his first travel book in 1831:

> "Oh, travel! travel! that is the happiest fate! And that's also why we all travel; everything travels in the whole universe! Even the poorest man possesses the mind's winged horse, and if it grows weak and old, death still takes it along on the journey, the great journey we all travel. The waves roll from coast to coast; the clouds sail across the great sky, and the bird flies along over field and meadow. We all travel, even the dead in their silent graves fly with the earth around the sun. Yes, 'to travel' is an obsession of the whole universe, but we humans are children; we even want to play at 'traveling' in the midst of the great natural journey that belongs to us and all things."[83]

A Visit to Portugal, 1866

But even Andersen reached his limits when it came to traveling. In spite of the fact that for many years he had dreamed of seeing America and personally confirming his overseas popularity, he never made it farther southwest than to Portugal. It was in the summer of 1866 that he finally accepted a standing invitation from the brothers Carlos, José, and Jorge O'Neill, who were the sons of the Danish Consul in Lisbon. In the 1820s they had lived in Denmark and met the young Hans Christian Andersen at the home of the Wulff family at Amalienborg, where the boys were visiting. The journey to the Iberian peninsula in 1866 took the author via Holland and France, where, as usual, he was feted and pampered, which he found very liberating. Perhaps this was because for the first time in many years, he was without the young men with whom he usually traveled; on many trips, they had proved to be more a burden than a blessing. Yet by the time Andersen reached San Sebastián, he could have used a younger, broad-shouldered traveling companion. It was then that his trials began, and with them came, of course, a steadily growing fear of exhaustion, assaults, food poisoning, and so on. The possibilities for death were almost legion in primitive Spain. When Andersen arrived in Madrid, his thoughts had already begun to circle around the next long stage of his journey, which would take him by coach across the arid plains of Extremadura, heading for Mérida and Badajoz. In a letter to Edvard Collin from Madrid, Andersen estimates the journey will take thirty hours. But in a new letter a couple of days later, as his anxiety has begun to increase, the journey through the Spanish hell is suddenly calculated to take more than forty hours. Yet the peculiar blend of childish helplessness and grown-up energy and courage, which characterized the traveling Andersen all his life, was reflected in the words: "I can't believe that I'll endure it, but to turn around is utterly against my nature. I'm taking this route; I dread it and I submit to it absolutely."[84] Good advice was precious to Andersen, and what he called "my double nature, fear of danger and the desire to try it."[85] Alone in the midst of the Iberian peninsula, he prayed that fate would be merciful; he sent a thought to the Turkish god and wrote resolutely to Fru Henriette Collin: "La ila ilallah! says the Turk, and submits!" [86]

Yet not all three of the O'Neill brothers could reconcile themselves to the Danish author's relaxed and indolent conduct as a guest during his visit to Portugal in 1866. At the end of July, Andersen spent two weeks in Sintra at the home of José O'Neill, who was constantly pestering the Dane to fulfill his obligations as a modern tourist. Andersen should take in as many of the sights as possible in this romantic pilgrimage destination of Sintra, which Lord Byron had once made so famous with his sojourns in the city's palaces, villas, and hotels. But Andersen had no wish to "gallivant around like an Englishman," as he said. He preferred to take his own slow and quiet route. Every single day he would start his walk down the road where there was a steep path up to the fairy-tale castle "Palacio da Pena," which was Sintra's landmark. It was said to have been built at the vantage point where King Manuel, in 1499, had caught sight of Vasco da Gama's fleet when he was returning home from India. The colorfully radiant castle had a magnetic effect on the Danish author as it stood there at the top of the mountain, glittering red and blue and chalk-white in the sunlight:

> "Beautiful and picturesque, King Fernando's summer palace, once a cloister, rises up on the mountain slope. The road leading up to it starts with cactuses, chestnuts, and plane trees and ends with birches and firs, where it winds its way among the wildly scattered boulders. From up

there you can see far out toward the mountains beyond Tajo and out to the mighty ocean."[87]

But shouldn't Andersen see something other than the castle? José O'Neill asked him this question every day, and he continued to exasperate the Danish author by wondering what he was thinking of saying back home in Denmark when people asked whether he'd seen anything of Sintra besides the king's palace. "I'll say no!" was Andersen's reply. And he put José O'Neill even more firmly in his place by telling him a story about the Englishman who once, at the top of Mont Blanc, crawled all the way up onto his guide's shoulders so that he would be able to boast that he'd climbed even higher than all the other tourists. It is questionable whether O'Neill understood the insinuation.

While he was in Portugal in 1866, Hans Christian Andersen clearly enjoyed being his own master and not at anyone's beck and call, rushing from place to place in between meetings and dinner engagements—something that he could do with ease and to which he was accustomed. Both his current situation in life and the tense political situation in Europe at the time prompted the Danish author to surrender to the moment and to the spirit in nature. Andersen was on the periphery, after all, on the outskirts of Europe where "the earth ends and the ocean begins," as it says in Portugal's great national epic *Os Lusiados*. And so he was also cut off from central Europe, which was filled with war and unrest. How would the war in Germany play out, and would France be drawn in? Was there truly any reason—other than a Christmas tree, gifts, and roast goose—for him to return home to Denmark in the fall? In Andersen's letters home to the Collin, Henriques, and Melchior families, it's apparent that he couldn't make up his mind how long he wanted to stay in Portugal, where he, like blessed Lord Byron, had found a paradise. The Danish author always referred to Sintra as an "oasis" in his letters, and in his diary entries for July 26 and 28, 1866, he states that "God's nature is sorely lovely here!" He also says it's as if all the regions of Europe have each "contributed a flower to this bouquet, formed by the oasis Sintra."[88]

At a Brothel in Paris

On August 14, 1866, Hans Christian Andersen left Portugal on board the ship *Navarro*, which had come from Rio de Janeiro and was now setting sail for Bordeaux. A couple of poems and epigrams, along with the drafts of two fairy tales, were all that Andersen had produced during his three-month stay in Portugal. His literary output was thus at an all-time low compared with what he normally produced from such lengthy sojourns in the countryside and out in nature. Immediately after his arrival in Lisbon in May, Andersen had indicated in a letter to Fru Ingemann the great expectations he had for his visit in Portugal, and he optimistically spoke of "a new wealth of memories." This presentiment turned out to be true. In his hatbox, Andersen brought home small shards of pottery from the Roman ruins on the Tróia peninsula near Setúbal, four-leaf clovers, big pieces of bark from a cork oak, a lime, several flower seeds for Fru Collin, and various snails in alcohol for Jonas. He also carried with him a great many impressions from a tremendously complex country and its gentle, friendly people, who had neither stolen the author's money nor robbed him of his innocence. The deeper significance of this journey in particular is evident in the last Portugal letter to Edvard Collin, which Andersen sent in August 1866, shortly before boarding the steamship that would take him across the Bay of Biscay. In the letter he takes stock of the previous three months: "I have much to tell you about this beautiful country, of which I have seen little and yet so much."[89]

This time he chose not to race around to pay obligatory calls on royalty and bask in the company of kings, princes, counts, and barons. Nor did he want to subject himself to insistent admirers at the salons, in trains, and in mail coaches. Instead, a solitary, meditative, calm, and unusually composed Hans Christian Andersen found the spirit in nature in the farthest corner of Europe. His sense of emptiness was suddenly gone, as it appears from a letter that Andersen sent to Dorothea Melchior in June 1866, in which he talks about the abandoned cloister right next to the O'Neill villa in Setúbal. He often climbed up there to sit in the shade beneath the big cork trees. He was able to find peace as he sat there, pretending to be a monk, feeling and thinking what so many young, handsome, and chaste men must have felt and dreamed at that spot over the years. Andersen often took along paper and pen on these little pilgrimages, but the blank pages remained untouched. As he wrote to Fru Melchior: "I feel captivated and enjoy it, but that too has its benefits."[90]

Andersen sought an entirely different sort of benefit from his travels to Portugal on his way back home when he spent twenty-four hours in Paris. There he purchased a sash for his medals, had a shave, and paid a call on Alexandre Dumas and his daughter. And in dignified solitude he went to a brothel. One evening, stimulated by the good red wine he had imbibed with his meal at the "Palais Royal," Andersen gathered his courage and threw himself into what he had for so many years both feared and longed for but from which he had always abstained, even though many men had tried to lure him to his ruin—most recently two of the O'Neill brothers in Portugal. After his visit to the Parisian brothel on August 30, 1866, Andersen turned to his diary late at night and confessed his sin:

> "During this whole trip I've been urged to pay a visit to a prostitute. No matter how tired I was, I decided to see one of these kind; I went into a house. A woman came who sold human flesh, four prostitutes appeared for me, they said the youngest was eighteen. I told her to stay, she was wearing hardly anything more than a shift, and I felt so sorry for her. I paid the Madam 5 francs, gave her [the girl] when she asked for it 5 francs, but didn't do anything, just looked at that poor child who uncovered herself completely and seemed astonished that I merely looked at her."[91]

The next morning Andersen once again donned his erotic blinders and continued on his homeward journey, as if nothing had happened. But something *had* happened. For the first time, all alone, Andersen had crossed the threshold of a brothel, paid for the goods, and tasted a bit of the sweetness of the female body, even though it occurred only in his eyes and afterwards nagged at his conscience: "Many Parisian thoughts, it's good that I'm leaving at once. The flesh is weak."[92]

During his stay in Portugal, Andersen was urged many times by Jorge O'Neill to try out the prostitutes of Lisbon, where it was possible to find passions and delights of every variety and for every taste. A few days after the author's arrival, O'Neill started alluding to these types of Lisbon pleasures: "I suppose you'll also want to screw . . . make the acquaintance of young people, who screw everybody."[93] O'Neill was just as stubborn as Andersen, and not long afterwards he once more drew the author aside and touched on this sensitive issue: Was it really true that Andersen didn't want to go to Lisbon to screw? Again Andersen had to turn to his diary and ask forgiveness for all his agitated thoughts: "After dinner [Jorge O'Neill] asked me if I wanted to screw, surely I was in need of it. It could be found in the city . . . Lay in a feverish sweat half the night and couldn't sleep, felt embarrassed in the morning about Georg [Jorge] and my own thoughts all night."[94] And two days later O'Neill again persisted with his suggestion to the lonely author from the cold north. After dinner O'Neill began talking once more about prostitutes, and at last Andersen spoke up and acknowledged his burning desire, but no more than that:

"I confided in him completely, said that I suffered from concupiscence, and he insisted on the necessity of cleaning out the pipes. I felt
dejected after this conversation. Had only cold water in my room in the
evening, probably good for the hot blood."[95]

The Danish word for "concupiscence" was known at the time from
the Bible and it was also used by the peasantry. According to the *Dictionary
of the Danish Language*, it has many meanings, including "fire," "rutting," and
especially "sensual desire."[96] In the sense that Andersen used the word in
1866, it means "lechery." This is how the author used it in other places in
his diary, for instance in 1833-34, when he was staying in Naples and was
very preoccupied with the sorts of things that a man had to do to be considered a man in the eyes of other males. Such things were apparently
going on behind the closed door of his traveling companion, Henrik
Hertz, in Naples. One evening Andersen knocked and was told in great
confusion to go away. Andersen thought about this a good deal in his diary:

> "Naples is more dangerous than Paris; there a person freezes, but here
> the blood burns. God lead me to what is most sensible and best; I don't
> regard this satisfaction as a sin, but I find it loathsome and dangerous with
> such creatures, and an unforgivable sin with an innocent creature. I am
> almost willing to agree with Hertz: Happy is the person who is married
> and does not commit concupiscence."[97]

Henrik Hertz was certainly no St. Paul during their stay in Naples.
And the sensitive, easily incited Andersen could not tolerate hearing Hertz
"talking lewdly," as he writes in his diary in 1834. Yet Hertz called
Andersen his "best friend" and said he was well aware that he "was an absti-
nent person." But he couldn't resist initiating the virginal author into various fiery scenes from city life in the shadow of a volcano, where a person's
concupiscence could be vented as much as possible. It was this lechery that
Andersen had confessed to O'Neill in Portugal, categorizing it as a torment. And so on his way home from Paris in 1866, Andersen decided to
investigate it. It would soon become apparent that the author's visit to the
brothel—in spite of his continued innocence—would exact a price beyond
the five francs. It made him feel that he had to return as quickly as possible to the city of cities. His official purpose was to visit the interesting
world exposition of 1867. Unofficially, he intended—with knowledgeable
and experienced guidance—to penetrate deeper into the labyrinths of
desire and see for himself what his concupiscence was all about. Over the

course of twelve months in 1867–68, he returned three times to the French capital. Even on his first visit in 1833, he described the city in a letter to his friend Christian Voigt as "the most lustful under the sun." Paris had not changed significantly over the years, except that there were more sodomites and places where men could meet and mirror their desire and longing in each other. "A dancing Adam without the fig leaf" was how Andersen described Paris and its visitors in a poem. He experienced the city as a carnival that allowed a person to lose himself in the Babylonian swarm of humanity on the boulevards and, under cover of the moment, do things that would be unthinkable back home in Copenhagen, with its narrow lanes and gossip mirrors at every window. Paris was a distorted paradise, filled with enticing and dangerous mirrors:

> Rushing, shifting, fatiguing, jumbled
> All around me—I am in Paris!
> Every day here is like a carnival day,
> A travesty of a new Paradise.
> Whitewashed graves with painted roses,
> Human souls in swaying reeds
> Dance around me, smiling, luring,
> Testify: "The moment, that is life!"
> The fig leaf is gone along with
> All that is ordinary in humankind.
> I am thinking of Babylon; Eden's
> Tree of Knowledge now grows in Babylon.[98]

The four visits to brothels that Andersen made during the period 1866–68 can all be considered primarily investigations and trial runs. After his first feeble visit attempted on his own in August 1866, Andersen returned in May 1867 along with Robert Watt, again driven by two parts desire and three parts curiosity:

> "After dinner I walked up and down in concupiscence, then suddenly went into a human shop; one was plastered with powder, the second ordinary; the third quite a lady. I spoke to her, paid 12 francs, and left without having sinned in deed, but certainly in my thoughts. She asked me to come back, said I was very innocent for a gentleman. I was so relieved and happy when I exited from that house. Many would call me a coward; is that what I am? Roamed the boulevard that evening and saw painted prostitutes sitting in the cafés playing cards and drinking beer and chartreuse."[99]

On his next two hastily improvised excursions to Paris—in September 1867 and in May 1868—Andersen again ventured into the "human shops" to purchase access to a woman. On each occasion he then proceeded to study the woman intensely while he talked to her. All four times the prostitutes were surprised, to put it mildly, by his passivity and kindness. They all tried to perform their job and do what they could to get this old, ugly man to take off his clothes and *faire l'amour*. But it never happened. Every single time Andersen would rush back to his hotel and enter a cross in his diary. Yet he would also—like Niels Bryde in the novel *To Be or Not to Be*— try to understand himself in light of a deed that was nearly as sinful. And like his alter ego and hero of his novel, Andersen would twist and turn everything demonic that stirred inside him, harnessing it all in words:

> "[Niels Bryde] acknowledged that something demonic was stirring inside him, but he listened to it, reasoning with himself that a person has to have courage to allow all the wild thoughts and forces within to gush out, has to be able to look at them and find the first bubbles of the source, understand the motives of his actions, even if they are vile; yes, know that! A person must manage, without fear, to penetrate that which is sacred to him, must be able to become intimate with every debauched thought, the sin itself, every vice, sense his penchant for it, know the power of his soul in that direction."[100]

That's also how it was for Andersen in connection with his four visits to prostitutes in the late 1860s. Each time he would label it in writing as a virtue that, fortunately, nothing had come of it but talk, even though the desire was also present—and to such a degree that he very nearly forgot his duty and his vow. Andersen described in his diary one evening how men as well as women had tried to lure him to his ruin: "I headed right for home [his hotel], with a feeling that I was protected from the rest of the world and myself; but for how long?"[101]

Was there some deeper purpose behind these visits? Did Andersen use these four brothel visits to search for more than an answer to the question of where the boundaries lay in terms of his own sexual desires? Perhaps these visits to prostitutes were not merely a matter of challenging the vow of chastity that he had given to God and was now putting to the test. There may have been something else enticing him: the social fate and individual life stories of the four girls. This was what the author would always end up talking about on each of his brothel visits, and perhaps their stories reminded him of his own murky family history on his mother's side. In these conversations carried out sitting on the edge of the bed, Andersen gained some insight into the situation and circumstances that his own maternal grandmother and aunt had experienced. This was something that his mother had witnessed firsthand, and it had also touched on Hans Christian Andersen's own childhood. Over the years, it was only in the veiled shapes of fiction that he had dared to approach this dark, shameful side of his past, which in his autobiographies was concealed under a romantic and idyllic layer. But in his literary works we enter the less well-known part of Andersen's life story. This was particularly the case in the novel *Only a Fiddler* (1837) and the fairy tales "She Was No Good" (1852), "The Marsh King's Daughter," (1858) and "The Wood Nymph," which was written during and after the author's first hastily arranged trip to Paris in 1867. It's a story about impoverished young women who sacrifice their bodies and souls on the altar of the big city and are transformed into mayflies.

For someone like Andersen, who traveled for the sake of discovery, his four visits to brothels in the late 1860s were also an expression of his boundless sense of interest and curiosity regarding strangers who might teach him something new about nature. Andersen always met plenty of people on his numerous trips abroad. On his ceaseless travels through foreign cultures in 19th-century Europe, he could see—without interference from anyone back home—his own reflection in much greater worlds. And he could observe firsthand various types of people and temperaments. The result of these observations fills most of his writings, transformed into poetry and prose, and culminating in something of a self-portrait in the fairy tale "Auntie Toothache." In this story we find the old but eternally inquisitive author in the figure of a grocery boy who plunders the filthy bins of reality to find traces of humanity on little discarded scraps of paper covered with handwritten words and notes. The grocery boy finds all possible forms of human testimonies, which he fishes out from the bin and pastes in his big, diverse, and random collection of human destinies. They are in a state of constant flux and transformation, especially as a narrative about human nature.

In the same way, Andersen's numerous trips and encounters with other people provided the author with essential breathing spaces in his occasionally quite painful life. His journeys away from Denmark almost always gave him temporary relief from the social, artistic, and especially the sexual repression and imprisonment that Andersen experienced in his native country. An openness toward and understanding of what was foreign, as well as a tolerance with regard to someone as different and eccentric as Andersen, were all greatly lacking in 19th-century Denmark. This was especially true among the elite and the upper social classes frequented by Andersen. People tended to judge him using the majority as a yardstick. Throughout Andersen's life, pedagogues were always quick to point out the faults and defects of his appearance, manners, art, and sexual identity. It's possible to get a real impression of the type of opposition he had to face most of his life by looking at the furious undercurrent of annoyance and indignation that flows through his three novels of education in the 1830s and continues on in his later novels, such as *To Be or Not to Be* in 1857 and *Lucky Peer* in 1870. Andersen never managed to escape the sort of people who insisted on civilizing sons of nature such as Antonio, Otto, Christian, Niels, and Peer, trying to make them more unequivocally masculine. But far from Denmark, out among strangers, Andersen found a freedom that was infinitely greater physically and psychologically than "the damp, gray, philistine city," as he in dark moments called Copenhagen. Everywhere in Europe during the Romantic period—in Paris, Rome, London, Berlin, and Amsterdam; in Weimar, Dresden, Hamburg, Venice, Florence, and Naples— Andersen saw himself in all the diverse manifestations of what it means to be human. And with this life-affirming mirror in mind, he would seek out the greatest and most crowded sites of the day—the boulevards, terraces, and promenades where people, in those days too, would gather to see and to be seen. Places like Regent Street, the Prater, Unter den Linden, the Brühl Terrace, the Corso, and the Champs-Élysées. These were the places where Andersen liked to stroll with his young male traveling companions in the flood of light from the gas streetlamps and lanterns. He would go to shops, to restaurants and cafés. And every single evening, if possible, he would also attend the theater—that flirtatious space where Amor, as described in the fairy tale "The Naughty Boy," always sits up on the great chandelier, burning brightly. People in the theater think it's just a lamp, but later they notice something else entirely. "Naughty, naughty Amor!"

The rest of Europe meant freedom for Andersen. There he found a much larger and freer human arena than in his native country, where people thought a sunset was only truly proper and beautiful if it was viewed from their own hilltop. Andersen gives this notion ironic expression in a witty little drama from 1868, *In the Vetturina*. In this play we hear about the average Dane in the person of Fru Svendsen from Nørrebro in Copenhagen, who has strayed into Italy along with her daughter and lap dog named Delle. On their way south through Europe, she complains that nothing measures up to Danish standards. In this excoriation of Denmark and the Danes, Fru Svendsen and Delle become the incarnations of a nation that is no longer interested in nature and thus has also lost contact with the rest of the world. Fru Svendsen is constantly cursing the wretched "tub" of a coach that they've been condemned to travel in, along with all the sinister-looking foreigners, who stink of garlic and oil. Or else they are cheaters and swindlers who, like the artist in one corner of the coach, just want to get their hands on Fru Svendsen's lovely daughter. And in Fru Svendsen's suspicious little Danish eyes, the Englishman in the other corner is a pompous ass who is "hobnobbing with the languages."

Unlike Fru Svendsen and Delle, Andersen wanted to go out into the world and be a Dane in a new, different, and more modern way. In the wake of the grand ideas about human beings, art, science, and religion that arose with the Enlightenment and high Romanticism, there was still, in Andersen's opinion, a call for freedom of the individual, in spite of incipient national bickering and unrest. During the 1830s, 1840s, and 1850s, he had found his own place and stage, which meant constant traveling and motion—in both reality and in his imagination. Like a child.

It is in light of this comprehensive tenderness and longing for the whole world—life far away on the globe and deep inside a person—that we should understand Hans Christian Andersen as "a traveler." His prayer to the world was: "Allow me to develop freely, in accordance with my own nature!" And "Take me as I am!" he implored. There was seldom room for that in his native Denmark.

Chapter Ten

The Man in the Moon (1870-1875)

"From America?" the author shouts to his housekeeper. His voice can be heard out in the entryway, where the two guests, who have not yet taken off their hats and coats, cast an inquisitive glance at each other, trying to hear more of the conversation on the other side of the wall. Suddenly the old woman appears before them and reports that the Councilor of State will see Herr Bergsøe and his American friend.

They step into a bright, narrow front room with two windows facing Nyhavn. In two corners of the room are busts of Hans Christian Andersen and Jenny Lind. Paintings and photographs in various sizes and in all kinds of frames hang on the walls. The tables and windowsills are crowded with potted plants and cut flowers in vases. From this flower room the guests continue on into the drawing room, which also has windows facing the street and canal. In the corner next to one window is the author's work area with piles of clippings, magazines and newspapers. Between the windows stands a console table with mirror. The many knickknacks and souvenirs on the shelf include a silver dock leaf, a Turkish fez, and a thick piece of bark from a cork tree. A faint scent of eau de cologne drifts from the green sofa, which stands in the center of the room behind an oval table covered with a tapestry cloth and with a porcelain bowl on top. Everything is done in the rococo style, framed by two tall bookshelves, with paintings and photos on the wall over the sofa.[1] In the midst of it all is Hans Christian Andersen, reclining in a flowered dressing gown with his head resting on a stack of pillows. He nods to his guests: the Danish author Vilhelm Bergsøe, and twenty-five-year-old Hjalmar Hjorth Boyesen, who is professor of Nordic languages and literature at Cornell University in New York, as well as editor of the Atlantic Magazine.

"So you've come all the way from America, Herr Boyesen? Well, nowadays the distance is a mere trifle. I have many friends in America. Do you know Horatz Scooder?"

"Horatz Scooder?" Professor Boyesen thinks for a moment. "No, I don't think I do."

"But surely you've heard of him. He's a very respected author!"

"It may well be that he is a respected man, but not an author," replies Boyesen. "I

know the names of most of the important writers in America, but I've never heard of Horatz Scooder."

"How strange," Andersen goes on, looking worried. "I heard that his books were supposed to be both charming and popular, and besides, he's translating most of my fairy tales into American English."

"Oh, you mean Horace Scudder!" exclaims Boyesen with a laugh. "Yes, yes, he certainly is a well-known author. I even have the pleasure of knowing him personally."

Relieved to hear that his translator is a well-known name, Andersen sinks back on the pillows. He now wants to know something about the modern America about which he has never managed to write. Would a Nordic elf know how to behave decently over there? Boyesen thinks this can certainly be done, and if Herr Andersen should one day honor his country with a visit, he offers to be his guide. If it's possible to avoid seasickness by being telegraphed across the Atlantic, then Andersen will gladly visit: "It's odd how distant America has become for me. I can easily imagine myself up on the moon, and I can picture all sorts of amusing things taking place there. But in the great, cold, and prosaic land to the west, the poetic imagination must starve to death from lack of material."

Boyesen disagrees with this and talks about bustling Manhattan and Broadway, which is so crowded with traffic that the police officers often have to escort elegant ladies across the street. Andersen sits up for a moment so that his long, thin legs are clearly visible. "Is that true?" he says, laughing. "I'd certainly like to see that, even though I would most likely get run over! Life over there must be simply colossal!"

Suddenly Andersen grows somber and wants to know why the Indians are treated so badly. Young Boyesen begs to differ with this opinion, and in his argument he makes use of Charles Darwin's theory about natural selection and the survival of the fittest. That angers Andersen. He calls Darwin a crazy, insignificant hack who merely imagines that he is descended from an ape: "It's so sad that people can't be satisfied with what God has taught them, but have to criticize His Word, as if they know better than He does. Useful inventions that make life easier and better—those I can approve of with all my heart, and scientists ought to restrict themselves to that sort of thing. But whenever anyone comes to me and wants to rob me of my faith in God and His Word, then I say to them: 'I beg your pardon, gentlemen, but I know just as much about this subject as you do, and I'm not about to accept you as my commander!'"[2]

And with that the conversation is over. And Hjalmar Hjorth Boyesen, who is in Europe to collect material for a couple of books about contemporary authors, continues on his way a few days later. His essay about Hans Christian Andersen is completed and published only after the Danish author has been dead for twenty years, and the American professor is himself at the end of his life. The essay starts with the words:

"Hans Christian Andersen was a unique figure in Danish literature and a solitary phenomenon in the literature of the world. Superficial critics have compared him with the Brothers Grimm; they might with equal propriety have compared him to Voltaire or with the man in the moon."[3]

*A*NDERSEN MET MANY PEOPLE during his lifetime, but he never managed to meet Charles Darwin. As young men in the early 1830s, both set off on journeys of discovery that dealt with human existence and would last for the rest of their lives. Andersen's literary course toward Fata Morgana was no less determined than Darwin's natural science expedition to the Galapagos Islands. Whereas the man of science stayed on land among the animal species in order to lead humans back to their cradle, the author traveled into the soul and explored the depths of the human psyche. Both asked the same fundamental questions: Who are we? Where did we come from? And where might we be going?

Andersen's knowledge of Darwin's theory of evolution came primarily from the young Danish author Jens Peter Jacobsen, who had written a series of articles about Darwin for *Nyt Dansk Maanedsskrift* in 1870.[4] This progressive journal was a forum for the ideas of a new era, especially the heated debate about whether humans had been created in God's image or in the image of an ape. The journal lay on the fairy-tale author's desk in Nyhavn. This was partly because in the same issue from October 1870 in which Jacobsen writes about Darwin, Andersen's latest fairy tale, "The Most Incredible Thing," was also published. The story deals with a spiritual barbarian who leaps onto the stage of life and vandalizes the eternal values.[5] While this wonderfully told story about the immortality of art insists on a worldview in which human evolution is placed in the hands of God, Jacobsen's series of articles in 1870-71 about Darwin propose exactly the opposite. His articles proclaimed that humans arose in a world without any form of divine guidance, and that everything came into existence through a battle with everything else. To Andersen's ears, this idea sounded like a terrible curse; nevertheless, it did fit with quite a few things he had experienced in his own life. Wasn't Andersen—the proletarian boy from Fyn who had been forced to starve and battle for life—a shining example of Darwin's theory of survival of the fittest?

No matter how reluctant he was to admit it, Andersen carefully read all about Darwin in *Nyt Dansk Maanedsskrift*. New theories about the organization of nature interested Andersen, who once long ago had promised H. C. Ørsted to create a literature for the new era, based on the discoveries and perceptions of natural science. But that was "back then," before 1860, when science and a belief in progress were still founded on equal parts fantasy and naïveté. In 1859, Darwin's *On the Origin of Species* was published in England, but by then Andersen had already been convinced for many years that, in spite of everything, there were limits to God's extraordinary management of human life. In the late 1850s, as he began to have doubts about many things, the ever-searching, skeptical author also adopted a critical view of Christianity. Yet he was even more skeptical of the scientific materialism that was then spreading with dizzying speed and soon would emerge as "The Modern Breakthrough." Andersen refused to accept a view of humanity as a mechanism utterly bereft of spirit—in spite of the new era's lovely sight of hot-air balloons, steamships, and trains. In his view, this would mean "a despairing existence in which immortality and even God disappear." And his growing skepticism about what is "modern" would then give rise to a *horror vacui*—a dread of the void. Along with his fear of having nothing to believe in besides money in the savings bank, this sense of dread began to appear between the lines of everything he was writing. All of these reflections, which had been temporarily put aside after his novel *To Be or Not to Be* appeared in 1857, once again came to the fore when Darwin's books were translated by Jens Peter Jacobsen into Danish in 1870. For Andersen, these were distressing ideas that disparaged all that was extraordinary in human beings, and it called for some kind of counterattack. This came two months before Andersen's death in 1875 and took the form of a poem, a call to arms that was critical of civilization. The poem, "Difficult Times," expressed what Andersen, once and for all, wanted to tell this Charles Darwin:

> Our era is now writing its book of wisdom;
> Will it be for good or for worse?
> It's terrible to be so clever
> That you don't believe in Our Lord!
>
> Oh, it would be better for anyone
> Who offends those less able-minded
> If a millstone hung around his neck
> and he lay deep in the sea.
>
> Now those abundantly clever know:
> God was created by human ingenuity,
> And the human being is "infallible,"
> An element is the source of life.

All we endeavored, suffered, endured,
Is extinguished with life's flame.
Into a fathomless void we sink.
Good and evil are one and the same.

Oh, eternal God, stay with us! Stay!
In You and of You all is given!
Grant us in grace "eternal life"
And memories of our life on earth![6]

No bust or painting of Darwin was ever put up in the home of the aging Andersen in Nyhavn. There wasn't even room for a tiny image of the natural scientist in a far corner of the huge folding screen on which the Danish author had begun to paste pictures during the winter of 1873-74. The images on the screen were supposed to represent all the people who had been of importance to Andersen and to the 19th century.

Andersen's folding screen, which must be regarded as the culmination of his work as a visual artist, is a movable and reversible collage presented in eight large chapters, each measuring 1.53 meters in height and 62.5 centimeters in width. It is in all respects a huge and unwieldy work which, during its creation in 1873-74, practically filled Andersen's small apartment. After it was finished, it stood in front of the author's bed in the third and innermost room of his apartment on the second floor at Nyhavn 18, which had a view of the Botanical Gardens that had been located behind Charlottenborg for many years, although by now the site was designated for development. The function of the folding screen, other than as decoration, was to hide the materialistic investment—a bed—which Andersen had been virtually forced to make by Fru Collin and Fru Melchior in 1866. It was an investment that he bitterly regretted. At the same time, the screen served as a movable folding wall with a series of large images from the complex and wondrous world in which Andersen had traveled so often, although during the past few years of his life he had to make do with lying in bed and reminiscing. The eight collages, four on each side, were arranged geographically as well as artistically and culturally, according to the countries, milieux, and worlds which throughout the century had contributed to shaping Andersen as a person and an author. Each area was separate, but in many places they overflowed their thematic and geographical frames and merged with other worlds on the folding screen, just as the author's own life had taken shape.

Collages of Words and Pictures

It was nothing new for Andersen to give a fairy tale concrete, figurative form by making paper-cuts or by creating a collage from small or large clippings from the day's newspapers and magazines. But because of his age and the rheumatism that made it harder for him to hold a pen for long periods of time, these types of collages began playing a greater and more vital role in Andersen's oeuvre. In the 1830s and 1840s, the numerous drawings he made with pen and pencil (approximately 300 in all) seemed to be his preferred means for expressing himself as a visual artist. The pen-and-ink drawings from his travels also served a photographic purpose. In the 1860s and 1870s, all his "paper-poems," as Andersen called his paper-cuts and collages, became an increasingly visible part of his work. This culminated in 1873-74 with the folding screen and a couple of large, imaginative paper-cuts intended for bazaars and good friends, including the Melchior family at their country home "Rolighed," where Andersen stayed for lengthy periods. There he had his own little apartment, and that was where he died on August 4, 1875.

Andersen's pictorial art gradually changed its focus from drawings to paper-cuts and collages, and over time he started "drawing" with his scissors. This had to do with a boom in the whole paper and printing industry during the 1840s. It meant that Andersen, as a traveling author, no longer needed to archive all his sensory impressions by making hasty drawings in the sketchbooks he had brought along, as described by the sculptor Jens Adolf Jerichau:

> "Andersen couldn't afford to buy pictures of the regions he had traveled through, but he always had paper and pencil at hand. And whenever, for instance, the *vetturina* would stop, he would immediately start sketching."[7]

Eventually Andersen had greater opportunities and could better afford to bring a little of the world back home from his journeys. By means of the new lithographic printing techniques, which had become more and more sophisticated since the 1820s, it was now possible to distribute portraits, popular genre and landscape images, cards, and teaching materials in great quantities all over Europe. This also meant that someone like Andersen, who loved to cut and paste, suddenly had access to an enormous number of pictures, drawings, and prints from far and near that could be used to spark a faulty memory after he returned home from a trip and wanted to reconstruct the "unforgettable" views and sights. Many of these pictures also became incorporated as elements in Andersen's collages in the relatively numerous one-of-a-kind picture books that he made in the 1850s and 1860s for the children of his friends.

"Things often wind up in the bin that shouldn't be in the bin." That's what it says at the beginning of the fairy tale "Auntie Toothache" from 1872. The story is itself a sort of literary collage in which various layers of text and narrative are placed inside of each other. It's a tale about the fact that great art most often arises from what at first is filled with pleasure and idyllic sweetness but later hurts like hell and can end up devouring a person. In short, it's a story about existential "cavities," as told by a student who, before he managed to become a famous writer, died of tooth pains and other ailments. He left all his manuscripts to his landlady, who sold them to the delicatessen owner for half a pound of green soap. The shopkeeper, in turn, intended to use all the papers to make paper twists for wrapping up coffee beans and salt herring. But his bookworm son—a real "paper-twist reader"—instantly fished the beautifully handwritten pages out of his father's bin and added them to his diverse collection of texts. And these pages form the majority of the narrative as we hear about them in a Cervantes-like frame story in "Auntie Toothache."

Andersen was also just such a "paper-twist reader." At his death he left behind an enormous quantity of paperwork, enough to nearly bury his residuary legatee, Edvard Collin. Much of this paperwork consisted of all sorts of collected and saved texts—not only his own but also letters and scraps of paper that had been sent or delivered to him, as well as clippings from newspapers, magazines, and journals. They formed great piles of paper that not only testified to the author's diligence with pen and paper but also reflected the fact that throughout his literary career, he had always paid close attention to what other people were writing, drawing, and printing. As previously discussed, much of what Andersen, the "paper-twist reader," found in various places would then become included in his fairy tales. Certain items would inspire him to retell a story, or they would be wholly or partially inserted into a larger frame narrative of his own invention. Andersen was amazingly clever at cutting and pasting, not only with scissors and glue pot but also with his pen. We find literary montages everywhere in his novels, plays, poems, and fairy tales. He was fully aware of this talent of his, and he wasn't shy about putting it into words—especially for children, who instinctively understood his desire to take things apart and then put them together in a new way: "Andersen, what a genius is he. / His paper-cuttings are the key!" That's what he wrote to one-year-old Astrid Stampe in the big, beautiful picture book he made for her in 1853.

We find traces of Andersen's scissors in many places throughout his writings. This is particularly true of his longer texts; in his novels and plays he often vigorously cuts and pastes people and settings, making such great leaps—often illogical and abrupt—in time and space that the reader occasionally both loses his sense of direction and runs out of breath. One pleasant exception is Andersen's first novel from 1829, *Walking Tour*, in which the most varied and contradictory items seem to be pasted together and inserted into this astonishing "bin" of a novel, which in many ways is typical for its time. The book is teeming with clippings, both large and small, from other literary genres. All jumbled together are poems, diary excerpts, dramatic fragments, aphorisms, and diverse little quotations from contemporary literature. There are also snippets from Greek and Latin classics, taken out of their original context and pasted into a more up-to-date frame, which creates both dissonance and harmony, depending on how the reader chooses to regard these textual collisions. But it's primarily in the brief and more supple form of Andersen's fairy tales that his literary collage technique fully comes into its own. In addition to "Auntie Toothache," we find superb examples in "The Door Key," "The Cripple," "The Snow Queen," "The Traveling Companion," "The Sandman," "Soup from a Sausage Peg," "The Marsh King's Daughter," and "The Galoshes of Fortune." Andersen inserts sections and narrative fragments from various genres and spheres into his text, making his fairy tales shift in space and time.

When discussing Andersen's refurbishing of the fairy-tale genre in the 19th century, it's essential to keep in mind the collage technique, which was a well-known stylistic feature of the literary arts during Romanticism. Time after time we see how this Danish world champion in creating illusions breaks the unity of his composition and in a matter of a few pages manages to pull the rug out from under the reader. The direction of both the form and content in Andersen's best fairy tales can almost never be predicted. The story may proceed up or down, out or in, forward or backward, in time as well as space, and along the way the reader continually comes upon boxes within boxes and layer upon layer of text. As it says of the professor's clever trick in the tale "The Flea and the Professor," when he makes his wife disappear during his magic show:

"He stuffed his wife into the table drawer, a big table drawer; there she crawled into the back drawer, and so she was not to be seen in the front drawer; it was like an optical illusion."[8]

Modern art books and reference works often say that the collage was something that the Cubists invented at the beginning of the 20th century. Then the Dadaists and Surrealists cultivated the art of the collage in the 1920s and 1930s, and modern Pop artists like Andy Warhol rediscovered it in the 1960s, using it as an artistic means of expression for their time. Yet even in the 19th century, people were creating images from a wide variety of materials, especially from other little printed pictures or fragments put together in new and surprising ways. This was something that had actually been going on ever since the printers found a way to reproduce text and images and thus provide the material basis for the collage. More than fifty years before the Cubists and Surrealists began cutting and pasting with newspaper fragments, colored paper, labels, and photographs, Hans Christian Andersen was actively making collages. And he was not the only one who cultivated this art form in the 19th century. Such a meticulously planned and ambitious project as the big folding screen that Andersen placed in front his bed also had its forerunners. In March 1873, Countess Wanda Danneskiold-Samsøe visited the old author in Nyhavn. On that occasion she gave him a small screen in a beautifully carved oak frame that she had made. Andersen was very enthused about the idea of placing pictures, especially small portraits, in such close proximity, and he wrote in his diary:

"Colored pictures on one side and non-colored ones on the other, cut out, pasted next to each other, merging as if forming a single image and yet an infinite number of them, they slid into one another like a strange dream. All arranged with taste and imagination."[9]

In other words, Andersen was inspired. And it's also possible that five or six years earlier, perhaps in connection with one of his trips to Paris in 1867-68, he was equally inspired by a big photo collage, "The Court of Napoleon III," which had been cut and pasted by the German painter and woodcarver Kaspar Braun in 1865. In this collage, hundreds of tiny human portraits were pasted close together, standing shoulder to shoulder and face-to-face—similar to the way they appeared on the marvelous folding screen that Andersen created eight years later.

Whether we look at the author's picture collages stretched across an entire screen or boiled down and concentrated on single pages in a picture book for children, the extensive collage art present in Andersen's works offers solid documentation for the author's unshakable faith in the fact that oral, written, and cut-out tales spring from the moment. That's why more than a hundred and fifty years later, so many of Andersen's collages that are scattered through the sixteen unique picture books that he made for children still seem incomparably fresh. Life seems to teem from many of these old images that Andersen created by pasting together train tickets, newspaper headlines, scraps of advertisements, postcards, and road maps. Often he would finish the pictures by adding a touch of watercolor paint in primary colors, or by pasting on top a bright violet, orange, or neon-green piece of paper that he had left over, to give a little more pizzazz to an image that had too much black and white. As Andersen explains in one of the five picture books that he made for Louise Collin's daughter, Agnete Lind, on a page where a shiny red scrap is glaringly juxtaposed with a uniformly dull newspaper clipping: "It is red, / It is sweet, / It is good there, the picture won't be drab!"[10]

What's special about a typical Andersen collage in his picture books for children is the way he manages to tell a story by using many different visual images but only a few, though very carefully chosen, words that attempt to bring together the wide range of visual elements in the collage. A small child looking at a picture book by Hans Christian Andersen could also get by with just looking at the images, making associations, and then constructing his own connections. Older children and childlike adults who were looking over the shoulder of the youngster could discover the author's intent behind the collage by reading the spare verses that were often added. For instance, what was a person supposed to make of a figurative paper-cut made from gold paper, with the author's scribbled handwriting in the center? Andersen offered his own answer: "Gold across, / a verse inside, / what a lark."[11]

Yet the author's own verses never provided all the answers. It was utterly essential for a collage-maker like Andersen, who was fond of children, that the young reader be a participant in and co-creator of the picture book. As it clearly says in *Astrid Stampe's Picture Book*, in which a great variety of images are placed on the page before the child, like a more or less random conglomeration of building blocks in the nursery: "From Italy's nature / You have here a piece of wall. / Here is a cactus, here a vine, / Put them together in your mind."[12]

Many Picture Books

Andersen made some of his best picture books together with Adolph Drewsen, who was the grandfather of the three Stampe daughters, to whom we will return shortly. Among the men of the Collin family, Drewsen was the one with whom Andersen got along best on a daily basis. In the 1820s, they had almost simultaneously made their entry into the self-confident and proud family—Andersen as a friend of the family, and Drewsen as the new son-in-law and husband of the family's eldest daughter, Ingeborg. The fact that the relationship between Andersen and Drewsen was so friction-free can also be explained in light of their shared joy for nature, children, and, in particular, cutting and pasting. Everything became synthesized in their joyous creation of picture books. In a playful letter from 1857, devised as an anonymous appeal to the world-famous creator of "the Agnete Literature" (Hans Christian Andersen) from "Your great admirer N.N." (Adolph Drewsen), the apprentice submissively asks his master for an appraisal of a picture book that N.N. has created on his own. In this connection, Drewsen anticipates a negative reply as he refers to the impending crushing condemnation from Andersen, and he calls his work "the wrong side of a story; because it's the story that creates the pictures, but here the opposite occurs and the pictures have created the story."[13]

This splendid formulation—"the wrong side of a story"—can be used to advantage regarding the sixteen picture books that Andersen made in the 1850s and 1860s. Unlike the author's literary works, and in spite of scattered little verses in the picture books, it's not the words but the collages that create the narrative in these unique works. This is quite apparent in one of the five picture books belonging to Agnete Lind. Thinking about his own difficult path through the theater world in 1820, Andersen chose to take the little girl by the hand and accompany her on the road out into life's great masquerade. "Preferably the Casino and not the Opera!" says the pleasure-seeking Agnete quite firmly, and the author does not contradict her. Then the two of them experience all sorts of strange things on their way to the theater. They hear about other performances, and their anticipation grows. But before the book and the journey are over, we suffer a great disappointment—as so often happens in life as well as at the theater—because the performance at the Casino is sold out.

"This Agnete Literature" is what Andersen himself called his picture book production, which began with the first books for Louise Collin's daughter in the early 1850s and at intervals, sometimes long and sometimes short, continued for the rest of the author's life, as new, dear children appeared. The picture books for Agnete Lind were unbound essay books that were far more fragile than the big, leather-bound books with fine handmade paper that Andersen gave to the daughters of Jonna and Henrik Stampe. Adolph Drewsen helped him to gather material and make clippings for the latter books. The images came from hundreds of newspapers and magazines of all different types, both domestic and foreign, including *Portefeuillen, Berliner Illustrierte Blätter, Alamanach Comique, Münchener Bilder, Le Charivari, Dagen*, and *Folkets Nisse*.

But the picture books for Agnete Lind were exclusively "collected, cut, and pasted by Hans Christian Andersen." That's what it says on each of them, and there is no question of the artistic copyright regarding the Agnete books, in which the young reader, from the very first page, is securely in Andersen's recognizable hands. As the author of picture books, he tried to be just as meticulously and perceptibly present in the collages as he was in his fairy tales, though without trying to steer them as much. And he never talked down to the children but always engaged them, for example by giving sweet little nudges and urging them to enjoy the reading, which was meant to be fun and not terribly serious. As always in Andersen's work, emotion and pleasure were foremost. Just listen: "Here's a bit of every sort, / Look, and read, and have some fun!" And halfway through the same Agnete book, it's finally time to show a little common sense: "Read and look at the picture book, / Do not toss it in the corner." And to round it off in a merry way, which probably amused the adult reader most, the picture book was evaluated by a cheerful, jovial critic, whom Andersen had cut out of a German magazine. There he sits, having himself a proper pint of beer: "A good glass of Bavarian beer he took, / and with it Agnete's picture book, / He drank and read, and looked and laughed too! / Yes, it's a good book, let me tell you!"

Humor was of great importance in the picture books that Andersen created. Merriment and lightness with regard to life's more serious matters were part of the pedagogical method. Anything that smelled of tragedy was quickly given a heavy dose of comedy. Under the picture of a terribly dour-looking man holding a stick, it says in *Astrid Stampe's Picture Book* from 1853: "Here goes to town a grieving man, / he walks with a furled umbrella in hand."[14] Oh, yes, in a book for children a person's inner umbrella should be just as optimistic and colorful as the Sandman's. Comedy could also be found in the age-old game of putting different heads on different bodies, or turning a picture or text upside down. For instance, in one of the Agnete books, Andersen seized the opportunity to cut a very exotic picture from the Tonga Islands out of the frame of its original article and then make the story his own. He pasted images of celebrating natives on a distant South Pacific island into a picture book along with a brief news report from a Fyn newspaper about the famous author Hans Christian Andersen, who had been a guest at a banquet given by the governor in Odense. Even in the more philosophical category of humor, which Andersen did not employ very often, he might suddenly pop up and show his teeth. For example, a satirical picture in one of the Agnete books has the headline "Aus dem Hundeleben" [From the Life of a Dog]. It shows dogs dressed up in human clothes, and the author's comment is: "The life of a dog—yes, how human it is."[15] And under a clipping that shows an old, rather stooped mother and her straight-backed young son trudging out of town, it says: "People walk for pleasure / and for their digestion, / they walk just to walk, / and because they must!"[16]

Any show of deference to strictly pedagogical, didactic methods was virtually never allowed to appear in Andersen's picture book production, especially not at the expense of any potential entertainment value. In the Agnete books in particular, it's quite evident that Headmaster Meisling's rebellious pupil from Slagelse Grammar School enjoyed the role of teacher and educator, in which he gave *emotions* just as much importance as *reason*; and once in a while he would take the liberty of letting creative chaos loose. But young Agnete Lind was of course supposed to learn something more substantial from Andersen the teacher—for instance, something about the plant and animal kingdoms, the history of religion, geography, and the art of poetry. Quite a number of the collages are composed of scraps from a book containing verses Andersen wrote about Danish poets. They came from his 1832 poetry collection titled *Vignettes for Danish Poets*. On one page of Agnete's book, fragments are scattered over the pink book cover from the first edition, to which Andersen added: "Verses / every which way. / These are not drafts, / But vignettes."[17]

Hans Christian Andersen created approximately sixteen picture books, and they are all one-of-a-kind. There was never any question of reproducing them, and most were put together in the 1850s and 1860s. He made them as new batches of children were born, baptized, and grew up among the families that he regularly visited, in the homes where he felt appreciated and welcome. For this reason the picture books should be viewed and read as an expression of the author's joy for these children and their families. And the books were received with particular joy by the children's parents, who realized they represented a gift and a gesture of friendship to the entire family. Various remarks in Andersen's diaries and letters from the 1850s and 1860s indicate that there may have been more picture books than the sixteen we know today. Half of the extant books were created for the daughters of two women belonging to the Collin family and their circle—Louise Lind (née Collin) and Jonna Stampe (née Drewsen)—whom Andersen had once swooned for in his own naïve and impulsive fashion.[18] In light of this fact, it might be said that eight of the picture books were intended for several little girls for whom Andersen, in theory, could have been more than a godfather. And the thought did occur to him while he was creating these marvelous books. This is especially evident in the charmingly coquettish playing with the role of narrator. Andersen was in his element in this veiled, in-between role of godfather, father, and happy fiancé to the four little girls. It was all in all an innocent but conscious role-playing, which gained further sustenance from the letters that a grateful Jonna Stampe wrote to thank the author on her daughters' behalf for the wonderful picture books:

> "My dear author and my dear friend! I have promised Immy [Rigmor] to write on her behalf to her godfather, who pleased her so much by sending her a crimson letter, which she showed to 'everyone' and then ending up tearing, so I took it away from her . . . we have to keep a sharp eye on her because she's an incomparable wildcat who suddenly runs off to all the horses and all the watchdogs. She still loves very much the figures that you cut out for her at Christmas, and she begs me to iron 'all the ladies' as soon as she sees a flatiron, because she once saw me smoothing them out in that way. Whenever she sees your picture in the book, she says so touchingly: 'That's Anser,' and then kisses it."[19]

The picture books for the three Stampe daughters at the Nysø estate were created in 1851, 1853, and 1859. They're different from the Agnete books not only in size and because of the fine leather binding, but they also have many more colorful paper-cuts, little verses, and rhymes that are the author's own creation—especially in *Astrid Stampe's Picture Book*. The Stampe daughters' books were also more expansive in their kaleidoscopic view of life outside the nursery, and they were quite advanced in terms of the underlying educational intent. The books constantly make clear to the Stampe children that the world is much bigger and more dangerous but also more exciting and challenging than what a child sees in the adults' drawing room or on the road outside the front door of the Nysø manor house. Andersen, as the collage artist, always keeps his eye on the horizon. Yet at no time does he forget that we are inside a picture book for Danish children, which is why he presents what is distant and foreign in relation to what is close at hand and familiar. For instance, he says of a picture showing an enormous fish against a landscape: "A whale close to Nysø Garden / He wants to come on land, he has a stomach ache."[20] This was how Andersen, as teacher, challenged the world view of the young Stampe children. He tried to prod their curiosity and sympathy instead of evoking dread or fear.

Untraditional and demanding. That's how Andersen's diverse teaching methods must be characterized in terms of his many godchildren. "Here you see the world very small, / Can you understand it all?" he asks the infant Astrid in 1853.[21] Astrid could hardly have done so. But this fascinating outpouring of pictures for her and her sisters consisted of approximately 1,000 in each book, including images of all kinds, from maps, landscapes, and city landmarks to historical events, portraits, studies of animals and flowers, as well as pictures of furniture and tools. In the years following the Stampe daughters' baptism, these books must have done their part to help the girls on their way in the world, which must have seemed terribly huge, even in such a tiny land as Denmark. It also must have been wonderfully reassuring to hold in their hands a "guide" by Hans Christian Andersen, who was fully aware of his obligations and responsibility as a storyteller. He knew when to stop in the midst of a chaotic stream of images, which provided the primary ideas in his collage and picture books. As it suddenly says in one of the books under a hand-colored picture of Vejle Fjord, seen from the south—after a couple of pages of swarming images and clippings: "You cannot fail, / here the road goes to Vejle!"[22] And when the young reader has once again presumably gone astray amidst the six or seven whirling collages, with clippings and words that shimmer before the eyes, the narrator is right there with his compass and overview: "If you can see it in your mind, / Kärnan tower in Sweden you will find."[23]

Writing with Scissors

There are many examples of wordplay in the picture books, such as the almost Zen-like verse: "On water the swan is beauty's mate / Up on land it has an awful gait."[24] Yet some of the greatest moments in these books occur when Andersen places two or more paper-cuts of various bright colors and sizes against the black-and-white background of the collage. It was almost as if he had sprinkled a great many little paper-cuts, torn scraps, and fragments of old clippings over the work, as he did with Astrid Stampe's book. And by doing so, Andersen gave his collage art a new dimension and depth. Suddenly all the modern materials of the day—newspaper head-lines, pictures, tickets, programs, sheet music, city maps, train schedules, and bills—were set off by rounder, softer shapes and figures from a much different era and world. A world in which Andersen's fairy tales also had their roots. It was precisely in this way that a particularly exciting dialogue arose in his collages, stretching from ancient, heathen times to the hyper-modern science and technology of the 19th century.

Andersen used his scissors as the spokesman for the age-old folk poetry; as such, it was a medium like the wise woman's eyeglasses and the ear trumpet in the fairy tale "What a Person Can Think Up" from 1869. In this story, a young poet from the city who has no imagination has to go out in the country and borrow the little old woman's magic tools, which will put some spark and fantasy into his pale modernity: "'It's a whole romantic story!' said the young man . . . 'Story on top of story! It spins and spins! It's all a jumble to me! I'm falling over!'" In the same way, from Andersen's scissors flowed a jumble of little stories, fairy-tale figures, and timeless representatives from a distant past, for which there was little room or understanding in the late 19th century. In 1873, at a dinner in Hannover, a German admirer who wanted to propose a toast to Andersen said that everything the Dane had created with pen, paper, and scissors was an expression of "the glory of poetry in our materialistic age."[25]

As far as the paper-cuts in the picture books were concerned, very few of them were originally created with the intention of placing them on a specific page in the book. As part of a collage, they were pieces in a game, and during the creative process they might well be moved around in the collage. This was how Andersen himself happened to explain it, more or less by chance, in *Astrid Stampe's Picture Book* in a little verse under a charmingly complex potpourri vase composed of no fewer than twenty-two little cutouts from eleven different types of colored paper. About this enchanting game—"the poetry of chance," as he liked to call it—Andersen writes: "Here is a vase of flowers, / It's Andersen's cutting and pasting!"[26] And in another place in the book, under a wide range of colored paper-cuts with reeds, ivy, ribbons, dancers, and swans, the author tries once again to gather the many different elements that he has scattered in his collage:

Andersen's poetry is what it's about
In cut-outs!
Colorful, peculiar it appears,
And all with shears.[27]

That was Andersen's own explanation of a particularly spectacular and jumbled spread in *Astrid Stampe's Picture Book*. And this is how we should view his paper art—as something ("colorful, peculiar it appears") which has close poetic ties to the rest of the author's art. It should not be simply separated out and placed next to his literary work. There are approximately 800 individual paper-cuts remaining today—from primitive figures and simple tableaux to the more ornamental and sophisticated designs. Certainly they represent a world unto themselves, but they also have their roots in the same rich, all-embracing author's imagination which in the 19th century revolutionized world literature with 150 fairy tales. This is why Hans Christian Andersen's many paper-cuts and drawings cannot simply be dismissed as an amusing pastime, a kind of therapy, or a game, as Andersen scholars have done for the past one hundred years. Nor can they merely be regarded as funny, entertaining illustrations for what most people consider to be the real and essential part of Andersen's work: the fairy-tale world of his written texts.

Andersen felt a natural inclination to draw and to "cut and paste"; it was as strong an urge as to write and to travel. He was always armed with pen and scissors, since he could always make use of them while he was waiting. And a sketch or a little, hastily improvised paper-cut could also help to start up a conversation with other people on the long journeys by mail coach and stagecoach. But the practical aspect also had its price, as Andersen experienced in the summer of 1836 when he was on his way from the Lykkesholm estate to Odense. He was joined by the actor Christian Foersom and H. S. Paulli, who would later become the choir-

master of the Royal Theater. "There was no room in the coach for my suitcase; it had to be put back on top, and while the others sat inside the coach,
I took out something for the journey. In my haste, my scissors ended up in
my billfold and in my back pocket. We drove off, the scissors slid out. I got
out at an inn where we wanted to have some mead. I got back in, and now
the scissors had turned around so I sat down and got a whole inch in me.
I could feel the blood running, and now I had to go inside and bathe my
backside with vinegar and water. Pauli brought the cup, and Foursom
squeezed the wound; what a splendid scene."[28]

But for the most part Andersen took up his scissors with joy. And after
he had folded the paper once or twice and started to cut along a vertical
or lateral axis, the whole process became a visual manifestation of how his
art sprang from nothing and could in a flash materialize in patterns, figures,
and landscapes. A paper-cut was often a whole little fairy tale, folded and
cut in several dimensions, with a great sense for the effects of depth and
contrast.

"From Andersen's shears / the fairy tale appears!" he once wrote to a
young friend, and with that he emphasized the element of improvisation
that was always associated with cutting and pasting. The sudden, unexpected
shapes and figures of a paper-cut were symbolic of the mighty forces inside
the author, which could swarm out of him in creative moments. For
instance, Otto Zinck, reminiscing about his childhood, recalled two drawings that Andersen had once made for him. One of them showed a regiment of soldiers in the process of marching out of the author's mouth. In
the other drawing, a group of grotesque human figures are squeezed together,
literally about to leap from his face.[29] Andersen was about twenty-five when
he made these drawings for Otto Zinck. But much later in his life we see
how he developed this bizarre form of self-portraiture by cutting out silhouettes in which human figures dance around the author's domed forehead, or they hang from or out of his capacious nose.

During the 19th century, many children encountered Hans Christian
Andersen with his scissors and paper in bourgeois homes in Copenhagen,
at various Danish manor houses, and at royal and princely estates throughout Europe. They might also find him visiting good friends such as
Kaulbach, the painter in Munich; the writers Elizabeth and Robert
Browning in Rome; as well as Charles Dickens in London. The children
saw him as someone who was full of imagination and fairy tales, and by

tapping on his high forehead or merely by picking up his pen or scissors, he could summon living things from the inanimate surface of a flat piece of paper. Whenever Andersen began turning the pieces of colored paper around the calm tips of his scissors as he talked, the children seated around the table knew that anything could happen. An improvised fairy tale might emerge that had some connection to the theme or motif of the paper-cut. Several times along the way, Andersen would stop to give the paper a new vertical or lateral axis that would break the symmetry and force new angles and perspectives. In many ways this corresponded to the tactics Andersen used as a storyteller, both orally and in writing, when he would cinematically proceed to "cut" the chronology or suddenly rearrange the composition and insert new points of view, scenes, or characters.

It was quite often a matter of a type of toy production when Andersen picked up his scissors. The result might be collage elements for a picture book, or he might create decorations for the nursery, in the form of paper dolls or amusing, movable figures. Or he might make the more clumsy but charming "windmill men," with the millhouse as the body and the wings of the mill forming the arms and legs. The windmill man often had an inviting ladder in front, leading up to a big door in the belly of the mill with drawers that could be opened and closed, and you could look in or out. With his wildly flailing arms, the windmill man could be set on the table or hung in the window, and—if it was a particularly festive and foilcoated windmill man—he could be hung on the Christmas tree. The toys that Andersen cut out also included theater sets, even entire theaters with curtains, orchestra pits, stage wings, and dancers. Or he might create Oriental palaces with slender spires and windows and doors that opened and closed, so the child's imagination could be allowed to come inside and have some peace and quiet for a while.

The collages in Andersen's picture books were overwhelmingly modern, making use of all manner of transitory contemporary materials. But with his paper-cuts, the author turns his attention to the distant past. He looks back to his childhood, to nature, and to the stereotypes of folk poetry, solidly rooted in the ancient world of legends and fairy tales, which had been such a lively part of the author's childhood on Fyn and had marked his upbringing. Andersen uses his scissors to cut his way, more or less consciously, back to the land of his childhood. As an extension of this, he occasionally takes a few steps further back in human history, to more amorphous and archetypal perceptions of human life. This is evident in the author's more naïve and rough paper-cuts, which in certain cases almost look as if they had been torn instead of being cut with scissors—and that was sometimes actually what happened if the material in question was the daily newspaper or a leaf from a rubber tree.

Some of these standing, sitting, leaping, and balancing fantasy figures are recognizable from Andersen's fairy tales, but many of them are also so grotesque and alien that we have to look further back in human history to find their roots. Andersen's scissors did not produce only sylphs, angels, swans, cheerful elves, and rows of hearts. They also created ominous trolls and witches, gnomes, fairies, mysterious mermen and sea hags, medusas, and other strange creatures. Some were half animal and half human, some half man and half woman, like the eight-legged orange crustacean in *Christine's Picture Book.*[30] Even though it wears a dress and is called "she," it has three faces, two of which are male. These figures come unquestionably from the deep layers of Andersen's imagination. They are creatures and plants that were associated with heathen ideas and primitive beliefs in powerful entities, which were also represented in the woodcarvings made by the author's paternal grandfather. They were all the "people with animal heads, animals with wings, and peculiar birds," as Andersen writes in *The Fairy Tale of My Life.*[31]

It is also down here, among the amorphous images of Andersen's imagination, that we find the source for another series of bizarre and exotic figures among Andersen's paper-cuts. They look like masks, fetishes, and prie-dieux from Inuit cultures in the Arctic regions, from African tribes, and from the peoples of Polynesia, where primitive art—orally narrated or sculpturally shaped—has always been highly valued and associated with a mythological, animistic view of life. Many of the paper-cuts Andersen made, including the long, thin devil-men and devil-masks, bear an astonishing similarity to the wooden gods that our European forefathers carved and worshiped during the Stone Age, and which have subsequently been found buried in the peat bogs. They were long, thin hermaphrodites, equipped with enormous genitalia and a single, crushed eye that was supposed to symbolize the god Odin, who gave one of his eyes to Mimer's well in exchange for eternal wisdom. In connection with this heathen aspect of Andersen's pictorial art, we also see his fascination with the Italian *commedia dell'arte* tradition and with the Greco-Roman fertility religion. He also draws on Danish chalk paintings from the Middle Ages, and all sorts of wonderful jumping-jack figures, Punch and Judy puppets, as well as gingerbread men and ginger-bread women, which he searched for, both as a child and as an adult, in all the markets of Europe.

By examining this often dark and mysterious side of Andersen's paper-cuts, we can also discover some fundamental roots to his fairy-tale writing. Edvard Lehmann, who researched the Danish peasant culture and had a particularly insightful view of Andersen's imagination, said in 1910: "Because half of his brain is that of a Papuan native, he can summon up in his writing precisely what the human race created in its infancy: fairy tales. Because fairy tales, like myths, are the first fruits here on earth. In Andersen they sprout anew. To Andersen it comes naturally; he does what no other writer in modern culture—even if he was a much greater writer—has been able to do: to create fairy-tale motifs. That's where he belongs, and he gives of himself."[32]

If we look at the 800 paper-cuts, both big and small, which stem mostly from the last twenty years of Andersen's life, we can sort them into two distinct main groups. The first is composed of an artist's sophisticated, neatly elegant paper-cuts, with their own easily recognizable mythology and diverse cultivated motifs from Andersen's fairy-tale world. They're all swans, angels, elves, ballerinas, Pierrots, Sandmen, trees, mills, gallows, hearts, and the like. To a great degree they were the result of a "salon art," intended to be shown, hung up, and admired by adults. This was true of both the large, detailed paper-cuts and the tiny, masterful miniatures, such as the famous rocking chair with its beautifully intricate back; it could balance on the tip of a finger. The second group includes the simple and primitive paper-cuts, which even today seem a more natural and rebellious counterforce to all the ingeniously bombastic sylphs and enchantingly arranged vines. This second group in Andersen's pictorial art is filled with silent, ponderous representatives from a much more shadowy and murky underworld. Here we find crude men and women wearing gaudy pirate clothes, demonic figures, and wild bestial creatures—gnomes, fairies, mermen, and sea hags. In their paper-cut state, they often look as if they were created by a busy sculptor or woodcarver who, instead of using his customary tools, has been given scissors that are much too small and elegant for his hand. But he did the best he could, sometimes even using his bare hands.

Bella Italia

The delicate and sophisticated versus the simple and primitive are two different aspects of Andersen's art that meet and collide in his collages and paper-cuts. This also occurred on the screen mentioned earlier, which stood in front of the author's bed during the last years of his life and which was a monumental attempt at gathering his life and work into a world-view. It was foldable and movable—very much in the spirit of a nomad. Andersen did not label the eight different panels, but they depict themes such as "Childhood," "The Theater," "Denmark," "Sweden-Norway," "Germany," "France," "England," and "The Orient." The folding screen presents a grand homage to all the cultures, art forms, landscapes, cities, people, and institutions that contributed to shaping and influencing the author's life. And the consistent, vertical axis in the composition of each panel gives the impression of an aristocratic outlook, which has a greater eye for heights and hierarchies than for breadth and the masses.[33] The top of each panel is crowned by sky, kings, military commanders and statesmen, as well as great, resplendent buildings and monuments. Below—like clusters of ripe grapes on the branches—are the representatives of culture and science, of whom Andersen met so many over the years. They now had their photographic likenesses pasted onto the screen in large groups of notables. And at the bottom, in cellars and caves, near the sea and on rocks, we see a few representatives of the impoverished, the drunken, and the criminal.

As a collage, the folding screen is an impressive work of art because its basic idea of reconstructing an author's divine flight through life is executed with such a strict, sharp eye for both the grand lines and the tiniest details. Andersen lays his cards on the table, so to speak: All right, here you have all the sources of my inspiration on a series of panels, and they may also be the key to understanding the fairy tale of my life! Yet this intriguing thought is quickly deflated when we discover that something is missing. There was one particular place and destination that attracted Andersen's lifelong attention, and which deeply inspired him on many occasions: "Bella Italia"! This was the country that attracted the author and his work at regular intervals over a period of forty years, and provided a great deal of material. From his very first lengthy trip abroad in 1833-34,

Andersen felt strongly connected to the land and people of Italy, as well as to the culture of the south. Over the years, he always longed to return. As he writes in 1836 to Henriette Wulff: "I am at heart a southerner, condemned to this Nordic cloister where the walls are fog, storms are the swaddling clothes, and the shackles—no travel money."[34] But for some reason there was no room for Italy on Andersen's external or internal screen in 1873-74. Instead, a different destination, "The Orient," was given prominence in a grand and separate chapter. This seems an exaggeration, even in something as fleeting as a collage, and even though Andersen knew *The Thousand and One Nights* by heart and had spent ten days in Constantinople in 1841. A survey of the author's life and work shows that, except for his trip to the Near East in 1841 and the travel book *A Poet's Bazaar*, there is not much Persian beauty or Eastern wisdom in Andersen's works. But why was "Bella Italia" not included on the folding screen?

You don't have to read many of Hans Christian Andersen's works to realize that Italy was a fascinating and disturbing force in the author's psyche all his life. There were few other countries that Andersen visited so often or with such pleasure. He was there at the age of 28 and 35; he returned when he was 41, 47, 49, and 56. He also visited Italy twice shortly before his death, when he was 67 and 68. All in all, he made eight trips over the course of forty years. During his first three visits, Andersen stayed in Italy for three to five months, and if we add up all the days, weeks, and months, the Danish author spent nearly a year and half of his life on the Italian peninsula. We can also try to add up this Latin attraction and inspiration in terms of fairy tales, lines of poetry, acts from plays, pages of correspondence, diary entries, and chapters from novels, starting with *The Improvisatore* in 1835 and going all the way up to *Lucky Peer* in 1870. It may not be as surprising to see how much Italy inspired Hans Christian Andersen as it is to realize that this infatuation and fascination with Italy was also based on outright fear.

"A trip through Germany and France holds basically nothing foreign: it's only beyond the Alps that the new world lies!" writes Andersen, using a jubilant exclamation mark in a letter from Milan in September 1833 as he heads for Rome for the first time in his life.[35] As mentioned, this was the new world to which Andersen would return many times, and it says a great deal about the Danish author's manner of traveling that each time he returned in a different way. It was as if he was always looking for a new route and new means of transportation to enter Italy. He would approach the country from the north, traveling by stagecoach, mail coach, and the so-called *vetturina* over various Alpine passes. Next time he might come by train from the west or northwest, via Milan and Genoa. And twice Andersen arrived from the northeast by steamboat, traveling from Trieste and going ashore at Ancona and Venice, respectively. He also tried departing from Italy by boat, going either south or north, toward either Malta or Marseille. This consistently deliberate attempt to try out various land and water routes both to and from Italy was typical of Andersen's habits and nature as a traveler. But it also reflects his geographical and cultural curiosity regarding a phenomenon such as "Bella Italia," which had to be seen and sensed from as many angles as possible. Even though Italy was not the country that Andersen visited most during his lifetime (that was Germany), the "new world" beyond the Alps still became a living framework around his difficult attempts to penetrate deeper into certain motives and conflicts within himself. There were aspects of himself as an artist and sexual being to which he did not dare surrender. Nor could he merely ignore or hide them, as he tried to do on the folding screen in 1873-74.

Italy was for Andersen, as it was for many other northern European artists during Romanticism, a symbol of the absolute beauty that is missing from a person's dark, cold life. This eternal sighing for the warmth of the south also contained a longing for all the sensuality and sexuality that an obedient and properly raised Protestant in the early 19th century had learned to keep in check. As far as Andersen was concerned, it quickly became apparent that there was also reason to fear this enchantment of Italy. The deeper a person penetrated into the idyllic country, the more snakes ended up crossing his path. Behind its deceptive glow, "Bella Italia" often became an importunate "Bella Donna" seeking the company of the stranger from the north; and she always had so many kinds of enticements to offer. As the Italian bride robber Rodrigo says with a merry laugh in Andersen's opera *The Wedding at Lake Como* from 1849: "Crush flowers / Enjoy love!"

The Wedding at Lake Como, which is also known in an earlier version under the title *Renzo's Wedding*, is one of many examples of the inspiration that Andersen gleaned from his trips to the south. There is not an ounce of travel description in the opera, and the mountainous region around Lake Como is limited to a two-dimensional stage set in the background. On the other hand, considering what a libretto will permit, there is tremendous depth to the opera's psychology. Here sex, love, and Catholicism are all

played out with great force, and most of the characters are sharply delin-
eated. We sense an inspired dramatist from start to finish, standing behind
his words and observing a culture permeated with the erotic urges of both
men and women, as well as a religion that is filled with paradoxes. As early
as 1849, Andersen noted on his trips south and remarked in his diaries that
men and women certainly did not hide their love in Italy. This was something he also noticed back in 1833-34, both on the shores of Lake Como
and in the passageways of the Uffizi in Florence, as well as in the parks of
Rome and especially in Naples, with its sinful city life in the shadow of the
volcano. It was particularly this erotically charged atmosphere, the farther
south he went in the country, that bound Andersen so strongly to "Bella
Italia" during that first visit in 1833-34. The young author was terribly fascinated by the dramatic natural landscape, filled with contrasts, as well as by
the inner nature of the people. "Italy's nature has entered my blood," he
writes in a letter on his way back to Denmark in 1834. At the time he is
also playing with the idea of never returning home: "If I had money I
would stay out here forever, never come home; only in the south can I
thrive, and I will put all my striving into returning there; that is the goal of
my future."[36] In the midst of this enthusiastic intoxication and on his way
home to his native land, the Danish author transformed himself into the
Roman boy Antonio in the first chapters of a novel, which the following
year would be given the title *The Improvisatore*. It was started in Rome,
amid a fierce longing for the Latin frame of mind that the author would
soon be leaving. The prospect of his encounter with the frozen North,
where—as Andersen wrote to his friend Christian Voigt—the year always
consisted of six months fog and six months ice-cold sunshine, called "summer," had made the pen glow in the hand of the improviser. Many years
later, in *The Fairy Tale of My Life*, Andersen summed up his mood as he left
the south for the first time:

> "My heart clung to Italy as a paradise that was lost to me, to which I
> would never return . . . My soul was filled with Italy's nature and its folk
> life; I felt homesick for that land. It seemed to merge with my own self,
> and quite extemporaneously a story emerged; it grew and grew, I had to
> write it down . . ."[37]

If we continue our survey of Andersen's Italian trips from 1833 to
1873, it becomes clear that the wild enthusiasm he felt in the beginning,
which has the character of an infatuation in his letters home to Denmark,
later diminished. With time, it came to resemble a strained marriage. But

in the beginning the relationship was unusually loving between the author from the north and the country to the south. "The south was my bride," Andersen states in 1840,[38] and back in 1835 he had written to Edvard Collin:

> "Oh, Eduard, if you had inhaled this air, seen all the loveliness, you would long as I do . . . the warm south, that is the bride I long for, her beauty enchants me, enthuses my soul. Oh, if only I could sell a rich man the years of my life; I would give him half to be able to live the other half in Italy."[39]

It would be too vague to speak of a classical, cultural journey of education to describe Andersen's first trip to Italy in 1833-34. In many ways it was a trip with such strong hallucinations that the windows in Andersen's various rooms with a view were at times thoroughly shattered. Many years later, when he wanted to recall in *The Fairy Tale of My Life* the whole vast, sensory and consciousness expansion he had undergone, this is what he said:

> "During my first visit to Italy, it was the nature and art alone that were so overwhelming, the true experience of that period . . . I practically reveled in the sumptuous nature that this land offered!"[40]

This has to be regarded as a form of rationalization after the fact. When Andersen, in his deferential autobiography, repeatedly claimed that on his first trips to Italy he primarily focused his interest on the landscapes and art treasures, it must be added that the young author was also very taken with the passionate way in which the Italian men and women lived their lives.

Eroticism in Naples

"It was the great pulse of the world that I heard," writes Hans Christian Andersen in his diary during his first visit to Naples in the early months of 1834. Another entry also confirms that one day, as he walked along the sea, he stopped to linger at the view before him, devoid of people. And the sea, in the author's words, lifted its great wings as coal-black smoke rose from Vesuvius into the blue sky. Yet the next diary entry reveals quite clearly that Andersen had also pressed his ear to flesh to hear the human pulse up close. At dusk he suddenly found himself in the middle of

a group of some of Naples' most insistent pimps, who wanted the foreign-
er to pay for the services of a *bella donna*. That same evening the author
wrote in his diary, "I can feel the climate affecting my blood; I felt a rag-
ing ardor, but resisted."[41] The incident was repeated two days later, this time
against the backdrop of an erupting Vesuvius, spraying great streams of lava
into the air. The symbolism was obvious. A crowd of pimps offered the
awkward Northerner everything from mature, buxom madonnas to pretty
children. Andersen, who was both curious and terrified, humbled himself
in his diary: "I felt thoroughly amorous, but resisted the temptation. If I
make it home innocent, I will remain so forever."[42]

Andersen extricated himself to the north by starting a novel that was
given the title *The Improvisatore* and was published a year after his trip. Here
we meet the author as the eternally innocent Antonio who, as an adult,
comes to volcanic Naples and encounters not only Vesuvius but also a fiery
and sensually sizzling beauty by the name of Santa. The voluptuous but
fallen woman with the ironic name sees in Antonio the great erotic challenge of her life. One day Santa tries to seduce Antonio, and she does so
with great caution and tenderness. At first she settles for caressing and kissing his forehead. Then, as she whispers a few sweet words in his ear and
puts her arms around him, Antonio loses all control of himself. This happens because a previously unknown, fierce desire is now awakened deep
inside his body:

> "My blood became like a flame, a trembling moved through my
> whole body; it felt as if my breath stopped. Never have I felt anything like
> it . . . I heard my own heart pounding, and a feeling of shame and reluc-
> tance arose in my soul; I turned away from her, that lovely daughter of
> sin."[43]

Antonio actually has a greater fondness for close, platonic relationships
with men. Yet he does have an erotic desire inside that can be awakened by
women, and his longings for love are not directed exclusively toward other
men. Antonio feels split, and he tries to harness this new experience, using
every means at hand and in his psyche. At the same time, in his heart he
tries to understand what sort of fierce desires and conflicting forces Santa
has aroused in him. Ascetic that he is, Antonio chooses to pursue the
woman and all that she has awakened in him from the secure distance of
fantasy and dream. In other words, he puts the brakes on his sexual desire
and freezes Santa's alluring beauty in what, for a voyeur, is an exciting state
called "sensual contemplation." That's how Andersen—very concisely—

describes Antonio's dilemma: "For me, it led merely to attentiveness, a sort of sensual contemplation that I had never before known. But this provoked a pounding of the heart, an anxiety, that made me shy and kept me at a distance from her."[44]

A short time later, Santa once again attempts to seduce Antonio, trying to talk her way to his naked body with tender words about the young man's marvelous improvising talents as she loosens the ties of his clothing and presses him to her bosom. But his new, clear limits with regard to carnal love withstand the test:

> "'No! No!' I cried and leaped up. My blood was like boiling lava. 'Antonio!' she shouted. 'Kill me, kill me, but don't leave me!' Her cheeks, her eyes, her gaze and expression were passionate, and yet she was so beautiful, a picture of beauty, painted with flames. I felt a trembling in all my nerves, and without replying I left the room, rushed down the stairs as if an evil spirit were pursuing me. Everything was flames outside, as in my blood. The air currents rippled with heat, Vesuvius was aglow with fire, the eruptions lit up everything around! Air! air! my heart demanded . . . I pressed my eyes closed, turned my mind to God, but it sank back; it was as if the flames of sin had singed its wings."[45]

Fleeing from the Fall, Antonio rushes down to the harbor and jumps into the nearest boat. Far out in the gulf, with a view of the city beneath the sputtering volcano, he can cool his burning body and survey the destruction, both internal and external. Never before has Antonio come so close to tasting the fruit of sin and being banished from the Garden of Eden. When he arrives on the other side of the bay, he resolves never again to get so close to a woman. He can look, but not touch or be touched. His genuine confessions and repentance are heard and accepted by the higher powers. Antonio is forgiven and immediately feels like "a child again in soul and thought."[46]

These passages from Andersen's breakthrough novel in 1835 are not meant to draw a smile from the reader. They were written in all seriousness, in the midst of a platonic era. In every respect, innocence is vital for Antonio, just as it was for Hans Christian Andersen throughout his life. The young artist's improvisational talent is based on the notion of being a virgin. It is in this pure, innocent state that Antonio wishes to live—to be seen, heard, and understood as a human being. For that reason, carnal love signifies the crossing of a boundary that will be fatal for the artist in Antonio. By sinking down and into Santa, he will—like the prince in the fairy tale "The Garden of Eden"—experience a fall and be cast out of the world on which his art depends and from which it draws.

But we would be greatly mistaken if we thought that Andersen, on his trips to southern Italy in 1833-34, 1840-41, and 1846, became so sexually frightened that he hid in his rented rooms or disappeared on long, solitary mountain hikes or spent whole days visiting dark and chilly museums. Nearly every day, especially in Naples, Andersen was out in the streets, making his way through the city. As he diligently notes in his diary, he was often strongly "affected" and "sensual in his blood" after these forays through the old Greek center of the city with its narrow, dirty streets beneath brightly fluttering white canopies of laundry. For Andersen, Naples was and continued to be the most dangerous city in the world. It was "more dangerous than Paris, because there you freeze, but here the blood burns," as Andersen wrote in his diary in 1834.[47] Two months after he left southern Italy and found himself in somewhat cooler Venice, he wrote in the same diary: "The Neapolitan passion again boiled in my blood, but there were no tempters here."[48]

One of the temptations to which Andersen surrendered on several of his visits to Naples was the secret room in the cellar of the Museo Nazionale. It was shown only to visitors who had obtained special permission. This little gallery, which Andersen called in his diary "Camera Obscœna," was filled with erotic art from the glory days of the nation. Here were phalluses in all possible sizes and angles of elevation; figures and sculptures with alluring sexual openings both in front and behind on women, men, children, and animals. It had all been discovered during the 18th and 19th centuries in connection with archaeological excavations of the inhabited areas surrounding Vesuvius. And judging by all the frivolous objects, Pompeii and Herculaneum must have been the Roman answer to Sodom and Gomorra, which had also been destroyed by fire and brimstone because God wanted to punish the inhabitants for their ungodly and immoral conduct. In Andersen's diary from 1834, we can see that he was not in the least scandalized by the bestial urges of the ancient Greeks and Romans, which were depicted so naturally and candidly on vases, amulets, oil lamps, sculptures, paintings, and bas-reliefs. And it was not just a matter of men and women in the missionary position; indecent relationships between hermaphrodites, sodomites, children, adults, and domestic animals were also portrayed in every possible advanced position and tableau.

Morally unperturbed, Andersen wandered among small phallic figures made of pewter, and giant penises with wings and bells, which had once hung and jingled like wind chimes in Pompeii and the surrounding area. There were truly "gripping signs" as the Danish author wrote in his diary:

> "Many bawdy pictures on plaster, various situations and manners in the performance of their desires. A lovely marble statue with a lecherous faun teaching a young man to play the reed pipe. A sepulchral monument with incomprehensible scenes, such as a priest, a goat & . . . & . . . In the room stood many priapuses, which pregnant women had apparently sat on."[49]

In 1834, Andersen had particular trouble finding the right words to describe a couple of figures with a lecherous faun. This is perfectly understandable if you take a look at the figures today in Museo Nazionale's collection of erotica from Pompeii. They include a faun, fifty centimeters tall, who has forced a goat almost as big down on its back and is roundly screwing the animal, which peers up at its conqueror with an expression of love and pleasure. It was a long way from these figures, both repulsive and fascinating, to the fairy tale about Thumbelina and her gentle dealings with beetles and field mice; Andersen wrote this story in the same year. But on his trip to Italy in 1846, the Danish author was compelled to go back to the locked cellar room. Just as he would later, in Paris in 1866-68, get closer and closer to the prostitutes with every visit, he now ventured a little closer to the heathen, bestial embraces in Naples, and concluded: "The satyr and goat in coitus are masterful, in terms of expression."[50]

Over the years, Andersen continued to cultivate this Italian sensuality, about which he had written a boldly honest novel in 1835—although from the safe distance of a voyeur. Italy became one big erotic museum. On his first visits, this entailed approaching and confronting all the invisible forces which Andersen, in a poem for Giuseppe Siboni, his old Italian voice teacher at the Royal Theater, collectively labeled "the southern fire and desire." On Andersen's first journey through the flames of the south, it was a matter of cautiously reflecting the sensual and sexual aspects of his own nature—aspects that attracted yet frightened him. Like Antonio in *The Improvisatore*, Andersen neither could nor wanted to surrender to these strong feelings. As William Bloch, Andersen's young traveling companion in 1872, so concisely expressed it several years after the author's death: "His fear of being mystified was stronger than his desire for the intriguing adventure."[51]

As the years passed, Andersen became the sort of aloof and blasé traveler that he caricatures in his little dramatic sketch *In the Vetturina* from

1868, which was originally intended as a prelude to a summer celebration for veteran visitors to Rome back home in Denmark. The play includes a well-traveled Englishman, who has seen it all and prefers to sleep his way through the Boot-country, although he wants to be awakened if anything remarkable happens outside the windows. He introduces himself with the words: "I love Italy in my mind, not in reality."[52] This brief remark reveals something of Andersen's own ambivalent relationship to Italy's culture and nature from 1850 to 1875. With time, he too retreated to the secure corner of the *vetturina*, allowing his body to rest while his spirit flew. In this way the Danish author—and platonic lover—could approach in relative safety this importunate country. He still loved "Bella Italia," but only in his thoughts, not in reality.

In a sense he ended up being punished for this aesthetic attitude on his last two trips to Italy in 1872 and 1873. Andersen had hardly crossed the Alpine passes of Brenner and Splügen with his young traveling companions, William Bloch and Nicolai Bøgh, before he began regretting his foray into the light and warmth of the south. He noticed at once an inner dread that Italy, like another *bella donna*, would close around him and demand that he—who over the years had gained so much from the south and still drew so heavily on Italy for his art—would now have to pay for it with either his virtue or his life.

In this woeful and abject manner, Andersen's forty-year Italian adventure came to an end. He turned his back on the sun and warmth, which he time after time had sought and praised in childishly exultant verses such as: "Hello, halla, hello, halla! / Down to Italia!"[53] That's how the idyllic watchword had sounded in the 1830s. But the end result in 1873 was unmistakable. In 1861, Elizabeth Barrett Browning had written a beautiful poem in Rome, "The North and the South," about the Nordic fairy-tale author's joyous relationship to the south, and vice versa. Yet "Bella Italia" no longer wanted anything to do with the perpetually innocent Dane who had taken and taken during his travels, but had never given anything of himself.

Innocence as Religion

"I take it that Andersen was something of an ascetic with regard to the sexual drive. In that case, his battle against this urge, in a man with such a strong imagination, doubtless contributed to the testiness of a hypochondriac."[54] This was written by one of the author's close friends, the physician Emil Hornemann, in a letter addressed to his cousin, Edvard Collin. At the time, Collin had started work on his book about Andersen and felt that he had need for a medical evaluation of Andersen's peculiar sexuality and his "paroxysms," as Edvard, for lack of a more precise term, called the attacks of eccentricity displayed by his author friend. Emil Hornemann was not just some random doctor expressing his opinion about Andersen's sexuality. For more than forty years he had been one of the two or three doctors who regularly saw the author. He was familiar with Andersen's physical as well as his psychological shortcomings. And he was the one, in particular, who treated all the symptoms of tenderness, itching, stinging, and pain exhibited by the author's body. As Andersen wrote in a song in the 1830s, when Hornemann became a physician and at the same time took on the author as his patient: "You always bring us help, / The big and the small, / If we have a swollen finger / If we have an aching toe, / Even if we hurt inside, / As everyone well knows: / You can ease our pain . . ."[55]

Yet Andersen's asceticism was more than just a sexual phenomenon. His abstinence went beyond the carnal and extended to the spiritual realm. Both his written works and his pictorial art reflect a comprehensive longing and thirst for the paradise that no adult can enter without being—as Andersen said—"childishly pure." But why were purity and chastity, which were very closely tied to his childlike psyche, so essential for Hans Christian Andersen? Because they provided an anchor and a sense of coherence for his view of life. They shaped his ethics and poetics and served many vital functions for Andersen, both as a private individual and a writer. Outwardly his childishness was a sort of armor against the numerous sexual temptations and perils; yet it was also the sword he used to fight his way into the world of art. This "childish purity" was an expression for the spiritual foundation and Romantic ideal on which his literature and pictorial art were based, and from which he drew his creative powers. To the very end of his life, Andersen clung to all that Niels Bryde, in the novel *To Be or Not to Be*, lacks: "Virginity! That is to say: spontaneity!"[56] For Andersen, the innocent state was both an existential and an artistic necessity. It was quite simply a matter of preserving a close, intimate relationship to playing, along with a joie de vivre—the principle of joy. As he wrote in the play *King Saul* in 1869: "There was a time, I see it in memory, / There was a time, it will never come again! / I clung to life with such a joy, / Like a child clings to his mother's breast. / The joy of my soul I could shout aloud . . ."[57]

As a man, Andersen's demonstrative innocence was also shaped by his sexual fears. As late as 1870, in the novel *Lucky Peer*, a demonic power emanates from the protagonist's erotic dream about elf girls who one night want to dance him into unconsciousness and slowly crowd close around him, "so that blood spurts from my forehead!"[58] But Andersen clung to his innocence and asceticism primarily because the world and nature of the child provided eternal inspiration and expression for the sources of his art that were constantly surging. Like many of the children and childlike adults we encounter in his works, Andersen refused to grow up. Instead, he wanted to stay on an island of innocence for the rest of his life. Here he had free, uninterrupted access to the imagination and realm of ideas, to games and joys, which were utterly essential for an improviser like Hans Christian Andersen. That's why it was so important for him to stage-set his life as one big platonic love affair, directed at numerous men and a few women: Edvard, Riborg, Christian, Ludvig, Louise, Henrik, Jonna, Jenny, Jonas, Harald, and many others. All these images of longing could keep him in a creative, dreamlike ecstasy that infused him with all the poetic energy and power he could want. It was a form of inspiration that had love at its core, although more as spirit than body or flesh, and there was never any thought of realizing or formalizing it. As Andersen writes in *O.T.* in 1836: "The first love of the pure heart is sacred! What is sacred can be intimated but not articulated—!"[59] Then the magic circle would be broken and the author would instantly be cast out of his creative paradise, stripped of all his imaginative forces, his poetic talents, and all the power of the world of poetry. Then there would be nothing left to write about or to cut from paper.

The notion of a person's right to play and experience joy formed the foundation from which Andersen's fairy tales grew and became known all over the world. As early as the 1820s, "a child's purity" became the fulcrum and power center of his life and work. Until his death in 1875, the author remained in some senses a child who, in the distant past, had abandoned his family and written off parts of his ancestry. And at the same time, with his consistent preference for the child's position, he turned his back on adult responsibilities and the obligations of the familial provider, which normally fell to husband and father. All his life he chose, instead, to be the son and brother. Andersen refused to grow up and age in the normal, bourgeois manner, and he never submitted to the traditional power structure of the family. For Andersen, he—the child—always came first. This point of view was especially manifest in his religion and faith in God.

★ ★ ★

The tenets of Andersen's faith cannot be easily formulated. His beliefs were of course marked by his upbringing and schooling, as well as by wise friends and his numerous trips abroad. At the same time, they were subjected to the author's highly impressionable imagination and shifting moods. "His relationship to God never ceased to be alive," Edvard Collin writes in his book about Andersen.[60] To this it must be added that his relationship to God was more magical than mystical, to the extent that Andersen never hid his view that only as a child can a person come close to God. This meant via feelings and faith rather than reason. "Faith is given, you cannot think your way to it!" as he said.

In many of Andersen's texts, the concept of "faith" is severely tested. For instance, the choirmaster in the novel *Lucky Peer* from 1870 tells Peer that it's impossible to have a clear conscience and run from one religion to another. You will sin either against the one you leave behind or against the one you accept. Peer thinks this is nonsense and replies: "You have no faith!," whereupon the choirmaster says that he certainly does, he has the God of his forefathers. "He lights the way for my feet and my understanding!" And to prove his faith even further, he immediately starts playing an ancient folk ballad.[61]

Andersen's own faith lies somewhere in between that of the choirmaster and Peer. In addition to the old folk beliefs based on heathen concepts, which can be found everywhere in Andersen's fairy tales, we also see more modern and foreign forms of belief in his writings. For example, his travel accounts are in many ways a series of confrontations with other religions and beliefs that either frightened Andersen or particularly attracted his attention. The Danish author often sought out these distant gods and used them to examine himself and his own culture.

An entirely different manifestation of the author's all-embracing and enormously practical faith in God can be found in Andersen's diaries. At regular intervals he would fall to his knees, clasp his hands, and pray to God with phrases such as: "Lord, do not forsake me!" "God, my God, give me faith!" or "God, lead me back untainted!" On such occasions his faith was both a crutch and a whip. This was either because Andersen, as he writes in a diary entry, had again been "a corporeal wretch" and masturbated; or because he generally feared for his life, given all the wars and cholera present in the world. One example of how—filled with fear and dread about the future—he turned to his God occurred during the bloody clash between Denmark and Germany in 1864. Andersen seriously feared that before long Denmark would end up under German dominion, and for a period this fear became a touchstone for his faith in God. Experiencing one of his most pessimistic moments during the war-filled summer of 1864, Andersen writes in his diary that God seems to have forsaken both him and his country. Then he voices his deliberations about putting his faith in the Virgin Mary in the future, if he receives no further specific signs or constructive help from the Lord Himself. It's possible to imagine that God was peering over the shoulder of the author as he wrote in his diary:

> "Religion is my light, my salvation, my faith. If I believe that God and Jesus are one, as the faithful would have it, then the Virgin Mary is the most chosen of human beings; in our humility before God, we may also pray to her to intercede for us. What thoughts I have. Lord my God! shine Your light into me and be merciful, and God, I am about to forsake You, whom I was able to cling to with my childhood faith."[62]

Even though Andersen grew up and lived in a Protestant culture and preferred to call himself a Christian, he often played with the idea of also being a Catholic, Muslim, Jew, or Buddhist. Like Christian in *Only a Fiddler*, Andersen wished to spread "the cloak of love over all sects," because—as he wrote in the novel—the Catholic song that is sung at Easter by Italian peasants up in the mountains contained just as much true Christianity as one of the hymns from the Danish church.[63] Similarly, it's quite typical of Andersen and his complex relationship to the divine that when he was alone in the Iberian peninsula in 1866, during the days before the perilous journey across the desolate Spanish plains to Portugal, he first seized upon Turkish beliefs: "'La ila ilallah! says the Turk and submits!" Then, on the following day, he prays fervently to his very Danish god: "Now there is nothing to do but let matters take their course. God will not forsake us!"[64]

We might say that Andersen's faith was globally based. Thirty years prior to the aforementioned journey across the Iberian peninsula, we encounter the same pragmatic attitude toward world religions in novels such as *O.T.* and *Only a Fiddler*. Otto Thostrup, the author's alter ego, says in *O.T.* that everything "that is sacred to the human heart is also sacred in every religion!"[65] This same religious relativism and human tolerance is revealed in *Only a Fiddler*. When Christian is a boy, he listens to the scriptures read aloud by his wise and heathen godfather, who knows so much about foreign peoples and various types of faith. One day the man gives his godson a brief lecture that is supposed to teach the boy about how important it is for a person to be tolerant of others, besides himself and his own God:

"There are many peoples on this earth! What we call sin, others may label as just. The savage eats his enemy, and his priest says: Now you will enter highest of all in heaven! The Turk has many wives, and his God promises him even more in paradise. One general receives honor and fame for what he does in a royal war, through injustice; while another who shows the same cunning ends up dismembered on the post! It all depends on custom and tradition. And who are we to say whether we follow the best, merely because we do what the majority does?"[66]

Childhood Faith

In other words, it is difficult and too limiting to define Hans Christian Andersen's religion as Christianity. He was instead his own theological faculty with an independent view of the big questions in life. He possessed a highly individual faith that refused to be imprisoned by rhetoric or rituals. This became quite evident in Andersen's legendary form of church worship when he was a guest at the Holsteinborg estate. There he always had at his disposal two rooms with direct access to the estate's church. Every Sunday he had the choice of the church service or a walk under the vault of the sky, where nature held its own sermon. If the author chose the garden—as he did, for example, on Sunday, June 14, 1874—Andersen would leave his hosts to their church worship. He would use the time instead to seek out and gather plants for one of his unusual bouquets in which branches, straw, and reeds from wild nature were combined with roses and lilies from the well-tended flowerbeds in the manor-house garden. These bouquets confirmed that God is present in nature, even in the smallest of things—and always on both sides of the estate's fence.

If Andersen chose to listen to the hymns and the pastor's sermon, he preferred to stay in his rooms, with the door slightly ajar. He would sit on a chair with his back or side turned toward the church and ongoing service. Then he would sit and listen. He preferred Brorson's hymns, such as "Up! all the things that God has wrought," rather than the pastor's sermon. In Andersen's opinion, certain pastors were an extremely disruptive element, at times even a direct and insurmountable obstacle in the relationship between people and God.

Andersen felt that religious arguments were in reality among the most edifying things for the soul. He speaks of the necessity for a person, at regular intervals, to receive some "spiritual tugs" in his life, so that his good sense won't crumble and be lost amid all the material delights.[67] It was precisely these types of "tugs" that had created Andersen's own complex faith, with its deep roots in an introspective childhood with close contact to his mother's prescient world and his father's free thinking. Many other views contributed to Andersen's religious sensibility. For this reason, his faith, if considered over an entire lifetime, is filled with a wide range of authorities and resources. In addition to the constant dynamic tension between the forms of faith and doubt held by his mother and father, Andersen was influenced by the thorough religious training he received at the grammar schools in Slagelse and Helsingør in the 1820s. He was also marked by his encounters with L. C. Müller in 1827-28, as well as various introductions to the nature philosophy of Romanticism as presented by H. C. Ørsted and B. S. Ingemann. Last but not least, the author's thirty trips abroad over a period of forty years also had an effect on shaping and coloring his faith. These strong impressions of the religious life of foreign peoples can be found everywhere in Andersen's literary works, his diaries, and his letters.

He never denied or completely let go of any of the sources of inspiration mentioned. They continued to offer a range of religious possibilities and productive approaches to the relationship between God and the individual. His father's skepticism, his mother's superstitions, the numerous essays he had to write in light of Krog-Meyer's religious catechism in the 1820s, as well as decades of pantheistic and scientific discussions with Ørsted and Ingemann—all of these things sharpened Andersen's religious temperament. His peculiar blend of a cultivated, childish naïveté and a mature, intellectual contemplation is most apparent in the novel *To Be or Not to Be* from 1857. This book depicts a modern person's constant wavering between faith and doubt. The novel was not the success that Andersen had hoped, although he did receive one weighty and enthusiastic letter from the philosophy professor F. C. Sibbern. The professor stated that Andersen, unlike his extremely confused protagonist, had always lived a peaceful, harmonious life without those sorts of bewildered scruples about God and the divine. Andersen offered this laconic comment in the appendix to *The Fairy Tale of My Life*, published several years after his death:

> "I did not have—as Sibbern believed and stated—a pious, dreamy child's temperament; I had undergone many religious struggles about faith and knowledge inside the secret chamber of my heart."

Although Andersen seldom went to church and preferred—as he said—the "unconscious church worship" out in nature, his faith was very much alive within him. His relationship to God was quite intimate—like that of a son with his father. In one diary entry the author spontaneously and typically exclaims: "If I had God here, I could press Him to my heart!"

Like H. C. Ørsted, Andersen supported a universal and easily accessible Christianity without the dead weight of strict dogmas. For example, Andersen had no interest in hearing about eternal damnation; in his opinion, there was no such thing as an unforgivable sinner. The punishment of hell was in Andersen's theological system both an unreasonable and unethical dogma. The notion that those who were ungodly and evil should burn for all eternity in the bottomless, stinking depths of hell was inconsistent with the consciousness of God's infinite goodness. In his fairy tale "A Story," Andersen has the wife of a fire-and-brimstone preacher say:

> "I am just a sinful person, but I could not bear it in my heart to let even the worst sinner burn eternally; so how could Our Lord allow it? He, who is so infinitely good and who knows how the Evil One comes from without and within. No, I can't believe it, even though you say so."[68]

A person had to be allowed to think for himself, not just regarding the question of hell and eternal torments, but also in terms of other religious issues. As Andersen once wrote in a letter to Ørsted, he found it far more blessed to *believe* if he also *knew*. He thought that the Lord could certainly tolerate being seen through the reason He had given to humans, and he went on: "I refuse to go to God with blindfolded eyes; I want them open, to see and to know. And if I should reach no other goal than the one who has only faith, my mind will still have become enriched."[69]

Here again we can sense the rationalistic temperament of his shoemaker father, along with his skepticism regarding Jesus and his miraculous deeds. The latter was something that Andersen himself encountered in the 1840s and 1850s when he read books by the religious historians David Friedrich Strauss and Ludwig Feuerbach, including *Leben Jesu* (1835) [*The Life of Jesus Critically Examined*] and *Das Wesen des Christenthums* (1841) [*The Essence of Christianity*], which had started a wave of aesthetic discussions all over Europe. For Andersen, these books must have sounded like a distant echo of his father's heretical thoughts back home on Munkemøllestræde around 1810. And at the heart of the aging Hans Christian Andersen's conflicted beliefs, we see traces of influence and inspiration from this criticism of the Bible. One topic of discussion was the idea that the gospels did not represent history but myth, and that faith therefore—from a phenomenological perspective—always expresses a person's own wishes. Taken to the ultimate conclusion, this meant that God was not a reality but a fiction who was always being created in a person's own image. In our imagination. These revolutionary ideas, which were of decisive importance for the secularization of the 19th century, can also be traced in the play *Ahasuerus*. The drama can be read as a religious self-portrait in which the author sees himself in Jerusalem's outcast, wandering shoemaker.

Like Ahasuerus, Andersen was a nomad with regard to worshiping a specific God in a specific sense and transfiguration. For the same reason, he was graced with a productive doubt, which serves certain believers well. Andersen saw the relationship between God and the individual person as a dynamic exchange of ideas and feelings, in which there was room for searching and criticism. And the space in which this encounter between God and the individual would take place was not the narrow confines of one belief system, but the vast, open landscape into which all people are born and undertake their life's journey—whether they call themselves Muslims, Catholics, Jews, or Protestants; whether they are a prince, a writer, or a shoemaker's son. We also hear this universal message in the play *The Moorish Girl* from 1840. In this story, the Muslim Miama meets the Christian Raphaella, and the two women, who for religious reasons should be natural enemies, instead develop a shared sense of sympathy and benevolence—something that the fundamentalism of both belief structures forbids them:

> For the first and perhaps last time
> We meet here in this world, why not
> Then part in friendship? I hold the belief
> That the Prophet's Paradise and Christ's Heaven
> Are, like Nature, merely one kingdom,
> And that the rose hedge of universal love
> Which blossoms there spreads in equal measure
> The same scent to the Christian as to the Moor.[70]

A God Dwells Within Us

Andersen believed in God, but that did not lessen his belief in himself. He often went his own way if there was any disagreement, in a metaphysical sense, about the course his life should take. In certain situations and phases of his life, he had good reason to feel blessed by the higher powers and to sense a divine goodwill. But even more often, a personal success—such as a major artistic breakthrough—came about because Andersen was the clever and industrious shaper of his own fortune. "Our fortune depends on our own firm will and outlook on life!" proclaims Naomi in *Only a Fiddler.* To a high degree, this creed was also Andersen's own. "We too must act and think," says Agnete in *The Wedding at Lake Como*, and she finds her way to the very heart of God's words about His relationship to human beings: "You too must act! In your action / Heaven will send down its help!"[71]

It was good to have God nearby, but the individual person's ability to take the initiative and grab an opportunity when it presented itself was in reality of equal importance in Andersen's liberal philosophy of life. Faith in Providence, as well as fatalism, individualism—and narcissism—all became combined in a higher, effective unity. Even though Andersen rarely doubted the Lord's fundamental solicitude for him, he still, just to be sure, had allied himself with a faith in destiny that could explain any eventual failure of Providence and offer help to the writer in distress. As a believer, Andersen wasn't taking any chances. In 1831, at the age of twenty-six, the author writes to Edvard Collin: "I have a fatalistic belief in Providence, although I seldom articulate it; whatever God has decided, will happen."[72] He had concealed in his sleeve this extra trump card, which he could play if both Providence and Fate ever failed him.

Andersen was enormously aware of his personal strengths. It was true that the gentle, kind Creator had given him and a few others a great many brilliant qualities, but, according to Andersen, it was the individual's own responsibility to make use of all these good basic gifts from above and below. This is expressed more clearly in the fairy tale "The Ice Maiden" from 1861. The main character, Rudy, is an orphaned but physically and psychologically strong little super-individualist. Using his formidable talents and indomitable will, he almost manages to climb all the way up to God. In this fairy tale we find the adage that was quoted in an earlier chapter. It might be a motto for the life, art, and beliefs of Hans Christian Andersen: "Our Lord may give us nuts, but He doesn't crack them open for us!"

Like any child keenly interested in who God is and what He means, Andersen never doubted the reality of the divine. "A god dwells within us," he wrote in *Ahasuerus* in 1847.[73] Even in a school essay from the mid-1820s that deals with the immortality of the soul and the resurrection of the body, he says that "God's voice speaks inside of us," and "heaven and hell dwell within the human being."[74] In young Andersen's numerous school essays we find the basis for most of his more mature concepts of God, who is described as "the invisible great one," and "the ruler,"[75] who is "all-perfect" and "all-wise."[76] And in the later essay that Andersen wrote for the prize competition at Copenhagen University, which he submitted in 1830, it's clear that even at the age of twenty or twenty-five, he had found answers to many fundamental religious questions. He had also formed his own explanation for what sort of precious material binds all religions together. It was a core that, according to the young Andersen, could be called a "childish spirit." In one of his best and most entertaining essays, which discusses the relationship between reason and emotion, this childish spirit is simply designated as the force behind human creation: "We see the childish spirit that animated the first humans, the mighty God, who so wondrously developed everything more and more. How childish are the ideas about the creation of the world."[77]

Andersen never gave up this perception that the earth's creation and the first humans came about in a children's room, springing from games and joy. In many ways he continued to shape this idea, first in his numerous poems around 1830, later in all the fairy tales, which began to be published in 1835. An early poem mentions, for instance, "the childish heaven," which the adult must constantly keep in mind if he wants to have a share of eternal life: "Oh Heaven is so vast, so vast! / A person feels quite small! / The grown-up becomes a child again; / As children we enter Heaven."[78] These first poems from 1830 are directly linked—especially via the fairy tales—to the novel *To Be or Not to Be* from 1857, in which it says: "It is the innocent who will reach the goal: the heavenly kingdom belongs to the children; the child's mind will reach it."[79] This direct link is again picked up in the final verse of one of Andersen's last poems, from February 1875, in which he turns to his own origins. With his hometown of Odense as a backdrop, he describes the child's eternal faith:

> I had a child's strong faith
> And Jacob's heavenly ladder,
> And I found the seeds that grow
> In the realm of fairy tales,
> Which reach into our childhood land
> And the garden of Paradise,
> To the shore of light, eternity
> Beyond the graves of earth.[80]

This type of naïve, inquisitive, and devoted religiosity that is associated with children became an emblem of faith for Andersen, giving him access to all different religions. This child's faith was the ability, with a little boy's or girl's supple and unpredictable imagination, to move in every direction from the narrow, straight ladders of orthodoxy. And it is no coincidence that Andersen, in *The Fairy Tale of My Life*, suddenly tells a story in which the author for once does not act as the child's advocate; instead, the reverse occurs. This episode takes place around 1830, when everyone was trying to correct the young man and artist. One day it got to be too much for a small child, as Andersen reports:

> "A present-day pastor from Jutland, who at the time was a university student submitting vaudevilles and critiques, could not resist the chance at a family gathering, at which I was in attendance, to scrutinize a few of my poems. A little girl, six years old, listened with astonishment to everything he found wrong; every word in my writing was reprehensible. And when he put the book aside and there was a brief pause, she picked it up and in her innocence pointed to a page, indicating the word 'and.' 'There's a little word left here!' she said. 'You haven't scolded this one!' He felt the blow of the child's words, blushed, and hushed the little girl."[81]

For Andersen, a child's faith was a magic wand that could appear at any time because it was waved by force of the emotions and not reason. This is what Gerda does at the end of "The Snow Queen," and the message is one that Andersen approved to the end of his days: "Unless you become as little children, you shall not enter the kingdom of Heaven." Gerda must be one of the most beautiful human figures in Andersen's works because she, as it says in the fairy tale, has a positive power in her heart, though she is not aware of it herself. It is one of the greatest emotional assets a person can have: the power of "a sweet and innocent child." Gerda is unable to reach Kai, who is a victim of ice-cold reason. She needs the help of extraordinary weapons, and a hundred years before Walt Disney's animations, we see in Andersen's fairy tale how the words of Gerda's pious prayer are transformed into a host of armed angels, who pour out of her mouth to take up the battle against the Snow Queen's deadly advance troops, dressed as razor-sharp snowflakes:

> "Then little Gerda said the Lord's Prayer, and the cold was so great that she could see her own breath. It came out of her mouth like a cloud of smoke. Her breath got thicker and thicker, forming into bright little angels that grew bigger and bigger as they touched the ground. All of them wore

helmets on their heads and carried spears and shields in their hands. There were more and more of them, and by the time Gerda had finished saying the Lord's Prayer, there was an entire legion around her."[82]

As the years passed, this child's faith became more and more important for Hans Christian Andersen. This was partially because he was aging, partially because all around him society was changing with disturbing speed and lack of foresight. The world was in the process of losing its innocence, and the only imaginable defense against the ungovernable materialism of the modern age was—in Andersen's opinion—the imaginative power that resided in the individual person. He describes it in *To Be or Not to Be* as: "The child mind that unconsciously clings to faith." In the 1860s and 1870s we often see how the author clearly steps forward in his literary works to preach the child's faith and seek religious dimension. This happens, for instance, in *He Was Not Born* from 1864:

"Our time! This miserable time, the least poetic of times! . . . Everything is enlightenment, clarity, an infinitely tedious mathematical calculation! The supernatural has been enlightened to death. The ghost appears only in *Hamlet*, not in reality."[83]

The Author and Death

One of Andersen's most beloved ghosts was Death. There are few figures in his works to whom he returns more often or examines from so many different childish angles. In the fairy tale "The Angel" from 1843, Death is a pleasant and helpful traveling companion:

"Every time a good child dies, one of God's angels comes down to earth, takes the dead child in his arms, spreads out his white wings, and flies over all the places the child loved, picking a whole handful of flowers to bring up to God, where they will bloom even more beautifully than on earth."[84]

Like the little child who has an eternity ahead of him, Andersen had an unshakable faith that a whole new form of existence awaited him when his spirit, at the appropriate time, would leave the husk of his body. On those occasions when he felt doubt about the soul's immortality, he would quickly revert to his child's faith, sometimes in a compelling fashion. In *The Fairy Tale of My Life* Andersen gives a vivid example of this sort of swift, effective alleviation and transformation of his nagging doubt. It was on a morning during the Christmas holidays at Bregentved estate. A thin layer of snow covered the flagstones around the obelisk out in the manor-house garden, and during his morning walk, Andersen used the tip of his cane to write in the snow: "Immortality is like the snow, / Tomorrow we won't be able to see it." Over the next days, there was a great thaw followed by a hard frost. By the time Andersen was once again able to go out to stretch his legs and pass by the obelisk on his morning walk, all the snow had melted except for the little area where he had written in the snow a few days earlier. Now only the word "immortality" was legible, and in his memoirs Andersen wrote of this icy, clear sign: "I was deeply moved by this incident, and my vivid thought was: 'God, my God, I have never doubted.'"

And so, with a wave of the magic wand in the snow, doubt is swept into the ground and skepticism is transformed to firm belief. At least if your name is Hans Christian Andersen. And the closer Andersen came to his own death, the more important and necessary it became for him—using more or less heavy-handed methods—to maintain his belief that he was on his way to a swift resurrection and not to a slow putrefaction. This was also the reason behind his sudden decision to change the ending of the fairy tale "Auntie Toothache" in the 1870s. The first version, from 1872, contains the pessimistic, Judgment Day statement: "Everything ends up in the bin." In the fall of 1874, while reading the proofs for the fifth and last volume of *Fairy Tales and Stories*, the old author decided to delete this unbearable sentence, giving the story a more optimistic ending:

> "The brewer is dead, Auntie is dead, and the student is dead, the one whose sparks of genius ended up in the bin: that's the end of the story, the story about Auntie Toothache."[85]

In spite of his great insight into the physical processes of nature—"the eternal cycle of things," as it's called in *To Be or Not to Be*—Andersen could not make himself impart the belief that we humans do not go to heaven but down into the bin and end up as organic fertilizer or burnable trash. As he cautiously had asked back in the 1830s in the fairy tale "The Galoshes of Fortune": "Will I merely come up as grass in Death's garden?" This question was later repeated, becoming a topic to be examined and discussed in *To Be or Not to Be* in 1857. In this novel the pious half sister of the scientific-minded Niels Bryde refuses to listen to the notion that the spirit does not go up to God when a person dies but instead becomes dispersed as various substances and gases, for the benefit of the plant and ani-mal kingdoms. Yet Niels knows better, and as the novel progresses he com-bines his faith and his knowledge into the High Romantic view that the human spirit benefits nature; and nature is God, after all: "'The great whole, the divine all,' exclaimed Niels, 'the ancient Pan, which the Greeks believed would be the last to survive the gods!'"[86]

In "The Story of a Mother" we find another example of an attempt to find a compromise to the difficult question about where the spirit ulti-mately goes when it leaves the human body. In this story, Death is employed as God's gardener in a hothouse here on earth, where he takes care of the flowers and trees that each represent a human life. This means that it's possible for us, while alive, to find the plant or flower that stands for our soul. Each plant will be pulled up by its roots when Our Lord tells His gardener to grab a shovel and dig us up so we can be planted in the garden of paradise. In keeping with the mild and promising transition to another form of existence, which is what death often is in Andersen's uni-verse, the moment of death is depicted as a gentle event, without any sort of physical pain or suffering. And so, in "The Galoshes of Fortune," there is talk of a person receiving a faint jolt in the heart and then "the liberat-ed soul flies off on the wings of electricity." And in "Peiter, Peter, and Peer" Andersen attempts to combine scientific and religious concepts in a uni-fied explanation of where we humans come from and are going. In this story life ends festively with "the great big kiss of death," which comes directly from Our Lord and is so filled with tenderness and solicitude that you simply disappear into the kiss, which feels like being dazzled by the sun, when everything goes black before your eyes.

In Andersen's universe death is not a painful and traumatic ending to a life but an optimistic and promising beginning. We find in Andersen the ancient, primitive belief of the human being as a seed that has to be buried in order to rise up from death. Throughout his works, he uses expressions such as "the life of death" and "the angel of renewal." He regards death as a release for the one who is suffering, and as a new chance for the one who has failed. "Our earthly life here is the seed of eternity," as it says in the poem "The Old Man," which Andersen wrote in the last year of his life. For the funerals of his friends and acquaintances, Andersen had writ-ten scores of poems that were read or sung either in the church or at the graveside. In a song written for the funeral of old Fru Collin in 1845, he wrote: "Oh Death, you are radiant and not a shadow."[87] It is this life-affirming view of death that extends throughout the author's life and work. Even as far back as 1822, in his *Youthful Attempts*, the seventeen-year-old Andersen expressed his unperturbed and almost expectant view of the end of life: "Death is sweet, death is the reward / For the anguish of life . . ."[88]

It can be said that Andersen had to believe in an eternal life; otherwise there would be no justice in his expansive beliefs. The concept of a promising life after this one provided meaning, in the most literal sense, to the harshness and cruelty of existence. For this reason the idea of eternity offered Andersen support for his belief in a merciful world order.[89] As Esther says in *To Be or Not to Be* about the injustice of life: "The mathematical calculation here can only be solved with the figure: *an eternal life.*"

At the age of ten, thirty, and seventy Andersen believed wholeheartedly in a heaven for the good and in a purgatory where those who were evil could, in a sort of in-between state, become good once again. In the frequently repeated ideas and speculations about life after death that are found in Andersen's art as well as in his letters and diary entries, the God in whom he believes is always ready to give the human being one more chance. And even one after that, if necessary. In "The Red Shoes" and "The Girl Who Trod on a Loaf" the two young sinners are severely punished within the framework of the stories—the first, with the amputation of her feet; and the latter, with eternal confinement in the company of the Devil's merciless great-grandmother. Yet both are given various opportunities to rehabilitate themselves until at the very end of the stories they are granted absolution through self-knowledge and the faith, hope, and charity of others. This is the red thread in Andersen's religiosity: All can be forgiven! As it is so beautifully expressed in "A Story," when the pastor with the harsh words and pitch-black views of God and His creatures is finally taken to task by the ghost of his deceased wife: "Look at human beings: even those who are evil possess a piece of God, a piece that will triumph and extinguish the fires of hell."[90] In other words, the evil forces in a person are always weak compared to the good, which come from God.

And there is good reason to draw attention to the "Devil" and all his powerful cohorts in a discussion of Andersen's ideas about eternity. As the Sandman confides in Hjalmar, people can also have too much of the good. In Andersen's theological system, the Devil is an inevitable part of his faith in Our Lord. As it says in *Only a Fiddler*, people must not be so blind in their faith that they see only God's cross and fail to notice the Devil standing behind it in the shadow. The mocking demon is part of the cross.[91]

As an artist and as a human being, Andersen never tried to avoid the subterranean powers. In fact, some of the best and most successful passages in his fairy tales take place in a perpetually dark underworld, where all sorts of trolls and demons come to life. Examples include the bog woman in her brewery and the Devil's great-grandmother, who embroiders lies and crochets curse words in "The Girl Who Trod on a Loaf"; as well as the troll whose favorite meal is the blue eyes of children in "The Traveling Companion." They all belong to this bottomless universe of sinister men and demonic women. They should never be discussed with malice; the necessity of their existence should simply be acknowledged. As the young Andersen writes in 1830:

> "Everyone speaks badly of Satan; they never recognize that he is merely fulfilling his duty. It is his job, after all, to seduce the children of humanity. He is the touchstone in this world; it is through him that we will be purified for the better; he is this struggle and flame, this *aspera* moving *ad astram*, and so he has here an important, meritorious role in the great drama of life."[92]

Much in Andersen's work deals with this division and struggle in the human being. His diaries, over a period of fifty years, are filled with attempts to record, investigate, and explain this "spiritual company of angels and demons," as it says in *To Be or Not to Be*. And when they could no longer be harnessed or contained in various artistic concepts—after the last fairy tale was written and the last paper-cut created—they swarmed out and made the last few years of the author's life a painful Elf Mound. The sun never fully came out again, and so, day after day, the mound with all its elves stood on glowing pilings.

Morphine

In 1873-74, as old age descended in earnest, bringing with it joint pains, colic, shivering fits, black stools, and jaundice, a cruder aspect of Andersen's refined and sensitive nature abruptly emerged. As he said one day to Henriette Collin when she was summoned to assuage his depression: "Oh, what am I going to do? I'm so filled with evil and hateful thoughts."[93] In a novel he once wrote of an aging but formally vital man that now it was as if the wind had rushed into his brain and was whirling around in there, as if inside an empty snail shell: "If my thought ever wanders out, it's like a sick man on crutches."[94]

To the author's own dismay, all sorts of sickly thoughts were now springing up from underground. They were distortions of human life, like the dead man experiences in the story "On Judgment Day." Accompanied by the angel of death, he ascertains that all living people look as if they're at a masquerade, and under their clothing they're carefully hiding something from each other: "One thing tore at another to make it visible, and then the head of an animal could be seen sticking out; in one person it was a grinning ape, in another a vile goat, a clammy snake, or a dull fish."[95]

In the same manner, in the years 1874-75, it was as if the myth of the lovable fairy-tale author, who had endured such terrible trials, now began to crack and reveal a more raw and primitive figure. The proletarian shone through more than ever before. Andersen became a difficult and embarrassing person to be with. He was quite aware that his personality was changing and that nature was claiming its due. Malice was no longer merely in the background or wings of his writings; it was something real that was stirring inside him: "The beast that we all carry; the beast that has become a solid part of the human being and that was jumping and leaping and wanting to get out."[96] Andersen found it tremendously difficult to age with grace and dignity. "Teach me, oh forest, to wither with joy" was never his favorite hymn, judging by the apparent reference in a diary entry: "For a whole day I sat indoors and indulged in caprices, rolled up in myself like a withered leaf, and that is not enjoyable." To paraphrase the author again, this time from an old novel: the soul, like a bat, was haunting the ruin of his body. And in a gloomy Christmas letter to Edvard Collin, Andersen writes in 1873: "If this is how old age comes, then it is quite terrible."[97]

The last years of Andersen's life were marked by behavior that was increasingly disgraceful and remarks that were wildly unrestrained. His diary provides a glimpse of the despair he felt when he looked in the mirror and saw his paternal grandfather, who once roamed the streets of Odense with flower wreaths on his head, beech branches stuck down his pants, and a horde of laughing boys following behind.[98] The same confusion and despair were beginning to plague Andersen, both in the company of strangers and when he was alone. He dreamed and fantasized about the endless number of women who over the years had set their sights on him. And the author who had always been so fastidious and vain no longer paid much attention to his appearance. Like the little story about the old, worn-out boots in *A*

Poet's Bazaar, Andersen had lost faith that a brush could give him back his youthful luster. For long periods of time he would stay home next to the stove. If he did pull himself together enough to go out, he might leave home without his false teeth and wearing a filthy, dented hat. In restaurants and *table d'hôte* at hotels abroad, where everyone dined together at one or more large tables, the guests would immediately recognize the famous Dane. And here too, Andersen attracted a good deal of negative attention, as Nicolai Bøgh mentions in his diary from the trip in 1873. For instance, the author would demonstratively cover his ears and complain loudly whenever the waiter would clatter the dishes, glasses, or silverware. Or he might decide to rinse off his false teeth in a water glass.[99]

Back home in Denmark, more and more people during the 1870s had their own cruel or ludicrous stories to tell about Hans Christian Andersen, whose ego had now become the permanent and absolutely invariable background for all his imaginings. As one of the last foreign visitors to his Nyhavn apartment in April 1875 characterized the old author's complete egocentrism during the last years of his life: "He had no immediate sense for the joys of others."[100] And as someone else wrote in Andersen's obituary:

> "It was almost impossible for him to think about anything but himself. He possessed in full measure the good heart that demands to share its happiness with others, but his weakness allowed him only rarely the joy of sharing the happiness of others."[101]

To an ordinary Copenhagen dinner party he might show up wearing around his neck his resplendent Mexican Order of Guadalupe medal and talk nonstop about the portrait that Carl Bloch was painting of him. "At the moment I think it looks like Goethe—though people say that I look so much like Schiller."[102] There were also rumors that an English lady who was staying with the Henriques family at their country estate of Petershøj in Klampenborg had actually seen Andersen, during one of his regular visits, open letters addressed to her. He was trying to find out whether the English had anything to say about him. Andersen apparently confessed to his embarrassing conduct, but he was more concerned and dismayed at the fact that there was no mention of him in the letters: "And here I thought the English were so fond of me!"[103]

Andersen's life had become sad, monotonous, and abnormally self-centered. Yet the diaries from his last years make for gripping and compelling reading because they present such a raw and honest picture of an old, ailing, and eventually morphine-addicted man in his daily struggle against annihilation. All of Andersen's negative thoughts about illness, death, and the ever-growing materialism of the times are constantly interspersed with a childish belief in a swift recovery of his health and an eternal life. This is also true of some of his last fairy tales, such as "What Old Johanne Told" from 1872, in which we hear about "Poor Rasmus" and the helpless way he throws out his arms as if to say "What good is it?" Juxtaposed with this torpid dreamer of a man is old Johanne with her more life-affirming advice: "Trust in yourself and Our Lord!"

Heaven and hell were at war with each other inside the aging Andersen. On the morning of an overcast day he might give up on everything and plan to commit suicide, but by afternoon, if his energy and the blue sky had returned, he could suddenly think about buying a house with a fountain, goldfish, and a green copper roof.[104] Or he might start planning the long trip to Montreux with Jonas Collin. Andersen ordered a new suit for the journey and had 200 calling cards printed while he sat at home in Nyhavn and proceeded to fold together a little account book and estimate the total travel expenses, including tips.[105]

During the last twelve months of Hans Christian Andersen's life— from the end of July 1874, when he returned home from the estates of Holsteinborg and Bregentved, and up until his death on August 4, 1875— he spent most of his time alone, in his apartment in Nyhavn, except when he had visitors. Yet he was also a frequent guest of the wealthy, hospitable Melchior family at their summer residence "Rolighed," which was located a short distance outside the city, close to Svanemøllen and Øresund. There the old author was pampered and nursed. Andersen was now plagued by coughing up phlegm as well as various fluid accumulations, which caused severe swelling in his arms and legs. And the rheumatism that had tormented all the joints of his body for many years had not gotten any better. "My body has grown so pitiful!" he remarks in his diary. There was no longer any medicine other than morphine that had any effect, even though all his life Andersen had tried just about everything: chloral hydrate, spirit of ether, valerian, raisins preserved in sugar and vinegar, bloodletting, sea baths, jet baths, Russian steam baths, sourdough under his feet, mustard on his wrists, Spanish fly across his throat, leeches on his neck, carrot wraps, milk gargles, rhubarb root, and many other things.

One of the remedies that over the years had a very positive and rapid effect whenever Andersen's whole body was feeling terrible had come from Theodor Collin and had to do with his hair: "Go over to Minet and have your hair curled!" No sooner said than done, and later a grateful author wrote in his diary: "*Eau chinine* and the comb also helped, and later in the day I was human again."[106] Of equal value for his mental health was the advice to get a shave, provided, of course, that the barber kept in mind who he had under his knife and didn't get too close to the author—as happened one early morning in May 1875, when Andersen was still groggy from the nighttime haze of morphine:

> "At dawn my sleep became heavier; nervously I got up. A new assistant barber arrived, he moved so close to me during the shaving that I would have pushed him away but was afraid of being cut; his eyes and gleaming white teeth had me feeling terrified, I was frightened by him, frightened of being assaulted, of evil people; I started having all sorts of crazy ideas and thought I was going to go mad."[107]

During the 1860s and 1870s, the Melchior family took over a large part of the familial obligations with regard to Hans Christian Andersen. As Bournonville expressed it, in the home of this Jewish family the author was surrounded by "sisterly and brotherly solicitude," and it was in the arms of this family that Andersen died in 1875.[108] The members of the Melchior family admired him as a brilliant author and pampered him like an ill, weak child. Andersen was fully aware of the sacrifices this entailed, and he showed his gratitude for the boundless kindness he received in this "home of the heart" by dedicating to the Melchior family his last, exceptional fairy-tale book in 1872. This book contained "What Old Johanne Told," "The Cripple," "The Door Key," and "Auntie Toothache." In addition, the family was acknowledged in various provisions of the author's will, and they inherited his big folding screen with the collage.

Andersen celebrated Christmas 1874 with the Melchior family at their home on Højbro Plads in Copenhagen. The marvelous holiday season had always played a prominent role in the author's literature, paper-cuts, letters, and diaries, ever since as a nineteen-year-old student he had raced along in Headmaster Meisling's horse-drawn coach from Slagelse to Copenhagen. It was always an icy cold journey, and young Andersen would seek shelter along with Fru Meisling and her four children under an eiderdown quilt, where they would play cards and sing. When the coach finally rolled into the capital, they would all be covered with feathers from a torn pillow—a white Christmas! Andersen had also spent a memorable Dionysian Christmas Eve in Rome in 1833. All the effusively happy and drunken Nordic artists, with vine leaves in their hair and ivy wreaths around their neck, had joined in to sing Andersen's Christmas song: "Let us, like the child, rejoice, / We are all children at heart." Afterwards they had planned an attack on Andersen's innocence, but the most virginal among them managed to escape amidst the crowds and ringing bells behind the church of Santa Maria Maggiore, where the baby Jesus was being carried in a holy procession.

Christmas was also special to Andersen because it was largely an improviser's holiday. At the estates and in the homes of the finer Copenhagen families, the stage for his art was set. Both as an author and a visual artist—with his lively words and busy scissors—Andersen was in his element during the Christmas season, when people would linger over meals and the theaters were closed. The author could devote himself to readings, Christmas games, amateur plays, and the so-called gift mottoes. This was a particular type of short verse that was attached to the Christmas presents, written with an eye to the gift itself as well as the recipient. For example, a knife for cutting open the pages of a new book was accompanied with the words: "With this knife you can cut open and look / at each idea in the body of the book." And on the outside of a package that turned out to hold a new copy of Andersen's latest fairy-tale collection it said: "Here you have the key, if I may offer a clue, / That opens the palace garden of his kingdom to you." The verses could also be mischievous and even slightly impudent—for example, if the future owner of a bound copybook was known to be quite messy: "That you should receive this is a crying shame, / Since the blots on the page will have you to blame." Andersen himself had certainly made his share of blots on the page at every Christmas since 1822. It was the winter solstice, which meant time for reflection—the culmination of the year, an ending and a beginning, what he was looking forward to . . . yes, what was that? Love, health, riches, and nature's renewal. Springtime and the arrival of the stork, and the author-bird's own annual flight to southern climes. Andersen diligently wrote in his diary during the Christmas season, and to the rural postman he delivered stacks of letters to be sent all over Denmark and abroad, with some of them going far out into the world. "Christmas is coming; childish, happy Christmas," Andersen writes to his sensitive friend in Weimar, Hereditary Grand Duke Carl Alexander, in December 1850.

But Andersen's last Christmas season was a sad affair. "Gray skies;

before you know it, it's dinnertime (12 o'clock) and the afternoon grows dark, so that it's evening by 3 o'clock."[109] Morphine was his only solace in his loneliness. His dreams at night were so lovely that even Headmaster Meisling had become amenable and acknowledged the brilliance of his difficult pupil. But when he woke up and looked at himself in the mirror, he could see nothing but illness and disease. The old author no longer had the energy to take part in the Christmas festivities that others wanted him to join. By eight o'clock on Christmas Eve in 1874, half an hour before the candles would be lit on the Christmas tree in the Melchiors' drawing room on Højbro Plads, Andersen asked to be driven back home to Nyhavn. There the two old Ballin sisters, who kept house for him, had lit a fire and set the table for Christmas supper. In peace and quiet Andersen spent the rest of the evening opening presents, and then sat back to examine his bounty: a rose bush, flowers, pots, framed portraits, woolen wristlets, writing implements, and three bottles of good port. He spent the days between Christmas and New Year's receiving visitors, counting his money, and calculating his fortune in the savings bank. During the last days of each year Andersen always tried to gain an overview of his material worth. Calculated in today's currency, the income of the sixty-nine-year-old author had made him a millionaire. Before Christmas substantial sums in royalties had poured in from both America and Germany, and more than 400 *rigsdaler* had been deposited in the bank by Edvard Collin. Even the smallest coin in Andersen's wallet was recorded, and then he threw himself into the Christmas spirit, later noting in his diary: "Yesterday gave the maid 2 *rigsdaler* as a Christmas present and errand boy 1 *rigsdaler*."

But that didn't mean he wasn't frugal, and of course his rooms weren't kept any warmer just because it was snowing and there was a fierce wind outside. Over at his desk in the corner it was only 53° Fahrenheit, and a flower vase with a stork pattern on the windowsill had shattered from the cold. Andersen mentions this in one of his Christmas letters, which were concerned with only four things: Andersen's Christmas presents, Andersen's health, Andersen's books, and the big statue of Andersen in the King's Garden, for which the public had begun to collect money. "It's not certain that I will live to see it; how long do I have from now until the grave?" he asks.

Not long. Andersen's suffering continued into the new year. Not even his seventieth birthday celebration and the awarding of the Commander of the Order of the Dannebrog, first grade, which was given to him by the king himself at Amalienborg Palace, could give the author any hope of getting well. By now he could neither read nor write, and all his thoughts circled more and more around death and himself. When the Danish-German author Edmund Lobedanz and his ten-year-old daughter visited Andersen in Nyhavn on April 24, traces of the birthday celebration from three weeks earlier were still apparent in the apartment, which resembled a mausoleum:

> "In the first of Andersen's rooms there was a platform and a carpet covered with flowers, a plaster bust of the author, wearing a laurel wreath; and all around it were countless gifts, even including, if I am not mistaken, cases holding medals. As I said, there was an air of homage in that room, which might have made many uneasy, and which would certainly have prompted satire, because here and there Andersen's naïve cult of his own persona seemed to have been taken a bit too far."[110]

The Last Journey

In early May 1875, Andersen attended a performance at the Royal Theater for the last time. Up in the balcony he fell asleep in the middle of the ballet *Arkona*, which "had absolutely nothing new to offer other than a lively little dwarf."[111] Later in the month, it was the seventieth birthday of the composer J. P. E. Hartmann. Andersen gave him a pair of delicate—and expensive—teacups. A few days later Jonas Collin came to take Andersen on an excursion to the zoo. They talked about their impending journey to Montreux and Menton, where they would spend the winter. During the first weeks of June it said "Bregentved" in Andersen's calendar, but the formation of a new ministry that required Count Frederik Moltke's presence in the capital intervened. Instead, on June 11, 1875, Andersen decided to go to "Rolighed."

The next day the Melchiors' carriage arrived to take him to the magnificent garden with a view of Sweden, Svanemøllen, and the open fields. Merchant Moritz G. Melchior walked across these fields every afternoon in the summer, on his way down to Øresund to swim after arriving home from a day of busy commerce in Copenhagen. The "Rolighed" estate, which resembled a miniature Rosenborg Castle, had a big dining room with a view of the water and an even bigger living room with an attached greenhouse and veranda. At the very top of the manor, on a covered balcony, the master of the house had set up several excellent telescopes so he could keep an eye on the merchant vessels, both his own and those belonging to others, as they passed Trekroner Lighthouse.[112] From another balcony of "Rolighed," in the summer of 1875, the old author could see no farther than to the trees that surrounded the big, luxurious garden where for five or six years he had picked countless numbers of flowers to create some of his fantastical bouquets and centerpieces. During those years "Rolighed" was famed for its table settings whenever Andersen was visiting. For instance, he might decorate the table with heads of cabbage in which he had stuck various straws and flowers from the garden. As he wrote on the fan belonging to the Melchior children: "The smallest leaf is a sorcery, / A living soul sits inside."[113]

But from his balcony in July 1875, the author could no longer see the difference between the beech, birch, elm, and oak trees. But he was still aware of the light and the wind, as well as the cries of the seagulls and the rustling leaves of the poplars. On Tuesday, July 25, 1875, he sat outdoors for nearly three hours. The following day he had to make do with the living room veranda, and on Thursday he stayed in bed. Fru Melchior brought him, as she did each morning when he was visiting in the summertime, a fresh flower from the garden. That day it was a white rose. Andersen grabbed her hand, squeezing and kissing it repeatedly, as he said: "Thank you and God bless you!" Then he closed his eyes again and dozed off. "His strength is visibly diminishing, and his face has sunken in and looks quite like a mummy. Poor Andersen!" wrote Fru Melchior in her diary.[114]

Over the next few days it became increasingly difficult to communicate with him, and he repeated himself over and over as Fru Melchior kept watch at his bedside. If she sat there too long, he would ask her to leave so he could be alone. On Monday, August 2, he seemed filled with new life— the way the stump of a candle suddenly flares up before it burns down into the candleholder. "Oh, how blessed, how lovely! Good morning, everyone!" Andersen said, shaking hands with Jens the servant. Later that day he asked Fru Melchior if she would please remember to make sure his artery was cut open if she should one day find him lifeless. He didn't want to risk being buried alive; in the past, whenever this fear happened to seize hold of him at bedtime, he would place a little note on the night table that said: "I only seem to be dead!"

There was good reason to fear death in 19th-century Denmark. Sometimes people were placed in their coffin and the lid was nailed shut while their heart was still beating. The Copenhagen city fathers had once—during the author's youth—considered building a big, central morgue where all the dead of the city would be brought and kept for one or two days before burial. There they would make sure that the deceased were actually dead, for instance by tightly tying little bells to their limbs, so that even the slightest movement would be recorded. And on the hour two trumpeters would blow their horns as loudly as their lungs and the brass would allow.

But not even a trumpet from Judgment Day was necessary in the case of Hans Christian Andersen. For a long time the author had been, as it says in one of his novels, "in transition to things," and on August 4, 1875, at 11:05 in the morning, he died. Jens the servant was the one who found him, lying in bed with a cup of gruel in his hand. Most of the contents had spilled out over him and the bedclothes. Jens immediately ran to the stairs and shouted: "The Privy Councilor is dead!" Fru Melchior, who had heard Andersen coughing in the night, now sat at his bedside for a long time while the servant removed the soup cup, wiped the dead man's mouth, arranged his clothing, and straightened the bed. Afterwards Fru Melchior contacted all his friends and acquaintances, summoned her husband home from the Stock Exchange, and finally put all the impressions and emotions of the morning into writing:

> "He died with a small sigh, which I find to be an indescribable joy for him, since he would hardly have had time to become aware of death . . . It is a great, blessed relief for me that he died here and not among strangers. I would not for all the world have been spared the sorrows and worries, and if I had listened to all the well-intentioned advice that people kept giving me with regard to a hospital and the like, I would never have forgiven myself if I had sent him away from here. The last 8-12 days he has been in a happy state, grateful and affectionate about all that has been done for him . . . I feel that all of us, but myself in particular, will miss him as a loyal, devoted friend. Peace be with his mortal dust!"[115]

On August 11, 1875, every seat in Copenhagen's Vor Frue Kirke was taken. Shortly after twelve noon, King Christian IX arrived with the crown prince, Prince Hans, and the rest of the royal family. They took their places to the right of the chancel, along with the Master of Ceremonies, the First Equerry, the Secretary of the Cabinet, the Privy Councilor, the Lord Chamberlain, the head of the king's aides-de-camp, and various chamberlains, commanders, and captains. In the front reserved seats were members of the Collin, Melchior, and Ørsted families; counts, barons, ministers, legislators, mayors, councilors, supreme court barristers, police chiefs, professors, representatives from the clergy of Copenhagen and the surrounding areas; and, last but not least—as it said the next day in the newspaper *Berlingske Tidende*—"practically all of the leading men from the world of art and literature."[116]

It was an amazingly colorful sight inside the huge cathedral room, where the black robes and white collars of the clergy were in sharp contrast to the gold and brightly colored uniforms of the foreign diplomats, flanked by all the marble apostles on pedestals in the dim light. And outside the church, the city was dressed in its finest. By early morning flags were flying at half-mast from all the buildings and the ships out in the harbor. Several hours before the funeral, crowds had begun to gather in the church square, and by the time the first tones sounded from the organ inside, Copenhagen citizens filled the streets all around Vor Frue Kirke—shoulder to shoulder and face after face, for as far as the eye could see. It looked like a scene from the author's big folding screen. There were rumors that many people had come from Odense, besides the official deputation, led by Bishop Engelstoft, Mayor Mourier, and Lotze the apothecary. There were foreigners from America, Finland, Sweden, Norway, Germany, and England, who had come to pay their last respects to Hans Christian Andersen. They brought palm fronds, elaborate lyres made from woven laurels, and great, heavy wreaths with white ribbons and inscriptions such as: "*Du bist nicht tot: Schloss auch Dein Auge sich—im Kindes Herzen lebst Du ewiglich.*"[117] [You are not dead: although your eyes are closed—in the hearts of children you live forever.]

The heavy oak coffin stood in front of the chancel, surrounded by floral-draped candelabras with mourning candles and covered with wreaths. Andersen had once said that when the day finally came, he would make sure that a little peephole was bored into the coffin near his head so that he—cold, stiff, and with his body starting to decay—could follow along with his own funeral. Then he would take a proper count and see who was in attendance. And as he confided to Edvard Collin and the young William Bloch: "To those who *aren't* in attendance, I will appear as a ghost, and I'm sure to be a terrifying ghost!"[118]

In honor of the occasion, the organist was Andersen's good friend, the composer J. P. E. Hartmann, who played a beautiful prelude and then struck up one of the author's old hymns about fearing and having the courage to undertake the last, long journey: "Make the pain brief in my transmutation,

/ Grant me all the courage of a child."[119] Then Archdeacon Rothe gave a sermon on the words of gratitude and hope: "The Lord giveth, and the Lord taketh away, blessed be the name of the Lord!" The archdeacon talked about Andersen's wondrous life and recalled the words of the apostle: "By the grace of God am I the man that I am, and I know that His grace has not been in vain."

If Andersen had been able to follow the ceremony through the peephole in his coffin, he would have seen seated on the front pew the grayhaired, somber Edvard Collin, who was now the residuary legatee of an enormous collection of documents as well as a solid fortune. He had been kept guessing to the very end, as Andersen, while staying at "Rolighed" in June and July 1875, had considered making various changes to his will. One day he suddenly inserted Moritz G. Melchior as executor, along with Edvard, who nevertheless retained his status as residuary legatee. It's true that Andersen and Edvard had grown apart during the last five or ten years, but the old love had not died. The size of Andersen's fortune was not news to members of the Collin family. Many of them had already taken loans from the author and owed him money at his death—including Edvard Collin.[120] All his life, Andersen had been remarkably thrifty, and even as a wealthy man, he was scrupulous with the size and state of his fortune. But he could also be quite generous. For instance, for two decades he had taken the young sons of his close friends and acquaintances on long, costly trips at his own expense. There are also lesser but by no means isolated examples of the author's generosity toward the family that had meant so much to him. In 1867, he writes to Edvard Collin on New Year's morning, commenting on the recently received annual report of his balance at the bank where his friend is the president. He then remarks that Henrik Stampe, who like Edvard Collin had borrowed a good deal of money from Andersen, according to the report was supposed to pay 5% in interest, which came to 50 *rigsdaler*. In Andersen's view, this seemed an exorbitant rate, and he stated that he wouldn't have peace in his soul if he accepted so much in interest when the loan totaled only 1,000 *rigsdaler*.[121]

From the last verbal confrontation between these old men, brothers, and friends, we can gain some idea of how vital their relationship still was at the end when Andersen lay ill out at "Rolighed," while Edvard Collin was at his summer residence in northern Sjælland and did not return to Copenhagen until his friend was dead. The incident once again occurred in writing. It all started in June 1875, when Andersen—with Fru Melchior as his secretary—reminded Edvard Collin of the usual annual report, which he didn't think he had received at the end of 1874. The reply that Collin sent from his summer residence "Ellekilde" on June 22, 1875, speaks for itself. On the one hand, he doesn't hide how annoyed he is at the perpetually bothersome Andersen, whom he was once long ago directed to treat as a friend and brother. On the other hand—and this should not be ignored—Edvard Collin signs his letter "Your oldest and constant friend":

"Dear Andersen!

I was just in the process of wheeling around manure when I received your letter, in which you confide to me your financial worries; I washed my hands and am replying immediately.

First, I must object to the notion that I supposedly neglected to present you with your balance sheet at the end of December 1874; this would be just as unthinkable for a businessman as it would be for a writer not to look at the newspapers to see how his work has been judged. Next, as you can imagine, I do not have your accounts out here, and I will not, as many another might do to seem important, inform others about the state of your income. For that reason, your accounts are in my vault at the bank.

. . .

I will not cite Methuselah; he belongs to myth. But even if you should reach the age of Drakenberg and thus have 50 more years to live, I can vouch for the fact that even if you travel every year, you will not ever suffer need. And as a guarantee for this, I will pledge Ellekilde Estate, with property and shore access.

. . .

Your oldest and constant friend, E. Collin"[122]

Andersen never managed to send a reply to this letter, which sounded so similar to one of the many songs that Edvard, over the years, had written for celebrations in the Collin family. Andersen could no longer muster his old fighting spirit, and in mid-July he made do with dictating a letter to Fru Melchior that was addressed to Edvard's wife. In this letter the deathly ill author talks about the bold travel plans that he and Jonas Collin had made, and that it would no doubt be necessary to take along to Montreux and Menton a servant who could help with the packing and unpacking, as well as the daily wrapping of bandages around the author's swollen legs.[123]

He never made it that far. Yet Andersen's last journey on August 11, 1875, did take him out of the city. And in the direction of Fyn. After the speeches, the church choir sang "Lovely Is the Earth," which then gave way to the sound of wind instruments playing Hartmann's "Funeral March for Thorvaldsen." Artists and students lifted the coffin with a cry of "Sleep well!" and then carried it out of the church, followed by standard-bearers. From the church square the great funeral procession slowly set off, as the bells of Vor Frue Kirke blended with all the other church bells in the city. In front drove a carriage filled with all the wreaths. Next came a procession of various singing associations, all on foot and carrying banners. Then the hearse with the wreath-covered coffin, followed by a great number of carriages. From Nørreport they continued across the embankment between the two lakes, Peblingesø and Sortedamsø, and onward along the uneven road to Assistens Cemetery beyond the grounds of Blågård. At the entrance, the funeral procession was greeted by a solemn song, and a color guard stood all along the way to the Collin family plot, where the pastor was waiting. Many swore that they heard a high, clear voice from inside the coffin:

> Farewell, each rose, fresh and red,
> Farewell, all my beloved!
> Lift me away, mighty Death,
> Although it is good to be here!
> Have thanks, O God, for what you gave,
> Have thanks for what will come!
> Fly, Death, across the sea of time,
> Away to eternal summer![124]

Notes

CHAPTER 1

1. Carl Otto: "Pennetegninger," *Tilskueren*, 1929, II (July–December), pp. 201–03. Carl Otto: *Af mit Liv, min Tid og min Kreds. En autobiografisk Skildring*, Copenhagen, 1879. Carl Otto: *Livserindringer fra mine Reiser*, Copenhagen, 1873.
2. Just Mathias Thiele: *Af mit Livs Aarbøger*, Vol. 2, Copenhagen, 1917, pp. 133–35.
3. Egon Friedell: *Kulturhistorie*, Vol. 2, Copenhagen, 1958, p. 303.
4. Hans Christian Andersen: "Indledning til Carnevalet (Casino 1853–54)," *Samlede Skrifter*, Vol. 11, Copenhagen, 1854, pp. 159–60.
5. Johan Gottfried Herder: "Von Ähnlichkeit der mittleren englischen und deutschen Dichtkunst." Quoted from Edvard Lehmann: *Almueliv og eventyr*, Copenhagen, 1910, pp. 20–21.
6. Hans Christian Andersen: *Mit Livs Eventyr*, in *Samlede Skrifter*, Vol. 21, Copenhagen, 1855, p. 35.
7. Georg Nygaard: *H. C. Andersen og København*, Copenhagen, 1938, p. 21, and L. Kruse: *Teatret*, Copenhagen, 1819, p. 228.
8. Roger Shattuck: *The Forbidden Experiment: The Story of the Wild Boy of Aveyron*, New York, 1980, pp. 192–207.
9. Emil Hannover: *C. V. Eckersberg*, Copenhagen, 1898, p. 122.
10. Otto B. Wroblewski: *Nørrebro i Trediverne*, Copenhagen, 1895, pp. 2–3.
11. Anne Scott Sørensen: "Blomsterpoesi – om Kamma Rahbek og Bakkehuset," *Nordisk salonkultur*, Odense, 1998, pp. 327–45. Troels-Lund: *Bakkehus og Solbjerg*, Copenhagen, 1920–22.
12. December 12, 1822. *H. C. Andersens Moder. En Brevsamling*, Odense, 1947, p. 13.
13. Hans Christian Andersen: *Mit Livs Eventyr*, in *Samlede Skrifter*, Vol. 21, Copenhagen, 1855, p. 35.
14. Thomas Overskou: *Den danske Skueplads*, Vol. 4, Copenhagen, 1854–64, pp. 312–14.
15. Hans Christian Andersen: *Mit eget Eventyr uden Digtning*, Copenhagen, 1942, p. 32.
16. Robert Neiiendam: *To kvinder i H. C. Andersens liv*, Copenhagen, 1954, p. 10.
17. *Illustreret Tidende*, July 11, 18, and 25, 1869. Published in Georg Brandes: *Kritiker og Portrætter*, Copenhagen, 1870.
18. Hans Christian Andersen: *Lykke-Peer*, Copenhagen, 2000, p. 35.
19. *H. C. Andersens Levnedsbog. Digterens Liv 1805–1831*, Copenhagen, 1926, pp. 44–45.
20. Paludan, Lauridsen, et al. (ed.): *Københavnernes historie. Fra Absolon til Weidekamp*, Copenhagen, 1987, p. 115.
21. William Bloch: *Paa Rejse med H. C. Andersen*, Copenhagen, 1842, pp. 12–13.

22. Marcus Rubin: *1807–14. Studier til Københavns og Danmarks Historie*, Copenhagen, 1892, p. 19.

23. *H. C. Andersens Levnedsbog*, Copenhagen, 1926, p. 39.

24. Hans Christian Andersen: *Kun en Spillemand*, in *Romaner og Rejseskildringer*, Vol. 3, Copenhagen 1944, p. 99.

25. Nicolai Bøgh: "Fra H. C. Andersens Barndoms- og Ungdomsliv," *Personalhistorisk Tidsskrift*, 1905, p. 63.

26. *H. C. Andersens Levnedsbog*, Copenhagen, 1926, pp. 34-35.

27. Hans Christian Andersen: *Mit Livs Eventyr*, in *Samlede Skrifter*, Vol. 21, Copenhagen, 1855, p. 18. H. Rosendal: "H. C. Andersens Barndom og første Ungdom," *Højskolebladet*, No. 13, Copenhagen, 1905, pp. 403-12.

28. *H. C. Andersens Levnedsbog*, Copenhagen, 1926, p. 60. Hans Christian Andersen: *Mit eget Eventyr uden Digtning*, Copenhagen, 1942, p. 42. Søren Chr. Barth: *Livserindringer*, Copenhagen, 1900, p. 205.

29. Hans Christian Andersen: *Mit Livs Eventyr*, in *Samlede Skrifter*, Vol. 21, Copenhagen, 1855, p. 19. Hans Christian Andersen: *Mit eget Eventyr uden Digtning*, Copenhagen, 1942, pp. 23, 34-35. *H. C. Andersens Levnedsbog*, Copenhagen, 1926, pp. 37-38, 52-53.

30. *H. C. Andersens Levnedsbog*, Copenhagen, 1926, pp. 61-62.

31. Ibid., p. 58.

32. Ibid., p. 61.

33. Nicolai Bøgh: "Fra H. C. Andersens Barndoms- og Ungdomsliv," *Personalhistorisk Tidsskrift*, 1905, p. 75.

34. Ibid., p. 74.

35. Birthe Johansen: "Balletskolen," *Det Kongelige Teater*, Copenhagen, 1995, p. 4.

36. August Bournonville: *Mit Theaterliv*, Vol. 3, Copenhagen, 1877, p. 48.

37. Hans Christian Andersen: *Mit Livs Eventyr*, in *Samlede Skrifter*, Vol. 21, Copenhagen, 1855, p. 44.

38. Carl Dahlén: *Armida. Heroisk Ballet i fire Akter*, Copenhagen, 1819. Frederick J. Marker: "H. C. Andersen as a Royal Theatre Actor," *Anderseniana*, 1969, pp. 280-81.

39. August Bournonville: *Mit Theaterliv*, Vol. 3, Copenhagen, 1877, p. 49.

40. Thomas Overskou: *Af mit Liv og min Tid*, Copenhagen, 1916.

41. Ibid., Vol. 2, pp. 11-12. Frederick J. Marker: "H.C. Andersen as a Royal Theatre Actor," *Anderseniana*, 1969, p. 283.

42. *H. C. Andersens Levnedsbog*, Copenhagen, 1926, pp. 69-70.

43. Ibid., p. 66.

44. Ibid., pp. 70-71.

45. Ibid., p. 72.

46. To B. S. Ingemann, Undated. *Breve fra Hans Christian Andersen*, Vol. 1, Copenhagen, 1878, p. 1. To Grundtvig, October 1820. *Gads danske Magasin*, 1911-12, Copenhagen, 1911, pp. 126-28; and The Royal Library, Laage Petersens Samling, no. 508.

47. The Royal Library, Ny Kgl. Samling 2451, læg I, E.

48. Georg Brandes: *Kritiker og Portraiter*, Copenhagen, 1870.

49. Hans Christian Andersen: *Mit Livs Eventyr*, in *Samlede Skrifter*, Vol. 21, Copenhagen, 1855, p. 49.

50. *H. C. Andersens Levnedsbog*, Copenhagen, 1926, pp. 68-69.

51. Hans Christian Andersen: *Mit Livs Eventyr*, in *Samlede Skrifter*, Vol. 21, Copenhagen, 1855, p. 51.

52. Hans Christian Andersen: *Scene af Røverne i Vissenberg i Fyen*, Copenhagen, 1941.

53. Georg Nygaard: *H. C. Andersen og København*, Copenhagen. 1938, pp. 41-42.

54. June 8,1826, *H. C. Andersens brevveksling med Lucie & B. S. Ingemann*, Vol. 1, Copenhagen, 1997, p. 26.

55. Hans Christian Andersen: *Skovcapellet. Det hidtil utrykte sørgespil fra 1821*, Copenhagen, 2000.

56. *Transskription af K.L. Rahbeks censur over H. C. Andersens indleverede tragedie Alfsol. September 3, 1822*, Odense Bys Museer.

57. *Transskription af H. Olsens censur over H. C. Andersens indleverede tragedie Alfsol. September 12, 1822*, Odense Bys Museer.

58. Johan de Mylius: *H. C. Andersens liv. Dag for dag*, Copenhagen, 1998, pp. 27-28.

59. Olaf Carlsen: "Da H. C. Andersen vilde paa Sorø Akademi," *Soraner-Bladet*, No.1-2, 1953. A detailed description of the events concerning the publication of Hans Christian Andersen's debut book can be found in Cai M. Woel's Afterword to *Ungdoms-Forsøg*, Copenhagen, 1956, pp. 153-89.

60. C. St. A. Bille and Nicolai Bøgh: *Breve fra Hans Christian Andersen*, Copenhagen, 1878, p. 2.

61. Ibid..

62. Hans Christian Andersen: *Mit Livs Eventyr*, in *Samlede Skrifter*, Vol. 21, Copenhagen, 1855, p. 57.

63. Tage Høeg: *H. C. Andersens ungdom*, Copenhagen, 1934, pp. 30-40.

64. Hans Christian Andersen: *Mit Livs Eventyr*, in *Samlede Skrifter*, Vol. 21, Copenhagen, 1855, p. 56.

65. Hans Christian Andersen: *Fodreise fra Holmens Canal til Østpynten af Amager i Aarene 1828 og 1829*, in *Samlede Skrifter*, Vol. 7, Copenhagen, 1854, p. 106.

66. Villiam Christian Walter: *Ungdoms-Forsøg*, Copenhagen, 1956, p. 9.

67. Ibid., p. 7.

68. Ibid., p. 8.

69. Ibid., pp. 14-15.

70. Ibid., pp. 28-29.

71. Harald Rue: "H. C. Andersen og folket," *Tiden*, No.4, 1947, p. 156.

72. October 3, 1822. *Dagens Nyheder*, November 29, 1931; and Elias Bredsdorff: "Spørg Ottilie . . . ," *Anderseniana*, 1983, p. 164.

73. Villiam Christian Walter: *Ungdoms-Forsøg*, Copenhagen, 1956, p. 102.

74. Ibid., p. 123.

75. Hans Christian Andersen: *Mit Livs Eventyr*, in *Samlede Skrifter*, Vol. 21, Copenhagen, 1855, p. 55.

CHAPTER 2

1. *H. C. Andersens Levnedsbog*, Copenhagen, 1926, p. 129.

2. Hans Christian Andersen: "Til min Moder," *Samlede Skrifter*, Vol. 15, Copenhagen, 1854, p. 3.

3. Hans Christian Andersen: "Sang ved Rector Meislings Indsættelse i Helsingør (Juni 1826)," *Samlede Skrifter*, Vol. 33, Copenhagen, 1879, p. 106.

4. Hans Christian Andersen: *Meer end Perler og Guld*, performed for the first time at the Casino Theater, October 3, 1849; in *Samlede Skrifter*, Vol. 14, Copenhagen, 1854, p. 119. Retold by Jens Andersen.

5. Hans Christian Andersen: *Mit Livs Eventyr*, in *Samlede Skrifter*, Vol. 1, Copenhagen, 1855, p. 74.

6. *H. C. Andersens Levnedsbog*, Copenhagen, 1926, pp. 123-24.

7.   August 9,1830. *H. C. Andersens Brevveksling mellem Edvard og Henriette Collin*, Vol. 1, Copenhagen, 1936, p. 61.

8.   Carl Roos: "Anderseniana. Fra Skoletiden i Slagelse," *Edda* 1917, p. 161.

9.   Ole Lund: *Smaabilleder fra Helsingør 1800–1830*, Copenhagen, 1900, p. 123.

10. H. C. A. Lund: *Studenterforeningens Historie 1820–70*, Vol. 1, Copenhagen, 1896, pp. 334-35.

11. Hans Christian Andersen: *Den skjønne Grammatica*, Copenhagen, 1999, p. 9.

12. Hans Christian Andersen: *Eventyrdigterens studenterkomedier samt "I Maaneskin,"* Copenhagen, 2001.

13. Nicolai Bøgh: "Fra H. C. Andersens Barndoms- og Ungdomsliv," *Personalhistorisk Tidsskrift*, 1905.

14. August 19, 1824. *H. C. Andersens Brevveksling med Jonas Collin den Ældre*, Vol. 1, Copenhagen, 1945, pp. 11-12.

15. J. P. Mynster in a letter to Jonas Collin, October 11, 1822. Quoted from Hans Brix: *H. C. Andersen og hans Eventyr*, Copenhagen, 1907, p. 219.

16. *Den Lærdes Bestemmelse. Fem Forelæsninger af Johan Gottlieb Fichte*, Fordansket af J. Collin, med nogle Tillæg af Forfatteren, Copenhagen, 1796. Jean-Jacques Rousseau: *Den unge Héloïse*, Oversætter og udgiver: J.Collin. Copenhagen, 1798-99. Carl Aaberg: "En administrator under enevælden," *Frederiksbog Amtsavis*, January 22, 1976.

17. Immanuel Kant: *Om Pædagogik*, Aarhus, 2000, pp. 22-23.

18. Niels Birger Wamberg: "Jonas Collin, potentat og velgører," *Guldalderhistorier. 20 nær- billeder af perioden 1800–1850*, Copenhagen 1994, p. 61.

19. Olaf Carlsen: "Da Andersen vilde paa Sorø Akademi," *Soraner-Bladet*, No. 1-2, 1953, pp. 6-8, 11-13.

20. Chr. Svanholm: "Saadan var Meisling!" *Berlingske Aftenavis*, April 1, 1950.

21. Kjeld Galster: *H. C. Andersen og hans Rektor*, Kolding, 1933, p. 82.

22. October 13, 1825. *H. C. Andersens dagbøger*, Vol. 1, Copenhagen, 1995-96, p. 12.

23. November 27, 1825. Ibid., p. 22.

24. Kristian Langdal Møller: "H. C. Andersen i Helsingør," *H. C. Andersen. Strejflys over hans Liv og hans Digtning*, Helsingør, 1968, p. 19.

25. September 15, 1825. *H. C. Andersens Brevveksling med Jonas Collin den Ældre*, Vol. 1, Copenhagen, 1945, p. 32.

26. December 19, 1825. *H. C. Andersens dagbøger*, Vol. 1, Copenhagen, 1995-96, p. 31.

27. October 20, 1825. Ibid., pp. 38-39.

28. May 3, 1826. Ibid., p. 44.

29. December 23, 1825. Ibid., p. 36.

30. May 7, 1826. *H. C. Andersens Brevveksling med Jonas Collin den Ældre*, Vol. 1, Copenhagen, 1945, p. 48.

31. July 2, 1826. Ibid., p. 56.

32. Hans Christian Andersen: "Fragment af en Reise fra Roeskilde til Helsingør," *Nyeste Skilderi af Kiøbenhavn*, No. 52, July 1, 1826, pp. 826-28. Johann Wolfgang von Goethe: *An Schwager Kronos. In der Postchaise den 10. Oktober 1774.*

33. September 2, 1826. *H. C. Andersens Brevveksling med Jonas Collin den Ældre*, Vol. 1, Copenhagen, 1945, p. 64.

34. Hans Christian Andersen: *Mit Livs Eventyr*, in *Samlede Skrifter*, Vol. 21, Copenhagen, 1855, p. 72.

35. November 20, 1825. *H. C. Andersens dagbøger*, Vol. 1, Copenhagen, 1995-96, p. 20.

36. Hans Christian Andersen: *Eventyrdigterens hidtil utrykte stile I*, Copenhagen, 1999, p. 10.

37. Ibid., p. 30

38. September 4, 1824. Bille and Bøgh: *Breve til Hans Christian Andersen*, Copenhagen, 1877, p. 146.
39. November 6, 1825. Ibid., p. 148.
40. Ole Lund: *Smaabilleder fra Helsingør 1800–1830*, Copenhagen, 1900, p. 119.
41. From after September 21, 1826. *H. C. Andersens brevveksling med Lucie & B. S. Ingemann*, Vol. 1, Copenhagen, 1997, p. 35.
42. Hans Christian Andersen: *Eventyrdigterens hidtil utrykte stile II*, Copenhagen, 1999, p. 26.
43. Ibid., p. 23.
44. *Museum. Tidsskrift for Historie og Geografi*, No. 1, Copenhagen, 1895, p. 379.
45. Edvard Collin: *H. C. Andersen og det Collinske Hus*, Copenhagen, 1929, pp. 61-64.
46. The Royal Library, Ny Kgl. Samling, 643. E. Gigas: "Et Minde fra H. C. Andersens første Ungdom," *Dansk Tidsskrift*, 1905, pp. 279-94.
47. Hans Christian Andersen: *Eventyrdigterens hidtil utrykte stile III*, Copenhagen, 1999, p. 51.
48. Edvard Collin: *H. C. Andersen og det Collinske Hus*, Copenhagen, 1929, p. 63.
49. December 26, 1825. *H. C. Andersens dagbøger*, Copenhagen, 1995-96, p. 39. The play mentioned is by C. J. Boye: *William Shakespeare*, Copenhagen, 1826.
50. January 24, 1826. *H. C. Andersen og det Collinske Hus*, Copenhagen, 1929, p. 43.
51. *H. C. Andersens Levnedsbog*, Copenhagen, 1926, pp. 87-88.
52. Ibid., p. 123.
53. January 4, 1827. Bille and Bøgh: *Breve til Hans Christian Andersen*, Copenhagen, 1877, p. 577.
54. Hans Christian Andersen: "Rime-Djævelen," *Samlede Skrifter*, Vol. 15, Copenhagen, 1854, pp. 9-10.
55. Ibid., p. 10.
56. Jørgen Skjerk in the Foreword to Hans Christian Andersen: *Slagelse-Digte*, Aarhus, 1974, pp. 9-10.
57. Otto Holmgaard (ed.): *Slagelsebogen*, Slagelse, 1968. Quoted from Jørgen Skjerk's Foreword to Hans Christian Andersen: *Slagelse-Digte II*, Aarhus, 1990, p. 14.
58. Hans Christian Andersen: *Slagelse-Digte II*, Aarhus, 1990, p. 45.
59. Hans Christian Andersen: "Til Frue Fuglsang," Ibid., pp. 27-30.
60. Hans Christian Andersen: "Naar Alnaturen slumrer," Ibid., p. 13.
61. Hans Christian Andersen: "Ynglingen og Oldingen," Ibid., p. 68.
62. Tage Høeg (ed.): "Tre ufuldførte historiske Digtninge," *Anderseniana*, 1935, pp. 29-58.
63. September 20, 1825. *H. C. Andersens dagbøger*, Vol. 1, Copenhagen, 1995-96, p. 4.
64. September 27, 1825. Ibid., p. 6.
65. Chr. Svanholm: *H. C. Andersens ungdoms-tro*, Trondheim, 1952, pp. 97-135.
66. Kjeld Galster: *H. C. Andersen og hans rektor*, Kolding, 1933, p. 22.
67. Hans Christian Andersen: *Eventyrdigterens hidtil utrykte stile I*, Copenhagen, 1999, p. 73.
68. Ibid., p. 74.
69. Hans Christian Andersen: *Eventyrdigterens hidtil utrykte stile II*, pp. 45-46.
70. October 20, 1825. *H. C. Andersens brevveksling med Jonas Collin den Ældre*, Vol. 1, Copenhagen, 1945, pp. 40-42. Printed in Hans Christian Andersen: *Eventyrdigterens hidtil utrykte danske stile III*, Copenhagen, 1999, pp. 9-12.
71. Hans Christian Andersen: *Eventyrdigterens hidtil utrykte danske stile III*, Copenhagen, 1999, p. 10.
72. Ibid., p. 11.
73. Hans Christian Andersen: "Poesien," *Samlede Skrifter*, Vol. 15, Copenhagen, 1854, pp. 1-2 (verses 1, 3, and 5).
74. January 16, 1824. Bille and Bøgh: *Breve fra Hans Christian Andersen*, Vol. 1, Copenhagen, 1878, p. 4.

75. Hans Christian Andersen: "Sjælen," *Samlede Skrifter*, Vol. 15, Copenhagen, 1854, p. 4 (verse 1).
76. Ibid. (verse 2).
77. March 1, 1826. Bille and Bøgh: *Breve til Hans Christian Andersen*, Copenhagen, 1877, p. 153.
78. August 25, 1826. Ibid., p. 571.
79. Kjeld Galster: *H. C. Andersen og hans Rektor*, Kolding, 1933, p. 43.
80. Hans Christian Andersen: *Eventyrdigterens hidtil utrykte stile I*, Copenhagen, 1999, p. 38.
81. Hans Christian Andersen: "Det døende Barn," *Kjøbenhavnsposten*, September 25, 1827. German translation by Ludolph Schley.
82. Hans Christian Andersen: "Det døende Barn," *Samlede Skrifter*, Vol. 15, Copenhagen, 1854, pp. 6-7.
83. The Royal Library, Ny Kgl. Samling, 643,8.
84. Hans Christian Andersen: *Skyggebilleder*, Copenhagen, 1986, p. 87.
85. *H. C. Andersens Levnedsbog*, Copenhagen, 1926, p. 120.
86. October 24, 1826. *H. C. Andersens Brevveksling med Jonas Collin den Ældre*, Vol. 1, Copenhagen 1945, p. 70.
87. December 27, 1825. *H. C. Andersens dagbøger*, Vol. 1, Copenhagen, 1995-96, p. 40.
88. Kjeld Galster: *H. C. Andersen og hans Rektor*, Kolding, 1933, p. 62.
89. Edvard Collin: *H. C. Andersen og det Collinske Hus*, Copenhagen, 1929, pp. 46-47.
90. October 28, 1867. *H. C. Andersens Brevveksling med Edvard og Henriette Collin*, Vol. 4, Copenhagen, 1936, pp. 43-44.
91. Hans Christian Andersen: "Svinene," *Samlede Skrifter*, Vol. 15, Copenhagen, 1854, p. 147.
92. Hans Christian Andersen: "Fragmenter af en ufuldført historisk roman 1824-25," *Anderseniana*, 1935, p. 39.
93. Hans Christian Andersen: *Fodreise fra Holmens Canal til Østpynten af Amager i Aarene 1828 og 1829*, in *Samlede Skrifter*, Vol. 7, Copenhagen, 1854, p. 87.
94. December 9, 1874. *H. C. Andersens dagbøger*, Vol. 10, Copenhagen 1995-96, p. 369.
95. Ole A. Hedegaard: *Fornedrelsens år. H. C. Andersen og Helsingør 1826–27*, Copenhagen, 1981, p. 144.

CHAPTER 3
1.   Evening 13 in Hans Christian Andersen's *Billedbog uden Billeder*, in *Samlede Skrifter*, Vol. 7, Copenhagen, 1854, pp. 131-33. Retold by Jens Andersen.
2.   The concept "nonsense-compote" shows up in one of Hans Christian Andersen's poems from his student days: "I en Stambog." See Hans Christian Andersen: *Slagelse-Digte II*, Aarhus, 1990, p. 38.
3.   Hans Christian Andersen: "Du skal lee!" *Samlede Skrifter*, Vol. 16, Copenhagen, 1854, p. 29.
4.   Hans Christian Andersen: "Hjerte-Suk til Maanen," *Samlede Skrifter*, Vol. 15, Copenhagen, 1854, p. 96.
5.   Hans Christian Andersen: *Den skjønne Grammatica*, Copenhagen, 1999.
6.   Hans Christian Andersen: "En Guddoms Tanke er Du, Poesi!" *Samlede Skrifter*, Vol. 15, Copenhagen, 1854, p. 70.
7.   Hugo Friedrich: *Strukturen i moderne lyrik*, Copenhagen, 1968, p. 36.
8.   Hans Christian Andersen: "Østergade," *Samlede Skrifter*, Vol. 16, Copenhagen, 1854, p. 137.
9.   Ibid., pp. 137-38.

10. Hans Christian Andersen: *Eventyrdigterens hidtil utrykte danske stile III*, Copenhagen, 1999, p. 94.

11. Ibid., pp. 95-96.

12. Harald Jørgensen: *Jonas Collin 1776–1861. Indflydelsesrig kongelig embedsmand og interesseret samfundsborger*, Herning, 2001. Niels Birger Wamber: "Den fødte Practicus," *Guldalderhistorier. 20 nærbilleder af perioden 1800–1850*, Copenhagen, 1994, pp. 58-67.

13. Hans Christian Andersen: "Lad Januari Atterkomst," *Samlede Skrifter*, Vol. 33, Copenhagen, 1879, p. 140.

14. December 29, 1845. *H. C. Andersens Brevveksling med Jonas Collin den Ældre*, Vol. 1, Copenhagen, 1945, p. 279.

15. February 8, 1846. Ibid., p. 287.

16. *H. C. Andersens Levnedsbog*, Copenhagen, 1926, p. 134.

17. Hans Christian Andersen: *Eventyrdigterens hidtil utrykte danske stile II*, Copenhagen, 1999, pp. 13-14.

18. Hans Christian Andersen's essays with L. C. Müller's corrections can be read in Hans Christian Andersen: *Eventyrdigterens danske stile III*, Copenhagen, 1999.

19. Hans Christian Andersen: *Mit Livs Eventyr*, in *Samlede Skrifter*, Vol. 21, Copenhagen, 1855, pp. 78-79.

20. Quoted from Ejnar Askgaard: "En akademisk borger," *Anderseniana*, 2000, p. 80.

21. Chr. Svanholm: "H. C. Andersens Stile og Müllers Rettelser," *Berlingske Aftenavis*, January 21, 1948.

22. Edvard Collin: *H. C. Andersen og det Collinske Hus*, Copenhagen, 1929, p. 47.

23. Hans Christian Andersen: *Eventyrdigterens hidtil utrykte danske stile III*, Copenhagen, 1999, p. 84.

24. Hans Christian Andersen: *Fodreise fra Holmens Canal til Østpynten af Amager i Aarene 1828 og 1829*, in *Samlede Skrifter*, Vol. 7, Copenhagen, 1854, p. 67.

25. Søren Chr. Barth: *Livserindringer*, Copenhagen, 1900, pp. 204-05.

26. Undated letter, from after November 18, 1828. *H. C. Andersens brevveksling med Lucie & B. S. Ingemann*, Vol. 1, Copenhagen, 1997, p. 39.

27. Hans Christian Andersen: *Fodreise fra Holmens Canal til Østpynten af Amager i Aarene 1828 og 1829*, in *Samlede Skrifter*, Vol. 7, Copenhagen, 1854, p. 107.

28. Ibid., p. 106.

29. Ibid., p. 107.

30. Georg Brandes: *Hovedstrømninger i det 19. Aarhundredes Litteratur. Den romantiske Skole i Tyskland*, Copenhagen, 1891, p. 15.

31. See Tage Høeg: *H. C. Andersens Ungdom*, Copenhagen, 1934, pp. 110-75.

32. Hans Christian Andersen: *Fodreise fra Holmens Canal til Østpynten af Amager i Aarene 1828 og 1829*, in *Samlede Skrifter*, Vol. 7, Copenhagen, 1854, p. 49.

33. August 8, 1847. *H. C. Andersens dagbøger*, Vol. 3, Copenhagen, 1995-96, p. 246.

34. Hans Christian Andersen: "Fodreise," *Samlede Skrifter*, Vol. 7, Copenhagen, 1854, p. 40.

35. Ibid., p. 30.

36. Ibid., p. 57.

37. J. L. Heiberg in *Maanedsskrift for Literatur*, Vol. 1, 1829, p. 169.

38. Thomas Overskou: *Den danske Skueplads, dens Historie, fra de første Spor af danske Skuespil indtil vor Tid*, Copenhagen, 1864. Jens Engberg: *Det kongelige teater i 250 Aar*, Vol. 1, Copenhagen, 1998, pp. 176-77.

39. Hans Christian Andersen: *Mit Livs Eventyr*, in *Samlede Skrifter*, Vol. 21, Copenhagen, 1855, p. 86.

40. *Kjøbenhavn-Posten*, No. 81, 1829, pp. 329-30.

41. *Maanedsskrift for Literatur*, Vol. 1, 1829, pp. 551-52. See also Kr. Langdal Møller: "Andersenske Drillerier. En Ungdoms-Kontrovers med Oehlenschläger," *Berlingske Tidende*, March 25, 1967.

42. June 2, 1831. *H. C. Andersens dagbøger*, Vol. 1, Copenhagen, 1995-96, p. 93.

43. May 5, 1831. Ibid., p. 60.

44. Hans Christian Andersen: *Skyggebilleder*, Copenhagen, 1986, p. 10.

45. Karl-Ludwig Hoch: *Caspar David Friedrich in der Sächsischen Schweiz. Skizzen. Motive. Bilder*, Dresden/Basel, 1996, p. 30.

46. Klaus Günzel: *Romantik in Dresden*, and Gregor J. M. Weber: *1798 in der Königlichen Gemäldegalerie zu Dresden.* Both articles are included in "Dresden und die Anfänge der Romantik," *Dresdner Hefte*, No. 58, 1999.

47. June 3, 1831. *H. C. Andersens dagbøger*, Vol. 1, Copenhagen, 1995-96. p. 94.

48. Kleine/Neidhardt: *Museum zur Dresdner Frühromantik*, Stadtmuseum Dresden, 1999, p. 10.

49. Johan de Mylius in Afterword to Hans Christian Andersen: *Skyggebilleder*, Copenhagen, 1986, p. 140.

50. Hans Christian Andersen: *Skyggebilleder*, Copenhagen, 1986, p. 90.

51. Ibid., p. 91.

52. Helge Topsøe-Jensen: *Omkring Levnedsbogen. En Studie over H. C. Andersen som Selvbiograf*, Copenhagen, 1943, pp. 64-65.

53. May 15, 1838. "H. C. Andersens Brevveksling med Henriette Hanck," *Anderseniana*, 1943, p. 249.

54. "My highly esteemed, cherished friend! I dare to call you this, although we have not yet had the occasion to meet each other in person; but during the happy hours when a friend who loves poetry read for me your lovely *The Improvisatore*, a bond of sympathy was created between us. This was for me in a surprising as well as agreeable manner later confirmed by the gift of *Agnete and the Merman*, and, in particular, through the little note on the cover, which so warmly conveyed your favorable thoughts of me. The friendliness of this way of thinking was also expressed there in the reasonable request of obtaining a few words in reply; and I can truly not comprehend how I could allow (almost) an entire year to pass before I fulfilled it." [translated from Swedish] (May 6, 1838. Bille and Bøgh: *Breve til Hans Christian Andersen*, Copenhagen, 1877, p. 27.)

55. July 7, 1830. *H. C. Andersens Brevveksling med Edvard og Henriette Collin*, Vol. 1, Copenhagen, 1933, pp. 31-35; and *H. C. Andersen og Henriette Wulff. En brevveksling*, Vol. 1, Copenhagen, 1959, p. 75.

56. Hans Christian Andersen: *Skyggebilleder*, Copenhagen, 1986, p. 118. Translation from German to Danish by Jens Andersen.

57. Ibid., p. 12

58. *H. C. Andersens Levnedsbog*, Copenhagen, 1926, p. 165.

59. August 18, 1830. *H. C. Andersens brevveksling med Signe Læssøe*, from manuscript, courtesy of Kirsten Dreyer.

60. "Two brown eyes I recently saw,/ in them lay my home and my world,/ there flamed cleverness and a child's peace; / I will not forget them for all eternity!" (Hans Christian Andersen: "Hjertets Melodier," *Samlede Skrifter*, Vol. 15, Copenhagen, 1854, pp. 72-73.)

61. H. Schwanenflügel: *Hans Christian Andersen. Et Digterliv*, Copenhagen, 1905, p. 42.

62. January 18, 1831. *H. C. Andersens brevveksling med Lucie & B. S. Ingemann*, Vol. 1, Copenhagen, 1997, p. 51.

63. Hans Christian Andersen: *Mit Livs Eventyr*, in *Samlede Skrifter*, Vol. 21, Copenhagen, 1855, p. 91.

64. Hans Christian Andersen: *Skibet*, Copenhagen, 1831, pp. 46–47.

65. Heinrich Heine: "En Yngling elsker en Pige," *Lyrisk Intermezzo*, Copenhagen, 1918.

66. Hans Christian Andersen: *Skyggebilleder*, Copenhagen, 1986, p. 37.

67. Hans Brix in the Foreword to *H. C. Andersens Levnedsbog*, Copenhagen, 1926, pp. 15–16. With regard to the "duplicitous courtship," see also Klaus P. Mortensen: *Svanen og Skyggen—historien om unge Andersen*, Copenhagen, 1989, pp. 62–63.

68. *H. C. Andersens Levnedsbog*, Copenhagen, 1926, p. 170.

69. Undated. Quoted from Hans Brix: *H. C. Andersen og hans Eventyr*, Copenhagen, 1907, p. 84.

70. Hans Christian Andersen: *Skyggebilleder*, Copenhagen, 1986, p. 16.

71. Ibid., p. 23.

72. Ibid., p. 29.

73. Ibid., p. 109.

74. Hans Christian Andersen: "Avis aux lectrices" (1830), *Samlede Skrifter*, Vol. 15, Copenhagen, 1854, pp. 18–19.

75. *H. C. Andersens Levnedsbog*, Copenhagen, 1926, p. 139.

76. Ibid., p. 21.

77. Ibid., p. 35.

78. Hans Christian Andersen: "Under Piletræet," *H. C. Andersens Eventyr*, Vol. 3, Copenhagen, 1919, p. 56.

79. Charlotte Bournonville: *Erindringer*, Copenhagen, 1903, p. 296.

80. Nicolai Bøgh: "Fra H. C. Andersens Barndoms- og Ungdomsliv," *Personalhistorisk Tidsskrift*, Copenhagen, 1905, p. 74.

81. Hans Christian Andersen: "Portnerens Søn," *H. C. Andersens Eventyr*, Vol. 5, Copenhagen, 1919, p. 14.

82. Ibid., p. 32.

83. January 18, 1831. *H. C. Andersens brevveksling med Lucie & B. S. Ingemann*, Vol. 1, Copenhagen, 1997, p. 51.

84. January 20, 1831. Ibid., p. 53.

85. April 21, 1831. Ibid., p. 57.

86. Hans Christian Andersen: "Hvad jeg elsker," *Samlede Skrifter*, Vol. 16, Copenhagen, 1854, p. 127.

87. Hans Christian Andersen: "Ung elskov," *Samlede Skrifter*, Vol. 33, Copenhagen, 1879, p. 17. Hans Christian Andersen: "Liden Kirsten," *Samlede Skrifter*, Vol. 12, Copenhagen, 1854, p. 109; Hans Christian Andersen: *Samlede Digte*, ed. by Johan de Mylius, Copenhagen, 2000, p. 577; and Hans Christian Andersen: "Ung Elskov," *Kjendte og glemte Digte 1823–1867*, Copenhagen, 1867.

88. March 1832. Letter to C. H. Lorenzen. Quoted from Johan de Mylius: *H. C. Andersens liv. Dag for dag*, Copenhagen, 1998, p. 46.

89. May 26, 1831. *H. C. Andersens dagbøger*, Vol. 1, Copenhagen, 1995–96, p. 77.

90. January 18, 1831. *H. C. Andersens brevveksling med Lucie & B. S. Ingemannn*, Vol. 1, Copenhagen, 1997, p. 52.

91. September 8, 1832. Letters from Hans Christian Andersen to Louise Collin, *Anderseniana*, 2002.

92. Ibid.

93. Rigmor Stampe: *H. C. Andersen og hans nærmeste Omgang*, Copenhagen, 1918, p. 163.

94. November 1, 1832. Letters from Hans Christian Andersen to Louise Collin (married name Lind), *Anderseniana*, 2002, pp. 13–14.

95. Hans Christian Andersen in a letter to B. S. Ingemann: "The review also says that the poem 'What I Love,' isn't natural, that I don't grasp so many emotions; but he has no idea about that!—I 'have tried to imitate Heine in unhappy love'; if only that were true!" (September 20, 1831, *H. C. Andersens brevveksling med Lucie & B. S. Ingemann*, Vol. 1, Copenhagen, 1997, p. 64.)

CHAPTER 4
1.   James E. Fremann: *Gatherings from an Artist's Portfolio*, New York, 1877.
2.   Emil Hannover: *Christen Købke. En Studie i dansk Kunsthistorie*, Copenhagen, 1893, pp. 96-97.
3.   February 25, 1834. *H. C. Andersens dagbøger*, Vol. 1, Copenhagen, 1995-96, p. 327.
4.   Ibid., p. 236.
5.   Edvard Collin: *H. C. Andersen og det Collinske Hus*, Copenhagen, 1929, p. 312.
6.   August 2, 1832. Th. A. Müller and H. Topsøe-Jensen: "Riborgs Broder. H. C. Andersens brevveksling med Christian Voigt," *Særtryk af Anderseniana*, Odense, 1948, p. 109.
7.   November 30, 1865. *H. C. Andersens dagbøger*, Vol. 6, Copenhagen, 1995-96, p. 336.
8.   "Since my relationship with him was never of the sentimental sort, my relationship to his memory cannot be of that kind either." (Edvard Collin: *H. C. Andersen og det Collinske Hus*, Copenhagen, 1929, p. 288.)
9.   October 3, 1865. *H. C. Andersens Brevveksling med Edvard og Henriette Collin*, Vol. 4, Copenhagen, 1936, p. 342. (Draft for letter No. 499.)
10.   August 10, 1832. Ibid., Vol. 1, Copenhagen, 1933, pp. 110-11.
11.   H. C. Andersen: *Fodreise fra Holmens Canal til Østpynten af Amager i Aarene 1828 og 1829*, in *Samlede Skrifter*, Vol. 7, Copenhagen, 1854, p. 74.
12.   Edvard Collin: *H. C. Andersen og det Collinske Hus*, Copenhagen, 1929, p. 306.
13.   Ibid., p. 306.
14.   Wilhelm von Rosen: *Månens Kulør*, Vol. 1, Copenhagen, 1993, p. 166.
15.   Wilhelm von Rosen: "H. C. Andersens forelskelse i Ludvig Müller," *Kritik 73*, Copenhagen, 1985, pp. 25-26; and Rosen: *Månens kulør*, Vol. 1, pp. 93-94.
16.   Ken Nielsen: *Gennem Maske og Ensomhed*, Dissertation from Copenhagen University, 2001, pp. 31-32.
17.   E. Anthony Rotundo: "Romantic Friendship: Male Intimacy and Middle-class Youth in the Northern United States, 1800-1900," *Journal of Social History*, Pittsburgh, 1989. Caroll Smith Rosenberg: *Disorderly Conduct: Visions of Gender in Victorian America*, New York, 1985, pp. 53-76.
18.   Marianne Berg Karlsen: *"I Venskabs Paradiis."* En studie i maskulinitet og venskap mellom menn med utgangspunkt i Conrad N. Schwach og Maurits C. Hansen 1814-42, Thesis in History at Oslo University, 1999.
19.   August 28, 1835. *H. C. Andersens Brevveksling med Edvard og Henriette Collin*, Vol. 1, Copenhagen, 1933, p. 239.
20.   Thorkild Vanggaard: *Phallóp*, Copenhagen, 1969, p. 160. Wilhelm von Rosen: *Månens kulør*, Vol. 1, pp. 112-13.
21.   The girl may also have been his childhood playmate Ane Elisabeth Hendrichsen (née Basse), whom the author visited in Odense when he was named honorary citizen in 1867. On that occasion he writes in his diary: "Little Ane, who was a boarder in my parents' home and with whom I refused to sleep on the bench." (*Anderseniana*, 1933, pp. 12-13.)
22.   Nicolai Bøgh: "Fra H. C. Andersens Barndoms- og Ungdomsliv," *Personalhistorisk Tidsskrift*, 1905, p. 64.

23. *H. C. Andersens Levnedsbog*, Copenhagen, 1926, p. 128.

24. Ibid., p. 81.

25. August 22, 1833. Th. Thaulow: "To H. C. Andersen–Breve," *Nationaltidende*, April 1, 1945.

26. Undated. *H. C. Andersens Brevveksling med Edvard og Henriette Collin*, Vol. 4, Copenhagen, 1936, p. 338.

27. Hans Christian Andersen: *O. T.*, in *Romaner og Rejseskildringer*, Vol. 2, Copenhagen, 1943, p. 252.

28. Ibid., p. 101.

29. Ibid., p. 102.

30. Ibid., pp. 138–39.

31. June 11–14, 1834. Kirsten Dreyer and Flemming Hovmann: "Et overset venskab. H. C. Andersens og Otto Müllers brevveksling," *Anderseniana*, 1993, pp. 33–34.

32. October 1, 1832. Ibid., p. 14.

33. Edvard Collin: *H. C. Andersen og det Collinske Hus*, Copenhagen, 1929, p. 47.

34. *H. C. Andersens Levnedsbog*, Copenhagen, 1926, p. 134.

35. Edvard Collin: *H. C. Andersen og det Collinske Hus*, Copenhagen, 1929, p. 47.

36. *H. C. Andersens Levnedsbog*, Copenhagen, 1926, p. 150.

37. Ibid., p. 145.

38. July 18, 1829. *H. C. Andersens Brevveksling med Edvard og Henriette Collin*, Vol. 1, Copenhagen, 1933, p. 5.

39. June 25, 1831. Ibid., p. 85.

40. May 19, 1831. Ibid., p. 69.

41. Ibid..

42. May 28, 1831. Ibid., pp. 73–75.

43. June 11, 1831. Ibid., p. 80.

44. June 25, 1831. Ibid., p. 85.

45. November 4, 1831. "H. C. Andersens Brevveksling med Henriette Hanck," *Anderseniana*, 1941, p. 17.

46. July 2, 1875. E. Marquard: "H. C. Andersens sidste Vilje," *Anderseniana*, 1939, p. 91.

47. Foreword to Bille and Bøgh: *Breve fra Hans Christian Andersen*, Vol. 1, Copenhagen, 1878, p. vi.

48. October 13, 1875. Quoted from E. Marquard: "H. C. Andersens sidste Vilje," *Anderseniana*, 1939, p. 75.

49. July 16, 1836. *H. C. Andersens Brevveksling med Edvard og Henriette Collin*, Vol. 1, Copenhagen, 1933, p. 256.

50. Wilhelm von Rosen: *Månens Kulør. Studier i dansk bøssehistorie 1628–1912*, Vol. 1-2, Copenhagen, 1993.

51. Johan de Mylius: "Var han ikke en stor Mand, saa var han dog en berømt Mand," *Anderseniana*, 2000, pp. 5–31. Bodil Wamberg: *De er den jeg elsker højest—venskabet mellem H. C. Andersen og Edvard Collin*, Copenhagen, 1999.

52. Among others, Johan de Mylius: "Var han ikke en stor Mand, saa var han dog en berømt Mand," *Anderseniana*, 2000, pp. 5–31.

53. C. Behrend and H. Topsøe-Jensen (ed.): *H. C. Andersens Brevveksling med Edvard og Henriette Collin*, Vol. 6, Copenhagen, 1937, p. 7.

54. July 3, 1836. Ibid., Vol. 1, Copenhagen, 1933, p. 253.

55. "If you laughed at me and called my feeling sentimentality, well, then you were . . ." (Edvard Collin: *H. C. Andersen og det Collinske Hus*, Copenhagen, 1929, p. 148.)

56. June 23, 1830. *H. C. Andersens Brevveksling med Edvard og Henriette Collin*, Vol. 1, Copenhagen, 1933, p. 26.

57.   August 18, 1830. Ibid., p. 65.

58.   August 24, 1832. Ibid., p. 115.

59.   Inga Nalbandian: *H. C. Andersen og de, der mishandlede ham*, Copenhagen, 1928.

60.   Edvard Collin's Foreword to *H. C. Andersen og det Collinske Hus*, Copenhagen, 1929, p. xi.

61.   Edvard Collin: *H. C. Andersen og det Collinske Hus*, Copenhagen, 1929, pp. 292-93.

62.   Douglas Murray: *Bosie: A biography of Lord Alfred Douglas*, London, 2000.

63.   Edvard Collin: *H. C. Andersen og det Collinske Hus*, Copenhagen, 1929, p. 289.

64.   July 5, 1835. *H. C. Andersens Bevveksling med Edvard og Henriette Collin*, Vol. 1, Copenhagen, 1933, p. 225.

65.   Hans Christian Andersen: *Mit Livs Eventyr*, in *Samlede Skrifter*, Vol. 21, Copenhagen, 1855, p. 91.

66.   Hans Christian Andersen: "Skilles og mødes," *Samlede Skrifter*, Vol. 11, Copenhagen, 1854, pp. 74-75.

67.   August 23, 1832. *H. C. Andersens Brevveksling med Edvard og Henriette Collin*, Vol. 1, Copenhagen, 1933, p. 113.

68.   August 7, 1832. Ibid., p. 110.

69.   August 9-10, 1832. Ibid., p. 112.

70.   Hans Christian Andersen: "Aarets tolv Maaneder," *Samlede Skrifter*, Vol. 15, Copenhagen, 1854, pp. 31-32.

71.   October 1, 1832. Kirsten Dreyer and Flemming Hovmann: "Et overset venskab. H. C. Andersens og Otto Müllers brevveksling," *Anderseniana*, 1993, p. 10.

72.   December 11, 1832. Ibid., p. 17.

73.   *H. C. Andersens Levnedsbog 1805–1831*, Copenhagen, 1926, p. 137.

74.   Søren Kierkegaard: *Enten–Eller*, in *Samlede Værker*, Vol. 2, Copenhagen, 1962, p. 335.

75.   November 4, 1831. "H. C. Andersens Brevveksling med Henriette Hanck," *Anderseniana*, 1941, p. 20 (the poem "Mol–Toner").

76.   Hans Christian Andersen: *Festen paa Kenilworth*, in *Samlede Skrifter*, Vol. 32, Copenhagen, 1876, p. 142.

77.   October 1, 1832. Kirsten Dreyer and Flemming Hovmann: "Et overset venskab. H. C. Andersens og Otto Müllers brevveksling," *Anderseniana*, 1993, p. 14.

78.   March 7, 1833. *H. C. Andersens Brevveksling med Edvard og Henriette Collin*, Vol. 1, Copenhagen, 1933, p. 119.

79.   February 16, 1833. *H. C. Andersen og Henriette Wulff. En brevveksling*, Vol. 1, Odense, 1959, p. 89.

80.   January 14, 1833. "H. C. Andersens Brevveksling med Henriette Hanck," *Anderseniana*, 1941, p. 57.

81.   Hans Christian Andersen: *Samlede digte*, Copenhagen, 2000, p. 328.

82.   March 13, 1833. *H. C. Andersens Brevveksling med Edvard og Henriette Collin*, Vol. 1, Copenhagen, 1933, p. 120.

83.   See letter to Otto Müller, December 11, 1932. *Anderseniana*, 1993, p. 18.

84.   Edvard Collin: *H. C. Andersen det Collinske Hus*, Copenhagen, 1929, p. 159.

85.   April 24, 1833. *H. C. Andersens Brevveksling med Edvard og Henriette Collin*, Vol. 1, Copenhagen, 1933, p. 122.

86.   August 7, 1833. Ibid., pp. 157-58.

87.   January 14, 1833. "H. C. Andersens Brevveksling med Henriette Hanck," *Anderseniana*, 1941, p. 60.

88.   June 11, 1833. *H. C. Andersens Brevveksling med Edvard og Henriette Collin*, Vol. 1, Copenhagen, 1933, p. 122.

89.   September 12, 1833. Ibid., p. 178.

90. August 14, 1833. Ibid., p. 164.
91. August 30, 1833."H. C. Andersens Brevveksling med Henriette Hanck," *Anderseniana*, 1941, p. 72.
92. September 12, 1833. *H. C. Andersens Brevveksling med Edvard og Henriette Collin*, Vol. 1, Copenhagen, 1933, pp. 177-82.
93. August 29, 1833. Ibid., p. 170.
94. Ibid., p. 169.
95. September 24, 1833. Ibid., p. 183.
96. Ibid., p. 185.
97. September 18, 1833. Ibid., p. 195.
98. September 24, 1833. Ibid., pp. 185-86, 188.
99. August 14, 1833. Ibid., p. 163.
100. Wilhelm von Rosen: *Månens kulør*, Vol. 1, Copenhagen, 1993, p. 268, and Vol. 2, pp. 443-44. Wilhelm von Rosen: "Den pæderastiske subkulturs opståen i København i 1860'erne," *Den Jyske Historiker*, No. 58-59, Aarhus, 1992, pp. 80-100.
101. December 18, 1833. *H. C. Andersens Brevveksling med Edvard og Henriette Collin*, Vol. 1, Copenhagen, 1933, p. 204.
102. Ibid., p. 205.
103. January 19, 1833. *H. C. Andersens dagbøger*, Vol. 1, Copenhagen, 1995-96, p. 279.
104. February 1, 1834. *H. C. Andersens Brevveksling med Jonas Collin den Ældre*, Vol. 1, Copenhagen, 1945, p. 109.
105. Hans Christian Andersen: *Agnete og Havmanden*, in *Samlede Skrifter*, Vol. 17, Copenhagen, 1855, p. 52.
106. Ibid., p. 17.
107. Ibid., p. 15.
108. Ibid., p. 24.
109. Ibid., p. 12.
110. Ibid., p. 24.
111. August 17, 1859. *H. C. Andersens dagbøger*, Vol. 4, Copenhagen, 1995-96, p. 356.
112. *H. C. Andersens Brevveksling mellem Edvard og Henriette Collin*, Vol. 1, Copenhagen, 1933, p. 164.
113. See Erik M. Christensen: "H. C. Andersen og den optimistiske dualisme," in *Andersen og Verden*, Odense, 1993, pp. 177-91.
114. Hans Christian Andersen: *Paa Langebro*, in *Samlede Skrifter*, Vol. 31, Copenhagen, 1876, p. 110.
115. May 26, 1833. *H. C. Andersens Brevveksling med Edvard og Henriette Collin*, Vol. 1, Copenhagen, 1933, p. 219.
116. July 5, 1835. Ibid., pp. 225-26.
117. July 16, 1835. Ibid., p. 233.
118. July 18, 1831, Ibid., p. 85.
119. Hans Christian Andersen: *Improvisatoren*, in *Romaner og Rejseskildringer*, Vol. 1, Copenhagen, 1943, p. 109.
120. Hans Christian Andersen: "Skandinavernes Julesang i Rom 1833," *Samlede Skrifter*, Vol. 21, Copenhagen, 1855, pp. 156-57.
121. December 24, 1833. *H. C. Andersens dagbøger*, Vol. 1, Copenhagen, 1995-96, p. 260.
122. *Improvisatoren*, in *Romaner og Rejseskildringer*, Vol. 1, Copenhagen, 1943, p. 84.
123. Ibid., pp. 71-72.
124. Ibid., p. 122.
125. Ibid., p. 84.

126. Ibid., p. 87.

127. Ibid., p. 19.

128. November 20, 1834. *H. C. Andersens Brevveksling med Edvard og Henriette Collin*, Vol. 1, Copenhagen, 1933, p. 222.

129. July 3, 1836. Ibid., p. 254.

130. July 16, 1835. Ibid., p. 235.

131. October 22, 1835. Ibid., p. 240; Hans Christian Andersen: "Til Henriette T.—paa hendes Fødselsdag," *Nytaarsgave fra danske Digtere*, Copenhagen, 1836, p. 100.

132. August 28, 1835. *H. C. Andersens Brevveksling med Edvard og Henriette Collin*, Vol. 1, Copenhagen, 1933, p. 238.

133. Ibid.

134. June 26, 1836. *H. C. Andersen og Henriette Wulff. En brevveksling*, Vol. 1, Odense, 1959, p. 229.

135. July 19, 1836. *H. C. Andersens Brevveksling med Edvard og Henriette Collin*, Vol. 1, Copenhagen, 1933, p. 259.

136. July 16, 1836. Ibid., p. 256.

137. July 19, 1836. Ibid., p. 260. The poem about the rose kiss in the summer of 1836 was not included in the letter's composition and argumentation merely by chance. This is evident from Hans Christian Andersen's later accounts of his sojourn at the Lykkesholm estate. The following summer, in August 1837, he was on his way back to the manor, and he says in a letter to Edvard Collin, who is about to celebrate his first wedding anniversary, that unfortunately the roses have finished blooming this year. And here, by all accounts, he seems to be thinking about the roses which, like Edvard Collin, can no longer be picked and caressed: "This year the roses have finished blooming; you know that last year I had them to kiss, like the nun her Infant Jesus. This year the roses are done; I'll have to see about finding something else." (August 11, 1837. *H. C. Andersens Brevveksling med Edvard og Henriette Collin*, Vol. 1, Copenhagen, 1933, p. 269.)

138. August 4, 1836. Ibid., p. 263.

139. Ibid., pp. 263–64.

CHAPTER 5

1.   "Anser" was the nickname that Rigmor, Astrid, and Christine gave to Hans Christian Andersen. He was the girls' godfather, and in the 1850s and 1860s he made regular visits to the Christinelund estate at Præstø. This was the residence of the girls and their parents, Jonna and Henrik Stampe. (Rigmor Stampe: *H. C. Andersen og hans nærmeste Omgang*, Copenhagen, 1918, pp. 132–33.)

2.   Hans Christian Andersen: "Alfernes Blomster. Et Folkesagn," *Portefeuillen for 1839*, January 20, 1839. The folk legend is retold by Hans Christian Andersen in verse; here, in turn, it is retold by Jens Andersen, quoting verses 2, 6, and 7 out of a total of eight.

3.   Alexander Wilde: *Erindringer fra før jeg blev Løjtnant*, Copenhagen, 1885.

4.   February 14, 1846. *H. C. Andersens Brevveksling med Edvard og Henriette Collin*, Vol. 2, Copenhagen, 1934, pp. 63–64.

5.   Edmund Gosse: *To besøg i Danmark*, Copenhagen, 2001, p. 76.

6.   Ibid., p. 77.

7.   A. Henriques: *Svundne Dage*, Copenhagen, 1929, p. 118.

8.   August Bournonville: *Mit Teaterliv*, Vol. III, Copenhagen, 1877, pp. 250–51.

9.   January 17, 1864. *H. C. Andersens dagbøger*, Vol. 6, Copenhagen, 1995–96, p. 180.

10.   William Bloch: "Om H. C. Andersen. Bidrag til Belysning af hans Personlighed," *Nær og Fjern*, VIII, 1878–79, No. 363, p. 4.

11.   Arthur Abrahams: *Minder fra mine Forældres Hus*, Copenhagen, 1894, p. 9.

12.   H. Topsøe-Jensen: "H. C. Andersen paa Holsteinborg. Blade af et Venskabs Historie," *Anderseniana*, 1938, p. 312.

13.   "Et rigtigt 'Andersensk' Eventyr," *Politiken*, March 30, 1930.

14.   Edvard Collin: *H. C. Andersen og det Collinske Hus*, Copenhagen, 1929, p. 299; and Aage Hansen: "H. C. Andersen læser op," *Aarhus Stiftstidende*, December 5, 1954.

15.   October 14, 1864. *H. C. Andersens dagbøger*, Vol. 6, Copenhagen, 1995-96, p. 140.

16.   Hans Christian Andersen: "Loppen og Professoren," *H. C. Andersens Eventyr*, Vol. 5, Copenhagen, 1919, p. 283.

17.   H. Topsøe-Jensen: "H. C. Andersen paa Holsteinborg. Blade af et Venskabs Historie," *Anderseniana*, 1938.

18.   Edvard Collin: *H. C. Andersen og det Collinske Hus*, Copenhagen, 1929, pp. 282-83. Hans Christian Andersen: *Bouts rimés*, Copenhagen, 1974.

19.   Edvard Collin: *H. C. Andersen og det Collinske Hus*, Copenhagen, 1929, pp. 271-72.

20.   H. Topsøe-Jensen: "H. C. Andersen paa Holsteinborg. Blade af et Venskabs Historie," *Anderseniana*, 1938, p. 311.

21.   Hans Christian Andersen: Forword to "Dödningen. Et fyensk Folke-Eventyr," *Digte*, Copenhagen, 1830, p. 105.

22.   May 14, 1835. *H. C. Andersens Brevveksling med Jonas Collin den Ældre*, Vol. 1, Copenhagen, 1945, pp. 120-21.

23.   Ibid., p. 122.

24.   Johan de Mylius: *H. C. Andersens liv. Dag for dag*, Copenhagen, 1998, pp. 60-62. *H. C. Andersens Brevveksling med Jonas Collin den Ældre*, Vol. 1, Copenhagen, 1945, pp. 122-23.

25.   August 7, 1836. *H. C. Andersens Brevveksling med Jonas Collin den Ældre*, Vol. 1, Copenhagen, 1945, p. 125.

26.   Johan de Mylius: *H. C. Andersens liv. Dag for dag*, Copenhagen, 1998, p. 63.

27.   New Year's Day, 1835. "H. C. Andersens Brevveksling med Henriette Hanck," *Anderseniana*, 1942, p. 104.

28.   February 10, 1835. *H. C. Andersens brevveksling med Lucie & B. S. Ingemann*, Vol. 1, Copenhagen, 1997, p. 103.

29.   Poul Høybye: "Chamisso, H. C. Andersen og andre danskere," *Anderseniana*, 1969, p. 400.

30.   *H. C. Andersens Eventyr*, Vol. 1, Copenhagen, 1919, p. 7.

31.   Ibid., p. 45.

32.   December 17, 1835, and Christmas Eve, 1835. *H. C. Andersens brevveksling med Lucie & B. S. Ingemann*, Vol. 1, Copenhagen, 1997, pp. 112, 114-15.

33.   Hans Christian Andersen: "Til de ældre Læsere," v-viii, *Eventyr, fortalte for Børn*, Copenhagen, 1837.

34.   *Dansk Literatur-Tidende*, No. 1, 1836, p. 10.

35.   *Søndagsbladet*, No. 20, May 17, 1835. *Dannora. For Critik og Anticritik*, Vol 1, 1836, pp. 74-76. *Dansk Literaturtidende*, No. 1, 1836, pp. 10-14. *Kjøbenhavnsposten*, No. 196, July 18, 1837.

36.   *Dansk Literaturtidende*, No. 1, 1836, p. 11.

37.   Ibid.

38.   *Dannora*, 1836, p. 74.

39.   Ibid., p. 76.

40.   Hans Christian Andersen: "Phantasus," *Samlede Skrifter*, Vol. 15, Copenhagen, 1854, p. 156.

41.   Hans Christian Andersen: "Keiserens nye Klæder," *H. C. Andersens Eventyr*, Vol. 1, Copenhagen, 1919, p. 148.

42.   E. Goodenough, M. Heberle, N. Sokoloff (eds.): *Infant Tongues. The Voice of the Child in Literature*, Detroit, 1994, pp. 5-6.

43.   For example: Peter Coveney: *The Image of Childhood* (London, 1957). George Boas: *The Cult of Childhood* (London, 1966). Reinhard Kuhn: *Corruption in Paradise: The Child in the Western Literature* (London, 1982). Sheila A. Egoff: *Worlds Within* (Chicago & London, 1988). Rosemary Lloyd: *The Land of Lost Content* (Oxford, 1992). Goodenough, Heberle, Sokoloff (eds.): *Infant Tongues. The Voice of the Child in Literature* (Detroit, 1994).

44.   George Boas: *The Cult of Childhood*, London, 1966.

45.   Friedrich Schiller: *Om naiv og sentimental digtning og Om det ophøjede,* Copenhagen, 1952, p. 57.

46.   Marianne von Herzfeld: "Goethe's Images of Children," *German Life & Letters. A Quarterly Review,* Vol. XXV, 1971-72, pp. 219-31.

47.   Peter Coveney: *The Image of Childhood*, London, 1957, p. 68.

48.   Hans Christian Andersen: "Den lille Idas Blomster," *H. C. Andersens Eventyr,* Vol. 1, Copenhagen, 1919, p. 50.

49.   V. J. Brøndegaard: "Lyd-malerier," *Fyens Stiftstidende*, March 15, 1953.

50.   Hans Christian Andersen: *Kun en Spillemand*, in *Romaner og Rejseskildringer*, Vol. 3, Copenhagen, 1944, p. 103.

51.   Ellen Key, *Barnets Aarhundrede*, Copenhagen, 1902.

52.   Finn Hauberg Mortensen: "I Familiens skød," *Andersen og Verden*, Odense, 1993, p. 123.

53.   Hans Christian Andersen: *Et Besøg i Portugal 1866*, Copenhagen, 1968, p. 50.

54.   Hans Christian Andersen: "Hvad man kan hitte paa," *H. C. Andersens Eventyr,* Vol. 5, Copenhagen, 1919, p. 194.

55.   Sophie Breum: "Byen og Æresborgeren," *Odense Bys Bog om H. C. Andersen*, Odense, 1905, p. 80, note.

56.   Georg Brandes: *Danske Digterportrætter*, Copenhagen, 1966, p. 217.

57.   Hans Christian Andersen: *Fodreise*, Copenhagen, 1986, p. 55.

58.   Hans Christian Andersen: "Dynd-Kongens Datter," *H. C. Andersens Eventyr*, Vol. 5, Copenhagen, 1919, p. 312.

59.   Hans Christian Andersen: "Boghveden," *H. C. Andersens Eventyr,* Vol. 1, Copenhagen, 1919, p. 26.

60.   Hans Christian Andersen: "De vilde Svaner," *H. C. Andersens Eventyr*, Vol. 1, Copenhagen, 1919, p. 218.

61.   Hans Christian Andersen: "Lygtemændene ere i Byen, sagde Mosekonen," *H. C. Andersens Eventyr,* Vol. 4, Copenhagen, 1919, p. 304.

62.   Jon Kehler: "Loppen og professoren," *Berlingske Aftenavis*, April 2, 1952.

63.   H. Trolle Steenstrup: "H. C. Andersen laante hos Patronio," *Fyns Social-Demokrat*, June 20, 1943.

64.   Fairy tales by Hans Christian Andersen that are based on or strongly inspired by folk legends include "Mother Elder Tree," "The Elf Mound," "Holger Danske," "The Elf at the Delicatessen," "The Elf and the Woman," "The Bell Deep," "The Wind Tells of Valdemar Daae and His Daughters," "The Girl Who Trod on a Loaf," "Anne Lisbeth," "The Bishop of Børglum and his Kinsman," "Hidden but not Forgotten," "Vænø and Glænø," "The Red Shoes," "The Marsh King's Daughter," "The Child in the Grave," and "The Snow Queen." Hans Christian Andersen stories that are based on folktales include "The Traveling Companion," whose source is the Fyn tale "Help for the Dead"; "The Wild Swans" is known in folk literature as "The Raven Princes"; "Little Claus and Big Claus" as "Big Brother and Little Brother"; "The Swineherd" as "The Proud Maiden"; and "Clumsy Hans" can be found in several popular versions,

such as "The Princess Who Was Not Allowed to Speak" and the variant from Fyn "Clod Hans."

65. Poul Martin Møller: "Om at fortælle Børn Eventyr," Torben Weinreich (ed.): *Lyst og lærdom. Debat og forskning om børnelitteratur*, Copenhagen, 1996, p. 24.

66. Hans Christian Andersen: "Hvad Fatter gjør, det er altid det Rigtige," *H. C. Andersens Eventyr*, Vol. 4, Copenhagen, 1919, p. 147.

67. Grethe Kjær: *Barndommens ulykkelige Elsker. Kierkegaard om Barnet og Barndommen*, Copenhagen, 1986.

68. December 26, 1837. *Søren Kierkegaards Papirer*, Vol. 2, Copenhagen, 1968, p. 99.

69. Grethe Kjær: *Eventyrets verden i Kierkegaards forfatterskab*, Copenhagen, 1991.

70. Sejer Kühle: *Søren Kierkegaards Barndom og Ungdom*, Copenhagen, 1950, pp. 106-07.

71. Ibid.

72. Wilhelm von Rosen: "H. C. Andersens forelskelse i Ludvig Müller og dennes forgæves forsøg på at få et ordentligt mandfolk ud af ham," *Kritik* 73, Copenhagen, 1985, p. 32.

73. *Søren Kierkegaards Papirer*, Vol. 1, Copenhagen, 1968, p. 74.

74. Carl Weltzer: "Søren Kierkegaard karikeret, kopieret og kanoniseret," *Dansk Teologisk Tidsskrift*, Copenhagen, 1948, p. 123.

75. Joakim Garff: *SAK*, Copenhagen, 2000, pp. 124-25.

76. Frithiof Brandt: *Den unge Søren Kierkegaard*, Copenhagen, 1929, p. 133.

77. Hans Christian Andersen: "Lykkens Kalosker," *H. C. Andersens Eventyr*, Vol. 1, Copenhagen, 1919, p. 185.

78. Carl Weltzer: "Søren Kierkegaard karikeret, kopieret og kanoniseret," *Dansk Teologisk Tidsskrift*, Copenhagen, 1948, p. 123. Hans Christian Andersen's manuscript of this brief poetry collection from 1828 is at the Royal Library (Ny Kgl. Samling 643,8).

79. *Søren Kierkegaards Papirer*, Vol. 2, Copenhagen, 1968, p. 286; and Joakim Garff: *SAK*, Copenhagen, 2000, p. 129.

80. Quoted from Joakim Garff: *SAK*, Copenhagen, 2000, p. 127.

81. Ibid., p. 128.

82. Søren Kierkegaard: *Samlede Værker*, Vol. 4, Copenhagen, 1901-1906, p. 344.

83. *H. C. Andersens Almanakker 1833–1875*, Copenhagen, 1996, p. 23.

84. June 15, 1852. *H. C. Andersens dagbøger*, Vol. 4, Copenhagen, 1995-96, p. 105.

85. Hans Christian Andersen: *En Comedie i det Grønne*, in *Samlede Skrifter*, Vol. 31, Copenhagen, 1876, p. 9.

86. Ibid., p. 10.

87. Ibid., p. 11.

88. *Søren Kierkegaards Papirer*, Vol. 3, Copenhagen, 1911, pp. 105-10.

89. Quoted from Joakim Garff: *SAK*, Copenhagen, 2000, p. 498.

90. Hans Christian Andersen: *Mit Livs Eventyr*, in *Samlede Skrifter*, Vol. 21, Copenhagen, 1855, pp. 198-99.

91. Hans Christian Andersen: *At være eller ikke være*, Copenhagen, 2001, pp. 189-90.

92. Joakim Garff: *SAK*, Copenhagen, 2000, pp. 129-30.

93. October 9, 1838. *H. C. Andersens brevveksling med Lucie & B. S. Ingemann*, Vol. 1, Copenhagen, 1997, p. 155.

94. *Søren Kierkegaards Papirer*, Vol. 2, Copenhagen, 1968, pp. 9-19.

95. Bruno Bettelheim: *Eventyrets fortryllelse—i psykoanalytisk belysning*, Copenhagen, 1991.

96. Hans Christian Andersen: *Billedbog uden Billeder*, in *Samlede Skrifter*, Vol. 7, Copenhagen, 1854, p. 156.

97. December 1837. Bille and Bøgh: *Breve fra Hans Christian Andersen*, Vol. 1, Copenhagen, 1878, pp. 396-97.

98.   November 25, 1837. "H. C. Andersens Brevveksling med Henriette Hanck,"
       Anderseniana, 1942, p. 207.

CHAPTER 6

1.   Hans Christian Andersen: "En geographisk Beskrivelse af det menneskelige Hoved.
      Ideer og Udkast (Nogle løse Blade af min Rejse-Mappe)," *Nyeste Repertorium for
      Moerskabslæsning*, July 7, 1832. Retold by Jens Andersen.
2.   Hans Christian Andersen: *En Digters Bazar*, in *Romaner og Rejseskildringer*, Vol. 6,
      Copenhagen, 1944, p. 346.
3.   November 20, 1843. *H. C. Andersens brevveksling med Lucie & B. S. Ingemann*, Vol. 1,
      Copenhagen, 1997, p. 191.
4.   Hans Christian Andersen: *Mit eget Eventyr uden Digtning*, Copenhagen, 1942, p. 107.
5.   P. L. Møller: *Kritiske Skizzer*, Copenhagen, 1971, p. 117.
6.   Heinrich Steffens: *Indledning til philosopiske Forelæsninger*, Copenhagen, 1803.
7.   May 27, 1840. *H. C. Andersen og Henriette Wulff. En brevveksling*, Vol. 1, Odense, 1959, p. 270.
8   February 1, 1839. "H. C. Andersens Brevveksling med Henriette Hanck,"
      Anderseniana, 1945, p. 326.
9.   April 3, 1839. Ibid., p. 342.
10.   Ibid., pp. 340-41.
11.   July 21, 1847. *H. C. Andersens Bevveksling med Edvard og Henriette Collin*, Vol. 2,
      Copenhagen, 1934, pp. 146-47.
12.   January 4, 1839. "H. C. Andersens Brevveksling med Henriette Hanck," *Anderseniana*,
      1945, pp. 313, 315-16.
13.   August 21, 1838. Ibid., pp. 266-67.
14.   Poul Høybye: "Hans Christian Andersens franske Ven Xavier Marmier," *Studier for
      Sprog og Oldtidsforskning*, Copenhagen, 1950.
15.   *Digteren H. C. Andersens Levnet, fortalt af ham selv. Til dels efter Marmiers franske Original
      ved K.*, Copenhagen, 1861.
16.   September 20, 1837. "H. C. Andersens Brevveksling med Henriette Hanck,"
      Anderseniana, 1942, p. 199.
17.   Nicolai Bøgh: "Bidrag til Kunstnerparret Heibergs Karakteristik," *Museum. Tidsskrift
      for Historie og Geografi*, Vol. 2, Copenhagen, 1891, pp. 83-84.
18.   Ibid.
19.   December 12, 1839. "H. C. Andersens Brevveksling med Henriette Hanck,"
      Anderseniana, 1945, p. 404.
20.   Ibid.
21.   September 8, 1830. Bille and Bøgh: *Breve til Hans Christian Andersen*, Copenhagen,
      1877, p. 515.
22.   Quoted from B. Grønbech: "Om 'Mulatten' og dens franske forlæg," *Anderseniana*,
      1978-79, p. 56.
23.   March 31, 1839. *H. C. Andersens Brevveksling med Edvard og Henriette Collin*, Vol. 1,
      Copenhagen, 1933, p. 271.
24.   February 6, 1840. "H. C. Andersens Brevveksling med Henriette Hanck,"
      Anderseniana, 1945, p. 427.
25.   February 16, 1840. *H. C. Andersens brevveksling med Lucie & B. S. Ingemann*, Vol. 1,
      Copenhagen, 1997, p. 168.
26.   Ibid.; and April 21, 1843. "H. C. Andersens Brevveksling med Henriette Hanck,"
      Anderseniana, 1946, p. 590.

27. Hans Christian Andersen: *Kun en Spillemand*, in *Romaner og Rejseskildringer*, Vol. 3, Copenhagen, 1944, p. 64.

28. November 4, 1838. "H. C. Andersens Brevveksling med Henriette Hanck," *Anderseniana*, 1943, p. 291.

29. March 15, 1840. "H. C. Andersens Brevveksling med Henriette Hanck," *Anderseniana*, 1945, p. 435.

30. Bo Grønbech: "'Mulatten' og dens franske forlæg." *Anderseniana*, 1978-79.

31. Nicolai Bøgh: "Uddrag af en Dagbog," *Julebogen 1915*, Copenhagen, 1915, p. 54.

32. February 20, 1840. "H. C. Andersens Brevveksling med Henriette Hanck," *Anderseniana*, 1945, p. 429.

33. Ibid.; and H. C. A. Lund: *Studenterforeningens Historie 1822–70*, Vol. 2, Copenhagen, 1896-98, p. 64.

34. Febuary 21, 1840. "H. C. Andersens Brevveksling med Henriette Hanck," *Anderseniana*, 1945, p. 431.

35. Hans Christian Andersen: "Fortale," *Maurerpigen*, Copenhagen, 1840, p. 8.

36. *H. C. Andersens og Henriette Wulff. En brevveksling*, Vol. 1, Odense, 1959, p. 276.

37. Nicolai Bøgh: "Bidrag til Kunstnerparret Heibergs Karakteristik," *Museum. Tidsskrift for Historie og Geografi*, Vol. 2, Copenhagen, 1891, pp. 86–87.

38. Niels Birger Wamberg: *H. C. Andersen og Heiberg*, Copenhagen, 1971, pp. 149-50.

39. Albert Fabritius: "H. C. Andersen og det Collinske Huus. Smaastykker fra den Collinske Brevsamling," *Personalhistorisk Tidsskrift*, 1941, p. 232.

40. Quoted from Niels Birger Wamberg: *H. C. Andersen og Heiberg*, Copenhagen, 1971, p. 127.

41. Albert Fabritius: "H. C. Andersen og det Collinske Huus. Smaastykker fra den Collinske Brevsamling," *Personalhistorisk Tidsskrift*, 1941, p. 234.

42. *H. C. Andersen og Henriette Wulff. En brevveksling*, Vol. 1, Odense, 1959, p. 273.

43. December 27, 1840. Ibid., p. 279.

44. September 16, 1845. *H. C. Andersens brevveksling med Lucie & B. S. Ingemann*, Vol. 1, Copenhagen, 1997, pp. 204-05.

45. Ibid., p. 204.

46. August 16, 1843. *H. C. Andersen Brevveksling med Jonas Collin den Ældre*, Vol. 1, Copenhagen, 1945, p. 227. Johan de Mylius: *H. C. Andersens liv. Dag for dag*, Copenhagen, 1998, pp. 93-94.

47. November 10, 1840. *H. C. Andersens dagbøger*, Copenhagen, 1995-96, pp. 49-50.

48. Ivy York Möller-Christensen: *Den gyldne trekant. H. C. Andersens gennembrud i Tyskland 1831–1850*, Odense, 1992, p. 133.

49. *H. C. Andersens Album* I–V, Copenhagen, 1980.

50. May 8, 1843. *H. C. Andersens Brevveksling med Jonas Collin den Ældre*, Vol. 1, Copenhagen, 1945, p. 212.

51. March 26, 1843. *H. C. Andersens dagbøger*, Vol. 2, Copenhagen, 1995-96, p. 335.

52. Quoted from Harald Rue: *Litteratur og Samfund*, Copenhagen, 1976, p. 36.

53. May 27 and May 31, 1865. *H. C. Andersens Brevveksling med Edvard og Henriette Collin*, Vol. 3, Copenhagen, 1936, pp. 183, 187-88.

54. March 25, 1843. *H. C. Andersens dagbøger*, Vol. 2, Copenhagen, 1995-96. p. 333.

55. March 28, 1843. Letter to Jonna Stampe, quoted from Edvard Collin: *H. C. Andersen og det Collinske Hus*, Copenhagen, 1929, p. 187.

56. April 27, 1843. *H. C. Andersen og Henriette Wulff. En brevveksling*, Vol. 1, Odense, 1959, p. 327.

57. Hans Christian Andersen: *Mit Livs Eventyr*, and *H. C. Andersens dagbøger*, Vol. 2,

Copenhagen, 1995-96, pp. 328-29; and Hjalmar Hjort Boyesen: "Erindringer om Hans Christian Andersen," *Illustreret Tidende*, XXXIII, 1891-92, pp. 318-19.

58.   *H. C. Andersens Album*, I–V, Vol. 1, Copenhagen, 1980, p. 291.

59.   N. W. Gade: *Optegnelser og Breve*, Copenhagen, 1892, p. 270.

60.   April 2, 1844. *H. C. Andersens Almanakker 1833–1873*, Copenhagen, 1996, p. 124.

61.   December 25, 1843. *Henrik Stampes breve til H. C. Andersen*, Manuscript, Odense Bys Museer.

62.   *H. C. Andersens Almanakker 1833–1873*, Copenhagen, 1996, pp. 114-28.

63.   January 23, 25, and "end of January," 1844. See Rigmor Stampe: *H. C. Andersen og hans nærmeste Omgang*, Copenhagen, 1918, pp. 101-11. There is quite a bit of confusion with regard to the dates and years listed on the letters in Rigmor Stampe's book. The letter dated January 23, 1844, is on pages 102-03; the letter dated January 25, 1844, is on pages 110-11; and the letter dated "End of January" is on pages 101-02.

64.   January 25, 1844. Ibid., p. 111.

65.   "End of January 1844." Ibid., pp. 101-02.

66.   May 3, 1844. Ibid., p. 112.

67.   June 6, 1844. Ibid., p. 113.

68.   July 4, 1844. *H. C. Andersens dagbøger*, Vol. 2, Copenhagen, 1995-96, pp. 406-07.

69.   June 24, 1844. Ibid., p. 397.

70.   June 26, 1844. Ibid., p. 399.

71.   Angelika Pöthe: *Carl Alexander. Mäzen in Weimars "Silberner Zeit,"* Köln/Weimar/Wien, 1998, p. 69.

72.   Ove Brusendorff and Poul Henningsen: *Erotikkens Historie*, Vol. 3, Copenhagen, 1936, p. 215.

73.   Ibid., p. 218.

74.   July 2, 1844. *H. C. Andersens Brevveksling med Edvard og Henriette Collin*, Vol. 2, Copenhagen, 1934, p. 5.

75.   Ibid.

76.   Ibid., p. 4.

77.   Angelika Pöthe: *Carl Alexander. Mäzen in Weimars "Silberner Zeit,"* Köln/Weimar/Wien, 1998, p. 71.

78.   Angelika Pöthe: *Schloss Ettersburg. Weimars Geselligkeit und kulturelles Leben im 19. Jahrhundert*, Weimar/Köln/Wien, 1995, p. 17.

79.   Ibid., p. 73.

80.   Ibid., p. 84.

81.   June 28, 1844. *H. C. Andersens dagbøger*, Vol. 2, Copenhagen, 1995-96, p. 401.

82.   August 29, 1844. Möller-Christensen (ed.): *"Mein edler, theurer Grossherzog!" Briefwechsel zwischen Hans Christian Andersen und Grossherzog Carl Alexander von Sachsen-Weimar-Eisenach*, Göttingen, 1998, p. 7.

83.   July 2, 1844. *H. C. Andersens Brevveksling med Edvard og Henriette Collin*, Vol. 2, Copenhagen, 1934, p. 3.

84.   November 5, 1844. Möller-Christensen: *"Mein edler, theurer Grossherzog!" Briefwechsel zwischen Hans Christian Andersen und Grossherzog Carl Alexander von Sachsen-Weimar-Eisenach*, Göttingen, 1998, p. 16.

85.   Angelika Pöthe: *Carl Alexander. Mäzen in Weimars "Silberner Zeit,"* Köln/Weimar/Wien, 1998, p. 69.

86.   Ibid., pp. 67-69.

87.   Charlotte Bournonville: *Erindringer*, Copenhagen, 1903, p. 296.

88.   July 23, 1834. *H. C. Andersens dagbøger*, Vol. 1, Copenhagen, 1995-96, p. 504.

89. December 19, 1845. *H. C. Andersens dagbøger*, Vol. 3, Copenhagen, 1995–96, p. 27.

90. Ibid..

91. On Christmas Eve 1845 at eight p.m. Andersen went to a merry celebration at the home of Fru Zimmermann, where he met a lady-in-waiting, a composer, and a painter: "Two angels stood with banners around the Christmas trees; I received a beautifully bound book for writing in and a lampshade; the ladies sang, I read a couple of fairy tales. Came home at 11 o'clock; everyone was asleep in the hotel, I quietly went to bed." (*H. C. Andersens dagbøger*, Vol. 3.) And later even Andersen believed the story. On Christmas Eve 1871 he writes in his diary: "It was quite pleasant on this lonely Christmas Eve; only once, in Berlin, when I did not receive an invitation from Jenny Lind, have I been alone."

92. December 24, 1845. *H. C. Andersens dagbøger*, Vol. 3, Copenhagen 1995–96, p. 31.

93. July 31, 1844. Ibid., p. 421.

94. December 22, 1845. Ibid., p. 29.

95. Jørgen Swane: "Søstrene Bardua," *Personalhistorisk Tidsskrift*, 1933, pp. 223–25. Petra Wilhelmy: *Der Berliner Salon im 19. Jahrhundert*, Berlin, New York, 1989, pp. 182–84, 599–604. Johannes Werner: *Die Schwestern Bardua. Bilder aus dem Gesellschaftskunst- und Geistesleben der Biedermeierzeit*, Leipzig, 1929, pp. 175–203.

96. Jørgen Swane: "Søstrene Bardua," *Personalhistorisk Tidsskrift*, 1933.

97. January 5, 1846. *H. C. Andersens Brevveksling med Edvard og Henriette Collin*, Vol. 2, Copenhagen, 1934, p. 46.

98. Hans Christian Andersen: *Mit eget Eventyr uden Digtning*, Copenhagen, 1940.

99. February 5, 1846. *H. C. Andersens Album* I–V, Kommentarbind 1, Copenhagen, 1980, p. 435.

100. November 24, 1843. *H. C. Andersens Brevveksling med Edvard og Henriette Collin*, Vol. 1, Copenhagen, 1933, p. 345.

101. June 13, 1831. *H. C. Andersens dagbøger*, Vol. 1, Copenhagen, 1995–96, p. 108.

102. Hans Christian Andersen: "Kongen drømmer," *Samlede Skrifter*, Vol. 13, Copenhagen, 1854, p. 98.

103. Ibid.

104. January 8, 1846. *H. C. Andersens dagbøger*, Vol. 3, Copenhagen, 1995–96, p. 42.

105. March 30, 1845. Möller-Christensen: *"Mein edler, theurer Grossherzog!" Briefwechsel zwischen Hans Christian Andersen und Grossherzog Carl Alexander von Sachsen-Weimar-Eisenach*, pp. 26–27.

106. January 9, 1846. *H. C. Andersens dagbøger*, Vol. 3, Copenhagen, 1995–96, p. 42.

107. January 15, 1846. Ibid., p. 46.

108. January 10, 1846. Ibid., p. 43.

109. June 10, 1841. Ibid., Vol. 2, p. 248.

110. January 27, 1846. Ibid., Vol. 3, pp. 51–52.

111. February 8, 1846. Ibid., pp. 58–59.

112. February 9, 1846. Ibid., pp. 59–60.

113. January 30, 1846. *H. C. Andersen. Brevveksling med Jonas Collin den Ældre*, Vol. 1, Copenhagen, 1945, p. 285.

114. February 27, 1846. *H. C. Andersen. Brevveksling med Edvard og Henriette Collin*, Vol. 2, Copenhagen, 1934, p. 72.

115. December 27, 1845. Ibid., p. 43.

116. March 24, 1846. *H. C. Andersens Brevveksling med Jonas Collin den Ældre*, Vol. 1, Copenhagen, 1945, p. 292. See also Ken Nielsen: "Andersen og Rasmussen," *Politiken*, May 12, 2002.

117. Julius Clausen (ed.): "Af J.L.Heibergs Teatercensurer," *Gads Danske Magasin*, Copenhagen, 1928, p. 291.
118. March 2, 1846. *Breve fra og til Johanne Luise Heiberg*, Copenhagen, 1955, p. 67.
119. Hans Christian Andersen: *Hr. Rasmussen. Originalt Lystspil i to Acter*, Copenhagen, 1913, p. 10.
120. April 2, 1846. "H. C. Andersens breve til Louise Collin," *Anderseniana*, 2002, p. 61.
121. August 20, 1846. *H. C. Andersens dagbøger*, Vol. 3, Copenhagen, 1995-96, pp. 171-72.
122. Hans Christian Andersen: *At være eller ikke være*, Copenhagen, 2001, p. 26.
123. Hans Christian Andersen: *Hr. Rasmussen. Originalt Lystspil i to Acter*, Copenhagen, 1913, p. 44.

CHAPTER 7

1. September 9, 1844. *H. C. Andersens Brevveksling med Edvard og Henriette Collin*, Vol. 2, Copenhagen, 1934, p. 13.
2. H. C. Andersen: *Bouts rimés*, Århus, 1974, p. 17. Kai H. Thiele: *En følsom rejsende. H. C. Andersen på Föhr*, Copenhagen, 1958. Hans Christian Andersen: *De to Baronesser*, Copenhagen, 1848.
3. Hans Christian Andersen: *Kun en Spillemand*, in *Samlede Skrifter*, Vol. 6, Copenhagen, 1854, p. 61.
4. Hans Christian Andersen: *Mit Livs Eventyr*, *Samlede Skrifter*, Vol. 21-22, Copenhagen, 1855, pp. 256-57.
5. September 9, 1842. *H. C. Andersens dagbøger*, Vol. 2, Copenhagen, 1995-96, p. 275.
6. July 5, 1842. Ibid., p. 273.
7. July 26, 1842. Ibid., p. 284.
8. December 10, 1843. *H. C. Andersen og Henriette Wulff. En brevveksling*, Vol. 1, p. 346.
9. April 27, 1838. "H. C. Andersens brevveksling med Henriette Hanck," *Anderseniana*, 1943, p. 238.
10. Eduard Boas: *Im Scandinavien*, Leipzig, 1845, p. 314.
11. Möller-Christensen (ed.): *"Mein edler theurer Grossherzog!"* Göttingen, 1998, p. 7.
12. February 21, 1846. *H. C. Andersens Brevveksling med Edvard og Henriette Collin*, Vol. 2, Copenhagen, 1934, pp. 67-68.
13. August 25, 1846. Ibid., p. 109.
14. August 15, 1846. Ibid., pp. 113-14.
15. Topsøe-Jensen: *Mit eget Eventyr uden Digtning. En Studie over H. C. Andersen som Selvbiograf*, Copenhagen, 1940, pp. 104-40.
16. Ibid., p. 122.
17. Ibid., pp. 30-31.
18. September 24, 1846. *H. C. Andersens Brevveksling med Edvard og Henriette Collin*, Vol. 2, Copenhagen, 1934, p. 121.
19. Adam Frederik Trampe (1750-1807).
20. Nicolai Bøgh: "Fra H. C. Andersens Barndoms- og Ungdomsliv," *Personalhistorisk Tidsskrift*, 1905, p. 60.
21. Bodil Stenseth: *Ægteseng og bordel. Om 1790'ernes seksualoplysning*, Copenhagen, 1997, p. 92.
22. Karl Larsen: "Den rigtige Indskrift," *Politiken*, March 30, 1930.
23. F. Hendriksen: *Kristian Zahrtmann. En Mindebog bygget over hans Optegnelser og Breve fra og til ham*, Copenhagen, 1919, pp. 168-71.
24. May 2, 1871. Jean Hersholt (ed.): *H. C. Andersen og Horace E. Scudder. En brevveksling*, Copenhagen, 1948.

25. H. G. Olrik:"H. C. Andersens 'fødested'" (in *Hans Christian Andersen*, Copenhagen, 1945, p. 23). Einar Askgaard:"Man gaaer først . . .," *Fynske Minder*, Odense, 2000, pp. 122-23.

26. H. G. Olrik: *Hans Christian Andersen*, Copenhagen, 1945, p. 33.

27. Karl Larsen:"Den rigtige Indskrift," *Politiken*, March 30, 1930.

28. Jonas Collin: "Litterair og Naturvidenskabelige Opsatser," The Royal Library, Den Collinske Samling, 121,4.

29. February 17, 1837. *H. C. Andersens brevveksling med Lucie & B. S. Ingemann*, Vol. 1, Copenhagen, 1997, p. 126.

30. Hans Christian Andersen: *De to baronesser*, in *Romaner og Rejseskildringer*, Vol. 4, Copenhagen, 1944, p. 276.

31. February 7, 1854. *"Mein edler theurer Grossherzog!"* Göttingen, 1998, p. 191.

32. January 21, 1854. *H. C. Andersens brevveksling med Lucie & B. S. Ingemann*, Vol. 2, Copenhagen, 1997, pp. 317-18.

33. Chapter 3 in Part 2 of *Kun en Spillemand* (Copenhagen, 1944, pp. 124-28). October 18, 1836."H. C. Andersens brevveksling med Henriette Hanck," *Anderseniana*, 1942, p. 143.

34. March 15, 1838. Quoted from Elisabeth Hude: *Frederika Bremer og hendes venskab med H. C. Andersen og andre danske*, Copenhagen, 1972, p. 26.

35. Grethe Hartmann: *Boliger og bordeller*, Copenhagen, 1949, p. 93.

36. Hans Christian Andersen: *Kun en Spillemand*, in *Romaner og Rejseskildringer*, Vol. 3, Copenhagen, 1944, pp. 125, 127.

37. Ibid., p. 126.

38. Grethe Hartmann: *Boliger og bordeller*, Copenhagen, 1949, pp. 48-49.

39. Einar Askgaard:"Man gaaer først . . .," *Fynske Minder*, Odense, 2000, pp. 123-24.

40. H. G. Olrik: *Hans Christian Andersen*, Copenhagen, 1945, p. 71.

41. Bodil Stenseth: *Ægteseng og borde*, Copenhagen, 1997, p. 169.

42. Hans Christian Andersen: *H. C. Andersens Levnedsbog*, Copenhagen, 1926, p. 56.

43. Einar Askgaard: "Man gaaer først . . .," *Fynske Minder*, Odense, 2000, p. 124. Otto Vilhelm Sommer:"Fodrejsen til Bogense og Omegn," *Anderseniana*, 1993.

44. Georg Hansen:"Kvinde og mand," *Dagligliv i Danmark i det nittende og tyvende århundrede*, Copenhagen, 1964.

45. S. F. Hafström: *Om Sædelighedsforholdene i det danske Folk, særlig i Bondestanden og Almuen*, Copenhagen, 1888, pp. 18-19.

46. Svend Larsen: "Barndomsbyen," *Anderseniana*, 1955, p. 59.

47. Ole Nederland: "Ægteskabelige og uægteskabelige forbindelser i 1600-tallets Odense," *Fynske aarbøger 2000*, Odense, 2000, p. 49.

48. Thestrup, Andersen and Oxenvad: *Mod bedre tider. Odense 1789–1868*, Odense, 1986, pp. 54-72.

49. H. G. Olrik:"H. C. Andersen og hans første Omgivelser," *Dagens Nyheder*, April 1, 1926.

50. Nicolas Gomard has been suggested as the possible father of Hans Christian Andersen, but the proof is based only on hearsay in the Gomard family and has been repudiated. (H. G. Olrik: *Hans Christian Andersen*, Copenhagen, 1945, pp. 40-45; and *Ekstra Bladet*, October 21, 1935, and *Berlingske Aftenavis*, July 22, 1936.

51. H. G. Olrik:"H. C. Andersen og hans første Omgivelser," *Dagens Nyheder*, April 1, 1926; and H. G. Olrik: *Hans Christian Andersen*, Copenhagen, 1945, p. 43.

52. Georg Hansen: *Sædelighedsforhold blandt landbefolkningen i Danmark i det 18. Århundrede*, Copenhagen, 1957, p. 108.

53. H. G. Olrik: *Hans Christian Andersen*, Copenhagen, 1945, p. 41.

54. Nicolai Bøgh: "Fra H. C. Andersens Barndoms- og Ungdomsliv," *Personalhistorisk Tidsskrift*, 1905, p. 63.

55. Julius Clausen (ed.): *H. C. Andersens Optegnelsesbog*, Copenhagen, 1926, pp. 30-31.

56. S. H. Clausen: *Odense og Omegn, en lexikalsk Beskrivelse*, Odense, 1863, p. 78. H. G. Olrik: *Hans Christian Andersen*, Copenhagen, 1945, pp. 96-97.

57. Hans Christian Andersen: *Billedbog uden Billeder. Sjette Aften*, in *Samlede Skrifter*, Vol. 7, Copenhagen, 1854, p. 123.

58. In the old days, images imprinted on the body were called *stigmata perpetua*. These tattoos were intended, in coded or symbolic form, to present information not only regarding a person's familial connections but also his social and class affiliations. As far back as the Middle Ages, primitive tattoos were used as a type of "mark of shame and disgrace," which whores were forced to display in a visible fashion so they could be kept separate from the finer ladies and virtuous maidens. (Rudolph Bergh: "Om Tatoveringer hos Fruentimmer af den offentlige og hemmelige Prostitution," *Hospitalstidende*, No. 38, 1902, pp. 947-55.)

59. Hans Christian Andersen: "Phantasier og Skizzer," 1831, *Samlede Skrifter*, Vol. 15, Copenhagen, 1854, p. 181.

60. Jens Jørgensen: *H. C. Andersen—En sand myte*, Aarhus, 1996.

61. Elias Bredsdorff: "Jørgensen og Andersen," *Politiken*, April 15, 1989.

62. November 18, 1848. *H. C. Andersen og Henriette Wulff. En brevveksling*, Vol. 1, p. 448.

63. November 14, 1869. *H. C. Andersens dagbøger*, Vol. 8, Copenhagen, 1995-96, p. 295.

64. H. G. Olrik: "H. C. Andersen og hans første Omgivelser," *Dagens Nyheder*, April 1, 1926.

65. *Fyens Avis. Onsdagen den 4. December 1867, 88. Aargang. Nr. 283*. Trykt af Chr. Milo, Odense, 1867.

66. "Hans Christian Andersen Optegnelse om hans far," The Royal Library, Den Collinske Samling 17,4°. Einar Askgaard: "Man gaaer først . . .," *Fynske Minder*, Odense, 2000, p. 118.

67. Nicolai Bøgh: "Fra Andersens Barndoms- og Ungdomsliv," *Personalhistorisk Tidsskrift*, 1905, p. 59.

68. Ibid., p. 71.

69. Ibid., p. 59.

70. H. G. Olrik: "Barnets Far og Mor," *Nationaltidende*, March 31, 1930.

71. Hans Christian Andersen: "Tanker over nogle forslidte Sko," *Nyt Repertorium for Morskabslæsning*, No. 24, Copenhagen, 1830, pp. 366-67.

72. Hans Christian Andersen: *Ahasverus*, in *Samlede Skrifter*, Vol. 17, Copenhagen, 1855, p. 105.

73. C. T. Engelstoft: *Odense Byes Historie*, Odense, 1880, pp. 360-69. Thestrup, Andersen og Oxenvad: *Mod bedre tider*, Odense, 1986, p. 159. "Odense gennem 125 Aar," *Politiken*, April 2, 1930.

74. Hans Christian Andersen: "Odense," *Samlede Skrifter*, Vol. 33, Copenhagen, 1879, p. 33.

75. Holger Rasmussen: *Fynske bindebreve*, Odense, 1960.

76. *H. C. Andersens Levnedsbog*, Copenhagen, 1926, p. 31.

77. Villiam Christian Walter (pseudonym for Hans Christian Andersen): *Ungdoms-Forsøg*, Copenhagen, 1956, p. 7.

78. Vilhelm Andersen: "Barndomshjemmet," *Odense Bys Bog til H. C. Andersen*, Odense, 1905, p. 47.

79. March 27, 1825. *H. C. Andersens Brevveksling med Jonas Collin den Ældre*, Vol. I, Copenhagen, 1945, p. 21.

80. Hans Christian Andersen: *H. C. Andersens Levnedsbog*, Copenhagen, 1926, p. 35.

81. Ibid., p. 37.

82. Ibid., p. 38.

83. Nicolai Bøgh: "Fra H. C. Andersens Barndoms- og Ungdomsliv," *Personalhistorisk Tidsskrift*, 1905, p. 61.

84. Ibid., p. 61.

85. N. I. Larsen and Johs. Jacobsen: *Blade af Skotøjfagets Historie i Danmark*, Copenhagen, 1936, pp. 23-24. Hans Heeland: *Skomageriets og Skotøjshandlens Historie i Danmark*, Copenhagen, 1926. Oxenvad et al.: *Mod bedre tider*, Odense, 1986, pp. 96-98.

86. Einar Askgaard: "Man gaaer først . . .," *Fynske Minder*, Odense, 2000, pp. 119-29; and H. G. Olrik: *Hans Christian Andersen*, Copenhagen, 1945, p. 94.

87. Hans Christian Andersen: *Mit eget Eventyr uden Digtning*, Copenhagen, 1942, p. 20.

88. Nicolai Bøgh: "Fra H. C. Andersens Barndoms- og Ungdomsliv," *Personalhistorisk Tidsskrift*, 1905, p. 62.

89. Hans Christian Andersen: *At være eller ikke være*, Copenhagen, 2001, p. 26.

90. Hans Christian Andersen: *Slagelse-Digte II*, Århus, 1990, p. 16.

91. June 10, 1840. "H. C. Andersens brevveksling med Henriette Hanck," *Anderseniana*, 1945, p. 462.

92. *Ordbog over det danske sprog*, Vol. I, Copenhagen, 1975, p. 838.

93. *Odense Byfogeds Arkiv*, Landsarkivet, Odense.

94. Georg Hansen: *Sædelighedsforhold blandt landbefolkningen i Danmark i det 18. århundrede*, Copenhagen, 1957, p. 37.

95. Oxenvad et al.: *Mod bedre tider*, Odense, 1986, pp. 114-15. Engelstoft: *Odense Byes Historie*, Odense, 1880, p. 438.

96. H. G. Olrik: *Hans Christian Andersen.* Copenhagen, 1945, pp. 58-59.

97. Hans Christian Andersen: "Kometen," *H. C. Andersens Eventyr,* Vol. 5, Copenhagen, 1919, p. 204.

98. Svend Larsen: "Barndomsbyen," *Anderseniana*, 1955, pp. 42-46.

99. Just Mathias Thiele: *Danske Folkesagn* I-IV. Hans Ellekilde: "Odense Bys Sagnoverlevering i H. C. Andersens Barndom," *Fyens Stiftstidende*, November 23, 1930.

100. Hans Christian Andersen: "Christian den Andens Dverg," *Anderseniana*, 1935, p. 61.

101. Sophie Breum to Vilhelm Andersen. *Odense Bys Bog til H. C. Andersen*, Odense, 1905, p. 47.

102. Hans Christian Andersen: "Hvad Gamle Johanne fortalte," *H. C. Andersens Eventyr*, Vol. 5, Copenhagen, 1919, p. 290.

103. Vilhelm Andersen: "Barndomshjemmet," *Odense Bys Bog om H. C. Andersen*, Odense, 1905, p. 46.

104. Edvard Collin: *H. C. Andersen og det Collinske Hus*, Copenhagen, 1882, pp. 291-92.

105. Hans Christian Andersen: *Slagelse-Digte II*, Århus, 1990, p. 70.

106. Hans Christian Andersen: *Eventyrdigterens hidtil utrykte danske stile II*, Copenhagen, 1999, p. 80.

107. July 11, 1832. *H. C. Andersens Brevveksling med Edvard og Henriette Collin*, Vol. 1, Copenhagen, 1933, p. 104.

108. August 3, 1832. Ibid., p. 108.

109. July 3, 1832. Ibid., p. 101.

110. February 27, 1833. Svend Larsen: *H. C. Andersens Moder. En Brevsamling*, Odense, 1947, p. 48.

111. December 16, 1833. *H. C. Andersen og Henriette Wulff. En brevveksling,* Vol. 1, Odense, 1959, p. 151.

112. Hans Christian Andersen: *Mit Livs Eventyr*, in *Samlede Skrifter,* Vol. 21, Copenhagen, 1855, p. 163.

113. Quoted from Hans Chr. Larsen: "H. C. Andersens slægts-puslespil," *Fyens Stiftstidende*, June 13, 1999, p. 9.

114. Nicolai Bøgh: "Fra H. C. Andersens Barndoms- og Ungdomsliv," *Personalhistorisk Tidsskrift*, 1905, p. 66.

115. Ibid., p. 67.

116. November 3-4, 1825. *H. C. Andersens dagbøger,* Vol. 1, Copenhagen, 1995, p. 14.

117. Svend Larsen: *H. C. Andersens Moder. En Brevsamling*, Odense, 1947, p. 48.

118. February 8, 1842. *H. C. Andersens Almanakker, 1833–1873*, Copenhagen, 1996, p. 78.

119. Hans Christian Andersen: *O.T.*, in *Romaner og Rejseskildringer,* Vol. 2, Copenhagen, 1943, pp. 97-98.

120. February 12, 1842. *H. C. Andersens Almanakker, 1833–1873*, Copenhagen, 1996, p. 79.

121. September 30, 1842. Ibid., p. 90.

122. H. G. Olrik: *Hans Christian Andersen*, Copenhagen, 1945, p. 75.

123. Grethe Hartmann: *Boliger og bordeller*, Copenhagen, 1949, p. 35.

124. February 9, 1842. *H. C. Andersens Almanakker, 1833–1873*, Copenhagen, 1996, p. 78.

125. Ejnar Askgaard: "Man gaaer først . . .," *Fynske Minder*, Odense, 2000, p. 119.

126. Grethe Hartmann: *Boliger og bordeller*, Copenhagen, 1949.

127. H. G. Olrik: *Hans Christian Andersen*, Copenhagen, 1945, pp. 66-75. Einar Askgaard: "Man gaaer først . . .," *Fynske Minder*, Odense, 2000, p. 121.

128. January 21, 1847. *H. C. Andersens brevveksling med Lucie & B. S. Ingemann*, Vol. I, Copenhagen, 1997, p. 207.

129. Quoted from F. J. Billeskov Jansen: *Verdenslitteratur*, Copenhagen, 1982, p. 222.

130. Ivy York Möller Christensen: *Den gyldne trekant*, Odense, 1992, pp. 204-25.

131. Ibid., p. 217.

132. October 1846. Bille and Bøgh: *Breve fra Hans Christian Andersen,* Vol. 2, Copenhagen, 1878, pp. 156-57.

133. July 22, 1847. *H. C. Andersen og Henriette Wulff. En brevveksling,* Vol. 1, Odense, 1959, pp. 388-89.

134. Undated. Charles Dickens to William Jeedan. Odense Bys Museer.

135. June 24, 1847. *H. C. Andersens Brevveksling med Edvard og Henriette Collin*, Vol. 2, Copenhagen, 1934, p. 138.

136. June 27, 1847. Edvard Collin: *H. C. Andersen og det Collinske Hus*, Copenhagen, 1929, pp. 244-45.

137. July 9, 1847. *H. C. Andersens dagbøger,* Vol. 3, Copenhagen, 1995-96, p. 222.

138. August 12, 1847. *H. C. Andersen og Henriette Wulff. En brevveksling,* Vol. 1, Odense, 1959, p. 395.

139. Elias Bredsdorff: *H. C. Andersen—mennesket og digteren*, Copenhagen, 1979, p. 235.

140. Ibid., pp. 236-37.

141. Willard Connely: *Count D'Orsay. "The Dandy of Dandies,"* London, 1952, pp. 456-58.

142. July 16, 1847. *H. C. Andersens dagbøger,* Vol. 3, Copenhagen, 1995-96, p. 230.

143. July 6, 1847. *H. C. Andersens Brevveksling med Edvard og Henriette Collin*, Vol. 2, Copenhagen, 1934, p. 144.

144. Elias Bredsdorff: *H. C. Andersen og Charles Dickens. Et Venskab og dets Opløsning*, Copenhagen, 1951, p. 24.

145. Edvard Collin: *H. C. Andersen og det Collinske Hus*, Copenhagen, 1929, p. 310.

146. August 30, 1847. *H. C. Andersens dagbøger,* Vol. 3, Copenhagen, 1995-96, p. 264.

147. August 8, 1847. *H. C. Andersens Brevveksling med Edvard og Henriette Collin*, Vol. 2, Copenhagen, 1934, pp. 152-53.

148. August 31, 1847. *H. C. Andersens dagbøger,* Vol. 3, Copenhagen, 1995-96, p. 266.

149. August 15, 1847. *H. C. Andersens Brevveksling med Edvard og Henriette Collin,* Vol. 2, Copenhagen, 1934, p. 158.

150. September 1847. Ibid., p. 162.
151. September 13, 1848. *H. C. Andersen og Henriette Wulff. En brevveksling,*Vol. 1, Odense, 1959, p. 440.
152. June 12, 1848. Ibid., p. 419.
153. Hans Christian Andersen: *Mit Livs Eventyr,* in *Samlede Skrifter,* Vol. 21-22, Copenhagen, 1855, p. 468.
154. May 20, 1848. *H. C. Andersen og Henriette Wulff. En brevveksling,*Vol. 1, Odense, 1959, p. 410.
155. May 29, 1848. *H. C. Andersens brevveksling med Lucie & B. S. Ingemann,* Vol. I, Copenhagen, 1997, p. 224.
156. May 13, 1848. *H. C. Andersens dagbøger,* Vol. 3, Copenhagen, 1995-96, p. 280.
157. September 18, 1848. *H. C. Andersen. Brevveksling med Edvard og Henriette Collin,*Vol. 2, Copenhagen, 1934, p. 185.

CHAPTER 8

1. March 17, 1851. *H. C. Andersens dagbøger,*Vol. 4, Copenhagen, 1995-96, p. 19.
2. Nicolai Bøgh:"Hvad H. C. Andersen fortalte. Nogle Meddelelser om hans Forhold til forskjellige historiske Personer," *Danmark. Illustreret Kalender for 1887,* Copenhagen, 1886, pp. 28-54.
3. August 3, 1850. Bille and Bøgh: *Breve fra Hans Christian Andersen,*Vol. 2, Copenhagen, 1878, pp. 246-47.
4. March 16, 1835. *H. C. Andersen og Henriette Wulff. En brevveksling,*Vol. 1, Odense, 1959, p. 211.
5. July 18, 1850. Bille and Bøgh: *Breve til H. C. Andersen,* Copenhagen, 1877, pp. 519-92.
6. June 24, 1836. *H. C. Andersen. Brevveksling med Edvard og Henriette Collin,* Vol. 1, Copenhagen, 1933, p. 247.
7. Hans Christian Andersen: *I Sverrig,* in *Romaner og Rejseskildringer,* Copenhagen, 1944, p. 13.
8. April 26, 1846. Bille and Bøgh: *Breve fra Hans Christian Andersen,* Vol. 2, Copenhagen, 1878, p. 150.
9. June 1851. *H. C. Andersens Brevveksling med Edvard og Henriette Collin,* Vol. 2, Copenhagen, 1934, p. 209.
10. *Chronik von Maxen,* Förderverein Museum Sächsische Land-Wirtschaft Rittergut Maxen, 1997.
11. May 15, 1854. *H. C. Andersens dagbøger,*Vol. 4, Copenhagen, 1995-96, p. 133.
12. Walther Killy: *Literatur Lexicon,* Bd II, München, 1989, pp. 376-77.
13. July 21, 1855. *H. C. Andersens dagbøger,*Vol. 4, Copenhagen, 1995-96, p. 165.
14. June 22, 1856. Ibid., p. 212.
15. July 9, 1855. Ibid., pp. 162-64. July 19, 1855. *H. C. Andersen. Brevveksling med Jonas Collin den Ældre,*Vol. 2, Copenhagen,1945, p. 104. July 19, 1855. *H. C. Andersen og Henriette Wulff. En brevveksling,*Vol. 2, Copenhagen, 1959, p. 229.
16. June 17, 1856. *H. C. Andersens dagbøger,*Vol. 4, Copenhagen, 1995-96, p. 210.
17. Ibid.
18. June 14, 1856. Ibid., p. 209.
19. July 26, 1856. Ibid., p. 227.
20. November 2, 1860. *H. C. Andersens Brevveksling med Edvard og Henriette Collin,*Vol. 2, Copenhagen, 1934, p. 384.

21. January 12, 1874. Bille and Bøgh: *Breve fra Hans Christian Andersen,* Vol. 2, Copenhagen, 1878, p. 690.

22. *H. C. Andersen Album I–V,* Vol. 1, Copenhagen, 1980, p. 43. Kommentarbind 1, p. 151.

23. Hans Christian Andersen: *Lykke-Peer,* Copenhagen, 2000, p. 17.

24. August 28, 1856. *H. C. Andersens dagbøger,* Vol. 4, Copenhagen, 1995–96, p. 236.

25. Hans Christian Andersen: *Lykke-Peer,* Copenhagen, 2000, p. 69.

26. Hans Christian Andersen: *Skyggebilleder,* Copenhagen, 1986, p. 111.

27. November 6, 1840. *H. C. Andersens dagbøger,* Vol. 2, Copenhagen, 1995–96, pp. 46–47.

28. March 8, 1846. Ibid., Vol. 3, p. 73.

29. Quoted from Gösta Zetterberg Törnbom: *Liszt,* Stockholm, 1956, p. 24.

30. Axelline Lund: *Spredte Erindringer,* Copenhagen, 1917, pp. 66–67.

31. May 31, 1852. *H. C. Andersens dagbøger,* Vol. 4, Copenhagen, 1995–96, p. 86.

32. Guy de Pourtalès: *I Kometens Tecken. Franz Liszt,* Uppsala, 1930, pp. 131–32.

33. September 5, 1857. *H. C. Andersens dagbøger,* Vol. 4, Copenhagen, 1995–96, p. 287.

34. Olaf Carlsen: "H. C. Andersen og Familien Kaulbach," *Aarhus Stiftstidende,* May 12, 1944.

35. Josefa Dürck-Kaulbach: *Erindringer om Wilhelm von Kaulbach,* Copenhagen, 1917.

36. Quoted from Olaf Carlsen: "H. C. Andersen og Familien Kaulbach," *Aarhus Stiftstidende,* May 12, 1944.

37. June 19, 1852. *H. C. Andersens dagbøger,* Vol. 4, Copenhagen, 1995–96, p. 99.

38. June 19, 1854. Ibid., pp. 150–51.

39. Sophie Rützow: "Der kleine Andersen ist da!" *Münchener Mosaik,* Vol. 3, 1940, pp. 345–46.

40. May 22, 1856. *H. C. Andersens dagbøger,* Vol. 4, Copenhagen, 1995–96, pp. 202–03.

41. Hans Christian Andersen: *I Sverrig,* Copenhagen, 1944, p. 121.

42. Hans Christian Andersen: *At være eller ikke være,* Copenhagen, 2001, p. 222.

43. Ibid., p. 161.

44. Ibid., p. 187.

45. December 27, 1855. *H. C. Andersen og Henriette Wulff. En brevveksling,* Vol. 2, Odense, 1959, p. 250.

46. July 16, 1856. *H. C. Andersens Brevveksling med Jonas Collin den Ældre,* Vol. 2, Copenhagen, 1945, p. 155. See also Elias Bredsdorff. *H. C: Andersen og Charles Dickens. Et Venskab og dets Opløsning,* Copenhagen, 1951, pp. 38–39.

47. July 5, 1856. Quoted from *H. C. Andersens Album I–V,* Copenhagen, 1980. Kommentarbind 1, p. 360.

48. April 3, 1857. Ibid., p. 127.

49. Quoted from Elias Bredsdorff: *H. C. Andersen og Charles Dickens. Et Venskab og dets Opløsning,* Copenhagen, 1951 p. 124.

50. Nicolai Bøgh: "Hvad H. C. Andersen fortalte. Nogle Meddelelser om hans Forhold til forskjellige historiske Personer," *Danmark. Illustreret Kalender for 1887,* Copenhagen, 1886.

51. July 21, 1857. Quoted from Elias Bredsdorff: *H. C. Andersen. Mennesket og digteren,* Copenhagen, 1979, p. 271.

52. *Fædrelandet,* July 11, 1857.

53. Quoted from Elias Bredsdorff: "H. C. Andersen serveret skarp sovs (engelsk sovs)," *Anderseniana,* 1978–79, pp. 11–12.

54. Hans Christian Andersen: "Et Besøg hos Charles Dickens," *Samlede Skrifter,* Vol. 28, Copenhagen, 1868, p. 33.

55. Hans Christian Andersen: "Et Besøg hos Charles Dickens i Sommeren 1857," *Berlingske Tidende,* January 24 to February 2, 1860.

56. May 21, 1860. Elias Bredsdorff: *H. C. Andersen og Charles Dickens. Et Venskab og dets Opløsning,* Copenhagen, 1951, p. 136.

57. August 10, 1857. *H. C. Andersens Brevveksling med Edvard og Henriette Collin*, Vol. II, Copenhagen, 1934, p. 289.
58. August 8, 1846. Ibid., p. 105.
59. Hans Christian Andersen: "Et besøg hos Charles Dickens," *Rejseskitser*, Copenhagen, 2003, p. 116.
60. Claire Tomalin: *The invisible Woman. The Story of Nelly Ternan and Charles Dickens*, London, 1991.
61. July 11, 1870. *H. C. Andersens dagbøger*, Vol. 7, Copenhagen, 1995-96, pp. 380-81.
62. December 12, 1860. Ibid., Vol. 4, pp. 463-64.
63. December 22, 1860. Ibid., p. 474.

CHAPTER 9
1. Hans Christian Andersen: *Kun en Spillemand*, in *Romaner og Rejseskildringer*, Vol. 3, Copenhagen, 1944, p. 128.
2. Ibid..
3. Rigmor Stampe: *H. C. Andersen og hans nærmeste Omgang*, Copenhagen, 1918, pp. 225-26.
4. Ibid.. (verse 6).
5. Hans Christian Andersen: "Jonas Collin," *Dagbladet*, September 2, 1861. *Samlede digte*, Copenhagen, 2000, pp. 568-69.
6. Rigmor Stampe: *H. C. Andersens og hans nærmeste Omgang*, Copenhagen, 1918, p. 17.
7. *Familie Viser Skrevne af Edvard Collin I–II*. Volume 1 covers the period from 1832 to 1857 and contains songs no.1-70, as well as a Foreword and commentary. Volume 2 covers the period from 1858 to 1876 and contains songs no.71-124, as well as commentary and other texts by Edvard Collin, including a play. The two volumes are bound in leather with gold type, and they measure 25 cm x 20 cm. Private collection.
8. In *H. C. Andersen og hans nærmeste Omgang* Rigmor Stampe discusses the first volume of Edvard Collin's song book, which goes up to 1857; she quotes from both the songs and Edvard Collin's comments (Copenhagen, 1918, pp. 211-63). Copies of Adolph Drewsen: "Familieviser. 1847" and "Viser m.m. til den Collinske Familie," which contain songs through the years by Edvard Collin, H. C. Andersen and other family members can be found at The Royal Library (Ms.micro 2826 / Ms.micro 2849). Also in The Royal Library are Edvard Collin: "To Hæfter med Afskrifter" (Den Collinske Samling 119,4°) and "Edvard Collins Familieviser" (120.4°). See also Jørgen Skjerk's numerous transcriptions of these songs in, for example: *H. C. Andersens Collinske Fødselsdagsviser* (Aarhus, 1983), *H. C. Andersen. En rest fra Drewsens visebog* (Aarhus, 1988), and *H. C. Andersen og Edvard Collin* (Aarhus, 1985).
9. *Familie Viser Skrevne af Edvard Collin I–II*, private collection, Vol. 1, No. 66.
10. Ibid., Vol. 2, No. 123.
11. Ibid., Vol. 1, No. 60.
12. *Adolph Drewsens Visebog*, The Royal Library, Ms.micro No. 2849.
13. July 4, 1874. *H. C. Andersens Brevveksling med Edvard og Henriette Collin*, Vol. 4, Copenhagen, 1936, pp. 295-96.
14. June 19, 1871. Ibid., pp. 178-79.
15. December 4, 1869. Ibid., p. 115.
16. January 1, 1865. *H. C. Andersens dagbøger*, Vol. 6, Copenhagen, 1995-96, pp. 174-75.
17. April 7, 1864. Ibid., p. 35.
18. New Year's 1866. *H. C. Andersens Brevveksling med Edvard og Henriette Collin*, Vol. III, Copenhagen, 1936, pp. 360-61.

19. Hans Christian Andersen: "Paa Ungdommens friske Rosenblad." Verse-vignette printed as introduction to Robert Watt: *Igjennem Europa. Reisenotitser*, Copenhagen, 1866.

20. March 2-3, 1864. *H. C. Andersens dagbøger*, Vol. 6, Copenhagen, 1995-96, p. 20.

21. Hans Christian Andersen: *Da Spanierne var her*, in *Samlede Skrifter*, Vol. 32, Copenhagen, 1876.

22. February 29, 1864. *H. C. Andersens dagbøger*, Vol. 6, Copenhagen, 1995-96, p. 19.

23. Hans Christian Andersen: *Kun en Spillemand*, in *Romaner og Rejseskildringer*, Vol. 3, Copenhagen, 1944, p. 66.

24. Ibid., p. 225.

25. Hans Christian Andersen: *Ahasverus*, in *Samlede Skrifter*, Vol. 17, Copenhagen, 1855, p. 134.

26. Ibid., p. 135.

27. For example, William Bloch: *Paa Rejse med H. C. Andersen*, Copenhagen, 1941; Nicolai Bøgh: *"Velkommen til en lykkelig Reise." Paa Rejse med H. C. Andersen 1873*, Copenhagen, 1998; and *H. C. Andersen og Jonas Collin den yngre. En brevveksling 1855–1875*, Copenhagen, 2001.

28. Hans Christian Andersen: "Til Jonas Collin," Stambogsblade XI, *Samlede Skrifter*, Vol. 33, Copenhagen, 1879, p. 77.

29. Hans Christian Andersen: *Paa Langebro*, in *Samlede Skrifter*, Vol. 31, Copenhagen, 1876, p. 140.

30. August 20, 1861. *H. C. Andersens dagbøger*, Vol. 5, Copenhagen, 1995-96, pp. 112-13.

31. Jonas Collin (ed.): *H. C. Andersens sidste Leveaar*, Copenhagen, 1906, p. 45.

32. Jonas Collin: "Litteraire og Naturvidenskabelige Opsatser," The Royal Library, Den Collinske Samling 121,4°.

33. August 25, 1861. *H. C. Andersens Brevveksling med Edvard og Henriette Collin*, Vol. 3, Copenhagen, 1936, p. 59.

34. June 2, 1870. *H. C. Andersen og Jonas Collin den yngre. En brevveksling 1855–1875*, Copenhagen, 2001, p. 168.

35. Hans Christian Andersen: *I Spanien*, in *Romaner og Rejseskildringer*, Vol. 7, Copenhagen, 1944, p. 309.

36. Ibid., p. 219.

37. September 12-13, 1862. *H. C. Andersens dagbøger*, Vol. 5, Copenhagen, 1995-96, pp. 218-19.

38. November 2, 1862: "In the garden three holes had been dug for the purpose; there Jonas and I sat in the moonlight beneath a laurel tree and did what we could; it was a strange privy." *H. C. Andersens dagbøger*, Vol. 5, Copenhagen, 1995-96, p. 280.

39. Hans Christian Andersen: *I Spanien*, in *Romaner og Rejseskildringer*, Vol. 7, Copenhagen, 1944, p. 218.

40. November 25, 1863. *H. C. Andersens dagbøger*, Vol. 5, Copenhagen, 1995-96, p. 434.

41. November 17, 1863. Ibid., p. 429.

42. Hans Christian Andersen: *I Spanien*, in *Romaner og Rejseskildringer*, Vol. 7, Copenhagen, 1944, p. 205.

43. Ibid., p. 199.

44. December 5, 1862. *H. C. Andersens dagbøger*, Vol. 5, Copenhagen, 1995-96, p. 318.

45. August 24, 1862. Ibid., pp. 204-05.

46. September 17, 1862. Ibid., pp. 225-26.

47. March 28, 1862. Ibid., p. 378.

48. December 20, 1863. Ibid., p. 451.

49. P. Helveg Jespersen: "Da H. C. Andersen samlede Snegle til Jonas Collin," *Dyr i Natur og Museum. Aarbog for Universitetets zoologiske Museum*, 1945-46, pp. 87-105.

50. April 23, 1861. *H. C. Andersens Brevveksling med Edvard og Henriette Collin*, Vol. 3, Copenhagen, 1936, p. 7.
51. November 29, 1869. Ibid., Vol. 4, Copenhagen, 1936, pp. 112-13.
52. December 23, 1869. *H. C. Andersen og Jonas Collin den yngre. En brevveksling 1855–1875*, Copenhagen, 2001, p. 159.
53. January 3, 1870. Ibid., p. 163.
54. December 30, 1863. Ibid., p. 115.
55. Jonas Collin (ed.): *H. C. Andersens sidste Leveaar*, Copenhagen, 1906, p. 49.
56. March 1, 1870. Ibid..
57. November 7, 1871. *H. C. Andersen og Jonas Collin den yngre. En brevveksling 1855–1875*, Copenhagen, 2001, p. 182.
58. May 27, 1868. Ibid., p. 151.
59. June 18, 1870. Ibid., p. 172.
60. September 5, 1867. *H. C. Andersens dagbøger*, Vol. 7, Copenhagen, 1995-96, p. 341.
61. Hans Christian Andersen: *Paa Langebro*, in *Samlede Skrifter*, Vol. 31, Copenhagen, 1876, p. 61.
62. April 26, 1863. *H. C. Andersen og Jonas Collin den yngre. En brevveksling 1855–1875*, Copenhagen, 2001, pp. 88-89.
63. December 29, 1861. Ibid., p. 49.
64. January 2, 1862. *H. C. Andersens dagbøger*, Vol. 5, Copenhagen, 1995-96, p. 141.
65. P. Hansen: *Den danske Skueplads*, Vol. 3, Copenhagen, 1891-96.
66. February 13, 1862. *H. C. Andersens dagbøger*, Vol. 5, Copenhagen, 1995-96, p. 147.
67. February 17, 1862. Ibid., p. 148.
68. November 18, 1869. *H. C. Andersens Brevveksling med Edvard og Henriette Collin*, Vol. 4, Copenhagen, 1936, p. 109.
69. March 5, 1862. *H. C. Andersens dagbøger*, Vol. 5, Copenhagen, 1995-96, p. 154.
70. March 6, 1862. Ibid.
71. August 27, 1863. *H. C. Andersens dagbøger*, Vol. 5, Copenhagen, 1995-96, p. 413.
72. July 27, 1864. Ibid., Vol. 6, p. 99.
73. It was August Bournonville who, in the 1857-58 season, obtained the first three-year contracts on the national stage for both Scharff and Juliette Prices. Elith Reumert: *Den danske Ballets Historie*, Copenhagen, 1922, p. 92.
74. November 7, 1871. *H. C. Andersen og Jonas Collin den yngre. En brevveksling 1855–1875*, Copenhagen, 2001, p. 183.
75. January 12, 1873. *H. C. Andersens dagbøger*, Vol. 10, Copenhagen, 1995-96, p. 7.
76. June 10, 1842. Hans Christian Andersen in a letter to Bernhard Cronholm. Quoted from Alfred B. Nilson: "H. C. Andersen och studentlifvet i Lund på 1840-talet," *EDDA*, 1926.
77. April 7, 1856. *H. C. Andersens breve til Fru Henriette Sophie B. E. Scavenius, født Moltke*, Odense Bys Museer.
78. August 13, 1850. *H. C. Andersens dagbøger*, Vol. 3, Copenhagen, 1995-96, pp. 425-26.
79. June 24, 1847. Ibid., p. 206.
80. December 4, 1840. Ibid., Vol. 2, p. 72.
81. September 15, 1836. Bille and Bøgh: *Breve fra Hans Christian Andersen*, Vol. 1, Copenhagen, 1878, p. 350.
82. December 5, 1833. Ibid., p. 165.
83. Hans Christian Andersen: *Skyggebilleder*, Copenhagen, 1986, p. 11.
84. April 30, 1866. *H. C. Andersens Brevveksling med Edvard og Henriette Collin*, Vol. 3, Copenhagen, 1936, p. 294.

85. Hans Christian Andersen: *Et besøg i Portugal*, Copenhagen, 1968, p. 86.

86. April 26, 1866. *H. C. Andersens Brevveksling med Edvard og Henriette Collin*, Vol. 3, Copenhagen, 1936, p. 292.

87. Hans Christian Andersen: *Mit Livs Eventyr*, in *Samlede Skrifter*, Vol. 34, Copenhagen, 1877, p. 148.

88. July 26 and 28, 1866. *H. C. Andersens dagbøger*, Vol. 7, Copenhagen, 1995-96, pp. 149, p. 151.

89. August 7, 1866. *H. C. Andersens Brevveksling med Edvard og Henriette Collin*, Vol. 3, Copenhagen, 1936, p. 331.

90. June 20, 1866. Quoted from Thelma Hanson: "Några minnesanteckningar om H. C. Andersen i Portugal av Adelaïde C. O'Neill," *Anderseniana*, 1969, p. 442.

91. August 30, 1866. *H. C. Andersens dagbøger*, Vol. 7, Copenhagen, 1995-96, p. 179.

92. August 31, 1866. Ibid., p. 179.

93. May 5, 1866. Ibid., p. 103.

94. July 10-11, 1866. Ibid., p. 138.

95. July 12, 1866. Ibid., p. 139.

96. *Ordbog over det danske Sprog*, Vol. 2, Copenhagen, 1975, column 1269-70.

97. February 26, 1834. *H. C. Andersens dagbøger*, Vol. 1, Copenhagen, 1995-96, p. 329.

98. Hans Christian Andersen: Paris. "Smaavers," *Samlede Skrifter*, Vol. 33, Copenhagen, 1879, p. 43.

99. May 5, 1867. *H. C. Andersens dagbøger*, Vol. 7, Copenhagen, 1995-96, pp. 280-81.

100. Hans Christian Andersen: *At være eller ikke være*, Copenhagen, 2001, p. 118.

101. April 30, 1867. *H. C. Andersens dagbøger*, Vol. 7, Copenhagen, 1995-96, p. 276.

CHAPTER 10

1.   The decor of Hans Christian Andersen's last apartment at Nyhavn 18 is described by Axel Bolvig in "H. C. Andersen som indretningskunstner" (*Politiken*, October 27, 1966) and Axel Bolvig in "Det gamle Sygehuus" (*Anderseniana*, 1968, pp. 285-98). The furnishings are described by Svend Larsen in "H. C. Andersens jordiske gods" (*Anderseniana*, 1953, pp. 274-96).

2.   Hjalmar Hjorth Boyesen: "Erindringer om H. C. Andersen," *Illustreret Tidende Nr. 27*, Copenhagen, April 3, 1892, pp. 318-19.

3.   Hjalmar Hjorth Boyesen: *Essays on Scandinavian Literature*, New York, 1972, p. 155.

4.   *Nyt dansk Maanedsskrift*, Copenhagen, 1871, pp. 97-122, 247-67, 537-51.

5.   Hans Christian Andersen: "Det Utroligste," *Nyt dansk Maanedsskrift*, Vol. I, Copenhagen, 1871, pp. 49-52 (was published in October 1870).

6.   Hans Christian Andersen: "Tunge timer," *Samlede Skrifter*, Vol. 33, Copenhagen, 1879, pp. 36-37.

7.   Nicolai Bøgh: *Erindringer af og om Jens Adolf Jerichau*, Copenhagen, 1884, pp. 185-86.

8.   Hans Christian Andersen: "Loppen og Professoren," *H. C. Andersens Eventyr*, Vol. 5, Copenhagen, 1919, p. 282.

9.   March 8, 1873. *H. C. Andersens dagbøger*, Vol. 10, Copenhagen, 1995-96, p. 43.

10. Hans Christian Andersen: *Agnete Linds Billedbog I*, p. 119, Odense Bys Museer.

11. H. C. Andersen and Adolph Drewsen: *Astrid Stampes Billedbog*, Copenhagen, 2003, p. 104.

12. Ibid., p. 49.

13. Quoted from Erik Dal's Foreword and Afterword to H. C. Andersen and Adolph Drewsen: *Christines Billedbog*, Copenhagen, 1984, p. 260.

14.   *Astrid Stampes Billedbog*, Copenhagen, 2003, p. 129.
15.   *Agnete Linds Billedbog I*, pp. 24-25, Odense Bys Museer.
16.   *Agnete Linds Billedbog V*, p. 59, Ibid..
17.   *Agnete Linds Billedbog I*, p. 13, Ibid..
18.   Four of the five picture books for Agnete Lind are in the Hans Christian Andersens House in Odense. Rigmor Stampe's picture book is in a private collection in the United States, while the picture books belonging to Astrid Stampe and Christine Stampe have both been published in Denmark (*Astrid Stampes Billedbog*, Copenhagen, 2003; and *Christines Billedbog*, Copenhagen, 1984). See Karsten Eskildsen's Afterword to *Astrid Stampes Billedbog*, Copenhagen, 2003, pp. 400-03.
19.   May 23, 1853. Odense Bys Museer.
20.   *Astrid Stampes Billedbog*, Copenhagen, 2003, p. 120.
21.   Ibid., p. 95.
22.   Ibid., p. 88.
23.   Ibid., p. 120.
24.   Ibid., pp. 67, 36.
25.   April 20, 1873. *H. C. Andersens dagbøger*, Vol. 10, Copenhagen, 1995-96, p. 70.
26.   *Astrid Stampes Billedbog*, Copenhagen, 2003, p. 110.
27.   Ibid., p. 87.
28.   July 19, 1836. *H. C. Andersens Brevveksling med Edvard og Henriette Collin*, Vol. 1, Copenhagen, 1933, p. 258.
29.   Otto Zinck: *Fra mit Studenter- og Teater-Liv. Erindringer*, Copenhagen, 1906, pp. 26-28.
30.   *Christine Stampes Billedbog*, Copenhagen, 1984, pp. 128-29.
31.   Hans Christian Andersen: *Mit Livs Eventyr*, in *Samlede Skrifter*, Vol. 21, Copenhagen, 1855, p. 9.
32.   Edvard Lehmann: *Almueliv og eventyr*, Copenhagen, 1910, pp. 164-65.
33.   Troels Andersen: "H. C. Andersens skærmbrædt—en collage?" *Billedkunst* No. 1, 1966, pp. 30-38.
34.   June 26, 1836. *H. C. Andersen og Henriette Wulff. En brevveksling*, Vol. 1.
35.   September 24, 1833. *H. C. Andersens Brevveksling med Edvard og Henriette Collin*, Vol. 1, Copenhagen, 1933, p. 190.
36.   June 26, 1834. "Riborgs Broder. H. C. Andersens Brevveksling med Christian Voigt," *Anderseniana*, 1948, p. 164.
37.   Hans Christian Andersen: *Mit Livs Eventyr*, in *Samlede Skrifter*, Vol. 21-22, Copenhagen, 1855, p. 185.
38.   Rigmor Stampe: *H. C. Andersen og hans nærmeste Omgang*, Copenhagen, 1918, p. 178.
39.   July 15, 1835. *H. C. Andersens Brevveksling med Edvard og Henriette Collin*, Copenhagen, 1933, Vol. 1, p. 226.
40.   Hans Christian Andersen: *Mit Livs Eventyr*, in *Samlede Skrifter*, Vol. 21-22, Copenhagen, 1855, p. 140.
41.   February 19, 1834. *H. C. Andersens dagbøger*, Vol. 1, Copenhagen, 1995-96, p. 316.
42.   February 21, 1834. Ibid., p. 318.
43.   Hans Christian Andersen: *Improvisatoren*, in *Romaner og Rejseskildringer*, Copenhagen, 1943, p. 180.
44.   Ibid., p. 190.
45.   Ibid., p. 201.
46.   Ibid., p. 202.
47.   February 26, 1834. *H. C. Andersens dagbøger*, Vol. 1, Copenhagen, 1995-96, p. 328.
48.   April 20, 1834. Ibid., p. 401.

49. February 27, 1834. Ibid., p. 330.

50. May 16, 1846. Ibid., Vol. 3, p. 111.

51. William Bloch: "Om H. C. Andersen. Bidrag til Belysning af hans Personlighed," *Nær og Fjern* VIII, Copenhagen, 1878, p. 3.

52. Hans Christian Andersen: *I Vetturinens Vogn*, in *Samlede Skrifter*, Vol. 32, Copenhagen, 1876, p. 116.

53. Hans Christian Andersen: "En lille Flugt til Rom den 8de Marts 1835," *Samlede Skrifter*, Vol. 33, Copenhagen, 1879, p. 113.

54. April 24, 1877. Letter from Emil Hornemann to Edvard Collin, Odense Bys Museer.

55. Hans Christian Andersen: "Impromptuvise 19, April 1832. Emil Hornemanns fødselsdag," *En rest fra Drewsens visebog*, Copenhagen, 1988, p. 9.

56. Hans Christian Andersen: *At være eller ikke være*, Copenhagen, 2001, p. 189.

57. Hans Christian Andersen: *Kong Saul*, in *Samlede Skrifter*, Vol. 30, Copenhagen, 1876, p. 135.

58. Hans Christian Andersen: *Lykke-Peer*, Copenhagen, 2000, p. 48.

59. Hans Christian Andersen: *O.T.*, in *Romaner og Rejseskildringer*, Vol. 2, Copenhagen, 1943, p. 128.

60. Edvard Collin: *H. C. Andersen og det Collinske Hus*, Copenhagen, 1929, p. 313.

61. Ibid., p. 68.

62. July 10, 1864. *H. C. Andersens dagbøger*, Vol. 6, Copenhagen, 1995-96, p. 86.

63. Hans Christian Andersen: *Kun en Spillemand*, in *Romaner og Rejseskildringer*, Vol. 3, Copenhagen, 1944, pp. 278-79.

64. April 26, 1866 and May 1, 1866. *H. C. Andersens Brevveksling med Edvard og Henriette Collin*, Vol. 3, Copenhagen, 1936, pp. 292, 295.

65. Hans Christian Andersen: *O.T.*, in *Romaner og Rejseskildringer*, Vol. 2, Copenhagen, 1943, p. 15.

66. Hans Christian Andersen: *Kun en Spillemand*, in *Romaner og Rejseskildringer*, Vol. 3, Copenhagen, 1944, p. 64.

67. Hans Christian Andersen: *At være eller ikke være*, Copenhagen, 2001, p. 211.

68. Hans Christian Andersen: "En Historie," *H. C. Andersens Eventyr*, Vol. 2, Copenhagen, 1919, p. 318.

69. August 3, 1850. Bille and Bøgh: *Breve fra Hans Christian Andersen*, Vol. 2, Copenhagen, 1878, p. 247.

70. Hans Christian Andersen: *Maurerpigen*, in *Samlede Skrifter*, Vol. 13, Copenhagen, 1854, p. 40.

71. Hans Christian Andersen: *Brylluppet ved Como-Søen*, in *Samlede Skrifter*, Vol. 12, Copenhagen, 1854, p. 179.

72. May 19, 1831. *H. C. Andersens Brevveksling med Edvard og Henriette Collin*, Vol. 1, Copenhagen, 1933, p. 69.

73. Hans Christian Andersen: *Ahasverus*, in *Samlede Skrifter*, Vol. 17, Copenhagen, 1855, p. 124.

74. Hans Christian Andersen: *Eventyrdigterens hidtil utrykte danske stile III*, Copenhagen, 1999, pp. 55-56.

75. Ibid., p. 41.

76. Ibid., Vol. 2, p. 72.

77. Ibid., Vol. 3, p. 10.

78. Hans Christian Andersen: "Phantasistykke i min egen Maneer," *Samlede Skrifter*, Vol. 15, Copenhagen, 1854, p. 94.

79. Quoted from Nicolai Bøgh: "Fra H. C. Andersens Barndoms- og Ungdomsliv," *Personalhistorisk Tidsskrift*, 1905, p. 79.

80. Hans Christian Andersen: "Odense," *Samlede Skrifter*, Vol. 33, Copenhagen, 1879, p. 33.

81. Hans Christian Andersen: *Mit Livs Eventyr*, in *Samlede Skrifter*, Vol. 21, Copenhagen, 1855, pp. 92-93.

82. Hans Christian Andersen: "Sneedronningen," *H. C. Andersens Eventyr*, Vol. 2, Copenhagen, 1919, p. 126.

83. Hans Christian Andersen: *Han er ikke født*, in *Samlede Skrifter*, Vol. 31, Copenhagen, 1876, p. 162.

84. Hans Christian Andersen: "Engelen," *H. C. Andersens Eventyr*, Vol. 2, Copenhagen, 1919, p. 28.

85. Hans Christian Andersen: "Tante Tandpine," *H. C. Andersens Eventyr*, Vol. 5, Copenhagen, 1919, p. 361.

86. Hans Christian Andersen: *At være eller ikke være*, Copenhagen, 2001, p. 99.

87. Hans Christian Andersen: "Fru Conferentsraadinde Collin født Hornemann," *Samlede Skrifter*, Vol. 16, Copenhagen, 1854, p. 188.

88. Villiam Christian Walter (Hans Christian Andersen): *Ungdoms-Forsøg*, Copenhagen, 1956, p. 104.

89. Fritz L. Lauritzen: "Religionen i H. C. Andersens eventyr," *Dansk Teologisk Tidsskrift*, Copenhagen, 1950, p. 154.

90. Hans Christian Andersen: "En Historie," *H. C. Andersens Eventyr*, Vol. 2, Copenhagen, 1919, p. 323.

91. Hans Christian Andersen: *Kun en Spillemand*, in *Romaner og Rejseskildringer*, Vol. 3, Copenhagen, 1944, p. 29.

92. Hans Christian Andersen: *Skyggebilleder*, Copenhagen, 1986, p. 104.

93. Edvard Collin: *H. C. Andersen og det Collinske Hus*, Copenhagen, 1929, p. 309.

94. Hans Christian Andersen: *Kun en Spillemand*, in *Romaner og Rejseskildringer*, Vol.   3, Copenhagen, 1944, p. 267.

95. Hans Christian Andersen: "Paa den yderste Dag," *H. C. Andersens Eventyr*, Vol. 2, Copenhagen, 1919, p. 362.

96. Ibid.

97. December 15, 1873. *H. C. Andersens Brevveksling med Edvard og Henriette Collin*, Vol. 4, Copenhagen, 1936, p. 273.

98. Nicolai Bøgh: "Fra Andersens Barndoms- og Ungdomsliv," *Personalhistorisk Tidsskrift*, 1905, p. 59.

99. Nicolai Bøgh: "Uddrag af en Dagbog. Ført af – paa en Rejse sammen med H. C. Andersen 1873," *Julebogen XIV*, Copenhagen, 1915, pp. 51-71. Nicolai Bøgh: *"Velkommen til en lykkelig Rejse." På rejse med H. C. Andersen 1873*, Copenhagen, 1998.

100. Edmund Lobedanz: "Erindringer om H. C. Andersen," *Nutiden i Billeder og Text II*, Copenhagen, 1877, p. 188.

101. Erik Bøgh: "Erindringer om Forfatteren til 'Den grimme Ælling,'" *Udvalgte Feuilletoner ("Dit og Dat") fra 1875*, Copenhagen, 1876, p. 203.

102. Elisa Bøgh: *Frederik Bøgh. En Levnedsskildring*, Copenhagen, 1887, pp. 298, 356-57.

103. E. Lehmann: *Almueliv og Eventyr*, Copenhagen, 1910, p. 158.

104. Nicolai Bøgh: "H. C. Andersens sidste Dage," *Illustreret Tidende*, XVI 1874-75, pp. 452-53, 456, 464-65.

105. Hans Christian Andersen: Beregning til Udgifterne til en Rejse 1875. The Royal Library, Den Collinske Samling 8,4°.

106. December 10, 1863. *H. C. Andersens dagbøger*, Vol. 5, Copenhagen, 1995-96, p. 440.

107. May 31, 1875. Ibid., Vol. 10. p. 455.

108. August Bournonville: *Mit Teaterliv*, Vol. III, Copenhagen, 1877, p. 253.

109. December 18, 1874. *H. C. Andersens dagbøger,*Vol. 10, Copenhagen, 1995-96, p. 374.

110. Edmund Lobedanz: "Erindringer om H. C. Andersen," *Nutiden i Billeder og Text II,* Copenhagen, 1877, pp. 181, 188.

111. May 5, 1875. *H. C. Andersens dagbøger,*Vol. 10, Copenhagen, 1995-96, p. 443.

112. Nicolai Bøgh: *Moritz G. Melchior. 22. Juni 1816–1 9. September 1884,* Copenhagen, 1885, pp. 15-20.

113. Axelline Lund: "Erindringer om H. C. Andersen," *Husmoderens Blad* X, Copenhagen, 1905, p. 111.

114. July 29, 1875. *H. C. Andersens dagbøger,*Vol. 10, Copenhagen, 1995-96, p. 480.

115. "H. C. Andersens Yndling fortæller om Digteren. Samtale med Frøken Melchior," *Aarhus Stiftstidende,* April 2, 1930.

116. *Berlingske Tidende,* August 11, 1875.

117. Ibid.

118. William Bloch: *Paa Rejse med H. C. Andersen,* Copenhagen, 1942, p. 93.

119. Hans Christian Andersen: "Psalme," *Samlede Skrifter,*Vol. 16, Copenhagen, 1854, pp. 196-97.

120. Johan de Mylius: "Var han ikke en stor Mand, saa var han dog en berømt Mand," *Anderseniana,* 2000, p. 15.

121. January 1, 1867. *H. C. Andersens Brevveksling med Edvard og Henriette Collin,* Vol. 4, Copenhagen, 1936, pp. 1-2.

122. June 22, 1875. Ibid., p. 327.

123. July 13, 1875. Ibid., p. 328.

124. Hans Christian Andersen: "En Digters sidste Sang," verse 2, *Samlede Skrifter,*Vol. 16, Copenhagen, 1854, p. 198.

Bibliography

PRIMARY SOURCES
Hans Christian Andersen's literary works, diaries, letters, manuscripts, and drafts.

REFERENCES
Samlede Skrifter, First edition, Vol. 1-33, Copenhagen, 1853-79.

H. C. Andersens Eventyr, Vol. 1-5, edited, with notes, by Hans Brix and Anker Jensen, Copenhagen, 1919.

Romaner og Rejseskildringer, Bind 1-7, published by DSL, ed. H. Topsøe-Jensen, Copenhagen, 1943-44.

Hr. Rasmussen. Originalt Lystspil i to Acter, ed. E. Agerholm, Copenhagen, 1913.

H. C. Andersens Levnedsbog. Digterens Liv 1805–1831, ed. Hans Brix, Copenhagen, 1926.

Mit eget Eventyr uden Digtning, ed. H. Topsøe-Jensen, Copenhagen, 1942.

Walter, Villiam Christian (pseudonym for Hans Christian Andersen): *Ungdoms-Forsøg*, Copenhagen, 1956.

VARIOUS ANTHOLOGIES AND COLLECTIONS
OF THE WORKS OF HANS CHRISTIAN ANDERSEN

H. C. Andersens Optegnelsesbog, ed. Julius Clausen, Copenhagen, 1926.

"Fra en Digters Værksted. H. C. Andersens Optegnelsesbøger," ed. H. Topsøe-Jensen. Reprint from *Fund og Forskning*, Copenhagen, 1962.

Slagelse-Digte, ed. Jørgen Skjerk, Århus, 1974.

Bouts rimés, ed. Jørgen Skjerk, Århus, 1974.

H. C. Andersen som hjemme-digter, ed. Jørgen Skjerk, Århus, 1977.

Fra Rim-Smedjen, ed. Jørgen Skjerk, Århus, 1981.

H. C. Andersen som hus-poet, ed. Jørgen Skjerk, Århus, 1981.

H. C. Andersens Collinske Fødselsdagsviser, ed. Jørgen Skjerk, Århus, 1983.

H. C. Andersen og Edvard Collin. Nogle hidtil utrykte viser m.m., ed. Jørgen Skjerk, Århus, 1985.

H. C. Andersen og Henriette Collin den ældre, ed. Jørgen Skjerk, Århus, 1986.

H. C. Andersen og Ingeborg Drewsen, f. Collin, ed. Jørgen Skjerk, Århus, 1987.

"Amors og Digterens Luner" og "Sangerinden," ed. Jørgen Skjerk, Århus, 1987.

En rest fra Drewsens visebog, ed. Jørgen Skjerk, Århus, 1988.

"Fy" eller "de heldige Sennopsblade." En børnekomedie, ed. Jørgen Skjerk, Århus, 1988.
En rest vers fra Nicolai Bøghs protokol samt tre danske stile, ed. Jørgen Skjerk, Århus, 1988.
"Horace Vernets Maleri." Et Tableau, ed. Jørgen Skjerk, Århus, 1992.
Eventyrdigterens "Tryllefløjten"—udkast, ed. Jørgen Skjerk, Copenhagen, 1997.
Eventyrdigterens Prologer og Epiloger, ed. Jørgen Skjerk, Copenhagen, 1998.
Den skjønne Grammatica, ed. Jørgen Skjerk, Copenhagen, 1999.
Eventyrdigterens hidtil utrykte danske stile I–III, selected by Jørgen Skjerk, Copenhagen, 1999.
Skovcapellet. Det hidtil utrykte sørgespil fra 1821, ed. Jørgen Skjerk, Copenhagen, 2000.
Samlede digte, ed. Johan de Mylius, Copenhagen, 2000.
Eventyrdigterens studenterkomedier samt "I Maaneskin," ed. Jørgen Skjerk, Copenhagen, 2001.
Digte der ikke kom med i eventyrdigterens "Samlede Skrifter," ed. Jørgen Skjerk, Copenhagen, 2003.

PICTURE BOOKS AND ALBUMS

H. C. Andersens tegninger til Otto Zinck, Vol. 1-2, ed. Kjeld Heltoft, Odense, 1972.
H. C. Andersens Album I-V, ed. K. Olsen, H.V. Lauridsen, and K. Weber, Copenhagen, 1980.
Christines Billedbog, ed. Erik Dal, Copenhagen, 1984.
Astrid Stampes Billedbog, ed. Karsten Eskildsen, Copenhagen, 2003.

LETTERS

Breve til Hans Christian Andersen, ed. C. St. A. Bille and N. Bøgh, Copenhagen, 1877.
Breve fra Hans Christian Andersen, Vol. 1-2, ed. C. St. A. Bille and N. Bøgh, Copenhagen, 1878.
H. C. Andersens Breve til Therese og Martin R. Henriques 1860–75, ed. H. Topsøe-Jensen, Copenhagen, 1932.
H. C. Andersen og det Melchiorske Hjem. En Brevveksling, ed. Elith Reumert, Copenhagen, 1925.
H. C. Andersens Brevveksling med Edvard og Henriette Collin 1828–75, Vol. 1-6, ed. C. Behrend and H. Topsøe-Jensen, Copenhagen, 1933-37.
"H. C. Andersens Brevveksling med Henriette Hanck 1830-1846," by Svend Larsen, *Anderseniana* IX-XIII, 1941-46.
H. C. Andersens Brevveksling med Jonas Collin den Ældre og andre Medlemmer af det Collinske Hus, Vol.1-3, ed. H. Topsøe-Jensen, Copenhagen, 1945-48.
"Riborgs Broder. H. C. Andersens Bevveksling med Christian Voigt," by Th. A. Müller and H. Topsøe-Jensen, Reprint from *Anderseniana*, 1948.
H. C. Andersen og Horace E. Scudder. En Brevveksling, ed. Jean Hersholt, Copenhagen, 1948.
H. C. Andersen og Henriette Wulff. En brevveksling, Vol. 1-3, ed. H. Topsøe-Jensen, Odense, 1959.
H. C. Andersens breve til Mathias Weber, published by The Hans Christian Andersen Society, ed. Arne Portman, Copenhagen, 1961.
H. C. Andersens breve til Carl B. Lorck, published by Odense City Museums, ed. H. Topsøe-Jensen, Odense, 1969.
"H. C. Andersens breve til Robert Watt 1865-74," ed. H. Topsøe-Jensen, in *Fund og Forskning*, 1971-72.
H. C. Andersens brevveksling med Lucie & B. S. Ingemann, Vol. 1-3, ed. Kirsten Dreyer, Copenhagen, 1997.

"Mein edler, theurer Grossherzog!" Briefwechsel zwischen Hans Christian Andersen und Grossherzog Carl Alexander von Sachsen-Weimar-Eisenach, ed. Ivy York and Ernst Möller-Christensen, Göttingen, 1998.

H. C. Andersen og Jonas Collin den yngre. En brevveksling 1855–1875, ed. K. Dreyer, Copenhagen, 2001.

DIARIES AND CALENDARS

H. C. Andersens Dagbøger 1825–1875,Vol. 1–11, published by DSL under editorship of K. Olsen and H. Topsøe-Jensen, Copenhagen, 1971.

H. C. Andersens Almanakker 1833–1873, ed. H. V. Lauridsen and K. Weber, Copenhagen, 1990.

H. C. Andersens sidste Leveaar. Hans Dagbøger 1868–75, ed. Jonas Collin, Copenhagen, 1905.

SECONDARY SOURCES

Books, bibliographies, journals, indexes, dissertations, and major articles.

Anderseniana 1933-2002 (Complete table of contents for the years 1933-1998 can be found in *Anderseniana* 1999, published by Odense City Museums, ed. Einar Askgaard and S. B. Madsen, Odense, 1999.)

BIBLIOGRAPHIES

Jørgensen, Aage: *H. C. Andersen-Litteraturen 1875–1968*, Aarhus, 1970.
Jørgensen, Aage: *H. C. Andersen-litteraturen 1969–1994*, Odense, 1995.
Nielsen, Birger Frank: *H. C. Andersen Bibliografi*, Copenhagen, 1942.

Andreasen, Uffe: *Poul Møller og romantismen*, Copenhagen, 1973.
Askgaard, Einar: "Man gaaer først saa gruelig meget Ondt igjennem . . .—om H. C. Andersens slægt," *Fynske Minder*, Reprint, published by Odense City Museums, Odense, 2000.
Bang, J. P.: *H. C. Andersen og Georg Brandes, samt andre H. C. Andersen-Studier*, Copenhagen, 1936.
Bang, Ole: *Store Hans Christian: H. C. Ørsted 1777–1851*, Copenhagen, 1986.
Bencard, Mogens (ed.): *Krydsfelt. Ånd og natur i guldalderen*, Copenhagen, 2000.
Bloch, William: "Om H. C. Andersen. Bidrag til Belysning af hans Personlighed," *Nær og Fjern*,VIII, 1878-79.
  Paa Rejse med H. C. Andersen. Dagbogsoptegnelser, Copenhagen, 1942.
Boas, George: *The Cult of Childhood*, London, 1966.
Bohr, Niels: "Tale på hundredeårsdagen for H. C. Ørsteds død," *Fysisk Tidsskrift*, 1951.
Bournonville, August: *Mit Theaterliv*,Vol. 3, Copenhagen, 1877–78.
Boyesen, Hjalmar Hjorth: *Essays on Scandinavian Literature*, New York & London, 1895.
Brandes, Edvard: "H. C. Andersen. Personlighed og Værk," *Litterære Tendenser. Artikler og Anmeldelser*, Copenhagen, 1968.

Brandes, Georg: *Søren Kierkegaard. En kritisk Fremstilling i Grundrids*, Copenhagen, 1877.

Kritiker og Portræter, Copenhagen, 1885.

"Den romantiske Skole i Tyskland," *Hovedstrømninger i det 19de Aarhundredes Litteratur*, Copenhagen, 1891.

"Romanerne om Geniet," *Samlede Skrifter*, Vol. XVIII, Copenhagen, 1910.

Brandt, Frithiof: *Den unge Søren Kierkegaard. En række nye bidrag*, Copenhagen, 1929.

Bredsdorff, Elias: *H. C. Andersen og Charles Dickens. Et venskab og dets opløsning*, Copenhagen, 1951.

H. C. Andersen og England, Copenhagen, 1954.

H. C. Andersen. Mennesket og Digteren, Copenhagen, 1979.

Breitenstein, Jørgen, et al.: *H. C. Andersen og hans kunst i nyt lys*, Odense, 1976.

Breum, Sophie (ed.): *Odense Bys Bog om H. C. Andersen*, Odense, 1905.

Brix, Hans: *H. C. Andersen og hans Eventyr*, Copenhagen, 1907.

Brostrøm, Torben and Lund, Jørn: *Flugten i sproget*, Copenhagen, 1991.

Brust, Beth Wagner: *The Amazing Paper Cuttings of Hans Christian Andersen*, Boston, 1994.

Brøgger Suzanne: "Skum eller Havhexens Opskrift," in *Den Lille Havfrue. H. C. Andersens eventyr fortolket i tekst og billeder*, Copenhagen, 1991.

Brøndsted, Mogens: *H. C. Andersen og avisen*, Odense, 1972.

Bøgh, Nicolai: "Fra H. C. Andersens Barndoms- og Ungdomsliv," *Personalhistorisk Tidsskrift*, 1905.

"H. C. Andersens sidste Dage," *Illustreret Tidende*, XVI, 1874–75.

Bøgh, Nikolai: *"Velkommen til en lykkelig Reise." På rejse med H. C. Andersen 1873*, Copenhagen, 1998.

Böök Fredrik: *H. C. Andersen*, Copenhagen, 1939.

Christensen, Erik M.: "H. C. Ørsteds optimistiske dualisme," *Guldalderstudier. Festskrift til Gustav Albeck*, Copenhagen, 1966, pp. 11–46.

Collin, Edvard: *H. C. Andersen og det Collinske Hus*, Copenhagen, 1882.

Coveney, Peter: *The Image of Childhood*, London, 1967.

Delcourt, Marie: *Hermaphrodite. Myths and Rites of the bisexuel Figure in classical Antiquity*, London, 1961.

Deren, Coke van: *The Painter and the Photograph—from Delacroix to Warhol*, Albuquerque, 1972.

Detering, Heinrich: *Åndelige amfibier: Homoerotisk camouflage i H. C. Andersens forfatterskab*, Odense, 1991.

Dreslov, Aksel: *H. C. Andersen og denne Albert Hansen*, Copenhagen, 1977.

Duus, Jørgen: *Silhuetter. Skygger påa væggen*, Copenhagen, 1998.

Duve, Arne: *Symbolikken i H. C. Andersens eventyr*, Oslo, 1967.

Enquist, Per Olov: *Fra regnormenes liv*, Copenhagen, 1981.

Friedell, Egon: *Kulturhistorie III. Romantik og liberalisme. Imperialisme og impressionisme*, Copenhagen, 1978.

Friedrichsmeyer, Sara: *The Androgyne in Early German Romanticism*, 1983.

Galster, Kjeld: *H. C.: Andersen og hans rektor*, Kolding, 1933.

Galster, Kjeld: *Simon Meisling—H. C. Andersens Rektor*, (in *Vor Ungdom*, 1932–33).

Garff, Joakim: *SAK*, Copenhagen, 2001.

Gjelten, Bente Hatting: *H. C. Andersen som teaterconnaisseur*, Copenhagen, 1982.

Goodenough, Heberle and Sokoloff (eds.): *Infant Tongues: The Voice of the Child in Literature*, Detroit, 1994.

Gelsted, Otto: *Den græske tanke*, Copenhagen, 1958.

Gosse, Edmund: *To Besøg i Danmark*, Copenhagen, 2001.

Grønbech, Bo: *H. C. Andersen. Levnedsløb—Digtning—Personlighed*, Copenhagen, 1971.

Handesten, Lars: *Litterære rejser*, Copenhagen, 1992.

Hansen, Claes Kastholm: *Den kontrollerede virkelighed. Virkelighedsproblemet i den litterære kritik og den nye danske roman i perioden 1830–1840*, Copenhagen, 1976.

Hedegaard, Ole A.: *Fornedrelsens år. H. C. Andersen og Helsingør 1826–27* (1981).

Helweg, Hjalmar: *H. C. Andersen. En psykiatrisk Studie*, Copenhagen, 1927.

Hekma, Gert: "Sodomites, Platonic Lovers, Contrary Lovers: The Backgrounds of the Modern Homosexual," *Journal of Homosexuality*, Vol. 16, New York, 1988.

Henriksen, Aage (ed.): *Ideologihistorie I. Organismetænkningen i dansk litteratur 1770–1870*, Copenhagen, 1975.

Heltoft, Kjeld: *H. C. Andersens Billedkunst*, Copenhagen, 1969.

Hetsch, Gustav: *H. C. Andersen og Musiken*, Copenhagen, 1930.

Holbeck, H. St.: *H. C. Andersens Religion*, Copenhagen, 1947.

Holm, Kjeld (et al.): *Søren Kierkegaard og romantikerne*, Copenhagen, 1974.

Hude, Elisabeth: *Henriette Hanck og H. C. Andersen. Skribentinden og digteren*, Odense, 1958.

Fredrika Bremer og hendes venskab med H. C. Andersen og andre danske, Copenhagen, 1972.

Høeg, Tage: *H. C. Andersens Ungdom*, Copenhagen, 1934.

Jacobsen, Hans Henrik: *H. C. Andersen på Fyn 1819–75*, Odense, 1968.

Johansson, Ejner: *Andersens ansigter*, Copenhagen, 1992.

Jørgensen, Jens: *H. C. Andersen. En sand myte*, Århus, 1987.

Jørgensen, Johannes: "H. C. Andersen," *Essays*, Copenhagen, 1906.

Karlsen, Marianne Berg: *"I venskabs paradiis": en studie i maskulinitet og vennskap mellem menn med udgangspunkt i Conrad N. Schwach og Maurits C. Hansen 1814–1842*, thesis in history, Oslo, 1999.

Kierkegaard, Søren: "Af en endnu Levendes Papirer," *Samlede Værker*, XIII, Copenhagen, 1906.

Kjær, Grethe: *Barndommens ulykkelige elsker. Kierkegaard om barnet og barndommen*, Copenhagen, 1986.

Eventyrets verden i Kierkegaards forfatterskab, Copenhagen, 1991.

Kjølbye, Bente: *Kærlighedens mange ansigter. H. C. Andersen, Jenny Lind og Felix Mendelssohn-Bartholdy*, Copenhagen, 2002.

Kofoed, Niels: *Studier i H. C. Andersens fortællekunst*, Århus, 1967.

H. C. Andersen og B. S. Ingemann. Et livsvarigt venskab, Copenhagen, 1992.

H. C. Andersen—den store europæer, Copenhagen, 1996.

Kuhn, Reinhard: *Corruption in Paradise: The Child in Western Literature*, Hannover & London, 1982.

Kyrre, Hans: *Knud Lyne Rahbek, Kamma Rahbek og Livet paa Bakkehuset*, Copenhagen, 1929.

Langdal Møller, Kr.: *H. C. Andersen. Strejflys over hans liv og digtning*, Helsingør, 1968.

Larsen, Svend and Topsøe-Jensen, H. (texts and selection of illustrations): *H. C. Andersens eget Eventyr i Billeder*, Copenhagen, 1952.

Larsen, Svend and Topsøe-Jensen, H. (eds.): *H. C. Andersen. Mennesket og Digteren*, Odense, 1955.

Larsen, Svend (ed.): *H. C. Andersens moder. En brevsamling*, Odense, 1947.

Larsen, Karl: *H. C. Andersen i Tekst og Billeder*, Copenhagen, 1925.

Lassen, Erik: *H. C. Andersen og herregårdene*, Copenhagen, 1993.

H. C. Andersen og de kongelige, Copenhagen, 1996.

Laurin, Carl G.: *Barnet i liv och kunst*, Stockholm, 1938.

Lauring, Palle: *H. C. Andersens Kors*, Copenhagen, 1981.

Lederer, Wolfang: *The Kiss of the Snow Queen: Hans Christian Andersen and Man's Redemption by Woman*, Los Angeles & Oxford, 1986.

Lehmann, Edvard: *Almueliv og eventyr*, Copenhagen, 1910.

Lilleør, Katrine: *Det guddommelige Eventyr.* Fønix,Vol. 15, 1991, pp.53-65.

Lloyd, Rosemary: *The Land of Lost Content: Children and Childhood in Nineteenth-Century French Literature*, Oxford, 1992.

Lobedanz, Edmund: "Erindringer om H. C. Andersen," *Nutiden i Billeder og Text*, II, 1877–78.

Lund, Ole: *Smaabilleder fra Helsingør 1800–1830*, Copenhagen, 1900.

Mellemgaard, Signe: *Kroppens natur. Sundhedsoplysning og naturidealer i 250 år*, Copenhagen, 1998.

Mortensen, Finn Hauberg:"I familiens skød," *Andersen og verden*, Odense, 1993, pp. 115-30.

Mortensen, Klaus P.: *Svanen og Skyggen—historien om unge Andersen*, Copenhagen, 1989.

Johan Thomas Lundbyes kærlighed, Copenhagen, 2000.

Mylius, Johan de: *Myte og roman. H. C. Andersens romaner mellem romantik og realisme*, Copenhagen, 1981.

Naturens stemme i H. C. Andersens eventyr, Odense, 1989.

H. C. Andersen—Papirklip, Copenhagen, 1992.

H. C. Andersen. Liv og værk. En tidstavle 1805–75, Copenhagen, 1993.

H. C. Andersens liv. Dag for dag, Copenhagen, 1998.

Mylius/Jørgensen/Pedersen (eds.): *"Andersen og Verden." Indlæg fra den første internationale H. C. Andersen-konference*, Odense, 1993.

Møllehave, Johannes: *H. C. Andersens salt*, Copenhagen, 1985.

Lystig og ligefrem. Andersens alitterationer, Copenhagen, 1995.

Møller, P. L.: *Kritiske Skizzer fra Aarene 1840–47*, Copenhagen, 1847.

Möller-Christensen, Ivy York: *Den gyldne trekant. H. C. Andersens gennembrud i Tyskland 1831–1850*, Odense, 1992.

Nelson, T. G. A: *Children, Parents and the Rise of the Novel*, Newark, 1995.

Nielsen, Erling: *H. C. Andersen*, Oslo, 1962.

Nyborg, Eigil: *Den indre linie i H. C. Andersens eventyr. En psykologisk studie*, Copenhagen, 1962.

Nygaard, Georg: *H. C. Andersen og København*, Copenhagen, 1938.

Nyström, Anker: *Om Homoseksualitet og Hermafroditisme*, Copenhagen, 1920.

Ochsner, Bjørn: *Fotografier af H. C. Andersen*, Odense, 1957.

Olrik, H. G.: *H. C. Andersen. Undersøgelser og Kronikker 1925–1944*, Copenhagen, 1945.

Oxenvad, Niels: *H. C. Andersen. Et liv i billeder*, Copenhagen, 1995.

Paludan, Helge (et al.): *Københavnernes historie. Fra Absalon til Weidekamp*, Copenhagen, 1987.

Poulsen, Henrik G.: *Det rette udseende. Fotografernes H. C. Andersen*, Copenhagen, 1996.

Prince, Aliston: *Hans Christian Andersen. The Fan Dancer*, London, 1998.

Reumert, Elith: *H. C. Andersen som han var*, Copenhagen, 1925.

Ringblom Hilding: *H. C. Andersen og trådene til Grundtvig,* Them, 1986.

Rosen, Wilhelm von:"Venskabets mysterier," *Anderseniana*, 1980.

"En havfrue. Om H. C. Andersens forelskelser i mænd," *Politiken*, March 22, 1981.

"H. C. Andersens forelskelse i Ludvig Müller," *Kritik*, No. 73, Copenhagen, 1985.

Månens kulør. Studier i dansk bøssehistorie 1628–1912. Bd. I–II, (Vol. I, pp. 323-70), Copenhagen, 1993.

Rose, Jaqueline: *The Case of Peter Pan*, London, 1984.

Rosenblum, Robert: *The Romantic Child. From Runge to Sendak*, London, 1988.

Rubow, Paul V.: *H. C. Andersens Eventyr. Forhistorien—Idé og Form—Sprog og Stil*, Copenhagen, 1927.

Rue, Harald: *Litteratur og samfund*, Copenhagen, 1937.

"H. C. Andersen og Folket," *Tiden. Tidsskrift for aktivt Demokrati*, Copenhagen, 1947.

Scavenius, Bente (ed.): *Guldalderhistorier. 20 nærbilleder af perioden 1800–1850*, Copenhagen, 1994.

Guldalderens verden. 20 historier fra nær og fjern, Copenhagen, 1996.

Schwanenflügel, H.: *Hans Christian Andersen. Et Digterliv*, Copenhagen, 1905.

Smidt, Claus M. and Winge, Mette: *Hen over torv og gade. Mennesker og huse i Guldalderens København*, Copenhagen, 1996.

Spink, Reginald: *Hans Christian Andersen and his World*, London, 1972.

Stampe, Rigmor: *H. C. Andersen og hans nærmeste Omgang*, Copenhagen, 1918.

Svanholm, Chr.: *H. C. Andersens Ungdoms-Tro*, Trondheim, 1952.

Fra H. C. Andersens eventyrverden, Oslo, 1975.

Svendsen, Erik: "'Han duede ikke,' Om H. C. Andersen og biedermeier," *Anderseniana*, 1994, pp. 5–35.

Sørensen, Peer E.: *H. C. Andersen & Herskabet. Studier i borgerlig krisebevidsthed*, Århus, 1972.

Sørensen, Villy: *Digtere og dæmoner*, Copenhagen, 1959.

"De djævelske traumer. Om H. C. Andersens romaner," *Hverken—Eller. Kritiske betragtninger*, Copenhagen, 1961.

Thelle, Mette (ed.): *H. C. Andersen som billedkunstner*, Fyns Kunstmuseum, 1996.

Thiele, J. M.: *Af mit Livs Aarbøger 1795–1826*, Copenhagen, 1873.

Thiele, Kai H.: *En følsom rejsende. H. C. Andersen på Før*, Copenhagen, 1958.

Topsøe-Jensen, Helge: *Mit eget Eventyr uden Digtning. En Studie over H. C. Andersen som Selvbiograf*, Copenhagen, 1940.

Omkring Levnedsbogen. En Studie over H. C. Andersen som Selvbiograf 1820–1845, Copenhagen, 1943.

H. C. Andersen og andre Studier, Odense, 1966.

Buket til Andersen. Bemærkninger til femogtyve Eventyr, Copenhagen, 1971.

Vintergrønt. Nye H. C. Andersen Studier, Copenhagen, 1976.

Uldall, Jens Th.: *"Her løb jeg om med Træsko paa." Historien om H. C. Andersens eventyrlige barndom*, Odense, 2002.

Ulrichsen, Erik: *H. C. Andersen og Hjertetyven*, Copenhagen, 1991.

Uttenreiter, Poul: *H. C. Andersens Tegninger*, København & Flensborg, 1925.

Wad, G. L.: *Om Hans Christian Andersens Slægt*, Odense, 1905.

Wamberg, Bodil: *De er den jeg elsker højest—venskabet mellem H. C. Andersen og Edvard Collin*, Copenhagen, 1999.

Wamberg, Niels Birger: *H. C. Andersen og Heiberg*, Copenhagen, 1971.

Wanscher, Vilhelm: "H. C. Andersens Fortællekunst," *Liv og Kultur*, I, Copenhagen, 1907.

Weinreich, Torben (ed.): *Lyst og lærdom. Debat og forskning om børnelitteratur*, Copenhagen, 1996.

Winge, Mette and Niels D. Lund: *Litteraturens børn. Barndomsskildringer i dansk litteratur*, Copenhagen, 1994.

Woel, Cai M.: *H. C. Andersens Liv og Digtning*, Vol. 1-2, Copenhagen, 1950.

Wullschlager, Jackie: *H. C. Andersen. En biografi*, Copenhagen, 2000.

Ørsted, H. C.: *Aanden i Naturen*, Vol. 1-2, Copenhagen, 1850-51.

Ørsted, Mathilde (ed.): *Breve fra og til H. C. Ørsted 1–2*, Copenhagen, 1870.

SELECTED LIST OF WORKS BY HANS CHRISTIAN ANDERSEN
WITH ENGLISH TRANSLATIONS OF THE DANISH TITLES

Agnete og Havmanden	*Agnete and the Merman*
Ahasverus	*Ahasuerus*
Astrid Stampes Billedbog	*Astrid Stampe's Picture Book*
At være eller ikke være	*To Be or Not to Be*
Billedbog uden Billeder	*A Picture Book Without Pictures*
Bruden fra Lammermoor	*The Bride of Lammermoor*
Brylluppet ved Como-Søen	*The Wedding at Lake Como*
Christian den Andens Dverg	*Christian II's Dwarf*
Christines Billedbog	*Christine's Picture Book*
Da Spanierne var her	*When the Spaniards Were Here*
Das Märchen meines Lebens ohne Dichtung	*The True Story of my Life*
"De røde Skoe"	"The Red Shoes"
De to Baronesser	*The Two Baronesses*
"De vilde Svaner"	"The Wild Swans"
"Den flyvende Koffert"	"The Flying Trunk"
"Den grimme Ælling"	"The Ugly Duckling"
"Den lille Havfrue"	"The Little Mermaid"
"Den lille Idas Blomster"	"Little Ida's Flowers"
"Den lille Pige med Svovlstikkerne"	"The Little Match Girl"
"Den lykkelige Familie"	"The Happy Family"
"Den standhaftige Tinsoldat"	"The Steadfast Tin Soldier"
"Den store Søslange"	"The Great Sea Serpent"
"Den uartige Dreng"	"The Naughty Boy"
"Det døende Barn"	"The Dying Child"
"Det nye Aarhundredes Musa"	"The Muse of the New Century"
"Det Utroligste"	"The Most Incredible Thing"
"Drengen og Moderen paa Heden"	"The Boy and Mother on the Heath"
"Dryaden"	"The Wood Nymph"
"Dynd-Kongens Datter"	"The Marsh King's Daughter"
"Dødningen"	"The Ghost"
"Elverhøi"	"The Elf Mound"
En Comedie i det Grønne	*A Comedy in the Open*
En Digters Bazar	*A Poet's Bazaar*
"En Historie"	"A Story"
"Engelen"	"The Angel"
Et Besøg I Portugal	*A Visit to Portugal*
Eventyr, fortalte for Børn	*Fairy Tales, Told for Children*
Festen på Kenilworth	*The Banquet at Kenilworth*
"Flyttedagen"	"Moving Day"
Fodreise fra Holmens Canal til Østpynten af Amager i Aarene 1828 og 1829	*Walking Tour from Holmen's Canal to the Eastern Point of Amager in the Years 1828 and 1829*
"Gartneren og Herskabet"	"The Gardener and the Lord"
"Gjenfærdet ved Palnatokes Grav"	"The Apparition at Palnatoke's Grave"
"Grantræet"	"The Fir Tree"

Index

Illustration Credits

SECTION 1

1. Painting by J. F. Møller: "Giuseppe Siboni," 1829, Private collection.

2. H. C. Andersen's travel pass, *H. C. Andersen's Album*, The Royal Library.

3. Watercolor by H. G. F. Holm: "Parti af Kgs. Nytorv Ca. 1850," Copenhagen City Museum.

4. Paper-cut, theater set, Odense City Museums.

5. Copperplate by Johs. Britze, based on a drawing by Johannes Riepenhausen: "Adam Oehlenschläger," 1809, The Royal Library / Gyldendal Publishing Company.

6. Lithograph, "Jonas Collin den ældre," *H. C. Andersen's Album*, The Royal Library.

7. Collage, *Christine's Picture Book*, Silkeborg Art Museum.

8. Painting by unknown artist: "Simon S. Meisling," Odense City Museums.

9. Photo by Knackstedt & Co.: Bredegade in Slagelse, ca.1910, Slagelse Archives.

10. Painting by C. W. Eckersberg: "H. C. Ørsted," 1822, Denmark's Technical Museum, Helsingør.

11. Painting by J. P. Møller: "Udsigt over Kronborg, Helsingør og Sundet," 1825, Denmark's National Museum of Art.

12. Etching by C. F. Bartsch, 1850, based on a drawing by Heinrich Hansen: "Den collinske gård," Odense City Museums.

13. Photo of Riborg Voigt, Odense City Museums.

14. Painting by Adam Müller: "Henriette Wulff," 1827, Private collection.

15. Drawing by unknown artist: "Henriette Hanck," Odense City Museums.

16. Painting by Wilhelm Marstrand: "Louise Collin," 1833, Odense City Museums.

17. Drawing by Wilhelm Marstrand: "Edvard Collin," The Royal Library.

18. Collage, *Christine's Picture Book*, Silkeborg Art Museum.

19. Drawing, *Corsaren*, No. 364, September 10, 1847.

20. Paper-cuts of red windmill-man and a clown with tray on his head, Odense City Museums.

21. Lithograph by C. Barth: "Adelbert von Chamisso," Odense City Museums.

22. Drawing by Wilhelm Marstrand: "Søren Kierkegaard," ca. 1850. Otto Marstrand: *Maleren Wilhelm Marstrand*, Copenhagen, 2003.

23. Collage from *Christine's Picture Book*, Silkeborg Art Museum.

24. Lithograph based on a painting by David Monies, 1844. Henning Fenger: *Familjen Heiberg*, Copenhagen, 1992.

25. Etching based on a drawing by J. V. Gertner: "Christian Molbech," The Royal Library.

26. Lithgraphs by A. L Noël, based on paintings by Richard Lauchert: "Hertugfamilien," Stiftung Weimarer Klassik.

27. Paper-cut of the king and the poet, Graasten Slot 1845, The National History Museum at Frederiksborg Palace, Hillerød.

Section 2

28. Lithograph, based on a drawing by F. Richardt, 1845, Odense City Museums.

29, 30. Photos of the house on Hans Jensens Stræde and the house on Munkemøllestræde, Odense
City Museums,

31. Drawing of Odense, created in 1839 by N. F. Juel, The Royal Library.

32. Photo of Andersen's Honorary Citizen certificate, Odense City Museums.

33. Photo of the Ørsted family, 1849, Gyldendal Publishing Company.

34. Lithograph, "Maxen and its grounds," *H. C. Andersen's Album I-V*, The Royal Library.

35. Photo of Franz Liszt by F. von Hanfstengel, Private collection.

36. Collage from *Agnete Lind's Picture Book V*, Odense City Museums.

37. Engraving by G. Luderitz, based on Wilhelm von Kaulbach's painting "The Angel,"
Odense City Museums.

38. Photo of Gads Hill, Private collection.

39. Photo of Charles Dickens with his daughters Mammie and Katie, 1860–65, Elias Bredsdorff:
H. C. Andersen og Charles Dickens. Et Venskab og dets Opløsning, Copenhagen, 1951.

40. Photo of H. C. Andersen and Jonas Collin, the younger; Bordeaux, January 9, 1863,
Odense City Museums.

41, 42. Photos of Harald Scharff and Lauritz Eckardt, photographer J. Löwy (photo on left) and
photographer Motzfeldt (photo on right), 1860–63, The Royal Library.

43. Photo of traveling gear, Odense City Museums, Frederick P. Henry: "Reminiscences of
Hans Christian Andersen," *The General Magazine and Historical Chronicle XXXI*, p. 47–49, 1929.

44, 45. Photos by M. Verveer of Hans Christian Andersen, Den Haag, March 21, 1866,
Odense City Museums.

46, 47. Hans Christian Andersen's folding screen, with views of two panels from both sides,
Odense City Museums.

48. "Paper-cut by H. C. Andersen for Fru Melchior, née Henriques, 1874," Odense City Museums.

49. Paper-cut of a miniature rocking chair, Odense City Museums.

50. Lithograph of Holsteinborg, Odense City Museums.

51. Photo by Hansen, Schou and Weller of Hans Christian Andersen sitting at the window,
May 21, 1874, Odense City Museums. Nicolai Bøgh: "H. C. Andersens sidste Dage,"
Illustreret Tidende, August 22 and 29, 1875.

52, 53. Photos of Dorothea and Moritz G. Melchior, Odense City Museums.

54. Gouache by Sally Henriques of "Rolighed," Private collection.

55. Drawing of Hans Christian Andersen's funeral, August 11, 1875, *Illustreret Tidende*, No. 830,
August 22, 1875.